A Fragile Movement

Recent Titles in
Contributions in Sociology

American Ritual Dramas: Social Rules and Cultural Meanings
Mary Jo Deegan

Multiculturalism and Intergroup Relations
James S. Frideres, editor

Homelessness in the United States: State Surveys (Volume I)
Jamshid A. Momeni, editor

Explorations in the Understanding of Landscape: A Cultural Geography
William Norton

Postmodern Social Analysis and Criticism
John W. Murphy

Suburbia Re-examined
Barbara M. Kelly, editor

Impossible Organizations: Self-Management and Organizational Reproduction
Yohanan Stryjan

Religious Politics in Global and Comparative Perspective
William H. Swatos, Jr., editor

Invisible Victims: White Males and the Crisis of Affirmative Action
Frederick R. Lynch

Theories of Ethnicity: A Critical Appraisal
Richard H. Thompson

Population and Community in Rural America
Lorraine Garkovich

Divided We Stand: Class Structure in Israel from 1948 to the 1980s
Amir Ben-Porat

A Fragile Movement

THE STRUGGLE FOR NEIGHBORHOOD STABILIZATION

Juliet Saltman

CONTRIBUTIONS IN SOCIOLOGY,
NUMBER 86

GREENWOOD PRESS

New York
Westport, Connecticut
London

Library of Congress Cataloging-in-Publication Data

Saltman, Juliet.
   A fragile movement : the struggle for neighborhood stabilization /
Juliet Saltman.
      p.   cm.—(Contributions in sociology, ISSN 0084–9278 ; no.
86)
   Bibliography: p.
   Includes index.
   ISBN 0–313–26490–2 (lib. bdg. : alk. paper)
   1. Discrimination in housing—United States.   2. Neighborhood—
United States.   I. Title.   II. Series.
HD7288.76.U5S26   1990
363.5′1—dc20   89–11940

British Library Cataloguing in Publication Data is available.

Library of Congress Catalog Card Number: 89–11940
ISBN: 0–313–26490–2
ISSN: 0084–9278

First published in 1990

Greenwood Press, Inc.
88 Post Road West, Westport, Connecticut 06881

Printed in the United States of America

The paper used in this book complies with the
Permanent Paper Standard issued by the National
Information Standards Organization (Z39.48–1984).

10 9 8 7 6 5 4 3 2 1

CONTENTS

The National Level: National Neighbors;
Conclusions; Implications for Social Policy and
Strategies for Social Change

ABBREVIATIONS

AMHA   Akron Metropolitan Housing Authority
BHCA   Blue Hills Civic Association (Hartford)
BHN   Belmont-Hillsboro Neighbors (Nashville)
BTNA   Butler-Tarkington Neighborhood Association (Indianapolis)
CDBG   Community Development Block Grant
CHRB   Community Housing Resources Board
CN   Crenshaw Neighbors (Los Angeles)
DOJ   Department of Justice
EI   Education/Instruccion (Hartford)
EMAN   East Mount Airy Neighbors (Philadelphia)
FHA   Federal Housing Administration
FHCS   Fair Housing Contact Service (Akron)
GPHC   Greater Park Hill Community (Denver)
HEW   U.S. Department of Health, Education & Welfare
HUD   U.S. Department of Housing & Urban Development
MO   Movement Organization
NAACP   National Association for the Advancement of Colored People
NCDH   National Committee Against Discrimination in Housing
NHS   Neighborhood Housing Services
NI   Neighbors Inc. (Washington, D.C.)

NN   National Neighbors
OHFA   Ohio Housing Finance Agency
OPEN   Fund for an Open Society
PLGNA   Prospect-Lefferts Gardens Neighborhood Association (Brooklyn)
SPCA   Sherman Park Community Association (Milwaukee)
SWAP   Senior Workers Action Program
UDAG   Urban Development Action Grant
UE   Urban Edge (Hartford)
UPON   United Promotion of Our Neighborhood (Akron)
USE   Useful Service Exchange (Akron)
VAMA   Voluntary Affirmative Marketing Agreement
VISTA   Volunteers In Service To America
WCA   Nineteenth Ward Community Association (Rochester)
WMAN   West Mount Airy Neighbors (Philadelphia)
WSN   West Side Neighbors (Akron)

PREFACE

I wrote this book because of curiosity and passion. Both of these are directly linked to my experience of living in Akron's west side for over thirty years. When I founded West Side Neighbors in 1967, two years after founding Akron's Fair Housing Contract Service, only the passion was at work. It still is. I strongly believe that racially integrated living is good—for the people who experience the richness of diversity, for the neighborhoods that have it, for the city, for the metropolitan region, and for the country. I believe integrated living represents the finest of what this society is all about—or should be, and could be. I believe racial integration is not only good, but is necessary. I do not think this will be a worthy society without it. I am certain this is so, because of what I and others know of the costs of segregation (Leadership Council 1987).

When I compared the twenty-year struggle for fair housing and integration maintenance in Akron—both of which I intimately experienced—I concluded that integration maintenance was the tougher battle. It is easier to attain integration than to maintain it, I slowly and painfully came to realize. When I saw the monumental forces and obstacles that daily confronted little, volunteer West Side Neighbors, I wondered how long they and their neighborhood could go on.

And when I saw that the battle was being lost on Akron's west side, I became curious. Was it really true, as others claimed, that racial integration in this society was just a transitional stage on the way to total resegregation? Were there any examples of really successful stable integrated neighborhoods in this country? What happened to this movement that started in the fifties? I had to find out. At this time, I was on the board of directors of National Neighbors, and began to better understand how that movement organization (MO) operated on the national level and how the whole movement functioned.

I confess that when I started this research, I thought sadly that I would not find any success stories. I was surprised and delighted when I did. My research questions then changed from, "What happened to the neighborhood stabilization movement?" and "Can racially integrated neighborhoods remain integrated?" to "Can we identify the factors that lead to success or failure in maintaining racial integration?" I think I have found some of those factors, but my sample is a nonprobability one. There are surely other factors at work that I have not identified.

This is not a quantitative study, though I use much statistical material, and numbers are extremely important in this research. Because this is a social movement, I try to capture the feelings, the hopes (often dashed), the fervor, and the passion I found wherever I looked. But I also have to take a hard look at structural matters and conditions far beyond the local neighborhood. I think the history of this movement is rooted in the history of the country, and this in turn is reflected in each local history on the community level. This is why I trace over time the events of urban renewal, public housing, school segregation, and race relations in each community.

But this book is not about events as much as it is about people, and their dreams, their visions of a better way of life than segregated living. It is about daily struggle and the constant confrontation of obstacles. It is about the pitting of the little folks against the monumental institutional forces that push against them. And it is about how hard it is to change established norms that have developed through hundreds of years of racism and segregation. I am still stirred by James Farmer's words, delivered in his deep, resonant voice at a National Neighbors regional conference in Akron in 1975: "An integrated society will not automatically happen. We've got to take deliberate counter-measures to create that kind of society. . . . It won't create itself. . . . And many of these counter-measures that we must take will have to be extraordinary measures . . . because in a way, we are jumping upstream . . . running against the prevailing trend [of segregation]."

This book is about "extraordinary measures," and about "jumping upstream." I offer it with much admiration and respect for all those caring people who were and are involved in this struggle.

PLAN OF THIS BOOK

I have divided the book into four parts. Part I contains only Chapter 1, which offers perspectives on social movements in general and the neighborhood stabilization movement in particular, and presents the analytical framework and methodology for my study. I was guided in this study by theoretical perspectives from three sociological fields—race relations, social movements, and urban community. Because these three perspectives are so intertwined throughout my analysis, I go into some detail here to explain them.

I examine this movement on two levels—the community level and the national level—through a study of movement organizations on each level, and their interaction. For readers who might not want all the living, breathing details of how movement organizations have functioned for over twenty years, it is possible to get the essence of the book by reading just the first and last chapters—1 and 9. But much of the drama would then be missed.

Part II analyzes the community level through three models: success, failure, and conditional. This section presents five detailed case studies (Chapters 2 through 6) and ten briefer profiles of urban and suburban movement efforts (Chapter 7). Here is where we see this movement as a needed social invention in different times and places, propelled by some common forces sweeping through each community across the country.

Part III concerns the national level of this movement, and offers a detailed analysis of the development of National Neighbors, the only national organization devoted to the goal of integration maintenance. Here in Chapter 8 we see not only the national MO's development through time, but also the interaction between the national organization and the local MOs that created it. We see, too, that many of the organizational struggles on the local level are repeated on the national level. And we recognize that the national climate affects both levels in the same way, and ultimately gravely affects the whole movement. Recurring and controversial ideological and structural movement issues are discussed.

I summarize all the above in Part IV, Chapter 9, where I draw some conclusions, and suggest some policy implications of this study. Finally, I offer a strategy for maintaining racial integration in urban neighborhoods based on my findings. I do not know of any other sociohistorical analysis of this movement, and I present it with the hope that it will be a contribution to knowledge generally and to integration maintenance efforts specifically. I even dare to hope that someone out there may try some of the suggested policies, just to see if they work.

ACKNOWLEDGMENTS

I am grateful to all the respondents and helpful residents in the local communities I visited. They gave generously of their time; they opened their homes to me; they shared their perceptions and feelings; they gave me their old organizational papers and records; they helped me locate valuable materials and other valuable people.

In Indianapolis, I specifically thank Marilyn Blackmon, Rodger Coleman, George Geib, Mark Gross, Doris Hicks, Ruth and Mabel Hicks, Gil Holmes, Peg Kennedy, Lucy and Bob Riegal, Lillian Robinson, Pat and Gene Selmanoff, and Phyllis and Steve West. I will not forget that within twenty minutes after I—a total stranger—first phoned when I got to town, Marilyn Blackmon and the Riegals drove up to my hotel and took me out to supper. I also thank the helpful staff at the public library, the state library, the Indiana Historical Society, and the *Indianapolis Star*.

In Rochester, I thank Carolyn Argust, Wyoma Best, Bea Harris, Roe Jameson, Diane Larter, Doris Meadows, Dana Miller, Carol Mulhearn, Jerry and Kathy O'Neill, Ruth Scott, Sue Segalman, Al and Kathy Settee, Dick Shroyer, Bill and Barbara Sullivan, Armin and Margaret Weiss, and the staffs of the city planning department, the Rochester public schools, and the *Rochester Times-Union*.

In Milwaukee, thanks to Ace Backus, Mike Brandt, Rita and John Conway, Bill Fogarty, Fred and Diana Freiberg, Carol and Charles Holton, Marilyn Johannsen, Gordon Kacala, Lila Kelly, Carol Malone, Dennis McGuire, Don Noel, Mindy Brudno Rayson, Ray Richardson, Ryan Sattler, Joan Stanford, Terre Valent, Alderman Bob Weber, and the staffs of the city development department, the *Milwaukee Journal*, and the University of Wisconsin.

In Hartford, where I cried, many thanks to Bob and Martha Belliveau, Bill Brayfield, Mary Collier, Jesse Collins, Ralph Dumas, Boyd Hinds (now deceased), Linda Kelly, Howard Klebenoff, Jim Mason, Jim Miller, Dottie Payne, Gerri Porter, Bob Sadler, Rhea and Phil Starr, Geri Sullivan, Patricia Sweet, Allen Taylor, Margaret and Bill Worthington, and the staffs of the Connecticut Historical Society, the *Hartford Courant*, Hartford public library, and Hartford public schools.

In Akron, I did not have to ask for many materials since they were mostly in my files and basement. But I am thankful and grateful for people who wrote their thoughts on the occasion of West Side Neighbors' twentieth anniversary. I used some of these in this book. I also used results of the 1979 and 1982 interviews on Akron's west side, and thank all those who participated in that work. Many thanks to West Side Neighbors for sharing some of the files of minutes of twenty years of board meetings. And thanks to the University of Akron library archives for lending me back some of my own early materials on West Side Neighbors.

In Washington, D.C., and Cleveland, Ohio, I thank Susan Learmonth and Chip Bromley for giving me access to the National Neighbors files and records, and for helping me gain access to the local groups.

I am grateful to Kent State University for granting me a sabbatical leave in the spring of 1984, so that I could do the field research for this book. I am also grateful to Dean Gene Wenninger of the research office of Kent State for the travel grant that helped me during the sabbatical semester. I thank Dean Bittle at the Stark campus of Kent State University for granting me a small teaching reduction each semester since 1984. I thank the secretarial staff of Stark campus for the xeroxing help with all of those reams of paper. And I thank the Dean's Committee for the travel grant in 1986 that got me to Gavle, Sweden, where I gave a paper at the International Research Conference on Housing Policy. The paper I gave there was based on this research, and the feedback I got at the conference was most valuable.

At Kent State, also, I am most grateful to Dr. Sid Reid of the library's Institute for Bibliographics and Editing. He allowed me to use their scanning machine, which reads printed matter and converts it to computer disk, after a burglar in 1987 took away two of my chapter disks, along with my computer. Insurance replaced the computer, but the disks would have been totally lost if not for Sid Reid's scanning machine.

I am most appreciative of the grant from the National Science Foundation and the Smithsonian Institute, given through the American Sociological Association, which enabled me to go to India in August 1986, where I gave a paper at the New Delhi conference of the International Sociological Association. Each time I talked about my research for this book, I received valuable comments, suggestions, and ideas. Though I did not always use them, they did make me think and were helpful as I waded through all the mountains of material assembled for this book.

Finally, I am grateful to my husband Bill, who lived through not only the five years of research and writing for this book, but also the many prior years of my involvement in two social movements on both local and national levels— the fair housing movement, about which I wrote ten years ago, and this one. He deserves all the awards for standing by, supporting, listening to the hopes and dreams and schemes, to many complaints, and sharing all the pain and the little bits of glory. For this, and much more, my love and appreciation go to him. Our children, now grown, are the living legacies of movement involvement. They, and all those other children of this movement, will shape the future. This book is dedicated to them.

Part I

PERSPECTIVES

1

ANALYTICAL FRAMEWORK

More than 80% of Americans live in segregated neighborhoods. What do we know about the 20% who do not? One social movement specifically and deliberately was formed to maintain racially integrated neighborhoods. What happened to it? This is a sociohistorical account of that social movement, the neighborhood stabilization movement, which grew out of the civil rights movement of the 1950s. In all the vast literature on the civil rights movement, there is nothing that systematically describes the sociohistorical formation, development, and results of this neighborhood movement.

I am defining neighborhood stabilization as the organized effort to maintain racial integration in urban neighborhoods. The participants in this movement sought—and still seek—neighborhood integration as a way of life. What they confronted, however, were massive institutional forces propelling their neighborhoods toward resegregation. The struggle that engulfed them is the story I try to capture here.

Three theoretical strands are woven together in this analysis, directly stemming from the nature of this movement. These guided me throughout my research and analysis. First, race relations theory provides a meaningful framework for analyzing the movement. Second, social movements theory offers an important analytical tool in studying the movement's origins, structure, process, and impact. And third, urban community theory helps to explain neighborhood transition and the linkage of the neighborhood and its organization to the larger community and society. All three perspectives sharpen our analysis of the process of neighborhood change, and further extend our understanding of this movement's dynamics and results. I do not know of any other study that combines these three approaches.

In this chapter, I will first present the three theoretical frameworks which guided my analysis. Then I will review the sociohistorical national context in which this movement developed. I will explain the general study of social movements, and how it relates to my specific analysis of this neighborhood stabilization movement. Here, I will present the analytical models I use for examining case studies of success, failure, and uncertainty (conditional), and I will define my terms. Finally, I will explain the methodology of this study.

THEORETICAL PERSPECTIVES

Race Relations Theory

I am using "theory" to mean anything from simple explanations to complex sets of interrelated propositions. In the field of race relations, a number of theories have developed explaining what happens when different groups migrate and come into contact, and how the intergroup contact leads to patterns of social interaction. "Migration is the basic factor underlying all racial contacts and subsequent relations" (Lieberson 1980: 375). Whether the migration was voluntary or involuntary is a critical factor in those subsequent relations. And which group initially had the greater power profoundly affects those relations. Thus, beginnings are important and history is everywhere. "The modern notion of race is a byproduct of slavery and colonialism, which gave rise to racism; racism . . . has its roots in a particular historical situation" (Francis 1976: 279).

Other theories are concerned with the persistence of those initial patterns: "Social events have a life of their own; once established, the customs persist long after causes vanish. . . . The patterns observed now were at least in part created by earlier events" (Lieberson 1980: 8). Still other theories relate to the change or disintegration of intergroup relations: "In the sociological study of race relations, the objective is to explain how patterns of racial differentiation emerge, how they are maintained through time, and how they are transformed or disintegrate" (Barth & Noel 1980: 432). Issues of social control and intergroup conflict are also critical aspects of race relations theories. We can collapse all of these attempts to explain race relations into three types of theories: social-psychological, power-conflict, and structural-cultural. Each emphasizes a different aspect of race relations; none is adequate alone. I have found all of them helpful in analyzing this movement, and briefly review them here.

Social-psychological perspectives, though less appealing to me as broad explanations of race relations, are useful in dealing with the phenomenon of perception. And perceptions are vital in understanding the very concept of race and of the intergroup relations flowing out of it. "What people *think* and *feel* about race affects behavior very much indeed . . . ideas about race can be one of the most fruitful causes of human misery" (Mason 1970: 1–3). So perceptions are indeed linked to outcomes. And the costs of segregation in our society are rooted in perceptions, which in turn are rooted in history.

"To seek for regularities at the sociohistorical level is to look for broad tendencies, trends, and recurrent sequences of events in such a way that they have a verifiable relationship to 'times when and places where' " (Schermerhorn 1970: 190). This is central to my study. Equally important is my belief that perceptions and their outcomes can be changed, but effectively only through structural changes in society.

Power-conflict approaches suggest that intergroup relations can best be understood in terms of differences in power. Richard Schermerhorn (1970) has suggested that when two different groups first come into regular contact, the least likely condition to prevail is equality. The initial differences in the power of the two groups will affect all their subsequent interactions and relations. "Within the American social structure, race relations are power relations" (Blalock 1982: 102). Moreover, conflict between groups is seen as sometimes inevitable, and often even desirable, to bring about constructive change. "There are times when integration can only occur in and through conflict, and conversely, other times when conflict is necessary to reach a new order of integration" (Schermerhorn 1970: 57–58). But whether conflict occurs depends on other factors such as degree of power differentials, extent of resources, and the type of society.

Power-conflict theories can be divided into Marxist and non-Marxist approaches, with Marxist views emphasizing economic factors as the basis of power differentials, and non-Marxist views taking a multidimensional approach to differences in power. I use a multidimensional view in this study. For example, I apply this statement to the neighborhood stabilization movement: "Race relations inherently are power contests between dominant and subordinate groups. This is true even though these relationships may appear to be smooth-running and free of overt conflict" (Blalock 1982: 101). In the case of the racially integrated neighborhood in this social movement, I see the subordinate group as the neighborhood and its organization, the dominant group as one or more of the institutional forces in the city at large.

Structural-cultural theories bridge the conflict and social-psychological approaches by suggesting that people learn the appropriate norms of relating to members of other groups. These norms are learned within the institutional arrangements of their community and society. As Lieberson observes, "There is a latent structure to the race relations patterns in a given setting, with only certain parts of the structure observed at a given time" (Lieberson 1980: 375). Robin Williams has observed: "Less obvious than segregation and discrimination are the many operating practices for intergroup behavior that arise in all communities. These are community patterns that define whether or not intergroup situations are appropriate and acceptable" (Williams 1964: 116).

When established, the norms lead to institutional racism. This operates as an impersonal web of discriminatory practices, even in the absence of personal prejudice. It effectively denies equality to members of certain groups in the major institutions of society: housing, education, justice and law enforcement, and employment. Robert Crain has noted, "In the absence of all [job] discrimination... American Negroes would still suffer the consequences of racial segregation in housing, voluntary associations, and informal social relations. These consequences are not merely psychic or social in character; they can be measured in crude monetary terms as well" (Crain, see Pettigrew 1980: 301).

Earlier, Harold Baron referred to the web of institutional racism:

The seemingly impersonal institutions of the great cities have been woven together into a web of urban racism that entraps black people much as the spider's net holds flies— they can wiggle but they cannot move very far. There is a carefully articulated interrelation of the barriers created by each institution. Whereas the single institutional strand standing alone might not be so strong, the many strands together form a powerful web. (Baron 1969: 144)

Social Movements Theory

In my earlier study of the fair housing movement, I waded through all the scholarly writings that defined a social movement (Saltman 1978). A final synthesis yielded a simple working definition, which I use again here. From social movements theory we see that a social movement is a voluntary association with four characteristics: change-oriented goals, geographical scope, organization, and duration.[1] This distinguishes the movement from other associations like garden clubs and corporations, which—though they may be enduring—do not have goals focused on societal change.

Movements are social inventions, since they are new ideas involving human interactions. They often emerge in a community or organization without any direct outside influence. This suggests that human beings have great creative resources that enable them to independently develop such needed social inventions (Whyte 1982).

Movements may be revolutionary or reform, depending on the extent of societal change they seek and the tactics they use to achieve change. They are typically studied through an examination of their phases of development. Jo Freeman (1983) suggests that the tension between spontaneity and structure gives a movement its unique nature: "When one significantly dominates the other, what may one day be, or may once have been, a social movement is something else" (Freeman 1983: 2). It is clear, however, that movement spontaneity must be organized to be effective.

Movements operate through movement organizations (hereafter referred to as MOs), which can be studied comparatively to see how they maximize their results. These organizations confront two fundamental problems: the mobilization of resources and the accomplishment of goals linked to change. In this study, we will see how different MOs in this movement have functioned, and what the results have been of their various strategies. This comparative analysis is the heart of the matter; it is critical to our eventual understanding of the factors of success and failure in this movement.

Both classical and more recent social movements theory focus on external social control factors affecting a movement's success or failure. Whereas classical movement theory emphasizes grievances and ideology among movement supporters, the newer perspective—resource mobilization theory—focuses on the process by which people with or without grievances are mobilized into social movements. Both approaches also recognize that a movement's internal structure makes a great deal of difference in its success. Whether it is inclusive or exclusive, whether segmentary, polycephalous, and reticulate, or centralized and bureaucratic, makes a difference and has an important effect on movement outcomes. Finally, both approaches recognize that movements are dynamic and malleable, and they respond at all times to the interplay of internal and external forces (Zald & McCarthy 1977; Roberts & Kloss 1979; Freeman 1983; Wood & Jackson 1984).

Throughout this interplay is the constant reminder of the importance of social and historical context. The past exerts a tremendous influence on intergroup relations and the extent of institutional racism. Only knowledge of this sociohistorical context can explain the particular intergroup relations and MO dynamics in each of the communities studied.

The neighborhood stabilization movement illustrates the concept of the "quotidian," pertaining to the routines of daily life. Support for a movement will peak when daily life is disrupted (Roberts & Kloss 1979). In each community studied, this disruption was a common one. Urban renewal dislocation brought blacks to new neighborhoods. This was the common precipitating factor leading to MO formation on the local level. But, reaching further back and drawing on race relations theory, we see that racism was responsible for the initial concentration of blacks in those neighborhoods that eventually became marked for urban renewal.

Using a combined classical and resource mobilization approach, we will examine the sociohistorical context of each urban neighborhood, the inception of each MO, its goals, structure, and strategies over time, and its impact. Since race relations are inherently power contests between dominant and subordinate groups, we will analyze the process of mobilization, the use of resources, and the effectiveness of tactics used by each MO. I will show that each of the MOs and the entire movement was directly affected by national events and developments occurring in the civil rights movement. Changes in that movement were brought about largely through political and legal means. On the local level, the neighborhood stabilization movement also used political strategies to persuade institutional decision makers to act in ways that would help the MO achieve its goals. Sometimes they succeeded.

Urban Community Theory

Finally, urban community theory further strengthens our analysis of this movement. The concept of community has its origins in ideas presented by nineteenth-century social philosophers such as Tönnies and Durkheim. Though these offered antiurban perspectives, focusing on the disorganizing and disintegrating aspects of urban life, they remain an important source of modern urban theory.

More recently, some community studies have focused on the nature of the ties and social networks that bind people to an area and to each other, even in the heart of dense, modern, seemingly impersonal cities (Fischer 1976; Taub et al. 1977; Wellman & Leighton 1979). The concepts of the "defended neighborhood" and the "community of limited liability" are relevant here. The "defended neighborhood" (Suttles 1972) is a local area threatened by social change, and mobilizing in its own defense. Roland Warren has observed: "Local communities are . . . the end of the line, the place where the impact of structures and processes in the national society gets felt by people in their daily lives. No community is an island, and the more one becomes involved in purposive change at the local level, the more likely one is to become aware of the genesis of many local problems in the larger society" (Warren 1977: 250).

The "community of limited liability" (Janowitz 1961) refers to limited and variable local attachments in urban communities depending on such factors as age, sex, class, family composition, and length of residence. "The question becomes not simply whether local sentiments are still significant, but for whom and for what reasons" (Hunter 1981: 65). This type of community has often been created by external agencies—local developers, planning offices, real estate interests, booster organizations, and so on—which have given it a name, created its boundaries, and maintained its official identity. The residents of this type of symbolic community may, however, become interdependent through the efforts of a local voluntary organization or community press. We see that in this movement.

Concepts of community power structures are helpful in identifying and understanding interlocking leadership networks in American communities. Vertical and horizontal dimensions of these structures reveal the complex external forces that impinge on neighborhoods and affect their life or death. The vertical pattern refers to ties to the larger society and culture; the horizontal pattern refers to the relation of local units to each other (Roland Warren 1963, 1977). Both have a significant impact on neighborhood development, reminding us again of the historical role of government as an influence on race relations, and the various ways in which governmental, political, and legal issues affect the course of events in any local community.

One of the persisting topics of urban research has been neighborhood change, or "succession." Three differing perspectives have emerged, offering divergent views of the future of racially changing neighborhoods. The first and most traditional approach—the orthodox view—I call "degenerative," since it sug-gests the inevitability of neighborhood decline after racial change has occurred (Molotch 1972; Wilson 1983). Wilson, for example, suggests that racial change in urban neighborhoods is "typically accompanied by two response patterns among whites . . . white flight . . . and avoidance. . . . To the extent that these response patterns occur, stable integration in the urban neighborhoods is not possible" (Ibid: 316).

The second approach I call "interactionist," since its focus is on the rela-tionship between social support networks and neighborhood preservation (Hunter 1974; Ahlbrandt & Cunningham 1978; Fischer 1976). This perspective does not accept the inevitability of decline in racially integrated neighborhoods, and suggests the possibility of neighborhood stability through social support networks (Suttles 1968, 1972). Consistent with this approach is the theory that organizations can create a sense of community when none exists in racially changing neighborhoods: "We found that this conscious 'social construction of community' has led to the creation and maintenance of a local community organization whose structure and activities are mechanisms which heighten both the social and symbolic 'sense of community' for its local residents" (Hunter 1975: 549).

A third and more recent approach, which I support, is an interventionist one. This view suggests that racially integrated neighborhoods may stabilize if sufficient resources and institutional networks are mobilized for collective action early enough (Galster 1987; Keating et al. 1987; Saltman 1984, 1986; Helper 1986; Lee 1985; Taub et al. 1984; Orfield 1984). Taub et al., for example, write:

Ecological facts do not, in fact, unidirectionally determine neighborhood outcomes. Corporate and individual decisions always intervene and sometimes modify the connec-tion between ecological circumstances and neighborhood outcomes. . . . What is clear is that interventions can and do work, and that they sometimes do so in situations that might be considered unpromising on the basis of historical understandings. (Taub et al. 1984: 187)

Other recent research also casts doubt on the orthodox view of inevitable neighborhood succession from white to black:

What I find most striking about the figures . . . is that a substantial number of mixed neighborhoods did not become appreciably blacker . . . more than one-fifth of the tracts became whiter or remained racially stable from 1970 through 1980. . . . Based on the recent experiences of racially mixed areas in the largest U.S. cities, then, succession hardly seems the inevitable, irreversible process that social scientists have traditionally thought it to be. (Lee 1985: 352).

From this comment, we can not know to what extent neighborhood stabilization may have been caused or influenced by organized efforts. This is something we will try to analyze here. Let us turn now to an examination of the national scene that gave rise to these efforts—the neighborhood stabilization movement.

SOCIOHISTORICAL NATIONAL CONTEXT

This movement arose during the civil rights movement of the 1950s. In fact, the same situational factors that gave rise to the fair housing movement (Saltman 1978) were present for this sister movement of neighborhood stabilization. Racism, migration, segregation, urban renewal, dislocation, discrimination, relocation, and denial of housing choice were some of the painful common spurs of these two movements. If we are to use race relations theories of migration and initial contact between groups, we must go back to slavery. Certainly, blacks in this country are the only minority group to arrive here in chains. This situation of involuntary migration has, indeed, made a difference—to blacks, to whites, to neighborhoods, communities, cities, and to the entire society.

The institution of slavery in America stained whites as well as blacks (Bennett 1966). The brief ten "golden years" following the Emancipation Proclamation were not enough to overcome the hundreds of years of prior domination and bondage. When the Northern troops were removed under the Hayes order, quick reversion to earlier patterns of oppression swept the country.[2] This, coupled with Southern economic decline, paved the way for the migration—this time voluntary—of blacks from the South to the North.

Mobility trends of whites and blacks play a vital role in this movement's dynamics. The impact of these trends, along with the racism that generated them, have resulted in residential settlement patterns marked by increasing racial segregation throughout the country up to this moment. Let us examine these patterns and the migration trends linked to them.

Migration, Racism, Segregation

One hundred years ago, 90% of all blacks in the United States lived in the South. Today, about 50% of U.S. blacks are in the South; the other 50% have migrated to the North, primarily to the twelve largest metropolitan areas in the country. This was one of the most dramatic migration streams in the nation's history. Scholars have seen migration in terms of push and pull factors, that is, "the push of limited social and economic opportunities at the place of origin, and the pull of promised opportunities at the place of destination" (Taeuber & Taeuber: 1965:12).

Three major waves of migration, beginning during World War I, brought blacks to urban cores across the country. The third and largest wave took place during and after World War II. Like the other two, it was a response to perceived economic opportunities and an escape from the social, economic, and political repression of the South. Settlement patterns of blacks have frequently been compared with those of other migrants to Northern urban areas. Foreign migrants, too, settled earlier around the central cores of cities. Such areas were easily accessible to places of employment, to transportation, and to transient and moderate-cost housing. But as soon as some occupational and economic stability was reached, foreign settlers moved away from central city cores as quickly as they could.

Black migrants inherited the blight left by earlier city migrants, and also settled in and around the central cores of cities. But here the parallel ends. Blacks were not able to leave the blighted areas as readily as the earlier migrants. There are four reasons for this. First, blacks arrived in northern urban centers at a later time in history, when occupational skills and training were already beginning to be necessary for economic opportunity and advancement. Second, blacks had to contend with the past history of slavery as an institution. This resulted in a slave psychology of whites and a continuing inferior status for blacks. Third, black visibility precluded any easy absorption. Whereas the accent of earlier migrants could be lost or modified, and cultural patterns could adapt to the dominant culture, blacks could not change the color of their skin. Thus technological, historical, and cultural factors, coupled with a fourth factor of increasing covert and overt discrimination, have forced blacks to remain primarily in and near the central areas of decay and blight. "No ethnic or nationality group currently exhibits levels of segregation as high as those for blacks . . . the segregation of these groups declined rapidly over time, while those for blacks have remained at exceptionally high levels" (Kain 1987: 78).

These areas of inner-city blight came to be marked for urban renewal and land clearance in the late 1940s, at the very time that blacks were migrating toward them in largest numbers. Well-documented is the fact that of three possible reasons for continued black confinement to ghettos—poverty, choice, and discrimination—it has been and is primarily discrimination that has forced blacks to remain in ghetto areas.[3] Forced by urban renewal, discrimination, and lower incomes to seek housing in ever-shrinking ghettos marked by increasing density, blacks shifted from one ghetto area to another between 1950 and 1970.

At about the same time that blacks were migrating in the largest numbers to the urban centers of this country, other factors were at work encouraging whites to move away from those centers. Though bigotry may have been responsible for the exodus of some whites from central city neighborhoods, the major reason for their moving away to the suburbs was that better housing opportunities were available to them. The federal government, through its sins of omission and commission, was largely responsible for this situation.

More than 13 million new homes were built in suburban areas for returning veterans and other moderate-income families after World War II. But these new homes, federally financed with FHA and VA mortgage assistance, were not available to all people. Federal Housing Administration building programs and policies on new housing construction in suburban areas covertly and overtly excluded minorities from access to such housing.[4] In addition, state courts upheld many discriminatory ordinances passed by local and state governments during these years, making the legacy of discrimination complete. Thus, the resultant past and current patterns of residential segregation are a direct outgrowth of federal malfunctioning.[5]

If we add to this the racist policies and effects of lending institutions, appraisers, insurance companies, and the real estate industry, we begin to see the total background for understanding racial segregation in housing in this country. The practice of mortgage "redlining" in racially integrated and transitional neighborhoods, for example, has been well-documented (Saltman 1980: 20–33). This is a contributing factor in the eventual total resegregation of such neighborhoods. The extent of racial discrimination in the real estate industry was documented nationally for the first time in the 1978 HUD-NCDH Audit (HUD 1979), and locally across the nation since 1969 (Saltman 1979, 1977). Even with partially analyzed data, which excluded racial steering, the HUD Audit showed that blacks in this country could expect to encounter discrimination in housing sales 62% of the time, and in rentals 75% of the time.[6] The first results of that nationwide audit were announced on the tenth anniversary of the passage of the 1968 federal Fair Housing Act.

Some urban and race relations scholars have claimed that the most serious domestic problem of the nation is the social and physical separation of blacks and whites.[7] Segregated housing has led to segregated schools, shopping areas, and recreational facilities, spawning a divided society, with the hostility, mistrust, and discord that characterize such a society.

What is important here is the persistence of these policies and practices until this moment, despite the passage of laws upon laws designed to correct them. The power of the norms, the difficulty of breaking the "cake of custom," is what is so critical to the understanding of any social movement—in particular, this neighborhood stabilization movement that we are studying.

One example of real estate appraisal policies and practices illustrates this well. Appraisals are critical because they guide lenders in their decisions on mortgage lending. Appraisal manuals contained strongly negative racial references from 1932 until 1977, when revision orders were issued by the Department of Justice (American Institute of Real Estate Appraisers 1977). One early reference in appraisal manuals was to a realtor's rank ordering of minority groups according to their effect on property values (Hoyt 1933). This realtor's list ranked groups in descending order, from most desirable to least desirable, with blacks at the bottom. But what is even more significant is the fact that the "bible" of appraising, still in use in 1975, continued to have this forty-year-old list (McMichael 1952). Though more recent appraisal literature has avoided explicitly negative racial references, the principles of homogeneity and conformity have continued to guide the individual appraiser's and lender's judgments and perceptions of neighborhood risk. And by the time the national appraisers' institute was forced to revise their manuals in 1977, hundreds of urban neighborhoods across the nation had been devastated by disinvestment and redlining. Especially vulnerable were those neighborhoods that were racially integrated. They were defying the norm, and they paid the price for their nonconformity.

The substantial research on residential segregation in this country indicates four general factors that have generated and maintained residential segregation in this country: (1) government policies and practices related to urban renewal, public housing, and suburban development; (2) the inadequate supply of low- and moderate-income housing dispersed throughout the metropolitan area; (3) suburban zoning regulations; and (4) racial discrimination in the housing industry by real estate companies, lending institutions, builders, appraisers, and individual owners and landlords.

The long history of segregation in housing is thus the result of past discriminatory practices, in which all of these—the private housing industry, and federal, state, and local governments—were active participants. These discriminatory practices have been traced from 1866, when the first open housing law was passed, to 1968, when the constitutionality of that earlier law was reaffirmed by the Supreme Court. This was several months after Congress passed its first federal open housing legislation, Title VIII of the 1968 Civil Rights Act.

During the 102 years it took to reaffirm legally the basic human right to shelter, three racist textbooks for the national real estate industry were published by 1923 and reconfirmed as late as 1950. Federal Housing Administration manuals from 1935 to 1940 insisted on discriminatory practices in instructions to builders of new housing developments. Federal banking agencies urged similar practices, and approved racially restrictive covenants in deeds during a sixteen-year period when more than 11 million new homes were built. State courts upheld many discriminatory ordinances passed by local and state governments during these 102 years, making the legacy of discrimination complete. The latest studies of racial segregation in housing in this country show no abatement.[8]

When the Supreme Court gave its historic 1968 decision on open housing, *Jones v. Mayer*, it linked housing segregation to slavery:

Just as the Black Codes, enacted after the Civil War to restrict the free exercise of those rights, were substitutes for the slave system, so the exclusion of Negroes from white communities became a substitute for the Black Codes. And when racial discrimination herds men into ghettos and makes their ability to buy property turn on the color of their skin, then it too is a relic of slavery.

The slave's protest against bondage and indignity has been echoed, in one form or another, continuously up to the present. We trace the civil rights protest briefly now, as additional background for understanding the origins and development of the neighborhood stabilization movement.

Protest, Response, Tango

Since the beginning of the modern civil rights movement in the 1950s,[9] one outstanding characteristic of the protest was its growing militancy into the 1970s. This twenty-year period coincided with the development of the neighborhood stabilization movement, first locally, and then nationally. If we look at the period from 1950 to 1955, which is when the first neighborhood stabilization groups began to appear, we see the backdrop for that emergent movement. Here is a brief overview of the national segregation climate at the time, and the beginnings of protest and victory in the modern civil rights movement. Here we also find the stirring of counter-movements.

In 1950, three Supreme Court decisions undermined the legal structure of segregation. In the McClaurin case, the Court ruled that a student, once admitted, cannot be segregated; in the Henderson case, it prohibited "curtains, partitions, and signs" that separated black dining-car patrons from whites; in the Sweatt case, it held that equality involved more than physical facilities.[10]

Additional legal and governmental actions paved the way for greater equity for blacks in the next five years. In 1951, racial segregation in Washington, D.C. restaurants was ruled illegal by the municipal court of appeals, the NAACP began its attack on school segregation, Illinois Governor Adlai Stevenson called out the National Guard to stop the rioting in Cicero, Illinois, when a mob of 3,500 tried to prevent a black family from moving into that all-white city, and President Truman named a committee to supervise compliance with antidiscrimination provisions in U.S. government contracts.

In 1952, the University of Tennessee admitted its first black student. In 1953, a bus boycott began in Baton Rouge, Louisiana, and riots recurring for three years began in Chicago, after black families moved into the Trumbull Park public housing project. The mayor assigned more than 1,000 policemen to keep order. In 1954, the Supreme Court ruled racial segregation in public schools unconstitutional, school integration began in Washington, D.C. and Baltimore, Maryland, and the U.S. Department of Defense announced the complete abolition of black units in the armed forces. In that same year, the first White Citizens Council unit organized in Indianola, Mississippi. In 1955, the Supreme Court banned segregation in public recreational facilities, the Interstate Commerce Commission banned segregation in buses and waiting rooms involved in interstate travel, and the bus boycott began in Montgomery, Alabama, touching off a wave of bus boycotts elsewhere.

From 1955 to 1965, the civil rights movement reached a peak of vigor and cohesion. Though separatism as a philosophy appeared throughout black history, its reappearance in 1966 led to the gradual deemphasis of the long sought-after goal of integration by a small, youthful, and vocal minority of black people. And though the national civil rights movement was no longer as unified as it had been, the momentum of the movement continued into the 1970s with additional legal, political, and judicial decisions that aided the goals of equal access and racial integration.

Examining the national climate for civil rights during these years shows the coexistence of the same two elements noted above: persisting segregation and discrimination against blacks at the same time that the push for equality was beginning to show some positive results. This is the tango of civil rights: one step forward and two steps backward. For example, in 1957, after the biggest civil rights demonstration ever staged by U.S. blacks in Washington, D.C., Congress passed the first civil rights legislation since 1875. In that same year, Nashville's new elementary school, containing one black child (and 388 whites), was destroyed by a dynamite blast. But three weeks later, in Little Rock, Arkansas, nine black children were escorted to high school by soldiers. And two months after that, New York City became the first city to pass a law banning racial discrimination in housing.

During the 1960s, the tango continued but the pace escalated. Among the dramatic events of this period, several stand out as critically important for this study. But for each gain, a heavy cost was paid. In 1962, President Kennedy issued an executive order barring racial discrimination in federally financed housing. He followed this with a national TV address in which he said that segregation was morally wrong. In 1963, 250,000 people marched on Washington protesting racial segregation and discrimination, and John Kennedy was assassinated. In 1964, Congress passed a civil rights bill that included public accommodations and fair employment provisions, and the murdered bodies of three civil rights workers were found in Mississippi.

The summers of 1965 to 1967 were heated with riots in Atlanta, Omaha, Detroit, Los Angeles, San Francisco, Chicago, Cleveland, and Milwaukee. The year of 1966 was also the year of Vietnam, the division of the country over it, and the new phrase: Black Power. Riots continued into 1968, with one hundred killed, 2,000 wounded, and 11,000 arrested in thirty-one cities across the country. The assassination of Martin Luther King in 1968 spurred Congress's passage of a civil rights bill eliminating discrimination in housing in 80% of the nation's housing. In that same year, the Supreme Court upheld the constitutionality of the 1866 Civil Rights Act barring racial discrimination in housing. Thus it took 102 years to confirm the basic human right to shelter.

Richard Nixon took office as President in 1969, antiwar demonstrations proliferated, and presidential advisor Moynihan proposed "benign neglect" of race issues. His advice was accepted by the President. This was the beginning of the wind-down of the civil rights movement, which continued to lose momentum into the 1980s and then heavily and deeply during the presidency of Ronald Reagan.

But some small gains did occur in the 1970s, along with the growing losses. Even as the war in Vietnam continued to plague the country and weaken the civil rights push, school desegregation continued in more than 200 Southern school districts. The Supreme Court in 1971 issued four unanimous decisions supporting school desegregation, a federal judge ordered black schools of Richmond, Virginia, to merge with white schools of two suburbs in 1972, and an appeals court reversed that order six months later. President Nixon continued to criticize court-ordered busing, and in 1973 submitted a budget that cut and eliminated over one hundred antipoverty, housing, and educational aid programs. In 1974, he resigned after the country watched nationally televised Watergate hearings. His successor Gerald Ford, who did nothing for civil rights, was replaced by Jimmy Carter, who briefly revived some interest in racial issues. His daughter, Amy, began attending a public school in 1976 that was predominantly black.

Whatever social and economic progress for blacks has occurred in this country took place in the 1960s and early 1970s, despite deep resistance to it. Some occupational mobility resulted. In 1960, for example, 25% more white than black men held white-collar jobs. For women, it was 41% more white than black. By 1983, this declined to a 14% difference for men and 17% for women. But black males are still highly concentrated at the bottom of the occupational status ladder, and the vast "underclass" of blacks has scarcely been touched by these gains. In education, we also see some gain in years of schooling for blacks. The gap between blacks' and whites' average years of schooling has decreased from three years in 1960 to less than six months today. But even blacks with the same years of schooling as whites do not earn comparable incomes. In the political world, more than 5,000 blacks now hold local elective offices, including over 250 mayors, in some of the nation's largest cities. But relatively few of these elected officials live in white or even slightly integrated neighborhoods. And few of them send their children to predominantly white schools.

These modest gains were eroded in the 1980s, when the earlier "benign neglect" under Nixon was replaced by deliberate abandonment under Reagan. Studies of racial segregation in housing, for example, show continuing isolation of blacks from whites in the nation's metropolitan regions. "Every investigation uncovers evidence that old impediments to free choice of residence by blacks continue" (Taeuber and Taeuber 1975). Though there was a brief time during the early 1970s when the new federal fair housing law was beginning to be implemented vigorously by the Department of Justice and HUD, it was over all too soon. Under the Reagan administration, the Department of Justice not only was inactive in housing discrimination cases, it even tried to reverse earlier policies which had attempted to reduce housing segregation. Especially significant and ominous is the dramatic increase in cases of racial violence across the country during the 1980s.[11]

So we see that the national civil rights struggle has run an uneven course; despite court rulings and legislation clearly outlawing virtually all types of racial discrimination, past patterns persist. These patterns and practices have resulted in racial and economic separation in every metropolitan area of the country. The ending of these patterns—the breaking of these norms and the establishment of new patterns of inclusion and diversity—was and is the primary goal of the neighborhood stabilization movement.

NEIGHBORHOOD STABILIZATION AS A SOCIAL MOVEMENT

Studying Social Movements

This movement, and my analysis of it, can best be understood by first understanding social movements in general. Recent scholarly analyses suggest, in fact, that neighborhood change can most effectively be studied through a social movements approach (Schwab & Ringel 1988; London et al. 1986). Earlier, we defined a social movement as having four components: change orientation, organization, scope, and duration. But each of these involves much more. The fact that a movement is organized for change suggests an organization, a structure, an ideology, a strategy, and an outcome.

Leaders and followers, peripheral members and supporters all play a role in a movement's organization. Movement organizations, through which movements are analyzed, have different levels of commitment among their participants. Exclusive membership demands maximum commitment, activity, and participation; inclusive membership has minimum levels of commitment (Zald & Ash 1966). These different levels of commitment are related to types of goals, the possibilities of their achievement, and the movement's eventual impact on the social environment.

The problem of commitment has been examined by John Wilson (1973). He sees that members of a movement have different motivations; they are not a monolithic uniform group. He suggests that we can imagine movement participants in an onion-ring formation, in which commitment lessens as the outer circles are approached. Wilson claims that when an individual joins a movement he or she does not necessarily make a commitment to the group, but must be persuaded to do so. Sympathy can be transformed into commitment by participation in tactics.

The act of joining is facilitated by friendship ties between the members of the movement and the potential recruit. Interpersonal contact through favorable channels, then, is as important as ideological appeal, since people who join movements do so partly because people in the groups they already belong to have joined. Thus, participation in one group eases entrance into another.

Once commitment is gained, however, it must be sustained, and this is a chronic difficulty that movements face. One reason for this is that there is bound to be disappointment over the lack of immediate achievement of the movement's objectives. Another is that the movement may operate in a hostile environment that challenges the movement's right to exist and the integrity of each member in it. The ideology of a movement is the foundation of group cohesion and solidarity.

Ideology, one of the critical elements of a social movement, refers to the underlying shared values of a group—its reason for existence. It is "the principles and action programs on which the members have reached a general agreement" (Heberle 1951: 7). The beliefs of any social movement reflect "the unique situation of the social segments that make up its base" (Gusfield 1968: 447). These beliefs represent a shared experience, and this experience is relevant only to the particular segment of society that has experienced it. So the ideology seems valid to that segment, and meaningfully prescribes solutions to problems they perceive, and justifies change. Ideas and doctrines are conditioned by the historical situation in which the ideas were conceived.

Ideology includes goals and is related to tactics. Goals may be explicit or implicit, general or specific, and immediate or ultimate. According to Rush and Denisoff (1971), an ideology sets the goals and defines the characteristic nature of a movement. They refer to movements as ideological organizations, and claim that ideology is interwoven with the type of social change that the members of a movement want. It is, then, a guidepost to the future, as well as being grounded in the past.

John Wilson (1973) suggests that ideology is a vital bridge between attitude and action, and claims that ultimately the ideology is the carrier of the ideas that mobilize people into action. Action, in social movements, is what is referred to as strategy, tactics, or program. Strategy is the general program for achieving the goals of the movement, and tactics refer to the specific ways of carrying out the program or strategy. Wilson claims that tactics provide the real meaning of the movement, and are the main source of involvement for the followers. For those outside the movement, it is the tactical behavior that gives the movement its identity.

Movements have three primary strategies open to them—persuasion, bargaining, and coercion—but no movement relies solely on any one of these strategies: "Movement leaders must make sure they are not boring their audience (the public, and internal supporters), and thus the popular demand for ever-new tactics places enormous burdens on a movement's leaders" (Wilson 1973: 232). According to Wilson, there is no such thing as the successful tactic—it depends on the movement circumstances, its resources, and the opposition it encounters. Tactics must, however, advance the movement toward its goals and yet sustain the followers as a united group. Specifically, tactics should be comprehensive, simple, and flexible.

Strategies in social movements are of critical importance. Robert Lauer (1976) develops a useful typology of strategies, based on three factors: who implements the change (the movement or the larger society), how much force is required for the change (nonviolent or coercive/violent), and the target of the change (individuals or the social structure). He then suggests how movement ideology and interaction with the larger society relate to the choice of one or more of six different strategies: educative, small-group, bargaining, separatist, disruptive, and revolutionary.

In considering strategies one must consider not only those of the movement, but also the responding ones of the target group or those in opposition. Three negative responses have been identified as cooptation, suppression, and discreditation. Rush and Denisoff (1971) offer prognoses as to which types of movements are most susceptible to each of these responses, and they further relate these to the types of society in which the movement exists—pluralist or elitist.

Factors outside the movement that affect the tactics chosen have also been considered by Zald and McCarthy (1973, 1977, 1987). They refer to tactical dilemmas, which are related to five factors that limit strategic choices: the values of the adherents, the values of the public, the relationship to authorities, the activities of the authorities, and the relationship to goals. They offer a resource-mobilization perspective on social movements, based on organizational use of people, money, and support in the achievement of movement goals. These are linked to the potential for cooperation and conflict between movement organizations and with the community at large.

Many classifications of types of movements are related to the particular kind of ideology or strategy that characterizes a movement. Movements may differ in goals directed toward changing individuals or society, they may differ in the extent of change sought, and they may differ in the means of attaining that change. Typical classifications are reform versus revolutionary (King 1956); reactionary, conservative, revisionary, or revolutionary (Cameron 1966); regressive or expressive or reform or revolutionary (Rush & Denisoff 1971); nonviolent, quasiviolent, and violent (Cameron 1966). Roberts and Kloss (1979: 39) note the relationship between reform and revolution, and point out its complexity: "Sometimes reforms are used to prevent revolution; in other cases they have paved the way for deeply radical change. Many . . . have argued that most revolutionary movements, of necessity, shift to reformist goals after a time because of the natural inability of the masses of people to remain mobilized over time."

Movement classifications may also differ according to how the movement grew structurally. Those that developed from separate groups merging into one large organization are called centripetal. But those that grew from one central group spinning off new groups are centrifugal. Other structural differences refer to the nature of the organization and its governance. One such classification refers to segmentary, polycephalous, and reticulate movement structures (Gerlach 1983). The segmentary movement consists of a range of diverse groups that develop independently; the polycephalous type lacks a central leadership and has many competing leaders; the reticulate type has diverse groups organized into a network. These typical movement structures are seen by Gerlach as effective in producing social change and surviving in the face of institutional opposition. Survival itself has most recently been analyzed by Carl Milofsky (1988: 15), who suggests that structures are less important than other factors in predicting organizational survival. Specifically, he claims that neighborhood groups with strong ideologies are most likely to survive.

Stages or phases of movement development have long been studied by scholars in the field of social movements. These are referred to as the life cycle or the natural history of a movement. The usefulness of this type of analysis was noted by Turner and Killian (1957), who saw it as emphasizing process, permitting prediction, and allowing discovery. Other scholars have emphasized three additional methods of studying the development of a social movement: the cross-sectional method, seen from a variety of perspectives; the comparative method (Lang & Lang 1961); and the value-added approach (Smelser 1963). The value-added approach, in contrast to the natural history type of study, suggests not only a sequence of stages but also which of the prior stages are necessary conditions for the later ones. Three phases of movement development, according to Smelser, are the incipient phase, the phase of enthusiastic mobilization, and the phase of institutionalization.

The "careers" of social movements were analyzed by King (1956), who saw movements having four stages of development: social unrest, popularization, formal organization, and institutionalization. Two significant dimensions of change suggested by him are successive internal alterations and reciprocal relations toward the external society. King considered the purposes and consequences of social movements in terms of accidental influences, manifest and latent consequences, and social change.

Also using the concept of "careers," borrowed from Dawson & Gettys (1934), were Lang and Lang (1961), who saw the beginning phase of a movement as a period of unrest with an agitator as the typical leader. Then comes a period of popular excitement, in which the vision of a prophet or the objective defined by a reformer spreads by contagion. This is followed by a stage of formal organization, headed by an administrator, with the beginnings of a division of labor, formal criteria of membership, and so on. Finally comes the stage of institutionalization, when the movement—now bureaucratized—is represented by a statesman.

Lang and Lang saw social movements as creators of and responders to changes in social conditions. Turner and Killian (1957) considered both stability and change as conditions promoted by collective behavior. The new ideas of one period become the old ones of the next; thus, institutionalization combines human tendencies toward both routinization and ideological innovation. They noted that a movement may persist for some time, even with a decline. Loss of power, program, or membership may be followed by transformation, stabilization, and continued existence. Conditions that keep a movement alive include the desire of the leadership for maintenance of prestige, and the desire of the membership for continued participation gratification. They saw the conservatizing aspect of movements as universal. They suggested that any movement arises out of prevailing societal values, and is therefore a link to conventional values.

Most social movement scholars refer to the eventual institutionalization of a movement, signalling its transformation from a change-oriented organization to one that is either routinized and stable or dead. Some emphasize the oligarchic tendencies of movement organizations. All scholars see movements as linked to social change, but few have developed ways of analyzing the impact of social movements. This is because the concept of success or effectiveness presents such difficulties: "How is one to distinguish the creative and constructive elements of social movement(s)? Unless we play gods ourselves we cannot finally and definitively hand out the prizes at some kind of historical judgment day" (Wilkinson 1971: 152).

Here we are faced with the most difficult task of examination and interpretation, for success of an organization is traditionally measured in terms of goal realization, and goals themselves are often vague and diffused, as well as being both professed and operative. Likewise, effectiveness and efficiency are difficult to operationalize and even more difficult to interpret.

Etzioni and others have suggested that comparative analysis is a fruitful approach to use in analyzing success.[12] This would involve comparing performances in relation to those of similar organizations, rather than in terms of an ideal for the prototype of that organization. In this way, other issues are recognized besides goal attainment, and might include such indexes of success as productivity, strain absence, and flexibility. Success and effectiveness, then, can be analyzed in terms of factors other than just goal attainment.

Killian (1964) claimed that some movements leave little mark on society, but even those that die may have a great effect. The movement that fails may leave behind the seeds of another movement. He contended that success cannot be measured in terms of values being actually realized, since values have something of the nature of myths. One way, however, in which a social movement may contribute to social change is by forcing the established structure of society to come to terms with it and its values. Institutionalization may also symbolize success and may accompany acceptance of movement values. In the continuous formulation, revision, and reformulation of values and norms in the process of a movement's development, social change is produced.

Studying social movements, then, involves an examination of growth patterns or natural history or life cycle. We look for the external influences that are significant in the genesis and development of a movement. We can best understand a whole movement through studying two levels: the national organization, and the local level, with its movement organizations. Internal organizational features such as leadership, membership, ideology, and strategy are of importance in considering the development of a movement and its ultimate impact. We can consider the impact of a movement in terms of manifest and latent consequences, and we will see the movement itself as both a product and producer of social change. With this as a guide, we are now ready to consider the neighborhood stabilization movement.

The Neighborhood Stabilization Movement

Long before a national organization was formed, a few scattered local groups in different parts of the country were trying to maintain racial integration in their own neighborhoods.[13] This movement, then, is an excellent example of a centripetal type of growth. It was the local groups that formed the national group—National Neighbors—in 1969, a full twenty years after the earliest local group began (Chicago's Hyde Park-Kenwood Community Conference). In fact, as we will see, for some years most of the local groups did not even know that any others like themselves existed. This movement is a true grass-roots movement. Though it lacks a central controlling administrative organization, it is change-oriented, it does have organization, it has durability, and it is national in scope.

The specific movement of neighborhood stabilization is presented here as an offshoot of the general civil rights movement. As such, it is a reform movement rather than a revolutionary one, since it does not seek the total alteration of the economic or political system. It does, however, attempt to change the norms of racial separation in local communities. In that sense, and in view of the long history of racism in this country, it may be more revolutionary than at first seems evident. It uses combined methods of persuasion, coercion, and bargaining to achieve its goals.

I examine this movement through studying movement organizations on both the local level and the national level. The local level includes five detailed case studies, and ten much briefer profiles of urban (7) and suburban (3) efforts. These show the geographical scope and strategic diversity of the movement. On the local (case study) and national levels, I analyze six aspects of organizational development: the sociohistorical context, inception, structure, goals, program, and impact. I look at each of these, explained in greater detail below, during three phases of organizational development: mobilization, maturation, and institutionalization. This enables me to note changes and adaptations during different phases of each movement organization's existence. I did not know, however, which were the beginnings and ends of the phases of development for each MO until I had carefully studied the MO's history and changes over the years. Only then was I able to make a judgment as to when one phase had ended and another had begun. So the dates of the phases are different, of course, for each MO studied.

The sociohistorical context on the local level refers to the historical setting and founding of the city in which the neighborhood effort is located, the city's general demographic and economic profile, its history of urban renewal efforts, public housing programs and locations, school racial composition and desegregation efforts, and the general trends of race relations in the city. I chose these factors after careful study of the literature on race relations and urban development, because they are so relevant to the study neighborhood's efforts in maintaining racial integration.

In thinking of the sociohistorical background for this movement, I must here acknowledge the role played by the earlier formation of the fair housing movement in 1949. There is little question of the importance of this movement in nurturing local neighborhood integration groups.[14] Some sources have suggested that neighborhood stabilization groups preceded open housing groups, and indeed provided the impetus for their formation. It is a fact that stabilization of one area cannot be effective unless there is an open housing market in the entire community or region. But it is equally true that an open housing group cannot work effectively unless stabilization of integrated areas occurs. So they are two sides of the same coin, and regardless of which type of group forms first, each soon comes to recognize the necessity of the other.

I also must point out the important role played by fair housing developers and real estate practitioners who assisted in the creation of racially integrated communities. Morris Milgram has devoted his life to such development ventures, and Stuart Wallace has done the same in the real estate world.[15] These efforts are not, however, included in this analysis because they are of a different nature from the grass-roots type of social movement.

For structural and internal organizational aspects on both levels, I include membership requirements and recruitment efforts, representation of the target population, committee structures and purposes, governance, funding, and staffing. I examine these during each of three phases of organizational growth and development: mobilization, maturation, and institutionalization.

I also examine the goals and program for each MO through the three phases of organizational development. Here I am interested in any difference between stated goals and operational ones, between the stated goals and the actual results of the program carried out by the MO, and between the stated and operational goals at one time period versus another one throughout the three phases of organizational development. I was struck by the similarity of program efforts in each of the communities, long before they knew about each other through annual National Neighbors conferences. I should not have been surprised by this, however, since the same forces were at work in each community, generating many of the same human responses to them.

The impact of the MO, on the local level, is analyzed in terms of four factors: (1) the extent of racial integration maintenance, (2) quality maintenance, (3) sense of community, and (4) organizational influence, each of which is examined over time during the three phases of organizational development. On the national level, also, I analyze impact through a twofold study over time of the national MO's influence on its member groups and on national decision makers.

In this research covering the whole movement across the country, I found various types of neighborhood and organization combinations. From these I developed three analytical models: first, the live movement organization (MO) and the successfully maintained integrated neighborhood, which I am calling *Model A, Success*; second, the dead MO and the predominantly black neighborhood, which I call *Model B, Failure*; and third, the live MO and the neighborhood that is transitional or has become predominantly black, which I am calling *Model C, Conditional*.

My use of the term failure does not mean that this is no longer a viable neighborhood. I use the term in a double sense, however, to mean that the

MO did not succeed in achieving the goal of integration maintenance, and that it did not survive. The only example of the failure model that I offer is Hartford's Blue Hills and its MO. There are surely other examples of failure in this movement; I do not analyze them here.[16]

The term conditional, as in Akron's west side and four of the profiles across the country, refers to the fact that the MO still survives, even though its goal has not been attained. And this does not mean that the goal is forever beyond reach. What humans have wrought can be undone and altered. My somewhat more detailed analysis of Akron's conditional effort is justified, I think, because of the special nature of this model. It may represent the most typical movement model in this country to date, and it may show most clearly the interplay of institutional forces on the neighborhood effort in this movement.

My detailed examples of movement success are in the three cities of Indianapolis, Indiana; Rochester, New York; and Milwaukee, Wisconsin. I also point to success in three briefer urban profiles and all three suburban ones. I use the term success to mean that some measure of stable racial integration has been achieved in the community, and that the MO is still alive. In no way do I mean to imply, however, that this success is a permanent condition. The reason for the title of this book—A Fragile Movement—is precisely because I see any success as tentative. It could be quickly eroded, toppled, or wiped out at any time by any number of single or combined institutional decisions and forces.

Let us talk of numbers, now, as we must. Integration is a process, not a number. We know this, and yet the numbers are what count in people's perceptions. And perceptions are at the heart of this subject; they can and do make or break this movement. How many blacks? How many whites? And for how long? Let us consider a continuum of integration, ranging from slightly integrated to moderately and then substantially integrated. Numbers can be assigned to each level, relating these to the proportion of blacks in a whole city. These could then be found for any neighborhood, or census tract. For example, if a city had 22% black population, any neighborhood that had more or less than that proportion could be ranged on the integration continuum from below the city average to substantially above it. How far above it would indicate the degree of integration all the way up through substantially integrated to resegregated. Others have used similar approaches; still others have developed alternate measures and interpretations. Orfield (1984), for example, in his analysis of Chicago refers to integrated tracts, transition tracts, panic tracts, black tracts, and white tracts, each numerically defined and indicating some degree of process.[17]

In the case of a 22% black city average, as in Akron, using the above continuum it would be possible to refer to any neighborhood below 9% black as predominantly white, from 10–21% as slightly integrated, from 22–39% as moderately integrated, from 40–69% as substantially integrated, and from 70–100% as predominantly black or resegregated. This would be a continuum of five levels of integration; it could be applied to any neighborhood in any city, depending on the citywide average of percentage black. But this, of course, obscures so much of the underlying process.

I have used such numerical indicators when doing computer analyses of mortgage lending data, where I had to distinguish between black and white neighborhoods for analytical purposes. I have also used numbers when analyzing public housing and other types of housing and school segregation. I remain uneasy about numbers as applied to this movement, however, because of my preferred view of integration as a process. This view suggests that as long as both whites and blacks in relatively similar proportions are moving into a neighborhood, it is integrated. I am comfortable with this, and less comfortable with precise numbers, though I acknowledge that I must sometimes use them. "Tipping points" I do not include in this study, since there is no universal application of this concept.[18]

Then there is the question of stability. For how long are given racial proportions maintained? The federal government (HUD) has defined racial impaction as more than a 10% change in black population in a decade, or an area being more than 40% black. Others have developed alternate measures.[19] I use decades and rely on census tract data to determine stability trends in neighborhoods. But the numbers often mask much of the dynamics of neighborhood change.

In this book, when I refer to integration maintenance I am not using the term integration to necessarily mean cohesion or welding of groups. Rather, I use integration as a synonym for pluralism meaning two or more diverse groups living peacably together in a common territory and sometimes joining in common effort. The maintenance of integration—the preservation of diversity or pluralism—is seen throughout this study as achieved through choice-expanding programs, that is, those that broaden the living choices of both whites and blacks. Each of our examples shows how this can be done through a broad array of creative strategies. In no way should integration maintenance restrict or limit choice for anyone. However, the strategies for achieving integration maintenance are not always seen by others as choice-expanding. This is a major recurring controversial issue of this movement, as explained further in Chapter 9.

In addition to the detailed case studies of success, failure, and uncertainty, I also examine briefly several other typical MOs across the country to indicate the diversity and geographical scope of this movement. These briefer profiles include municipally funded suburban efforts, in contrast to the other urban neighborhood efforts in the heart of larger cities. Each of these could well have been a case study of noteworthy achievement, but space and time limitations bound me.

METHODOLOGY OF THIS STUDY

This book is based on field research and interviews, census data and documentary review, historical analysis, and some participant observation on both local and national levels.[20] William F. Whyte (1982) suggests that the study of social inventions—which movements are—involves major changes in research methods and theory development. Contrary to the traditional research approach, the study of social inventions begins with field observation. It is followed much later by research design, and ends with an evaluation of the social invention. In this evaluation, we need to search for the underlying principles of social dynamics causing social change, Whyte claims, and we need to use these insights to help solve human problems. I have tried to apply some of his wisdom here.

Knowing that Akron would be one of the local efforts studied in depth, I chose the four other case study communities so that they would be comparable to Akron. The four other case study neighborhoods and their organizations were selected according to six criteria based on comparability of age, continuity of movement effort, size of community, type of community, region, and purpose. Thus they all represent long-standing neighborhood stabilization groups in medium-sized cities in Northern or Midwestern industrial areas, whose original purpose was stabilization as here defined. They were from fourteen to twenty-eight years old at the time of my initial field visit in 1984, and all were founding members in 1970 of National Neighbors—the only national organization devoted solely to neighborhood stabilization.

During the spring and summer of 1984, I made four field visits to the neighborhood study sites in Indianapolis, Rochester, Milwaukee, and Hartford. I had never been to three of these cities before: Milwaukee I had visited once briefly as a guest speaker. What I had learned in Akron and in other research the previous twenty years helped me to search quickly and adequately in new places. Each visit lasted one week and was preceded by letters and phone calls to past and current organizational leaders in each community. Names were obtained from the office of National Neighbors in Washington, D.C., which sent letters to the local leaders informing them of the purpose of the visit.

During each field visit, I taped interviews with organizational and community leaders and residents, past and current. I also took notes on some shorter, spontaneous interviews.[21] Interviews were from one to three hours long. I used the same open-ended interview schedule for each one, which is reproduced in Appendix B. Snowball techniques were used to secure additional names of salient respondents.[22]

Primary historical materials were collected in each study community, including MO newsletters, correspondence, minutes of meetings, annual reports, brochures and other printed material. In addition, visits were made to local governmental planning departments to secure census data, school data, and other pertinent information concerning the city and its neighborhoods. Finally, many hours were spent in the library of the local newspaper securing copies of newspaper articles about the neighborhood, its organization, and the city's development over the past two decades. I took photos of the study neighborhood, showing the condition of streets, housing, business district, and facilities in each area.

The visit to Hartford posed many problems in record collection, since the local organization was not functioning any longer and earlier records had been mislaid or destroyed. Just when I thought I had located an important collection of organizational materials in a former resident's basement, I found out that the new owners had thrown them away as trash.

I wrote to people who had left the area and moved out of state, and finally located someone who had the needed early materials and was able to send them to me. I am indebted to Professor William Brayfield, professor of history at the University of Hartford, who shipped to me two large cartons of valuable materials. And I am most grateful to Margaret and William Worthington, who gave me names and addresses of former BHCA leaders and also told me about Vincent Bolduc's earlier dissertation relating to BHCA and Blue Hills. I then had to find out how to locate him, in order to find out the name of the dissertation. All this eventually happened, but it took months.

I accumulated forty tapes of interviews, each ninety minutes long. This required six to eight hours of transcription for each hour of tape. I arranged for the transcriptions to be made by two transcribing classes of students at a local community college. These were done during the two semesters of 1984–85, and resulted in 2,100 pages of unedited transcripts.

Several respondents in each community received my first draft of the chapter about their city and neighborhood. I sent these so that I could learn of any errors of fact that I might have made, to get some early feedback before I proceeded. Responses varied from simple notes saying, "Sounds good," "You captured us," to long essays about how and why certain events took place, with only two disagreeing with my interpretations and conclusions.

I have changed all names of local respondents, to preserve their privacy.[23] I have also changed my own name as a participant in Akron's MO. On the national level, I have retained the actual names of nationally known public figures. All quotes are, however, strictly authentic in the actual words of the respondents, as they spoke them. Any judgments, interpretations, and conclusions are my own, unless noted otherwise.

On the national level, I also analyze the MO—National Neighbors—through a study over time of their records, correspondence, reports, board minutes, and newsletters. In addition, I used interviews and annual conference reports and records to round out my information.

I raise two central questions in this sociohistorical analysis of the neighborhood stabilization movement: (1) can racially integrated neighborhoods remain integrated? and (2) can we identify the factors that lead to success or failure in maintaining racial integration? I answer, with qualifications, "Yes," to both questions. I am using comparative in-depth examples of success and failure in movement development and maturation in multiple U.S. neighborhoods, but I realize full well that there is so much more that I could have done. Others will, I hope, continue this exploration and broaden it.

NOTES

1. How long is long? The concept of duration, from social movements literature, suggests only that a movement endures beyond a single point in time. This distinguishes a movement from mere collective behavior, which not all scholars do (Saltman 1978, ch. 1).

2. Two most dramatic examples of this return to oppression are laws that made it a crime for black and white persons to look out of the same window at the same time, and that made it a crime for storage textbooks used by white children to touch the textbooks used by black children (Woodward 1963: 84–89).

3. Among the many scholars presenting evidence supporting this view are J. Farley 1987; Darden 1987; Taeuber and Taeuber 1965, 1979; Willie 1979; HUD 1979; Kain & Quigley 1975; Pettigrew 1975.

4. Abrams (1965: 61–62) cites discriminatory sections of FHA manuals.

5. Public housing policies and practices and VA and FHA loans were also notoriously racially discriminatory and segregative.

6. This is based on four homeseeking visits.

7. Among those holding this view are Miller 1965; Darden 1987; J. Farley 1987; Taeuber and Taeuber 1965, 1979; and Willie 1979.

8. Noel & Wertheim 1987; Tobin 1987; Goering 1986; R. Farley 1984, and many others confirm this.

9. I and others (Freeman 1983: 10) date this from 1955, with Rosa Parks's defiance of bus segregation in Montgomery, Alabama.

10. The chronology of events from 1950 to 1964 is adapted from Bennett 1966 (398–412). From 1964 to 1977, events are adapted from *Encyclopedia News Annuals* and *Encyclopedia Britannica Book of the Year*. After 1977, major sources include Hochschild 1984; Farley 1982; Willie 1979; and Wilson 1978.

11. This has been noted in such daily publications as the *New York Times*, and by others: Anti-Defamation League special reports, the National Institute Against Prejudice and Violence, and the newsletter of People for the American Way. A 1986 Center for Democratic Renewal report cites 2,919 racially motivated incidents between 1980 and 1986.

12. Among these are organization scholars Marvin Olson (1989), John Campbell (1976), Peter Rossi (1972), and fieldwork scholars William F. Whyte (1984) and Robert Yin (1984).

13. Chicago's Hyde Park-Kenwood Community Conference is the first local group I know of; it was organized in 1949. By 1965, the first movement newsletter appeared, the *National Newsletter for Interracial Communities*, which linked a few other scattered groups.

14. *Trends in Housing*, a major fair housing movement publication of the NCDH, devoted an early issue to "The Challenge of the Changing Neighborhood" (Jan.–Feb. 1960) and a later one to "Keeping Integration" (Nov.–Dec. 1965). The NCDH also published a significant article on maintaining stable integration in their *Fair Housing Handbook* (1963).

15. OPEN was founded by Milgram and James Farmer to provide mortgage incentives for integrative moves. Milgram was one of the first integrated real estate developers in the country, who hired Wallace as an early sales employee. Wallace later founded Fair

Housing Inc. in Cleveland, the first such professional real estate agency there and possibly anywhere (See Milgram 1977).

16. Several suburban efforts that failed to preserve integration but still have organized groups are New Rochelle, New York; Forest Park, Illinois; and Maywood, Illinois. In each of these, however, municipal support did not begin until the communities were already substantially integrated. These would all be examples of Model C (Conditional). The only suburban effort that is a failure (black neighborhood, nonsurviving MO) that I know of is Inglewood, California. As for city neighborhood MO efforts, there must be many more than Hartford's that did not survive, but I do not know of them, nor does NN. This would be an important research effort to pursue.

17. Integrated tracts, according to this definition, must have had at least 5% black or Hispanic population in 1970, but not more than 50%. The leading minority group cannot have increased by more than 20% during the 1970s, and there cannot have been more than 60% combined black and Hispanic population in 1980 (Orfield et al. 1984: 15). Additional concepts of integration are found in Galster 1987; Obermanns 1980; Taub et al. 1984; Helper 1979; and Bradburn et al. 1971.

18. John Goering has most recently testified that the "tipping" phenomenon in the racial transition of neighborhoods is extremely complex and influenced by many variables; thus, "it is incorrect to postulate an iron law of demographic change as the key to the process of racial transition" (Affidavit, Starrett City vs. U.S.A., 1986; 1978). Others who do use the tipping point concept are Clark 1987; Schelling, 1972.

19. See Orfield et al. 1984.

20. I had few guidelines on how to study a social movement when I first developed a methodology for analyzing the fair housing movement more than ten years ago (Saltman 1971, ch. 1; 1978, ch. 2). I was gratified to find that others have made use of this methodology, and acknowledged it (Freeman 1975). But the major guideline for studying both of these movements—fair housing and neighborhood stabilization—came from my own involvement in these movements, which helped me know what to look for. That involvement included several changing roles over the years: local founder, board member, committee member, sociologist, consultant, national Board member, and, always, participant observer.

21. Some interviews were unplanned, such as the one during the street fair in Rochester where I learned much from an MO member I bumped into, and another one in Rochester when I was walking down the street and stopped to talk to someone cutting hedges who turned out to be an ex-member of the MO.

22. Snowball techniques refer to nonprobability samples conducted in stages. In the first stage a few persons having the requisite characteristics are identified and interviewed. These persons are used as informants to identify others who qualify for inclusion in the sample. The second stage involves interviewing those persons, who in turn lead to still more persons who can be interviewed in the third stage, and so on (Bailey 1978).

23. A few local names are retained if they are public figures or their statements are a matter of public record.

Part II

THE COMMUNITY LEVEL

MODEL A: SUCCESS

2

INDIANAPOLIS: BUTLER-TARKINGTON NEIGHBORHOOD ASSOCIATION

"Sometimes an irritant—but always a force to be reckoned with"

"It was like you were vigilantes with the zoning changes. . . . You had to be on your toes every minute"

"I would say we've achieved our original goal"

SOCIOHISTORICAL CONTEXT

We will understand the study neighborhood and its Association better if we know something of the city and its sociohistorical past concerning race relations. Indianapolis is the capital of Indiana, the seat of Marion County, and the largest city in the state, with almost 500,000 people, of whom 22% are black. Often called "the crossroads of America" because so many lines of nationwide traffic intersect in the city, Indianapolis is a manufacturing and banking center. Located 180 miles from Chicago and 100 miles from Cincinnati, it ranks twenty-sixth in population among U.S. cities. It is the home of Butler University, Indiana

All chapter quotes are from transcripts of taped interviews, conducted in Indianapolis during March 17–23, 1984, unless otherwise noted.

University–Purdue combined regional campuses, the John Herron Art Museum, the Indianapolis Motor Speedway, the Indianapolis Convention Center, Botanical Gardens, Bush Stadium, and the world's largest Children's Museum.

An orange-covered booklet, prepared by the city, refers to Indianapolis as "A City of Dynamic Neighborhoods." The booklet features sixteen city neighborhoods, including the Butler-Tarkington study neighborhood, each served by a neighborhood association. On its cover is this nostalgic message: "Neighborhoods. . . . They're what we grew up in. Think back. Your neighborhood was people . . . friends. And it was more. It was where you built your hopes and dreamed your dreams. It was a place to feel secure . . . to feel at home. . . . Indianapolis."

Ben Allendale, university professor and long-time resident of the Butler-Tarkington (BT) neighborhood, described Indianapolis as "a kind of overgrown village . . . there is a rural ideology that's permeated this state and town. . . . You do your own thing with your neighbors, your immediate community, but you don't necessarily organize on a citywide basis unless you're driven to it."

Until the late 1840s Indianapolis remained a small town, important only as the seat of the state government. It did not acquire the legal status of a city until 1847, when the Madison and Indianapolis Railroad was completed. Until then, business in the city had been almost entirely local, with the entire cost of city government only $7,554. Ten years later, annual expenses were up to $80,172, and by 1870, city expenses were $405,016 (Thornbrough 1965).

George Sackman, city official, said: "I think basically you're talking about a very conservative Midwestern community where there are racial problems . . . you don't have riots in the streets, but there are many minorities who still feel very strongly that they are in a city that is run by white people who pull things off and leave blacks out." Indianapolis's past race relations provides the background for this observation.

Though nearly all churches in the city supported the North in the Civil War and proclaimed slavery a sin, there was almost total segregation in those churches after the war. Though the state of Indiana was the first to establish free public schools, school laws before 1869 expressly stated that public schools were open to white children only. The state supreme court had ruled that black children could not attend public school with white children, even if they paid their own tuition. Black children were educated in private schools operated by blacks themselves with the help of some white religious groups, especially Quakers. Though Governor Oliver P. Morton and his successor strongly urged legislation to provide public schooling for blacks, as did the state teachers association and the state superintendent, traditional white supremacy arguments prevented this until 1869.

In 1869, a state act was passed requiring separate schools for blacks "where their numbers were large enough to justify such a school." By 1873 all counties in the state had separate schools, and in 1877 the law was amended to allow "colored children to attend school with white children where there were no separate schools." So the law permitted segregation, but no longer made it mandatory. By 1908 there were eight black high schools in the southern part of the state, which were added on as "departments" to existing elementary schools. In 1916, there were seventy-six black men and 168 black women employed as teachers in black schools throughout the state.

The proportion of blacks in Indianapolis rose during this time from 8% in 1880 to 11% in 1920, most having come there after the Civil War from Kentucky and other parts of the South. This was one of the highest ratios in the major Northern cities of the United States at that time (Phillips 1968). Indianapolis then had 300,000 people and was viewed as "a somewhat blurry but authentic mirror of Hoosierdom at large" (Madison 1982). A 1931 issue of *American Magazine* chose Indianapolis as the typical city in which to find the typical American family. The *Indianapolis News* agreed, pointing to the large native-born population, central location, high proportion of home ownership, and so on. The belief that Hoosiers were generally alike, that they avoided extremes, that they held on to past traditions, that they represented what was best about America—all this was a theme running through the history of the state from 1920 to 1945. "This Indianapolis idea affected nearly every feature of public life in the state even while the sentiments and realities on which it was based were challenged and changed" (Madison 1982).

Some of the challenges and changes that belied the "best of America" theme were the rise of the Ku Klux Klan in the 1920s, the changing technology of agriculture, the devastation of the Depression, and the social upheaval of World War II. The growing number of blacks was also one of the changes and challenges. During the 1920s the state's black population increased by 39%, compared to a 9% increase in white population. By 1930, blacks were 12% of Indiana's population and the KKK reached its peak of support in that state.

The state's and the Hoosier City's reputation for friendliness, neighborliness and tolerance did not often extend to blacks. Racism and segregation were common experiences for most blacks in Indiana. Discrimination was found in every facet of life in the state, intensifying after World War I with further growth in the black population. "Theatres, parks, cemeteries, restaurants, hotels, beaches, pools, orphans' homes, hospitals, newspaper society columns, the state militia and other places and institutions in many Indiana towns and cities excluded blacks or assigned them separate places" (Madison 1982). In larger cities blacks created their own institutions, such as the Senate Avenue YMCA in Indianapolis.

During the early 1920s, as the number of blacks in Indianapolis continued to increase, frightened whites increased their demands for segregation in the schools. In late 1922 the school board proposed that a new high school be built for blacks, who opposed such segregation and filed suit against the school board. They lost the suit, the school was built, and in 1927 the school board announced that every black high school pupil in Indianapolis had to attend that school. This policy lasted until 1949, when the state passed a desegregation law. One fight blacks did win was changing the name of the high school from Jefferson to Crispus Attucks, which they argued was more appropriate for an all-black school.

Segregated housing in Indianapolis was reinforced in 1926 by the passage of an ordinance prohibiting blacks from moving into white neighborhoods without the written consent of a majority of neighborhood residents. After the local NAACP battled it in court, the ordinance was declared unconstitutional. Though described as "the only significant legal victory against segregation in the state during the 1920s," this did little to reverse existing housing segregation. In 1937, one of the first public housing projects for blacks in the country was built on Indiana Avenue, in the heart of the city's major black neighborhood. With federal funds, seven additional new housing projects were later built—all segregated—located in all-black neighborhoods in the northwest part of the city. This was not far from the Butler-Tarkington neighborhood, which contained the governor's mansion.

World War II brought some changes in race relations to Indianapolis. Before 1941, nearly all skilled jobs were closed to blacks. But during the war, they were needed as workers, and this prompted the formation of the Indiana Plan of Bi-racial Cooperation in 1942. Though this plan opened up some employment opportunities for blacks, housing opportunities remained blocked. When urban renewal began to clear hundreds of acres of land with black-occupied homes on it, their displacement path was clearly marked—northward.

Among the massive urban renewal projects in Indianapolis that contributed to black displacement was a new university complex on the west side, merging Indiana University and Purdue University's regional campuses (IUPU). The IUPU complex contained a medical center, housing the largest medical school in the country, a dental school, and a nursing school; the largest law school in the state; an art school; the oldest physical education school in the country; a social work school; and an undergraduate college with schools of business, engineering, and physical sciences. The 14,000 students on this extensive campus took the place of thousands of black households, who pushed northward in their search for housing. As university professor Ben Allendale recalled: "When we came here in 1961 the med center was buying up land all around there—it was black people living there and they'd been moving north in this area steadily. . . . Some of their housing had all been torn down—when we came here there were several square blocks of what had been largely black populated areas."

Other urban renewal projects that displaced additional thousands of black households were a block-long federal building, a 24-million-dollar convention and exposition center covering two whole city blocks, a new bridge, and seven spokes of wide concrete highways. Mary Gowen, long a resident of B-T, remembered one of the highways: "The highway took the 31st Street area . . . people were displaced, it was a black neighborhood, very lovely . . . from Clifton Ave. and Thirty-first Street . . . also back of the General Hospital and IUPU."

Racial discrimination in Indianapolis's housing was still pronounced in 1978, when the nationwide HUD audit tested the equality of housing opportunities (HUD 1979a). The audit coordinator for the area including Indianapolis said, "We found considerable discrimination in Indianapolis, with blacks treated less favorably than whites 15 out of 30 times when seeking apartments, and 37 out of 50 times when seeking homes to buy" (*Courier-Journal*, Lexington, Kentucky, April 20, 1978). In a more recent interview, the coordinator said: "Some of the more flagrant discrimination acts occurred in Indianapolis. . . . I found here the greatest gap between reality and perception. The audit took more time there than anywhere else in my region because the white coordinator was not sensitive to the black tester's needs. She was defensive about her findings. Finally, we had to import testers from Fort Wayne to finish the survey" (phone interview, C. Schrupp, April 4, 1984).

One important governmental change in the Indianapolis area, with far-reaching consequences for blacks and our study neighborhood, was the 1969 consolidation of the city and country governments into "Uni-Gov." This was a bold experiment in municipal government that resulted in Indianapolis's rise in city size ranks in the 1970 census from twenty-sixth to twelfth in the nation. The unit is governed by a mayor and city-county council of twenty-nine members, four elected at-large, the others elected from twenty-five council districts. This eliminates the usual city and county duplication and overlapping of services, departments, and boards, which are now consolidated into six administrative departments.

Originally, Uni-Gov did not provide for a metropolitan police force, fire department, or school district. A historic, successful lawsuit in 1971 challenged the omission of the schools from this plan, with significant consequences for the maintenance of neighborhood integration in Indianapolis. First filed in 1968 by the NAACP and the Department of Justice, the complaint was later revised to cite the location of Indianapolis's public housing projects as also contributing to school segregation in the city.

Ultimately, after thirteen years of protracted legal struggle, both the schools and public housing projects were ordered to desegregate and to disperse throughout the county. This metropolitan remedy had significant and positive consequences for the maintenance of racial pluralism in Indianapolis's neighborhoods. But before and during the legal struggle for desegregation, black displacement by urban renewal continued. Among the thousands of displaced blacks pushing northward were a few who moved to the bottom section of the Butler-Tarkington neighborhood.

INCEPTION

The first black families who moved to the all-white Butler-Tarkington neighborhood as a result of urban renewal were not well received. Bertha Moore, longtime black supporter and leader of the neighborhood association, said: "This I knew just from history—that some black families were not received well. There were even cross-burnings and negative things that were being done when the people moved in. . . . So the Butler-Tarkington Neighborhood Association (BTNA) was formed to make a smooth transition—to make the newcomers feel welcome and to try to establish a bridge between the two races and between the old settlers and the newcomers."

Founded in 1956, the BTNA still exists today, retaining their original goal. That goal, as stated in their constitution, was "to achieve an ideal racially integrated, beautiful neighborhood in that part of Indianapolis north of 38th Street, west of Meridian Street, south of 56th Street, and east of Route 421 and the Water Company Canal, whichever is the farthest east." By the time this purpose was formally embodied in a constitution, however, the organization had already existed for over eleven years.

Four families—two black and two white—are considered the founders of the organization, meeting together in the early spring of 1956 in one of their homes. An Earlham College professor served as advisor and also recruited several students to assist the fledgling committee during its first two years. When they first met to consider forming an organization, the founders realized the difficulties of having a neighborhood association devoted to the daring concept of interracial living. This was daring in 1956 anywhere in the United States, and was especially daring in Indianapolis, where segregated living had long prevailed in a town that considered itself Southern.

The four founding families of the BTNA at first met in response to some negative white reactions to the increase of black residents in their neighborhood. Their second meeting, however, was in response to a nonracial neighborhood issue requiring immediate action. The one park in their area, Tarkington Park, neglected for some time, was threatened by a proposed conversion to a parking lot for adjacent businesses. This prompted the group of four families to organize immediately as the Butler-Tarkington Neighborhood Committee, with their first focus of action the retention of Tarkington Park. They drafted and circulated a petition with 800 signatures to the park board asking that the park be retained as a playground. The park board responded positively, and was eventually persuaded by the new committee to clean and develop the park as a playground, to equip it, and finally to furnish staff supervision for the playground. This first victory—one of many over the next twenty-eight years—set the pattern for the organization, which began to meet monthly and widen its activities.

The group established committees to study zoning enforcement, urban planning and development, and other urban issues relevant to the neighborhood. One of these issues concerned panic selling of homes and methods of preventing it. Early proposals for dealing with this problem included the development of block groups to encourage residents to remain calm in the face of "natural Negro residential expansion" (*Indianapolis Star*, June 17, 1958). The block group formation was a controversial issue among black residents, who responded first with silent disapproval, then with open antagonism. This sounded too much like other black groups they had known, which were designed to "keep Negroes out." Also, black participants were seen as Uncle Toms by some of their black friends because of their interracial associations with the new neighborhood committee. These cross pressures made black participants wary and uncertain about the motives of the new group.

Despite these difficulties, the group of twenty to thirty residents continued to meet monthly, established their first steering committee, and planned their first public meeting for June 1958. The first major expense of the group was twenty dollars to mail the letters announcing the public meeting. Held on June 8, 1958, the meeting drew over one hundred people who came to hear a speaker from the Metropolitan Planning Commission talk about urban planning. The first news article about BTNA and their meeting referred to it as "a new interracial group whose purpose was to improve and maintain the neighborhood between 38th and 52nd Streets and Route 421 and Illinois" (*Indianapolis Star*, June 17, 1958).

Despite this success, the issue of block groups continued to divide the committee, and the group discontinued its meetings over the summer of 1958. Many thought the committee had disbanded. But in the fall of 1958, a few members began to renew their meetings—without the original founders. New officers were elected and the group slowly rebuilt its organization, though attendance was sparse—as few as ten per meeting. Gradually the group enlarged. The statement of purpose was reevaluated and retained intact. New committees were formed; study groups presented information on programs from other cities, and slowly the organization became reestablished around the issues they discussed with increasing vigor. Some of these issues were: "How to welcome new neighbors, how to maintain constructive relations with neighbors who were not used to home ownership, how to cope with juvenile delinquency . . . no complete answers were found" (BTNA history 1968).

Attendance at meetings grew to fifty to eighty persons, and by the summer of 1959 a second public meeting was held, articles of incorporation were developed, and dues were established (one dollar per member). The first newsletter was published in 1960. At that time, the BTN Committee officially became the BTNA. One year later, BTNA was incorporated and the neighborhood's northern boundary was extended two blocks to 54th Street. Only one other change in their boundaries occurred in 1965, with another two-block northern extension, to 56th Street.

STRUCTURE

From 1960 on, the heart of the organization was its committees. The earliest ones were: zoning, municipal services, recreation, public information, program, membership, finance, and hospitality. These changed over time in response to changing issues and needs. Two committees added very early—by 1963— were housing and education, followed by long-range planning. Later, the zoning and municipal services committees were combined into a conservation committee.

These remained the basic functioning units of the organization throughout its history. Their charge was "to work together on any problem facing residents of the area, to develop procedures for checking on zoning law violations, and to assure the maintenance of proper municipal services and recreational facilities" (constitution, 1967).

The policies of the organization were set by a board of directors (changed in 1973 to "managers"), consisting of six officers and all committee chairs, which were appointed by the president with the approval of the board. The officers were elected annually by the members at a spring or summer meeting. Board meetings were held monthly in neighborhood churches or other facilities, and were open to all members, as were committee meetings. All meetings were announced in the association's newsletter published ten times a year.

A one-page constitution was approved in 1967 by both board and membership. An earlier draft of this constitution (March 27, 1967) shows that very few changes were made. One change, however, revealed some inner conflict and a potential source of future difficulties which did, in fact, later surface. In the draft preamble, BTNA was referred to as "a group of persons interested in achieving an ideal racially integrated beautiful middle-class neighborhood." The words "middle-class" were first inserted, and then removed, suggesting some differences of opinion concerning the actual status of the neighborhood, as well as the image projected by this phrase.

Related to this is an important change that occurred in 1972 in the method of electing board members. The BTNA, already sixteen years old, actively sought greater geographical representation of the area by having board members elected from specific neighborhood areas, so that the board would reflect more closely the actual economic and racial composition of the entire area. However, this remained an elusive goal and as hard as they tried, they were never able to get enough participation from the southern black portion of the area.

The annual membership drive was usually door-to-door, involving hundreds of volunteer workers recruited as block representatives. These block workers were specifically assigned to their block for the purpose of soliciting contributions from residents of the block. The BTNA area was divided into eleven neighborhoods, with a coordinator for each. This drive required months of planning and a few weeks of execution.

The BTNA remained a volunteer organization throughout their existence, with no staff and no external funding. Occasional part-time staffing did occur, but was short-term. Some of the part-time staff was through student aid from nearby universities, and some other staffing occurred through a small foundation grant for a youth recreational program in the schools. But essentially BTNA was totally volunteer, unfunded and unstaffed, operating through their board and committees. They had no office until September 1970, when a room was donated by one of the churches in the area. Once the office was established, volunteer help was sought to answer the phone, keep records, and so forth. This is when part-time student aid began to be used.

Over the years, the need grew for a coordinator or executive director, but such staffing was never obtained. Though occasional attempts were made to secure outside funding for this purpose, such funds were never granted. The minutes of one meeting ended wistfully with: "The Board was asked to consider the great need for a salaried Executive Secretary in a BTNA central office in the future" (minutes, Oct. 5, 1965). Again the following month, the minutes of a general meeting referred to "current plans to try to finance and obtain the service of a full time or part time executive director" (November 23, 1965). A report to the board from the finance committee the following month indicated that they had met to discuss the development of a grant proposal to foundations "for the purpose of employing professional staff to work under the direction of the board and its various committees."

The need for a paid executive continues to be reflected in the 1967 constitution, which contained a clause about it.

The expressed need for a paid director or coordinator continued until 1970: "We are waiting to obtain a $15,000 grant to fund an Executive Director and office" (financial committee report, Aug. 1970). Such a grant never came, and this contributed to a rising sense of frustration among some in the group. Others were pleased to avoid the bureaucracy and relinquishment of control associated with paid staff.

The exasperation and impatience of some of the board members is revealed in minutes concerning the development of a brochure. Some of the members could not understand why it was taking so long to get the brochure together: "Mrs. E probably voiced the sentiment of most board members when she said that a brochure has been under discussion for so many years that the pressing need is to get *something out now*" (minutes, March 1, 1966). How long it takes volunteers to do anything, and how very slowly things progress!

We have noted that in 1972 an important change occurred in their system of electing board members. They were to be elected from specific neighborhood areas, so that the board would reflect more closely the actual economic and racial composition of the entire area.

The change in board structure may have been generated by growing internal and external criticism of the association, as the minutes of board meetings show from 1970 to 1972. For example, a suggestion was made that "membership meetings might be held less frequently, with more emphasis on attendance at the meetings" (minutes, Sept. 28, 1970). Apparently, interest was waning and not many people turned out for the general meetings.

The least interest and participation seemed to be from the southern section of the BTNA area, which was all-black. A report on the membership drive indicated that twenty blocks had no workers, and these were mostly in the southern section. Further internal awareness of inadequacy: "Some block clubs are springing up in the area, apparently to cope with local problems. This would indicate that BTNA has not reached out effectively enough to the people in these areas. We should study how we can be of service" (minutes, Nov. 2, 1970). One board member, who was the public relations chair at the time, also expressed her concerns: "I am concerned about the image this Board creates. I believe that participation—real grass-roots participation—correlates with image and . . . such participation is lacking, especially in the southern part of the neighborhood. I wonder if part of the problem is that we turn off a lot of people by subtly telling them that we are better than they are. . . . What is communicated to someone without the right credentials who wants to become active?" (minutes, May 8, 1970).

Internal criticism peaked in May 1970, when two student workers presented their evaluation of BTNA to the entire board. The evaluation was based on their observations while working with the organization from October 1969 to May 1970. First they praised the organization for moving "from nonexistence to a thirteen-year-old well organized association . . . with a substantial amount of reputational and actual power in the city and county" (evaluation, May 8, 1970). They acknowledged the "wide range of human and economic resources of the residents," and the "dedicated hardworking people who keep the organization alive and viable." Then they discussed the goals of the organization, noting that "the existence of BTNA is a goal in and of itself . . . fostering representation, communication and participation" in a decision-making process that affected their lives and neighborhoods. They cautioned that "specification goals must be fitted into this structure and philosophy, and not vice-versa." And they urged continuous expansion of resources, "human and otherwise," rather than just relying on what was readily available.

Then they singled out for deeper analysis two committees with easily identifiable goals: the conservation committee and the housing committee. Referring to the conservation committee, they raised these questions: is its purpose to conserve, to slow deterioration, or to improve the neighborhood? What is it that the committee is supposed to conserve? They recommended an examination of its goals, with specific definitions, and a priority listing. Then they examined the housing (and integration) committee's stated goal of "achieving a beautiful and integrated neighborhood." They noted that since the origin of BTNA, portions of the area had changed from a predominantly white neighborhood to a predominantly black one. The students raised these questions: can the now-minority whites learn how to live as a minority, and can the blacks learn how to live as a majority and assume the major leadership role? "Is it not the responsibility of the committee to see that this process occurs? Do the majority now want integration? Is the neighborhood really integrated? What of the north-south division?" (evaluation, May 1970).

The searching critique then addressed the issue of change and flexibility. The students observed that the BTNA was slowly moving from a volunteer organization to a service organization, with many of its services becoming contractual and needing a paid director; they saw this as a sign of growth and progress. But they also saw in these changes the need for change in the organization's structure. Especially they referred to the need for the structure to be adequately representative: "The membership must consist of all segments and groups of the neighborhood." Also, the institutional members—businesses, churches, schools, the university, and so on—needed to be more actively involved, with increased communication. Board roles and responsibilities needed clearer delineation. As BTNA moved toward becoming a service type of organization, contractual agreements might be necessary. This would require structural provisions for making legitimate requests, demands, and agreements.

Five suggestions were offered for the board's consideration: training sessions for organizational participants; increased use of ad hoc committees for specific tasks and issues; establishment of a block organization system to foster communication and broader representation; employment of an executive director skilled in community and neighborhood organization; and supporting legislative measures giving neighborhood groups political authority.

Serious board discussion followed this evaluation. Members raised questions about the mechanics of block organization. Existing block clubs were not as effective as they could be. How could this be improved? But the most critical question concerned the inadequate representation of residents on the board, at meetings, and in the organization generally—especially those from the all-black southern sections of the area. Why was this so? One response was that the BTNA "had become viewed as an elite group, so many people are reluctant to participate." Two other views: BTNA "cannot do much for the southern end," and "BTNA has not extended itself sufficiently to recruit the non-participants" (minutes, May 8, 1970).

Also raised was the question of BTNA's effectiveness in dealing with crises over the years. Board members noted that many of the problems were the same as those that faced the organization twelve or thirteen years ago, when they first started. They recalled that the BTNA had to contend with a series of crises "from its very inception." Maybe BTNA had not been as persistent as it could have been: "People often talked but did not accomplish." Improvement of follow-up was seen as necessary: "seeing that a matter is not dropped until it has been settled." The need for a director was again voiced and seen as vital for coordinating block organization and recreational programs for youth.

Finally, the board developed a list of five priorities: hiring a coordinator or executive director; organizing an effective block structure; obtaining more adequate representation; acquiring a centrally located neighborhood facility; and support of Minigov—a proposed new city political structure giving increased authority to neighborhood groups. Ranking of these was left for another time. Though the first two goals were not achieved, the third was earnestly attempted and the last two were obtained. The third goal—more adequate representation—was sought through the change in the board member elections. Despite this change, however, the goal of increasing participation from the southern black portion of the area was ever sought and not achieved throughout BTNA's existence.

At the same time that the provocative student evaluation was presented, the public relations chair also offered a critique of the BTNA board and organization. Her criticism focused on the elitist image of the board in the community. She referred to the "legalistic structure of the organization . . . committees, board, motions, importance of word arrangements in innumerable statements (such as this!) . . . more and more people have had it with traditional structures" (minutes, May 8, 1970).

She raised the question of BTNA's effectiveness:

Does BTNA do anything? What has been accomplished for the schools? For youth? What is wrong with "Lighted Schools" [the after-school recreation program sponsored by BTNA]? We have the resources and seem unable to manage them. . . . How effective is BTNA in coping with the downtown bureaucracy? We do put on public meetings, halfheartedly. We scramble to get a program together monthly which may or may not be any good—the important thing is to have a program for the members. And a few faithful people come every month to these showcases of something. How many Board members bother to come? . . . The outstanding characteristic of BTNA is that we are loathe to change . . . our slowness to change is what newcomers notice—and part of it is because of the ponderousness of the structure of BTNA. Also we seem uneasy about taking a chance—about being responsible for something which might fail. Better nothing than failure. . . . The rest of the world is changing—stability will never return—if we don't keep up, we are lost. (minutes, May 8, 1970)

We must recall that 1970 was a difficult time for all groups devoted to racial integration across the country—it was the peak of black separatism.

Finally, she spoke of the need for more social rather than work-related activities:

We must become proficient at building personal relationships with people who are quite different from us. We will have to change ourselves, both individually and as an organization, before such relationships will be possible. . . . The immediate output of a committee is not as important as building personal relationships. Nor are a few triumphs over the downtown bureaucracy as important in the long run. They will be meaningless if we cannot get along together, trusting each other enough to be honest, ultimately loving each other. Integrated neighborhoods such as ours are laboratories for inter-group relations. . . . If we can't make it, can anyone?" (minutes, May 8, 1970).

They did make it, but as we will see, their successful survival was due more to external than internal factors.

The BTNA's development over the years is revealed in a review of the changes in memberships and financial assets. The articles of incorporation, drawn up in 1959, called for dues of one dollar for each member. This was largely used for mailing costs, with other operating income coming from additional voluntary donations. By the fall of 1961, there were sixty paid members, with an increase to 245 just three months later after a public meeting. A 1962 mail solicitation for dues resulted in contributions of $148, but the BTNA budget for that year called for $550 in contributions and $200 in dues. By June 1962 membership went up to 335, and increased to 407 by October 1963. One year later the membership figure was 480. These figures represented households rather than individuals, so the actual count of paid members was higher. In 1965, BTNA reported $2,285.27 in receipts from members, of whom 191 were new and 315 were renewals (BTNA history, 1968.)

The first step toward institutional memberships was taken in 1966, with four churches and a religious seminary in the neighborhood being the first institutional members. The March 1966 membership was 350 families, with a goal of 200 more set for June 1966. That year's membership drive enrolled 500 families as members, a total of 900 individuals. By the fall of 1967 this increased to 1,500, with revenue surpassing the proposed budget figure of $2,200. At this time some new categories of membership were established, which recognized different amounts for different types of memberships: $1 per person, $5 per family, Supporting—$10 per family, Sustaining—$25 per family.

By 1969 the budget had increased to $7,770, approximately $3,700 more than any proposed budget prior to that time. There were 2,043 members by June 1970, representing 1291 families, a gain of 347 families over the previous year. In 1971 bonding of the treasurer was arranged for $5,000. In 1973, the paid members were 1,134 with $4,887.75 in dues, an increase of 15.7% over the previous year. This number of households represented 35% of all households in the BTNA area. Most of the revenue raised was from door-to-door solicitation rather than fund-raising events.

In November 1973, the new name "board of managers" was adopted for use by those directing the activities of the organization. Their meetings continued to be held monthly, open to all residents and now based in one church which had donated office space. We have seen that the number of paid memberships varied according to the zeal and skill of whoever was the volunteer coordinator of the membership drive. Eventually, though they continued their membership drives, the organization came to consider all residents as members, whether they contributed financially or not.

The time of the membership drive changed in 1980 after the 1979 drive "ran into trouble with bad weather and year end holidays" (newsletter, Sept. 1980). Though the number of paid members decreased over the years—down to 819 households in 1982, which was almost half of what it was ten years earlier— assets and revenues were higher than ever before. The March 1984 treasurer's report listed $10,000 in a certificate of deposit, $6,766.05 in a money market fund, and $4,539.22 in savings and checking accounts. By 1983, the BTNA had set up a finance committee to recommend to the board the disbursement of funds to other groups in the area on written request. Was this a measure of success, indicating a decline in the need for BTNA? Examining its programs over the years may offer an answer.

Before turning to the BTNA's goals and program, we note these comments from the BTNA president as their twenty-fifth anniversary approached: "We don't look for outside grants, with the associated strings attached. We have no paid staff, so all our income is spent on programs and projects directly concerning our neighborhood" (newsletter, Nov.–Dec. 1980). Again, one year later: "Would you believe that the BTNA is twenty-five years old? Not as a formal organization, but as a small group of committed people determined to have a successfully integrated neighborhood with nice homes. . . . Since BTNA is a group of volunteers, we cannot provide many direct services, but we can help neighbors help themselves and to help each other" (newsletter, Sept. 1981).

Clearly, the need for a paid coordinator or executive director had waned long before then. The BTNA, almost thirty years old, remains the typical long-term volunteer group, with not much efficiency and—some think—not much effectiveness. One former board member, Ben Allendale, described their management style:

There is no place to keep things. We had a card table in the parish office that we used as our headquarters for quite some years. And they also gave us a room at Fairview Church for a while—but the point is it has all been volunteer . . . and you see it is handed on or not handed on—the box of files and papers gets transferred to whomever . . . and it has been very haphazard.

Though their office efficiency may have been somewhat haphazard, their goals and program over the years were quite stable and orderly, as we see next.

GOALS

The BTNA's goals remained fairly constant throughout their first quarter-century of existence, though their program changed in response to changing needs and issues. The organization's major goal is explicitly stated in the preamble of their constitution: "to achieve an ideal racially integrated beautiful neighborhood." This goal was stated in the president's platform at the time of the organization's incorporation (newsletter, Dec. 1961) and formally adopted by BTNA on June 14, 1967, nine years after their informal initial formation.

A later brochure described the organization as "founded in 1956 to conserve and improve the neighborhood by promoting cooperative efforts among residents, schools, churches and civic groups." The brochure went on to refer to "this inter-racial association" as actively fostering better communication among its residents in order to prevent intergroup conflicts and promote democratic living. Finally, the brochure cited keeping the quality of the neighborhood high as a goal of the BTNA, as well as developing a sense of community among the residents. The means to achieving these goals were: "to work together on any problem facing residents of the organization, to develop procedures for checking on zoning law violations, and to assure the maintenance of proper municipal services and recreational facilities."

By the early seventies, the purpose of the BTNA was slightly but significantly amended by the addition of the concept of "maintenance." In its brochures and flyers, the group's goal was now stated as "achieving and maintaining a racially integrated, beautiful neighborhood." This is, of course, a reflection of the changes in racial composition in the BTNA area, with increasing minority proportions. Again, in a membership flyer in the early 1980s, which refers to nearly twenty-five years of growth, the BTNA was described as "dedicated to continued maintenance of a high standard of living in the area."

In their twenty-fifth anniversary celebration leaflet, the BTNA purpose was listed as "lessening neighborhood tensions, eliminating prejudice and discrimination, defending human and civil rights secured by law, combating community deterioration and juvenile delinquency, and the conduct of educational and charitable programs all within the neighborhood." These purposes were continually stated throughout the seventies and up to the present. Thus, over the years, though the goal of the organization remained substantially the same, there was recognition of the changing realities within their neighborhood. Adaptation to and acknowledgment of these changes was reflected in public written statements of purpose that appeared throughout three decades of the organization's existence.

Various committees prepared written statements of policy, which provided a link between goals and subsequent programs. The housing integration committee's policy statement is one early example. In it, the committee noted first that their policy was supported by the general policy of the BTNA: "To use all of its efforts to maintain and preserve an attractive and stable racially integrated residential neighborhood" (housing integration committee policy statement, Nov. 16, 1966). They then noted that their policy was supported by both black and white representatives at the BTNA's monthly meetings.

The committee's statement began with the hope that their policy would be "an effective, morally fair and legally sound" way of achieving the goals of the organization and the residents of the neighborhood. The stated policy was "to promote uniform integration" throughout all the blocks of the neighborhood and "to prevent any further blocks from remaining segregated" (all-white or all-black). The organization was to also work through a fair housing subcommittee to open up other areas of the county to minorities.

An addition to the statement noted that increased housing demand by blacks would affect the various neighborhood blocks differently. Blocks with less than 25% nonwhite residency would not become unstable. But blocks with more than 25% nonwhites should be surveyed as to their reactions. "If it appears that the stability is threatened (40–50% non-white), the Association will use its efforts . . . to work with the residents of this block to insure the continued racial integration of the block" (housing integration committee policy statement, Nov. 16, 1966). Though a 1968 general area survey did ask about moving plans and reasons for it, no results were available from these questions. There is no indication that BTNA ever used such data in their attempt to maintain racial balance in their community.

But the minutes of an August 1968 meeting indicate that the housing integration committee proposed short-term loans, second mortgages, and other financial incentives to enable white families to buy homes on "critical blocks" in the neighborhood. The committee was charged by the board to "find a group of families willing to incorporate" to carry this plan out (minutes, Aug. 6, 1968). The proposal was to be discussed with a representative from the Ford Foundation. There is no record of any follow-up action on this proposal for incentive payments for pro-integrative moves—perhaps the earliest in the nation.

Also discussed at the same meeting was the possibility of cooperating with the geographically adjacent neighborhood organization, Meridian-Kessler, to employ a full-time person to promote housing integration in the northern section of the city. Eventually the Meridian-Kessler group did hire such a person, but BTNA was not involved, and never did employ a full-time staff person.

In January 1969, a new housing policy statement began with these words:

The BTNA area has been faced over the last 15 years with a gradual increase of all-Negro blocks, one-by-one, from south to north across the neighborhood. About 60% of the households in the total area are Negro. The blocks south of 46th St. are with few exceptions all-Negro. In the entire neighborhood, no blocks remain all-white. The basic problem at this time is to make the rate of white move-ins greater than the rate of Negro move-ins. (housing policy, 1969)

The general policy of BTNA was then restated: "To maintain and preserve an attractive and stable racially integrated residential neighborhood." Next, the earlier housing policy—to promote integration and prevent segregation—was reiterated "to open up housing opportunities for minorities in other parts of the county" (housing policy, 1969). These stated policies were greatly aided by the announcement of a three-year grant of $60,000 from a local foundation to Neighborhood Housing Opportunities, a nonprofit corporation organized to promote integrated housing throughout the county. Thus, other organized efforts bolstered their own throughout the metropolitan area.

In keeping with these policies, BTNA's action plan was to attract white families to live in the area. Negro families would be "welcomed warmly at all times, but Negro families considering moving into the area will be informed of its present predominantly Negro racial imbalance; these families will also be urged and assisted to seek to buy homes in predominantly white blocks within but especially outside of BTNA's boundaries." The statement ended with provisions for amendments to the policy, which could be filed by residents, and an annual review by the board of directors. It was unanimously approved on January 20, 1969. By 1971, the policy statement included this change: "Negro families contemplating moving into the area will be informed of the current racial distribution and past trends. Educational efforts will be undertaken to promote the value of integrated living in other sections of Marion County." No additional housing policy statements or amendments appear in later BTNA records.

An education policy was established in 1968 by the education committee, and approved by the board of directors and BTNA members. The policy statement began with the firm belief that the success of the organization in achieving its main goal depended to a great extent on the schools serving the neighborhood. Two reasons were given to support this belief. The first was that school boundaries, education standards, and the degree of school integration "strongly affect the degree of integration in housing patterns." The second was that the "degree of excellence in educational standards is a strong selling point in attracting prospective buyers to a neighborhood." The task set for the education committee was "to achieve the highest possible educational standards in the BTNA schools" by working directly with the appropriate educational and governmental groups. They listed four criteria they would use to measure achievement: integration level ("approximately equal to that found in the metropolitan area"); student-teacher ratio (as low as recommended by "respected national educational groups"); curriculum (including minority contributions to history); and facilities ("the best available").

A later public statement about schools appeared in June 1970, and was sent to key educational officials and the two local newspapers. This statement praised the strengthening of academic programs at the BTNA area high school, Shortridge, later closed under the citywide desegregation plan. The introductory paragraph of the statement reaffirmed the earlier education policy and even more clearly explained it: "We believe that integration in these schools is highly desirable for two reasons: it strengthens the educational potential in these institutions, and it helps to maintain neighborhood stability" (minutes, June 1, 1970).

Now we will examine BTNA's program to see how and whether their stated goals and policies were actually carried out.

PROGRAM

We can divide BTNA's development into three phases: early development or mobilization (1956–63), maturation (1964–72), and institutionalization (1973–). In over a quarter-century of existence, BTNA's four major concerns consistently were: housing integration, school integration and quality, zoning variance opposition, and youth recreational opportunities. One other concern arose periodically; that was crime. Additional ongoing organizational activities were membership drives, publicity, and community social events. Very often the events and the publicity (the BTNA newsletter) focused on one or more of the four major concerns. Membership drives were, of course, essential to the survival of the organization. As we analyze the three phases of BTNA's development, we find the four major concerns surfacing with differing intensity over the years.

Housing

Organizational leaders described the beginnings of BTNA as being based on practicality and neighborliness, but the issue that first drew the founders together was neighborhood integration. When the increase in black residents produced some incidents and problems leading to BTNA's formation in 1956, early meetings included discussion on methods to arrest panic selling. One method proposed was the establishment of block organizations, which we already noted as a point of controversy.

In May 1961, two homes owned by blacks in an otherwise all-white block in the BTNA area were vandalized and defaced. The BTNA worked quickly to relieve tensions and to befriend the black residents, and largely as a result of their efforts three other nearby homes that were for sale at the time were later sold to whites. By 1962, BTNA faced two major problems: "the continual threat of panic selling and depreciating real estate values" (BTNA history, 1968). A film series in the summer of 1962 attempted to deal with some of these issues by showing such films as "Property Values and Race," "High Wall," and "Burden of Truth."

During their second, or maturation phase (1964–72), BTNA established a housing information service, with a BTNA phone operating out of a volunteer's home. The primary purpose of the service was to refer prospective buyers to real estate agents approved by BTNA, and to give BTNA area residents information on housing. In 1965, the housing integration committee formed four subcommittees: (1) Stability—which was to hold block meetings to encourage residents to stay and tried to deter panic selling; (2) Advertising—which was to produce and distribute a new brochure to promote the area and attract new residents; (3) Referral—which was to follow leads provided by the advertising group and refer them to sellers; and (4) Greater Indianapolis Housing—which was to work with city and county government, private units, and the Indianapolis Real Estate Board to achieve open housing throughout the county, "thus easing the possibility of reaching racial balance in the B-T area" (BTNA history, 1968).

In 1967 these activities were embodied in a housing policy, "to stabilize the integration pattern." Publication of short ads began in the Sunday *Indianapolis Star* real estate section and in two national magazines, *Saturday Review* and the *New Republic*. These ads were designed to attract prospective white buyers with catchy headlines such as "Join the Flight from Suburbia." The BTNA was mentioned by name and the housing referral service phone number was given. When people called, a personal guide service consisting of twenty volunteers was called into action. The guides were prepared to show the community to potential buyers and "vouch for the advantages of living in the area" (BTNA history, 1968). During the summer of 1967, a staff member of the state Civil Rights Commission was appointed to work with BTNA to assist them in their integration stabilization efforts.

In 1968, BTNA made an arrangement with one realtor to work only in the BTNA area. This was later expanded to include several other agents. The agreement with them involved supplying them with access to all potential buyers uncovered by the recruitment and advertising campaigns. The BTNA maintained a brokers list, which was distributed to potential buyers. In return, the agents would spend almost all of their time trying to place buyers in the BTNA area and increase the number of potential buyers.

By 1968, BTNA had organized a federation of neighborhood civic associations to promote stable integration in central Indianapolis. The brochure distribution efforts were not as successful as hoped for (annual report, 1970), though continuing placement was to be attempted in personnel offices of major employers in the region. One of the organization's real estate agents commented at the time that "racial balance seems stable and property values are good" (newsletter, Nov. 13, 1970). She reported forty-two sales in the BTNA area during the previous six months, with eight pending, and twenty-eight homes available. Names and phone numbers of three agents were listed and continued to run in the newsletter until June of 1971. After that, only the housing committee chairperson's name and phone number were given as a reference for those wanting to sell their homes. A news item in 1972 noted that "demands for housing in our neighborhood are constant and growing," and that "large numbers of prospective buyers and renters" were available from the housing committee chair (newsletter, Oct. 3, 1972).

By 1973—the beginning of BTNA's third phase of development, institutionalization—the concern for housing integration was listed as only fourth out of eight possible concerns in a survey of residents, with the overall ranking as follows: crime, need for a youth center, community spirit, integrated housing, high school education, trash pickup, primary education, cable TV. In 1976, the housing committee was listed as the housing referral committee, and within a year a new name and phone number were given for residents to contact if they had property to rent or sell: "Calls came in daily requesting rentals in our area" (newsletter, April 1977). By 1980, no housing or referral committee was listed in the newsletters. Also in 1980, however, a major thoroughfare in the neighborhood was declared a "historic preservation area." This important boulevard was lined with large mansions and trees, and included the governor's mansion. Perhaps a housing and referral committee was no longer needed.

In the August 1982 newsletter, committees of housing and conservation had been combined, and a chairperson was being sought. Again in October 1982, members and chairpersons were sought for six committees, including housing and conservation. Clearly, housing integration was of diminishing concern to the organization by this time.

One reason for this may have been that a Neighborhood Housing Service had operated in the B-T area from 1977 to 1981, but was then unfunded. The reason for the discontinuation of funding was that the B-T area was declared too prosperous to qualify for this program—a nonprofit corporation making low interest loans for repair and rehabilitation of housing. The program, however, was expanded on a citywide basis in 1982, with a small southern portion of the B-T area included.

After 1980, no further housing activities of the organization were mentioned in BTNA newsletters or city news items. While one indicator of organizational decline is committee inactivity, it can also be an indicator of success. In the case of the BTNA housing committee, it was a mark of success: By this time nothing much more needed to be done in order to maintain stability in the B-T area—just eternal vigilance.

Schools

Though the 1968 BTNA history does not mention schools or education as a major concern of the organization, the minutes of board meetings and newspaper articles show that much attention was given to racial balance and quality of the schools. This was especially true in the second phase of BTNA's development—the years before the citywide desegregation suit was first settled in 1971.

School board elections, for example, are emphasized in a 1964 newsletter: "The most important single issue in the May primary . . . is the election of the Indianapolis School Board. Policies adopted by this Board will determine the quality of education of Indianapolis's children for the next six years—half the public school life of your child! Vote! Vote! Vote!" (newsletter, April 1964). The BTNA's keynote speaker for their eighth anniversary dinner the following month was a schools administrator from St. Louis.

The organization's first public item addressing the issue of racial balance in the schools appeared in the October 1964 newsletter. Headed "Racial Imbalance: Fear or Frontier?" the article had four paragraphs discussing de facto segregation at Shortridge High School—the only high school in the B-T area. The article raised the question of what to do "about this catastrophic problem in racial imbalance," which remained unsolved despite "meetings, impassioned pleas, proposed plans." The real problem was the quality of education at the high school, and the real question was: "Could there be quality education with only a 40% white enrollment? . . . or 20? . . . or 10?"

Members of BTNA had pledged themselves to proving interracial communities could be harmonious and productive on all levels regardless of the degree of racial imbalance. So the new frontier of racial concern was the question of whether white families could continue to live harmoniously and creatively in a predominantly black community. Their answer to this question was: "We believe they can, and will continue to work together in this situation, trying to prove what this city and the world must eventually learn—mankind must learn to live together, or we will die together" (newsletter, Oct. 1964).

Nine months later, the Indianapolis school board announced plans to make Shortridge High School a citywide Academic School (college prep), with admission based on achievement records. The BTNA held a general meeting to discuss the issue. With one hundred people attending, a three-member panel discussed three questions: (1) What is quality education such as we seek for the community of Indianapolis? (2) What is the past, present and future of the Shortridge geographic neighborhood in relation to our concern for an integrated neighborhood? and (3) From the BTNA view, what are the problems and implications of the school board decision to make Shortridge an academic high school?" (minutes, Nov. 16, 1965). The panelists were from the Mayor's Commission on Human Rights, the Indianapolis public schools, and BTNA. At this meeting, after the discussion, it was decided that the education committee and executive committee would prepare a position paper on the schools issue. That position paper, widely circulated, made three points: it praised the school board's decision to make Shortridge an academic high school, noting that without this the school would soon have become "all-Negro and all the residential area with it"; it protested the assignment of three elementary schools (one, School 43, was in the Butler-Tarkington area) to another totally segregated and overcrowded all-black high school (Crispus Attucks); and it called for more public discussion and community participation in "vital policies" (BTNA schools position paper, Dec. 2, 1965).

The minutes of a board meeting held shortly after the position paper came out note that a unanimously carried motion called for BTNA to "oppose with all its resources the redistricting of School 43 as a feeder school for Crispus Attucks" (minutes, Dec. 7, 1965). By February 1, the school board had declared an open enrollment policy for Elementary School 43—BTNA's efforts had been convincing and successful. Mindful of their manners, they sent a letter of appreciation to the board.

For the next ten years, BTNA was deeply involved in the Indianapolis school desegregation efforts, both voluntary and, later, court-ordered. They sent each school board member and key administrators subscriptions to the national publication *Integrateducation*. They were represented on all task forces and committees eventually formed by the school board to study and prepare citywide desegregation plans. They held public meetings with education experts featured as speakers, they held luncheons and dinners for combined school faculty and administrators, they formed coalitions with other community groups to take joint action and develop joint positions.

A strong resolution issued in 1969 restated BTNA's support of school integration and offered four recommendations calling for full integration of all city schools in 1971, with community involvement. It also opposed a specific plan offered by the U.S. Department of Health, Education and Welfare and stated its readiness "to prevent implementation of that plan by legal means" (resolution, May 17, 1969). This statement was presented at the next meeting of the school board, and at a general BTNA membership meeting on June 2, 1969.

On January 27, 1970, the school board announced its decision to phase out Attucks and Shortridge high schools in order to achieve racial desegregation. By then the law suit against the schools had been in court two years. Redistricting of the remaining high schools would have Butler-Tarkington area elementary school students assigned to another high school. The program was to begin in the summer of 1970—one year before the court decision came in. The BTNA issued a statement to the school board commending them for their efforts to desegregate the city high schools. The statement praised their plans for human relations programs, involving all participants—students, staff, and parents. The BTNA reaffirmed their willingness to assist officials of the schools in their efforts to establish a fully integrated school system.

The entire February 1970 issue of the BTNA newsletter was devoted to schools and their integration. At that time the racial composition of Shortridge high school was 65% black and 35% white. One of the two elementary schools in the BTNA area, number 86 was declared a "naturally integrated" school (40% black), and was the only public school exempt from the busing that eventually occurred throughout Indianapolis. Many BTNA members and supporters believed it was their housing integration efforts that made and kept that school naturally integrated.

Again a mark of success, B-T area residents' concerns for education in 1973 were fifth (high school) and seventh (elementary schools) out of eight community concerns. One meeting in 1973 was devoted to the status of Shortridge High School. By 1980 the education committee was combined with the recreation committee. No further references to schools were found in newsletters through 1984. The education and recreation committee was in need of a chairperson and members in a 1982 newsletter, and there were no references to schools in the last newsletter studied (Jan.–Feb. 1984).

By the early 1980s, education was no longer a paramount issue for the BTNA. One Indianapolis Star article in 1983 referred to the planned reopening of Shortridge as a junior high school, and BTNA's support of that action. From 1973 to 1984, only four city newspaper articles related to BTNA and schools, compared to eleven in the period from 1964 to 1972. So the greatest program activity devoted to schools occurred in the second phase of BTNA's development—prior to the legal decisions that eventually desegregated the entire school system on a countrywide basis. But even in 1984, discussion of the schools generated more emotion and heat than any other topic. Particularly the closing of Shortridge High was seen as a traumatic event. Its imminent reopening as a junior high was heralded by all respondents as a boon for the Butler-Tarkington neighborhood and for all their children.

Zoning and Long-Range Planning

The single most time-consuming long-term task of the association in all of its years of existence was the preparation of a land use subarea plan for the Butler-Tarkington area. This seven-year study and plan development was done in cooperation with city planning staff, and was finally approved in 1970 by the Metropolitan Planning and Development Commission of Indianapolis.

The land use subarea plan was most significant for the BTNA and the neighborhood's eventual success. It paved the way for all later zoning and land use monitoring by the association, providing a set of goals for the use of land and facilities in their own area. In all subsequent years, everytime zoning changes were proposed for the Butler-Tarkington area, the association successfully blocked them by citing the land use plan and showing how the proposed change would be inconsistent with it.

The plan grew out of the efforts of the long-range planning committee of BTNA, first formed in 1963. Long before the plan was conceived, a zoning issue was so important that it played a major role in the early formation of BTNA as an organization. We have noted that the second meeting of the organization in 1956 was devoted to discussion of the endangerment of Tarkington Park—the only park in the area. This park, neglected for some time, was in jeopardy because of some neighboring businesses wanting to obtain the park for a parking lot. This is what prompted the fledgling group "to organize immediately as the BTN Committee." A petition to the park board requesting the development of the park as a playground was drafted and circulated; "Thus the committee had arrived at a focus for action, a reason for existence" (BTNA history, 1968). By December 1956, over 800 signatures had been obtained, and the park board decided to maintain the park intact. Later the park board was persuaded to appropriate funds to "clean up the play area, equip it, and provide playground supervision."

This was the first of many actions and victories for BTNA relating to zoning variances. At BTNA's second meeting, "committees were established to study park development, zoning ordinances and their enforcement, and to acquire study materials pertaining to urban problems" (BTNA history, 1968). They did their homework well, as all their subsequent zoning activities indicate.

The very first BTNA newsletters in 1960 showed great concern for zoning. Almost the entire second issue of the newsletter was devoted to the subject of revised zoning laws and their implications for the area (newsletter, Nov. 1960). During the first phase of BTNA's development, attempted zoning changes occurred again in 1962. A plan to build two apartment houses in a single-family neighborhood of Butler-Tarkington was opposed by the organization, and the application for the zoning variance was finally withdrawn by the applicant. The newsletter item describing this was headed "Retreat In Good Order," and noted:

Granting of such variance unquestionably would have been contrary to the best interests of the B-T area—one of single family residences. . . . One of the organization's most vital functions is safeguarding the neighborhood against zoning violations and variances which would serve as a hole in the dyke and result in an ensuing flood of deteriorating property values. (newsletter, Feb. 1963)

The article then praised the BTNA zoning committee for doing a "remarkably fine job." Though the chairperson of that committee reported no further pending applications for zoning changes at that time, they soon reappeared.

In April 1963—the beginning of BTNA's second phase of development—another petition for a zoning change was submitted. This was for a twenty-nine-unit apartment building at the same location as the previous year's request—but this time by a different builder. The BTNA again mobilized support for a protest, and again won a dismissal of the petition. Eventually, however, that site did become the location of a twenty-four-unit apartment building, despite BTNA's unanimous opposition. In November 1963, a zoning variance was granted for this purpose, representing one of BTNA's few failures regarding zoning changes.

The type of opposition organized by BTNA at the zoning board hearings included attendance by organizational leaders, residents, and representatives from other neighboring institutions, such as Butler University. In addition, letters were written to the zoning board explaining BTNA's "policy against any variances which would alter the basic character of their community—one of single family residences" (newsletter, April 1963).

One BTNA zoning decision made by the board of directors was reversed by the membership, and placed the president of the organization in the awkward position of representing the organization in a decision he did not agree with. In April 1963 a home in the Butler-Tarkington area was to be bought and converted to a greenhouse by a theological seminary. The seminary was about to erect a $5 million complex on a sixteen-acre site, and needed the greenhouse for the complex. The board's decision to support the zoning change was reversed by the membership at a general meeting; the president of BTNA carried out the wishes of the members and opposed the variance.

The long-range planning committee began its preliminary work toward an area land-use plan with a survey in 1965 to "measure the success of integration in the BTNA area" (minutes, Oct. 5, 1965). The survey was also designed to learn the attitudes of residents toward various levels of integration. It was to be conducted by students from Butler University and the Christian Theological Seminary, both located in the area. By the fall of 1967, the committee was so burdened it advertised twice for a volunteer secretary. The second ad stated that the committee would relax the age requirement to over 85 and double the salary to twice the gratitude of the committee (newsletter, Sept.–Nov. 1967).

In cooperation with the Metropolitan Planning Department, a senior university student in community planning worked with the committee to develop the land use plan, beginning in December 1968. A second survey was conducted to determine what the residents wanted for their community. A series of neighborhood meetings took place in December, developing goals for the land use plan. Additional meetings of committees were devoted to discussions of the proposals which emerged from the public meetings. The comprehensive plan attempted to identify all problems within the neighborhood—social, economic, and physical.

In the fall of 1969, a draft of the plan was presented at a general meeting. A series of six neighborhood meetings followed, with the planning student (now an associate planner with the Metropolitan Planning Department) and committee members discussing the specific needs and problems of each neighborhood as identified by the residents. The results of the 1968 survey were also presented. A second draft of the plan was to incorporate some of the discussion results.

Not all residents from all six neighborhoods participated. The long-range planning committee expressed concern that the southern, predominantly black, part of the BTNA area had very little involvement. One newsletter item was headed "South BTNA, Please Speak," and announced a special public meeting reviewing the plan and urging BTNA residents, "especially of the southern part of the area," to come and express their views of the plan (newsletter, Jan. 1970). This meeting followed by only two weeks an all day session on the plan for the board and the planning committee.

The revised plan was presented to the board early in March of 1970, and to the general membership several weeks later. A vote was taken in April by the board, which unanimously recommended that BTNA members request adoption of the plan by the Metropolitan Development Commission. On May 2, members cast seventy ballots, sixty-nine for the plan and one against it. The plan was then presented to the planning and zoning subcommittee of the Metropolitan Development Commission, which recommended adoption as part of the County Comprehensive General Land Use Plan.

In May 1970, the committee turned its attention to implementation of the plan, which included task forces organized to acquire a community center and the construction of a low rise apartment building in a commercial area. On July 1, 1970 the metropolitan commission approved the plan without change. Democracy works slowly.

Immediately after the acceptance of the plan, BTNA faced four requests for zoning changes: a fraternity house, expansion of an existing sorority house to hold seventy people, a variety store, and apartment house construction. These were successfully thwarted by BTNA, on the grounds that they would have varied the land use plan they worked so hard to develop. In 1971 the preservation of a major residential boulevard was assured with the designation of the street as a historic area by the state legislature. The BTNA played a role in that decision and was overjoyed at the passage of the Meridian Street Preservation Act.

From 1973 to 1984, thirteen articles appeared in the city newspapers referring to BTNA attempts—mostly successful—to thwart zoning changes. In all the zoning variances they opposed in those years, they were able to point to the land use plan as a concrete reason for resisting changes. The BTNA generally won their point, and requests were usually withdrawn or not passed by the zoning board.

Complementing the land use plan and zoning change opposition were neighborhood conservation efforts. These were also an integral part of the BTNA maintenance and vigilance efforts. A separate conservation committee handled such matters as litter, street lights, business deterioration, abandoned cars, stray dogs, housing repairs and rehabilitation, and safety. Eventually the task of block organization was given to them, but this never became a major effort of BTNA or the committee. The processing of residents' complaints was done by this committee, with an average of five a month. One special effort in 1976 concerned opposition to planned utility poles—each one 92 feet tall—going through the area. Of twenty-six newspaper articles on BTNA that year, sixteen were about the group's opposition to the poles. Their vigorous organized protests succeeded in rerouting the poles.

Recreation

A fourth major effort of BTNA throughout their existence was the development of recreational programs for young people in their area. As early as 1961, a program was begun by the BTNA recreation committee to provide evening recreation at one of the two public elementary schools in the neighborhood. The recreation committee's chair, a social worker, commented on the reasons for doing this: "There's been a real lack of organized recreation programs in this neighborhood. If we succeed in developing a really good program, we're going to help keep a lot of kids from getting into trouble" (newsletter, Dec. 1961). By 1963, the evening program was running three nights a week, with attendance ranging from forty-three to 320 a night. Activities for boys and girls included volleyball, kickball, relays, ping-pong, chess and checkers. The two supervisors' salaries were paid by the park department. In 1962, BTNA donated one hundred dollars to help support a baseball team for youngsters in the neighborhood. This made it possible for them to compete in the city park department sports program. In that same year, BTNA held a general meeting on the subject of the gap between ideal and practice of racial equality in the Boy and Girl Scouts organizations. Baseball was again sponsored by BTNA in the summer of 1963, when one of their two teams won the city championship. By 1967, BTNA's goal was to sponsor ten teams. A newsletter item called for financial sponsors and coaches: "Let us know whether you're rich or have coaching ability" (newsletter, April 1967).

The possibility of establishing a recreation center for youth in the area was first explored by BTNA in 1963 when they formed a special committee to consider this. The president said he felt a recreation center was one of the most promising ventures that could possibly be undertaken by them (newsletter, Feb. 1963). A 1966 professional report of recreational needs in the area indicated that the area was high in recreational facilities, but the programs needed much development and improvement. Professional staffing was needed to train and supervise volunteers. A question was raised at the end of the report: "Recreation for what?—The answer seems to lie in the direction of providing meaningful relationships—the creation of community experience. The quality of relationships must remain the concern of the association . . . rather than the numerical increase of activities" (church liaison committee report, Jan 4, 1966).

A Mott Foundation grant of $5,000 was obtained in 1969 by BTNA for an evening recreation program in the schools, called Lighted Schools. The grant was to be channelled through another existing recreation program, called Upswing. At this time, BTNA's recreation committee became the recreation and youth committee.

By 1969, almost half the entire annual budget of BTNA—$3,075—went to the recreation and youth committee, including $600 to junior baseball teams. This led to a conflict within the organization over priorities. The minutes of a board meeting show that the conservation committee "wishes to go on record as opposing unanimously further expenditures by BTNA to hire recreation directors" rather than hiring auxiliary policemen to patrol specific areas in the neighborhood for safety (minutes, Aug. 4, 1969).

Efforts to secure a recreation center for the neighborhood continued, and a youth association was formed to help with fund-raising events. Financial assistance to summer baseball teams also continued, despite the priorities conflict, and became an integral part of BTNA membership drives. For 1970, BTNA's budget requests increased to $7,777, of which $3,307 was for the recreation and youth committee. But staffing problems developed with the Lighted Schools program, the coordinator was asked to leave, and a replacement had to be found. Organizational confusion arose as to the relationship of BTNA to the Lighted Schools advisory council, which had a number of representatives on it. Channels of communication were a problem as to finances and staff, and the BTNA board was uncertain as to how to resolve these issues satisfactorily.

A site for a community center was incorporated into the area land use plan, and by June 1970 plans were under way for a resolution asking the Metropolitan Development Commission to authorize the city to acquire the designated property for a community center. This property contained two acres and a former fraternity house, long neglected and vacant.

The BTNA annual report for 1969–70 stated that the recreation and youth committee had five priorities that year: Lighted Schools, tutoring, summer recreation programs, junior baseball, and jobs for youth (in cooperation with five neighborhood churches). Of these, two were not carried out—tutoring and jobs for youth—because of lack of time and participating members. The others occupied all of the time of the committee. Activities reported for the Lighted Schools program included some adult programming, a basketball tournament for neighborhood youth, a talent show, a drug abuse program, and the standard types of youth recreation activities.

In September 1970, BTNA received a funding request from the Lighted Schools program for $10,200. Two months later, they requested the use of the organization's church office for the program. The board granted permission on a trial basis, for daytime use only. The funding request was delayed pending an evaluation of the program. By March 1971, the Lighted Schools program was scheduled to be withdrawn from the BTNA neighborhood because of "cutbacks in funds and the high cost of the program for benefits derived" (minutes, March 1, 1971). The program was to continue in twelve other schools, supported by other foundations and Model Cities funds.

Summer recreation programs continued to occupy the recreation and youth committee, in cooperation with neighborhood churches, the park department and the university. When the chair of the recreation committee resigned in April 1971, the board reconsidered the goals and functions of the committee. They asked the former chair to help the committee write a complete job description for the committee chair. Their view on the function of the committee was "primarily to coordinate and facilitate the work of the churches, city agencies, and other interested groups in effectively serving the neighborhood together" (minutes, April 1971).

All committee structures were reorganized in 1971–72, and what once was the recreation and youth committee became Youth Projects. They soon began searching for a young minority person to be a part-time organizer of youth programs in conjunction with the schools serving the area. The 1971–72 projected budget for BTNA was $11,700, of which almost half was allocated for youth projects. This was the largest single budget item.

A youth center was set up in 1972 in cooperation with Indianapolis Settlements, Inc. The BTNA was represented on the board, along with other neighborhood representatives and representatives from the settlements. The center's activities included evening and after-school programs for first graders through high school. The youth center became the Butler-Tarkington MultiService Center in March 1973; its activities expanded to include bowling, ballet classes, arts and crafts, jobs for youth, drama, music, and—finally—tutoring.

A survey of residents in 1973 indicated that area residents rated the youth center as the second most important issue they wanted the BTNA board to concern itself with; the first was crime. Others in rank order were: (3) community spirit, (4) integrated housing, (5) high school education, (6) trash pick-up, (7) elementary education, and (8) cable TV.

The MultiService Center expanded in November 1973 with the addition of a veterans outreach center. The center's name and area of service were changed in 1981, becoming the Martin Luther King Center, with its service area covering the entire north central portion of Indianapolis. Ten articles about the center appeared in BTNA newsletters from 1976 to 1983. A brand-new facility was built for the center in January 1984.

A new focus of activity for the recreation committee in 1979 and 1980 was the desegregation of an all-white private country club located in the northern section of the area. A new organization, called the Coalition to End Racial Discrimination, Inc., was formed in August 1980 to protest racial discrimination in membership policies at the club. The protests, with strong support by BTNA members, included demonstrations in front of the club. The BTNA played a major role in the eventual desegregation of that institution, which opened its doors to black members for the first time in September 1981. Petitions, marches, demonstrations, and a lawsuit finally led to an out-of-court settlement, and the acceptance of eight black and biracial families as club members.

Three other major aspects of BTNA program activities were social events, membership drives, and the newsletter publication. These were constant throughout all the years of the organization's existence, and took up a great portion of the time and energy of members. Social and community events, including public meetings, accounted for forty-nine of the 186 newspaper articles about the organization in the years 1958 to 1983. This was 26% of all the articles printed about the BTNA, and the highest percentage of all categories of articles. The remainder of the articles over the years were devoted to other types of programs (rat control, crime prevention, housing rehabilitation) and articles of general interest about the organization and its development as the oldest neighborhood organization in Indianapolis.

Newsletters in the third phase of the organization's development (1973–84) noted that BTNA each year gave small grants to other organizations. This indicates that the association no longer had any pressing needs of its own. Was this a sign of success or fatigue? Let us examine this in the next section.

IMPACT

We will use four criteria to assess the effectiveness or impact of BTNA. Each of these factors is relevant to the goals of the neighborhood stabilization movement: (1) maintenance of racial pluralism; (2) quality maintenance; (3) sense of community; and (4) organizational influence. These four factors were evaluated through census data, interview transcripts, visual surveys and photographs, news content analysis, organizational minutes, and published reports. Thus the analysis of impact is both quantitative and qualitative.

Integration Maintenance

First, to what extent have racial integration and stability been maintained in the Butler-Tarkington area? Census data over three decades indicate these have been achieved (see Appendix A, Table 2), even though the level of racial pluralism is not the same throughout the study area. Clearly, there are really three neighborhoods in the area (see Figure 1). Of these, one—the bottom, southern portion—is not integrated and never was, having been a primarily black area when the organization began. The other two neighborhoods—moving northward—are moderately and slightly integrated, having gradually increased their proportion of blacks over twenty-eight years of the organization's existence. In 1940, all the area's black population was in the southern tract, which ironically also contained an enormous cemetery, Crown Hill. As already noted, black migration within the Butler-Tarkington area has been northward, propelled by land acquisition by medical and educational institutions and other urban renewal since the 1950s.

Between 1960 and 1970 the greatest racial change occurred in the middle tract, which went from 15% to 29% black. The upper tract changed slightly from zero to 5% black. By 1980, the central tract had increased to only 34% black, and the upper tract showed another 5% increase in black population. Thus, over twenty years, racial integration was maintained even though the integration level was not the same throughout the three portions of the area.

Stability was also maintained, as data concerning housing occupancy reveal. In 1980, 55% of all residents had lived in their housing units ten years or more. Only 6.6% of the owners and 41% of the renters had moved into their units in the fifteen preceding months. Ten years earlier, only 40% had lived there ten years or more, which was slightly higher than the county rate of 38%. Thus, not only was racial integration maintained, but neighborhood stability was achieved.

School data are not as helpful in assessing neighborhood integration maintenance, since the schools began modifying their attendance zones when the lawsuit was first filed in 1965. This continued during and after the court-ordered countywide desegregation plan in 1975. But a brief review of the racial composition of the two elementary schools and one high school in the Butler-Tarkington area shows some of the changes that occurred in the schools.

In 1965, elementary school 43, with 1,000 students, was 100% black. It was located in the southernmost tract of the area. School 86, in the upper tract, had 518 students, of whom 33% were black. In 1966, the proportion of blacks in School 86 increased to 40%, and in 1967 it was 42.5% The city proportion of black students in 1967 was 32.8%. Shortridge Junior High School was 92% black in 1965, 93% in 1966, and 96% in 1967. Its total number of students increased in those three years from 348 to 710. This school was later closed, with BTNA deeply divided over this issue. By 1980, 26% of Butler-Tarkington students in grades K–12 were enrolled in private schools, similar to the national average.

Though racial integration was maintained in the area since the inception of BTNA, to what extent was this due to the efforts of the association? Most of the respondents in this study were quite emphatic and positive in their answers to the question, "Do you think BTNA succeeded in its original goal?" John Burns, a white university professor and former board member, said:

Well, the original goal was to create a stable multi-racial neighborhood. And, obviously, they did so. I think they have headed off blockbusting . . . it is not likely that anyone is

ever going to be able to intrude a sudden, destructive element in the neighborhood. . . .
Now I would consider that a definition of clear success.

Elsie Bernivan, a white attorney and organization leader, also pointed out successes:

Probably years ago the major success was to keep realtors from steering or scaring. . . .
We have this realtors' agreement that signs not be posted in a changing area and that
no solicitation be permitted. . . . We are reversing the patterns because the values have
gone up . . . basically we stayed stabilized.

Anne Morris, former president of BTNA and a black teacher, agreed: "I think
that we kind of have the feeling that we solved the problem of stabilization in
all of the neighborhoods . . . one of our main successes would be that—and being
an effective agent for racial harmony."

Ben Allendale, one of the earliest BTNA members, corroborated this positive
view:

The property values have gone up so much . . . a real estate agent . . . told us that the
houses in general have been selling faster and turning over faster here than in comparable
neighborhoods . . . I would say we have a stable, integrated neighborhood of high quality
. . . and there certainly are harmonious racial relationships.

Bill Gerber, a former Meridian-Kessler (adjacent neighborhood) resident who
recently moved to Butler-Tarkington, said: "A house in B-T with a for sale sign
in front of it is still relatively rare, and the sign is there a very short time."
George Harris, a black resident and organization leader, spoke of change and
success:

Initially, of course, the issue would have been flight. . . . That I don't think is any longer
an issue in the community. . . . It remains a very attractive and sought-out place to live.
But while it is integrated, there is really a division along economic lines, which also
happens to be pretty much racial. . . . I suspect, though, that the black end has been
there all the time.

Finally, Dot and Al Hunt—two well-known organization and community
leaders, white—offered an explanation for the integration maintenance of the
neighborhood. They spoke of BTNA's early fair housing efforts in organizing
other neighborhood groups in the city and suburbs to declare their neighborhoods
"open to all." They continued:

[Then] other areas of the city opened up for black people to move to, and it became an
"in" thing for white people to live in B-T. Whether we had anything to do with it, or
whether it would have happened anyway—we don't know . . . but blockbusting seems to
have really died down. I really see this area as being integrated racially, and by age and
economic level too.

When asked what obstacles the association had faced, these two respondents
immediately said: "The largest one was the real estate community." And when
asked whether they thought that was still a major obstacle, they said:

I would still. Because when a major firm such as Eli Lilly will bring an executive to town, the realtor is not going to bring that family to B-T unless that individual says, "I've heard about B-T, I plan to live there, find me a house there." And we still have problems with personnel departments of companies not sending people here . . . so we still have some of these same problems—but we've tried to work a lot of them out. . . . So I would say we've achieved our original goal—the association has been a tremendous success.

Quality Maintenance

To what extent has the quality of the Butler-Tarkington neighborhood been maintained? Overall, respondents' answers to this question were positive, but there was acknowledgment of the deterioration of some business areas and of some of the area's southern portion, which was predominantly lower-income and black. Visual inspection confirmed this. Elsie Bernivan spoke of BTNA's work in trying to maintain quality: "The major successes have been in the area of stopping commercial encroachment and working on housing conservation— working with code enforcements, bringing houses up to standards without alienating people." She also said they had had a Neighborhood Housing Services program for a few years, but when the funds ran out they were not renewed, because the area did not have enough "poor" and deteriorating structures to qualify. The southern portion was lower-income; this was where the need was, and where past housing improvement efforts were concentrated. She said more funds were needed there.

In answer to the question, "What do you think is the single most important need of the area today?" Elsie Bernivan and many other respondents mentioned commercial revitalization. Ben and Jean Allendale, long-term residents, spoke of deteriorating business areas:

Generally, overall, they're going downhill. Even ten years ago it was at that point. The neighborhood association never did work very hard trying to get support for this—we never did go out trying to raise money for it, we weren't very aggressive. In general, what has gone is both business and industry.

Other respondents spoke of the work of a new development group, MACO, in revitalizing the 38th St. corridor, a major business strip, and were hopeful that it could improve. George Harris felt that at least one business area had improved, as did Anne Morris, another black leader: "In one instance there is a business area that has become more vital in recent years, decidedly more vital. There are several new businesses there—in fact, six new ones within the last three or four years. [Did BTNA solicit these businesses?] No, but we encourage our members to support them—we are very active in supporting new businesses."

The feeling that BTNA had not adequately addressed the issue of commercial area deterioration was also expressed by Dot and Al Hunt, who felt that allowing another group (MACO) to take over this task was a serious omission of the association. A city official, Robert Cathcart, confirmed the view of BTNA's weakness in the commercial areas: "My guess is that we've done more through those other groups [MACO and East Side Community Investments] than all of the previous years combined."

Though residents showed concern over their business areas, they were consistently proud of their housing quality. The Hunts, for example, felt there had been a continuous progression of quality maintenance. When asked how the neighborhood might have changed physically over the years, they said: "It's bound to have aged . . . but as far as upkeep . . . I think we're on a real upward thrust." They pointed to BTNA's long struggle with proposed zoning changes, and their successes in staving them off, as contributing to the quality maintenance of the area.

It was like you were vigilantes with the zoning changes—You had to be on your toes every minute. And someone was always trying to change things—away from the direction that you were in. This was 1970. . . . [And you won all those zoning cases?] We didn't lose any, I don't think. . . . We were demanding that they hold the sub-area plan.

The Hunts also spoke about the significance of getting Meridian Boulevard declared a historic preservation area. This was done legislatively by securing passage of a Preservation Act for that specific boulevard, a main artery in the BTNA area: "Nobody understands how important that was—that formed a backbone for two neighborhood organizations to really strengthen their areas. It really had a rippling effect."

The contrast in quality between the residential and commercial areas of the Butler-Tarkington neighborhood is revealed in census statistics. From 1960 to 1968, the number of deteriorating homes rose from 88 to 388, mostly in the southern end of the area. Special repair funds were then focused on that area, through BTNA efforts. By 1980, of the 3,273 housing units in Butler-Tarkington, 79.2% were owner-occupied. This rate of owner occupancy was 21% higher than for the city as a whole. The median value of owner-occupied homes was $37,800 in B-T compared to $26,800 for the city as a whole. Rents, however, were somewhat lower—$137 in Butler-Tarkington, compared to $150 for the city. Of the rentals, 61.3% in the area were black-occupied, compared to 33% for the city. For commercial structures, however, the picture is very different: in 1970 49% of these structures in the B-T area were identified as "deteriorating." Most of these were in the lower black tract. Census data of 1980 showed no significant change (U.S. Census, 1960, 1970, 1980). To balance this, one formerly deteriorating business area had revived in the northern, slightly integrated tract.

Sense of Community

To what extent has BTNA created a sense of community in their area? We have already noted that of the 186 city newspaper articles about the association over a twenty-five-year period, forty-nine were about social and community events arranged and sponsored by the organization. These included public meetings, community dinners, house tours, study groups, concerts, and other special events. All of these activities provided some sense of community within BTNA boundaries. In addition, all households in the BTNA area—over 3,000—received the association newsletter, since all came to be considered members whether or not they contributed financially to the organization.

Yet there was broad agreement among respondents that the three geographic segments of the area were not well integrated socially, especially the lower segment. This area was seen as all-black, though census data showed it to be 80% black. Also generally acknowledged was the fact that the organization itself was no longer holding as many community events as it used to. In all the comments made in hundreds of pages of transcripts of interviews in 1984, only one respondent felt that the association was still as social and sociable as ever. When asked the question, "Has BTNA changed any over the years?" Anne Morris—another black resident and former association leader—answered; "We're not as social. We don't do as many social events. [Why do you think that is?] I don't know why really . . . unless everybody is busy, involved with their own thing."

The Hunts—two long-term association leaders and residents—gave their view of BTNA's effectiveness in providing a sense of community:

We no longer have those monthly meetings that were informative, and that brought people together. . . . Maybe we have one or two events a year—an annual meeting and a pitch-in dinner. [Why do you think this is happening?] First of all, I think our lives are more complicated even than they used to be fifteen years ago. Maybe less crisis. We're less crisis-oriented at the moment—we don't have anything major. In those early formative days and years there seemed to be a greater need of coming together. That's particularly true when you are trying to bring blacks and whites together for the first time.

The tangible evidence—through records and news clips—is of a greater number of events during phase one and the first half of phase two, with some waning towards the end of phase two and into phase three.

Though the association did struggle with the problem of north-south social, racial, and economic divisions, they were never able to resolve the situation. Their greatest success in providing a sense of community was in the central portion of their area, and especially among those limited numbers who participated in the management of the affairs of the organization. Even here, recent years have shown less enthusiasm. The association was becoming tired, and their original mission was perhaps no longer an appealing issue of the 1980s. They may also have succeeded so well that not much was left for them to do.

Influence

What influence did BTNA have on institutional forces and decision makers? In each of their major program areas—housing, schools, youth recreation, and land use—we have seen that BTNA sought to influence institutional policies and practices with varying degrees of success. In housing, the housing information service, the agreements with exclusive Butler-Tarkington real estate agents, the public relations materials and news publicity, and the countywide efforts to promote open housing all had an early impact on the real estate practices in the area. This, of course, was greatly reinforced by passage of federal open housing legislation in 1968, which charged local city and county commissions with implementing the law.

The BTNA's early efforts with the schools established their role as a watchdog in the area, and as a strong supporter of system-wide integration. The association in phase two successfully prevented the feeding of its black elementary school into the all-black high school, and instead achieved open enrollment for the elementary school. Though this was essentially a symbolic victory—since it did little to change the actual racial composition—it was, nevertheless, an important indicator of how the school board regarded the association and bowed to its pressure.

The association's work with recreational programs and facilities for youth was very strong in their first two phases, resulting in phase three in the securing of a major facility serving the area. Their recent effort to desegregate an all-white country club in the northern sector was successful, showing ongoing concern of the association and ongoing recognition of the organization's clout.

Finally, their work with land use was almost totally successful. In all their years, virtually every time the association tried to block zoning changes, they won. The BTNA's early (phases one and two) involvement in the development of a land use plan for their area was significant, since it paved the way for all later zoning and land monitoring—providing an enduring set of goals for the use of land in their own area. It became easy for them to thwart some suggested changes by pointing to the land use plan and showing how the proposed change would be inconsistent or harmful to the plan. Generally, then, in all four program areas, the association presented a unified and strong image and succeeded in influencing key decision-makers.

Respondents expressed their views of the association's influence in varying ways. The Hunts said: "We know that we have the ear of the city administration . . . we know that when we come forward with an idea or a plan we're going to be listened to . . . we know that because we've had feedback from other people." They recalled one public hearing in city council chambers, which showed how they were able to mobilize residents to support their zoning requests when needed:

For that fight we had at least 250 people in the chambers—we covered our whole area and we had a whale of an integrated turnout, with busloads of people—and we also encouraged crying children and wheelchairs . . . why not, we know that zoning is partly a dramatic show . . . it was amazing. I was just flabbergasted at how many people showed up that night. . . . I had never seen a turnout as strong as that on any issue. This was 1973.

The issue was the adjacent university's proposal to acquire Butler-Tarkington homes for sorority and fraternity residences. The university lost.

George Harris, black leader in the association, felt that BTNA was "seen as very active, involved, articulate, organized as part of the community. I think they have been appreciated . . . sometimes as an irritant, but always as a force to be reckoned with." The Allendales, former leaders in the association, agreed: "From what we pick up, we think this is still true. . . . They [BTNA] are very much respected by the city officials as being the neighborhood association for this area, the spokesperson, coordinator, as a competent and responsible group . . . so I think they do have good contact with city officials and they respond."

Bill Gerber, who moved to Butler-Tarkington after living in the Meridian-Kessler neighborhood, referred to another type of influence BTNA had had: "I know, as a founder, that the Meridian-Kessler Neighborhood Association chiefly patterned themselves after BTNA, which by that time had results to show. They were nine years old then—this was 1965."

Finally, Elsie Bernivan—president of the association at the time of the interview—modestly reflected: "I think we are well perceived by the city. We have some very influential old families that are living in the area, and I think we probably have more political clout than we realize. We're not politically astute. We're getting there, but we're not as sharp as we could and should be. But I think we're seen as effective . . . we do get in there and talk to people."

Generally, BTNA's record is an impressive one, showing effective lobbying by the organization and persistent concerns for the neighborhood. The association throughout its existence has presented a unified strong and stubborn image and succeeded in influencing key decision makers. Since some of those influential decision makers lived in the Butler-Tarkington area, their responsiveness was not surprising.

FACTORS OF SUCCESS

Now, finally, how can we account for the successful survival of BTNA? What were the factors that contributed to their success? And what can we project into the future—for the association, and for the neighborhood? We can divide success factors into two types—internal and external. Internal success factors relate to the structure of the organization and its participants. External factors include the neighborhood's physical environment—its location, facilities and amenities—and its social environment, that is, other institutional relationships affecting the neighborhood, and political conditions involving city government-neighborhood relations. Additional significant external factors include the city's economic base, and the court-ordered citywide school desegregation program, which ultimately involved not only schools but public housing as well. As we will see, some of the internal and external factors are intertwined.

Internal

There was nothing in the structure of the organization that was unusual for this type of organization. Unlike the other two movement organizations representative of this model, however, the Indianapolis MO has remained unfunded and totally voluntary throughout its long existence. The BTNA's attempts to ensure geographical representation on their governing board were not very successful. Most of the work of the organization throughout its history was done by residents of the area's middle tract, which was moderately integrated. The involvement of residents of the other two tracts—primarily white and primarily black—was minimal. The organization's structure, then, was not a significant factor in its successful survival.

Another internal feature, however, was significant. The organization was blessed with an abundance of talented, dedicated people. This was largely a result of some external features of the neighborhood that attracted such residents. A major private university (Butler) is an integral part of the area, located in its central tract. It is a major stabilizing force, with its acres of wooded grassy campus and its auditorium, which serves as the home of the Indianapolis Symphony. In addition, the Children's Museum—claimed as the largest in the world—and a leading theological seminary are in the heart of the Butler-Tarkington neighborhood. These facilities and amenities are clearly outstanding. They originally attracted professional people to the neighborhood, who then provided rich human resources for the neighborhood association. "The quality of leadership in the association has remained high—we've been used to being sure of active talented people here." This was a typical comment from respondents, confirmed by nonresidents as well.

Ben and Jean Allendale, two of the earliest BTNA leaders, spoke of the combination of internal and external factors that made the area a lively one:

We are surrounded by a cultural presence. The [Children's] Art Museum across the street is internationally known, then there's Butler University with its Century Hall having marvelous plays, and over here's the Field House, and then in the summer next to that is the Summer Outdoor Theatre. So we've got the culture here. . . . We can walk down the block to drop into the symphony, and can walk over to the art museum . . . It's very affordable for university people, symphony people, art museum employees. So there are a number of factors that tip the balance in favor of the neighborhood.

If there had not been a BTNA, would some of these stabilizing things have happened anyway? The answer: "My feeling now is that the neighborhood might not have made it without BTNA. I see it as having held the fort at least for

five years until other things turned in our favor. . . . If other parts of the city
hadn't opened up for blacks, I don't think we could have done it [remained
integrated and stable] . . . because people in the neighborhood weren't opposing
the migration of blacks, and the natural force was simply to have blacks move
into this neighborhood."

The cultural presence and abundant amenities of the B-T neighborhood are
clearly outstanding. They have certainly contributed in large measure to the
stabilization of the neighborhood. But these are external to the organization
itself.

External

An additional helpful external factor was the role of the city in promoting
neighborhood organizations and facilitating interchange and positive relationships with them. This factor was acknowledged by several respondents. The
city, for example, participated for a nominal fee in a neighborhood statistics
program with the U.S. Department of Commerce. As a result, each of sixteen
Indianapolis neighborhoods and their organizations received total family and
area statistics for their entire neighborhood, making it possible to analyze trends
and do comparative analyses. In addition, the city assigned program planners
to work with each neighborhood organization, so there was constant liaison
between the neighborhoods and the city planning department. The Hunts described the city's role in encouraging and helping the 120 neighborhood organizations in the city:

They are active ongoing groups. . . . The mayor has a neighborhood council and they
were meeting monthly . . . they are an advisory council to the mayor, and he in turn
tells them what's happening. He has one assistant in charge of neighborhood relations.
. . . He finds out what people are really interested in. . . . The planning people of the city
have gone to these different areas that have modest neighborhood associations and worked
with them on developing city plans in specific detail for every block in the neighborhood.

Several respondents pointed out the fact that the adjacent Meridian-Kessler
neighborhood, which shared a common boundary (Meridian St.) and some
shopping areas, had an active neighborhood association. This also eased some
of the burdens of both groups by providing double energy and resources devoted
to mutual concerns. Some rivalry existed between the two groups, which may
have been healthy in spurring each other on. The BTNA, as the older group
and the acknowledged model for the other one, may have been motivated to
continue to set an example. They did, however, have one shortcoming—no
staff. Some comparisons between the two groups surfaced in the interviews.
Robert Cramer, a city official, said: "I think BTNA was perceived as a little
less sophisticated in their leadership than MK—but they were working together
. . . MK has managed, though, to do a membership project and fund raising and
all kinds of other things."

Bill Gerber knew both groups well: "I had the impression around 1980 that BTNA might phase out—some said at that time that it wasn't as strong as it had been. But now I find it better than I had envisioned . . . they have a president who is doing a good job, I think. Now, Meridian-Kessler may be stronger, with a little bit of different emphasis—a lot depends on who is in a position of leadership."

Patti Kimble, a leader in the Meridian-Kessler group, also felt that BTNA was somewhat weaker: "I don't think they have a paid staff person . . . and my feeling is—that they are fairly disorganized. We are perceived as having much more weight, much more strength, much more organization. It's really hard to get hold of someone there [at BTNA]. In fact, they had an all-neighborhood meeting that they didn't even have people come to because the dates had been messed up."

When asked whether they thought BTNA had suffered because of a lack of paid staff, Al and Dot Hunt had different opinions. Dot thought they had not suffered, and had in fact gained because "staff makes people depend on them instead of themselves." Al thought lack of staff had hurt BTNA, and had benefitted the Meridian-Kessler group.

There is little question about paid staff providing some relief to organization leaders. But there is some question about whether this is needed now for BTNA. Perhaps the time for this help is gone, perhaps the volume of organizational activity has waned. Some respondents seemed to feel that BTNA was not doing very much any more.

Laurie and Phil Roberts, active leaders in the organization a few years earlier, had this to say:

I think it has a lot less intensity. When we came here it hung together very socially too. Like everybody would gather around and there were a lot of parties and that. . . . We used to have more social events—now only one or two a year. I think people were more ideological . . . now there are business transfers, people are getting older, and there's been some fleeing too.

Ben and Jean Allendale also spoke of some waning: "The general level of activity is not as strong, and I think that is because of the ceased threat. The second thing is that the leadership group may be somewhat more conservative . . . and there's no paid person, it's all volunteer."

The current president, Elsie Bernivan, confirmed the aging of BTNA and the need for paid staff. Longingly, she said:

I'd really like to see BTNA have a staff person—I'd really love to have them represent the organization—someone we could send to the mayor's advisory task force meetings— we really ought to have someone there—it's very hard on a volunteer to say do and go and have at such and such a time. But I don't want it to be that the organization becomes "them." The organization should still be "us." But even a part-time person, someone who could do the newsletter . . . it's hard to get something together. . . . I wish we had a higher profile—more visibility.

George Harris also spoke of the aging of BTNA: "I think it's probably hard to struggle to be as active and as meaningful and as creditable as it was early on. [Why?] I don't know, I think there may have been a stronger sense of commitment on the part of people—more than there is now. . . . The single most important need? . . . Making sure the quality remains."

Anne Morris, another black leader of BTNA, said when asked about the future: "I think it [the neighborhood] is going to just stay as it is—a very pleasant place to live." Historian John Burns said: "I would say I think the organization is a victim of its own success in that now they have the problem of figuring out what else can you do."

It is a fact that the BTNA is now serving as a conduit for small grants going to other groups in need. The president, Elsie Bernivan, spoke of this: "A lot of our money goes to supporting various other groups and services . . . our money goes to support the services we can't provide, but we feel should be continued—so our rule is it has to be serviced within the neighborhood for the benefit of our residents. . . . Give us your funding requests, and then we go from there."

The twenty-fifth anniversary program of the association, printed in 1981, had these words: "BTNA was founded to achieve an ideal, racially integrated, beautiful neighborhood. Today it is a vigorous and vital force in building and maintaining an outstanding quality of life for its residents." Now, there may be some qualifications to these words. The BTNA is no longer quite as vigorous as it once was. The neighborhood is not exactly ideal, since one-third of it is almost all-black, and some of the commercial areas are run-down. But the organization has surely been a vital force in achieving and maintaining a high-quality, stable, integrated community. And even if it did nothing else but serve as a watchdog and continue to distribute small grants for worthy programs in its neighborhood, this would perhaps be an appropriate and graceful way for a middle-aged organization to spend its golden years.

In conclusion, the organization played a critical role in preserving the Butler-Tarkington area as a desirable integrated community. But three other forces external to the organization were essential in the success of this neighborhood's stabilization. The amenities and facilities of the neighborhood, the city's role, and the school desegregation program were the three major external forces in the neighborhood's success and the organization's survival. Without these, it is not likely that either the neighborhood or the organization would have successfully survived.

The amenities and facilities of the neighborhood were vital in two ways. First, the facilities served as an attraction for skilled, professional dedicated people to the neighborhood—to live, work, and recreate—and these were constant valuable resources for the organization. Second, the amenities projected an image of desirability and value for the neighborhood, and this made it easier to preserve it and maintain its quality.

The second force—the city's role—was to enlist very early the participation of organizational leaders and members in the planning process and development of the long-range land use plan for their neighborhood. This enabled the organization to constantly have a reference point for any perceived challenges to the plan, and it enabled them to effectively resist such challenges throughout their second and third phases of existence.

The third force—the school desegregation program—was extremely important in removing the racial identifiability of neighborhood schools in Indianapolis. School desegregation legal rulings also succeeded in preventing additional public housing from being built in or near existing racially integrated neighborhoods. As one resident put it: "If blacks move into an integrated neighborhood they are going to be bussed out. If whites move in, they can stay in the neighborhood school. So it behooves blacks to move to any one of those other township schools because then they are going to be 'naturally integrated' and won't have to be bussed."

The city's school desegregation program had a significant positive impact on the neighborhood. Very early—even before 1965, when the lawsuit was first filed—as soon as the intent to file suit against the board of education was publicized, the school administrators began to adjust school attendance zones and modify school programs to improve racial balance in the schools. Citywide bussing began in 1971, when the case was first settled, and the neighborhood school was no longer a meaningful concept in Indianapolis.

The result of this was that residents in any neighborhood of the city could expect two things: racially integrated schools everywhere, and neighborhood schools nowhere. This effectively removed one stigma from racially integrated neighborhoods, since their schools were no more racially identifiable than those of any other neighborhood. Thus families could be encouraged to move to pluralistic Butler-Tarkington, for example, and not worry about having their children attending racially isolated schools there. In fact, this more than anything else enabled BTNA's housing information service and affirmative marketing programs to succeed.

Another positive by-product of the school desegregation court order was the addition of the issue of segregated public housing four years after the first case was settled. This ultimately led to a metropolitan remedy for both the schools and public housing: the public housing authority was enjoined from building any more housing units anywhere within the city of Indianapolis. The case was in and out of court for over ten years, but the final remedy was most beneficial to the Butler-Tarkington neighborhood. It not only removed the identifiability of its neighborhood schools, it also removed the possibility of further impact from public housing projects.

Not all respondents agreed with this assessment; some believed the court order had caused white flight to either private schools or the suburbs. However, the proportion of the area's school-age children attending private schools in 1980 was 26%, and this included Catholic schools. This was not significantly different from the countywide and national averages for private school attendance.

In conclusion, though BTNA played a critical role in preserving the B-T area as a desirable, stable pluralistic community, three other external forces were essential to their success. The amenities of the neighborhood, the city's role, and the school desegregation program were those forces.

The Butler-Tarkington neighborhood was blessed in having these three external forces to guarantee the successful efforts of the neighborhood organization that served it. The work of the organization, vigorous as it was, was a necessary but insufficient condition of success. The external factors, too, were necessary but may have been insufficient by themselves to ensure success. Without the organization's early work in preventing zoning changes and promoting affirmative marketing of their area, the neighborhood might have been totally resegregated long before the schools were desegregated. This would have made it extremely difficult, if not impossible, to maintain racial pluralism and achieve eventual stability in the area. Thus, the timing of the internal and external factors made it possible for the neighborhood and its organization to succeed in achieving a stable, pluralistic, high-quality neighborhood. Without these factors, it is not likely that either the neighborhood or the organization could have successfully survived, given the long history of racism in the city.

3

ROCHESTER: NINETEENTH WARD COMMUNITY ASSOCIATION

"Where diversity is not only tolerated, but celebrated"

"I can't remember when I last saw a vacant house in the Ward"

"We are known as the strongest community association in the city"

SOCIOHISTORICAL CONTEXT

Once known as a mecca for immigrants, Rochester's location on the Genesee River and the New York State Barge Canal near Lake Ontario's southern shore explains why. A mill, built in 1789 on a clearing around a hundred-foot waterfall called Upper Falls, was the reason for the early attraction of workers and settlers to that spot. The falls still generate electricity for the city. This area became a permanent settlement in 1812, largely through the efforts of Nathaniel Rochester, a New Englander. It was incorporated as the village of Rochesterville in 1817, and was granted a city charter as Rochester in 1834.

Quotes in this chapter are from transcripts of taped interviews conducted in Rochester during July 29–August 5, 1984, unless otherwise noted.

The community was first famous for its flour milling and was known as "the Flour City." In the mid–1800s it developed into a nursery products center and became known as "the Flower City." After the Eastman Kodak Company located in Rochester, people called it "Kodak City." Rochester claimed by the 1960s to be the "City of Many Industries," and at that time—with 800 manufacturing plants—it led the world in the manufacture of photographic film, cameras, optical goods, dental equipment, thermometers, mail chutes, and enameled steel tanks.

More recently, as a leader in optics and lasers, Rochester—seventy miles northeast of Buffalo—has claimed to be a high technology center. It is the home of the University of Rochester, founded in 1850, the Rochester Institute of Technology, founded in 1829, as well as Xerox Corporation, Bausch & Lomb Corporation, and the Kodak Company, all of which provide cadres of skilled researchers, professionals and technicians in the scientific and technological fields.

Also the home of the Eastman School of Music, Rochester is now the third largest city in New York state, with 241,700 people. It has a leading symphony orchestra, the Rochester Philharmonic, and Botanical Gardens, a Museum of Arts and Sciences, the Memorial Art Gallery, an International Museum of Photography, a chamber orchestra, the Seneca Park Zoo, an opera theater, and Stasenburgh Planetarium. Two newspapers are published in the city; eight radio stations and three TV stations broadcast from Rochester.

The Genesee River divides the city into two almost equal parts, connected by twelve bridges. Rochester, with one of the best park systems in the country, is on a broad level plateau in the heart of the picturesque Genesee Valley. Among its landmarks is the Mt. Hope Cemetery, one of the oldest Victorian cemeteries in the nation, which contains the graves of Susan B. Anthony and Frederick Douglass. Douglass, the famed ex-slave, orator, and writer, published the *North Star* in Rochester—a leading antislavery newspaper in mid–nineteenth-century America.

In 1984, Rochester celebrated its sesquicentennial, "while scrambling to complete an urban renewal program that has changed its face without solving all its problems" (*Akron Beacon Journal*, June 17, 1984). It was this urban renewal program, begun decades before, that caused the demolition of whole neighborhoods and waves of human dislocation. It also led to the formation of the Nineteenth Ward Community Association (WCA), twenty years ago.

"Urban Renewal has changed the shape of the skyline and the face of virtually every neighborhood in this city. Construction has closed streets, turning the city into a constantly changing labyrinth of detours and dead ends. One resident of a ramshackle neighborhood has posted a reminder for any overly enthusiastic demolition expert. With its misspelling, it has become part of the town's lore. 'I sill live here,' the sign says" (*Akron Beacon Journal*, June 17, 1984).

I saw that sign and didn't know whether to laugh or cry. About a mile away is a vast central city wasteland called Exchange Street. On it is the sole survivor of earlier land clearance and renewal projects—a one hundred twenty-year-old landmark called Earl's Grill. It has remained alone there for ten years. But it, too, is slated to go soon to make way for new town houses. One patron said about the impending demolition of the grill, "It may be a step forward for progress, but it makes me cry in my beer" (*Akron Beacon Journal*, June 17, 1984).

A brief review of Rochester's demographic trends will show more clearly the impact of its urban renewal programs. The major black migrations to Rochester were in the 1950s and early 1960s. In 1950, Rochester had only 7,590 black people, or about 3,000 families. This was 2.3% of the city's population at that time (332,448). Some of these black residents had lived in the city a long time, others had come more recently in a wave of black migration from the South during and after World War II. Since 1950, Rochester's black population has grown nearly sevenfold, quadrupling to 31,751 (10%) in 1964, and increasing further by nearly 20,000 to a total of 51,115 in 1970. That was 17% of the city population. By 1980, the black population was 26% of the total city population, partially explained by the 20% loss of the city's white population between 1970 and 1980.

Enticed by Northern labor recruiters, and encouraged by reports of prosperity in the North, whole families of Southern blacks came to Rochester in the fifties and early sixties. The migration to Rochester from the South continued into the sixties, when the riots of 1964 rocked that city and the entire country. Why did the riots occur in Rochester? How did this come to happen in the city that was home from 1847 to 1872 to Frederick Douglass, who said of it: "I know of no place in the Union where I could have located . . . with less resistance, or received a larger measure of sympathy and cooperation. . . . I shall always feel more at home there than anywhere else in this country" (Douglass 1966: 151–52).

The answers lie in the history of urban renewal in Rochester, coupled with the legacy of racism and segregation that existed there—so typical of other Northern urban "meccas." And Frederick Douglass did indeed encounter the forerunners of this legacy one hundred years before, despite his nostalgic words above. He also wrote that public school segregation in Rochester then was so blatant that he had to withdraw his children from the public schools to give them a decent education (Douglass 1966: 149–52). We will discuss Rochester schools separately after we consider racism, the riots and urban renewal in that city.

Racism in Rochester—as in other American cities—was reflected in the areas chosen for land clearance: poor black neighborhoods. And of course the fact that they were areas of black concentration and confinement further reflects the racism of the community. Waves of black migration from the South created two major black enclaves in the center of the city. The two major areas of settlement for blacks in Rochester were the central east and the central west side, especially around Clarissa Street (west side) and Joseph Street (east side). These were the places torn apart by the 1964 riots. And these were the very areas later selected for further massive land clearance in renewal projects.

By 1964, when the Rochester riots broke out, many blacks had been displaced by so-called urban renewal six and seven times, shunted into ever-shrinking ghetto areas. Decent housing in Rochester was hard to find, and unemployment was widespread in black neighborhoods: "People spent a lot of time sitting on the stoop. . . . Lots of families had a room and a Murphy bed . . . we were tired of rat infested homes, of having no jobs, of being discriminated against" (Rochester Democrat-Chronicle, July 22, 1984).

Old news articles from the Rochester Democrat-Chronicle show the chronology of urban renewal events that led to shrinking ghettos and to the riots. A later article, "Who Killed Our Neighborhoods?" confirms them (Democrat-Chronicle, July 7, 1974). Beginning in 1939, the headlines tell the tale: "Clearing of Ormond Area" (Feb. 7, 1939); "Demolitions Set Despite Protests" (Aug. 22, 1963); "Higher Kennedy Towers Requested" (Jan. 18, 1964); "Downtown Face Lift" (Jan. 28, 1974); "Downtown's Face Keeps Changing" (Jan. 28, 1974); "City to Get $60 Million for Renewal" (Aug. 22, 1974).

During these years, Rochester cleared land for a new civic center, two downtown arterial belts, public housing (racially segregated), parking decks, malls, a War Memorial with a 7,500-seat sports arena and auditorium, a 240 car pigeonhole garage "with a dashing checkerboard front" (Times-Union, March 12, 1952), a riverfront park, and a "spectacularly successful 500 car multi-ramp garage . . . raking in money so fast that the million dollar investment should be liquidated in fifteen years. . . . Another ramp garage is under construction, a third is on the drawing board, and there may be a fourth" (Democrat-Chronicle, Sept. 8, 1957).

From 1952 to 1977, nearly $220 million was spent on nine urban renewal projects covering nearly three square miles. Rochester had the thirteenth largest urban renewal program in the nation, though it was only the thirty-fourth largest city. All three levels of government spent the $220 million trying to wipe out blight, and—though not trying to—creating more blight. They moved 4,350 families—one out of twenty-three—and relocated 911 businesses, putting 420 of them out of business. They built three parks, three elementary schools, two hotels, three office buildings, two parking garages, rebuilt streets, and put in new sewer and water lines. They left 110 acres of vacant land. They also built public housing; the first was a 392-unit high rise project, Hanover House, built in 1952 at Joseph and Herman streets.

Public housing for the poor, always racially segregated, was built for families in black areas or the elderly in white areas, and maintained as separate projects. The areas of public housing projects were racially identifiable as black or white throughout the 1960s and 1970s. Late in the 1970s, efforts were made to desegregate some of the units, as well as some leased and scattered-site housing. But by then, whole neighborhoods and their schools were racially segregated.

Comments about Rochester's urban renewal programs show their impact on neighborhoods, and on blacks in particular. Blacks charged that urban renewal was a black removal program, designed to destroy black neighborhoods. They said displaced blacks ended up in substandard housing in other parts of the city. They also said that cleared land stood vacant for years, waiting for funds to become available for housing. Typically, the city's first urban renewal project—completed in 1959—cost $55.4 million, and moved 850 families, of whom three-fourths were black and poor. The third ward, once the most elegant in the city, had 540 homes torn down for urban renewal. "Vacant land is nearly all that's left of a neighborhood once called 'the hill of liveliness' " (Mangione 1974: 7). Even a director of the city Housing Authority acknowledged: "Today we have a complete shift to the preservation of neighborhoods. The way we did it then was a complete antithesis of that—it was the destruction of neighborhoods" (Democrat-Chronicle, Dec. 25, 1977).

Three days and nights of violence in July 1964 reflected the tensions, the pent-up frustrations, and the deep exasperation of those living in crowded, blighted, segregated neighborhoods. Ironically and tragically, one of the causes of their plight—urban renewal—also became the proposed remedy. City officials claimed that further urban renewal in the riot areas "would cleanse the business districts of Joseph and North Clinton Avenues and the residential neighborhoods next to them" (Democrat-Chronicle, Dec. 27, 1977). To be called the Upper Falls project, this was heralded as a five-year plan for one block at a time. Since everyone wanted to sell, though, it became a two-year plan, and the area quickly became a ghost town. The adjacent neighborhoods received the displaced people and became the new targets for blight, overcrowding, and future land clearance. By the mid-seventies, an additional $100 million had been spent for urban renewal projects in the areas where the riots had occurred.

President Nixon's moratorium on housing construction in the seventies affected housing plans. Of 5,076 housing units torn down, only 2,973 new ones were built—about three for every five torn down. The moratorium left the city with 110 acres of vacant urban renewal land, of which about eighty-two acres were meant for housing. By this time, the vacancy rate in the city was 10%, so there was no longer an urgent need to build.

As in other cities, Rochester's demographic changes—brought about by urban renewal displacement, relocation, and public housing site selection—affected the neighborhood schools, which in turn affected the neighborhoods. Though the Rochester public schools first began to maintain a racial census in 1966, their recognition of the extent of racial isolation in their schools was evident as early as 1963. And this recognition was encouraged and aided by the state of New York, which in 1960 issued a statement claiming that racial isolation in the public schools was harmful (State of New York 1960).

The Rochester statement was actually a resolution, adopted unanimously by the school board on August 27, 1963 as their "Policy on Racial Imbalance in the Public Schools," and it shows their awareness of the problem. Four clauses affirmed their belief that schools should prepare children for life in a democratic society, that this depended on the degree of cultural interchange in the schools, that improved racial balance would help this interchange as well as increasing pupil motivation and achievement, and that six Rochester schools were racially imbalanced (ranging from 70–95% black in 1962).

The resolution called for the development of plans for significantly reducing racial imbalance in those schools where it existed. The plans were to be implemented by the superintendent of schools no later than September 1964, and could include any or all of these eight methods for achieving improved racial balance: redrawing district boundary lines; school pairings; establishing junior high schools; changing feeder patterns of primary to secondary schools; open enrollment plans; closing schools or portions of them; building new schools; and creating school groupings within the city.

These plans were the first of a long sequence of board actions intended to overcome the negative effects of racial isolation of children in the public schools of Rochester. In February 1964, a voluntary open enrollment program began in which 495 minority children from six inner-city schools voluntarily transferred to eighteen outer-city schools having few minority students. A home school zone plan was initiated in 1965 in which children were free to transfer to any of three schools in a zone. A total of nine schools were involved, with 231 children participating.

That same year an urban-suburban transfer program was begun, with minority students volunteering to attend white suburban schools. Twenty-four first graders from a predominantly black city school transferred to a suburban elementary school. In 1966, open enrollment was expanded to the secondary school level, with 230 seventh graders from three black schools transferring to three white high schools. In addition, some schools were closed and new ones were opened, with racial balance as the stated reorganization goal. At that time, minority students were 28.7% of all those attending Rochester public schools.

Despite these efforts, by 1978 minority enrollment in Rochester schools was 56.2%, having nearly doubled in twelve years. In those twelve years, school administrators continually monitored their plans and modified them periodically, as needed, in keeping with the major goal of racial balance. In 1967, the board of education issued a statement in response to a national report of the U. S. Commission on Civil Rights. The Rochester board called for regional approaches to the reduction of racial isolation, but committed itself to continuing to develop and use programs locally to reduce isolation (Rochester board proposals, March 16, 1967). Some of these efforts included classes for the gifted in inner-city black schools, a reverse open enrollment plan, and the creation of a citywide magnet junior high school, the World of Inquiry school.

The state of New York's education department consistently reinforced these local efforts. A 1968 report, "Integration and the Schools,"outlined state policy and thirteen recommendations for action. It said: "This condition [racial segregation] must not be tolerated in a democratic society. Effective solutions must be found even if they require major changes. . . . This statement . . . is a reaffirmation of the determination to see that segregation in education is eliminated" (State of New York, 1968).

During the 1971–72 school year, the board of education implemented a districtwide reorganization plan designed to provide improved quality of education as well as racial balance in nearly all schools. But the following November, a new board was elected, which rescinded the reorganization plan and restored the earlier voluntary open enrollment plan, along with the urban-suburban transfer of minority students. Thus the Rochester struggle for racial balance and equal educational opportunity in the public schools continued over the years, while the proportion of minority children increased steadily in the district.

By 1976, ten elementary schools had minority enrollments of over 90%, with 39% of all black children having no interracial school contact. At the same time, five elementary schools were 90% or more white, with 3,300 children denied the opportunity for interracial contact. Only 4.9% of all the students in 1976 participated in the open enrollment plan, which was modified then to insure that all voluntary transfers contributed positively to racial balance in the schools. Before then, no racial count was taken of those transfers. The 1976 modification did result in some racial balance improvement in twenty-three out of the forty-six elementary schools and seven of the twelve secondary schools. Over 800 minority students participated in the urban-suburban transfer program.

Despite these constant efforts to improve racial balance in Rochester schools, 1,500 students left the school system in 1978 (Times-Union, Sept. 13, 1978). This prompted a citizen group to survey parents as to their reasons for withdrawal, and to present their findings to the school board. Though further modifications in the plan resulted from this study, the school district in 1979 came under review by two federal agencies: the Civil Rights Division of the Department of Justice, and the Office of Civil Rights of HEW (Times-Union, April 17, 1979). By this time there were at least three different citizen groups involved with school improvements—a Citizens Task Force on City/School District Finances, Better Education Today, and the Coalition for Accountability in Rochester Education. All vied with each other for support, publicity, and response from school officials.

A 1980 five-page resolution by the school board contained six clauses referring to past actions relating to racial balance efforts, and called for yet another revision of its school zone and transfer policies (resolution, April 11, 1980). A change in school superintendents at this time did not reduce the programs for achieving racial balance. Memos and reports from school administrators indicate constant monitoring, reassessment, and revisions of school racial balance programs during the past twenty years.

One resident who had two children in the Rochester schools said at the end of an interview, "I never took a school bus, and Emily [daughter] has never not taken a school bus." When I asked him if he thought having the open enrollment system was a benefit for his integrated neighborhood, the nineteenth ward, he said: "Absolutely I do—because it means you're not locked into one choice and you can use the public school system and not go to a private school, and you don't have to move outside the ward to get the school choices you want" (J. O'Donnell). In fact, one of the external reasons for the success of the Nineteenth Ward Community Association in maintaining stable integration is the school program for racial balance. Let us turn now to that organization, and see how it began, and what it did, and why it succeeded.

INCEPTION

Clergy from eleven different neighborhood churches in the nineteenth ward of Rochester were the catalysts for neighborhood action in 1965. Responding to changes in their area resulting from massive urban renewal relocation, block-busting, and white flight, about seventy-five residents and church leaders gathered on July 19, 1965, at Calvary Baptist Church to discuss their concerns. A steering committee was formed to develop a statement of purpose. The following month, on August 30, some 300 residents of the nineteenth ward came to the same church to approve that statement of objectives. Chaired by a minister, the steering committee of twelve also included two other clergymen who labored together to draw up the first statement. These words reflect their earliest concerns:

Unless a nineteenth ward community council is soon formed to take positive steps, the deterioration of the nineteenth ward community, due to mass exchange of property ownership, unchallenged requesting of zoning variances, and lack of provision for parking facilities will accelerate. The deterioration will result from the employment of "block-busting" techniques on the part of certain real estate salesmen and brokers, including the use of racial issues to induce panic selling. (Bush & Weiss 1979: 1; Meadows 1984: 15)

The original objective was to form a community council to take preventive measures to deal with the above factors and any new situations that might develop. The overall goal was "to preserve the nineteenth ward as a desirable residential community, open to all who could afford to maintain a home." In addition, they hoped to provide a model "for the possibility of a racially integrated community within a stable residential area." They went on to define a "stable community" as one in which the homes were mostly one- or two-family residences, and in which the buying and selling of property was "for reasons other than panic and speculation."

The two earliest structural subdivisions of the steering committee were finances and membership, and constitution; the first two program committees formed were education and public relations, and issues and actions. The latter was subdivided into four others: building and maintenance, real estate, social actions, and parking/zoning/planning. In September 1965, over 400 people came to the neighborhood high school to discuss the objectives of the new group and additional community needs. One month later, another informational meeting was held in another church location.

One of the founders and first chair of the issues and actions committee recalled the early days of the association: "What started all this was real estate problems with block-busting—and after the ministers and some of the people got together, we passed the hat and I guess we got around thirty dollars. That was the first treasury or funding that we ever had. And from the first meeting came three or four others and a few temporary committees" (Ron Jarvis).

This founder and early activist of the Nineteenth WCA pointed to three specific real estate problems that plagued the neighborhood and united the residents with a common grievance. The three real estate practices were: using racial issues to encourage panic selling in the neighborhood; encouraging black prospective buyers and discouraging white buyers from looking at homes in the neighborhood; and encouraging buyers to use property for speculation rather than residence (Meadows 1984: 16).

The early meetings revealed that real estate practices were not the only issue. Three other problems that concerned residents in those early days were the noise from airplanes flying to and from the airport (on the western border of the ward), school curriculum and racial balance issues, and the need for youth services. These, along with real estate practices, continued to be the main problems of the association during the next twenty years.

One of the first comprehensive newspaper articles about the nineteenth ward organization referred to the association having banded together to keep the neighborhoods stable and to have a voice in guiding any changes in the ward. By 1969—the time of the article—the nineteenth ward had changed in ten years from an all-white area to about 10% black. The article noted that change in this way: "Twenty-five years ago, it was one of Rochester's most desirable neighborhoods [meaning all-white]. . . . People just don't want it to become all-black and leave them as the only white. . . . They've seen it happen" (*Democrat-Chronicle*, April 13, 1969).

This did not happen to the nineteenth ward, and the association's work for twenty years may have been a prime stabilizing factor. We turn now to an analysis of their structure over three phases of their development.

STRUCTURE

Phase One: 1965–70

From their inception, the association divided the nineteenth ward into geographical districts. These divisions, conceived by the membership committee, grew from twenty-two to twenty-six, and then to twenty-eight. City election district boundaries were used, with some modifications to allow neighbors on the same street to be in the same district. Organizers were recruited for each of the twenty-two districts first designated. The organizers were charged with securing members for the fledgling organization, and their efforts produced 700 members by the end of the first year of the organization. Each district elected a representative to the council of delegates, the group's governing body. The Rochester group was unique among those studied here, in that it specified total geographical representation for its governing body from the beginning. However, examination of meeting minutes indicates that delegate council meetings often had only half the districts represented, and that less than half of the institutions were in attendance.

Each of the ten local churches in the nineteenth ward pledged to pay part of the salary of a part-time staff worker to handle the secretarial tasks for the organization. Thus, two months after their formation, the association had a part-time staff worker assisting them. Throughout their existence, the WCA retained a part-time staff person to handle secretarial work and assist in the administration of the committees, board, and council of delegates. This was another important factor differentiating the Rochester neighborhood association from the others studied in this book.

The Rochester group also carefully separated their budget and staff for daily business from other funding and staff secured for special projects. These did not even appear on the organization's treasury reports. Until 1972 (Phase 2), the WCA had no office; in 1972 they set up an office in a storefront on one of the neighborhood's few business streets.

Their early method of securing funding was also unique. Ron Jarvis—a founding member and first chair of the issues and actions committee—explained how their first funded youth project was organized:

We had volunteers helping run storefront youth centers for a time . . . but we recognized we needed some kind of a professional. So we started looking and interviewed about fifteen people and we settled on Ted Amber, a minister from Detroit. We said we can underwrite your paycheck for the next three months. . . . Your first job is gonna be to fund your own salary. What we needed was a person who could sit down and write to the Ford Foundation and all these places and develop grant money. . . . Well, before he got through he was up to around the $300,000 mark.

This first director of the WCA's youth center went on to work for the city's youth division, then the county's youth department, and finally ended as the state director in charge of all youth programs.

The association's council of delegates—consisting of representatives of the twenty-six districts and neighborhood institutions—first met monthly to resolve community issues, and met annually for a full membership convention. Later, when attendance began to wane, the constitution only called for four delegates' meetings a year. All delegates had alternates from their district who could represent them when they were absent. Chairs of standing committees were also important and served as advisors to the council, and later were members of the council.

But the real power of the organization lay in the executive committee, and especially in the president. The president appointed all committees and their chairs, with the approval of the executive committee—consisting of five officers, the immediate past president, and two council representatives. All were elected by the council for one-year terms, but eligible for reelection in subsequent years. Only the president was limited to two consecutive terms.

From 1965 to 1968, three successive part-time staff workers worked for the association out of their homes, doing much of the needed telephoning, typing, and mailing. They were aided by college students as summer volunteers, recruited through the campus ministries of the council of churches. During this early part of phase one, most officers and committee chairs remained the same, giving much continuity to the organization. Continuity was also provided by having new delegates receive training for their roles in special annual training sessions, taught by several experienced council members. A delegates' manual, prepared in 1968 by a former president and then current officer, was given to each delegate, committee chair, and officer. This training and orientation for council members continued throughout the association's existence, and is an important factor in their continuity and success. Delegates' actual responsibilities, however, were not spelled out until phase two, when this became necessary for organizing and recruiting in unrepresented districts. As in the other cities studied, the areas with least representation and participation were predominantly white or black.

By 1969, the organization saw the need for quarterly financial statements; this was, in fact, made a constitutional amendment at that time. "The annual statement was no longer sufficient as expense and incomes grew" (Bush & Weiss 1979: 11). At this time family memberships were three dollars a year and individual memberships were two dollars. Additional income was raised from special events. Though each event brought modest returns, together they made up a sizable portion of the association's income. However, this was beginning to be too small an amount to handle the volume of work the association was doing by then—mostly through their youth and real estate committees. In December 1970, at the end of phase one, the treasurer reported almost $500 in unpaid bills.

Although the report of memberships in the association was 700 one year after they first organized, the number fluctuated over the years. In 1968, only 230 households paid dues to the WCA, in 1969 over 500 were members, and by 1970 749 households were dues-paying members. Three new membership categories were added at that time, bringing added revenues to the group's treasury: sustaining, contributing, and participating merchants. Ten merchants were listed as participants in 1970, with the numbers growing over the years. The specific numbers of members in any one year reflected the particular skills and successes of the chairperson of the membership committee for that year.

The association's first full-time staff person was hired in September 1969. Two months later, the new youth director obtained a $5,000 foundation grant and $500 donation for a mimeograph purchase. A state grant of $10,800 followed for a youth film project. A second state grant of $23,700 was obtained for the project in December 1970. These were the first of many grants the director succeeded in getting for the youth project, including a large one from the National Institute for Mental Health. Within a year of his arrival, the new director submitted his proposal to the federal government for a quarter of a million dollars for the youth project. He got it. His own salary at that time was $10,500 a year, and the two new youth workers he hired each received $7,500 a year (minutes, Oct. 14, 1970).

One important constitutional change that occurred towards the end of phase one, in November 1969, modified the system for selecting district delegates. It now allowed delegates to be on the council who "have a legitimate interest in the District," instead of the earlier requirement of coming from a district having ten paid memberships (Bush & Weiss 1979: 16). This change was made to allow strong workers to help weaker districts. The WCA's history notes, "It has caused some concern since." We have already noted that some sections of the nineteenth ward were more difficult to organize than others. These were generally the blacker and poorer sections, as in other cities studied. Since people came to represent those areas who did not live in them, a potential source of conflict and misunderstanding was built into the organization's structure with this 1969 amendment.

The charge that the association was white-dominated and middle-class has plagued them throughout their existence. Though they have tried consistently to recruit blacks into the council, on committees, and into leadership positions— and often succeeded—they have never been able to erase the image of themselves as a predominantly white group. This, of course, has made it even more difficult to successfully recruit blacks. Typical was this observation from a long-term leader of the association (white): "One thing we have regretted is that we have not had greater black participation in the WCA. . . . We've always . . . tried to pay attention to that—to try to reach out and improve. . . . We've actually had proportionately more blacks as leaders than those who were members" (Carrie Amber). Much earlier—fifteen years before—a news article quoted the president of the WCA admitting the association had trouble recruiting blacks. He said then that many blacks thought it was a white neighborhood protection group. At that time it had about fifty black members out of 1,200 (Democrat-Chronicle, April 13, 1969). Clearly, the problem never went away.

Phase Two: 1971–78

Early in this phase, the need for an office for the association itself, apart from the youth project, was actively expressed for the first time by the office coordinator. In November 1971, a temporary office was established in one of the neighborhood churches, and one month later, a new association office opened on one of the main business streets of the area. A part-time bookkeeper was sought, and a new part-time office coordinator was hired. She stayed two years, and was replaced by another office coordinator who remained throughout phase two, again giving much-needed continuity and stability to the changing organization. The search for a storefront office continued, however, and it was not until 1974 that the hoped for storefront was secured.

The youth project went through tremendous changes during this second phase of WCA's development. The changes were all in the direction of more and more funding and expanded programs. The project's staff grew from one to thirteen, with two additional people hired as liaison workers with the public schools. Grant receipts for the youth project during the first ten months in 1973 were $167,523.35, and these continued to grow.

In June 1974, the highly effective youth project director left the project after four and one-half years for a position with the county youth board. Though a capable replacement was found, the youth project was never again as successful as it had been, and was soon plagued with staff turnover and administrative problems. In April 1977, the youth project was merged with another agency "after a huge investment of energy on the part of the Executive Committee, Youth Committee, and Youth Project staff, who found this a difficult and emotional issue" (Bush & Weiss 1979: 40). This project had lasted eleven years under WCA direction. Longtime association members referred to the youth project in interviews with affection and nostalgia, recalling it as the first funded project of the association. They found it difficult to relinquish their authority over it.

A wide variety of other funded programs had begun during phase two, however, and these were able to take the place of the youth project. In 1971, for example, a senior citizen service program was organized with aid of a $6,000 foundation grant which continued for the next two years. This was followed by other foundation grants of $7,000 for the seniors program. A two-year Ford Foundation grant of $50,000 for a schools promotional effort was awarded in 1976. Toward the end of phase two, the WCA received a state grant of $30,000 for a preservation program of housing services and research. In a related effort to fight foreclosures and abandonment, they began actively to seek funds in 1978 from the city, state, and private foundations to implement this program.

Community events and the membership drives continued to supply funds for the operating expenses of the association, apart from the special funded projects. An annual income of $19,963.78 for operating expenses in 1972 rose to $23,900 by 1979—all raised by volunteer activities. By the end of phase two, a two-page printed explanation guide was prepared for interpreting the association's monthly financial statements.

Membership levels fluctuated, again depending on the energies and skills of the drive leaders. In 1971, thirty-eight businesses were participating merchants; in 1973 the number increased to forty-seven. General memberships ranged from an all time high of 1,100 in 1973 to a low of 600 in 1977, increasing by 160 new memberships in 1978. A 1974 survey of ward residents by WCA revealed the need for greater outreach efforts to secure memberships. Telephone campaigns were begun for association promotion and member recruitment. In October 1977, the delegates council authorized an annual finance campaign, to be conducted in coordination with the annual convention. Sixty percent of the revenues were to be allocated for operating expenses of the association, and 40% were to be reserved for "innovative program development" (Bush & Weiss 1979: 42).

The WCA formed an important new committee in 1975, when the delegates council directed the president to appoint a long-range planning committee (minutes, May 21, 1975). At its first meeting, the following month, the six-member committee adopted an acronym for its group: PACE '76, relating to the four major phases in that process: planning, allocation (of financial and human resources), campaign (financial), and evaluation. The " '76" referred to the first year of the second decade of association service to the community.

Chaired by the former first director of the youth project, the committee developed a work plan and a one-year timeline. The committee expanded to twenty-one members and put over 1,000 person hours into this process. Their final thirty-three-page report was written with a dual purpose: to support perceived needs in the nineteenth ward with recommendations; and to document the process the committee used to reach their recommendations.

Two surveys were conducted by the PACE committee to help them decide what the community's needs were. One was a direct mail questionnaire sent to all 589 association members; the other was a random telephone survey of 272 residents of the ward. Responses from the two surveys were combined to produce the perceived needs of the community. In addition to the surveys of residents and members, the committee held personal interviews with representatives from churches, merchants, neighborhood institutions, and local and regional government agencies. They also used secondary data sources, including demographic data, government documents, and planning reports. Two final major needs for the nineteenth ward emerged from all these sources: safety and property preservation.

After survey and interview results were compiled, seven groups of residents were formed as "think tanks" and were asked to produce five solutions to the expressed needs. Two community consultants provided advice on the decision-making model, which also included training sessions for the group leaders. Short-range and long-range goals were produced, along with one-year cost estimates. The results were included in the final report, which became a standing future resource for the association in subsequent years.

This detailed planning process was in later years streamlined into one Planning Day, which ranked problems by priority, offered methods of dealing with them, and referred them to the delegates council for final determination of neighborhood needs. In 1978, for example, such needs were found to be: (1) physical appearance, (2) human feelings and perceptions, (3) commercial viability, and (4) institutional practices.

Three constitutional changes were made in 1974, allowing nonresident memberships, modifying the duties of the treasurer, and creating the position of two new delegate representatives to serve on the executive committee. These reflect the ever-present need to better represent the community in decision making.

Again in 1976 the bylaws were amended, this time to include a planning and evaluation committee as a permanent standing committee, replacing the former PACE. Later in that same year, another constitutional change was approved by the membership, which extended the boundaries of the WCA to the rear lot line of properties on border streets and moved the northern boundary line further north, from Chili Avenue to West Avenue. Organization of this new northern wedge-shaped area began with a membership solicitation campaign.

During this second phase the association was involved in continuing organization of unrepresented districts and training of delegates. A memo to the executive committee noted four duties of a delegate: (1) Arrange for the distribution of the association newsletter to every home in his/her district twice a year (May and October); (2) attend delegates council meeting each month, with alternate when possible; (3) organize and host a district meeting at least once a year in October (for election); and (4) be the contact person for all residents in district on any matters of concern.

In 1972, former verbal reports by committee chairs were dispensed with in favor of written reports from each committee. Folders of committee reports were prepared for all members at the annual convention. Thus the formalization of the association was under way early in phase two. A prophetic note is found in the Agenda of a Delegates Council meeting set for July 1972:

We want to assess the financial opportunities opened by our tax exempt status and our growing sophistication in attracting money from government agencies and private foundations. . . . This discussion raises fundamental issues about the nature of our Association. Some people argue . . . that too many large programs will make us overly bureaucratic and that lots of money from outside sources will dilute the volunteer spirit which had made us so successful. (Handwritten note, Agenda for Delegates Council, July 1972)

This growing formalization and organizational complexity of the WCA was also recognized in 1973 by the formation of a social committee, set up as an offshoot of the public relations committee. The establishment of the social committee seemed to be an attempt to provide a counter-trend to the growing bureaucratic tendencies of the organization. Further reflection of perceived impersonality and unconcern of the association is found in 1977, when a small group called the Arnett Area Alliance began to deal with problems in one neighborhood that the association was apparently not handling.

Organizational complexity in phase two was accompanied by some volunteer fatigue. By February 1974, the growing burdens of the volunteer newsletter editor resulted in her replacement by a new editor. Turnover in editors continued throughout the rest of phases two and three. Other examples of some fatigue at this time are seen in committee chair resignations: the chair of the schools committee and the chair of the parks and recreation committee. Each left their positions vacant, leaving gaps hard to fill.

Phase Three: 1979–

Early in 1979, the housing preservation project (noted above) opened in a satellite office, using a $30,000 state grant. Two foundation grants of $11,500 were also received for the project. The WCA's new rehabilitation corporation, FOR–19 (Focus on Rehabilitation in the Nineteenth Ward), also at this time received funding of $65,000 from the local Community Chest, which enabled it to hire staff to buy, rehabilitate and resell abandoned homes in the ward. Additional funding was sought from federal, state and local government agencies, which was granted in 1980. A city grant of $35,000 and a $67,647 federal grant further strengthened the project and expanded its activities and staffing. In 1981, a state grant of $45,000 was also awarded for the preservation program. By the end of 1981, the state funding for the preservation project increased by 42%. That project then expanded to include businesses, and increased staffing required a larger office and a new location. So in phase three, WCA maintained three offices: one for their operation, and two others for each of these two projects.

Action taken to deal with administrative matters involved increasing amounts of time and energy by executive committee members, who already were attending numerous association meetings each month. In addition, a newly funded project was added to their growing list of program concerns: Trends, funded by the state, city, and a foundation to provide home security, primarily for the elderly. A comment from one resident and delegate reveals the growing administrative burdens: "Seventy percent of all meeting time of the board, executive committee and delegates council is spent on personnel matters regarding funded projects— such as how to deal with grievances" (Don Sawyer).

A twenty-one-page personnel policies manual prepared by the association (not dated) shows the extent of the Association's involvement with administrative details, as does a two-page document labeled "Greviance [sic] Proceedings" (WCA Grievance Document, Oct. 20, 1982). The minutes of another executive committee meeting in 1983 contained only one out of six agenda items that was *not* related to administrative details relating to the funded projects.

By June 1983, the demands of the executive committee were so great that a special volunteer oversight committee for the preservation project was proposed. This was to be a four-person committee including the association treasurer. The committee's responsibilities would include total program administration: hiring and firing decisions; job description preparation (with the staff manager); hearing employee grievances; reviewing program reports from the staff manager; providing measurable goals and objectives for the program and manager; evaluating the manager; providing special training; preparing with staff all funding applications and budgets; monitoring the financial status of the program; and revising and approving monthly financial reports.

What is truly remarkable is that four people were indeed found who were willing to devote the necessary time and effort to serve on this new committee (minutes, Jan. 18, 1984). Minutes from that meeting also indicate renewal of state funding for the preservation program, with additional foundation and corporate financial support.

However, at that time the association and both of their funded projects got into serious trouble when a $50,000 federal and state tax liability was discovered. A flurry of meetings of the executive committee took place, with association officers trying to understand how this could have happened without their annual audits spotting the bookkeeper's oversight. The association was stung by a news article that appeared with this headline: "19th WCA Owes More Than $50,000 in Back Taxes" (*Democrat-Chronicle*, March 31, 1984). A special commission was set up by the WCA to determine the causes of the problem and to recommend actions for resolving it. They found that the problem was caused by cash flow difficulties in the FOR–19 project, which resulted in nonpayment of taxes in 1981 and 1982. In those years a thorough financial audit was not made, and the errors were not discovered. But by June 1984 all the taxes were paid, with interest. The FOR–19 project, however, was phased out earlier than the WCA had planned. The preservation program continued undaunted, and even received an additional new $499 grant from the Junior League.

By 1982, the association operated their office and volunteer activities with a budget of $24,012.80 for the year. Detailed financial reports and breakdowns were available for distribution, indicating ongoing support and strength. The major sources of funding for WCA's operating expenses continued to be membership drives, finance campaigns, and the Square Fair—all carried out independently of the funded projects. The association office, part-time staff, and other affairs were kept strictly separate from the funded staffed projects. But the responsibilities of maintaining all of these separate operations weighed heavily on WCA leaders. One resident and volunteer said: "The bookkeeper now keeps track of seventeen different accounts at the Preservation office" (Dana Morris).

One sign of reaction to the growing complexity of the association's programs in this phase was the formation of a WCA human relations committee, "which will deal with neighborly things such as block parties" (minutes, May 9, 1983). This seemed a clear bid for some homey, nonbureaucratic ventures. And along with the increased complexity came some fatigue. Three signs of fatigue found in WCA records were the trouble in organizing the Citizen of the Year dinner, and the difficulty in obtaining anyone to chair the Square Fair: "A chair person is needed by February 15 if Square Fair is to occur this year" (minutes, Jan. 18, 1984)—they finally did find three people—and the continuing turnover of newsletter editors: "Where Is That New Editor?" (newsletter Jan. 1984).

That newsletter issue listed thirty-four volunteers as having put it together. Despite changes in editors and volunteers, however, WCA's newsletter, *Update*, continued to be published and distributed monthly. But conducting their annual finance drive became too much of a chore, and was not done in 1983. The finance committee recommended that the drive not be held that year, but rather that emphasis be placed on the upgrading of memberships and obtaining higher levels of contributions (minutes, April 4, 1983).

Thus, the glamor and glory of all the funded programs has also brought anxieties, administrative burdens, fatigue, and some burnout. We turn now to an examination of those programs during the three phases of WCA's development, as well as of the goals that led to them.

GOALS

The original goals of the WCA were stated in their first constitution and newsletter. Though the words were modified in 1970, their basic intent remained the same throughout the association's existence. The first version of the constitution listed three objectives of the association: to preserve and further develop the nineteenth ward as a desirable residential community; to promote civic pride in the nineteenth ward, and to do everything that is morally and legally right to achieve these ends (WCA constitution, Nov. 29, 1965, and newsletter, March 15, 1966).

"Just What Can the Community Association Do for Me?" was the heading of a major article in the association's first newsletter. In this article, following the list of three objectives noted above, were more detailed explanations of the goals and objectives of the new organization:

The 19th WCA is *designed to maintain vigilance against the evils which cause decay of a community.* These evils are clear cut and evident. They include block-busting, disregard for zoning laws, untidyness and carelessness on the part of individuals and, most important of all, well meaning irresponsibility and ignorance on the part of the average citizen who does not try to stop these other evils. (newsletter, March 15, 1966; emphasis added)

Ron Jarvis, a founder of WCA, recalled the early days and the first stated goals a little differently: "The original goal—we were primarily concerned directly with the integration situation and the way it was being handled. That was goal number one. We wanted to stop the so-called block-busting tactics, and we wanted to open up the area to blacks." Cindy O'Donnell had another view: "I think the basic desire of having a prosperous community with good city services, good schools—that's the goal at a very simplistic level."

The early goals of the WCA were publicly referred to by their public relations director in a news article that appeared toward the end of phase two. According to this public relations spokesperson, the goals were: "To stop the blockbusting, stabilize the population growth, stop the busting up of large houses into apartments, and to keep the owners on the premises" (*Democrat-Chronicle*, May 27, 1976).

The only constitutional goal change—and a most important one—made in the history of the association took place in 1970. The executive committee and all standing committee chairs developed four goals for the association as an alternative to the three original objectives noted above. These were presented and approved at the November 1970 annual members' convention. The new goals were:

(1) Create a conscious multiracial community *where individual and cultural differences are not only tolerated but celebrated,* and where people share a sense of community, (2) insure that the community, through the Association, determines the kinds of high quality services it needs from public and private institutions, (3) encourage resident home ownership and oppose any threat to the residential character of the community, and (4) recognize our relationship and responsibility to the total metropolitan community. (convention minutes, Nov. 1970; emphasis added)

The president of the WCA wrote about the goal amendment in the next issue of the newsletter: "These objectives reflect a shift in emphasis from property values to human values that is taking place in the Association" (newsletter, Nov. 1970). Though the emphasis on property values continued nevertheless throughout the existence of the organization, these goal changes did three important things for the association. First, they explicitly named racial integration as a goal for the first time; second, they specified action areas of concern; and third, they linked the neighborhood group to the larger metropolitan community. Each of these was reflected in the program of the association over the next two phases of their development.

The goals and general spirit of the WCA at the end of phase one are most clearly revealed in a keynote speech given by Art Sansom, the outgoing WCA president, to the 1970 members' convention. He spoke of some misunderstandings in the larger community about what the WCA stood for. They had been called radical by reactionaries and reactionary by radicals. Sansom said he thought the WCA provided each of them the unique opportunity to be for something. And that something was "how do we deal with fear in general, and black-white fear in particular."

He then pointed out that by moving to the nineteenth ward, and choosing to remain in it, they had chosen to deal with a given set of problems. For those who were ready to be for something, there were these alternatives: emphasizing human dignity rather than demeaning it, knowing who you are and being it:

These alternatives provide for the future of the 19th Ward. . . . James Baldwin said it most eloquently when he wrote these words, "The moment we cease to hold each other, the moment we break faith with one another, the sea engulfs us and the light goes out". . . . [The] famous musical tragedy "West Side Story" has a note of hope in the finale: "Some day, somewhere, we will find a new way of living. We will find a way of forgiving— somewhere there's a place for us, a time and a place for us." Now has to be the time and the 19th Ward has to be the place . . . for us. (convention minutes, Nov. 1970)

This spirit, and the goals that motivated it, were retained throughout WCA's existence. Let us now see how they implemented both spirit and goals.

PROGRAM

One early action taken by the fledgling WCA had a profound influence on their spirit, program, and strategies. Ron Jarvis recalled this significant action: "When the Nineteenth WCA was about five months old, they called in an Alinsky-trained organizer to help. He was a minister and he came for six months and instructed the group on strategies and tactics for achieving their goals. He also founded FIGHT [a black organization]. He told us if we survived the first five years, we'd be there forever." Some elements of this early training remained with WCA's first leaders, and were transmitted to later ones. We can see the Alinsky effect in WCA's courage, willingness to take risks, and stubbornness, all of which are shown in their program.

The main efforts of the association were focused on youth recreation, real estate practices, housing rehabilitation, and schools. We will examine each of these below, and trace their development throughout all three phases. One other issue—the nearby airport and its negative effect on the area—was the subject of many early meetings of the group, and it surfaced periodically throughout all three phases of WCA's development. An airport subcommittee was actually formed in the earliest days of the association. The Social Actions Subcommittee, part of Issues and Actions, was the forerunner of the youth committee, which by 1970 had reorganized into six subcommittees. During phase one (1964–70), much time was also spent on organizational structure, development, and community events.

Youth

Phase One. The chairperson of the Social Actions subcommittee organized the first WCA youth group in the nineteenth ward, the "Nineteeners." To meet their needs, the association rented a storefront as a gathering place for young people in March 1968. This was called the "Bakery," and was the first organized youth project developed by the association. Several months of cleaning, painting, decorating, electrical work, and other improvements were necessary before the doors of the Bakery opened. One volunteer who lived close by was the "Keeper of the Key." The WCA's informal history refers to these early days: "Those were exciting times at the 'Bakery.' Nightly groups of 75–100 gathered. The teenagers cleaned, painted and decorated. Much effort resulted in a fun place in which to gather. . . . The transformation of a dirty storefront into an attractive meeting place was as important to the youth as having a place to use" (Bush & Weiss 1979: 8).

The responsibility of the youth committee's Chair at that time grew tremendously. Not only was he responsible for providing supervision and guidance for the hundreds of young people attracted to the Bakery, but he also had other increasingly pressing problems concerning personnel, maintenance, and finances. Sixteen years later, that volunteer chair fondly recalled the early days of the youth project: "We were loaded with kids—boys and girls . . . we were like a magnet. They spread the word themselves. . . . What the kids basically wanted was somebody to talk to and relate to. That's all the structure they really wanted. It got them off the streets and we had a tremendous success" (Ron Jarvis).

Toward the end of phase one, a full-time youth director was sought and hired, coming in September 1969 to begin a long relationship with the association, as noted above. Under the direction of the new youth director, funding proposals were submitted in the next few months to a dizzying variety of private and public sources, most of which awarded sizable grants to the youth project over the next few years. The grants grew, even after the director left. By 1970, the end of phase one, the youth committee had expanded to six subcommittees, added six young people to represent youth, and began to work with parolees returning to the nineteenth ward.

Phase Two. In 1972, the WCA youth project received a prestigious NIMH grant, which—in addition to the other state and local funding— brought the total project's funding close to $200,000. With its staff increased to thirteen, it opened an office, a second drop-in center (the "Agency"), and developed a film called "Blessed is the Rain" with forty youth. In cooperation with a new WCA seniors program, the youth project sponsored a Hire-A-Teen program in 1973, and also employed a youth worker to do group counseling with children and adults having problems affecting school adjustment.

As noted earlier, the youth project bid farewell in 1974 to its first director, who moved up to regional and then state administrative levels. After he left, the project suffered constant staff turnover and finally merged in 1977 with the Children's Hospital—to the sorrow of many WCA members, and the satisfaction of others who were dismayed by the faltering program.

Real Estate/Housing Maintenance

Phase One. The first stated concern of the association when they began was real estate practices, as we noted earlier. This concern was voiced in the earliest objectives of the group, which called attention to the need to take positive steps to avoid deterioration in the nineteenth ward. Such deterioration was attributed to "block-busting techniques on the part of certain real estate salesmen and brokers to induce panic selling" and racial steering. One of the most effective programs of WCA was their real estate service.

This began with a general membership meeting on May 18, 1968, which was devoted to discussion of a successful real estate listing and referral service in Laurelton, New York—a racially integrated community. After this service was described to the WCA, members voted to establish a similar service in the nineteenth ward. The real estate service operated out of the youth center's storefront, using a different phone number, and was staffed by volunteers evenings and weekends. One volunteer became the WCA's first real estate center clerk.

In the first year of the service, eighteen homes were sold, for an average price of $18,000, comparing favorably with the average realtor's selling price in the ward of $15,000 at that time. This took away $19,440 in commissions from realtors, and this fact was used as a bargaining point to persuade real estate agents and brokers to modify their practices. Two college students, assigned to assist the real estate committee in the summer of 1968, wrote a promotional folder used by the real estate center and assisted in a survey of new homebuyers. Their study of one hundred new nineteenth ward homebuyers showed that 64% of the buyers were white, with one realtor controlling 44% of the white buying market, and fourteen other realtors also selling to whites. Nineteen additional realtors were selling to blacks. These facts helped the real estate committee plan their strategy, which included block meetings on streets panicked by heavy real estate solicitation.

The WCA's real estate committee asked residents of those streets to sign cease and desist orders against soliciting realtors and affidavits testifying about current real estate practices. Residents were also encouraged to place signs in their windows reading "This home NOT for sale." When solicitation continued, WCA—armed with signed petitions and affidavits—appealed to the New York State Attorney General and Secretary of State for a general cease and desist order protecting the entire nineteenth ward against solicitation.

In June 1969, the New York secretary of state publicly agreed to put the whole ward off limits to realtor solicitation if enough signatures were obtained on resident petitions. Forms were circulated by WCA throughout the ward, and several hundred signatures were secured before the deadline of July 1. One month later, a news item announced that 650 real estate brokers were barred from soliciting in the nineteenth ward (*Democrat-Chronicle*, Aug. 22, 1969).

During this period, an article about the nineteenth ward was followed by an editorial praising the work of the association. The editorial referred specifically to the WCA's real estate center as working in the ward's best interest to achieve a stable neighborhood (*Democrat-Chronicle*, April 13, 1969; April 16, 1969). By this time, the WCA's real estate service was advertising in the classified section of the city newspaper, and WCA used the service as leverage in trying to get the board of realtors to establish a joint planning and grievance committee. Though the board refused, WCA members felt that "the success of the real estate service did more to change real estate practices in the 19th Ward than anything else" (Bush & Weiss 1979: 15).

By the end of 1969, the real estate center had thirty-six homes listed with it, and was recognized as a growing stabilization force in the community. And as a result of all the real estate complaints coming from the WCA, a citywide real estate advisory panel was established in April 1970, chaired by the WCA's first president. The WCA's real estate committee rejoiced three months later when the city council passed a series of zoning reforms, including the banning of "Sold By" signs by real estate firms or individuals. The committee had argued many hours before the council about the deterioration of an area that could be caused by those signs. All their efforts paid off.

Phase Two. The real estate service announced in 1971 that its three years of sales in the nineteenth ward had topped the million-dollar mark (Bush & Weiss 1979: 28). This was a loss of nearly $70,000 in commissions for the real estate industry—an important negotiating tool for the WCA, as we've noted, in their effort to bring about reform in real estate practices.

To promote the nineteenth ward as a desirable neighborhood for prospective homebuyers, and also to instill pride in its residents, WCA held its first house tour in 1971. This became an annual event and a major fund-raiser for the organization. In response to increasing resident turnover, "I'm Staying" signs appeared in many area windows in 1972, and WCA appointed a director of newcomers to greet new residents of the ward.

The real estate service reported a banner year for 1972–73, with $1,441,800 worth of properties sold. This represented 24.5% of all properties sold in that time period, a remarkable feat for a volunteer effort. In the first five years of the service, they sold $3,361,350 worth of homes in the nineteenth ward. Rental property listing was considered in 1973, though not actually implemented until 1978, and cease and desist orders were again circulated in the ongoing effort to stop solicitation by real estate agents.

By 1973, the real estate committee had undertaken a vigorous inspection of homes in the ward and found hundreds of violations. "Poor conditions of roofs, siding, chimneys, driveways, fences, gutters, and junked cars were among the violations cited and reported to city officials" (Bush & Weiss 1979: 28). This effort was named "City–19" and expanded to a cooperative venture with city building inspectors to find external code violations in the nineteenth ward.

The real estate service dwindled between 1974 and 1978, then revived under new leadership. During that period, however, even with weak leadership the service and real estate committee managed to generate some positive action and results. A slide-tape show about the advantages of living in the nineteenth ward was prepared by the real estate committee in 1974; their promotional efforts were greatly aided by an article that appeared in *Reader's Digest* about the nineteenth ward. Other articles appearing in the local press at that time also presented positive images of the area and the association.

In 1975, they participated in an audit of real estate practices co-sponsored by the Urban League and four churches in addition to WCA. The results, sent to the U. S. Department of Justice, showed racial steering and racial discrimination in 75% of the tests made on one large real estate company. In 1976 they produced a film on the benefits of city living, intended for the use of the real estate service and committee. The WCA entered the film in a local contest to give it greater exposure, and to their surprise and delight it won the first prize of two hundred dollars.

News articles about WCA's real estate service again appeared in 1978, noting that buyers and sellers using the service saved money by selling without an agent's 6% fee. With new leadership, the revived real estate service in 1978 held an open house for all houses listed with them, and also established a clearing house service for rental properties. An aggressive advertising campaign began, and FHA and VA foreclosed homes were listed with the service for the first time.

Still another new real estate project was announced in two news articles in the summer of 1978. This new project was a public relations program (affirmative marketing) to attract more homeseekers from the suburbs to the nineteenth ward. Using $6,000 from city Community Development Block Grant funds, WCA hired a market consultant to develop mailing brochures promoting the nineteenth ward as a desirable place to live. In addition, the association provided a "welcome package" of information on the neighborhood. This was a result of recommendations of the Mayor's Task Force on Housing Abandonment that city neighborhoods should be marketed to "stem the tide of housing abandonment in Rochester" (Democrat-Chronicle, Aug. 8, 1978; Times-Union, Aug. 24, 1978).

During this period, WCA was not able to meet all nineteenth ward residents' needs, as we noted earlier. The formation in 1977 of the Arnett Area Alliance in one section of the ward stung the WCA into recognition of their failure to meet that area's needs. This may have actually been a catalyst that moved the WCA to form their preservation program and later their rehabilitation project.

An offshoot of WCA's real estate committee was formed in 1977 as a "housing task force." Charged with working on the problem of boarded-up houses which had proliferated in the area, the task force formed a citywide coalition of community groups with the same concerns. The following year the task force met with state VA officials and negotiated an agreement with them that would greatly increase the speed of rehabilitation and marketing of VA foreclosed homes. This was the forerunner of the FOR–19 corporation, formed by the association late in phase two and fully operative in phase three. The task force also formed a new bank investment group in 1978 to begin discussions with one bank about neighborhood reinvestment strategies, after they had studied trends of vacant houses and foreclosures in the ward.

The task force and other WCA members met for many months to discuss the feasibility of developing a nonprofit housing rehabilitation corporation to bring substandard housing up to code and back on the market. In June 1978, the delegates council voted approval for the incorporation of such a group, with the 19th WCA as the sole member. Named Focus on Rehabilitation 19, Inc. (FOR–19), they began negotiations with several potential funding sources to obtain initial operating capital, which was not received until phase three.

A 1978 revitalization task force in a northwest corner of the nineteenth ward organized resident participation and discussion for three months to develop a three-year plan for the best use of $2.8 million of the city's community development funds for that area. The work of the housing task force was recognized in 1978 when its chairperson was named WCA's Citizen of the Year, later to become WCA's president. At the end of phase two, a WCA housing task force leader prepared a graphic display of planned preservation programs of housing services and housing research, soon funded by the state.

Phase Three. Housing and related issues continued to occupy much of WCA's time in their third phase, with their two housing projects receiving increased funding each year. Complementing the funded housing programs was the volunteer housing task force, which continued to monitor vacant homes and press for bank reinvestment in the area. During 1979, the task force held meetings with ten banks and received a commitment from one of them for $500,000 in conventional mortgages allowing rehabilitation costs as part of the appraised value of the home. Task force members also were successful in convincing HUD, the VA, the city, and lending institutions not to board up vacant houses in the area. Their research showed that boarded vacant houses had more vandalism than unboarded ones; government and bank executives believed them.

The preservation program, begun in 1978 at the end of phase two, made it possible for the association to keep detailed records of housing transactions in order to monitor trends in home sales. Their findings showed that property values in the nineteenth ward, after a period of decline in the early seventies, began to stabilize in the mid-seventies. After two years of the program's accomplishments in housing and commercial rehabilitation, the average selling price of a nineteenth ward home increased 36%: from $19,742 in 1978 to $28,815 in 1980. In the city at large during that same time period, the average selling price increased only 17%.

The preservation program, in addition to its research component, offered the following services to residents of the nineteenth ward: Lend-a-Tool Library, in conjunction with a Home Repair Network; information on special materials grants for home repairs; street improvements; commercial revitalization; housing promotion; and energy audits. In its first year, 287 free energy audits were completed, 191 ward homes made major improvements, and the total investments made were almost $309,000. A national President's Award for Energy Efficiency was given to the program in 1981.

During 1982 and 1983, almost $930,000 in public and private grants and loans were spent on improving one hundred homes in the nineteenth ward. In addition, twenty-two homes were improved through the special materials grants of the preservation program. Commercial improvement used $143,000 for twelve businesses. A Junior League grant of $499 was given for the maintenance of the Lend-a-Tool Library in January 1984, and additional grants of $1,450 for the tool library came from a local foundation and corporation.

In its second year, the preservation program added a new funded component— FOR–19, described above as an outgrowth of the earlier WCA task force on vacant homes. FOR–19 was a nonprofit housing rehabilitation corporation, which completed and sold its first rehabbed house late in 1980. A news article heralded the work of the new corporation early in 1981, calling the nineteenth ward a "bright spot" (*Times-Union*, Feb. 2, 1981). Vacant houses in the ward were reduced by 20% from 1978 to 1980, from 155 to 118, as a result of the association's efforts. The director of the city's Property Conservation Bureau referred to the nineteenth ward as having "one of the most active community groups. When you have a highly interested neighborhood group, you have a better neighborhood. I applaud their efforts" (*Times-Union*, Feb. 2, 1981).

The new rehabilitation corporation was formed to buy and rehabilitate vacant homes and then sell them to low-income families. With grants totalling $100,000 from the city and a private foundation, they prepared a work plan calling for twelve houses to be rehabbed in eighteen months. Their strategy was to select key houses on certain streets: "We've found that once you rehab a vacant house and make the outside pretty, the neighbors will start fixing up their houses," said the project's rehab specialist. He compared their efforts with those of HUD, and claimed the corporation did a better job in terms of time and appearance. "We think we can 'turn around' a house in six months, where it takes the federal government about two years to get a vacant house back on the market." A WCA leader added: "We're more concerned about preserving the character of the house and having it blend in with the rest of the neighborhood. . . . By keeping the neighborhood attractive, more people will want to live here" (*Times-Union*, Feb. 2, 1981). WCA leaders gave credit to the city for its interest in the vacant house problem. They cited the city's homesteading program, a rehab loan program offered by one of the banks, and city efforts in rehabbing and selling tax-foreclosed houses. The head of the Property Conservation Bureau said the nineteenth ward's interest in vacant houses was "catching on" around the city (*Times-Union*, Feb. 2, 1981).

One factor in the city's interest in housing was Bob Sorenson, a city planning department neighborhood specialist who lived in the nineteenth ward. Formerly a WCA employee in their preservation program, he told of his work with WCA, and noted the extent of the city's support:

The city has been generous with rehab grants—our grant program is based on income, and if you own the house and don't have much income you can get $3,500 or up to a $6,000 grant for home improvement. . . . The city has about *five and a half million in outright grants for housing repair*. All of this has helped to stabilize the nineteenth ward. (emphasis added)

Some signs of trouble with the rehab project appeared one and a half years after it began: the construction manager resigned, leaving a critical gap in the corporation's work. Also, the city's community development department had sent a letter to FOR–19, indicating dissatisfaction with their fulfillment of a city contract (minutes, June 1, 1982). The corporation was terminated in 1984, a few months earlier than anticipated, when $50,000 in tax arrears were discovered. Their office was sold to raise some of the money needed for the payments.

Shortly after FOR–19 ended, WCA announced their application for an $80,000 state grant for an expansion of their preservation project to include commercial revitalization. This continuing project, plus a newly funded crime prevention project, were the funded programs of the organization at the end of phase three. Their funding future was somewhat insecure by then, with grants applied for on a year-to-year basis (minutes, June 14, 1984).

Schools

Phase One. In the fall of 1968, WCA—then three years old—held a general membership meeting to enable the Rochester school board president to answer questions raised by nineteenth ward residents about school reorganization. This meeting was followed by others in which residents and WCA members aired their concerns. At that time, 34% of the children in the Rochester public schools were black. But in the nineteenth ward, the black percentage in the schools ranged from 5% to 84%.

The schools remained a constant issue in the association during the next decade, while the major means used by the school board to promote racial balance was voluntary open enrollment and urban-suburban transfer of minority students. The schools as a WCA concern was referred to over and over in interviews with residents and association members and leaders. Many referred to it as an organizational issue that failed—the association did not get what it wanted in the public schools. One observation shared by many was: "All the other programs to improve the neighborhood might fall flat unless we have a healthy public school system." Healthy meant racially balanced.

By February 1969, WCA's constitution had been amended to add the schools committee to the list of permanent committees. The following fall, an impassioned speech to the school board by WCA's schools committee leader Art Sansom reflected ward residents' concerns at that time. They were irate about racial imbalance in the Rochester schools, and especially in their ward. They were very upset about the board's rescinding a previous decision on school reorganization—in effect for only one year—which had brought improved racial balance to the nineteenth ward's public schools. In anger, many of the parents in the ward and on the WCA schools committee had participated in a 1969 boycott of the schools—a first in the history of Rochester, and a first for many of the schools committee members, who had never been in a picket line before (remarks to school board, Sept. 4, 1969).

Sansom became the next president of the WCA. A few months after his passionate speech, in December 1969, the superintendent of the Rochester schools presented a plan for the reorganization and desegregation of the city's public schools. This plan was enthusiastically supported by the association, which had two of its leaders involved in an advisory planning council that helped to develop the plan. The WCA sponsored a public meeting the following month to inform residents about the plan. A ward-wide distribution of their newsletter in February 1970 also gave residents detailed information through a series of questions and answers prepared by WCA. The entire issue of the newsletter was devoted to the school plan. Early in February 1970, the WCA president again addressed the school board, offering strong support for the re-organization plan before they officially approved it. His remarks reflected the race-consciousness in the city and in the country at large at that time (remarks to school board, Feb. 1970).

When a past president of the WCA was elected to the school board, WCA members and supporters felt confident that the new school reorganization plan would continue to be implemented. It was, for one year, with excellent results for nineteenth ward schools. But when a new school board was later elected, another vote upset the plan, to the great dismay of WCA members and nine-teenth ward residents.

Phase Two. The schools committee worked vigorously at the beginning of this phase in support of the newly reorganized school system. This school re-organization plan was to have had a positive effect on racial balance in the nineteenth ward schools, and WCA's schools committee offered much assistance in curriculum improvement, expansion, and innovation. One item in the WCA history confirmed this: "Due to the efforts of our Schools Committee, Madison High offered 98 new courses in English, business, history, math, languages, and other areas" (Bush & Weiss 1979: 25).

Unfortunately, with the reorganization in effect only one year (1970–71), rumors foretold the undoing of the plan. News articles and headlines in *Update* reflected the association's anxiety and concern. One *Update* article, headed "Ward Association Wants Picketing Stopped," told of nightly picketing of the home of one of the board of education members—a former WCA president and supporter of the reorganization plan. Nightly demonstrations provoked con-frontation, with name-calling, loud chanting, noise-makers, and the wearing of white sheets. One of the neighbors, a WCA member and leader, said: "I've been driven out of my home state of Mississippi by people like this, wearing sheets, and I have no intention of being driven out of Rochester" (newsletter, June 18, 1971).

Association leaders and volunteers responded to the stormy and tenuous school situation by conducting and publicizing a survey of 1,100 homes in the nineteenth ward showing the extent of community support for the reorganization plan. Despite their findings (*Times-Union*, Dec. 20, 1971), and despite public pleas to keep the plan, a school election resulted in five new school commis-sioners, who swept in on an antibusing platform and rescinded the plan. The WCA warned that rescinding the plan would lead to racial and socioeconomic resegregation in the schools. In fact, it did.

For the next few years frustration with the schools was so intense that WCA's school activities sharply decreased. Not until 1975 was there any visible, renewed association participation in school matters. This came about through a Ford Foundation grant of $50,000 awarded to WCA for two years to improve the public image of schools in the nineteenth ward. The project, called the Schools' Community Communication Project—a subdivision of the youth project—was designed to "help create a stable interracial neighborhood." A news article about the grant quoted WCA's vice-president as hoping that the newly funded publicity program would alleviate the misgivings that people have about city schools: "A neighborhood will remain integrated only so long as people have confidence in their school system," she said (*Democrat-Chronicle*, Oct. 23, 1975).

With the Ford Foundation grant, WCA and their schools committee were reactivated. They prepared a slide-tape show on two schools, held lunches and meetings with teachers and principals, lobbied for high-quality administrative appointments and school budget maintenance and expansion, and held public forums on educational issues (Bush & Weiss 1979: 39). When the grant expired, the schools committee again became rather inactive until the very end of phase two. Then, WCA's president presented to the delegates council data on the test scores of elementary schools pupils from the nineteenth ward, showing that sixth grade scores in reading and math had been substantially below (one to three years) the national norm for the last four years (Delegates Council, December 1978). This sparked a resurgence of schools activity in phase three.

Phase Three. In 1979, anxious parents organized an Education Resource Network, which held an Education Planning Saturday in the ward's Wilson Junior High School. They brainstormed the problems facing the junior high school and its students, and they formed five subgroups. They produced a paper prepared to stimulate discussion and action, enabling the school to provide a reasonable educational alternative for the majority of junior high students in its feeder pattern. At that time, August 1979, only 40% of the seventh and eighth grade students in the feeder pattern attended that school. The WCA committed $1,000 from their treasury to strengthen these "vital efforts" (Bush & Weiss 1979: 49). By the end of phase three, a total academic change had occurred in the junior high school of the nineteenth ward, and the racial isolation had dropped from 80% to 60% minority in a few years. The school was turned into a magnet high school, which reattracted both white and black students.

Despite the success of the new magnet program at Wilson High School, parents in the nineteenth ward were still unhappy about "bright flight." A news article headed "Fighting Bright Flight" described a group of thirty parents, teachers, and administrators who wanted special academic programs put in their elementary schools to reattract bright students going elsewhere. The parents, "working under the auspices of the nineteenth WCA," complained that "the reputations of their four elementary schools have deteriorated to the point that many of the brightest children, white and black, are going to other city schools, to private or parochial schools, or even to the suburbs" (*Times-Union*, Feb. 21, 1984). At that time, the racial composition of the four elementary schools in the nineteenth ward ranged from 64% to 87% black, showing some improvement over previous racial imbalance.

The parents also wanted a grammar school for the seventh and eighth grades, and protested that no other section of the city had that problem—no grammar school and no traditional high school. More than 2,000 students from the nineteenth ward were being bused to other high schools throughout the city and county, and half the elementary children attended school outside the ward at that time. More of these were white than black. The school board promised, as a beginning, to add enrichment programs in two of the ward's elementary schools in response to the parent group's protest. The struggle continues.

Other Activities

Phase One. In addition to these activities focused on youth, real estate, housing maintenance, and the schools, WCA was active during their first phase in blocking zoning variances, rerouting truck traffic, arranging for the removal of junk cars, fighting for tax reassessments, forming a coalition of neighborhood groups (Metro-Act, later the Community Organization Coalition), clean-up and fix-up campaigns, facility planning, securing recreational maintenance, reporting code violations, promoting tree planting, obtaining zoning reforms, and sponsoring community events.

The community events sponsored by the association included an annual Citizen of the Year dinner, begun in 1969, the annual Square Fair, which began as an art show in 1968, neighborhood exhibits held periodically, and car washes, bake sales, paper drives, dances, and the annual delegates convention. Mimeographed newsletters were sent to all ward residents—about 8,000 households— once or twice a year, and to members quarterly.

Phase Two. In this second phase of their maturation, the association was involved in a wide variety of other programs—some old, some new—reflecting enduring or changing issues and concerns. The airport surfaced periodically as a crisis issue. Both old and new community events were frequent and successful, providing an ongoing sense of community for the nineteenth ward, as well as some profit for the maturing organization. Newsletters changed from quarterly to monthly publication, but with fewer ward-wide distributions.

By the middle of the second phase, WCA had come to be known locally as the most powerful neighborhood group in the city, and nationally as one of the fifty most effective groups in the country. They hosted the 1973 National Neighbors annual conference, and sent a family of ambassadors across the country to study other integrated neighborhoods, with the aid of a Ford Foundation travel grant.

During the seven years of the second phase, forty-four articles about the association appeared in city newspapers, compared to a total of six during the first phase. The work of the association was recognized and helped by a mayor's proclamation declaring May 1971 to be Nineteenth WCA Month and recognizing the association's "serving as a model of an urban, integrated neighborhood" (mayor's proclamation, May 11, 1971).

Foundation grants helped WCA provide new senior citizen services in 1971. A 1972 community forum encouraged seniors to express their wishes and needs for activities and services. Additional foundation grants helped WCA establish its Hire-A-Teen program in 1973, through which teens could be hired by senior citizens to help with household chores for two dollars an hour; half the fee was paid through the WCA. Income tax assistance was offered to seniors in 1974.

WCA also continued to sponsor some fun-loving, purely social events during this phase. Typical events sponsored by the association in that time period included annual house tours, winter ice-skating parties, summer camping weekends (begun in 1971), annual delegates conventions, annual Square Fairs, Citizen of the Year dinners, outdoor concerts, summer film festivals, Newcomer's Welcome picnics, Thanksgiving dinners, dances, bake-ins, park festivals, the Merchant of the Year award program (begun in 1977), the Dollhouse Show, annual paper drives, and an annual marathon (begun in 1978).

Other programs and issues the WCA was involved in during phase two were improved street lights (1971); a babysitting registry; a recycling center (1971–76); two neighborhood health centers; maintenance of recreational facilities; tree and flower planting (1971); highway control; a truck traffic ban on selected streets; unleashed dog control; zoning variance monitoring; noise and traffic airport control; crime prevention (Citizens Patrol, begun in 1975); business street revitalization (1975); library assistance; older home maintenance printed information (1976); Welcome Neighbor packet distribution (1977); coalition building with other neighborhood organizations on selected issues; improved city services; and a shoppers' survey on residents' preferences.

Phase two ended on a high note when the nineteenth WCA was singled out for recognition by the National Commission on Neighborhoods. The commission, created by Congress under President Carter, chose fifty neighborhood organizations across the country for special case studies. The WCA was one of them, and was cited as one of the strongest neighborhood groups in the country (*Times-Union*, July 29, 1978). They sailed into their third phase with an impressive record behind them, and new funding for new programs ahead of them.

Phase Three. The beginning of this phase was highlighted with a week-long celebration of city living, in cooperation with the Rochester Board of Realtors. This marked the first such venture in the city ever sponsored by the Board of Realtors. "Homecoming Week" was designed to encourage home buying in the nineteenth ward and other city neighborhoods by showing city neighborhood facilities and resources, open houses, a home-buying seminar, theater productions, school personnel meetings, a walking tour conducted by the League of Women Voters, a parade, a breakfast, and culminating in the annual WCA Square Fair (*Democrat-Chronicle*, June 1, 1979).

A newly funded crime prevention project, TRENDS, was an outgrowth of earlier volunteer neighborhood safety programs begun in the summer of 1976. Then called ACT (Against Crime Together), it consisted of a telephone network, first tried in an eighty-block area, with neighborhood volunteer watchers.

From 400 members the program grew to 8,000, and then spread throughout the city. Crime figures in Rochester show the program's impact. In 1976, the year ACT was formed, there were 33,127 larcenies; by 1981 these had dropped by half to 15,168. In the same period, burglaries dropped from 13,646 to 7,827, murders from forty-five to thirty-eight, and robberies from 1,377 to 1,246. The program was praised nationally in an article in *Good Housekeeping* in November 1982.

ACT continued while the newly funded TRENDS project began as a service for senior citizens. The service provided for lock installation, newsletter printing and distribution, police inspections of home security systems, continuation of ACT phone chains, and research and monitoring to assess the program's impact. Publicized as the Reassurance Project, it was designed to especially reassure low-income elderly of the security of their homes and neighborhood—particularly in the nineteenth ward.

Other program activities of WCA during phase three were: monitoring of group home locations, which had proliferated in the nineteenth ward, with 15% of all those in the city located there; street and lighting improvements; human services planning (with a United Way grant shared by two other groups); business area clean-up; a new human relations committee "to deal with neighborly things such as block parties"; tax reassessment; a continuing but changed real estate service, including a new participating realtor program (adapted from Akron's UPON project in 1981); airport noise, safety, and pollution; improved traffic patterns; postal service facility retention; vacant lot maintenance; footbridge planning for access to the University of Rochester through an Associated River committee; and AB–19, a special target area improvement program. A membership form from this phase lists eighteen WCA committees activities for volunteers to get involved in, plus fifteen skills that volunteers could assist the organization with, as well as five added types of volunteer help: access to van or truck, locate goods or services at cost, substitute office staff, office help, home assistance.

Community events held by WCA in phase three were continuations of previous ones. But the various dinners, drives, and fairs were beginning to be more and more difficult to do. The WCA was getting tired. When members of the executive committee were asked by the president to state their number one priority for 1983, one member—an early president—had none, and suggested that that might be the problem. Had they run out of ideas? In an interview, this was also expressed with a somewhat anxious smile by another past president: "We seem to be searching for direction now—not exactly sure of what to put our efforts into" (Carrie Amber).

Another executive committee meeting three months later heard a recommendation by the finance committee that no fund drive be held that year, but that emphasis be placed instead on the upgrading of memberships with higher contributing levels (minutes, April 4, 1983). The following month, the minutes report discussion of the difficulty in organizing the Citizen of the Year dinner.

Holding the event at a party house was suggested as one way the evening could be fun "rather than an evening of work" (minutes, May 9, 1983). And the establishment of the new human relations committee "to deal with neighborly things such as block parties" also indicates a need to unwind and regroup. The January 1984 *Update* was searching for a new editor, with a farewell from the old one and the outgoing president. But the delegates council meeting reported in that issue seemed to have been totally involved in decisions relating to the funded programs—personnel code changes, grievance procedures, oversight committees, and personnel changes (newsletter, Jan. 1984).

Despite these signs of fatigue, WCA ended their third phase blessed with human resources. Even if they never did another thing, they could take great pride in what they had accomplished in the past two decades. Twenty-seven articles about the association appeared in city newspapers in the six years of phase three, slightly under the average of those in the previous phase, but a creditable number nevertheless. Further analysis of those articles shows that twenty of them were in the years 1979 to 1981, while only seven appeared from 1982 to 1984. Some slowdown of public relations, but hardly a dying group. The organization was past middle age, somewhat weary, but still vigorous and healthy. Their greatest asset was their people—rich in skills, intelligence, creativity, and dedication.

IMPACT

Considering the four factors outlined earlier, we can judge the impact of the nineteenth WCA on their neighborhood and community. As for a fifth factor—survival—we know they have succeeded in staying alive, and are even flourishing. We will come back to this at the end of our account, as we try to analyze the reasons for their successful survival. What about the other four factors?

Racial Pluralism Maintenance

First, to what extent have they been able to maintain racial integration? From census tract and block data, school data, visual assessment, and interviews we can evaluate the extent of integration maintenance in the nineteenth ward. The census data show that the racial composition of the ward changed from zero black in 1940, to 10% black in 1960, to 14% in 1970, to 49% in 1980 (see Table 1 and Figure 1).

For the city of Rochester during this time, the change in minority proportions was from 17% black in 1970 to 26% black in 1980. Thus the increase in the nineteenth ward was 34%, compared to only 9% for the entire city. Though this is a significant increase, the area is still an integrated one. However, according to the HUD definition of impaction, the nineteenth ward would be considered impacted—that is, having more than a 10% increase in the previous decade or being more than 40% black.

A closer look at the six census tracts within the nineteenth ward shows a range of black population from 2.5% to 27.3% in 1970, changing to a range from 21.6% to 69.6% black in 1980. A further breakdown of the change in each tract during that decade shows a range from 19.1% to 42.3% increase in black population. Three of the six tracts were predominantly black by 1980, though some residents and city officials maintained that the increase peaked in 1978 and that the numbers have remained stable since then: "One of the things I'm going to caution you about in looking at trends . . . is that the black population in the ward peaked around 1978 and has been stable or declining actually since then. So it hasn't been a steady increase between 1970 and 1980" (Bob Sorenson). In the absence of interim census data, we cannot verify this claim.

Population declined by 11% in the nineteenth ward between 1970 and 1980. But this figure masks the actual dynamics of the demographic changes during that decade. The population loss was in the white population only, decreasing almost 50% from 20,112 in 1970 to only 10,425 in 1980. The black population in the ward rose in that period from 3,496 to 10,469.

School data have already been reviewed, and normally—as with most interracial communities—would show greater proportions of blacks in the schools than in the neighborhoods. However, the long-term administrative programs for racial balance in Rochester have altered the schools' racial composition considerably, so that they do not reflect the degree of racial enrollment typical for that neighborhood's racial composition.

Despite the maintenance of racial integration in the nineteenth ward residents knew that outsiders perceived their neighborhood as being black. One of WCA's founders spoke of this: "The majority of the people—I know from experience— say, 'Oh, yeah, you live in the ghettos. You live in boogieville' " (Ron Jarvis).

Members and leaders of WCA believed their earlier work with the real estate service, preservation program, and housing rehabilitation was responsible for the eventual maintenance of integration in their area. Though we have no way of knowing the extent to which any process of resegregation may have been slowed by their work, their perceptions enabled them to view their neighborhood quite differently than did outsiders. They were optimistic about the future, and proud of the past. One resident, also a staff member, spoke confidently:

I don't see any more blockbusting for the next few years. People in general and realtors are aware of the appreciation of our properties more than before—so . . . I think the neighborhood's future is brighter now than it has been for many years—the housing looks better, and people have reset their values and now enjoy city living. (Charlotte Moran)

Another resident, a teacher and historian, also spoke of rising housing values: "We don't have the real estate service any more because we don't need it. I think that the improvement of value has done this. . . . The physical appearance of this neighborhood has appreciated considerably because of our preservation program" (Dana Morris). Bob Sorenson, city employee, former WCA staff member, and current resident, spoke of the diversity of residents:

It's a very unusual mix of people . . . and in many cases they're living side by side. . . . One of my favorite statistics is that we have a group of census tracts which has among the highest number of heads of households with graduate degrees, and we also have the highest number of heads of households who are high school dropouts. It's a real strange neighborhood.

Quality Maintenance

To what extent has WCA maintained the physical quality of their area? This has already been answered in some of the comments made about the first factor, integration maintenance. We have not, however, dealt with the businesses in the nineteenth ward. Several streets are considered shopping or business streets in the ward, though the association consciously tried to keep it primarily residential, and worked early for zoning designations that would accomplish that.

The various business streets in the ward have not had the same kind of development over the years; some have fared much better than others. In 1984, the general perception by residents and myself was that one street, Thurston Road, was experiencing a revitalization, but that the others were not, and needed it. A grant proposal had just been written for the WCA, applying for a renewal and increase of state funds for the preservation program, to allow for staffing to work on commercial revitalization in the area.

One resident pointed to the differences in the business areas:

Thurston Road has some businesses that are new—those are recent, within the past year and a half. Gelato [an ice cream shop] is there to stay, and the new Peaches [restaurant] is doing well—have you tried their eggplant? That's not the business district that's in real trouble. The one that is in real trouble is Genesee Street, and part of Chili Avenue is a big problem. As for Arnett, they've gone through a number of changes in the major store there and they've begun to have vandalism. (D. Morris)

One resident and WCA leader referred to one business street—Genesee, the eastern boundary of the WCA area—as "probably still the shakiest and shows the least amount of evidence of new businesses and improvements. It is in a way the most vulnerable—because the greatest concentration of both poor and minority residents is to the east of Genesee Street" (Carrie Amber).

The president of WCA told of the improvement of Thurston Road, where the WCA storefront office is located:

Over the last few years as people moved into the neighborhood because of the increase in housing values, Thurston Road has seen a resurgence as a retail center. I think the association played a role in all that through the preservation program—giving information to people on grants and loans available for repair of homes—and a lot of that has now spilled over to the businesses. (David Mantell)

Another resident spoke of WCA's role in neighborhood preservation:

The thing is that the real estate committee formed a city-wide coalition and put a lot of pressure on HUD and VA to rewrite their policies—to improve the time between when they took over the property and when it went back on the market. So all of this has helped make people's perceptions of the ward more positive. (Cindy O'Donnell)

A review of the data pertaining to the kinds of families moving into the nineteenth ward in the past decade will help us better understand the changing neighborhood's appearance. Since 1970, the nineteenth ward lost 11% of its population, while the city as a whole lost 18%. The population over age sixty-five decreased by about one-third, compared to 16% for the city. For young adults, however—the age group from twenty-two to thirty-four—the nineteenth ward increased by 18%. Household size has decreased, as it has in the rest of the city.

Regarding income, the average household income in the 19th Ward was $17,343 in 1980, close to the citywide average of $17,805. It ranked eighth out of thirteen neighborhood planning districts in the city on income level. Those living in poverty were 9.4%, compared to 12.6% for the city as a whole. The dependency ratio was ninety-eight, compared to ninety-one for the city (number per one hundred persons aged twenty to sixty-four). Regarding education, 47% had less than a high school education in the nineteenth ward, compared to 50% for the city. Unemployment was 8% in the ward, slightly above the city rate of 7.1%. For teen pregnancies, the ward ranked eighth in the number of pregnancies (slightly below the city average), tied for fifth in abortions, and was sixth in the number of out-of-wedlock births to teenagers.

Owner occupancy was 63% in the ward, with the median value of owner-occupied homes $24,810, compared to $25,700 for the city as a whole. One of the ward's six census tracts was cited as showing problems in three social service aspects: public assistance under sixteen years of age, venereal disease, and infant mortality. One increase for the nineteenth ward was greater than any other section of the city: between 1970 and 1980 there was a 266% increase in the number of single parents with children under eighteen. This had been 4% of the district's population in 1970, but rose to 17% by 1980. For the city as a whole, the increase was 82% since 1970. The citywide proportion of all households having single parents with children under 18 was 13.4%, or 4% less than in the nineteenth ward.

Considering some of these sobering changes in the past decade, we might conclude that the WCA has done reasonably well in the maintenance of the physical quality of their neighborhood. Visual inspection of the area, supplemented by photographs, revealed a mixed level of physical quality. Generally, the area is a pleasant one, with large, older, attractive homes on many streets. Some streets, identified by census data, residents and observation as having more black households, had a greater number of two-family and multifamily dwelling units. They were also not as well-maintained. One corner had a large unit of run-down double units. The Arnett and Genesee business areas were dilapidated with vacant, boarded-up buildings. And just two blocks away from the desirable Sibley Tract were several deteriorated, unkempt homes on Post Avenue.

How the area may have looked ten years ago we do not know. And how it might have looked without the association's constant housing efforts we also do not know. But it seemed to me that the residents' perceptions of their area— almost totally positive—were more due to their knowledge of the hard work of the association than may have been justified by the actual physical appearance of the neighborhood. It is very nice in some places, but not so in others. Perhaps, however, this is par for most neighborhoods.

Sense of Community

To what extent has the association provided a sense of community? A 1984 news item announcing the eighteenth annual Square Fair referred to it as the "longest consecutively running neighborhood festival in the city" (*Democrat-Chronicle*, June 17, 1984). Other community events sponsored by the association also serve to draw people together—certainly in the planning and organization of the events as well as in the participation at the event. Hundreds of people each year attend the association's annual fair and house tour. Smaller numbers are involved in other events such as the annual dinner, delegates convention, picnics, and so on. There is no question about the sense of fellowship generated among those who are a part of these events and the work of the association.

But how representative are these people of the entire ward? Certainly they are mostly white, and only a fraction of all those who live in the community. This is one of the consistently mentioned weaknesses of the organization by those who are closest to it. Typical comments about the lack of representa-tiveness of the association are these:

The association has over the years had a hard time attracting a substantial black mem-bership. . . . I think there's a perception in the black community that . . . the way the meetings are run . . . that kind of formal structure . . . maybe they couldn't compete on that level—that they were shut out. Also, many were working two jobs just to keep their house. Are you going to do volunteer work in the evenings? . . . And blacks might think why do I want to get involved in time and headaches, and what will it do for me, and how will my friends perceive me for being involved in it? (John O'Donnell)

From a black leader, then president of WCA:

I think a failure of the association is that it hasn't eliminated the perception that it has only one type of people—white. When that perception has been in effect for so many years I would consider that a failure of the association. . . . Sometimes there are two wage earners in black families which doesn't allow either one really to participate—no time, no energy. And if you look at the things we work on—if blacks had a choice to work on issues that primarily benefited black people or issues that benefit the neighborhood in general, many would choose the black issues. There are many in the neighborhood who do that—so we don't get them. They can't do both. (David Mantell)

Yet, an analysis of the programs WCA has been involved in over the years does show an acute awareness of needs of low-income households, in predominantly black neighborhoods of the nineteenth ward. And their efforts to attract more blacks into WCA have been constant throughout their existence. Their eagerness to give them leadership positions in the association is reflected in this comment: "I remember one year they had someone black as a vice-president who had only been on the board for only two weeks—which I thought was a terrible embarassment—to nominate someone for office because of one thing only—being black" (Dana Morris).

Some of these sober reflections are balanced by others which testify to the positive feelings of neighborliness in the community:

After we rented here, we looked to buy in a block where we could feel there was solidarity. There were many neighbors who shared the same values and we have been very pleased with our choice. . . . You know you're not an isolated family. There's a whole lot of people who feel the same way I do—I'm talking about solidarity on the block. . . . The association and the committees and activities I think have made people feel that there are ways to solve problems. (Cindy O'Donnell)

One black resident, a professional, thought the nineteenth ward was a great place to live: "When we came here and you said the nineteenth ward it was something special, something was happening there, and of course it was an integrated community so you felt welcome" (Wanda Brent).

Another resident and WCA leader, white, shared this view: "We are a small community—when something happens, people know about it—I think we've been a model with our Against Crimes Together program—that's done with block meetings and phone trees, so crime is not really a problem in the nineteenth ward" (Carrie Amber). A young white professional and WCA supporter said: "This community gave me a lot of support—my friends, the church. . . . We are known as the strongest community organization in the city" (Dana Morris).

Finally, one resident and business owner spoke of the nineteenth ward as a folksy community: "This community is almost like a small country town with very little happening in one morning that probably isn't known all over by the afternoon. . . . It is really interesting. I think it is very family oriented. Plus it has a strong community feeling, and I suppose the association has had a lot to do with it" (Charlotte Moran).

Influence

Our fourth measure of impact is organizational influence. How much influence has the organization had? What impact has it had on decision-makers who affect the neighborhood? We can evaluate this through newspaper articles, newsletters, reports, minutes, interviews, and reflection. Of the twenty-seven news articles about the WCA during phase three, nineteen were directly related to their funded and volunteer programs, five were about their community events, and three others were related to miscellaneous issues, such as the airport, a racial vandalism incident, and the schools. One major impact of the organization has been on the neighborhood itself and its people, as we have already seen from the comments above.

A second significant impact has been on several institutional forces that affect the neighborhood: the real estate industry, appraisers, the banks, the local government, the regional housing agencies of the federal government (FHA and VA), the police, and the schools. From interviews with city officials, organizational participants, and residents, we can see the effects of the organization over twenty years of its existence. Respondents were all asked their views on the successes and failures of the organization and the future of the neighborhood. Those views differed, but all pointed to the impact of the real estate service and preservation program, as well as the earlier youth project. A few cited the crime prevention program.

Ron Jarvis, folksy founder and early leader, spoke of WCA as a catalyst:

Well, I think our notable accomplishment has been the zoning. I think our going from the various R classifications up to an R–1 [residential] and forcing the city to enforce that has been very important for the neighborhood. There was a time when we were considered the most powerful association in the U.S., and we have been patterned and copied many times over. . . . City Hall had a lot of respect for us. . . . We've been a catalyst. . . . When we'd come in to the city council with a proposition they would say, "Look out, they mean business." They knew.

Lifelong resident John O'Donnell also pointed out the impact WCA had on elected officials: "I think in the early days the city and the county were very unresponsive to neighborhood organizations. I think the Nineteenth Ward Association was one of the leaders in getting city and county officials to recognize citizen input, and they were very effective in getting what they wanted." Wanda Brent, a black professional woman who moved to the nineteenth ward in 1979 said:

When we came they were established and they had a reputation as being very aggressive about the area being an integrated one. Quite frankly, they were the first and one of the most aggressive neighborhood groups in the city of Rochester—especially in the field of education citywide . . . they had a reputation of being forward moving and vigorous.

Another long-term resident and association supporter and earlier leader, Dorothy Linger, spoke of the group's effect on the city:

Part of the association's activities that I always considered the strongest one was its advocacy for services—to make sure city services did not decline in the area, which often comes with a change in the racial population. . . . They used their power against deterioration of buildings by citing violations, they made sure streets were repaired, and garbage was collected.

The WCA's activity and influence on the schools was acknowledged by all those interviewed. Most of them noted some failure as well as success. Carrie Amber, WCA leader and past president, recalled how hard it had been to work on the schools:

There's a very active parents group at Wilson Junior High [now a magnet school]. That school would never have survived if it hadn't been for WCA volunteers. . . . The schools have been the hardest thing, and the thing where people got burned out the most. I mean there are people who were on fire—really on fire—about the schools when we moved here. They gave their heart and soul; they really worked on that issue. . . . It makes you angry at the school district for the way they have done their changes . . . it's made it more difficult for this neighborhood.

When asked what she thought WCA's failures had been:

I think absolutely of the schools. . . . We couldn't accomplish what we wanted. . . . But I think the problems with the schools have also been due to forces beyond our control. The funding formulas for the schools and the constraints for balance within the school population. . . . But at the same time I say the schools have been a failure, we have to keep fighting the battle. . . . WCA is continuing to work with the schools even though they had a lot of blows and burnout. . . . New people have come along magically.

Dorothy Linger, an earlier WCA president and schools committee leader, told of her own involvement and anger about the schools:

The largest anger I have ever had was against the school district for allowing this crap to go on. . . . Now a few of us at Wilson have started to agitate for academic reforms. . . . We had a lot of skilled people in the area. People who fear nothing. . . . These are basically association people or people who are or have been active with them like myself. And we looked into data about testing levels, who is going out of the neighborhood to which schools, and we were able to influence the new principal there.

The recently revived school activity in the nineteenth ward and earlier failures were also mentioned by John O'Donnell: "I think that getting Wilson going [as a magnet high school] was a big success. That parents group at Wilson is highly active and many of the people in the group are also active in the association.

The WCA school committee tried for years—tried all kinds of different approaches—and I think they had an impact when they got to Wilson."

The greatest influence the WCA seems to have had, referred to over and over in interviews, is on the real estate industry. That influence, led by the volunteer real estate committee, and later the housing task force and preservation program, resulted in the gradual rise in housing values in the nineteenth ward. Proudly, residents and association members spoke of some of these efforts and their positive consequences. News articles corroborated these residents' perceptions, some of which are offered below.

Bob Sorenson, former WCA staff member and current city planning department staff member, recalled the early years of WCA's housing programs and their impact:

They started their own real estate service. . . . If I had to pick a single indicator of how a neighborhood is doing I would pick housing value. In the mid-seventies our average selling price was way below the city-wide average. After five years we're now able to say our sales prices are a little above the citywide average—between forty-two and forty-five thousand dollars. So it takes a long time to generate that kind of momentum.

Carrie Amber, past WCA president and long-term resident, also pointed to the rise in housing values in the ward:

We came here in '68. Over the years there was a dip in housing values which bottomed out in the early seventies. . . . But by the late seventies we were really seeing an upswing, and I very much attribute the work of the association to that. . . . Having our own real estate service, working for zoning changes, monitoring code violations . . . and we worked very hard with HUD and FHA about their foreclosed property. . . . The housing values have certainly appreciated—higher than any other neighborhood.

Again comments on the rise in values from Dana Morris—teacher, mother, and WCA supporter: "This house has tripled in value. . . . I think what made it happen was a combination of things—the preservation program, ending of foreclosed properties, fixing up vacant houses, filing code violations—it was all really an obscene situation, and the association stopped it."

Finally, John O'Donnell confirmed the role of WCA's programs in changing the actual and perceived quality of the neighborhood:

The real estate service started out in some confrontational way with the brokers—but these mellowed over the years and I think toward the end there was fairly good cooperation with them. The service was finally discontinued because it no longer was necessary. The housing market had changed . . . and the perception of the ward had changed and the realtors changed. . . . The interesting thing is that much of this is psychological . . . although a lot of it is due to the market. Perceptions are more important than anything.

FACTORS OF SUCCESS

We turn now to the reasons for the survival and success of the WCA, and divide these again into internal and external factors, recognizing, however, that each affects the other. One internal reason for WCA's successful survival is their early achievements. There may be no greater generator of energy and commitment than accomplishment itself. The association won some victories early, and this was a superb motivator in propelling them forward. Two important internal factors in their early and later achievements have been their leaders and their structure. Five significant external factors are the location of the neighborhood, the city's economic base, the state of New York's programs and policies affecting schools and neighborhoods, the city's responsiveness to neighborhood groups, and the school administration's citywide open enrollment plan.

Internal

The structure of the organization seems to have been a contributing factor to its survival and success, though not conducive to broad participation. The association was originally designed to be representative of every geographical district in the ward. This structure has been retained, but in practice the important decision-making and planning is done by the executive committee—a handful of eight people—with great power vested in the president. Though the delegates council is officially responsible for final decision-making, in practice it is the executive committee that does the initial brainstorming and planning. Sometimes they are joined by committee chairs, who with them form a "cabinet." This, however, is a structure and practice that evolved independently of the constitution.

The result of this is that a small group of planners—skilled and farseeing—run the organization, and run it well. Another human factor that has aided this process is the part-time staff person employed as office coordinator. We noted earlier that since their inception, the association has been fortunate in having the neighborhood churches contribute to the salary of a part-time office coordinator. What this has done from the earliest days of the organization is free the leaders from menial tasks and allow them the time and energy to devote themselves to policy formation and program development. Though the budget of the association rose from $4,000 to $30,000 over twenty years, they did raise most of that money themselves, except for the paid office staff funded by the neighborhood churches. But the seemingly small factor of office assistance has been an important one in allowing the leaders to focus their abundant talents on program and policy development.

As we have seen, the association decided very early to hire someone to run their youth project. They chose wisely, for their new director—charged with securing his own funding—was able to secure vast amounts of funding in a relatively short period of time. This was one of the greatest early accomplishments of WCA. But they had the foresight to begin writing funding proposals for a number of other projects very early in their development, so that by the time the youth project was well under way, others had begun to take its place when it finally merged with another institution. Again, the constant backup of office staff, though part-time, has freed the leaders for planning and development work throughout their organization's existence.

Most of the respondents interviewed for the study spoke of the excellent leadership of WCA, but some also noted the luck of the organization concerning external factors. John O'Donnell was one of those; he referred to a healthy economic climate in the city, and the good housing stock in the neighborhood as two lucky factors for WCA:

The association was very successful. I think that without it a lot of things would not have happened here . . . they came along at the right time, they did an awful lot of work, they had a lot of smart people who devoted an awful lot of time. . . . They were also just lucky too . . . Rochester has had for years the lowest rate of unemployment in the whole state of New York! There are a lot of healthy companies in town and the area. And the other thing is, there is a great variety of housing stock in terms of styles and prices [in the ward] . . . It's a very attractive neighborhood.

Carrie Amber emphasized the commitment of WCA's supporters: "One of our major successes is the renewal of people committed to the goals of the association . . . this commitment to an integrated stable neighborhood. . . . The other success, I think, is a measurable thing—we are no longer experiencing undervalued property, we don't have a lot of vacancies, and our housing stock has remained in good shape."

She also spoke of WCA's emphasis on recruitment of leadership replacements, another example of the wisdom of their leaders in preparing for their own orderly departure: "We tell every committee chairperson, 'One of your tasks for this year is to find your replacement even if they don't replace you next year.' " Another example of good organizational management was the practice of having each committee responsible for a project prepare a summary folder and evaluation to pass on for the next committee's reference.

Other comments about the calibre of WCA's leadership are related to the external factor of proximity of the university and other institutions of the city: "We've benefited tremendously from employees at the university—faculty and staff—who often had more flexible schedules and could do volunteer work" (C. Amber).

External

External factors relating to the city's economic health and the dispersement of public housing were cited by respondents as contributing to WCA's success: "Generally, the picture in Rochester's employment has been good. On the whole, we have been relatively less severely hit than other places. Our area is very good for jobs" (Bob Sorenson).

The ward did not become the site of public housing projects during WCA's existence. This was a most helpful factor in allowing WCA to develop their programs successfully. An examination of all public housing locations in Rochester reveals only one small, twenty-unit structure for the elderly in the nineteenth ward, constructed in 1970. An association leader spoke of the issue of public housing in the ward and WCA's position on that issue:

About five years ago [1979] the housing authority was beginning to put scattered-site public housing in the nineteenth ward. Our main objection to that was that it would undo all that we were trying to do at that time with upgrading housing. So we strongly and astringently objected to that, and the city agreed with our point of view. And at that time there was a vacancy on the authority's commission and I was appointed as a commissioner. (C. Amber)

Two important points are made here: first, the city agreed with WCA's position; and second, a WCA leader was appointed to the housing authority's commission. Both of these situations were extremely helpful to WCA's success.

Among the other external factors accounting for WCA's success and survival are the state and city policies and programs. The state policy was supportive of racial balance in schools as early as 1960, and also provided numerous funding opportunities for neighborhood nonprofit groups such as the nineteenth WCA. City policies and programs also were supportive of neighborhood groups and maintenance.

One small but important difference between Rochester and Akron, for example, relates to housing repair funds. In Rochester there were always substantial outright grants for repairs in all portions of the city, rather than just in selected target areas, as in Akron. These Rochester grants were individually from $3,500 to $6,000, and for the entire city $3 to $5 million a year for repair grants all over the city as well as in selected target areas (City of Rochester Dept. of Community Development, Housing Rehabilitation Programs, 1984).

Another helpful city policy in Rochester was its subscription to the neighborhood statistics program of the U.S. Census. This is an arrangement where the census data is broken down into neighborhood segments, and made available to the city for trend analyses, monitoring, and so on. The city must pay for this service, and Rochester does. Akron does not.

The city of Rochester's prosperous economic base is also a factor aiding the work of the neighborhood association. Had there been a major recession or massive unemployment here in the eighties as in many other communities (including Akron), the success of WCA's programs might have been seriously threatened. As it was, the economic development and maintenance of the city was a reinforcement to the economic development and maintenance of the nineteenth ward as a neighborhood.

Finally, the school's open enrollment policy is an important factor in stabilizing the nineteenth ward as an integrated neighborhood, though not all ward residents thought this was a good plan. John O'Donnell, for example, spoke of some of the problems of this policy:

One of the problems with open enrollment is that school friends tend to be inaccessible except to talk to on the phone, or it's a car ride, or when you're older you can take city buses. But it's a long bus ride across town. . . . From a kid's point of view with somewhat limited mobility, there's an advantage in neighborhood schools.

Though the open enrollment program took away some of the joy and convenience of strictly neighborhood schools, and though many area residents wished for a better plan, it was ultimately helpful to the neighborhood by allowing options to parents who believed in integrated living but not in racially isolated schools. They were enabled to stay in the neighborhood while sending their children to schools out of the neighborhood. At the same time, state policies supported twenty years of constant efforts by the local schools to improve plans for racial balance. These are ongoing, and the nineteenth ward and all other sections of Rochester will be the better for them.

This is quite different from Akron, where the state is quiet and the local school officials refused to acknowledge there was a problem for twenty years, faced two lawsuits, were forced to make some changes, but still refuse to deal with the virtually all-black school cluster in the West Side Neighbors area. This is sure death for that area as an integrated neighborhood.

THE FUTURE

What of the future of WCA and the neighborhood? Most comments were optimistic, some were cautiously so about the organization, and a few were somewhat negative:

I think the significant change is going to be the fact that the people moving into the neighborhood now are people who are able to afford investing large sums of money into these older homes . . . in many cases it involves two salaries, two working people. Now whether or not these people are going to have the time to do the kind of volunteer work we've always had is a real question. (Dana Morris)

This respondent also referred to a shift in political power from the city to the region, because of the highway system:

Another important change that is occurring is . . . that most of the political power now is going to the region rather than the city. . . . The city's been choked off by this freeway system. People are bypassing the city, getting out to their suburban homes as quickly as possible, and that has great impact on the small businesses in the community. . . . Many have closed up and moved to suburban shopping malls.

Then she spoke of the association again, and referred to lack of clear future goals: "We don't really have any more enough main issues of concern. . . . It's no longer clear what they should be doing in the future."

Also speaking about the lack of clear goals, and the anxieties about continuing to recruit new volunteers, was Carrie Amber, past WCA president and sixteen-year resident:

We've been sort of struggling with what's our mission of the eighties. I feel probably our committees are less active now, there are fewer people active on the committees than we were at earlier times . . . it's been hard for us in the last four years to rally the forces. . . . We haven't had the same kind of blatant problems. It was really easy to get a lot of people out when there were boarded-up houses. The problems now are less visible. . . . As for the neighborhood, for the future we are going to continue to be a stabilized neighborhood.

Citing possible external factors that could affect the nineteenth ward in the future, John O'Donnell referred to school funding: "One thing that could have a big impact other than a recession or depression is the school funding . . . through the state constitution it's tied to the city taxing power and budget. . . . If anything happens to the budget, the city schools essentially could collapse financially—and that would have a big impact on people with children anywhere in the city." Then he spoke of the future of the WCA:

So now, about the future of the association? In some sense, it has achieved its goal. And I don't expect it to disappear. . . . So often, I'm sure you've seen it, organizations die because they really don't have a strong purpose. I really don't know what will happen. . . . If we had gotten to today without having an association, I'm not sure it would be founded. But I think its momentum will keep it going even if there is a lower level of urgency.

Ron Jarvis, still a resident but no longer active in the association, drew an organic analogy when asked if he thought the association had changed much over the years:

Yes, I think it's a lot weaker . . . I think it's no different than the human body. . . . I think that it's tired, it's old, it's burned out. But the foundation is there. And it would indeed rally if another crisis came around. . . . There's enough there, and there's enough old-timers around that they, I'm sure, would jump in.

When asked if the organization might die out, he said he didn't think so. And in response to the question of whether it was as much needed as it once was, he said, "Yes." To the question of whether he thought some of the problems were still the same, he said: "Some. I don't consider block-busting the same. . . . I thought that was a dead horse. . . . Although you begin to wonder. . . .

Again this year, I noticed in certain areas the results of canvassing, because only one real estate agency has signs up."

From Don Sawyer, a young, white resident and active WCA member:

I don't think the Association has the strength and vitality it used to. There are no more crises. In reality, one or two people from the districts show up at the annual convention . . . The real power is in the executive committee and the staffed programs . . . we are losing some committed newcomers. They're moving in for economic reasons, not ideological ones. The association needs to involve these or they will lose a valuable source of volunteers and members.

Finally, we have two different assessments of the neighborhood reflecting black and white views. The white view was negative; the black view was positive. Art and Karen Sansom, in their early forties, white, are long-term residents and WCA leaders—he a past president, she a volunteer on the school committee. Both are now employed by the city—he as assistant budget director, she in zoning and urban planning:

The future of the neighborhood? . . . (She) I'm scared. I'm worried about the schools and the lack of social integration. The association is weaker than it was, and the ward is now politically divided into three legislative districts. That makes it harder to have an impact. (He) The successes of the association are neighborhood stability and excellent property values now. The failures are the schools.

Art and Karen Sansom offered their views of the single most important need of the area: "To be perceived as a multiracial area, and for something dramatic to happen on Arnett Road [business strip]. The association is not doing enough on this. . . . Our area is perceived as black working class by city officials and school officials."

But Rae and Bill Sherman had a different view. In their early fifties, black, she a past WCA president and now an elected city representative, they thought the nineteenth ward was the "in" place to live:

The future of the neighborhood? . . . Very positive, it's the "in" place to live. The association? That will depend on how they involve newcomers and renters. They'll need a freshness of outlook and continuity. . . . Their annual events have been dwindling. . . . The neighborhood is seen by non-residents as a more affluent area, with a lot of envy. I don't think it's seen as a black area—not like the third and twenty-first wards.

As one earlier respondent remarked: "It depends on who is doing the looking." But generally, both white and black respondents in Rochester saw the nineteenth ward as continuing to be a stable, integrated neighborhood in the future, and all acknowledged the role of the association in bringing it to that position.

Their work, spirit, and vision of the future were aptly symbolized at the Street Fair they sponsored in 1984. There, displayed on the sidewalk in front of the neighborhood hardware store on Thurston Road, was a large basket of baby dolls—black and white, together.

4

MILWAUKEE: SHERMAN PARK COMMUNITY ASSOCIATION

"So we accomplished a lot mainly because we didn't know it was impossible"

"But it's all so fragile"

"I just hope that people here recognize how valuable what they have is . . . and they will take care of it to nurture it, value it"

"I mean there are 40,000 people . . . you are talking about a small city"

SOCIOHISTORICAL CONTEXT

Milwaukee, with 741,324 people, is one of the world's largest centers for making heavy machinery; it also has one of the largest brewing industries in the country. Sometimes called "the nation's safest city," it won the national accident prevention contest of the National Safety Council several times. It is also known for honest and progressive government and a low crime rate.

Situated on the Milwaukee River, its design is a checkerboard pattern, with Wisconsin Avenue dividing the city's north and south sides and Lake and Capitol

Quotes in this chapter are from transcripts of taped interviews conducted in Milwaukee during April 20–27, 1984, unless otherwise noted.

drives. Milwaukee is the home of Marquette University, Concordia College, Milwaukee Downer College, the University of Wisconsin-Milwaukee campus, the Milwaukee School of Engineering, two art galleries, two art schools, and over seventy parks. It is sometimes referred to as Cream City because of the color of the bricks that were made there in earlier days.

City of "beer, bratwurst, and gemutlichkeit," Milwaukee in 1967 had open housing marches led by Father Groppi, with children chanting as they marched, "I just want to testify what the white man has done to me" (Aukofer 1968). Let us see what was done here, and what led to the formation in 1970 of the Sherman Park Community Association.

In 1836, when Milwaukee was founded, it was a village of fifty houses "seething with bustle and activity" (Still 1948). As a fur trading post, it was set on the mouth of the Milwaukee River close to where it joined the Menomonee River, the Kinnekeneck River, and Lake Michigan. Two rival settlements on each side of the river were consolidated as one village in 1839 and eventually chartered as a city in 1846. The earliest data on ethnic background, first available in 1848, showed that immigrants made up over half of Milwaukee's population. This grew to two-thirds of the 20,000 people by 1850, with Germans the predominant group, followed by Irish. By 1870, native born Wisconsinites were 40% of the population, then served by a wheat, brewery, and hog economy.

The first black settler came in 1835, with about twenty black families living there by 1845. In 1860 this had only increased to ninety-two families. The northward movement of blacks during and after World War I was not as marked in Milwaukee as in some other Midwest cities, because many northbound travellers stopped in Chicago—only a half hour away—and stayed there. Between 1910 and 1920 Milwaukee's black population doubled; it tripled during the twenties, and increased 18% in the thirties. But with all this growth, blacks were still only half of 1% of the total population in the city.

The reaction to this increase was not positive, as a very small 1924 news article reveals. Headlined, "Proposes City Negro District," the article began: "Milwaukee will have a 'black belt' if the Real Estate Board can find ways and means to make it practicable." Two other sentences followed, explaining that the board, at its weekly Tuesday luncheon, discussed the "advisability of restricting the negro population in a certain area of the west side. The members say that the negro population is growing so rapidly that something will have to be done" (Milwaukee Journal, Sept. 16, 1924).

By 1940, Milwaukee, with 8,821 blacks forming less than 2% of the city's population, still had a smaller proportion of blacks than twenty-two of the twenty-five largest cities of the nation. At that time, Milwaukee blacks lived in a square mile on the northern and western edges of the city's business district. The living area of blacks was four blocks long and three blocks wide. The population density there was twice the average for the city. The city was as segregated as any Southern town, with restrictive covenants and "understanding" maintaining residential segregation.

When Milwaukee's Mayor Daniel Hoan appointed a committee early in 1940 to study black housing in the city, the committee reported that building spacing, heating, and sanitary facilities were below average. By the end of the Depression, more than half the homes in the city that were "unfit for human habitation" were occupied by blacks (Aukofer 1968: 34). The city then began to demolish all below-standard buildings in the city—a program which had no target date, and was still going on in the late sixties.

With World War II and worker shortages, blacks were recruited to Milwaukee's industries. Many plants that had been totally segregated began to hire blacks, but when military contracts ran out at the end of the war, 1,500 blacks were out of work. Blacks could not buy homes or rent outside of the inner core area. Black servicemen had to go to a black USO. There were no black high school teachers in the city. By 1950, blacks were 3% of Milwaukee's people, with 21,772 blacks living in the city.

In the next ten years the black population grew to 8.4%, with 62,458 black people living in a somewhat expanded inner core of the city. As the boundaries of this inner core bulged westward and northward, whites fled. By 1967 the black population rose to almost 90,000, which was then 12% of the city's population of 774,000. That 12% lived in 5.5% of the total land area in the city, making Milwaukee one of the most segregated cities in the country. An FHA study in 1967 showed, however, that 320 black families lived outside the inner core, most of them on the northwest side of the city in an area that came to be known as Sherman Park—our study site.

Perhaps even more than segregation and ghetto conditions, it was urban renewal that led to the Milwaukee riots of July 1967, which left three dead, one hundred persons injured, and 1,740 persons arrested. This was known as the long hot summer across the nation, and though it may have been oddly termed in Milwaukee's climate—where summers are short and cool—it did happen there too. Compared to Detroit, however, Milwaukee's riot "was a puff of smoke" (Aukofer 1968: 7). Though it only lasted five hours, it was followed by a curfew of nearly ten days.

It started on North Third Street in the heart of the ghetto. That summer, an area of the ghetto was scheduled for demolition as part of the city's ongoing urban renewal program. Called Kilbourntown Three, it was the most neglected spot in the city with many vacant houses, broken windows, and gutted buildings. By that time Milwaukee had planned twenty-two urban renewal projects aimed at clearing slums or rehabbing inner core neighborhoods. This was one of them, though most others were still on paper. One that was completed had 600 apartments, but typically the rents were too high for those who had been displaced. Public housing was available, but it was segregated because southside political leaders had refused to permit any in their all-white area.

Other urban renewal, however, had taken place. Between 1959 and 1969 freeways were expanded, new apartment buildings replaced old mansions, the old train depot was replaced by a new Union Station, the Civic Center was expanded with a new twenty-eight-story Marine Plaza and other new high rise office buildings, there was a new post office five blocks long, a Center for the Performing Arts, the nation's fourth largest natural history museum, a state office building, an underground parking pavilion, with a treed, fountained and benched park above it, a new zoo, and a triple-domed conservatory in Mitchell Park. All this urban renewal activity brought Milwaukee a three-foot trophy in 1969 from the National Congress on Beautification, which declared Milwaukee the grand winner of American cities in the National Clean-up, Paint-up, Fix-up beauty contest (Wells 1970: 269).

As the downtown clearance and renewal got under way, the neighborhoods began to feel the reverberations. And soon, the neighborhoods came to be slated for their own kind of renewal, beginning with building demolitions. Some of the neighborhood clean-up began with the clearing out of old buildings in the third ward. This started much the internal migration of blacks, and continuing urban renewal and displacement resulted in continuing black movement west and north.

While all the displacement and movement was occurring, as a result of urban renewal, three other institutional forces were affecting blacks and their own and surrounding neighborhoods. Employment, housing, and schools each contributed to the denial, discontent, and despair of blacks in Milwaukee. Added to the continual shunting about of blacks as a result of urban renewal, these three factors were the critical additional ones leading to the riots of the sixties in Milwaukee.

Employment of blacks was a serious problem, as in other cities. Estimates of black unemployment in the city in 1967 were two to three times higher than for whites. Though many businesses and industries in the area claimed they had ended racial barriers, they complained that qualified blacks could not be found. Indeed, housing segregation, poor education, and discrimination qualified blacks primarily for low-level jobs—which were quickly disappearing.

Schools in Milwaukee provided additional space for overcrowded black children by additions to existing schools. The effect, of course, was to confine black children to racially segregated schools in black neighborhoods. Of forty-four new schools constructed between 1950 and 1965, only two were in areas where black enrollment was over 50% (U.S. Commission on Civil Rights 1967: 51). When white schools became overcrowded or were closed down for remodeling, the school system for many years had bused white children to receiving schools, which absorbed them routinely. This practice was known later as "intact busing."

The practice changed in 1957 when the school system began busing black children to predominantly white schools. There, however, the receiving schools kept the black children in separate classrooms. In one instance, a number of black children lived closer to their white receiving schools than to the black sending school where they were officially enrolled. Despite this, they were required to walk to the sending school to board the bus. A simple boundary change could have enabled the children to enroll officially in the receiving school, and busing would not have been needed at all.

In 1964, lunch was given for the first time to the black children in a receiving white school. But after proposals were made to fully integrate the black children into the receiving school, the school board declared busing to be educationally undesirable and discontinued busing from two black schools. In order to eliminate the busing but accommodate the students, the board leased an unused Lutheran school in the area to accommodate the 290 students. The school, Meinecke, became 99% black. At that time there was available space in eighty-four elementary schools that were 90% or more white. In these schools the average percentage of capacity used was 73.7%. Several citizens and parent groups rented a bus, and under the board's free transfer plan, they transported over one hundred students from overcrowded schools to nine suburban schools.

A thirty-eight-year-old black attorney and a thirty-nine-year-old white former nun formed an unlikely team in 1964, leading the fight against de facto segregation in the Milwaukee schools. Both relative newcomers to the city, they organized boycotts, sit-ins, and demonstrations for two years. The attorney, Lloyd Barbee, was chair of the Wisconsin NAACP when he first raised the issue of segregation with the Milwaukee school board in 1963.

At that time, Milwaukee kept no racial statistics on the schools, adhering to what they claimed was a "color blind" policy. But the NAACP conducted its own survey and found fourteen schools that were more than 90% black, four others that were 60–90% black, and four more that were about 50% black. Though their approach to the committee was moderate, the proposals were radical for their day: Barbee told the committee that NAACP would engage in direct action if the school board did not take definite steps to reduce school segregation.

Among the proposals he suggested were clear-cut policies on student transfers, rezoning, site locations for new schools, and teacher and administrator reassignments. Two weeks later, the committee's response was that these proposals "would abolish the neighborhood school system as it operates here" (Aukofer 1968: 52). Soon there was a total impasse between the school board and the civil rights groups. In March 1964, the state NAACP and the Milwaukee CORE chapter formed the Milwaukee United School Integration Committee, with Barbee as chair. Known as MUSIC, the group organized subsequent boycotts of the black schools and established 312 Freedom Schools for the children.

"Intact busing" had already been the cause of mass picketing of schools in protest against this policy. To most members and supporters of the civil rights organizations, the intact busing issue was the most flagrant and visible example of the school board's maintenance of a segregated school system. Three days after the first school boycott on May 18, 1964, the new committee adopted an open enrollment policy, with all other proposals rejected. The school board later officially adopted this policy, also rejecting all others. Protests against intact busing went on into 1965, with picketing and human chains blocking school buses. But the school superintendent continued his claim that it was "administratively unfeasible" to integrate the classes.

In June 1965, Barbee filed a federal court suit on behalf of black and white parents of school children, charging the Milwaukee school board with operating a segregated school system. The case was supported by the national NAACP and did not come to trial for eight more years. The state of Wisconsin during this time weakly encouraged local school authorities to take action to alleviate racial imbalance, but did not make this an enforceable requirement. In March 1966, for example, the State Superintendent of Public Instruction issued a statement on de facto segregation, saying that "lack of opportunities for some form of integration is harmful to the white community as well as it is to the colored community" (U.S. Commission on Civil Rights 1967: 233).

Meanwhile, more boycotts and demonstrations took place, with a new response from the school board. Deluged with letters, statements and proposals from religious, academic, civic, labor, and political organizations, the school board now responded that de facto school segregation was caused by housing patterns. Since the school board was not responsible for housing patterns, it had no responsibility to solve the problem.

The active struggle for open housing in Milwaukee was preceded by an NAACP Youth Council protest in 1966 against the all-white FO Eagles Club. In Milwaukee, membership in the Eagles Club—the second largest one in the nation—was almost a political necessity. Every class of white people belonged, including most members of the city's political power structure: seventeen judges, ten county supervisors, the district attorney, the county treasurer, ten city aldermen, the city attorney, city treasurer, and city clerk. The NAACP youth picketed the Eagles Club in protest against public officials belonging to a segregated club, and their picketing was followed by a bombing of the Milwaukee NAACP office.

Before the Eagles Club demonstrations ended, housing became the next focus of the Youth Council's actions. They picketed absentee owners of ghetto properties to call attention to run-down housing. Since lack of open housing had produced the ghetto, they soon began to campaign for an open housing law. Their biggest demonstrations occurred over this issue, and the issue eventually rocked the city of Milwaukee and drew national attention to it.

We have already noted that few Milwaukee blacks lived outside the city's inner core. The Wisconsin state legislature had passed a weak open housing law in 1965, but it covered only 25% of the housing in the state, and only about one-third of the housing in Milwaukee. In the city, eighteen of Milwaukee's nineteen aldermen had turned down open housing laws four times, including six white aldermen with black constituents. In the summer of 1967, the Youth Council picketed the homes of these aldermen, led by Father Groppi. The aldermen resisted, responding that they had not voted for a local open housing law because the state already had one. This was the last demonstration before the riots of 1967.

After the ten-day curfew was over, the Youth Council—again led by Father Groppi—marched across the bridge to the all-white southern section of Milwaukee holding fair housing banners. Thousands of tense white spectators flanked the streets and then pressed into the marching youth, shouting and screaming hate-filled words. One hundred twenty-five police in riot gear calmed the crowds, and the youth returned on the bridge to their safe north-side ghetto. A second night of marching followed, with the same white spectator crowds, who this time swarmed over the marchers and threw eggs and garbage at them. Police again dispersed the crowds and the young marchers returned, only to find their youth office—"Freedom House"—had been burned by a fire bomb.

The following night, at a gathering of several hundred open housing supporters in the office, the police came to disperse the group. Pandemonium broke out, with some demonstrators refusing to go, others singing and chanting "We shall not be moved" (Aukofer 1968: 122). Fifty-eight persons were arrested that night, and the issue of open housing was briefly replaced by one of freedom of assembly. The mayor had banned night marches and demonstrations, and the issue attracted national attention. Milwaukee became the "Selma of the north," and sympathizers from all over the country poured into the city to march with the Youth Council. More than 2,300 people walked fifteen miles on September 10, 1967, and a new counter group was born—Milwaukee Citizens for Closed Housing. Fanned by this hostile group, supporters of open housing grew, but the mayor remained firmly opposed, saying that an open housing law would promote white flight.

Finally, one tiny northern suburban village—Bayside—became the first in a string of suburbs in the Milwaukee area to pass an open housing law. In the months that followed, other suburban communities passed open housing laws, with twelve Milwaukee suburbs having open housing laws stronger than the state law. On December 12, 1967, the Milwaukee city council passed an open housing law that was the same as the state law. By the spring of 1968, seventeen communities had passed open housing laws, 200 days of marches had taken place, President Kennedy had been shot, Martin Luther King had been shot, and President Johnson had signed the federal open housing law of 1968. The next day after the signing, the mayor of Milwaukee announced that he would recommend immediate enactment of a city open housing law modeled after the new federal law.

Even this, however, did not halt racial discrimination in housing in the city of Milwaukee. Against this background of racism and bitter struggle, and fanned by urban renewal displacement and resulting white flight, Milwaukee's neighborhood stabilization movement organization—the Sherman Park Community Association—was founded.

INCEPTION

An informal nine-page history of the Sherman Park Community Association (SPCA) refers to seven couples as the founders of the organization in the autumn of 1970. The author of this brief history was one of the founders, and the last narrative page of the history states that it was "compiled with affection and nostalgia, ten years after the formation of the group" (Johannsen 1980: 7).

The seven couples met, this "handful of northwest side residents . . . following weeks of conversation about concerns over the future of their city and their neighborhood" (Johannsen 1980: 1). They felt that only through neighborhood organization could they form a "powerful and cohesive association" that would have an impact on decisions and events affecting their residents. At that time, of the 49,572 people living in the Sherman Park area, only 3.3%—1862 people—were black. They all lived in the eastern third of the Sherman Park area, closer to the inner core of the city, from which many had come when displaced by urban renewal.

Three major concerns about recent events and decisions prompted the discussions of the seven founding couples: (1) rapid racial change of an adjacent neighborhood, Atkinson-Teutonia; (2) two proposed freeways to be constructed in their area; and (3) school boundary changes and internal school problems. These three events were viewed with much heat and emotion by the residents of the Sherman Park neighborhood. The rapid racial change of the Atkinson-Teutonia area was attributed to racial steering and block-busting in the real estate industry—"the manipulated housing market" (Johannsen 1980: 1). The proposed freeways were seen as a threat to "cut up the west side with barriers that would isolate businesses, churches, and schools from their neighborhoods and promote racial segregation." And the "severe" school problems were seen as a result of faulty school board decisions: "Radical change of the Washington High School boundaries in May, 1970 had altered the racial and socio-economic make-up of the school—but the school Board had refused to address the academic and human relations problems that were thus created" (Johannsen 1980: 1).

Each of these issues was the focus of the first three standing committees set up by the new board of the SPCA: housing, expressway, and education. Despite the realities and urgency of these three issues, the first news article about the new organization ignored the issues. The first public statement of SPCA declared that the group was not formed in response to any threat, but to improve the quality of life in the fifth ward on Milwaukee's northwest side. The article, written by the group's first president, defined the boundaries of the Sherman Park area as North Avenue, Keefe Avenue, Thirty-fifth Street, and Sixtieth Street. The number of residents in the area was given as 25,000 people. In fact, there were almost twice that number (U.S. Census 1970, 1980). Until the formation of SPCA, there had been no geographical entity called "Sherman Park." That neighborhood received its name and identity with the formation of the movement organization.

STRUCTURE

We will analyze the organizational development of SPCA over three phases: phase one (1970–74), which was totally voluntary; phase two (1975–79), in which they had an office, staff, and three grants; and phase three (1980–present), in which they had a new office, more staff and multimillion dollar funding. When SPCA began, and throughout their first phase, a board of volunteer directors and the three standing committees noted above conducted the work of the organization. During that time, the membership grew from two dozen to one hundred. The first year's financial statement showed a total annual budget of $1,247, received from membership fees, newsletter ads, and "substantial church donations" (Johannsen 1980: 3). Most of that money was spent publishing the newsletter, which was distributed free. Board and committee meetings were held in members' homes, and public meetings were held in church halls. "The idea of an office and staff wasn't even dreamed about" (Johannsen 1980: 4).

In 1975, the organization received its first substantive funding, a United Way grant of $23,000. An office was established in one business district, and a part-time office coordinator was hired, plus one community organizer. One year later, in 1976, SPCA received a Ford Foundation grant of $15,000 to develop a Neighborhood Affirmative Marketing Program. Total funding in 1976 was $40,000, including membership dues and other donations. At that time, two staff people and one office coordinator were SPCA's paid employees.

During 1976, SPCA wrote a funding proposal for a housing rehabilitation program in cooperation with the Milwaukee Building Trades Council (AFL-CIO). The program, called the Sherman Park Plan, was funded in the summer of 1977 for almost $400,000. Twenty-three people were needed to staff the new program, which was set up as a development corporation with a separate advisory board made up of housing committee and SPCA members. By 1978, there were deep tensions and conflicts, which are revealed in the records of SPCA. The loss in 1977 of both a skilled executive director and a board president was devastating to the organization. By 1984, eight executive directors had come and gone. Let us see what led to this incredible turnover.

In keeping with these new structural expansions, SPCA revised their constitution in 1977, establishing four operational committees and five other standing committees. The four operating committees were executive, finance, personnel, and membership/program. The standing committees were business, education, housing, neighborhood safety and security, and senior citizens. By this time, the housing committee had been subdivided into two separate funded programs, explained further below.

Also reorganized in the 1977 constitution was the board election procedure. The new procedure called for an annual election of ten board members for two-year terms, with five more members to be appointed for one year by the president "to balance the racial, age, sex, socio-economic and geographic composition of the Board with that of the Sherman Park area" (newsletter, Sept. 1977). At least one-third were to be members of racial minorities. No board member could serve for more than four consecutive years. At least eight general membership meetings were to be held each year, with an annual meeting designated for the month of May.

The 1977 constitutional revision reflects tensions and the need to further define board roles. The major changes proposed—the new method of electing board members to improve racial balance, and the mandate of one-third minority—were a clear response to growing charges that the board was unrepresentative of the area it served. In addition, the executive officers were to have more defined responsibilities: the first vice-president would chair the personnel committee (plus two board members, and two other non-board members), the second vice-president would chair the membership and program committees, and the treasurer would chair the finance committee and be responsible for financial planning. So, with increased scale came greater complexity of structure and greater tensions and anxieties.

Meanwhile, the affirmative marketing program changed its name and funding source after the Ford Foundation grant expired at the end of a year. The new name of the program was the Housing Information Service, and the new funding source was the state department of housing and development. This program and the rehabilitation program, plus the United Way program, had twenty-six full-time and ten part-time employees, and a director. As staff increased, volunteer committees were assigned staff persons to work with them and assist them. This was a welcome aid; it also presented some problems.

In October 1977, annual committee reports began to reveal tensions concerning program conflicts and board-staff relations. One such report came from the neighborhood safety and security committee, which had been established in March 1977 and had begun to develop procedures for forming block clubs. Disagreements had arisen over goals and objectives, however. Most of the committee felt that block clubs could discuss issues unrelated to safety, but some felt that safety should be discussed at every block meeting. "There is some concern that the Safety Committee is being 'used' to organize blocks because SPCA wants block clubs" (annual reports, Oct. 4, 1977).

The staff person assigned to work with that committee stated in the report that there were also disagreements as to whether the committee or the block residents should determine the agendas and choice of printed materials for block distribution. Apparently a majority of the committee and the staff person felt that the block leaders should make these choices. "Disagreements about these issues have taken up so much time that several very interested committee members are questioning whether their time is being well spent." The difficulties within this safety committee must have been too great to overcome, because by 1978 no such committee was listed in the SPCA annual reports.

Another committee showing difficulties in staff-committee relations was the ten-member education committee. Their 1977 annual report, also written by a staff person assigned to the committee, stated that some months of fruitless discussion had occurred: "The first nine months of the year have been characterized by meetings where discussions went around in circles and little concrete action was taken. The development of committee objectives [in August and

September] should help alleviate some of the problems" (SPCA annual reports, Oct., 1977).

This report also indicated some role confusion and fears of overdependence on staff, and finally referred to the difficulty of finding committee members and volunteers who were not already affiliated with or employed by the public school system of Milwaukee. The "complexity of the school desegregation issue" was linked to the problem of attracting and retaining committee members.

Open acknowledgment of the organization's lack of demographic representatives was made internally and externally. A 1978 internal staff memo on the need for community organizing refers to "the recognition by some SPCA members that the Association is not truly representative of the entire, diverse population of the community. SPCA is, indeed, predominantly white, middle-class and . . . professional in composition and leadership" (memo, Sept. 12, 1978). The memo went on to state a long-range goal of organizing around issues of major concern to minority, low-income and older adult residents of the Sherman Park area. In this way, it was hoped that a broader cross-section of residents would be involved in the activities of the association. An action plan was outlined that included a survey of the concerns of residents in the eastern third of the area, which was predominantly black.

Two days later, the board and staff received excerpts from a report of the National Commission on Neighborhoods, based on a visit made by the commission the previous summer. The memo accompanying the excerpts from the report said: "These provide an interesting insight on how an outsider with no vested interest in the Association views it. They also provide a basis for us to take a look at the Association and where it is going" (memo, Sept. 14, 1978). Some of the salient excerpts noted that leadership in SPCA was comprised mainly of "white professionals, most of whom live on N. Grant Blvd."—the integrated portion of the area. This indicated "a lack of outreach . . . a stagnation of community resources and a segregation of leadership development." Also, the organization did not have "the block organization that provides a turnover of leadership." Decisions were made "by a small group and communications between them are sporadic." The SPCA had developed "into a program and service association rather than an organizing block structure," and it did not have "a history of confrontation or block leadership orientation." The association tended to be "shortsighted and cluttered with short-term problems," and had not pursued "a strategy over time other than the Freeway issue." There was, finally, a word of praise for SPCA: "The organization has developed a moral fabric with a sustaining outlook, i.e., the permanent commitment for an integrated community" (memo, Sept. 14, 1978).

A news article at this time referred to SPCA's president as saying that conflicts between paid staff and volunteer board and committees had arisen because areas of responsibility had not been clearly defined. "In the last three years we have gone from a Ma and Pa operation to a corporation. . . . But Ma and Pa are still on the Board and want to get in there and play with the cash register and stock the shelves." The article also said the executive director—the group's second—had recently resigned because of "a lack of clarity and accountability regarding the administration of the association" (*Milwaukee Journal*, Sept. 12, 1978). The president referred to the conflict as growing pains, and said the association was in the process of redefining their direction and expectations for staff members.

A special SPCA board meeting was held September 20, 1978, to discuss the national commission report and to set future directions. In fact, it was not until January 1979—four months later—that the board was able to deal with this. But at this special board meeting other issues were more pressing, as the minutes of that meeting show. The first item on the agenda was a personnel item—the relationship between committees, staff, and the executive director. The personnel committee was charged with clarifying personnel policies and considering some changes. The second agenda item was sexism in the association. Because of the amount of discussion generated by this issue, the agenda item concerning SPCA's future direction was tabled—the very reason for the meeting.

A small paragraph on page two of the minutes of that meeting was revealing: "There was concern expressed that we were no longer dealing with issues but rather spending all our energies fighting among ourselves" (minutes, Sept. 20, 1978). Also in the minutes of that important special meeting was an announcement: "We will be moving October 15 . . . and volunteers are needed." The move was to a larger storefront office, after three years in the smaller first one.

A few months later, an important structural change took place. In March 1979, SPCA established a redevelopment corporation as a subsidiary of the organization. It was seen as the newest committee, with the SPCA board electing the board of the redevelopment corporation, consisting of nine members. The four areas of activity were: housing rehabilitation, housing acquisition, storefront conversion, and commercial redevelopment.

A news article two months later referred to the group's rapid growth having "spawned bureaucratic problems, a decrease in volunteer enthusiasm, and conflicts among board members, volunteer workers, and paid staff." The article also noted a second resignation of the executive director, who had resigned earlier but had then agreed to stay on after board discussion and persuasion. This second resignation was final, and the article quoted the director as saying: "We have to define the right mechanism for translating our noble beliefs into everyday life" (*Milwaukee Journal*, May 1, 1979).

With the establishment of the separate subsidiary corporation, the group hoped to resolve some of its internal problems. The SPCA would spend less time on administrative details and could devote more time to issue advocacy. In fact, it took them over three months of discussion and planning to reach this point, as the idea was first broached by the ex-Director in a board report dated December 14, 1978. It was repeated in a December 20 memo from the executive committee to the board. This memo was titled "Need to Establish Future Direction for SPCA," and along with the need for a separate subsidiary corporation it stated two other needs: more social events bringing neighbors together, and better representation of the resident population. Each of these was addressed in the constitutional changes noted above.

The Sherman Park Redevelopment Corporation was incorporated in September 1979, and a ten-person board began functioning the following month. The corporation had twelve full-time staff, and the Sherman Park Plan had an annual budget of over $300,000. Communication was to be maintained between the SPCA and corporation boards through monthly reports and quarterly joint meetings. A year later, they found this was not enough, and SPCA requested that the corporation assign one of their board members to the SPCA board (minutes, Oct. 23, 1980). Clearly, this had become a cumbersome, difficult, and troubled arrangement.

By March 1983, two documents were distributed to SPCA board members indicating that serious internal problems were still present. The first was a report prepared for the SPCA board by the Milwaukee Management Support Organization (MMSO). The second was a report to the board from a staff member who was a community organizer.

The MMSO was a nonprofit private management group that was asked by the SPCA board to conduct a study of the organization's structure, goals and programs. This request was made at the suggestion of the past executive director upon his resignation (for the second time). Two MMSO volunteers interviewed committees, staff, and board members during a five-week period in February 1983. Their report, based on these interviews, identified primary issues and problems and presented some options on their resolution.

The issues and problems cited included a loss of direction by SPCA; a lack of priorities; poor internal communication; confusion as to the roles of board and staff concerning policy-setting; weakening of volunteer involvement; decrease in membership and fund-raising activities; and inadequate response to neighborhood change as seen in program focus and board representation.

Many options were suggested for the SPCA board and members to consider as a means of reducing or resolving some of the problems identified above. Among these were: total analysis and reconsideration of the organization's goals, objectives, priorities and programs; development of a long-range plan of goals and objectives (two to five years) and a short-range one (one year, with periodic reconsideration); and structural modification of board committee/staff relationships. This structural change was enormous: it called for monthly committee reports to the board, staff assigned to each committee, a board representative on each committee, periodic meetings of all committees, administrative matters delegated to executive committee, requirement of all new board nominees to have prior service on a program committee, staggered three-year terms of board members to avoid high turnover, restructuring of committees to reflect changed programs, restructuring of staff to divide the executive director's responsibilities and to assign half to an associate director, and staff assignments of the tasks of volunteer recruitment and involvement, membership drives, and special fund-raising events.

Some of the program changes suggested for consideration included crime prevention and direct services for youth and the poor, reflecting the demographic changes in the Sherman Park area. The report concluded with the recognition of the pride in SPCA's past accomplishments, its strength, and its commitment. "It is this strength that will carry SPCA through its present crisis and renew its purpose and effectiveness" (MMSO report 1983).

The SPCA's next director lasted seven months. Her successor had just begun in 1984 when I visited. A few months later I learned that there were administrative problems with the new director—who had no prior administrative experience—and that the personnel committee was working with her to correct these. She, too, was gone by the end of the year, and replaced with another— and another. Despite the earnest attempts by SPCA to improve their structural difficulties, their rapid increase in complexity seemed too much for them to handle.

A second report revealing SPCA's internal problems named another reason for their troubles. This report identified the "root cause" of the internal crisis as the rapid change in the racial and economic composition of the population of the Sherman Park area. "It is this contradiction between the dreams of the '70's and the facts of the '80's that this report seeks to address." The author, a staff member and community organizer, presented a statistical picture of what was happening to the Sherman Park community using data on race, age, income, housing, and crime. He offered some projections for the future and discussed the implications of these projections for SPCA, their programs, and for the Sherman Park community as a whole. The purpose of the report was "to help the Board of Directors decide on the direction for SPCA. I hope this report can serve as part of an assessment of the needs of the majority of residents and give a few ideas on how to meet them" (Hagedorn 1983: 1).

The major thesis of the report was that Sherman Park was really three distinct neighborhoods, one mostly black and poor, one mostly white and middle-class, and one that was integrated and in between the other two, and changing: "The term 'Sherman Park' as defining a single community . . . is at this time misleading. The factors that shaped a slowly integrating, predominantly white middle class community in the early seventies have radically changed" (Hagedorn 1983: 1).

Questions raised in the report related to which sections of the neighborhood SPCA wanted to concentrate on serving, what the issues of each section were, what the factors were that affected the quality of life in Sherman Park, what changes SPCA could make to better reflect the demographic changes of the past decade, and what issues SPCA could handle best. Finally, the question was asked, "If SPCA is unable or unwilling to represent all segments of the community, how will the unrepresented segments be served?"

The report ended with the observation that the identity crisis being experienced by SPCA could be overcome, since the people of Sherman Park "want to live a better life and are willing to do something about it. For SPCA, the crucial decision is to grasp the best role for itself in the eighties" (Hagedorn 1983: 14). Let us now examine SPCA's stated goals and the program conducted during their three phases of existence, and see if they adapted their program to the changing needs of the changing community.

GOALS

The brief SPCA history states that there was complete agreement on one basic goal: "SPCA would take a strong stand supporting racial integration in every area of its work" (Johannsen 1980: 2). Specifically, the association would consistently encourage and maintain the racial integration of its area as "a desirable and enriching part of urban life." It would strongly encourage residents to remain in the area, would welcome new residents and invite them to join the organization, and would fight illegal real estate practices (block-busting and steering) through "every possible legal channel."

The first news article written by the SPCA president lists the beliefs of the new group: (1) a "beautiful" socioeconomic mix in a healthy urban environment; (2) integration; (3) good schools; (4) neighborhood stores rather than large shopping centers; (5) being part of a community (*Milwaukee Journal*, Aug. 19, 1971). One other belief expressed in that article was that answers would not be found in "giant federally funded programs run by top heavy administrations and monitored by power hungry politicians." Yet, six years later—as we have seen—SPCA found itself involved in a bureaucratic structure with almost half a million dollars in funding for a housing rehabilitation project.

Brochures written, printed, and distributed by SPCA reinforced the basic goal of integration. One dating from the mid-seventies refers to the SPCA as "over 700 members who come from a variety of backgrounds, but share a commitment to their multi-racial urban community." A later one stated: "Members of the SPCA believe that our future lies in encouraging people of all races, religions, and national origins to come together."

Though a 1976 application for Ford Foundation funding stated that SPCA members "celebrate the richness and vitality" of their neighborhood, it then referred to two critical neighborhood situations that residents were "being forced to confront": integrated housing patterns were not a reality in all parts of the area, and there had been a visible decline of home maintenance efforts throughout the area. Two reasons offered for the decline in home maintenance were: the large proportion of elderly living in the Sherman Park area—the highest percentage (almost 30%) of any neighborhood in the entire city; and extensive absentee ownership (over 50%). The lack of total integration was attributed to practices of racial steering (proposal to Ford Foundation, 1976).

Another application for funding from a different source stated the primary SPCA goal as

to serve and promote the interests of the neighborhood as well as the uniqueness and diversity that exists in Sherman Park. Members . . . believe that our future lies in encouraging people of all races, religions, and national origins to come together to meet our common goals of good quality education, beautiful homes and streets, and preserving the most attractive, convenient and interesting place to live in Milwaukee. (application to OPEN, 1977)

The purpose of SPCA, as stated in the bylaws adopted seven years after their founding, was: "to identify and publicize the advantages" of the area; "to educate the Milwaukee community" about these advantages; to improve communications inside and outside the area concerning schools, housing, safety, businesses, and other community needs and concerns; and "to explore and promote innovative projects which will initiate action designed to promote integrated urban living" (bylaws, Aug. 1977).

More specific goals, which supported SPCA's general goal, were also stated by SPCA's various committees. In 1978, eight committees existed and their purposes were explained in eight pages of an SPCA document. The business committee's purpose was to evaluate the needs, problems and prevailing attitudes of local merchants in order to revitalize and regenerate interest and increased profitability within the business community. The arts and recreation committee's purpose was to act as a stimulant and catalyst for arts and recreation activities available to west-side residents. This committee was formed in 1978. The purpose of the community regeneration committee was to ensure resident participation in any land use planning affecting Sherman Park neighborhoods, with consideration of the ideals of integration, racial equality, and neighborhood determination in such plans. This grew out of the earlier anti-freeway efforts of 1970, which led to the formation of SPCA.

The education committee's purpose was to promote quality, integrated education for Milwaukee, to keep the community informed of and to support educational programs in area schools, to act as a resource to individual parents, parent groups and school administrators in the area and its schools, and to develop supplementary educational activities for neighborhood children. The purpose of the membership and program committee was to plan and sponsor community events involving area residents. The newsletter committee's purpose was to prepare and distribute a monthly newspaper to 2,000 recipients.

Two committees that were forerunners of funded programs noted above were the Housing Information Service and the Sherman Park Plan. The purpose of the information service was to preserve and integrate the community through a listing service of units for sale or rent, an elderly outreach program to assist elderly with needs and services, and an absentee ownership program, with an annual housing maintenance survey of code violations. The Sherman Park Plan's purpose was to deal with housing maintenance and rehabilitation problems in the area through making home repairs and providing employment in skilled trades for minorities.

Both of these committees were outgrowths of the housing committee, one of SPCA's first and most enduring committees. The earlier goals of the housing committee were even more explicit than the later ones. Cited in a 1977 funding application were two objectives of the committee. "Perhaps those specific objectives that are most important to SPCA are those articulated by the Housing Committee . . . 1) equal access to housing through support of legislation to eliminate discriminatory practices in selling, lending, and zoning, and 2) encouragement of vigorous and sensitive code enforcement in dealing with housing deterioration." An additional statement of belief by the housing committee referred to the Sherman Park area as a "viable integrated neighborhood . . . important in a metropolitan setting where segregated housing patterns persist. Therefore, we commit our energy and resources to maintain and enhance SP as a lively and vital community with good housing available to all people" (application to OPEN, 1977).

Analysis of 124 city newspaper articles about the organization since 1971 showed five that were specifically related to SPCA goals. The first one was cited earlier. In 1972, the second article relating to goals quoted SPCA's president as saying the organization was trying to combat block-busting and panic sales of homes in the area as black families move in. He said: "We are trying to promote the positive aspects of the neighborhood and encourage white people to stay." The article was headed, "Stability with Integration Praised," and it referred to an interfaith event, attended by over 300 people, where the SPCA was praised by one of the clergy speakers (*Milwaukee Journal*, March 13, 1972).

One year later, an article headed "Neighborhood Group Walks Narrow Path" referred to the SPCA goal of wanting their area to be a "multiracial, multiethnic community for rich people, poor people—whoever wants to live there" (*Milwaukee Journal*, April 16, 1973). In 1978, the board held a series of meetings to assess its role in the community and to set directions for the future. An article headed "Sherman Park Group Feels Pains of Success" referred to internal problems and a need for a redefinition of directions and expectations. The major goal referred to at that time by the president was "to develop a broader more integrated membership base that better reflected the total community and the concerns of minorities, elderly, and low income families" (*Milwaukee Courier*, Dec. 28, 1978).

In 1980, the organization was again publicized as developing new goals in response to its serious internal difficulties. An article headed "SPCA Outlines Its Goals for the Future" cited seventeen goals developed by the organization— then ten years old—at a town meeting held by the SPCA board for area residents. An analysis of the seventeen goals, however, reveals them to be restated objectives related to the overall original goal of promoting and preserving their integrated neighborhood. Included were these six: to encourage business and economic development in the Sherman Park community; to promote economic and racial integration; to develop and support programs that meet the needs of the elderly; to increase broad and diversified association membership; to carry out ongoing evaluation of association programs and activities; and to develop long-term financing for the association in an effort to achieve self-sufficiency.

The committees of SPCA were charged with developing the means for attaining the goals. In 1983, another SPCA board retreat was held to assess its goals and objectives. By this time, eight executive directors had come and gone.

Content analysis of twenty-nine monthly newsletters from 1976 to 1984 revealed a fairly steadfast goal. As stated in the constitution and brochures, this goal was printed in each newsletter. One abbreviated goal statement appeared in the May 1976 newsletter, printed in a box headed "SPCA Officers and Statement of Purpose." The statement was: "The SPCA is a neighborhood organization whose purpose is to serve and promote the interests of the neighborhood as well as the uniqueness and diversity that exists in SP." All other newsletters had the expanded statement of purpose which, as already noted above, went on to say: "Members of the SPCA believe that our future lies in encouraging people of all races, religions and national origins to come together to meet our common goals of good quality education, beautiful homes and streets and preserving the most attractive, convenient and interesting place to live in Milwaukee."

One variant of this statement was found in the February 1977 newsletter, under the heading "What Is SPCA?":

The SPCA is a neighborhood organization on Milwaukee's west side. SPCA consists of citizens who associate to discuss issues, develop strategy, and decide on common action in order to improve the overall quality of life in this community. Members of the SPCA understand the importance of effecting public policy and share in the responsibility for shaping the future of their community. Through this active participation in public life and by their unwavering dedication to racial integration, members of SPCA are actualizing their commitment to a more democratic and pluralistic society. (newsletter, Feb. 1977)

The next issue, and those thereafter until 1980, restated the expanded version of the original statement of purpose.

In 1980, hard times reduced the volume of the newsletter and changed its format. No statement of purpose appeared until December 1981, and then it was the expanded earlier statement. This continued until July 1983, after which it vanished. By 1984, a member-resident of the area, and a former staff member, said: "I don't know what the goals of the SPCA are any more. I think they're very ambiguous" (Frank Felber). A review of the structural changes of SPCA over the years has already revealed the strains and problems they faced. Now let us examine their program to see to what extent they were able to translate their goals into action.

PROGRAM

In all the years of SPCA's existence, they have consistently addressed three major concerns: the freeway, housing (including fair housing and rehabilitation), and schools. An early news article corroborates this: "The organization has concentrated its activities on freeways, schools, and real estate firm activity" (*Milwaukee Journal*, April 16, 1973). In later years, seniors and crime were added to SPCA's program concerns. If we divide the SPCA's existence into three periods—early development (1970–75), maturation (1975–79), and institutionalization (1980–   )—we can analyze their program development over those three periods.

The Freeway

The opposition to the construction of Park West and Stadium North freeways was one of the first tangible issues that drew the residents of Sherman Park together. Beginning in 1972, the battle to oppose construction lasted five years. It ended in the offices of the federal Department of Transportation with the rejection of an environmental impact statement. This statement was written by Milwaukee County after a court order made four years earlier. "It took the County four years to write that document and even after all that time and effort, they were unable to convince the federal government that the Park West was worth building. . . . The DOT said the Park Freeway West will have significant adverse impact, particularly in the severance and disruption of established residential communities along the project route" (newsletter, Feb. 1977).

The decision of the DOT was identical to the views which SPCA and another group, the Westside Citizens' Coalition, had been expressing for years. In fact, both groups had filed a lawsuit in 1972 in an attempt to stop the construction of the proposed freeway. The struggle was fought by a small number of dedicated residents and their equally dedicated lawyers. During the five years of this political and legal battle, a growing number of state and local politicians came to support the views of the SPCA and the Westside Coalition. By the time the simple final rejection memo from Washington arrived, those politicians who aligned themselves with the SPCA position included three senators, sixteen assemblymen, half the county board, most of the city common council, and one congressman.

As soon as the news was received, amidst the jubilation were immediate plans to create a citizens' task force to plan for the redevelopment of the freeway land. The SPCA held a public meeting on February 17, 1977, to begin the planning process. One of the leaders of the struggle summed up the situation this way: "I honestly think that this is one of the greatest things that happened here since SPCA got started . . . no money, no clout, no organizers, we were opposed by labor, business, the press, everybody. Yet, the [freeway] won't be built, and maybe that area can thrive again" (newsletter, Feb. 1977). The expressway committee of the SPCA became the Community Regeneration Task Force. By 1984, a new attractive housing development was on its way to completion in the vast empty area formerly reserved for the freeway.

Housing

The SPCA's housing program had three separate aspects: fair housing, affirmative marketing, and rehabilitation. Of all the newspaper articles about the organization, the housing program was the one referred to most often: 32% of the 124 articles about SPCA since 1971 were related to housing issues.

One of the first actions of the housing committee was to get the city's council to pass an ordinance in 1971 prohibiting the use of "for sale" signs, except by owners. This was done in response to the panic selling tactics used by local realtors in integrating neighborhoods such as the Sherman Park area. The SPCA's housing committee joined forces with another neighborhood association (Capitol Neighbors, now defunct) when block-busting became a critical issue in both groups' neighborhoods. They believed that the sight of "for sale" signs in the community had the "unsettling and detrimental effect of encouraging people to sell, thus abandoning the neighborhood and, in many cases, the city" (proposal to Ford Foundation, 1976).

In the spring of 1976, the housing committee began a real estate audit to test for racial steering. An earlier research report had concluded that Milwaukee, though the northernmost of the large cities in the U.S., had the highest degree of suburban segregation. It held the "dubious distinction of being one of the most segregated large areas in the nation" (report, May 19, 1977). This situation prompted the audit.

One year after the real estate audit began, SPCA filed a formal complaint with the U.S. Department of Housing and Urban Development against four major real estate companies in Milwaukee. The complaint, filed in May 1977, charged discriminatory housing practices, including racial steering and differential treatment of homeseekers on the basis of race. In addition, the complaint stated that those discriminatory practices caused and perpetuated the segregated housing patterns throughout metropolitan Milwaukee. The complaint was based on an audit of forty-two visits made by black and white home buyers during a fourteen-month period.

Meanwhile, during the audit, SPCA's housing committee prepared a proposal to the Ford Foundation for the funding of a Neighborhood Affirmative Marketing program. This program was designed to do four things: inform the community of unethical real estate practices in Sherman Park; promote the advantages of living in the area as an integrated community; transfer absentee-owned houses in the white section of Sherman Park to young minority families who would live in and maintain the properties; and assist elderly persons owning duplexes in these areas in selling these to young minority families. The elderly would then rent their current unit from the new minority owners at a reasonable rate. In January 1977, the Ford Foundation gave a $15,000 grant to SPCA to conduct this program.

The housing committee came to recognize in the early months of the program that unless they expanded the program to include the entire Sherman Park area, their efforts would be addressing only a fraction of the area's problems. Plagued with such problems as racial steering, block-busting, redlining, absentee ownership, and the decline of home maintenance efforts, SPCA began the housing information service in September 1977. This was an expansion of the Ford Foundation program to the entire Sherman Park area, and a broadening of its goals and objectives. They also began to search for other funding sources to replace the Ford grant when it expired at the end of one year. They successfully secured funds from a local foundation and the state of Wisconsin department of local affairs for a total of $25,000, plus $2,250 from a local bank and corporation. The four goals of the program were: eliminating discriminatory practices in the Sherman Park neighborhood, desegregating the segregated areas, strengthening and maintaining the integrated areas, and encouraging home maintenance efforts.

The program was implemented through the provision of a variety of services, including lists of homes and apartments for sale or rent in the area, information on housing repair programs available to residents, referrals to cooperating brokers and attorneys, and special assistance to families making pro-integrative moves, such as low-cost appraisals, attorneys' closing fees, and escort service. From the first Ford Foundation grant of $15,000, the grant amounts for this program grew to $27,250 and then to $48,587. The staff increased from one and a half to two full-time and three part-time workers. In a typical year, 289 families were counseled on buying or renting housing, twenty-nine actually bought or rented, and half of these were pro-integrative moves. This was not enough to change the segregated living patterns of Milwaukee.

To deal with the intense problems of illegal real estate practices, some of the early leaders of SPCA organized a fair housing group to deal with racial discrimination in housing throughout the metropolitan area. The Milwaukee Fair Housing Center was incorporated in 1977. It has become one of the most vigorous fair housing agencies in the nation. But this, also, was not enough to change the segregated living patterns of Milwaukee—though it did increase the entire city's awareness of fair housing as a vital issue.

An ongoing activity of the housing committee was an annual housing maintenance survey conducted throughout the area by volunteers organized and trained by the committee. The survey identified building code violations on all properties in need of repair. Owners were not only notified and urged to repair the properties, they were also offered assistance with repairs. Noncooperating owners were reported to the city's building inspection department.

Concern over the number of low-income, elderly and handicapped residents who could not afford to maintain their homes led to SPCA's development of the Sherman Park Plan, first funded in 1977. This program provided free skilled labor to eligible homeowners for home repair, while at the same time providing job training to minority youth and women. Thus the plan simultaneously improved the Sherman Park area and offered employment. Approximately forty-five to fifty homes a year were rehabilitated under this program, funded by

CDBG and CETA federal-city grants of almost half a million dollars. This program became so complex that, as we have already noted, a separate corporation was eventually formed in 1979 to handle administrative matters relating to the staff of almost twenty-three persons. The average age of the homeowners assisted under the plan was seventy-one, the average annual income was $6,400, and the average number of working hours on each rehabbed home was 250. This was and is the most heavily funded program of SPCA.

Education

The purpose of the education committee was to promote quality integrated education, to inform the community of educational programs in area schools, to support those programs, and to develop supplementary educational activities for neighborhood children. According to the brief informal history of SPCA, the education committee—among the most active since SPCA began—exerted a significant influence on Milwaukee school board policies. By pressuring the school board, the education committee was able to form a Citizens Council, which developed into Citizens United for Education. This organization was able to effect major changes at one junior high school, bring about the demise of another, and the relocation of a third as the first citywide specialty school. Also achieved was the conversion of still another school into a four-year high school specializing in computer technology. In addition, the education committee was instrumental in reducing racial tensions at the area high school after it was desegregated. Though SPCA did not file the suit (this was done two years before they began), they supported it and those involved in it. They also supported and campaigned for four people from the community who ran for the school board, and won.

When the Milwaukee school system was desegregated by court order in 1976, SPCA's education committee developed comprehensive plans for the desegregation program, many features of which were included in the final plan approved by the school board. A 1976 newsletter article about the schools, headed "Desegregated Schools—Good For Integrated Areas," stated that the desegregation of the Milwaukee schools was one of the best things that could happen to the Sherman Park area: "The SP area can now continue to attract both black and white families who want to live in a quality integrated area. Now the % of desegregation in the schools does not have to be a factor when buying a house." (newsletter, Oct. 1976).

Two years later, the education committee testified in federal court against the proposed school board desegregation plans because they were not citywide, not comprehensive enough, and because they placed the entire burden of busing on black children. The committee became active in the monitoring of the school desegregation program, as well as in the Coalition for Peaceful Schools, which was dedicated to quality integrated education throughout the city.

Seniors

The senior citizens committee first became active in 1976 when they began working with older neighbors to foster social contacts and provide informational services. We have noted above that Sherman Park had the highest percent of people age sixty and over of any neighborhood in Milwaukee County. A special SPCA membership rate of two dollars—other rates were five dollars and more—was offered to Sherman Park seniors in a May 1976 newsletter. This included the newsletter subscription and voting privileges. That newsletter listed senior citizens as one of seven organizational activities for volunteers (the others were housing, business, newsletter, education, fund-raising, and clerical). A "Seniors Corner" began appearing in the newsletter soon after as a featured article. An early article described a Sunday afternoon meeting of seniors in the SPCA office with "socializing, summer salads, and discussion" (newsletter, Aug. 1976). A decision was made at that meeting to hold monthly senior meetings from then on.

Later, the senior program became part of the housing service, as noted above, with a grant from the state Department of Aging. In 1977, 392 elderly residents of Sherman Park were individually contacted as part of the Elderly Outreach program. This was established to inform elderly residents of illegal real estate practices such as block-busting and steering, and how to deal with them. The program developed after neighborhood surveys conducted by SPCA revealed that many homes of the elderly were badly in need of repair, and that the elderly were often victimized by real estate agents trying to induce them to sell quickly. Social service and housing information were provided as well, including transportation to facilities and agencies, housing rehabilitation, food emergencies, and home health care.

One newspaper article referred to the Elderly Outreach program positively, and with humor: "Senior citizens are encouraged with warmth and friendship because as one young resident said: 'They're people too, and I plan one day to be one' " (*Milwaukee Courier*, Oct. 2, 1978). Senior citizens was one of five standing committees named in SPCA's 1978 constitution. In SPCA's 1980 reorganization and board restructuring, the elderly were again included in its revised goals: "To develop and support programs that meet the needs of the elderly." The senior citizens committee was listed on the newsletter's organizational activity sheet in January 1980. In November 1980, the newsletter included a notice asking for volunteers to assist in services to the elderly with another agency, Family Services of Milwaukee.

A town meeting held by SPCA in 1981 drew residents who expressed concerns of the elderly about crime. At that same meeting, another relevant concern was expressed about underrepresentation of the elderly on the SPCA board. By 1982, SPCA had joined other neighborhood groups in Milwaukee in a citywide elderly crime prevention program sponsored by the Milwaukee police department. This program was an escort service for the elderly, assisting them with shopping and banking tasks, and serving as a deterrent to assaults. The SPCA was also a member of the citywide Senior Action Coalition of sixty-seven different community organizations with an interest in the problems of the elderly. As such, an SPCA representative attended monthly coalition board meetings.

The SPCA developed some fifty block watch groups in 1982 as a safety measure for the area. The elderly escort program was publicly praised in a 1983 news article, which noted a 20% reduction in crimes against the elderly since the escort program began (*Milwaukee Journal*, Jan. 6, 1983). But two months later, an article described Sherman Park residents as "taking to the streets in an effort to stop burglars and prevent muggings" (*Milwaukee Journal*, March 10, 1983). Actually, SPCA had been concerned with crime since 1977, when they formed the first block club to discuss ways of promoting safety. At that time they also established the Whistle Stop and Block Watch programs, and made phone directories available to all block residents. They also established a safety and security committee as an organizational activity. But they were not able to sustain the block and safety activity adequately, until they made this a focus for the elderly.

Thus, SPCA programs focusing on the elderly developed midway during phase two of their history, but changed over the years from mere social outreach to information about illegal real estate practices, to home repairs, and finally to crime prevention. These changing concerns reflected quite accurately what was happening in the racially transitional area of Sherman Park.

Other Program Activities

Other types of SPCA program activities were social events and meetings, membership drives, newsletter publication and distribution, cultural events, and youth recreation, including the Sherman Park Kickers, a kids' soccer team. The Kickers began in 1976 and contributed many teams to the city league. An annual dinner meeting included an Integration Award, given to a person who had contributed significantly to the advancement of integration in Milwaukee. The first recipient, in 1976, was an attorney, Lloyd Barbee, who had represented the plaintiffs in the Milwaukee school desegregation case. The award dinner was held in the grand ballroom of a major hotel, with tickets costing $12.50 per person.

Cultural and recreational events became a special SPCA interest in 1978 when they formed the City West Arts and Recreational Council. The goal of the council was "to act as a stimulant and catalyst for arts and recreation activities available to westside residents" (Johannsen 1980: 7). One of their projects was the publication of a monthly community activity calendar in the SPCA news-letter. Other projects included concerts, art shows, a film series, and increased live entertainment in west-side clubs. August was the month for an annual Sunday afternoon SPCA picnic held in Sherman Park, with games and prizes for all ages. A giant potlock food table was available for five hours. A welcome committee visited newcomers with gifts and information about the neighborhood and SPCA. An annual tour of homes began in May 1979, drawing hundreds of visitors to the "architectural variety and quality of housing" in Sherman Park (Johannsen 1980: 9).

Despite all these activities, both volunteer and funded efforts to preserve their neighborhoods, SPCA leaders often wondered whether they were making a difference. One poignant comment from a leader reveals their thoughts:

We have struggled with the private and government forces which chew up older neighborhoods in the name of progress and free enterprise. We have brought suit against major realtors for racial steering and against the transportation planners who tried to carve us up with a freeway. We have received grants of federal funds intended to help save this part of the city. And we wonder today whether we are succeeding. Because despite a solid track record and a reputation for success, we recognize that each day may find us falling behind. (statement to city council, John Gelman, March 28, 1984)

Let us turn now to an analysis of SPCA's impact.

IMPACT

Integration Maintenance

To what extent has the Sherman Park area been maintained as a racially integrated community? We see from Table 2 and Figure 1 (Appendix A) that Sherman Park's black population in 1970 was 5%, and that by 1980 it was almost 34% of the total population. In 1970, only three Sherman Park census tracts had black people living in it. By 1980, all seventeen tracts in the area had some black households. These were not evenly distributed, however, as further examination shows. In the eastern portion of Sherman Park, with 23,343 people in seven tracts, 62.8% were black in 1980. The western portion, with 17,502 people in six tracts, was only 3.7% black. And the central portion, with 11,977 people in four tracts, was 20.8% black in 1980. At that time, Milwaukee's overall black population was 23.1%.

Thus, though Sherman Park was racially integrated, the level of integration was very uneven. All respondents acknowledged that Sherman Park was, in fact, three neighborhoods divided according to racial composition. One university professor, a nonresident, also referred to the three sections and to recent changes: "The eastern third of the SPCA area is all black...they [SPCA] delayed the process, but it's now growing blacker" (Dan Norris). Some pointed out, however, that SPCA had consciously included the eastern portion within the boundaries of their work area, and had even expanded the boundaries to include neighborhoods with higher proportions of black occupancy.

A current staff member, black, saw SPCA positively: "One of the things I think is real significant is the fact that SP is the only community that I know of that had a very specific and very deliberate plan for welcoming in people of other races" (Catherine Mellon). And a former staff member said: "I knew they were committed to . . . a stable integrated neighborhood. They were committed to keeping the housing in good shape. Also I knew that that neighborhood was liberal, both black and white." Asked if she had the impression that there was predominantly white leadership in the organization she replied: "I did not have that impression before I came to work for them, but I found it out afterwards" (Janet Stouffer).

A former association leader and current resident spoke of the struggle to maintain racial diversity in Sherman Park:

The neighborhood I live in is now 75% black. When I moved into this home eight years ago, it was probably in the vicinity of 30% black. . . . I think that if I were going to predict down the road which way we're going, I think that I'm going to wake up in a few years and find myself living in a 99% black middle-class neighborhood, which is clearly not what I'd like to see. I'd like to see an integrated neighborhood where white demand is allowed to function as strongly as black demand. . . . I don't see it happening, given all the odds and forces working against it right now. (Frank Felber)

One former SPCA president and long-term resident told, wistfully and hesitantly, of the inner struggles of remaining in the neighborhood:

We still find ourselves here, but we keep thinking that after fourteen years it is time for a change . . . and where do you go? And somehow we've been here so long—we've been preaching a certain type of lifestyle and it seems somewhat inconsistent to go to an all-white suburb, or even a suburb out of the city . . . but a lot of the people who have left here have. (Robert Sedwick)

This respondent's wife had been mugged in the neighborhood park, his house robbed, and his son's bicycle stolen. I had been informed by others that they might move because of these events, but it didn't seem imminent when talking to him. He felt guilty for contemplating moving, and said so later: "So somehow you just come to the point where you say that it is all part of it . . . and you continue to stay here."

Newspaper articles over the years referred to misconceptions about SPCA's goals. One article in 1973, headed "Neighborhood Group Walks Narrow Path," quoted SPCA's president explaining the difficulties: "If we talk about stability, blacks think we are trying to keep them out. If we talk about integration, we make some whites nervous. They think we are trying to bring blacks in. So we just talk about what a good place to live SP is" (*Milwaukee Journal*, April 16, 1973). This article referred to the SPCA as "essentially a group of white liberals" that had been "forced to deal delicately with racial questions."

Misconceptions about the organization's ideology and tactics continued throughout the years. A 1977 news article, headed "Integration Plan Biased," described a critical report of SPCA's newly funded affirmative marketing program, saying they were trying to steer minorities toward buying homes in one part of the Sherman Park area (*Milwaukee Journal*, May 12, 1977). This was shortly after SPCA had filed suit against four real estate firms for racial steering. Twelve days later, SPCA publicly replied to these charges and defended the program by saying it was an attempt to provide housing opportunities for those who had been denied them in the past (*Milwaukee Journal*, May 24, 1977).

A more positive 1978 news article, headed "The Sign Says It: Integration Works," ended with this note: "Several years ago the neighborhood was given up as going to the dogs because blacks were moving closer and closer. . . . But older residents joined with the newcomers and built on a community pride that would compare with any in the county" (*Milwaukee Journal*, April 23, 1978).

A former city alderman who lived in and represented the SPCA area said he thought the city was causing white flight in the area:

It's a segregated city, and SP is getting blacker, with more white flight. There is Section Eight concentration there, plus leased housing concentration, and more units of public housing are going into the North Avenue area [the southern border of the area]. They should spread this out to other areas. . . . This is why the city gave $20,000 of CDBG funds to SPCA for a mobility assistance program. (Bert Westin)

Quality Maintenance

To what extent has the neighborhood quality been maintained over the years? Some 1980 census household statistics are revealing and address this point. The median family income for the entire Sherman Park area in 1980 was $17,000, slightly above the city's median of $16,060. But again, the three sections of Sherman Park were quite different. The eastern segment had a median family income of $13,500; the central segment had $20,800 as its median family income; and the western segment's median family income was $20,000. Thus, we see that the eastern section—predominantly black—was substantially lower, while the other two sections were higher than the citywide average. Since public housing units were beginning to be concentrated in the eastern section, the lowered income would be expected.

Similarly, examining rates of owner occupancy, we see that though the average for Sherman Park was 52.4%—higher than the city average of 47.2%—this was not the case with the eastern section of SP. There, the rate of owner occupancy was slightly below the city average, with 46.1% owner occupied. The central and western sections had 55.1% and 57.1% respectively.

The percent of elderly in Sherman Park as a whole was 13.5%, 1% higher than the city average. The eastern section of the area was 8.3% elderly, the central section was 15.6%, and the west section was 19%. The proportion of youth under eighteen was reversed, with 27% for the city, 30.3% for Sherman Park as a whole—39.2% for the eastern section, 26.2% for the central section, and 21.2% for the western section. Female heads of households for the city

were 35.5%, for Sherman Park a bit higher at 37.4%. But the eastern section
had 44.1% female-headed households, the central portion 34.2%, and the west
32.7%.

These figures, along with the fact of increasing concentration of subsidized
housing in the Sherman Park area would suggest the possibility of some deterioration. Visual inspection confirmed this in some of the business sections, but
not in the housing. The housing generally looked well-kept and in good repair.
Some of the business sections looked run-down, with vacant stores and shoddy
exteriors. Interviews reinforced these perceptions.

In answer to the question, "Have you noticed any physical changes in the
area—residential or business?" two residents who had recently returned after an
absence of several years said:

I guess I'd have to say it was a change downward. It was just starting to go down before
we left—just starting to slide, but it has slipped considerably. . . . Yes, there's been some
deterioration. . . . But in terms of the general neighborhood, it looks real good. There
are spots that look better. . . . Partly this is because of the organization [SPCA] and partly
because of the economy. Lots of people decided to stay put and keep up, fix up, rather
than leave. (Carla and Chester Harris)

Dan Norris, university professor and nonresident, spoke of housing values: "The
housing values in SP have not inflated as in other areas, because of its racially
transitional nature." And a young attorney, resident and association member,
talked about abandoned houses in the area: "We've [the housing committee of
the SPCA] identified thirty-nine houses in the eastern section which are abandoned VA homes . . . all were foreclosed, and the VA holds on to them one
year before they resell . . . and has no legal obligation to repair during that time.
. . . This leaves all those homes in limbo. . . . This is our problem" (Donna
Felber).

A founder of SPCA, still a resident, referred to the impact of urban renewal
on the business district and the change in types of businesses in the area: "Well,
it started out—the deterioration was first noticeable on North Avenue because
the freeway was going in and they tore down 4,500 housing units. So that had
to have a huge impact. . . . You remove all those people from that business
district and the little grocery stores can't make it, the little drug stores can't
make it, and the dry cleaners can't make it, and all of a sudden you start getting
empty store fronts" (Margaret Johnson).

Also referring to business area decline was Robert Sedwick, a business executive and longtime resident and Association member and ex-leader: "Our
business strips here are in very bad shape, and they continue to get that way."
When asked to describe the decline, he replied:

Well, I think a couple of things. Obviously, the suburban shopping centers have pulled
the good merchants away and given them storefronts at the main shopping centers. The
downtown revitalization has hurt the neighborhood—it's great for downtown but it has

hurt these strips. And thirdly, obviously our neighborhood is becoming a poor neighborhood as the transition continues. People who move up that ladder choose to leave. . . . Blacker and poorer are moving in to the community.

Many respondents spoke of SPCA's efforts to rehabilitate housing, especially in the eastern, predominantly black section. One special program to identify homes in need of repair was a volunteer street survey, as noted above. One resident, a black association leader, described it as "a very important thing to come out of the housing committee . . . we're going to help with it, we'll go around and check the houses for code violations" (Tracy Vale). When asked how they decided where to go, she replied: "They tell you where to go. The committee gets it together. There've been years where they have a hundred people out doing the spring survey." She then explained that there was a training session with a building inspector, who showed films on what to look for; then the volunteers were given packets and sent out. They were given two weeks to complete their survey assignment, which included a form listing various code violations to check. Owners who had violations were sent a letter informing them of the survey results on their home, and were asked to call the association if help was needed to correct the violations. Other violations were reported to the building inspection department.

With some pride, she told of an absentee owner of many buildings who was taken to court by SPCA for multiple neglected violations. Then she added, "The economic situation in the neighborhood must be less today than it was some years ago. . . . I would guess it's going down from the east to the west. . . . But it doesn't have to be deteriorating as much as it is today. . . . The city is going to have to pay closer attention."

Two residents, one a former staff member, the other an association leader, described the association's projects addressing neighborhood deterioration. The Sherman Park Plan, a rehabilitation program run in cooperation with tradesmen, was designed to upgrade homes of people in need, and to bring women and minorities into the building trades. "The Redevelopment Corporation handles this now—we also run ads in our newsletter which is distributed to all the households in the area now, saying this is what the plan does—if you think you are eligible, fill in this form and we will talk to you about it" (Margaret Johnson).

One former staff member recalled earlier efforts and results: "We started to work on the problem of absentee ownership, and we identified two people who owned dozens of properties in neighborhood duplexes. We set out to push the building department inspectors to tackle them, and when they failed to do this we went to the media. . . . We did drive out two of the absentee landlords in the neighborhood" (Frank Felber).

A news article confirmed SPCA's militancy in correcting housing deterioration. Headed, "Suit Pushes for Repairs on Building," the article stated that the SPCA, several block clubs, and the city had filed suit under a little-used state law asking that an apartment building be declared a public nuisance and that all needed repairs be made. The article also noted that the owner had been fined and jailed the year before for code violations on another property (*Milwaukee Journal*, Oct. 7, 1980).

Sense of Community

To what extent has the association maintained a sense of community in the Sherman Park area? One Milwaukee city planning director did not believe that a sense of community was possible in Milwaukee, according to a news article which appeared in 1973: "The neighborhood is a fiction" (*Milwaukee Journal*, April 16, 1973). He said city studies had shown the concept of neighborhood as a cohesive social unit could not be applied to Milwaukee. A vice-president of SPCA was also quoted in that article, supporting somewhat the planner's contentions: "In the Milwaukee culture we tend to be very private people. We value our turf." The article went on to state that the quest for privacy worked "against the development of a sense of neighborhood and cohesion," and ended with an announcement of the SPCA's intent to organize block parties to combat "this sense of isolation."

One might say, however, that every time a neighborhood newsletter is received, and every time a neighborhood function takes place, a sense of community is being nurtured. Al Billey, longtime association supporter and United Way grant-giver, spoke about this as "bringing the people together where they are, communicating with each other."

A founder of the association, still a resident, offered a special piece of information relevant to sense of community: "Do you know this area was never known as the Sherman Park area before we made it the Sherman Park area? . . . because it was just a dinky park and nobody knew anything about it. We gave it that identity which is a nice feeling." This respondent also spoke of the association newspaper as fostering a sense of cohesion within their large neighborhood of 10,000 households: "We gave it out free in all the stores—like beauty shops, barbershops, drug stores, places where neighborhood people went—and members got it in the mail, the churches got some, and so we had a circulation of about 4,000. About 90% of our budget then went for the newsletter" (Margaret Johnson).

Block organization was referred to as a positive SPCA action, which started late in its development because of a hostile environment:

I think it has been helpful from the crime prevention standpoint and in getting people to know each other . . . There are a lot of block clubs in the area right now. I think it's a helpful thing in an integrated area because people are often fearful of who their neighbor is and they have to get to know each other. (Frank Felber)

As a counter-balance to these positive reflections on the association's role in providing a sense of community were three recurring negative themes. One was the continual recognition of the three-way division of Sherman Park along racial lines, a second was the growing fear of crime, and a third was the waning of some of the association's community events. All three of these would indicate some weakening of a sense of community, or cohesiveness, in the Sherman Park area.

A news feature on SPCA in 1978 noted the decrease in participation. Titled "SP Group Feels the Pains of Success," the article referred to only seventy-five members, "a decrease in volunteer enthusiasm and participation, a lack of minority and working class members, a structure that borders on the bureaucratic, and conflicts between board members and paid staff" (*Milwaukee Journal*, Sept. 12, 1978). But the last paragraph in the two-page feature concluded with a slight note of hope:

No longer characterized by fear and flight, SP now attracts people who like the area's older homes and want to live in an integrated urban neighborhood. But, many say the major challenge still facing the Association is that of creating a genuine community for all who live in this west side neighborhood, giving new meaning to the group's slogan— "Since we're neighbors, let's be friends."

Influence

To what extent has the SPCA influenced key decision-makers that affect their neighborhood? Newspaper articles, newsletters, minutes, reports, interviews, and reflection show that the SPCA has been an innovative aggressive force in the Milwaukee metropolitan area. Action in each of their program concerns has had an impact on the institutional networks involved: freeway blockage, housing discrimination, housing deterioration, and school desegregation.

Of 124 newspaper articles concerning the SPCA in their first fourteen years of existence, 32% were concerned with housing—deterioration and the efforts of the group to stop it, affirmative marketing of the Sherman Park area, and racial discrimination in housing. Of these articles, 23% related to community events or recreational activities sponsored by SPCA, 14% were about general aspects of the organization, and 9% related to the schools.

A brief review of some of the newspaper headlines over the years show the kind of impact the association had. From 1976: SPCA Preparing Survey of Housing Conditions; Buildings Repaired; SPCA and Milwaukee Bldg. & Constr. Trades Council Join Forces for Housing Rehab Program; SPCA Members Polled for Greenlining Strategy; Westside Com. Org.'s Boost Area. From 1978 and 1979: SPCA Housing Rehab Program Progress; Bldg. Inspectors Defend Extension; W. Side Group to Buy Homes/Redvlpt. Corp. Begins; House Renovation Puts Smile on New Owner's Face; Com. Gr. Buys Duplex; Renovation Project Turns Out a Winner. From 1980–1983: SPCA Wants Property Declared Public Nuisance; SPCA Housing Survey to Identify Homes Needing Repairs; $10,000 to SPCA to Find 100 New Units; Housing Survey to Begin; Housing Survey Results. Thus, the work of the organization in reducing housing deterioration was widely publicized, and indicated success.

The SPCA's efforts in stopping real estate discrimination were headlined in a major lawsuit filed in 1976 against four major real estate firms. Though this did not eliminate racial discrimination in housing, it did jolt the real estate industry in the Milwaukee area into consciousness about their practices. Out of this suit came the formation of the Milwaukee Fair Housing Center, which has grown into one of the most effective such agencies in the country. Some of the leaders of SPCA were also the founders of the center. Catherine Mellon, a current SPCA staff member, confirmed this: "SPCA was responsible for spinning off the MFHC, which is very active."

The whole issue of school desegregation was a critical one for the SPCA. Recognizing that they could not maintain their struggle for an integrated neighborhood without integrated schools, they played an active role in the formation of school policy. Though SPCA did not file the lawsuit against the schools (since they didn't even exist until two years later), they supported the suit and those involved in it. They also supported four people from the Sherman Park community who ran for the school board and won. The political impact of SPCA was described by ex-president Bob Sedwick: "Over the years, I think that the organization has become very respected in that no one can take a stand without considering our community association . . . they [SPCA] developed a lot of say in how this neighborhood is run."

One impact SPCA had on the real estate industry was securing the passage of the ban on "for sale" signs in Sherman Park. Several respondents spoke about this as a major victory, with four years of enforcement making it more effective.

The SPCA's success in blocking the proposed freeway through their neighborhood has already been discussed. This was followed, some years later, by their success in securing a high-quality housing development on the vacant land originally cleared for the freeway. Known as Parc Renaissance, the development was hailed by the association's supporters, who had all along urged its construction. Referring to the press's change in attitude about this, Margaret Johnson recalled with glee: "All of a sudden we became these great heroes. Now they thought we were terrific, but earlier both papers were pro-freeway and felt we were terrible trying to stop progress and keep people from getting downtown faster."

Finally, a measure of impact is the amount of funding the SPCA has managed to secure. Phenomenally, they increased their funding from a modest $30,000 to almost half a million dollars in one year. Frank Felber, former SPCA staff members, described this: "It was tremendous growth during that period. Very exciting things, it was growth, it was staff, and it was success on a number of fronts . . . which accounts for a lot of the changes that occurred at that time. Almost too much to handle."

One other indicator of impact should be noted. Two awards were given to the SPCA in 1975, one from B'nai B'rith for its outstanding community work, and one five months later from the Milwaukee County commission on human relations for their efforts to maintain integration in Sherman Park.

Though SPCA's impact within the neighborhood has already been shown through their programs, the impact of their newsletter should also be noted here. The SPCA newsletter was distributed in ever-increasing numbers over time, though not in a steady progression. Beginning with a distribution of 3,000, they went down to 2,000 in 1978, up to 4,000 in 1979, down to 1,000 in 1980 because of a budget crisis, and finally up to 18,000 in 1984. This was a gigantic increase, brought about by staff management of advertising which gave sufficient revenues to have the paper pay for itself. This type of mass distribution was bound to have a significant impact on the residents of the area, as well as on city officials and other key leaders who also received it.

FACTORS OF SUCCESS

Finally, we ask what has contributed to the survival of the organization, and what has led to its success? And are there some qualifications to that success? What can we project into the future for the association and for the Sherman Park neighborhood? We will again refer to internal and external factors in this analysis, with internal factors relating to the organization itself, its programs, and its participants. External factors will include physical, environmental conditions of the neighborhood; social-political conditions involving institutional relationships and governmental or organizational conditions; the city's economic base; public housing placement; and the school desegregation program.

Internal

Beginning with the participants themselves, we conclude they had zeal and courage. Founder Margaret Johnson described the fear and panic at the time of the formation of the organization:

There was pressure from realtors all over, and this was very blatant—there was no subtlety whatsoever . . . the only purpose was to frighten people. Blocks were being contacted by telephone, every doorknob was being hung with something. It was just saturation. Things were said like, "Your house is never gonna be worth this much again, can you afford to lose money on your house?" At that time there was very little specific on the books [concerning fair housing] . . . one of the first things we felt was fear. Fear is kinda like measles. It just feeds on itself and then it spreads. . . . So we thought we've got to have communication, and we started a newsletter. . . . We had this handful of people, all very dedicated and hard-working. We made an awful lot of racket. . . . If we had stopped to think about it, perhaps we would have been overwhelmed at everything that had to be taken on. . . . But . . . people were angry, and anger is gonna fuel a lot of your energy to get you going. So we accomplished a lot mainly because we didn't know it was impossible.

They not only had energy and courage, they also were dedicated. In addition, they had the priceless ingredients of intelligence and creativity. They were able to seize the appropriate moments and turn them into the best possible results for their agreed-upon goals. They also were able to get funding at the right time, and to use that funding to secure more funding for the programs they saw as most relevant to their goals. This was true for the first phase of their development, 1970–74, and up to the middle of their second phase of development, in 1977. After that, there were serious board-staff difficulties that affected productivity and morale. All respondents acknowledged this, some more strongly than others.

These structural difficulties were discussed above, and we have seen how devastating they were to the organization. A leadership vacuum was also hurtful to the organization in 1977, just before their funding glories turned into troubles. One of the staff members at the time, Frank Felber, described the situation:

Shortly after I left as director, the president moved out of town. Then there was not the leadership or knowledge or expertise left after we and some of the others went. There were still many good people left, but the leadership was not as consistent and clear as it was when we were there. What happened after that is that the organization went through a good half dozen executive directors, a good half dozen presidents . . . for I guess seven years. And there's been substantial turnover even on the board.

Thus, we see that some of the internal aspects of the organization were extremely positive—their people during the first seven years, their ability to secure enormous funding, the programs; and some are negative—the staff problems and structural difficulties, their weakened leadership, and their lack of clear-cut goals during the late seventies and early eighties. However, much hope for the future remains.

External

Turning to external factors that impinged on the organization, we first must remember the historical context. Felber provided the backdrop for the organization's environment: "No neighborhood could maintain itself as an integrated entity and have any stability whatsoever as long as the rest of the metropolitan area was basically a segregated one. . . . Sherman Park is not an island; it resides in the center of a metropolitan area that is one of the most segregated in the country."

We also must be reminded of the 1924 news article that described the setting up of a "black belt" designed by the realtors' association. So, the Sherman Park neighborhood, like all neighborhoods, is a product of its history. The fact that it is divided into three sections along racial lines, and has remained so for so long, is no accident. This is part of the real estate design dreamed of sixty years ago, and so meticulously implemented over the years. Even as late as 1984,

HUD had to order the Milwaukee housing authority to integrate its public housing projects, of which some scattered sites were increasingly located in the Sherman Park eastern sector.

Other neighborhood factors that are negative in the Sherman Park community are the concentration of subsidized housing, the business area deterioration, the many duplexes in some sections, and the fact that there are no special amenities in the neighborhood. Even the park that bears its name is seen as "a dinky park." The housing stock remains of good quality, and a few streets are quite attractive. The rest of the area is pleasant, but mediocre. If we add to this the economic base of the general metropolitan area, which is declining, and troubled employment, we have some serious negative factors that do not offer much hope for the future of the neighborhood.

Balancing these, however, are four positive external factors. The city of Milwaukee began a vigorous neighborhood development program in 1977, with much recognition of the need for infusing special programs to the city's neighborhoods. This was late for Sherman Park, but a hopeful sign nevertheless. A 1979 news article confirms the city's belated but growing interest in Sherman Park. The headline was "Sherman Park Key, Former Mayor Says," and the article reported that the ex-mayor had stated that "the survival of the SP area represents one of the most crucial tests facing the city in the years ahead" (*Milwaukee Journal*, March 29, 1979).

Second, the United Way in Milwaukee has a unique interest in assisting neighborhood organizations, and seems likely to continue unless the SPCA becomes disastrously incompetent. Another likely continuing funding source is the state, with which SPCA has established cordial ties. Thus the future of the organization seems for some time secure. Third, the school desegregation program for the city—though not the best—at least removes the burden from the neighborhood of having racially identifiable schools. Because of this, affirmative marketing programs for the neighborhood have some chance of success. Finally, the presence of a vigorous fair housing center in the city is a significant positive force that can only be good for the Sherman Park neighborhood, as well as for the entire metropolitan region.

THE FUTURE

Respondents addressed their concern for the future, recognizing some of these issues, and raising others. One of the SPCA founders worried about the future:

Some of the newer people on the board don't realize the perils . . . We are still faced with the need to maintain the housing stock, and we must maintain good public education . . . but the problem is Milwaukee itself . . . there's a permanent loss of industrial jobs— we don't know what impact that will have on this community, because we are part of the larger area. . . . Generally, I'd say SPCA has had major successes in all areas, and our failures have not been entirely our failures. They have been failures to be able to change the larger society, which continue. . . . I don't think we could have done a whole lot more than what we have done. But it's all so fragile. . . . Unless we have crises I don't honestly believe they [SPCA] will mobilize the volunteers . . . they used to do everything in the old days. (M. Johnson)

Janet Stouffer, a former staff member said: "That was the worst job I ever had in my life." Why?

I think the main problem or the biggest one is that in the seventies SPCA really made a name for themselves . . . so SPCA became a mini-City Hall for the people who lived there. There were extremely high expectations, they demanded many things, and the boundaries are extremely large. I mean there are 40,000 people . . . you are talking about a small city . . . so it was frustrating—and very sad. . . . Do I think they succeeded? Well, no we did not succeed totally, but we sure slowed down the process of resegregation. I believe that, and that is not all that bad. They bought time.

Bert Westin, a former city alderman for the area agreed: "Even though SPCA hasn't been able to stop the process of racial transition, they did slow it down. They worked hard, and still are—but there are a lot of forces working against them."

A current association leader felt that the Sherman Park area would be "a strong, vibrant community in years to come. The real key is to maintain the current housing stock. Today there is a real significant future here, with lots of challenges to the neighborhood association. Without SPCA the chances of integration maintenance would be greatly reduced" (Bud Fowler).

Two members of the United Way allocations committee gave their views of the organization. One said: "They have not done grass-roots development. They're different from other neighborhood groups, their block clubs came much later. The group is in trouble. There is concern over their administrative ability. Their funding will not be increased. I think it will be maintained" (Matt Best). The other committee member said: "As long as I'm on, they'll still get their money. But yes, there are some problems with their operation" (Al Billey).

Finally, the observations of Frank Felber, a former association leader and current resident, offer a sober assessment of the past and future of the Sherman Park area and the SPCA:

I find it difficult to articulate what the goal of the present organization is. It's very ambiguous. . . . [Do you think they succeeded in doing what they set out to do?] Yes, if you look at the whole term of the organization from the beginning to the present . . . I would say we accomplished some things. If nothing else, we effected a very smooth transition for minority residents moving into this area. We paved the way and broke down a lot of the hostility that I think would have been there very strongly were it not for the efforts of SPCA to open the doors here. Stopping the freeway can only be viewed as a positive development; the school desegregation thing, despite its problems and limitations, did some positive things for schools in this neighborhood. I think the efforts to contain the absentee ownership in the neighborhood were pretty successful, even though we still have the presence of absentee owners in the neighborhood. Starting the Fair Housing Center was great, but . . . it cannot possibly effectuate the kinds of changes that would preserve SP as a balanced integrated living environment. [What would it take to do that?] I think it would take a massive infusion of monies, both in terms of enforcement of fair housing laws and of affirmative housing programs. There are still institutions which treat this neighborhood and all integrated or minority neighborhoods differently when it comes to providing services than predominantly white neighborhoods, and those institutions need to be taken on in a serious way and challenged to adopt more affirmative practices. . . . Until we systematically deal with all those institutions on the public policy levels and in a legal manner, I don't think that we will see the changes occur. [What of the future of the neighborhood?] I think that certainly the racial composition will continue to change. The emphasis on integration will probably continue for some time. There will be people, voices in the neighborhood, that will support the issue of integration. But I do see white flight continuing in the area. I do see steering continuing, and I do see disinvestment continuing in the area. But this is probably one of the older integrated neighborhoods in the city. I just think—I hope—that people here recognize just how important that is and how valuable what they have is . . . and they will take care of it to nurture it, value it.

We will see. In 1988, Milwaukee reached an out-of-court settlement with surrounding suburbs for a metropolitan school desegregation program, with $5 million awarded to the Fair Housing Center for a simultaneous five-year regional housing mobility program. This will surely help Sherman Park's future, and benefit the entire city and region.

5

HARTFORD: BLUE HILLS CIVIC ASSOCIATION

"What happens to a dream deferred?"

"I drive through every day . . . it reminds me, painfully, repeatedly, of the best and busiest years of my life"

"We were all working our hearts out, trying to make that integrated neighborhood work"

"The work never ended . . . people can't sustain that kind of fervor for very long"

Keney Park sign: "Closed from dusk to dawn"

INTRODUCTION

When I first called the BHCA phone number given to me by the National Neighbors office, I was told it was no longer a working number. Hoping this was a mistake, or a temporary disconnection, I called the reference librarian at my local library to find out if there was a listing in the Hartford phone directory

Chapter quotes are from transcripts of taped interviews conducted in Hartford during June 3–9, 1984, unless otherwise noted.

for the association. She said there was a Blue Hills Citizen Action group listed and gave me that number. When I called the number, a voice with a Hispanic-sounding accent responded and answered my question about BHCA by saying they were no longer in existence. I asked how long this group had been there, and the answer was vague; "Oh, a few years."

I had other Hartford names to call, so I proceeded to do this. But a number of names and phone numbers that I called got the response of "no longer a working number." I was uneasy when I went to Hartford, but at least I knew that some of the Blue Hills people were still around.

One of the first things I noticed in the Hartford newspaper, the *Courant*, when I got there on June 3, 1984 was an announcement of a meeting—open to the public—of the Citizen Action group I had spoken to earlier. I decided to go. It was held in St. Justin's Church meeting hall, in the heart of the Blue Hills neighborhood. About sixty people were there, mostly black, with a few white city officials and organizational leaders. Concerns expressed related to safety, housing maintenance, and business strip problems. The atmosphere was unenthusiastic and depressing. Maybe it was the heat (about 92 degrees); more likely it was my fear that my initial anxieties had come true. This group was definitely not the BHCA, though it had the same initials and worked in the same neighborhood. The BHCA I knew about was surely dead, and Blue Hills was no longer an integrated community. My task, then, was to find out what happened.

SOCIOHISTORICAL CONTEXT

From a small river town in 1819 with thirty-eight unpaved streets and 6,000 inhabitants, Hartford grew to become a major Eastern city of today with 135,000 residents. Known as the insurance capital of the nation, it has three of the largest insurance companies in the world. It is the capital city of Connecticut, and is thought by some to have "a cultural sophistication to complement its corporate competence" (*Magazine*, March 1984: 165). It is the proud possessor of a new downtown thirty-eight-story office building that is the tallest skyscraper between New York City and Boston. What happened between 1819 and today? What made Hartford grow?

The first people to find Hartford a desirable place to live were the Dutch, who built a fur-trading post on the Connecticut River in 1633. Three years later, English Puritans came to settle in the area and eventually prevailed. For almost 200 years, typical Connecticut Yankees were of British extraction and staunch members of the Congregational Church. But they "were not eager to welcome folk of different backgrounds": the vote in 1637 was limited to "respectable, landowning, churchgoing, white, Puritan Englishmen," as was typical in colonial America (Grant & Grant 1969: 57, 58).

Hartford's early economy was based on the Connecticut River. Until about 1820 it relied on trade from the West Indies, but when the steam engine came into general use after 1820, it brought more trading vessels, more commerce, the first large factories, and more people to Hartford. The newcomers settled mostly to the north and south of Hartford's center, and below the area that is now Main Street. The west, now Bushnell Park, was a vast marshland, unsuitable for housing. Eastern movement was blocked by the river.

With the coming of the railroad in 1838, additional commerce and long-range development occurred. The railroads opened up inland trading with other parts of the country, and manufacturers began to find Hartford a prime location for their operation. At this time the wealthiest people of Hartford lived in the downtown area. They stayed there until it began to be overcrowded by the immigrants who flowed in after 1840. The poorest people of Hartford, including blacks, lived on the fringes of the downtown area in the streets surrounding the state capitol. The land in that area was not considered valuable then, because it was isolated from the central business district, and inconvenient for easy access to and from work.

Between 1850 and 1860, transportation improvements changed the face of Hartford's residential neighborhoods, and after the Civil War Hartford grew rapidly as an important center of merchandising, manufacturing, insurance, and finance. Wealthier residents moved out of the downtown area in large numbers. Factories came to be located near the railroad, which ran through the center of the city. And housing for the factory workers was built near the factories. This explains why some of Hartford's neighborhoods contained such heavy concentrations of ethnic groups—early and later immigrants. But it does not explain why the north end of Hartford came to be a densely populated black ghetto.

The first black family to settle permanently in Hartford came in 1765. Others followed, and by the time of the Civil War about 700 blacks were living in the city. The estimated black population in Hartford in 1865 was about 1,000, scattered through several parts of the city. There was no ghetto then or in 1870, when a city directory no longer listed blacks separately. The largest number of black people lived on the east side of Hartford, close to where they worked, or they lived in three other sections of Hartford, then considered outlying—including the swampy area around the capitol building. In 1870, only 21.4% of Hartford's blacks lived in the city's north end, and "there seemed to be an accepted place for blacks in Hartford society" (Pawlowski 1973: 27), though their opportunities for education were limited, as was their participation in politics and social life.

One reason they gradually lost this place in society was the influx of white European immigrants. A significant change in the national origin of newcomers began to take place after 1885, as in the rest of the country. The earlier immigrants had come from northern Europe and the British Isles; most of them later came from southern or eastern Europe and French Canada. Thus the relatively homogeneous Connecticut Yankees changed to a much more heterogeneous group. By 1910, almost one in three Hartford residents had been born abroad, coming not primarily from Ireland as in the past, but rather from Germany, Italy, Poland, Spain, and Portugal.

Job competition was keen when the Irish and other groups came in large numbers between 1860 and 1920. The economic position of many Hartford blacks then began to wane, as the ghetto formation in the north section of Hartford grew. By 1900, over 45% of the city's blacks lived in the north end of Hartford. Though it was then still a racially integrated area, "certain streets or residences on these streets were racially segregated. Thus . . . the beginning of the north end ghetto could be seen even before World War I" (Stave 1979: 33).

The first wave of Southern blacks began to move in to Hartford around 1915, after they had been recruited by Hartford labor agents sent by the city's business leaders. Moving to Hartford for "a new life" (Pawlowski 1973), they were very poor, rural people who flocked into the north end, drawn by the black churches located there. "There was also evidence that business interests in Hartford had selected the area of lower North Hartford for southern blacks. The idea was to limit them so that in the small area there would be a high potential for collecting high rents, and low potential for blacks to mix with whites" (Pawlowski 1973: 28).

Hartford city directories between 1915 and 1920 indicated that black business owners and workers lost their jobs at a tremendous rate, being replaced by Irish, Polish, and Jewish immigrants.

After the jobs went the land, the houses, etc. Legal and social pressures were applied to raise taxes and threaten foreclosures. The result was that in Post World War I Hartford it was clearly established that North Hartford was where blacks—all blacks—would live and the south end would be for whites. (Pawlowski 1973: 27)

Of the few blacks still living in south Hartford then, most were in public housing projects, which as late as 1950 had portions set aside as black sections.

Black population jumped from 1.8% to 3% of the city's total by 1920. But the greatest increase in black population in Hartford, as in other Northern cities, was during the years after World War II. Their percentage doubled between 1950 and 1960, from 7.1% to 15.3%, and almost doubled again between 1960 and 1970. By 1970, Hartford's 44,000 blacks made up 28% of Hartford's population.

The city's urban renewal plans and practices also affected population movement within the city. During the 1950s, the city's urban renewal program cleared 190 acres of land immediately adjacent to the downtown area. More than 1,200 households and 750 businesses had to relocate:

The speed and magnitude of these changes had a negative impact on the city's neighborhoods which had whole new populations placed on their doorsteps almost overnight.

By the end of that decade Hartford lost more than 15,000 residents and numerous businesses. . . . The combination of better highway systems, suburban housing opportunities and urban blight resulted in an exodus of moderate and upper income residents and the further concentration of urban poor. (Hartford Planning Department 1983: 3)

Bob Harris, a former state representative, later director of a community development program in a poor black neighborhood, described Hartford's urban renewal program as three waves, starting in 1950. Originally, he said, these three waves came from decisions of the Chamber of Commerce, the former Travelers Insurance and CIGNA Insurance companies, the Hartford National Bank, and other corporate leaders.

They decided they were going to clean up downtown and with the city fathers—the politicians and city council—they created the urban renewal project called Constitution Plaza. They knocked down Front and Market Streets which were black and Italian areas, and through restrictive real estate practices the poor Italians went south and the poor blacks went north. That sent the first wave of blacks out of downtown and up into an area which then was the second phase of urban renewal [now the Hartford Graduate Center]. That wave then meant two other waves . . . then both those waves went as a third wave up into South Arsenal . . . that took from 1950 to about 1963 or 1964 . . . which created this wave of displacement.

He went on to explain how inadequate relocation provisions were for those who were displaced:

There were no displacement regulations then, nothing beneficial at all for poor people. . . . What was going on was further resegregating, double segregating of race and poverty then. . . . Public housing was scattered but segregated—oh, yes, it remains so today . . . so what happened is waves of people where shunted through the north end of Hartford by the real estate industry as it block-busted and rolled things over. . . . And that is basically how the Blue Hills Civic Association got started. . . . They saw it happening right in their neighborhood and decided to do something about it.

During the decade from 1960 to 1970, forty-eight acres of land were cleared by urban renewal, and eighty-two acres by school building programs, resulting in the displacement and relocation of 3,400 households and 900 businesses. Two residential areas were virtually eliminated. One of these, North Meadows, had already lost 775 acres earlier for Constitution Plaza, forcing 2,800 people to other neighborhoods. Thus the city fathers disposed of their land and people, and paved the way for neighborhood change and racial and economic resegregation.

Demographic changes in Hartford between 1960 and 1970 are reviewed in a city publication (Hartford Planning Commission 1978: 3) which notes profound racial change: 25,000 whites left the city and 21,000 nonwhites replaced them during that decade. Of the eighteen neighborhoods in Hartford, seven experienced 83% of this change. Blue Hills, our study neighborhood, was one of the seven, as was the adjacent neighborhood, Upper Albany. Five neighborhoods with sharp increases in minority population also had income declines. Blue Hills and Upper Albany were among these.

The Blue Hills neighborhood had the third largest population change in the city, with 4,800 nonwhites replacing 4,282 whites. Income in Blue Hills during that decade, which had exceeded city, state, and national averages in 1960, failed to sustain that level by 1970. It did exceed the citywide average, however, and its level of owner occupancy remained high, despite the decrease in stability. Thus, though Blue Hills still attracted homeowners in 1970, they were primarily nonwhite and lower in income than their predecessors. The Hartford commission report commented on the effects of Hartford's urban renewal:

What the data do not show is the tragic physical deterioration and loss of neighborhood commercial enterprise, so vital to positive neighborhood organization and identity. The data also fail to show the emotional scars from social unrest which culminated in the civil disturbances of the late 1960s. . . . The whole effect on existing neighborhoods was clearly dramatic, creating rapid changeover in population, fear of economic loss, mistrust and anger. Ultimately this led to the demise of both the neighborhood fabric and program strategies themselves. (Hartford Planning Commission 1978: 7)

Of course, these demographic changes markedly affected the racial composition of the schools, which in turn had a dramatic impact on the neighborhoods. This was especially true in the north end of Hartford, where Blue Hills is situated. When the historic 1954 *Brown v. Topeka* school desegregation case was decided by the Supreme Court, Hartford's public school population was primarily white. The minority proportion in the entire city was only 7.1%. By November 1965, the *Hartford Times* reported a school population of 57.4% white and 48.6% nonwhite.

One scholar has noted that segregation in Hartford

was probably the most severe in Connecticut. According to a study done by the Civil Rights Commission, in 1963 Hartford had fewer blocks with blacks and whites as neighbors than any other city in the state. The great bulk of the Afro-American population took up residence in the north end of the city. The north end is a small area of 120 city blocks walled off for the most part by the railroad tracks, Keney Park, and the City's business area. (Champ 1975: 2)

Here we should add one more boundary of the north end black belt of Hartford— the massive public housing projects that form the western boundary of Blue Hills. At this time, in the early 1960s, the national civil rights movement, including the drive to desegregate schools, affected Hartford and pressured its city officials. White flight had begun, housing and schools were increasingly segregated, central city businesses were declining, and some government and local groups were pressing for compliance with recent court decisions and other equity regulations.

An open enrollment plan was adopted by the Hartford Board of Education in 1963, with little impact on racial and economic imbalance. Next, the board of education commissioned a Harvard University study of the Hartford schools, in response to growing pressures in the community for desegregation. The Hartford Board of Education turned to the Harvard Graduate School of Education for advice on a school building plan that would also address the issue of growing racial isolation. The Harvard Report, published in 1965, recommended the reorganization of the system into seven middle schools with grades five through eight, and the building of two new high schools, all of which would reflect citywide racial distribution (Harvard University 1965). Thus, the Harvard plan offered an interlocked, far-reaching educational program for the city for the next decade.

It was not accepted by the board of education. Instead, the board modified and compromised all of the detailed recommendations and suggestions over the next ten years (Champ 1975), generating three lawsuits. One of their compromise programs was a regional school desegregation program, Project Concern, which began in 1966 as a two-year experimental program financed with federal, state, and local tax dollars, as well as private foundation funds. The initial budget was $90,000. Two hundred sixty-six minority children began participating in the program, which first involved five suburbs surrounding Hartford. The children were randomly selected from eight Hartford elementary schools having 85% or higher minority enrollments. By 1970–71, sixteen communities and a total of 101 public, parochial, and private schools, were educating 1,549 Hartford children, with a 96% voluntary acceptance rate by Hartford parents of the chosen children.

By 1971, the program had been extended to the junior and senior high school level. However, the original Harvard plan called for 6,000 minority students to be bused to suburbs within a fifteen-mile radius by 1974. This never happened. What was done was admirable, but the scale was too modest to seriously affect the Hartford school problem. Though Thomas Pettigrew referred to Project Concern as "the most interesting racially oriented project under Title III" (Hartford Public Schools 1967: 12), another educator lamented: "But the predominantly black schools remained behind as black as before" (Champ 1975: 12). Rather than achieving desegregation of Hartford schools, Project Concern— with its one-way busing—did achieve integration on a small scale in white suburban schools of the Hartford metropolitan region. For those who participated in this, the results were compelling. A twenty-year study tracing the lives of those involved in Project Concern, and comparing their lives with those of the minority children who remained in the black city schools, dramatically indicates the differences (National Institute of Education 1986).

The Quirk Middle School finally opened in September 1972. This was Hartford's largest city school experiment in integration. It was also the most controversial, for it attempted to bring white students into a school located in a nonwhite area. Originally intended as a four-grade school, it actually served just the seventh grade. Originally projected as opening with 35.2% white pupils, 34% black, and 31% Hispanic, it actually opened with 62.5% black, 18.8% Hispanic, and 18.8% white. By 1973, the minority percentage was 73.8%, and in 1980 it was 87.7% black. Another integration attempt that failed.

A third middle school never materialized, and the second one had a minority percentage in 1973 of 97.6, which by 1980 was 99.1% black. The three city high schools showed similar trends over the same seven years, ranging from 26.7% to 62.6% black in one, 71.6% to 85.2% in the second, and 98.7% to 99.7% in the third. This third high school was the one in the Blue Hills neighborhood, newly opened in 1974—but too late for desegregation of the school or the neighborhood.

In March 1970, the Hartford Board of Education adopted a voluntary desegregation plan designed to reduce racial isolation over a three-year period. They continued to modify their system frequently as population shifts were noted. Their voluntary plan involved a middle school program, redistricting of two high schools, and Project Concern within the city schools. In 1976 another reassignment plan was instituted involving five elementary schools, and in 1979 a funding proposal for a city magnet program for two high schools was developed, but remained unfunded. Finally in 1980, the board of education revised its student transfer policy to consider racial balance as a factor before allowing any transfers in the district.

Between 1973 and 1980, enrollment of whites in Hartford public schools declined from 26.9% to 15.8%, the number of Hispanics increased from 23.9% to 37.2%, and that of blacks decreased slightly, from 48.9% to 46.4%. Currently, Hartford serves 24,674 students in twenty-five elementary schools, two middle schools, and three high schools, with a citywide racial composition of 46.4% black, 15.8% white, and 37.2% Hispanic. This composition, however, is not maintained in many of the individual schools, which continue to be predominantly either white or black.

Hartford schools made national news in 1985 when three black parents were charged with felonies for sending their children to suburban schools, using false suburban addresses. One defense lawyer said: "They never intended to steal anything—just get their kids an education." Another defense lawyer said conditions in the Hartford schools—inferior education and drugs—were responsible for the parents' actions (*New York Times*, May 12, 1985).

In an annual summary of its desegregation efforts, the Hartford Board of Education wrote that it was committed to providing equal educational opportunities to the city's students. However, the task was becoming increasingly difficult "as financial support . . . continues to decline." They claimed that their plan would

ensure compliance with the [state] Racial Imbalance Regulations. These regulations, however, do not address the existing demography of urban school districts which now serve a majority of minority students. Because of this phenomenon, the Hartford Public School system is a segregated system which will continue to exist until metropolitan remedies are included in strategies developed by state officials to reduce this isolation. (Hartford Schools 1981)

In 1980, the Hartford Board of Education was notified by the State Board of Education that five of its schools were out of compliance with the state's racial imbalance law. In April 1981, another plan for improving racial balance in Hartford Schools was adopted after "the emotional level of our community approached the boiling point" (Hartford Schools 1981: 24). The Hartford Board of Education at this time also recommended amending the state racial imbalance law, which we now briefly review.

Passed in 1969, the Connecticut racial imbalance law required annual reports of school racial composition from local boards of education. Stipulated as racial imbalance was a range of twenty-five percentage points below or above the proportion of blacks for the whole district. The law mandated a corrective plan from the local board within 120 days after notification by the state board. Technical assistance from the state was offered. Fifteen specific provisions for the plan were outlined, along with approval mechanisms, and monitoring of implementation. The purpose was "to guide and assist local and regional boards of education in developing plans to comply with the legal requirements for eliminating racial imbalance in the public schools" (State of Connecticut 1970: 11).

On October 2, 1984, the Hartford Board of Education submitted two proposals for amendment of the racial imbalance law to the State Board of Education. One proposal would have exempted cities with minority student enrollments greater than 75%, the other called for a regional approach to racial balance wherever it was impossible to achieve racial integration in a school district with too large a minority population. Also at this time, deep concerns were expressed by the Board about federal and state funding cutbacks affecting the Hartford schools. One Hartford educator commented earlier: "It is hard to end any discussion of school desegregation [in Hartford] on a happy note . . . it is impossible to be at all optimistic . . . when it comes to dealing with our most critical domestic dilemma" (Soifer 1975: 21).

This critical dilemma was also seriously affected by the state financing of education. Nationwide, Connecticut ranked fourth from the bottom in the percentage of municipal educational costs paid by the state. Connecticut's school aid program has been called "perhaps the worst in the nation in terms of basic design" (McEachern 1976: 57). A stark picture is given of the inequities in the state education finance system by comparing five of the richest and poorest towns in Connecticut. In 1973, for example, the richest towns were able to spend much more per pupil, with only 23% of the poorest towns' school tax rate. "The problem is that pupil educational outlays are an increasing function not of local tax effort but of the town's local property wealth" (McEachern

1976: 57). The state provides more aid per pupil to the wealthiest districts ($287) than to the poorest districts ($254).

This inequity was the basis of a lawsuit, *Horton v. Meskill*, decided in Hartford County Superior Court in December 1974 and then appealed to the Supreme Court. A 1972 report of the state Tax Reform Commission found that "the public school finance system is inequitable, inherently unequal, may be unconstitutional, and economic segregation is becoming markedly worse" (Brayfield & Brayfield 1975: 26). An earlier task force, formed in 1968 to study regional problems, had suggested that compensatory education was the solution to the problem, and that relief should come from more state funds (Brayfield & Brayfield 1975: 25). The relief did not come.

Such was the background for the formation in Hartford of the Blue Hills Civic Association (BHCA) in 1962, an example of a neighborhood stabilization group that failed. It failed to achieve integration, it failed to stabilize, and it even failed to survive as an organization. Why?

INCEPTION

In 1962, a proposed zoning change led to a group of Blue Hills residents coming together to protest a planned medical building on Blue Hills Avenue. This group presented their views at a City Council hearing, "and as a result the Council voted against the zoning change eight to one. It was then decided to form an association to promote a more positive approach to this area" (Bolduc 1976: 50).

Twelve people went to the first organizational meeting, held on December 11, 1962 in the Blue Hills branch library. They continued to meet there for most of the next sixteen years. Two of the founders commented on their reasons for wanting to form an organization. One said that such a group

should make a stronger and closer knitting of the residents. . . . It should not be a crank organization, but one with a very positive approach with committees going down to City Hall to attend Council rezoning and replanning meetings, and acting as watch dogs as to what would affect this neighborhood. This would be a non-political organization with absolutely no politics involved. (Bolduc 1976: 50)

Another founder said:

The primary purpose would be to keep the members informed as to just what is going on in this area which would affect them. . . . An association would be more effective, and City Hall would be much more apt to listen to such a group. . . . Such an association would lend prestige to the area, and could be instrumental in making the area more attractive. (Bolduc 1976: 50)

Only about four meetings a year took place in the next three years until September, 1965. Much time was spent at these meetings on organizational development and procedures: elections of officers, obtaining new members, establishing the boundaries of concern, and so on. Meetings were usually held in neighborhood homes, with eight to twenty people present.

The major concern of the first three years was zoning issues, which involved some monitoring of the city council. An association newsletter article notes that the reason for forming the BHCA was "undesirable zoning changes" (newsletter, Nov. 1971). The group believed that the neighborhood should remain residential, and it was opposed to any attempts of the business community to develop the area for commercial purposes. In addition, the group held two contests: landscaping in the spring, and holiday decorations at Christmas time.

One analysis of these first few years suggests that the early Blue Hills groups responded to outside pressures on their neighborhood from local businesses or government. However, the infinitely more pressing problem of racial change, at first ignored, gradually worked its way into the center of the neighborhood concerns. "Since the early Civic Association . . . did not address this complex issue . . . other residents felt they could and should" (Bolduc 1976: 51). And they did.

"Since 1962, there have been two Civic Associations, both formed because of racial invasion" (Bolduc 1976: 48). According to this view, the original association existed till 1965 and was less active, more conservative, and either ignored the racial transition or covertly combated it. "In 1965, a decidedly more liberal Association came into being in the midst of an internal conflict, which resulted in a 100% turnover in membership. This newer, highly action-oriented Civic Association was conspicuously the product of the changing character of the neighborhood" (Bolduc 1976: 48).

By 1965, the Blue Hills neighborhood was about 30% black. A new elementary school had just opened on the western boundary of the neighborhood, which led to a shift in school districts. Also, there were a series of racial incidents in the high school on the eastern end of the neighborhood. "These incidents finally forced the CA to face the race issues and the inevitably heated internal conflicts had to be resolved. In . . . a sudden flurry of meetings and activity in the fall of 1965, the CA took on many new active members . . . and for the first time openly mentioned the 'race issue.' " The organization had been and was at that time still all-white. They recognized, however, that "greater Negro participation should be encouraged" (Bolduc 1976: 52).

In the fall of 1965, the organization changed in leaders, membership, and direction. For the first time, the issue of race was openly discussed. In particular, they called attention to the extent of racial change in the neighborhood and the fact that the organization was all-white. This is the only organization studied that did not begin with a goal of integration maintenance. This is also the only organization studied that died. We turn now to an analysis of BHCA's structure during their three phases of organizational development. Phase one we mark from 1962 to 1965, and then with changed goals and leadership from 1965 to

1968. Phase two, with some funding, was from 1969 to 1975. Phase three, the truly final one, was from 1976 to 1980.

STRUCTURE

Committees

The earliest six committees of the BHCA were zoning and neighborhood improvement, housing, education, membership, parks and recreation, and newsletter. In phase two, a senior center committee was formed in 1971 to oversee the newly funded Senior Center. A youth services committee was formed in 1974, and continued throughout the remainder of the organization's existence. All of these were developed and maintained during the first two phases of BHCA's development, except for the housing committee, which went through a double spin-off process in phase two.

In the summer of 1969, early in phase two, the housing committee formed a separate Housing Services Corporation with its own legal identity. This was primarily a housing rehabilitation sales program, formed to relieve the housing committee of its growing work load. It grew out of the original real estate listing service of the housing committee, announced in the first issue of the BHCA News, in May 1968. Staffed by volunteers who were active BHCA members, the corporation dissolved in 1972 after much conflict (see Program below). A new separate corporation was formed called Urban Edge, which was a real estate nonprofit fair housing program, again created and staffed by a few BHCA active members. Urban Edge continued throughout phases two and three of the BHCA, and even outlived it. By 1984, however, it too had stopped functioning.

Newsletter

Since 1968, the newsletter was the major vehicle of communication between BHCA and the neighborhood of 3,000 plus households. A simple mimeographed two-page newsletter was the format during 1968, which was the first year of distribution. Five thousand three hundred copies of the newsletter were printed and distributed to all households and businesses and library branches in the Blue Hills neighborhood. Even this simple newsletter soon came to be too much for volunteers to handle, as early minutes indicate: "it is necessary to explore other methods of printing the newspaper because it is too much for one volunteer to do" (minutes, Oct. 15, 1969).

In 1969, early in phase two, a grant of $7,990 from the Hartford Foundation of Public Giving enabled BHCA to develop a professionally printed newspaper, which was delivered free to all households in the Blue Hills neighborhood. Two years later an additional $1,000 grant from a Hartford bank further strengthened the printing and distribution of the paper. By December 1969, the news ads were bringing in seventy dollars and the paper was beginning to become self-supporting. The January 1970 issue had eighty dollars in ads, "but it was suggested that too much stress not be placed on advertising" (minutes, Jan. 19, 1970). The ads ranged from two to nine during 1970 to 1974, and increased to a peak of eighteen in 1974. In 1972, the paper expanded to eight pages, and eventually became completely supported by local advertising.

The newsletter was published six to ten times a year (not in the summer) during the BHCA's first two phases of development, and more and more irregularly during the third phase. The continuous preparation and distribution of the newsletter took an enormous amount of time, and was handled entirely by volunteers. Some articles were signed by individual BHCA members, others were not. Photographs were in almost all issues, showing people at various community events, or places referred to in the articles. The news format generally included items related to functioning committees, most notably recreation, schools, housing, and neighborhood improvement (which sponsored a "house of the month" photo). News of library, church, and other community events, as well as organization meetings and occasional public issues, were also presented. The organization was most visible through its newspaper, and when the organization stopped functioning, the thing most missed about it was the newspaper.

Membership

The membership committee was formed in 1965 to conduct annual membership drives. Before then, dues had been five dollars. When the leadership and ideology changed in 1965, dues were reduced to one dollar in an attempt to increase members. The membership drives were organized through street and area coordinators, and sometimes touched off block parties on several streets. The neighborhood was divided into seven districts, with one captain for each, and up to twenty block and street coordinators. Each volunteer called at the preassigned homes, introduced her/himself as a neighbor, and handed out information packets on the association and neighborhood. Each district held a "meet your neighbor" social hour during the year, which was the culmination of the drive. One board member in 1969 gave out 250 flyers to the people in his district, inviting everyone to meet over coffee and doughnuts at his home on a Saturday morning. Such zeal did not recur often in the following years.

At the beginning of phase two, in 1969, a change in the bylaws expanded membership to institutions: They could become nonvoting members with an annual payment of ten dollars. It was further decided to try to include the two surrounding massive public housing projects as members. A decision was also made to retain as members those who had not renewed their memberships. In 1971 dues were dropped completely, and every resident of Blue Hills was automatically considered a member of the association. The highest number of dues-paying members was reached in 1970, with 900 households listed. Though financial drives continued even after the 1971 change in membership status, they never again reached that number of financial supporters. By 1974, the number of families who contributed financially to BHCA was down to 180.

The tasks of the street and area coordinators were not limited to membership drives, however. One agenda for a 1969 membership meeting listed the responsibilities of street coordinators as: (1) sending a welcoming letter to new residents; (2) serving as liaison between residents and board; (3) encouraging and arranging block meetings or parties; and (4) soliciting members according to prescribed procedure. This procedure included cards, decals, comment forms, and committee forms to be presented to residents with an invitation to join. Invariably, each year there were streets with no coordinators. The minutes of November 18, 1970, for example, show twenty-two streets with no coordinators. And invariably the task of covering these streets fell to board members, already overworked and overinvolved in other board and committee business.

One complaint that surfaced early in phase two at a street coordinators' meeting was to recur throughout the second and third phases. That complaint was about the connection between BHCA and politics: "Board members engaging in contacts for political reasons should not mix in BHCA activities at the same time" (minutes, Oct. 8, 1969). The board then decided that ads from political candidates would not be accepted in the BHCA *News*, even though they recognized that it was through the political process that decisions were made that affected the neighborhood.

Office

The BHCA office opened on September 7, 1969; a grand opening celebration and a news article in the *Hartford Courant* publicized the event. The foundation grant that enabled the newspaper to be professionally printed and mass-distributed also funded the office. Staffing for the office, however, was unfunded, and thus only possible through volunteers. This was immediately a problem, and eventually led to the turnover of the office to the two offshoots of the housing committee, the Housing Service Corporation and Urban Edge. The first stationery with the BHCA logo appeared in December 1969, with an attractive house in a circle centered next to the name of the organization.

The problem of staffing the office arose as soon as the office was obtained: "BR will ask PR if she will set up a volunteer staff for the office during the week beginning September 7. RS moved that the office be open six hours every Saturday and every Sunday, with Board members taking three-hour shifts on a rotating basis" (minutes, July 23, 1969). By December, only three months after the grand opening, one board member "questioned the necessity of an office when it is vacant so much of the time" (minutes, Dec. 17, 1969). Occasionally, school art exhibits were displayed in the office, but board members had to be there to open and close the doors for parents and visitors who came to see the art exhibit.

Early in 1970, the board discussed the possibility of hiring a part-time secretary to staff the office and help with committee work. The money would have come from excess funds accumulated from advertisers who bought space in the BH *News*. However, there was not enough support from the board for using that money for part-time staffing, even though they had drafted a funding proposal that included the need for full-time staffing.

One month later the board again faced the issue of the office when a board member "questioned the use of the BHCA office, especially since the grant will end next year and the rental of the office will then cost $2,000 a year" (minutes, March 1970). A three-person committee was formed by the board to study long-range plans for the office. One board member "questioned if the Foundation would allow the Association to use the money for a purpose other than the office" (minutes, March 1970). So they were uncertain about how their funding source would perceive their underuse of the office, and worried that this might curtail the funding.

Early Fatigue

Had they realized how helpful part-time staff could have been, and had they made a commitment to securing such staff, they might have avoided or at least delayed the fatigue and burnout that eventually overcame them. In February 1970, three committee chairs resigned simultaneously from three critical committees: education, membership, and neighborhood improvement. Two months later, the president announced his resignation. Meeting minutes report his saying that being president required

a great deal of time and effort—much more than he can give. He felt that the neighborhood was going through an extremely critical time and that it required a President who could devote much more time. Board members discussed what could be done to help relieve the President's many chores, but as it was late (11 P.M.) the Board decided to call a special meeting... to discuss any changes in organization and structure. (minutes, April 15, 1970)

At the special meeting, held two weeks later, the president reported on the vast number of meetings he had attended as president, and called for a rearrangement of committees and officer responsibilities. He complained that the vice-presidents were so busy with other duties that they were unable to relieve the president. One board member, whose earlier proposal for reorganization had been resisted, questioned the necessity of BHCA to the area. The board reacted defensively to this: "Most felt a definite loss would be experienced in the whole community, since the Association has so many things to its credit. . . . Most of all, the Association has been a catalyst in the neighborhood and in the city. The Board agreed it is as representative as it can be and has become a mini city hall" (minutes, April 27, 1970).

Some board members acknowledged that some structural problems existed.

Communications between board members and the president were seen as inadequate, the duties of vice-presidents were unclear, and the "pooling of talent and time was essential" but hadn't been achieved well enough. A number of suggestions were made for improving the situation, including greater involvement of the membership, less committee involvement of vice-presidents so they could better assist the president, less board involvement in committee operations, and more announcements of open committee meetings in the *News*. But the only suggestion that was immediately implemented was the one about announcing open committee meetings. Other structural changes occurred slowly or not at all. A comparison of the first bylaws with 1976 revised ones indicates no substantive structural changes.

Proposal

An important item appeared in the minutes of December 16, 1970, though at the time no one may have recognized its significance. The BHCA board was presented with a written proposal from the city social service department and the Commission on Aging to establish a Northwest Senior Center. This center would be under the supervision of BHCA. The board appointed an ad hoc committee to study the proposal. The committee included elderly from the adjacent public housing project, Bowles Park.

The following month, the committee recommended that BHCA accept the responsibility for the center, the fourth in the city, and set up a five-member advisory committee to hire a program director and supervise the center's operation. The center could become an all-purpose one in the Blue Hills area, it would provide a needed valuable service one year at a time, and it would honor neighborhood control. The question then raised was: could five people be found to serve? (minutes, Jan. 13, 1971). The question now is: how could anyone possibly have known that this senior center would ultimately be the only remnant left of the once-vital BHCA? We turn now to a brief review of the finances, the leadership, and the bylaws revisions of BHCA, which may help us begin to understand what happened.

Finances

The earliest budget proposed by BHCA's board was for October 1, 1968 through September 30, 1969. This budget projected a need for $550 to cover postage, office supplies, space rental for meetings, printing, and miscellaneous. Income projected was $400, with a deficit of $150 (minutes, Jan. 15, 1969). At the end of phase one, the treasurer's report noted thirty-one dollars left in the treasury following a $400 payment for 3,700 brochures. They were doing better than they had expected.

At this time, funding proposals were being prepared for grant requests from foundations. Three items were suggested for the grants: the newspaper; the office, including supplies, equipment, and staff; and educational programs for the schools. The board divided the proposal projects into these three areas of concern, and assigned a different board member to prepare each. In addition, they assigned a committee of four to oversee all the proposals. At this time, the first suggestion was made for the use of an office for a real estate listing service (minutes, Dec. 9, 1968).

In July 1969, the treasury contained $1,139, including $500 for an elementary school summer reading program conducted by the BHCA, the Early Childhood Learning Center. At this time the board decided to keep grant money for specific purposes separate from the organization's general account (minutes, July 23, 1969). The first sizable grant came in 1969 from the Hartford Foundation, which gave $7,990 for the BHCA's newspaper and the office. The newspaper grant was a continuing one.

In November 1969, after careful preparation and much revision, BHCA applied for a three-year grant of $161,600 for a nursery school, community center, executive director, and secretary. This proposal was submitted to three foundations: Ford, Sears-Roebuck, and New World. When all three rejected the proposal that same month, the board immediately sent the proposal to three additional foundations. All rejected it. By January 1970 the Board decided to reexamine the proposal to consider some changes. At that time, the treasury showed $633.30 in expenses, $52 income, and a balance of $47.

In January 1970, the board discussed the advisability of raising membership dues to two dollars annually. This was to be one of the bylaw changes. At this time BHCA had 801 members. Nine months later, BHCA's savings account had $3,768.73, their checking account had $140.52, and all bills were paid (minutes, Oct. 1970).

A second sizable grant—$15,500—came to BHCA in February 1971, for the operation of the senior citizens center. This, too, was an ongoing, renewable grant. At this time, also, Hartford business leaders gave a $1,000 grant to BHCA's housing corporation for promotional ads. Two years later, two additional grants were given to BHCA for newsletter addressing equipment. Two months after these were received, BHCA also got a $12,500 one-year federal grant from LEAA for a youth worker. In addition, they raised $6,000 for their summer reading improvement program. These contributions came from four insurance companies, one foundation, two banks, one corporation, several PTAs, families, and the BHCA treasury.

In January 1974, BHCA faced several disasters. Their youth coordinator quit, they needed a recreation worker for their preschool program, and most significantly, Urban Edge—the spin-off from the housing corporation—took over the BHCA office and the grant for the promotional ads. In the spring and summer of that year, BHCA received $100 from a foundation for a landscaping project, and two anonymous gifts of $275. But their big grant of $14,887 came for their summer reading improvement project. Everything they were doing, however, was done by volunteers. In December 1974, they wrote another proposal for a

$35,000 grant to pay for an executive director, a secretary, and an office. This proposal was sent to fifteen foundations in the area; all rejected it.

Meanwhile, the funded senior citizen center continued, though its directors began to show much turnover. In the spring of 1975, BHCA requested $19,228 for their summer reading program, which served 150 children. They also requested and received contributions for a community garden that they sponsored. After this date, only the senior center continued to submit funding renewal proposals. No other records exist of BHCA trying to secure additional funds. By 1980, they were defunct. Was there something in their governance that led to the death of this organization?

Leadership

Five out of ten chapters of a 1976 doctoral dissertation on the BHCA are devoted to an analysis of the oligarchic nature of the organization: "The BHCA is oligarchical in nature simply because it is a formally organized association, and all such associations, Michels asserts, eventually become oligarchical" (Bolduc 1976: 66). Though the dissertation author obviously accepted European sociologist Robert Michels' "Iron Law of Oligarchy," I found BHCA no more oligarchic in nature than any of the other neighborhood organizations studied in this or other research.

The dissertation explores the extent of minority control of the organization, noting the minimal participation of residents at monthly and annual meetings. Dues-paying members ranged from 100 to 400 persons, with a high point in 1970 of 900 families, as we noted above. "In all their programs, only a small fraction of the target population was actually reached, and involvement varied greatly" (Bolduc 1976: 71). About 3% of the residents were involved with the organization, ranging from active participants to marginal ones. Yet this extent of involvement is typical for civic associations, according to established research on voluntary associations. And it is certainly typical for movement organizations in the social movement literature.[1]

A content analysis of twenty issues of the BHCA newspaper from 1972 to 1974, or 72% of all published issues, showed thirty separate articles publicizing membership drives and encouraging participation from nonactive residents. "Thus to the extent that the Association is oligarchical, it is not so by either the design or wishes of the current leaders" (Bolduc 1976: 73).

One of the reasons offered by Michels for the organizational phenomenon of oligarchy was the accumulation of expertise by persons doing various specific tasks. This is suggested in the dissertation as one of the reasons for the oligarchic nature of the BHCA. Certainly the newspaper editing and ad procurement, the summer reading program, and the preschool program—all took special skills that were not easy to acquire, and were difficult to find in many other persons even if they might have been willing to assume such tasks.

The Bolduc dissertation summarizes its findings with the statement that

BHCA, like most formal organizations, was dominated by a handful of individuals who represented a very small proportion of the neighborhood. They were well-known to each other, and to peripheral members, they worked up to forty hours a month on association business, and often attended two or more meetings a week relating to association matters. Their names appeared continually in the BHCA newspaper and at gatherings. They had higher incomes and education than most people in the neighborhood (Bolduc 1986: 81).

Those in leadership roles were difficult to replace because of their accumulated skills and knowledge. Though the association consistently encouraged and sought broad-based participation in its affairs, it rarely got more than 4% of the residents to participate. Other scholars have shown that racially integrated neighborhoods have lower rates of participation in neighborhood organizations than racially homogeneous ones.[2] By 1974—the end of phase two—Blue Hills was 73% black, and had a higher proportion of two-wage-earner households than majority populated areas. This, too, reduced the numbers of willing participants in the neighborhood organization.

An analysis of bylaws revisions over the years shows a persistent grappling with these issues and problems, and an earnest attempt to broaden the base of involvement in the organization. As early as November 1969, one revision permitted nonvoting institutional members, and called for the expansion of the board from fifteen to eighteen members. In October 1970, the service of board members was limited to three successive terms. And by May 1972, a revision called for at least six elected board members who had not served in the previous year. These were clear efforts to encourage new participants. As in the other neighborhood groups studied, these efforts did not often succeed.

Bylaws Revisions

Bylaws revision generally signals some dissatisfaction with the functioning of an organization. They indicate that someone has questioned the existent structure or operation of a group, and believes it could be improved. Extensive revisions of BHCA's bylaws occurred in January 1976. They did not result in any major structural organizational changes but they did indicate internal distress.

The revisions defined further the expanded geographical boundaries of the Blue Hills area, clarified the organization's relationship with other associations, clarified the definition and role of voting members and their dues, and changed the time of the annual meeting. They added one officer and clarified the election procedure of officers, changed the length of term of the board of directors, added a provision for removal of board members with three consecutive absences, allowed for proxy votes of directors (signs of waning attendance), eliminated ex officio committee members, eliminated the need for cochairmen for each committee (it was hard enough to get one), and they clarified constitutional amendment procedures. By then, the organization was dying.

Waning

In the spring of 1976, obvious signs of fatigue and burnout were affecting even the BHCA summer reading program. A front-page article describing the March 1976 public meeting said that an ad hoc committee working on the reading program "felt they have too few individuals and too little time before this summer to obtain funding and get a program operational" (BHCA *News*, April 1976). Therefore, the usual source of funding for this program, the Hartford Foundation, had not even been approached. The article began with the observation that attendance at the March meeting was less than usual, "though the issues were important, exciting, and as usual—exhausting." That issue of the *News* also contained a letter from a distressed BHCA president, written in response to a negative article about Blue Hills that had appeared in a local weekly publication.

Two months later, another front-page article was headed "BHCA Meetings Indicate Lack of Needed Help" (*News*, June 1976). Ironically, the lead article on the front page of that issue was headed "City Housing Values Up 23%," and the third remaining front-page article was "Target Site Named for NHS Program." This referred to a Blue Hills area selected for housing rehabilitation in a new neighborhood housing services program. So, even while positive events were occurring for the neighborhood, the organization was in deep trouble.

The article about BHCA revealed a lack of interest and participation in the monthly meetings. An April meeting was described as "brief, poorly attended," with a featured rat control "program which never happened. The meeting started with three board members present, two or three others later to appear. Only one or two nonboard persons attended. The most significant issue was the questioning of the continued existence and value of the BHCA itself, its relationship and relevance to the BH community" (*News*, June 1975).

Also in that June issue, several other news items indicated serious organizational and neighborhood problems occurring simultaneously with positive programs and events. An editorial, "BHCA Needs Help!" referred to vacancies on the board, and limited or no membership on committees. It called for the "time, energy, and commitment" of residents to fill these. The editorial page also noted the resignation of the previous editor "because of a lack of time."

An angry letter to the editor again berated the recent article in the *Advocate*, a weekly newspaper which gave a negative, "scabrous portrayal of Blue Hills." The writer was offended by a photo of a boarded-up foreclosed house that accompanied the article, by publicity about "the peccadillos of 'youthful apartment dwellers' and 'teachers at Weaver High School,' " and by promotion of "unrest" and "distorted images" of the Blue Hills neighborhood. Anxieties about rising crime in the neighborhood were responsible for another article on community security, outlining procedures for increasing safety through block organization.

Balancing these three unhappy, anxious news items were three positive ones.

Headed "BH Pre-School Called Best in City," one article described and praised the children's program developed by BHCA. Another one was a large ad calling for a staff of three to head the new housing services program, which was to benefit a portion of the Blue Hills neighborhood. A third new item referred to a new women writers' collective formed in Blue Hills by a resident-librarian who was active in the BHCA, and whose husband had been an early president. A double page of the women's poetry made up the inner section of the June 1976 BHCA News.

Final Struggles

During the third phase of BHCA's existence (1976–80), only twelve issues of the News appeared in those four years, with different editors each year. After 1977, the monthly meetings were no longer held in the branch library but were held in the Mt. Sinai Hospital, and occasionally in the senior center.

An important structural change occurred in 1978: The BHCA executive committee decided to serve as the board of directors for the senior center. Written reports from the center staff would be submitted to the board. The minutes of February 2, 1978 indicate that by then the senior center was the only active year-round program of the organization. The only other program was the summer youth jobs program. Many board members were involved in other spin-off projects that were no longer run by BHCA. The president asked that board members involved in such projects prepare a list of all affiliated projects for the next board meeting. But the March minutes show nothing of this. The decision to have the BHCA executive committee serve as the board for the senior center was the death rattle of the organization. But they could not have known this.

During this third phase of BHCA's existence, there is continual evidence of difficulty in finding people to serve on committees. This is not surprising, since fatigue and burnout by this time would be inevitable for the old-timers—that is, those who hadn't moved away. For the newer board members, growing involvement in coalition efforts with other groups took more and more time and energy, and seriously depleted their remaining efforts for BHCA. Records of one board meeting in 1978 indicate coalitions had been formed or were in process for the following: a crime prevention committee with an adjacent neighborhood organization; a housing assistance fund; a housing advisory task force; a community center; the newspaper; property taxes; and neighborhood development. In addition to these, the sixteen board members were responsible for representation on the neighborhood housing services advisory group, the ongoing senior center, the summer jobs program, and the monthly newspaper. As if these were not enough, the board was also arranging a spring dance. Ironically, the theme of the dance was "Too Much Too Soon." At least the first half of that theme was appropriate for BHCA at that time.

The minutes of the next board meeting confirm this. Only nine attended.

At this board meeting, the president reported that the community center committee did not meet, the neighborhood improvement committee would need a new chair since the old one resigned "due to the demands of law school," the tax reassessment meeting was rescheduled, and five other committees had not met. The minutes of that meeting were taken by an acting secretary because of the absence of the regular one. On the president's handwritten agenda for the following board meeting was a list of seven potential new board members to fill vacancies on the board (minutes, March 2, 1978).

An April 1978 letter from the president to all residents of Blue Hills indicates a weary organization trying almost desperately to regain strength. The letter is a personal appeal for participation in the organization:

Many of you know . . . the strong tradition associated with the BHCA. I firmly believe that with your participation we can restore this tradition and make the Civic Association once again a strong community force. One cannot continue to sit back and ask, "Well, what are THEY doing?" The THEY is speedily dwindling, and in the final analysis must become you. . . . I make a special appeal to those of you who are elected Board members to attend the meeting (May 4, '78) and renew your commitments to the Civic Association.

Also in that April 1978 letter from the president was the opinion that BHCA should have just a few essential standing committees: education, political issues, community improvement, and housing. Yet, instead of cutting down the number of committees, a few months later the organization became part of another coalition group—a Keney Park Task Force to improve the neighborhood park in safety and maintenance.

The BHCA had two crises during the summer of 1978. One was the city's cut in funding for the summer youth jobs program, as noted in a letter of complaint from the BHCA president to city officials (est. July 1978). The other crisis was that they had to move their senior center. They were notified in August 1978 that they had to vacate the church-owned building the center was in; they had six weeks to find another facility. Their treasurer's report at that time showed $1,222.71 in the BHCA account, plus $450.34 for the newsletter, and $88 for the senior center.

The two-page, senior-center committee report of September 7, 1978 began: "During the pass [sic] three months, we . . . have been working . . . on resolving the pressing problem of maintaining the Center and develop [sic] a positive attitude with its members." The rest of the report was divided into two parts: Accomplishments and Problems. The accomplishments included the announcement that one member of the committee had "assumed the role of acting director in the absence of the director." The other four items listed referred to summer program activities and bookkeeping matters relating to the center. The problems were these three: the need to find a new place, the need to plan the fall program, and the need to fire the absent director and find a new one or an interim one.

Despite the waning interest and participation of members and residents, and their own board and committees, the organization struggled until December 1980 to maintain a semblance of structure, program, and open meetings. A list of standing committees in October 1978 showed nineteen board members assigned to five committees: neighborhood improvement, education, newspaper, recreation, and senior center. The senior center moved temporarily into a northwest boys club facility for four months, after which it moved in June 1979 into a small old frame house donated by Mt. Sinai Hospital. It still exists there.

The neighborhood improvement committee functioned as a part of the Neighborhood Housing Service program until it ended in July 1980. The minutes of one meeting show only one of the BHCA committee members present, with four others representing other groups and the NHS (minutes, March 15, 1979). A complaint letter dated May 9, 1979 to a neighborhood hardware store that had trucks and supplies cluttering the street is the last evidence of that committee's actions.

A letter from the president to board members about a meeting scheduled for May 3, 1979 reminded them that the bylaws allowed board removal for three or more unexcused absences. "If you are interested in continuing your *active* service on the Board . . . please attend" (emphasis in original). Another letter from the president in May 1979 requested assistance in grant-writing from a private regional planning group.

The only other evidence of any substantive BHCA activity from June 1979 to September 1979 is correspondence and documents relating to the renewal of funding ($24,890) for the senior center and the summer youth jobs program. The address on the correspondence was the president's home. The board's racial composition at that time was three white and nineteen black, reflecting the neighborhood's racial proportions. One final treasurer's report for June 1979 showed $1,101.65 in the bank at the end of that month, with June expenses of $400 for two delegates to attend the National Neighbors annual conference in Colorado, and $342 for the spring dance. Income was $520 from the dance.

An article in the *Hartford Inquirer*, a black press newspaper, announced the 1979 annual meeting of BHCA to be held September 6, 1979. The meeting was to include a dedication of their new office space in their newly acquired senior center home. Also on the agenda were election of board and officers, and bylaws changes. Readers were invited to submit their names for service on the board. The proposed bylaw changes were revealing. What they indicated was a recognition of the decline of the organization and a last attempt to pull it together.

Four changes were proposed, relating to boundaries of the Blue Hills area, voting of members at meetings, month of annual meeting, and duties of officers and standing committees. The newspaper article included several revealing comments relevant to each of the changes. The boundary change was to extend the southern boundary to a major street "but excluding the residents of that street who have, in fact, become a part of the UACO neighborhood" (*Inquirer*, Aug.

15, 1979). This referred to a thriving, heavily funded adjacent neighborhood group, Upper Albany Community Organization, which occasionally conducted some joint activities with BHCA. Some of the Blue Hills residents had come to identify more with the UACO group than with the BHCA.

Another proposed change dealt with members' voting at monthly board meetings—allowing every paid member to vote, whether or not they were board members. The article noted: "The change is consistent with the present situation whereby non-board members are the most regular attendees, and therefore, have, in fact, been the voice of the neighborhood." Here was public acknowledgment of the fact that the BHCA board was not functioning, and was not perceived as representative of the residents.

Finally, in referring to the proposed change defining duties of officers and committees, the article added, "including re-establishment of the Blue Hills *News.*" This was, again, public recognition of the malfunctioning of the organization. The last paragraph of the article was a last plea from the BHCA president: "Residents of Blue Hills, your involvement is essential. While issues . . . may not have yet reached the point criticality [sic], we need not—must not—wait for disaster before the decision is made to plan for, and participate in, our community life."

The meeting was held, and the bylaws were changed. But nothing happened to change the organization from being a weak remnant of the former thriving group. Of the four named standing committees, only the senior center committee functioned, and today the center is all that is left of the former BHCA.

The Last Two Newsletters

One final note on the newspaper completes our analysis of BHCA's structure. After November 1978, no more regular issues of the BHCA *News* appeared. One more issue in June 1980 and a final one in December 1980 were published as part of the Hartford Neighborhood News Network. The June 1980 issue's front-page article was headed, "We're Back!" It went on to say:

After a break of about a year and a half, the BH *News* resumes. . . . It is ironic that the Blue Hills community seems to have lapsed into silence at precisely the point when it has emerged as one of the most politically significant communities in the city of Hartford. Hopefully, the re-emergence of the *News* will serve as a catalyst for a reawakened concern for the issues affecting the neighborhood residents.

We know this did not happen.

This June issue contained several other significant articles. One other front-page article was headed "NHS Phases Out of Blue Hills," and a front-page photo showed the business strip of Blue Hills with completed, long-awaited improvements. The narrative under the photo said, "Some problems persist, though. Vacant rental space still exists, parking and traffic congestion are still a problem, and there have been complaints about drinking and loitering on the strip." The lead article of the issue was headed "National Neighbors Convene in Hartford," and BHCA was listed as one of the local sponsors, along with two other neighborhood organizations and a neighboring town (Bloomfield).

But the inside of the four page paper had a notable and prophetic article about BHCA, headed "BHCA Stands at the Crossroads." The new BHCA president was quoted: "There is an urgent need for people to volunteer to work through the BHCA. We also need more participation by current Board members. Out of 15, only 5 are presently actively involved in the Civic Association. Attendance at BHCA meetings has sharply declined in recent years, and this makes it very difficult for the organization to function."

The president pointed to two BHCA achievements over the past year: passage of a city tax differential bill, and efforts of Save Our Students—a group formed to upgrade the quality of the public schools. In fact, neither of these was a BHCA achievement. Both of these were large coalition efforts that took BHCA participants away from their own group into much broader based ones. The article ended with the statement that BHCA planned to continue to meet monthly throughout the summer.

But when fewer and fewer people came to the meetings, the president stopped having them. The organization functioned in name only, in order to receive the city funding for the senior center and summer youth job program. All other activity stopped.

Two other news items were of special interest in the June 1980 issue. In addition to the "home of the month" photo, there was an "eyesore of the month" photo. This was of a vacant house due to be renovated soon with financing for a new owner from the NHS and the Connecticut Housing Investment Fund. With the phasing out of NHS, however, other "eyesores of the month" might not be so fortunate in the future. An editorial also questioned the withdrawal of NHS and the implications for the Blue Hills neighborhood. One small additional item in this newsletter was "Blue Hills Community Garden Ready Soon"; this referred to the garden plots obtained years earlier by BHCA for Blue Hills residents. This was yet another small surviving element of its former energy.

The final issue of the Blue Hills News contained a notice of a BHCA monthly meeting scheduled for January 8, 1981 in the neighborhood hospital. The only other organizational news was a long article on senior center news. The front page was devoted to safety in the neighborhood, with the lead article about crime in the Blue Hills area and how residents could organize block watches to deal with this. Listed in the article were the names of twenty-five Blue Hills families whose homes or property had been burglarized in the past eighteen months: "crime here continues to climb" (News, Dec. 1980). Hardly positive public relations!

At the top of the paper: "Season's Greetings from the Blue Hills Staff." The only known staff at that time was the one at the senior center. No other news or newspaper has come from BHCA since then. We turn now to a review of BHCA's goals and program for more clues about the reasons for their death.

GOALS

The BHCA's application for incorporation contained the first formal statement of the goals of the new organization. These are repeated in the 1965 bylaws under purpose:

The objectives of the organization are, by collective action, to preserve and promote the welfare and best interests of the Blue Hills Avenue area of the City of Hartford; to educate the public as to both the assets and needs of the Blue Hills Avenue area; and to act as a responsible and representative civic organization to present the viewpoints and represent the interests of residents of the Blue Hills Avenue area before governmental officials and bodies.

Though no area boundaries are mentioned in the first bylaws, minutes of early meetings show them to be almost the same as the ones included in later revised bylaws: "From Westbourne Parkway, north to the Bloomfield line, west to Granby St., and east to Keney Park" (bylaws, 1976). The only change in the revised bylaws was the west boundary extended to "the west branch of the Park River." The later bylaws continued the same stated goals as in the first ones.

We noted above the change in the fall of 1965 in organizational membership, leaders, and direction. The new leaders and members brought a new ideological position and fervor to the association. "This resulted in a radical shift in both the problems that the Association would address and the actions they would pursue" (Bolduc 1976: 53). For the first time the issue of race was openly discussed—in particular, the extent of racial change in the neighborhood and the fact that the organization was all-white. The organization extended their areas of concern with this motion: "It was moved and seconded that the Association change its position from acting solely in zoning matters relating to the area and become more actively involved in any problem associated with the BH area" (Bolduc 1976: 53). School busing was then discussed and another motion was passed to establish study groups "with Negro parents" to study de facto segregation in the Hartford schools.

Deep internal conflict arose over the issue of race. Some of the early founders were opposed to the inclusion of blacks in the organization, if not the neighborhood. The new changed focus of racial inclusion on all levels was resented and resisted. So even though the stated goals were still the same—"to preserve and promote the welfare and best interests of Blue Hills"—the operating goals became very different.

A widely publicized letter sent by the next BHCA president to the Hartford Board of Education supported busing for racial integration and relief of overcrowding. The letter stated: "We have discovered that racially mixed schools and neighborhoods provide a very sound environment for educating our children in the values of a free and democratic society." A newspaper article quoted the letter further: "[The president] . . . noted the BH area has undergone a planned economic and racial integration among its residents recently, which demonstrates that this section of the city can remain a stable and attractive area where citizens of different background can live and work together for the common good and the future of our children" (*Hartford Courant*, Sept. 1, 1966). This statement was the first public one in which BHCA's ideology was similar to that of other groups in this movement.

When the first issue of the Blue Hills *News* appeared (two stapled pages, mimeographed on both sides), the beliefs of the leaders were clearly and openly stated. Again, these were consistent with those of other neighborhood stabilization groups. In describing their establishment of a new real estate listing service, the lead article stated that they believed their area had to serve as an example of one that was

determined to fight to remain integrated. Stabilization has become a key. Our motives must be clear. We are not stating that we cannot become more integrated. However, the Blue Hills area has moved well beyond what might, a few years ago, have been considered the "Tipping Point." Without tipping. With augmented programs to increase our own neighborliness and understanding, we believe ours can remain a stabilized, integrated neighborhood. However, we cannot, nor can the City, assume that there is not a tipping point for this area" (*News*, May 1968)

Thus the goal of stable integration maintenance was publicly stated in 1968. The BHCA's specific objectives were listed under a statement of purpose, also in the first issue of the newspaper. Included among these were the elimination of overcrowded classrooms, upholding and improving educational standards, enforcing building codes, opposing detrimental zoning changes, preventing commercial extension, improving the "avenues of communication," and opening housing opportunities in other city neighborhoods. Also: "The Association is on record as opposed to the establishment of a Mason-Dixon Line in Hartford."

From the order of citation, we can guess that the overriding concern at that time was the quality of the schools. The second major concern was zoning and code enforcement to maintain a quality residential neighborhood. A third concern for the improvement of interpersonal relations within the neighborhood was less emphatic than the final concern for equal housing opportunity throughout the city.

In 1969, BHCA's goal was perceived somewhat differently in a newspaper article announcing a foundation grant to the organization. The article referred to BHCA as a "volunteer neighborhood improvement agency" and noted that it was established "when panic selling of housing threatened sections of the Blue Hills area. The Association took steps at that time to promote an integrated neighborhood" (*Courant*, April 30, 1969).

By October 1969, early in phase two, questions arose within the board of directors as to the housing politics of the organization. Preparation of suggested policies was delegated to the housing committee chair, who brought them to the board for review the following month. The board, after lengthy discussion, tabled any decision till the following month. At the December meeting, members struggled with the issues of "integration and what is it, what is a balanced neighborhood, and whether housing concerns the people of the area" (minutes, Oct. 13, November 17, December 17, 1969).

The board was unable to resolve these issues and did not adopt a housing policy at that meeting. Though the minutes of December 17 noted that "the matter will be further discussed at the next meeting," the board did not discuss it at the next meeting and no housing policy was established for the organization. A few years later, the issue was raised again, and the board was then virtually ripped apart by the conflict over how to maintain integration. The chair of the housing committee suggested reorganization and long-range planning for the group in December 1969, but the board resisted that as well: "Discussion pointed out that the BHCA is a people's organization and the important thing was to initiate action rather than deciding organizational concepts" (minutes, Dec. 17, 1969). The president recommended "holding off further action on the proposal until the board members studied and digested it." But the records do not show that they ever discussed this again. If they had, their eventual burnout might have been avoided.

The reorganization memo to the board began with: "We are all aware of the rapid changes that have taken place in our neighborhood. These changes have been reflected in the Community Association (CA) and its Board. But I submit to you that the pace of changes has been so fast that we have not had an opportunity to examine our objectives and goals as an Association, and how we as a Board can best attain these goals" (memo, Dec. 1969). The three page mimeographed statement continued with a detailed plan for increasing the efficiency of the organization and its committees, for setting priorities and defining the long- and short-term goals and objectives, and for periodically reviewing past and future achievements and plans. The board was unable to deal with this.

Four months later, when the president announced his resignation because of lack of time and others' lack of time, the subject of reorganization, leadership, and goals came up again. Once more, the board was unable to deal with this: "Some stated that the problem of leadership depends largely on the President, but that specific problems existed, such as communications between Board members and the Presidents. . . . It was agreed that the duties of the Vice-Presidents were unclear. . . . The question of *set goals* arose, but most members felt this could not and should not be done. Anything done is a goal as it is necessary and meeting a need" (minutes, April 27, 1970).

In June, after two board members returned from a National Neighbors conference, the subject of goals resurfaced when the two delegates discussed two ideas stressed at the convention: "One, that the organization must not spread itself too thin. It was suggested that a goal be set, strategy planned and militancy employed, if necessary. Two, the association should have a definite purpose and know what it is trying to achieve. . . . The Associations with the greatest success were those with one or two specific goals—no more" (minutes, June 1, 1970).

The minutes indicate that the board then discussed its priorities and decided a long-range study was needed. Some members felt the issues were interrelated and "it would be difficult to separate committees and to narrow our outlook." The question was raised whether the BHCA was fighting hard enough to achieve their goals or whether they should become more militant. The housing committee chair again recommended that the board establish and define purposes, strategies, and tactics for the association.

One board member suggested that the board "go to a retreat for 2 days to enable us to better understand each other. Many members questioned if it would work" (minutes, June 1, 1970). Finally the same board member proposed that the weekend retreat be delayed till the new board took office in the fall. The board agreed, and passed a motion to have a fall board meeting deal with the purposes and priorities of the association. Such a meeting was not held. The housing committee chair moved to another city a few months later. The subject of reorganization was over.

One funding proposal in 1971 refers to BHCA ideology at that time: "The Neighborhood Improvement Committee of BHCA has worked toward solutions of many environmental and societal problems affecting the physical well-being of the neighborhood. It has sought to improve the quality of life to counteract the myth that multiracial neighborhoods invariably deteriorate" (proposal for recycling project, Summer 1971).

By 1972, the goals of the BHCA were even more simply stated: "The objectives of the BHCA are to promote a quality multi-racial neighborhood and represent the neighborhood before the various city governmental structures. This is accomplished by joint action of the residents of the neighborhood" (activities of BHCA, October 25, 1972).

Bill Sterling, a former board member active during BHCA's second phase (1969–75), referred to three phases of the organization: "First—to keep blacks out, second—to achieve integration, third—to have neighborhood stabilization—meaning economic upkeep." He believed there was a three-phase cycle of all nonprofit organizations—and he was not a sociologist. According to him, then, the third phase of BHCA was neighborhood maintenance.

The original stated goal of neighborhood preservation was certainly maintained throughout the life of BHCA as an organization. The later, secondary goal of neighborhood integration maintenance was no longer possible by phase three, since by then the neighborhood was predominantly black, as were the schools and the surrounding gigantic public housing projects. But even in phase two, the secondary goal was given to other spin-off organizations to achieve.

During the third phase, neighborhood maintenance and preservation was BHCA's only clear operating goal, as minutes of board meetings, news editions, and correspondence indicate. In addition, an increased emphasis was placed on political action and awareness. A new committee was even formed to deal with political issues. This may have been a reflection of the fact that two early BHCA leaders were elected as state representatives, who then appointed other BHCA early leaders as administrative assistants. Whatever the reason, the *News* from 1975 on contained a growing number of articles that were political rather than organizational or neighborhood-oriented. Now we turn to an analysis of BHCA's program during their three phases of development.

PROGRAM

As in other neighborhood groups in the movement, BHCA's program was accomplished through their committees and board of directors. The four major committees were housing, education, neighborhood improvement, and recreation. Later, as we noted above, youth services and the senior center became part of BHCA's program, and finally were the only remnants of the organization during their third and last phase.

Neighborhood Improvement

The neighborhood improvement committee was first called the zoning and neighborhood improvement committee, and was one of the original committees of BHCA, even before the active change in direction in 1966. During this early period, zoning changes were critical issues for the organization, and in fact were the major stated reason for its formation. Most of the zoning changes opposed by BHCA would have resulted in business expansion and loss of residential usage in Blue Hills. The association resisted these changes by securing cooperative lawyers who represented them before city officials. Between 1963 and 1968, these lawyers made twenty appearances at city hall in opposition to proposed zoning changes, their in-kind contributions were estimated at $4,000, and their results were all positive. None of the proposed zoning changes were ever made by the city.

During the second phase of BHCA's development, the emphasis of the neighborhood improvement committee shifted to neighborhood maintenance rather than improvement. Typical agenda items during phase two were stray dogs, trash and litter, abandoned cars, housing code violations, and street and curb problems. Action on these involved written or personal contact with city officials or residents, depending on who was creating the problem or could resolve it. Beautification of the neighborhood was an ongoing concern of the committee. In 1970, the neighborhood improvement committee, aided by a local foundation grant, publicized the sale of hundreds of lawn shrubs to Blue Hills residents at nominal cost. Classes were offered in lawn and garden care.

A 1972 BHCA activities sheet listed the following six items under neighborhood improvement: follow-up on problems regarding city services on trash removal and abandoned cars, traffic circulation and congestion, road repair, and code enforcement; encouraged merchants to keep their areas clean; human relations work between youth and merchants; special clean-up days; increased the number of trash cans at key spots; and replacement of mail boxes that the post office had removed.

In 1973, the committee began to feature in the *News* a photo and brief description of a praiseworthy "house of the month." This continued regularly throughout the rest of phase two. During phase three, the feature photo appeared irregularly in the *News*, and ironically changed focus in a final issue, in June 1980, when the photo appeared as the "Eyesore of the Month." Until then, the feature photo and article congratulated owners for their careful maintenance and noted that such homes were "a credit to their owners and the neighborhood." Members of the committee selected the homes to be featured, attempting to create and maintain a model for other residents (Bolduc 1976: 107).

Residents whose property showed signs of negligence—uncut grass, peeling paint, cluttered yard, and so on—received letters from the committee asking them to correct the problem in the name of community pride and upkeep of property values. The letter also offered suggestions for those with financial limitations. If no improvement followed, the committee referred the matter to the health department or other city offices for action. This activity declined in phase two, going from a high of forty letters a year in the late 1960s down to twelve a year in 1973.

Traffic flow was another concern of the neighborhood improvement committee, which coordinated complaints and suggestions of residents with appropriate city officials. They lobbied successfully to have several traffic control devices installed, and they sponsored a proposal in 1973 to build a new road rerouting city traffic away from the neighborhood. This was eventually accomplished, though city officials claimed they had been considering the change for several years.

Perceived increases in crime in the neighborhood led to requests from the committee for improved police protection and security. Theft prevention devices were publicized and distributed to Blue Hills residents by the committee during phase two.

A merchants association was formed by the committee in 1974, and together they initiated a shuttle bus service to help Blue Hills residents get to the stores and other facilities in the neighborhood. Though the bus was discontinued after four months of underuse, the merchants association continued, and was able to secure some needed street improvements a few years later. By this time, the neighborhood housing program had begun in the Blue Hills area; the neighborhood improvement committee was supplanted by the new program early in phase three.

Recreation

The recreation committee was extremely active throughout the first and second phases of the association. They were responsible for a large proportion of all the articles that appeared in the *News* on special events. This was true for all three phases, dwindling only in the last part of phase three, from February 1977 till the last *News* issue in 1980. A typical array of such articles included items about seasonal recreational events and programs, library news, an organizational picnic or dance, dance classes, films, dramatic presentations, poetry readings, youth activities, art displays, park activities, potluck suppers, and other special events.

One special annual event that was unique in the city and possibly the entire country was the Freedom Seder. Begun in 1968, this springtime community dinner was attended by several hundred black and white people, who shared the Jewish Passover story and traditional foods and music. It was celebrated, however, as a symbol of the universal struggle for freedom throughout human history. Freedom Seders continued throughout the second phase of the BHCA, commemorated with full-page photo spreads in the *News*. After 1973, the seders also honored Martin Luther King. The seders continued until phase three. The eight consecutive years of this annual event left one of the strongest organizational impressions on area participants, as interviews eight years later in 1984 revealed. Earlier, BHCA leaders had said: "It was the personification of what the neighborhood was all about—people from different backgrounds all struggling to be free" (Bolduc 1976: 153).

A 1972 fact sheet listed nine activities of the recreation committee at that time: family folk nights, Freedom Seder, creative dramatics program, adult recreation, square dance, work with parks and recreation department, work on Blue Hills recreation center, film workshop for high school students, preschool recreation program. Other activities organized or sponsored by the recreation committee included Christmas sings, carnivals, magic shows, musical activities, summer park programs, athletic events, and family picnics. Though attendance at all the social events was racially integrated, a recurring criticism was that some events were predominantly white or black. For example, the 1974 Seder "was heavily white dominated," as was the square dance and potluck supper that same year. One estimate was that less than 10% of those at the square dance and supper were black. "Sensitive to this criticism, the Recreation Committee immediately organized and ran a Spring Soul Dance two months later" (Bolduc 1976: 153). This was attended by 350 people, of whom about 60% were black.

Responding to parent demand, a preschool recreation program began in November 1970, early in the second phase of BHCA's existence. It was preceded by a successful Saturday school for toddlers (*News*, Jan. 1970). The preschool program was placed in the city's recreation center in the heart of the Blue Hills neighborhood, after BHCA learned that their office did not meet city fire standards. The program was sponsored and funded by the city, but BHCA coordinated all the volunteer parents. The program operated three mornings a week for two and a half hours and was for three- to five-year-olds, with some "precocious" two-year-olds.

When the preschool program began—"Pre-School Program Opens . . . at Last!" (*News*, Oct. 1970)—BHCA coordination insured that no more than eighteen children would be present each day. Any child within the three to five age group could come with a parent; if the parent could not remain for the entire play period, BHCA arranged to have a parent present for every five children. The City Parks and Recreation Department provided equipment and a staff person and the building.

By February 1971, the program began to fail because of underattendance. It shut down for a time, but then reopened: "Attendance must improve if it is to stay open" (minutes, Feb. 17, 1971). Considerable time and energy was given to planning and coordinating the program, with separate meetings arranged to do this. Six volunteer mothers' names and phone numbers were listed in the February 1971 *News* to handle various aspects of the program. The program "passed another crisis successfully when the program was extended until the end of May. Earlier, parents were notified that the program would close in March" (*News*, Feb. 1971). When concerned parents met with city officials and their councilman, the program was extended and officers were elected to run it. At this time, three librarians were regularly participating with story hours for the children, and parents whose children attended had to donate one morning a week at the recreation center, which expanded to four mornings.

By June 1976, the preschool program in Blue Hills was "called the best in the city," according to a feature article in the *News*. The free program was described as administering a subtle blend of "coax-compel-and comfort" to approximately twenty children aged two and a half to four from all over the city. The director of the program, a resident of Blue Hills, stated in a *News* interview that much of the success of the program was due to the cooperative participation of the children's parents, who were able to provide a one to three ratio with the children.

The program also drew praise from the city's supervisor of parks and recreation, who rated it "a well-developed success" (*News*, June 1976). This news article noted two successive budget cuts by the city. It mentioned that "the fight by BHCA to establish the Pre-School . . . succeeded in overcoming much of the city's bureaucratic pedantry." Also mentioned was the "unflagging dedication of the founders," who created a "solid foundation." Finally, the article ended with a warning to the community that it must continue to organize and "resist the psychology of politicians who would improve city finances by cutting its community services." This must not have happened, because that was the last reference ever made to the program in the *News* or in the minutes of the association. The preschool recreation program lasted for six good years.

Another concern of the recreation committee was the Blue Hills branch library. Since many recreational and educational events were held in the library, the association was the first to protest when funds were cut or programs were curtailed. When a major fire destroyed the branch early in phase two, the association organized public meetings with residents and city officials to plan the reestablishment of the branch library. They succeeded.

Teenagers' needs were also considered by the recreation committee. During phase one, the recreation committee sponsored and secured funding for a youth and teen recreation and education center, the Eugene L. Mansello Memorial Center. This functioned during the summer of 1968 and "was unique in its use of neighborhood young people in setting policy and planning program and leadership" (proposal for funding, 1968). Concern for teenagers continued throughout phases one and two, and on into phase three. A *News* item in phase two, headed "Help Plan Teenage Activities," referred to an open meeting sponsored by BHCA in the recreation center (*News*, Sept. 1972). A *News* editorial two months later described efforts to rehabilitate and revive the recreation center. These efforts eventually succeeded because of BHCA's persistence and pursuit of appropriate city officials.

By February 1973, the center was open six days a week, including Saturdays. Two months later, BHCA sought state funding for a youth worker from federal LEAA funds. In June 1973, a front page *News* announcement was titled "Youth Grant Secured" (*News*, June, 1973). The grant, from the State Planning Commission for Criminal Administration, was to be used to hire one full-time youth coordinator to work for "improved opportunities and services for youth in Blue Hills." The proposal for the funding, however, was more specific about the goals and objectives of the youth program. The major goal was to locate troubled youth and assist them with referrals to other existing youth service agencies. The program would initially be linked to the BHCA summer reading improvement program, which would be an important source of initial contact.

During the summer of 1973, a teacher at one of the Blue Hills public schools became the new youth coordinator. Six months later, a *News* item appeared headed "Youth Coordinator Quits." This was followed by the hiring of another teacher, who also left after a short time. During the tenure of the second youth coordinator, a youth employment service was developed, which provided a job clearinghouse for young people. When the youth coordinator's job ended, the jobs program continued as a summer program under the supervision of the BHCA board. Eventually this became funded in phase three as the Youth Jobs Program, and it continues today under other sponsorship.

By October 1974, BHCA's original youth program was officially ended, and they requested continued funding assistance for another agency working in the Blue Hills area with troubled youth up to age seventeen. For the remainder of phase two, BHCA continued to offer occasional recreational activities and field trips to teenagers in the Blue Hills area.

Housing

The earliest activities of BHCA were related to housing and the housing committee, which functioned actively from 1965 to 1969, when a housing corporation was formed. In 1965 "for sale" signs began to appear rapidly in portions of the Blue Hills area. To stem the panic selling, the new leaders and members of BHCA placed signs on their own lawns saying "This Home *Not* for Sale." This received widespread publicity, and was believed by members to have "dramatically reversed the selling trend in several key blocks" (*News*, Nov. 1971).

One of the first actions of the housing committee was the formation of a real estate listing service. This was, in fact, the subject of the lead article in the first *News* issue in May 1968. The service was begun to counteract the damage done by block-busting realtors who "black-listed" Blue Hills as its racial composition changed. To attract potential homebuyers to the Blue Hills neighborhood, a brochure was printed, called "A Way to the Future: The Blue Hills Neighborhood." Seven hundred copies of the brochure were distributed to major employers in the Hartford metropolitan area. The brochure stated the goal of integration, cited the advantages of living in Blue Hills, and provided phone numbers and addresses of members who offered personal follow-up. This consisted of meeting and talking to prospective Blue Hills homebuyers, showing them around the neighborhood, showing them available homes to buy or rent, and maintaining an up-to-date listing of Blue Hills homes on the real estate market. The committee claimed it was directly connected with the sale of forty-three homes in the Blue Hills neighborhood (*News*, March 1971).

But this may have been too costly in time and energy for the volunteer committee, for in 1969 the real estate service was given over to a separate newly formed housing services corporation. This corporation struggled with the real estate service and a housing rehabilitation program until 1972, when it dissolved after "the most bitter internal conflict in the association's history" (Bolduc 1976: 125). We examine closely the ideological issue underlying this conflict, for it may have been responsible for the association's eventual death, and it still plagues the entire movement.

First, let us analyze the basic philosophy of the initial real estate listing service. Formed in response to vigorous block-busting by realtors, the free volunteer service was established to encourage prospective homeseekers to move into the Blue Hills neighborhood. We note that at that time the Blue Hills area was 43% black, having increased from 10% black ten years earlier. The earliest statement about the new real estate service recognizes the difficulty of maintaining integration, and the fragility of stabilization, but it does not come to grips with the need for a specific strategy to achieve it. The statement refers to whites and blacks, but does not deal with racial groups as part of a planned strategy: "Many . . . people have been discouraged from buying here by real estate agents who warned prospective white families that this area will be the next ghetto. Many Negro families have contacted us to inquire whether or not the area is in fact becoming a ghetto and to inquire how the area would react to their living here" (*News*, May 1968).

The same inability to deal with a specific strategy for integration maintenance can be seen in a housing policy statement developed in November 1969. After noting the association's purpose of maintaining a stable and attractive neighborhood, this statement begins with an avowal of open occupancy:

It is a policy of the Association that . . . housing, both for purchase and for rental, be open to all persons without regard to race, religion or national origin. One of the values we seek to enhance is the opportunity for people of different backgrounds to live together in mutual respect. Any actions taken in the area of housing will always be performed in a manner that will support this goal. (housing policy, Nov. 1969)

The next paragraph attempts to offer a specific tactic for maintaining integration: "We also recognize that efforts should be made to maintain the integrated quality of life in the neighborhood. *This means that we will work to interest white families in living in the area.*" Immediately following this is a self-conscious explanation:

It is easy to misinterpret such a statement to say that it is opposed to open housing. In fact, the statement is an attempt to counteract the well-documented flight of white families out of the city, especially from areas that are integrated. If we want to maintain an open neighborhood, it must be open to all in fact, not just in theory. Affirmative action is required to attract and retain white families to the area generally, while at the same time we support open housing in every individual sale or rental. (housing policy, Nov. 1969)

This is followed by a list of four objectives to be achieved by the housing committee: (1) maintenance of lists of homes for sale or rent in Blue Hills; (2) referrals of homeseekers to such available housing; (3) joint efforts with real estate agents and others to attract families to the neighborhood; and (4) developing new programs to improve housing in the neighborhood.

A broader statement, which may have served as the basis for the one above, refers to eight specific goals of the housing committee, which were intended to "make the neighborhood attractive." In addition to the ones above, these included monitoring of properties to insure their meeting building code requirements, securing legislation requiring inspection of all properties and correction of any code violations before sale or rental, passage of regulations prohibiting "cold canvassing" in the area by real estate agents "to prevent residents from being disturbed by unfounded fear," and opposition to any expansion of low-income housing in the Blue Hills neighborhood "until other towns in the region have done their share in this regard" (housing policy, Nov. 1969).

The adopted housing policy did not refer to any of these specific goals, nor did it mention special efforts to preserve racial diversity in the area. And nowhere was there recognition of the need for regional open housing programs for blacks

as a way of spreading out the demand for minority housing. Instead, the Blue
Hills area continued to be the only hospitable neighborhood in the city for
upwardly mobile blacks, and their pent-up demand for housing resulted in continuing racial concentration in the Blue Hills neighborhood.

It was, however, the attention paid to white recruitment that caused the
bitter conflict within BHCA. In March 1969, the housing committee was expanded into the separate housing services corporation to offer an alternative to
traditional real estate agents, who continued block-busting and racial steering
in the Blue Hills area. The new corporation was to continue the advertising
campaign begun earlier by the housing committee (5,000 brochures extolling
the virtues of the Blue Hills neighborhood), and was to hire a full-time realtor
to sell homes in Blue Hills. Profits from sales were to be used for buying and
rehabilitating run-down properties.

The new corporation raised $2,500 to get the group started, and in early 1971
launched a vigorous advertising campaign. Flyers, bumperstickers, newspaper
space, and billboards were used, with two themes predominating. One emphasized the convenient location of the neighborhood: "Blue Hills Commuters
Don't." The other focused on the racial mixture of the neighborhood: "Want
to Live in an Integrated Neighborhood?" (Bolduc 1976: 123–125).

Members of the housing services corporation felt that blacks would be drawn
to the Blue Hills area with no special efforts needed by them. Therefore, if the
area were to remain integrated, whites needed special encouragement to move
in. The ads, therefore, were targeted for the white suburban population, even
though homes continued to be sold to blacks continuously. Some saw this as
an "affirmative action program for whites" and the resulting publicity drew much
attention in Hartford (Bolduc 1976: 123–125). One entire editorial in the local
newspaper was devoted to it (Hartford Times, June 19, 1971). In the editorial,
the author—Don Noel, a resident of the neighborhood—noted that though
Blue Hills was attractive to many black families who were welcome, it also
should be attractive to white suburbanites, "since only about one in four of the
families who move in are white."

The editorial continued by saying this was not a panic situation but that it
was a trend the community would like to change, since they found value in the
integration of race and religions. The recently formed Blue Hills Housing Services Corporation was cited as campaigning to attract more white suburbanites
to the neighborhood. Then the question was raised: "Are there any problems?
Of course, schools are a problem. They've been in a slump. But they're looking
up." The editorial minimized problems relating to parks and crime. Keney Park,
adjoining the Blue Hills neighborhood, was referred to as having "a handful of
tough kids who give the place a bad reputation, but they're a problem that can
be brought under control." Outsiders thought crime was a problem, but the
article claimed that burglaries were no higher in Blue Hills than in surrounding
suburbs. Finally, the editorial noted that the problems were not overwhelming,
or people would be moving out in droves—which they weren't. That came later.

Following the ad campaign that prompted the above editorial, members of the corporation sold twenty-three homes, mostly to whites from suburban areas. This is the point when, in May 1971, the focus on the white market fell under criticism within the BHCA. Several outspoken members asked for "a clarification of the corporation's racial policy" (Bolduc 1976: 125). Was preference being given to whites in the sale of homes? If so, some felt this was racist and could not be tolerated. Finally, shareholders withdrew their support and the corporation dissolved.

Emotions on this issue were heated:

Personalities became intimately involved and the issues became more confused. As in most cases involving race, strong moral overtones quickly came to the fore. Initially, the proponents of each view seemed to have an equal number of advocates. Yet, as the debates continued, an increasing number of Association leaders came to perceive the affirmative action of white recruitment to the neighborhood as tantamount to a quota system, and a quota system as tantamount to racism. (Bolduc 1976: 125)

The final vote of corporation shareholders had only five couples supporting the affirmative action program. Eventually these five families moved away, never quite regaining acceptance among their former friends and neighbors: "None of us ever felt completely comfortable in the neighborhood again" (Bolduc 1976: 126). It is not surprising that this issue tore the association apart. It continues to do so in the national movement and in the courts to this moment.

The housing committee was responsible for the monitoring of real estate activity in the neighborhood. Numerous letters of protest were sent to realtors who were badgering residents to sell "before the neighborhood gets any worse" (Bolduc 1976: 122). One real estate office was reported to have moved out of the neighborhood because of BHCA pressure. Two legal actions concerning housing were initiated by BHCA's housing committee. A block-busting suit was brought in March 1972 against one realtor, and a racial steering suit was filed in 1973–74 against eight real estate firms, with BHCA as one of several plaintiffs.

The block-busting suit was originally filed as a complaint to HUD on November 11, 1971, then referred to the Connecticut Commission on Human Rights and Opportunities, and finally to the Federal district court. When the agent gave up his real estate license, the court declared the case moot. It was the first use of fair housing law in the state of Connecticut (letter from attorney to HUD, June 5, 1972).

The racial steering suit was brought by Education/Instruccion (EI), still another splinter group formed in 1971 by formerly active BHCA members and residents. EI was a general civil rights group that conducted educational research. It organized an audit of housing opportunities for minorities in the Hartford area, consisting of sixty test cases of matched black and white and Hispanic-white testers looking for homes advertised by eight real estate companies. The tests were conducted by volunteers, almost all of whom were active members of BHCA. The many months of testing "revealed conspicuous racial steering among the realtors" (Bolduc 1976: 123). The charges, filed with the Department of Justice in 1974, were investigated by the FBI and were, of course, denied by the real estate companies (*Hartford Courant*, Feb. 21, 1974). A consent decree was issued in 1975, which required the companies to engage in fair housing practices and inform their staffs of provisions of fair housing law. No admission of guilt was needed for the decree by the Department of Justice.

Bob Harris, the former director of EI, a former BHCA member and Blue Hills resident and in 1984 one of the few remaining whites, said the Hartford newspapers would not print the story when first informed of the findings, because "they had so much money in real estate advertising" it would be bad for business. Finally, he said: "We ended up going to Associated Press and it went out through the AP wires and came back in with the AP heading and was printed in both papers the same morning to protect them. That's how sad the situation had become." He also complained that the State Human Rights Commission, formed to receive and act on discrimination complaints, was ineffective: "They're eighteen months backed up and wouldn't do anybody any good."

The housing committee of BHCA stopped functioning in 1972, after several former BHCA leaders formed Urban Edge as a nonprofit fair housing real estate company. The Hartford Neighborhood Housing Services rehabilitation program began in Blue Hills in 1974, initiated by another former BHCA leader; it continued for three years and went on to other cities across the nation. No other housing program or activity was undertaken by BHCA during their third phase of existence. We turn now to our last program analysis of BHCA—education.

Education

Even more vital and important than the early housing committee was BHCA's education committee. "The intense activity of this committee was a major contributor to the image of the Civic Association" (Bolduc 1976: 137). A 1972 fact sheet on BHCA listed education as the first major category of action for the organization, with nine specific educational actions the organization had undertaken: follow-through program in the elementary schools; multimedia center at one school; retention of resource teachers at two schools; saving the Blue Hills branch library when funding cuts threatened its existence; constant contact with the board of education to keep, improve, and encourage development of educational programs; volunteer teacher aide program; summer reading program; annual teacher orientation session; and school evaluation program.

These were all accomplished during the first two phases of BHCA's existence. After the spring of 1973, in phase two, the activities of the education committee dwindled, focusing on the ongoing summer reading program and the support of the branch library. By this time, the Blue Hills schools were almost totally black, ranging from 81.3% in the elementary schools to 93% black in the high school.

The summer reading program lasted only until 1976, after which general organizational decline led to no one being willing or able to write funding proposals to enable the program to continue. An April 1977 *News* article (phase three) announced that leftover moneys from the summer reading program would be used as mini-grants (seed money) to other nonprofit groups who requested it.

The BHCA's overriding concern with education and the public schools was linked to the association's goal of preservation of a high-quality racially integrated neighborhood. Since the schools were such a vitally important neighborhood facility, association leaders believed it essential to have high-quality education in its neighborhood schools. The earliest reputation of BHCA was as a school-oriented organization—"just a big P.T.A."—as minutes of a 1969 board meeting reveal (Bolduc 1976: 137).

The early newsletters and minutes of phases one and two show the extent of concern about maintaining the quality of education in the Blue Hills public schools. The first *News* issue had education as one of two front-page lead articles (the other one was on housing: "Free Real Estate Listing Service"). The education article was headed "Education Committee Obtains Commitment from U. of Hartford for Rawson and Twain." This referred to the newly established education committee, which had met with representatives from the local university to expand student-teacher placements in the three elementary schools serving the Blue Hills area, and to discuss a proposed educational park for Blue Hills. Continuing meetings were planned "to provide quality and integrated education to all students of the area in all schools" (*News*, May 1968). At that time, the schools of Blue Hills were already 70% to 90% black, though in the rest of Hartford's schools 45% of the students were black, 37% were white, and 16% were Hispanic (Hartford School Racial Statistics, 1971).

The second issue of BHCA's newsletter explained more about the proposed educational park. The lead article called "Education Outlook" was followed by one on the educational park: "What is it? What is the need? Why the urgency now? What are the results of inaction?" (*News*, June 1968). Three projected results of inaction were given, in answer to the third question raised above: schools will continue to be inadequate and overcrowded; the pattern of segregation now existing will be accelerated; and a school at the West High School site will be in a congested area and is very likely to become entirely segregated. These were prophetic warnings; they all came true. The educational park never materialized.

A 1968 letter from the education committee to local university educators and community leaders provides further evidence of how hard they tried to create this park. This letter, written at the end of phase one, reveals that the original prime goal of the education committee was to achieve racial integration in the Blue Hills schools through the park. When it became apparent that this goal would not materialize soon—and perhaps never—the group turned its attention to smaller, more attainable goals. In the seven years of its activity, it was able to make some significant contributions to the quality of education in the Blue Hills neighborhood. An early childhood learning center was established by the committee at one elementary school, as well as a Saturday school for toddlers. The local university's role in teacher training was expanded to all three elementary schools in Blue Hills. The committee recruited and sponsored a program of volunteer teacher aides in the three elementary schools, using more than thirty women volunteers at least one half-day a week to assist in classrooms or the library. This enabled the school libraries to be open more hours during the school week.

The education committee also established an assessment team, which devoted almost two years to an evaluation of the quality of education in the three Blue Hills elementary schools and the high school. The all-volunteer assessment team formed four committees to deal with five areas of major concern. They held hearings with pupils, staff, parents, and visited each school for at least three weeks, with scheduled meetings and discussions. Over seventy volunteers and community organization representatives undertook this long and painstaking research, headed by the BHCA's education committee chair. The team's findings were produced in a series of committee and individual reports, and the final twenty-page report was presented at two public meetings in January 1973, and then reviewed by the board of education and school administrators.

There is no evidence that any of their thoughtful, detailed recommendations were ever put into practice. Yet the work of the assessment team was highly regarded by other BHCA members and residents, and continued to be mentioned years later as one of the significant achievements of the organization.

The education committee's summer reading program was considered by many to be the most successful accomplishment of the committee and of BHCA. Beginning in 1969 with 30 children and volunteer aides, the program grew to an involvement of 150 children and an annual budget of $6,410. The summer classes taught reading to children needing remedial work through music, dance, and games, as well as through more traditional methods. They drew together human resources and facilities from several art centers, corporations, and the city's education and recreation departments. The volunteer efforts poured into the program were enormous. Besides the planning and implementation of the program, and writing the funding proposals, five women from the community each spent one morning a week working in the library, five others did music or art work with the children, and two public library staff members donated many hours to the program. The summer reading program lasted until 1975, when it died from general organizational fatigue, as we noted above. While it lasted, the results were clear and positive. They were good for the children, good for the neighborhood, and good for the organization. All lost when it ended.

The Final Phase

No articles about BHCA activity appeared in any of the city newspapers during the third phase of their existence. Analysis of the BHCA newsletters, minutes, and correspondence shows that the major activities of BHCA during their last four years were the publication of the *News*, the operation of the senior center, the summer youth jobs program, neighborhood improvement, and political participation on selected issues. The only recreational activity during this phase was one Freedom Seder (the eighth one, in April 1976 was the last) and one annual spring dance in 1979. Monthly meetings continued to be announced until December 1980, but these were sometimes not held, or were rescheduled because of poor attendance. Even membership drives stopped during this phase, with the last request for dues appearing in the November 1975 issue of the *News*.

The newspaper preparation, since its inception in 1968, consumed a tremendous amount of time and effort from a dwindling supply of volunteers. Throughout phase three, the *News* carried requests for help with the paper preparation. But the pleas were not successful, since only one other issue appeared—and then silence.

Early in phase three, BHCA joined nine other neighborhood groups in a "neighborhood strategy" for the use of federal Community Development funds for ten Hartford neighborhoods. Between $500,000 and $1.2 million were to be allocated for each neighborhood for housing rehabilitation and economic development. The BHCA worked with city staff to develop plans for the program in their neighborhood, and they helped publicize meetings for hearing residents' reactions.

When the neighborhood housing services program began its three-year program of housing rehabilitation in the Blue Hills and adjacent neighborhoods, some of the most active BHCA members served on the NHS board. This continued to drain the energies of the most dedicated members, though their efforts did result in neighborhood improvement. The resurfacing of one portion of a major street in the Blue Hills neighborhood was done through the combined efforts of the city, the NHS, and BHCA. This was cited as one accomplishment of the organization during the summer of 1978. They had few others to cite at that time.

News publicity on crime prevention increased and continued throughout the third phase. But no concrete organizational efforts were directed toward the reduction of crime. During 1978 some attempt was made to secure funding for such a program, in conjunction with an adjacent neighborhood organization, UACO. The records do not indicate any success with this attempt. News items show, however, that individual blocks organized themselves into security networks, but there is limited evidence that BHCA actually assisted with these efforts. The joint task force set up to improve the neighborhood park in 1978 included crime reduction as one of its goals. There is no evidence that this succeeded. The sign on the gateway to the large uninhabited park in the summer of 1984 reinforces this conclusion: "Closed from dusk to dawn."

The youth summer jobs program continued throughout the third phase of BHCA, and still was in existence in 1984 even though BHCA no longer functioned as an organization. The average number of young people participating in the annual six-week program ranged from seventeen to twenty-eight. After 1978, the program funding was given to the Blue Hills neighborhood through another community organization, South End Community Services. The 1979 contract stipulated the conditions under which BHCA—then barely functioning—was to administer the program, and called for the placement of at least seventeen youth in "meaningful summer employment." It also required the responsibility for collection of timesheets, distribution of paychecks, maintenance of records, and general supervision of the program. One or two volunteers from the Blue Hills neighborhood handled this program for the dying BHCA.

The senior center dominated the program of BHCA during their third and final phase, and remains the major tangible evidence of the organization's former existence. Of the eleven *News* issues that were published in the third phase, five contained articles about the senior center. This is more coverage on a regular basis than was received by any other single activity of the organization in phase three. One exception is the monthly announcements of BHCA meetings—which few attended.

We have already referred to some of the center staff and facility difficulties during the final years of BHCA. We now briefly describe the operating program of the center during phase three. A staff of six conducted the program: an executive director, a secretary-bookkeeper, and four activity workers—a ceramics teacher, a crochet teacher, a general crafts teacher, and a macrame teacher. In addition there were two janitors, one of whom also served as an escort. All but the janitors were women. The instructors and janitors were evenly divided racially (half white, half black: the director and secretary were both black. The facility was a small ramshackle two-story older home, with most of the activity downstairs and the office upstairs. About fifteen seniors came to the house daily for various program and social activities. Typical events included: workshops with crafts, cooking, plants and pottery; holiday socials, dances, trips to the theater, parks, and other places of interest; guest speakers; and specialized information on taxes, safety, health, and other topics relevant to seniors. The center was open five days a week from ten o'clock to four o'clock, with a hot lunch served daily for fifty cents. Volunteers were constantly sought. On the day I visited in June 1984, only two seniors were in the little house, and all the staff.

A content analysis of the eleven issues of *News* published from November 1975 to December 1980 reveals a decrease in recreational activities and events sponsored by BHCA, a decrease in articles relating to the public schools, an increase in political issues, and an increase in general articles not focused on the neighborhood or the organization. News items relating to housing were mostly limited to other organizations, and news items relating to neighborhood improvement focused increasingly on security, crime, and housing upkeep. All of these reflected the demographic changes in the neighborhood, and the organizational changes and its eventual burnout and death. We turn now to the impact of BHCA.

IMPACT

As with the other movement organizations, we will examine four factors in evaluating the success of Hartford's Blue Hills Civic Association. First, to what extent was racial pluralism maintained? Second, how well was the physical quality of the area preserved? Third, is there a sense of community in the neighborhood? And fourth, how much influence did the organization have? In the case of Hartford, BHCA can be considered a double failure: not only did they fail to maintain racial pluralism in their area, they also failed to survive as an organization. We will first examine these four factors, and will then analyze the reasons for failure.

Integration Maintenance

Looking at this factor, we have already concluded that BHCA did not succeed at all. Data on Blue Hill's racial composition, shown in Tables 1 and 2 and Figure 2 (Appendix A) are the basis for this conclusion. A neighborhood that is almost 90% black can not be considered an integrated one, by any standards. Could BHCA have done anything at all to have prevented the racial impaction of the Blue Hills area? And, if so, when might this have happened?

Prevention of impaction might have occurred in 1971 if the housing corporation had been encouraged to continue its policy of affirmative marketing. We recall that this policy came under severe criticism within the association, and that the active recruitment of whites to the Blue Hills area was seen by many organization leaders as a racist program. This caused the dissolution of the housing corporation, and the formation of a separate real estate group, Urban Edge. Not only did this end the affirmative marketing program—which might have succeeded in maintaining Blue Hills' racial integration—but it also diverted some of the best talents and energies away from BHCA to the new venture. Ultimately, however, both groups failed to maintain racial integration in the neighborhood.

What might have succeeded in 1971 was a well-coordinated effort to recruit whites to the Blue Hills neighborhood at the same time that blacks were given expanded housing choices elsewhere. This could have been done in conjunction with the Connecticut Housing Investment Fund, which was heavily funded to assist blacks in moving to the suburbs. Unfortunately, CHIF also had internal problems and conflicts, and eventually turned its focus to rental counseling, energy conservation, and the rehabilitation of existing units. Though its active counseling and mortgage assistance efforts helped over 1,900 minority families move to the suburbs throughout the state of Connecticut, this did not help the

Blue Hills area. Had BHCA and CHIF worked together, however, on a specific affirmative marketing program involving the Blue Hills area and the Hartford metropolitan region, the segregation in Blue Hills might have been avoided.

But there was no ongoing fair housing program of combating racial discrimination in the housing market. The two legal suits filed in the early 1970s were a mere ripple in the tide of housing discrimination, and without a sustained vigilant effort to combat this, racial steering continued and the dual housing market prevailed. The inevitable result was the further racial impaction of the highly vulnerable Blue Hills neighborhood. We must see the Blue Hills neighborhood, then, as one segment of a city and metropolitan area, with external forces impinging on it that might have been impossible to control by a neighborhood organization—even the most vigorous dedicated one—which BHCA surely was in their first two phases.

What were these forces? First, the enormous earlier urban renewal and land clearance programs in the heart of the city, forcing the displacement of thousands of minorities. Second, the documented existence of racial discrimination in the housing market, coupled with mortgage redlining resulting in racial concentration in specific areas of Hartford—notably, the north end, and the Blue Hills area. But these factors also existed in the other cities studied. So what was unique about Hartford? Here we cite a third and fourth force: public housing location, and school racial imbalance. Two massive public housing projects bordered the Blue Hills area, and their children were included in the Blue Hills neighborhood schools. And finally, the schools themselves, with city efforts at desegregation occurring too late and too little to avert racial impaction of the Blue Hills schools. Add to this a business strip that received attention too late to matter, and we have the death of an integrated neighborhood and the death of the organization fighting to keep the neighborhood and itself alive.

Quality Maintenance

How well preserved is the housing stock, the business strip, the park, and the general appearance of the area? Visual inspection and interviews with residents and nonresidents support the conclusion that the Blue Hills area is still pleasant-looking, with decent housing, and well-kept grounds. However, the small business strip is not well maintained, has considerable litter in full view in front of most stores, presents parking difficulties, and is generally unattractive. This, despite a supposedly successful revitalization and beautification program undertaken by the city in the later 1970s. In addition, the large Keney Park that forms the eastern boundary of the Blue Hills area appeared unkempt and quite deserted.

An examination of census data reveals some of the changes in the three tracts of the Blue Hills area from 1960 to 1980. Median income in 1960 exceeded city, state and national averages, but in 1970 it exceeded only the citywide average. Owner occupancy rates remained fairly stable at 55% with only a 4%

change, but there was a decrease of 17% in permanency as measured by population living at the same address five years or more. A stability index developed by the city Planning Commission rated Blue Hills in 1970 as zero on six measures: median income, incidence of poverty, home ownership, permanence of residence, racial change, and population change. The index ranged from minus twelve to plus twelve, with higher scores indicating greater stability. Blue Hills' life-cycle stage in 1970 was considered as "incipient decline," with movement toward healthy. In 1970 its population was 7% below poverty, and 42% black (Planning Commission Report, 1978). By 1980, the only substantial change was racial composition; other data showed a slight downward trend: 8.7% were below poverty, 10% of the homes were rated substandard, 53% were owner-occupied, and the population was 77% black.

Interviews with current and former residents offered mixed reactions to the question, "Has the general neighborhood changed in any way over the years?" Bob Bellows, current resident, thought that Blue Hills had rapidly deteriorated in the seventies, leading to significant numbers of abandoned houses. Harold Kilmer, a former resident, said: "There's some additional deterioration and yet there are still some of the most beautiful streets in Hartford." A third resident, Bob Harris, felt that the commercial strip had improved, but "now it's getting worse again." Dee Porter, a fourth resident, also thought the business strip had deteriorated in recent years, and the streets were "horrible—the streets are very bad, not just in Blue Hills, but everywhere in the city." As for housing quality, she felt it was stable, "but people work pretty hard around here to keep their property up."

Rita and Ed Schott, former residents who have come back to visit, said the business strip had deteriorated: "When we come back each year, we see it." But Bill Sterling, a former resident who had directed the NHS program, felt that the Blue Hills area "looks better than ever—NHS did this in one and a half years." Bert Benson, a current resident, thought the business area had deteriorated, but the general neighborhood still was of "good quality." The last president of BHCA, Roger Dunn, said he thought the nature of the businesses had changed and was "downgraded—people with different values were moving in and scared people away."

Still another ex-president, John Morton, said: "The business area has deteriorated. We used to have high hopes for it. But there's been arson there—and some good stores moved out and were not replaced by others." A nonresident noted, however, that Blue Hills housing prices had doubled in the last ten years. No significant differences in racial views appeared, and the overall conclusion was that the general neighborhood had retained its quality, with the exception of the business strip.

Sense of Community

How well did BHCA provide a sense of community? Here we find an unqualified positive record. If there was anything that BHCA succeeded in, it was this. Over and over again, respondents cited their feelings of fellowship and camaraderie when recalling their affiliation with the organization. We have already noted that the largest single category of newsletter items was recreational events sponsored by the organization. These were, of course, happenings designed to increase contact and sociability. But the planning and arranging of those events must have created even greater bonds among those participating.

From one respondent who moved to another town is this poignant note:

We have retreated from most neighborhood politics, citing age, energy, and past service. But we also know it is because we are not now (or probably again will be) in a neighborhood in which we can invest—excitedly, energetically, happily, fully—as we did in Hartford's Blue Hills. With few exceptions, our friends also left Blue Hills. But I drive through every day on my way to [work], which is located on the north edge of the old neighborhood. It reminds me, painfully, repeatedly, of the best and busiest years of my life. . . . As I remember it, our vision was fixed on a single lower middle-class neighborhood "in transition," which we thought could be made a model—whatever the rest of the city, state, nation, and world thought. I am not sorry we did so, for I doubt we would have had the energy otherwise, and we grew to know many people beyond our own professions and ethnic, racial backgrounds who will always be firm friends. (letter from Bob Bellows, Sept. 6, 1984)

Harold Kilmer, an early leader who also moved away, said: "There was always a battle, there was always a crusade. . . . What I miss—and a bunch of us who got together a couple of weeks ago were talking about this—what we all missed was the something special we shared about pulling together for what we all believed in and wanted. . . . We were all working our hearts out, trying to make that integrated neighborhood work."

A former president, still a resident (black), recalled: "When we came here in '72 there was a kind of community—the civic association at that time went to great lengths to welcome the people to the community . . . there were a number of different social gatherings—parties, events—a lot of introduction to the people, a real self-consciousness." He spoke of the value of living in an integrated community and recalled the neighborly atmosphere: "Those were the times, very important—the attempt to link specific Afro-American and Jewish traditions and liberation over a potluck supper and candles. So there was a real attempt—a serious one—to socialize and foster a sheer sense of community consciousness. Those were very special" (John Morton).

Ann and Roger Wellington, two long-term elderly residents, white and still there: "It was an opportunity for us to get to know black people and white people in an absolutely equal way. And we achieved something special with the Freedom Seder—with maybe 300 people in attendance." And from an early leader, Dee Porter, black, and also still living there:

It [the BHCA] sponsored some very tight bonding—because we went through so much together. And one of the things it's done for me was to help me build some relationships that are long-lasting. A good many of these people have moved all over the country, but they're still in contact. They never come to the East coast without coming here or calling to let me know they're here. And that's precious—always precious. . . . That was a very big plus—and nobody can take it away. . . . There were a lot of people coming in to Blue Hills. It was a changing neighborhood and people were moving up on the economic ladder. . . . I think all the social workers in the world came to Blue Hills, and all the attorneys too. Some graduating class must have turned out a thousand attorneys and a thousand social workers. And they all converged right here in Blue Hills. People were able to get personal help—advice, counseling. It was those kinds of things—big as well as small—that held the Blue Hills group together and made it work.

Finally, Rita and Ed Schott who left Blue Hills for a job transfer in 1974, at the height of BHCA's activity, said this in answer to the question, "Would you say the group has or has not succeeded in achieving its original goals?"

If we talk about survival, obviously not. If we talk about integration, certainly not. But if we talk about a wonderful sense of community among the fifty or eighty families that were active, yes! This was a dream and we worked intensely at it. Many of us learned skills and gained knowledge we never would have had otherwise. We've taken this to other communities and put it to work. Our children have the values we always hoped for, and that's certainly important. Blue Hills was very good for them—and us. There's an old Talmud saying, "If you save one person you save the world."

Influence

In the *Hartford Courant*, a leading city newspaper, articles about BHCA were sparse compared to the publicity received by other neighborhood stabilization groups elsewhere. From 1969 to 1973, only fourteen articles appeared about BHCA, and none after that. But an analysis of minutes, records, transcripts of interviews, and the newsletters of the association offer more positive evidence of organizational influence. This is especially true during the first two phases of the organization's existence. Also, the two spin-off groups from the association—Urban Edge and Education/Instruccion—were important in their influence on the real estate industry through their lawsuits, innovative structure, and publicized goals and achievements.

But the most compelling evidence of organizational influence is found in records of three major programs of the association: neighborhood improvement, education, and housing. In each of these, dedicated volunteers repeatedly contacted key decision makers and officials to express their concerns about issues affecting the neighborhood. They were able to prevent some major and minor decisions, change others, and bring about still others by influencing the appropriate officials relevant to the particular issue. It also helped to have some of those officials living in or being former residents of the Blue Hills area.

For example, the association in its first phase was able to block a Chamber of Commerce multimillion-dollar proposal for a low-cost housing project in Blue Hills. One early president described this with quiet pride: "Well, we blocked the Chamber of Commerce, and they were burnt. . . . It was the first time in their history that I know of that they and the city lost this huge battle. . . . Well, they learned that ultimately they had to come to us ahead of time" (Harold Kilmer).

We have already noted that every zoning change resisted by the association in its first phase was successfully blocked. This was done by the neighborhood improvement committee, which arranged for more than twenty city hall appearances by BHCA representatives between 1963 and 1968 in opposition to proposed zoning changes. The work of the neighborhood improvement committee complemented the efforts of the housing committee, which launched a valiant effort to promote the area as a desirable integrated neighborhood in BHCA's second phase. They did succeed in those early years in attracting young families to the neighborhood. Their successful "not for sale" signs campaign in the wake of real estate block-busting and racial steering tactics received prominent attention, and certainly produced some consciousness-raising throughout the metropolitan area. And their early attempts to set up a corporation to deal with housing rehabilitation eventually led to the selection of Blue Hills as one of the target areas for a pilot NHS program, later expanded to other cities and states.

Somewhat influential, also, were the two spin-off groups from the housing committee—Urban Edge, the nonprofit fair housing/integrated real estate company, and Education/Instruccion, the civil rights group that did real estate auditing and then brought a law suit against eight of the largest real estate companies in the Hartford area. This was followed by other discrimination suits in rental housing and against state and local agencies charged with racial discrimination in hiring and mortgage lending. But these two groups also did not survive.

One former president from the late seventies recalled the impact of those open housing activities: "We pulled the curtain on deeply entrenched racist real estate practices. I think it put a brake on such practices for a while" (John Morton).

In the areas of education, the association worked vigorously and constantly during their first two phases to achieve and maintain quality education. Though unable to obtain racial balance in the Blue Hills schools, they did support and work for the passage of a state law that changed the basis of state funding of education and became a model for other states as well. Earlier, a state school racial balance act was enacted, which the association sponsored and backed through one of their early leaders, who became a state representative. But by the time this was implemented, the Blue Hills schools were virtually all-black, and later city efforts were unable to effect any racial change there.

Political representation and clout from the Blue Hills neighborhood was plentiful, and this also helped the association receive some sympathetic response from city and state officials. We have earlier noted the growing emphasis on politics in the BHCA *News* during phase three. This was a reflection of the fact that former organizational programs were ending at the same time that political representation from Blue Hills was growing. By the end of the third phase, most elected Hartford city officials were black, and a substantial number of them came from the Blue Hills neighborhood as current or former residents.

FACTORS OF FAILURE

We have seen that BHCA did have a positive impact on the community—their own area and far beyond it. But they did not survive. Why, then, did Blue Hills fail—as an organization, and as an integrated neighborhood? Again, let us divide the factors into internal and external as we try to analyze the reasons for its decline.

Internal

We have already referred to burnout and fatigue when we discussed the organization's structure and program. This occurred early in the third phase of the association's existence. We have seen that by 1978, the organization was wearily and barely struggling to maintain a skeletal structure and program, and that by the time National Neighbors had their national conference there in 1980, the organization was quite dead.

One logical explanation for this might be that the neighborhood became overwhelmingly black, the original goal was then impossible to attain, and so there was no cause left to work for. But that is too simple. If we look at other neighborhood stabilization organizations we find that even when the neighborhood became predominantly black, the organization continued with a secondary goal of neighborhood maintenance and improvement—a perfectly respectable second aim for a neighborhood group. Why didn't BHCA do this?

One difference between BHCA and the other movement organizations studied is that this was the only organization that did not begin with the stated goal of integration maintenance. By the time new leaders and members openly acclaimed that goal in 1965, the neighborhood was already almost half-black, and the schools there were predominantly black. Though the zeal and commitment during their first two phases of organizational development were unsurpassed anywhere else, this came too late to bring stabilization to Blue Hills. Recognition of this did lead to deep burnout, fatigue, and discouragement. This, plus the fact that they were unable to secure funding for the staffing they so much needed for their monumental task, led to even more burnout of the already overworked and overburdened volunteer board and committees.

Dee Porter, still living in Blue Hills, thought the association

began to fade when the old crowd—the sixties and seventies group—began to move out. There was no reason for it to go down. There were other people in the neighborhood that could have taken the reins and carried it on. But when that sixties-seventies group moved out, we lost our energies . . . they were all burned out, they were tired . . . all that energy gone.

She also wryly commented on BHCA's life cycle: "In a nutshell. . . . From keeping blacks out, to neighborhood improvement, to *blah*." One current resident, Bob Harris, saw it a little differently: "The civic association went through a period where it was everything volunteer and then it got very sophisticated and had summer programs with money and there were grants and whatnot. Then when those fell down and there was nobody to do all that, everybody said we can't do it any more because there's no one being paid to do it. . . . Yeah, they got tired."

Another early leader, Harold Kilmer, who returned to the suburbs spoke of commitments and burdens: "People have to be willing to make a commitment to be involved in all kinds of educational and political neighborhood concerns. It puts a burden on them—but that's the problem. That's why a lot of people suffered burnout. They really did. Every day you faced a potential crisis, a potential battle."

Two early leaders who left at the height of BHCA's activity to take jobs in another state also spoke of burnout, leadership, and conflict:

There was such an intensity in this struggle and the work never ended. There was always more to do. People can't sustain that kind of fervor for very long. Because we were so anxious to encourage black leadership, we sometimes had elections of black officers who had no experience. Had we recognized the dangers of this for the organization, we might have guided them more—or maybe even not have been so set on having the black leaders. . . . Then, too, there was an internal split on whether to actively attract whites— the compromisers—or let come what may—the purists. (interview, Sept. 27, 1984)

Perhaps most important as a reason for burnout was the bitter internal conflict over affirmative marketing tactics, which further weakened the organization and caused the spin-offs of two other organizations. These, staffed by former BHCA leaders, seriously splintered the group and resulted in fragmentation of talent and energy. To add to this, rapid continuing white flight continually drained the remaining leaders and members of their friends, allies, coworkers, support— and hope.

One remaining white resident, Bert Benson, spoke of earlier conflict, and of how it felt to be racially isolated in Blue Hills:

That ideological split tore apart the organization in the early seventies. . . . I differed with some early leaders who were willing to steer blacks away in their effort to maintain integration. I stalked out of some board meetings saying, "I won't be a party to that." . . . I've wrestled with the issue of our kids being the only white ones left. I recognize the social isolation—but they are loners anyway, as are we, so maybe it doesn't really matter that so many others have left. We're not tied to the neighborhood socially anyway—and our friends have always included others outside the neighborhood.

The decline of the organization was seen by one early leader as the result of a combination of internal and external factors:

I think certain people put their lives in this for anywhere from five to eight years. Some of them reached burnout. Some of them, I think, got discouraged—I guess they just didn't see the city responding. Others saw the problems so interwoven with our state structure here, and just felt the state was not giving up resources to help any urban neighborhoods and there was no way we were going to win the battle.

Then he softly recalled:

Others . . . wanted to live here, but once their children finished schools, they didn't need a big house any more so they got out. Others moved out sadly. Some of them had bad experiences, I guess—some felt the battle had become hopeless and the neighborhood was losing its integrated character—and we were getting killed by real estate agents at that time. (Harold Kilmer)

One of the last active white members to move away, Ginny Satterwhite, had this reflection: "As the struggle ended to keep it [the neighborhood] integrated, interest in the organization waned. . . . In the late seventies crime became a growing problem. A few people kept the organization going then—but now the area, without the organization, is no longer a presence in the city." When her youngest child—a shy girl—had to confront the fact that she would be the only white child in her class at school, they decided to leave. This, of course, brings us to external factors, to which we now turn.

External

One of the earliest leaders spoke almost woodenly of the impossibility of maintaining integration: "Racial integration can't work. It's only a stage between all white and all black segregation. Whites won't accept it" (Bill Sterling). He, in fact, moved back to the suburbs, where his children had "at least some integration in the schools." He referred here to the city of Hartford's voluntary busing plan, Project Concern, in which black city students could attend white suburban schools.

Another respondent, a remaining white in Blue Hills, spoke negatively about the same Project Concern, believing it contributed to white flight out of Hartford:

The public schools became devastated because of Project Concern. This program was for the highest quality black kids to go to suburban schools—so what did that do to the Blue Hills schools? It left the dregs behind . . . Your best parents and best kids are taken out . . . and that really hurt us. I saw that with my own kids and their friends all along . . . It was an emotional tearing apart of the kids. . . . Just like stripping a plant to the point where there's nothing left in terms of friendships . . . That was upsetting. (Bob Harris)

A white older couple, still living in Blue Hills, spoke of the racial isolation in the Blue Hills schools: "I think that more recently people moved [away] because of the schools. The high school was once awfully good and it was predominantly white when it was built. After we moved here, white attendance just slid off the map. . . . Very bad—for white children" (Ann and Roger Wellington).

In addition to and related to the serious racial isolation in the Blue Hills schools, which was cited by those who moved away as the single most important reason for their moving, was the matter of school funding. The school funding base was inadequately structured, following state mandates (McEachern 1976). The implications of this weakness for Blue Hills are seen in several critical decisions made in the mid- and late sixties by the Hartford school board.

With a gigantic study team's recommendations before them offering details for keeping the city's schools racially balanced and academically enriched, the Hartford school board rejected the plan that would have achieved this. State funding difficulties were cited as the major reason for this rejection. Instead of adopting the plan, the school board spent the next ten years implementing piecemeal segments of the plan, avoiding others, and circumventing still others (Champ 1975; Brayfield 1975). The results of this for the Blue Hills schools were disastrous. By the time school officials seriously began to devise ways of achieving racial balance in the city schools, it was too late.

Another external factor cited by one respondent as a reason for BHCA's decline was the formation of a new organization in the late seventies at about the time that BHCA was beginning to wane. The new group was the Blue Hills Citizen Action group, the group I was referred to when I first came to Hartford. This was a local chapter of a statewide group, which operated with paid organizers and addressed consumer issues. By some, it was seen as a political arm of politicians, but others regarded it as a serious, hard-working consumer advocate group. One BHCA respondent described it "as active as BHCA probably ever was, and has taken its place. It's not a neighborhood based group. . . . It's not that buddy-buddy neighborhood oriented thing. They have organizers" (Bob Harris).

Finally, we have the fact that externally the Blue Hills neighborhood was surrounded from the outset by the most massive public housing projects in the city of Hartford. One-quarter of all public housing in Hartford was located in the Blue Hills neighborhood. Fourteen hundred residents, more than half of whom were black, were included in the BHCA target boundaries and in their school cluster. Inevitably, this was not helpful to the goal of integration maintenance in the neighborhood or the schools.

Analyzing the difference in the views of white and black respondents concerning the demise of BHCA, I found many similarities and two sharp differences. In their reaction to the question about BHCA's failure to survive, all of them referred to fatigue, and to the earlier intensity and endless work as volunteers. Both blacks and whites spoke of the failure of leadership in BHCA when the area became predominantly black. The remaining whites were tired, and the blacks had other priorities, or commitments to work and family.

The external obstacles—public housing surrounding the neighborhood, inadequate funds for the schools—were mentioned by whites only. And the racial isolation in the schools was referred to consistently, but only by whites, as the major reason for white flight. Blacks spoke of white flight a great deal, but did not cite the schools as a prime cause of this. Every white respondent spoke with heat and sorrow of the schools' racial isolation as the main reason for their moving or their friends and neighbors moving.

The Future

What about the future of the Blue Hills neighborhood? Most respondents saw Blue Hills stabilizing as a black community—low middle-class—with some political representation on local and state levels. They did not regard the citizens action group as a replacement of the BHCA, but saw it as an outside group dealing with various consumer issues—utilities, protection, services, and so on. One current black resident spoke of Blue Hills' current political clout: "One of the interesting things about what is happening is that Blue Hills is now one of the most influential political communities in the city. The majority of the black leadership comes from Blue Hills—this was not true ten years ago. . . . As for BHCA, I guess—finally, the vision of an integrated neighborhood just played itself out" (John Morton).

Most respondents had deep nostalgia and abiding affection for the old organization as they remembered it. One said the biggest single loss—the thing she missed most, besides the people—was the newspaper. But the last president, Roger Dunn, black and still a resident, said there was another weekly paper, the *West End Agent*, which was a profit-making venture paid for by advertising: "so now there's no need for ours—also they took away our ad sources." He also felt that the neighborhood "doesn't get the response we used to downtown—for crime or street repair. We can't seem to keep city hall on its toes to address the issues we have in common."

This respondent also felt that there was no more time to be active and do the work of the old association: "More of those kinds of people moved in, and people doing the work moved out, and this hurt us. No more professionals are left—both white and black moved to suburbia." His parting thought was: "I hope to revive the organization. My dream is to get back to what we were."

A nonresident and nonparticipant, Arthur Telford, gave the view from downtown: "By 1977 Blue Hills was already seen as an all-black neighborhood. But it now [1984] has the highest voting percent of any area of the city, and the family income is first or second highest in the city." Against the wall, on the floor of his law office—high up in Hartford's newest gleaming structure—was a large poster, unhung but framed. Its title: "What happens to a dream deferred?" That raisin in the sun was BHCA, I thought as I left.

Epilogue

My notes of June 9, 1984 were written just after I had completed my field work in Hartford. I offer them here because they are still relevant.

Yesterday seemed to tell the whole story—starting in the morning with Harold Kilmer, the early leader, who greeted me softly with, "So you came to hear about our Camelot?" (He is the one who moved in to Blue Hills the earliest of all those I interviewed—in 1963.) And ending with Ginny Satterwhite, the BHCA leader—and such a tireless worker—who most recently moved out of the Blue Hills neighborhood in January 1984. Her pain was obvious. It was mine, too. She said, with tears rolling down her cheeks: "I didn't want to move away. I really didn't. But we just couldn't send our youngest—a shy little girl— to a school where she would be the only white child." What happened in between, of course, is what I came to Hartford to find out.

This twenty-year struggle was surely a valiant one—with some of the early leaders forming other vigorous nonprofit advocacy groups for different specific programs. I see more of this in Hartford than any other place I've studied. Maybe that's the reason why the organization didn't survive—much zeal was siphoned off in other directions. There was also deep ideological dispute on how to achieve the maintenance of the neighborhood as an integrated one. This is not unlike the current controversy gripping the national leaders of the movement—to what extent is affirmative marketing seen as a curtailment or expansion of black housing opportunities and choices? We have clearer answers to this now, but in the late sixties and early seventies the issues were newer and sharper, with few models. In Hartford, it seems, the philosophical differences among the Blue Hills leaders at that time split the group and led to some of them moving away.

But I don't think it was the internal differences that led to the end of the organization. The end of the organization followed the end of the neighborhood as an integrated neighborhood. The external forces had a much greater impact, I believe. The forces of urban renewal relocation, public housing location, school racial imbalance, city services neglect, business area deterioration, racial steer- ing, mortgage and insurance redlining are each devastating enough to the main- tenance of neighborhood integration. But all together—which voluntary organization has the human resources and endurance to successfully combat them? Smaller suburbs of large cities are now in the eighties devoting full-time staffed municipal efforts to dealing with these mammoth forces—and ultimately this is what is required to succeed in this effort.

I thought today of city neglect—rooted in a legacy of racism and indifference— when I took photos of the Blue Hills two-block shopping strip. This was sup- posedly beautified fairly recently, according to some of my respondents. I saw no beauty. The planting of a few trees and some sidewalk and curb improvement does not provide beauty when surrounded by vacant stores, litter, and discarded cans and beer bottles. This little improvement here, though surely welcomed by residents, must have come too late—as with most cities (definitely Copley Road in Akron). Residents of integrated neighborhoods have to work so hard, and it takes so long—so many months and years—until they are listened to. And by then it's too late. The hope has long since gone.

That's what this movement, as all others, is based on—hope. When that's gone, the movement is over. An organization might survive, but not the movement. Why does the adjacent West End neighborhood have such a nice shopping strip? Why does it have such a variety of interesting stores? Why does it feel like a healthy neighborhood? Why doesn't the Blue Hills strip feel like one? How might this have been avoided? And when?

Postscript

From the *New York Times*, November 1, 1987:

Hartford Mayoral Race Focuses on City's Split Personality. . . . "It is a tale of two cities— a place to work. What I would like it to be is a place to live, also," said the Democratic black mayoral candidate Carrie Saxon Perry. Her view was shared by the Republican candidate Philip Steele: Too many office buildings . . . at the expense of where the people live. "The booming downtown should be helping our neighborhoods." Both focused attention on the two cities of Hartford—"the growing corporate center surrounded by neglected neighborhoods."

At the National Neighbors 1988 conference in Philadelphia, I saw Bert Benson from Hartford—one of the most thoughtful people there that I interviewed, and one of the last remaining whites in Blue Hills. He had come to the NN conference as an individual, since there was no group in Hartford any more. He came because "I needed to be with others who cared and were involved with this effort—and because I missed it." He came alone, as his wife was showing their house that weekend; it was up for sale. They decided to move because "nothing holds us here any more—not institutions, not the neighborhood, there is nothing to even walk to." He said Blue Hills was even more segregated now than when I was there four years ago.

Final Postscript

June 24, 1989: I have just learned that BHCA has revived! A letter from their new Board Secretary asks for all old materials used for this study. Delighted to send them. *Question:* Does this mean that BHCA is no longer an example of failure? Is it now a Conditional model? Doesn't MO survival (or revival) mean that positive change is now possible in Hartford?

NOTES

1. See, for example, Schwab 1982: 377; Zald & McCarthy 1987: 370–71; and Wilson 1973: 9, 306.

2. Census data (1980) show that blacks have double the number of two-income households compared to whites. This would suggest less time and energy for voluntary association participation. See Lieberson 1980: 51; Gist & Fava 1974: 362; Chapin 1974: 151–153; Keller 1968: 53–67. For an alternate view, see J. Williams et al., "Voluntary Associations and Minority Status," in Davis 1979.

6

AKRON: WEST SIDE NEIGHBORS

"Fighting to keep its dignity in the face of problems that threatened to turn the area into a slum"

"The best part of it has been the sharing of a vision with wonderful people"

"If we had known how hard a task it was, and what a constant struggle it would be, and the institutional forces we would have to confront—we might never have begun"

"Our sense of being part of something worthwhile, something significant— a statement to the world"

"Turnover is the biggest problem"

"I was solicited twenty-five times by real estate agents wanting me to sell"

Now we come home to Akron, where my own experience with neighborhood stabilization began with West Side Neighbors in 1967. Two years earlier I had been a founder of Akron's open housing group, the Fair Housing Contact Service. We learned quickly that in order for open housing to work in a community, a demonstration model of successful integration was needed. West Side Neighbors was to be that model for Akron. As I write this, plans are under way for the twenty-year anniversary celebration of West Side Neighbors. They are still alive. Whether they have succeeded, and to what extent, is still a matter of judgment. Let us examine their history, their goals and program, and their impact as we have done in the other four communities. But first, let us review their setting and sociohistorical background.

SOCIOHISTORICAL CONTEXT

The name Akron comes from the Greek word akros, meaning high place. This describes the city's location, lying across a ridge 950 feet above sea level in northeastern Ohio, and also its terrain, consisting of many hills. The city has much greenery and trees, and is quite lush in the spring and summer because of ample rainfall and moisture year-round. Fall is a lovely riot of color. Winter is a terrible three months of grey skies, freezing weather, and icy roads.

Akron was until a few years ago the largest rubber manufacturing center in the world, serving as the home of four of the world's largest tire and tube manufacturing plants. It was considered the rubber capital of the world. But when General Tire closed its plant in 1982, the city soon stopped producing tires. Now its five main industrial employers are service industries, retail trades, durable goods, nondurable goods, and rubber and plastic products. The city has an art museum, a symphony orchestra, an extensive public library system with seventeen branches, four hospitals, and a university of 28,000 students. The population of Akron is 230,000, making it the fifth largest city in Ohio. Blacks are 22% of the total population.

Though named an All-America City in 1980, not all perceive it as deserving of that title. Still, it does typify many American cities, so the title may be an apt one. As a community relations director put it: "We've got the same problems you have in Forsyth County, Georgia. They may not wear robes here, but they still discriminate." Since Benjamin Franklin Goodrich began his rubber plant here in 1870, Akron has been typical of blue-collar middle America. This is the home of the Soap Box Derby, more bowling alleys than other cities four times bigger, and an active Ku Klux Klan. It also is the place that abolitionist John Brown lived in during the 1840s, when northeast Ohio was filled with antislavery sentiment and action. Today they're called civil rights believers, and they still live in Akron too.

In 1825, the town of Akron was first proposed as a stop along the Ohio canal, since it was located at the highest point of the canal route. Though the canal route officially opened in 1827, Akron did not become a city until 1865—the year the Civil War ended. When a special 1865 census was conducted by the state of Ohio, the count then turned up 5,066 persons in Akron, sixty-six more than the number required to become a city. By the time the first rubber factory was built in Akron in 1870, the city's population was 10,000. Only 196 of them were black.

State statutes required separate schools for black children when there were more than thirty of them. These "black laws" were repealed in 1887, but that didn't bring about the end of racism in Ohio or Akron, as we will see. The black population in Akron grew slowly from 451 in 1890 to 525 in 1900 and 647 in 1910.

Racism in Akron was apparent in 1900, even though the black population was then only 1.2% of the total. When a black laborer was accused of molesting a six-year-old white girl, Akron authorities sent him to a Cleveland prison to avoid a local lynching. In protest, several hundred men stormed city hall and blew it up with dynamite. City officials had to call in the Ohio National Guard to quell the riot.

After 1900, the rapid growth of the rubber industry attracted many workers from the South, as well as from Europe. In the one year 1910, the rubber companies doubled their capacity. More than half the present population of Akron consists of people from Southern states, especially West Virginia, Kentucky, the Carolinas, Tennessee, and Alabama. This is an important fact for understanding race relations in this city. Of all the groups that flocked to Akron to build tires, the most extensive one was the Appalachians—most often known here as hillbillies. Many of the sons and daughters of Appalachian migrants live in the mostly white neighborhood of Kenmore, which is just below a mostly black neighborhood of west Akron—part of our study area.

From 1900 to 1930, Akron was the fastest growing city in Ohio. In 1900, only 525 black people lived in Akron, which then had a population of 42,000. Blacks were concentrated in two wards located in the central and east-central part of the city. When rubber companies doubled their production in 1910, the total population increased 202% in the next ten years—from 69,067 to 208,435. Of the newcomers, 100,000 were Southern whites and 5,000 were blacks. In that same decade, blacks doubled their presence in Akron, going from 1.2% in 1910 to 2.4% in 1920.

Some whites responded to this increase with renewed racist activity. During the 1920s, when the Ku Klux Klan was revived nationwide, Akron was a focal point of Klan activity. Three Akron Board of Education candidates in 1923 were endorsed by the KKK and were elected, and from 1925 to 1928 the Klan held a majority of board of education seats (Grismer 1952).

By 1930, the population of Akron was 255,040, with blacks making up only 4.3% of the total. The 11,080 blacks were situated in several areas of Akron at that time, with only one tract in central Akron having over 25% black population concentrated there. This was lowland area next to the Little Cuyahoga River, and was one of the least desirable areas of the city. Here were the coal companies, lumber yards, the railroad, and mud roads. Six tracts surrounding the central business district had 10–25% black population, and the remaining black people were dispersed throughout the city.

World War II brought a new influx of blacks to Akron, with rubber companies beckoning. Between 1940 and 1950 their number doubled—from 12,309 in 1940 to 23,878—a 95% increase. During this period, the housing shortage was acute for everyone, but especially for blacks, who did not have equal access to all areas. In 1940, blacks were confined to seven census tracts out of fifty-eight, despite the great increase in their population. One tract—the Howard Street area—had over 50% of the black population, and it grew from 50% to 74% black. This was due to the construction of a black public housing project, Elizabeth Park, in that area. Additional public housing projects increased housing segregation in Akron.

From 1940 to 1942, the Akron Metropolitan Housing Authority (AMHA) established three segregated public housing projects in the Akron area: Elizabeth Park, noted above, Edgewood Homes as a white project, and Norton Homes as a white project in Barberton, an adjacent city south of Akron. At the same time, the federal government established three racially segregated war housing projects in Akron: Hillwood Homes and Wilbeth-Arlington as white projects, and Ardella Homes as a black project. These were administered by AMHA from 1943 to 1953, then were formally deeded to AMHA in 1953. Akron news articles in 1946 referred to public confrontations between black leaders and the AMHA director, with one such verbal clash occurring at an annual dinner commemorating Brotherhood Week.

By 1950, AMHA operated eight public housing projects in Akron containing 3,400 family units. Each of the eight was operated on a segregated basis, and consisted of two permanent low-cost units for low-income families and six temporary projects for veterans with 2,300 units. The two permanent ones—Elizabeth Park, black, and Edgewood Homes, white—had 550 family units. Edgewood was built in a racially mixed neighborhood, where blacks' homes were demolished to make way for the all-white project. Though Edgewood Homes was later converted to a black project, the others have retained their racial identities to this time, affecting the schools and neighborhoods around them and ultimately the entire city of Akron.

In addition to public housing segregation, the private housing market also practiced racial discrimination, which increased racial segregation. In 1945, a two-day interracial clinic was held by the Akron Ministerial Association to hear a report on community resources for blacks. Topics included housing, employment, and schools. The report indicated that blacks felt rejected and discriminated against in housing and employment; this led to a community audit in 1950. The community audit, prompted by a concern for biracial progress stemming from the earlier interracial clinic, culminated in 1952 with a report, A Study of Discrimination in the City of Akron. The report analyzed seven aspects of interracial living, including employment, housing, and education. Again— as in the 1945 interracial clinic—both housing and employment showed serious discrimination.

In the years between 1940 and 1950, housing access to blacks was denied in specific areas of Akron. These were cited in the community audit and included Cuyahoga Falls—a northern suburb often referred to as Caucasian Falls. News advertisements of housing during this decade used the phrase "colored or white," meaning the homes were in a black neighborhood. Seventy-five such ads offering homes for sale appeared in the local newspaper, the *Akron Beacon Journal*, during a two-week period in March 1952, according to the community audit.

Though inequities in education were a minor part of the audit report, they were greatly magnified ten years later when the first of two separate lawsuits—fifteen years apart—was filed against the Akron Board of Education. The first suit, filed by the national NAACP in 1963, charged Akron school authorities with intentional segregation. Among actions cited were attendance zone changes and the creation of optional zones, which removed white students from racially integrated schools and allowed them to attend white schools. This resulted in increased racial segregation in the schools and neighborhoods involved.[1]

In 1968 the court ruled in favor of the schools, claiming that no intentional segregation had been proven by NAACP. The case was never appealed, and the lower court decision remained to plague Akron residents ever after—even entering the final decision in the second school lawsuit, filed in 1978. In those ten years, practices and policies of urban renewal relocation and public housing site selection further created and perpetuated residential segregation in Akron, with blacks mostly relocating in the western part of Akron. This is where West Side Neighbors began in 1967. We turn briefly to the chronology of those events.

From 1940 to 1960, the nonwhite population of Akron increased 208% from 12,309 to 37,636. During the same period, the white population of Akron increased only 9% from 232,482 to 254,457. Much greater was the increase of the white population in the suburbs. By 1960 the ratio of whites to blacks was seven to one in Akron, and fifty-eight to one in Summit County surrounding Akron. Residential segregation in Akron increased between 1940 and 1950, and again between 1950 and 1960, using the index of segregation developed by Karl and Alma Taeuber (1965). In 1940, blacks occupied only seven out of fifty-eight total census tracts. But despite their tremendous population increase from 1940 to 1960, blacks moved into only two additional census tracts during those twenty years. Moreover, the census tracts occupied by blacks contained the most blighted areas of the city (U.S. Census 1940, 1950, 1960).

Along with the flight to the suburbs, the period from 1940 to 1960 and beyond was marked in Akron, as in other cities across the nation, by a surge of urban renewal. The expansion of the University of Akron, the construction of an innerbelt expressway system, the enlargement of Akron General Hospital, the expansion of one of the rubber companies, and the land clearance in an area mistakenly called Opportunity Park were some of the urban renewal projects that affected the black population, forcing them to vacate these areas and seek new ones.

An analysis of the housing market in 1965 shows that 2,875 housing units were removed from the Akron housing stock from 1960 to 1965, an average of 550 units per year. Nine hundred units were removed for urban renewal, and 800 units were demolished to make way for an interstate highway system during that period. From 1965 to 1970, 3,000 more units were removed. Though a sharp increase in rental-unit construction occurred after 1960, the prices made them unavailable to those displaced by urban renewal.

Blacks and civil rights activists in Akron protested the housing situation on numerous occasions. In 1962 a new organization was formed as a study group concerned with the elimination of discrimination in housing. This group, of which I was a part, the Council on Housing Opportunities Made Equal in Summit County (HOMES) was the forerunner of the Fair Housing Contact Service. The HOMES group gathered and presented data to the Akron City Council in 1964 in support of a proposed fair housing ordinance. Several months of public hearings led to the passage on July 14, 1964 of an emergency fair housing ordinance, by a vote of eleven to two. The *Akron Beacon Journal* called this the city council's finest hour (Saltman 1978).

But immediately after this historic vote, organized real estate interests petitioned for a citywide vote on the fair housing law. Obtaining enough signatures for this referendum, the issue was placed on the November 1964 ballot. And barely five months after it was voted in, the fair housing law was voted out by 60,000 people. It may well have been the shortest length of time of any fair housing law in the country. This led to a five-year court battle testing the constitutionality of the referendum; which was finally won in the Supreme Court in 1969 (*Hunter v. Erickson*), reestablishing the Akron fair housing law. By this time, both the Fair Housing Service and West Side Neighbors had begun, and ghetto riots had rocked Akron. The riots occurred in the heart of an urban renewal area in August 1968; they were among the last to occur in the nation. Seven days of unrest resulted in a citywide curfew and national guardsmen patrolling the area.

Now we turn finally to the results of urban renewal relocation in Akron, which must be understood as part of the total local environment faced by West Side Neighbors when it began in 1967. Of 3,197 households relocated by Akron urban renewal projects between 1962 and 1972, 72% moved to twenty-two tracts on the west side of Akron. Of these, 68% were in the Buchtel and South High School attendance zones, with Buchtel High School located in the heart of the West Side Neighbors area. Seven tracts in the Buchtel zone received 851 of these households (54%), and six tracts in the south zone received 733 households (46%).

Relocation of black and white households was significantly different, however, and followed and exacerbated existing patterns of racial segregation in Akron. If we examine the racial breakdown and tract relocation for just one urban renewal project—the largest one, Opportunity Park—we can see the racial difference in relocation. Opportunity Park, with 409 white and 714 black households, accounted for 39% of all west-side relocation in Akron. From the Opportunity Park project alone, 366 families were relocated into the west side of Akron, to the Buchtel High School zone. Of these, 332 were black and only 34 were white.

For individuals displaced by urban renewal, the data are similar. Again, examining only the Opportunity Park project, a total of 705 individuals were displaced, of whom 426 were white and 279 were black. Where did they go? Seventy percent of the black persons were relocated on the west side, and 93% of the white persons relocated to white neighborhoods, including fifty who moved to white suburbs. Relocation into public housing units followed the same pattern.

The results of this urban renewal displacement are clearly seen by analyzing racial impaction trends in the city of Akron. A racially impacted area was defined by HUD in 1972 as being more than 50% black or having more than a 10% increase in black population in the past ten years. In 1960, only 27% of all racially impacted areas in Akron were on the west side. By 1970, 40% of all impacted areas were on the west side (Akron Department of Planning & Urban Renewal, 1975, 1972). Urban renewal relocation played a major role in increasing the black concentration on Akron's west side, and was a major impetus in the formation of West Side Neighbors in 1967.

INCEPTION

Three reasons are given by the founders for the formation of West Side Neighbors (WSN): reaction against racism, desire for neighborhood control, and the wish to serve as a demonstration model of integration. Racism in the city of Akron, as in the other cities we have examined, had resulted in racial concentration and segregation. Urban renewal then displaced huge black enclaves. West Side Neighbors, instead of waiting passively for events and outside forces to affect their neighborhood, wanted to control their own destiny. Above all, they wanted to provide a demonstration model of effective, integrated living—where blacks and whites could live, work, and play together in an attractive, stable, desirable community. They hoped "that a vital, active neighborhood organization could avert the typical resegregation pattern that often occurred in other integrated neighborhoods in many cities across the country" (WSN, A Brief History 1972).

The first public notice of any organized stabilization effort in Akron was in a six-line news item that appeared in July 1967. Headed "For Stability," the tiny article announced that a biracial, interfaith committee was at work in west Akron planning an open meeting of all residents interested in stabilizing the area's neighborhoods. The meeting was "tentatively planned for early September" (*Akron Beacon Journal*, July 20, 1967). What that notice did not say was how long such a group had been functioning, why it began, and who the participants were.

West Side Neighbors was actually the outgrowth of a neighborhood stabilization committee of the Fair Housing Contact Service (FHCS), formed two years earlier in 1965 (Saltman 1978). Founders of FHCS quickly came to realize that they could not effectively open new areas to blacks without having some examples of successful integrated living. The west side of Akron was to be such an example, and the stabilization committee of FHCS was formed when FHCS was one year old. What they soon recognized, however, was that the task required full-time massive effort, which they could not do. They also saw that it would best be done by residents of the west side area as a separate organization.

Two of the seven founders of West Side Neighbors were women on the FHCS board of directors, who had served on its stabilization committee and who lived on the west side. I was one of them. The remaining five founders were two ministers who had parishes in the west side, two west-side black community leaders, and a newspaper writer who also lived in the west side. The newspaper writer wrote an editorial, just a few days before the small public notice mentioned above, titled "Citywide Integration Vital" (*Beacon Journal*, July 17, 1967). In this editorial he spoke of the need for stabilizing west Akron neighborhoods, and of the efforts of FHCS toward this goal. His editorial was in response to an earlier public statement by Ed Davis—the only black city councilman—warning that Akron's west side could turn into a slum. Ed Davis was also a founding member of FHCS. Why did he make such a statement? Urban renewal relocation was the reason.

Councilman Davis warned of the increasing hordes of low-income families moving to the west side, at the very time that stabilization efforts were under way to make that area "a desirable integrated community" (WSN brochure, 1968). The editorial analyzed that situation, Davis's statement, and the community's response. The need for additional low-income housing dispersed throughout the metropolitan area was a major point made in the article, and the goals of FHCS' stabilization committee were explained in some detail.

"What is stabilization," the editorial asked. According to FHCS, it was "keeping a neighborhood racially integrated while continuing to attract white home-seekers to the area." In addition, it was "encouraging white families to move into integrated neighborhoods, and keeping existing white families from moving out because of fears and rumors" (*Beacon Journal*, July 17, 1968). The key to stabilization was the schools, and the maintenance of their racial integration and quality. The FHCS was quoted in the editorial as considering the 30% black enrollment "ideal" at west Akron's Buchtel High School. The editorial ended with the recognition that "in the end, however, stabilization in west Akron will depend on integration elsewhere. One cannot be very successful without the other." All participants came to learn this, and much more.

The seven founders who planned the first public meeting of west-side residents prepared 7,000 announcement flyers, which were distributed door-to-door by Boy Scouts. But they really expected only about fifty people to come. They set up fifty chairs in the Westlawn Church basement, where the meeting was to be held, and were astonished when 250 residents came. They had held three informal meetings since July planning this event, and they were delighted with the unexpected crowds. Their delight turned to chagrin when they found that many of those who came thought that stabilization meant keeping blacks out.

When the goals of the new west-side group became clear, about 150 people got up and left. Integration was not for them. Those who stayed were witnesses to the beginning of a bold, new, controversial—and often misunderstood—effort. As in other movement groups across the country, and in National Neighbors as well, the concept of stabilization was not clear to everyone. Confusion about its meaning arose periodically throughout the existence of the organization.

Four days after the first public meeting, a featured editorial appeared in the *Akron Beacon Journal*, titled "To Stabilize and Improve." It began with the statement that Akron's west-side area could become "one of the nation's model integrated communities if residents and property owners carry on from the exciting start they made Tuesday in forming a neighborhood association" (*Beacon Journal*, Sept. 23, 1967). The turnout of 250 people who came to the meeting was described as "a true cross-section of races, religions, and interests to discuss mutual concerns arising from the fact that the area is changing."

Another public meeting held one month later gave the new group greater organizational strength. A twenty-one-member steering committee was elected, and bylaws were adopted by 150 people who again gathered in Westlawn Church's basement on October 17. The bylaws established nine standing committees to conduct the group's program; dues were set at one dollar per person, and membership was unrestricted.

The group's geographical location was named as "west Akron's Copley-Delia-Slosson neighborhood," which clearly placed it as a biracial area. The area south of Copley Road, which included Slosson Street, was predominantly black, largely from urban renewal relocation. The boundaries of the WSN area remained intact throughout their existence. They were originally selected to coincide with the attendance zone of the high school serving the area: Buchtel High School: Mull Avenue on the north, Wooster Avenue on the south, the expressway on the west, and Portage Path and Exchange streets on the east. This area included some 10,000 households and covered over 200 blocks; it represented one-seventh of the city of Akron. This size could well have qualified it as a separate city. Many times over the years, in fact, some west-side residents wanted to secede from the union.

A news article about WSN's second organizational meeting gave the new group's purpose as, "to attain and maintain a stable, integrated community" and "to promote community harmony and improvements" (*Beacon Journal*, Oct. 18, 1967). In the next twenty years, they did try to achieve all of this. Luckily, when they began they had no idea how incredibly difficult it would be.

STRUCTURE

We turn now to an examination of how the group operated. Included in the structural aspects of the organization are their governance, membership, finances, meetings, representation, board, committees, and staffing. We will analyze these over three phases of organizational development: Phase one—a time of mobilization—I have placed from 1967 to 1975. My reason for selecting this cutoff date is that it marked the beginning of serious change in the group's activity, leading to a five year series of funded projects. Phase two—a time of maturation—is from 1976 to 1982, during which all the funded projects were conducted with staffing. Phase three—a time of institutionalization—is from 1983 to the present, during which WSN returned to an unfunded state and a time of reorganization.

Phase One: 1967–75

The biracial makeup of the founding steering committee was perpetuated in all subsequent boards of directors, with the black proportion becoming somewhat greater over the years. The first temporary steering committee had four black members out of twelve. The first elected steering committee had twenty-one members, of whom nine were black. Twenty years later, the 1987 board of directors had a black woman president and thirteen black members out of twenty-three. This was a consciously planned effort to maintain substantial black representation and involvement in the direction of the group's work. Three early constitutions show this intent.

The first guiding document stated that the governing body "shall be composed of a Steering Committee of 21, as broadly representative of community interests as possible" (proposed bylaws, Oct. 3, 1967). Though other changes were made in later documents, this phrase remained in all other governing bylaws and was reflected in all the printed literature of the organization.

This earliest document of the organization reflected an expressed wish of some of the founders, especially the clergy, that the organization be "welded by goal orientation rather than formal structure" (minutes, July 20, 1967). The one-page simple proposed bylaws contained only five brief sections concerning name, purpose, structure, membership, nominations, and elections. Nine standing committees were to be created, with chairs appointed by the steering committee to be elected from the floor. Membership was to be open to all who agreed with the purposes of the organization, listed simply as "to attain and maintain a stable, integrated community." Much of this simplicity was lost in the second guiding document of WSN.

The second written guide was presented six months later to the elected steering committee for approval. This second document—now five pages long—was called a constitution rather than proposed temporary bylaws, and it named the governing body a board of directors rather than a steering committee. The same number of members was given, but now the organization was referred to as a corporation that was to be biracial and interfaith (constitution, 1968). In this second document, the purpose was broadened to include six specific goals and all the additional changes and expansion dealt with organizational structure. Included in this structural section were details pertaining to the board of directors, its officers, its executive committee, the standing committees, and the members. A new section on amendments was also added in this second proposed governing document.

The third and final constitution was very similar to the second one, with minor changes made and approved by the steering committee one month later. This version served as the principal guide to the organization throughout its existence, though additional minor changes were suggested periodically. Had the founders been able to anticipate all that would happen to their group and neighborhood, they might have constructed a different type of document.

Though their constitution was very specific about the duties of each officer and about the purpose of the organization, it was not specific enough about the function of the executive committee and the method of electing future directors. Yet it was too specific about naming standing committees and dues categories, which had to be periodically revised. The constitution served the organization very well during the first phase of their existence, but in the second two phases, as leadership and organizational skills declined, the constitution was less and less helpful to the ever-changing board of directors. Interpretation of it sometimes became a point of dissension within the group, as they faced harder and harder obstacles to achieving their goals.

The constitutionally mandated method of electing the board of directors made no provision for geographical representation of the area, and it made no provision of mandatory retirement after a stipulated length of service on the board. This had two results: some neighborhoods in the WSN area were not represented, and some board members suffered burnout. As in some other cities we have examined, the Akron group was underrepresented in their board and membership by the predominantly white sections and by some black sections of their area. Much of the leadership came from the well-integrated portions of WSN's area, and adjacent neighborhoods. The peripheral geographical sections were much less involved.

Thus, the constitutional phrase urging that the governing body be "as broadly representative of community interests as possible" had no explicit mechanism for achieving this. The constitution merely stated that nominations for the board were to be made by a nominating committee made up of one representative from each standing committee. An unwritten policy, however, that was usually followed by nominating committees over the years was that the board should be composed of equal numbers of males, females, blacks, whites, and residents of both north and south of Copley Road (the Akron Mason-Dixon line, dividing white and black for many years). But in later years, it became more and more difficult to recruit anyone to serve on the board of directors, especially males of either race.

Because the constitution allowed unlimited reelection to one- or two-year terms on the board, a few of the original board members served as long as twelve years. Others who were elected subsequently remained for as long as nine years. None of these was able to sustain unlimited energy and enthusiasm, however, and their service and attendance at monthly board meetings waned considerably.

Though a 1970 constitutional amendment made it possible to remove any board member who had two consecutive unexcused absences, this was later interpreted to mean three absences. Thus, a board member who came to one out of three board meetings could remain. If they called in with some excuse, they could remain on the board indefinitely without attending meetings. This did not make for a very vigorous or effective governing body.

The only significant changes in the constitution, made in phase two, concerned quorums and dues and the executive committee. The original constitution called for a majority of board members to be present before any business could be officially conducted. This was changed in 1981 to make it possible for only one-third of the board to be present to conduct official business. The reason for this was obvious: dwindling attendance at meetings. And one reason for that was insufficient new blood on the board, resulting in fatigue and burnout by old members.

Two other constitutional changes in phase two removed the specific dues structure and expanded the executive committee. Each of these changes reflected organizational changes, which in turn reflected neighborhood changes, the most significant of which was the marked increase of blacks in three of the five census tracts of the WSN area (see Tables 2 and 3 and Figure 3, Appendix A).

West Side Neighbors was a totally volunteer organization for their first ten years. During this time, the board of directors set policy and the volunteer committees carried out the program. The minutes of board of directors' meetings during the first phase show a unification of thought and action. Though the constitution said little about the committees, they were the heart of the organization in the first two phases and worked zealously to implement the group's goals. The constitution created nine standing committees: "schools, publicity, neighborhood conservation, recreation, city services and safety, community education, finance and membership, block organization, housing" (constitution, 1968). Very few controversies arose between committees and the board during phase one. Suggestions made by each to the other were well received and generally accepted, though discussion was lively. The wish of some of the founders to have the group guided by "goal orientation rather than formal structure" did prevail in phase one.

Board meetings, held monthly in the homes of board members on Sunday evenings, were largely devoted to hearing committee reports. As committees grew, and as their work expanded and they needed more discussion, the meetings became longer and longer despite clear efforts to keep them short. As the neighborhood changed racially and economically, responding to this change required more and more group action and time and energy.

Though the board did not seriously begin to write and submit proposals for funding until 1976—the beginning of phase two—their awareness of their need for funding and staffing grew throughout phase one. When in their fourth year the board was offered free office space in the church of one of the founders, they were grateful but concerned about who would manage it (minutes, July 1971). Two months later, they discussed a fund-raising monthly paper drive, which they thought could support a part-time secretary to help in the church office. But the paper drive never materialized, so there was no money for a secretary. They remained in the church office, unstaffed, until the church was sold in 1977.

The need for some paid staff continued, as did the need for more funds. In 1974, they did get a small grant of $500 from IBM, for paint to assist hardship cases in fixing their homes. This was arranged by a board member who was an employee of IBM, and who later became WSN's seventh president. This is the only grant WSN received during their first phase of development, and even that tiny amount was hard to administer with no office help.

During WSN's first eight years (1967–1975), which I am designating as phase one, the structure of the organization and its operation remained much the same. Board meetings were held monthly in members' homes, later in the church office, then again in members' homes. Public meetings for residents and members were also held monthly in rotating church locations or other neighborhood facilities. The branch public library was a favorite public meeting spot since it was racially unidentifiable and located on Copley Road, then neutral turf.

Board elections were held annually in October, with constitutional provisions for half the board to remain, and half to be replaced. Committees were responsible for the program of at least one community (public) meeting, but later in phase one this was changed to having the vice-president totally responsible for the public meeting programs and arrangements. For the first four years, public meetings were held monthly. As attendance began to drop, summer meetings were eliminated. Later, winter meetings were eliminated. Finally, public meetings were held four times a year, twice in the early and late fall (before Christmas), and twice in the mid- and late spring (before the middle of June).

Finances of the organization were always slim pickings. The treasurer's reports during phase one show a general fund balance ranging from $278.28 in June 1970 to $2,450.44 in December 1975. All of their funds came from dues and contributions, augmented by special fund-raising events. During phase one, all treasurer's reports showed two accounts. One was the general fund for operating expenses, the other was the American Field Service Fund which was for a foreign student scholarship sponsored by WSN since 1968. An international dinner held each spring generated the money for the scholarship, which amounted to over $800 a year. This fund was usually larger than the operating fund for WSN, and sometimes this provoked negative discussion within the board—rare during the first phase.

Membership during phase one was larger than in any other phase. Over 700 families, representing 2,800 persons, paid dues to the organization during the first few years of its existence. This dwindled down to 500 at the end of phase one, however, and fewer later on. Dues were extremely low: one dollar per year for individuals, two dollars for families, ten dollars for organizations, and fifteen dollars or more for sponsors. Membership drives during phase one were somewhat haphazard, usually consisting of a mailed reminder and occasional door-to-door solicitation.

Three announcements made at board meetings toward the end of phase one heralded the beginning of a new phase of development for WSN. One small item tucked at the end of the minutes led to a large change: "Suggestion that research be started on 'housing repossessions' in West Akron, and that such information could be of real value to WSN" (minutes, Dec. 9, 1973). This led to WSN's first redlining study and annual mortgage lending reports.

The second significant announcement was the president's report "on a meeting held at Buchtel High School by the Summit County Criminal Justice Commission. At the meeting, it was announced that there remains a possibility of Federal funding for neighborhood groups that submit proposals on crime prevention projects in the West Akron area" (minutes, Nov. 9, 1975). This paved the way for the first funded staffed project of WSN.

The third announcement related directly to the first one, though it was made two years later: "Sara Milner asked if WSN would be interested in sponsoring redlining research to be done by university students at no cost to WSN. Motion passed that WSN sponsor such a program" (minutes, Dec. 14, 1975). This venture led to profound changes for WSN, and two additional projects funded by two private foundations, the City of Akron, and United Way.

Phase Two: 1976–82

Phase two was marked by two critical changes for WSN: serious pursuit and eventual receipt of funding, and inexperienced leadership. This was not a good combination. Until 1975, the board of WSN was made up of skilled and knowledgeable organizational leaders. Late in 1975, an inexperienced member reluctantly agreed to become president of the board, with the promise of much help from long-time and experienced board members, who were unwilling to assume a leadership role. This began a series of inexperienced presidents, who served sometimes reluctantly, sometimes eagerly, but never very ably during the next two phases. Some WSN presidents used their learning experience on the WSN board to go on to elected leadership roles in the community.

The first news of funding came with this announcement: "Bob Wendall reported that the crime program with the WSN, YMCA and the WHEN groups has been funded and that we will be responsible for coming up with a 5% matching fund ($1,500). This will be due in early fall, before the program begins" (minutes, March 14, 1976). So began the first funded project for WSN, under an incredibly awkward structural arrangement. Funded by the federal Law Enforcement Assistance Agency (LEAA) program, the money came to the state Department of Economic and Community Development, from which it was passed on to the county Criminal Justice Division, and then subcontracted to the local agency administering the program. If this was not cumbersome enough, the grant to Akron was funnelled through the local YMCA, and then down to two neighborhood organizations, of which one was WSN. The grant was for $29,345 for one year, and required a 5% match, as noted above.

WSN had no experience in running a funded program. They had never hired anyone before, they had never had budgets of more than $3,000 to handle, they had no knowledge of how to deal with staff, and they did not know anything about crime prevention. What they did was the best they could think of; they asked one board member who was knowledgeable in personnel matters to oversee the project. She was to work on a joint three-way administrative committee in conjunction with the YMCA and the other neighborhood group involved, WHEN (Wooster Hawkins East Neighbors, which WSN had helped to organize in 1969). The YMCA was to do all the paper work and recordkeeping.

The awkward name of West Akron Community Crime Prevention Project (WACCPP) was given to this program, which called for a staff of one director, two community organizers (one was part-time), and one part-time secretary. Most of the funds went to the salaries of the staff, with $2,700 for supplies. The program was an excellent one, and will be discussed more fully in the next section. Here we are concerned with the structural arrangements, which were unwieldy even for a most experienced organization.

Monthly administrative meetings were held with two representatives from each neighborhood organization and the administrator of the YMCA. The two WSN board members who attended both worked full-time, and also were expected to attend regular WSN monthly board meetings in addition to these project meetings. The WSN board heard monthly reports from these two representatives, but didn't feel directly involved with the project. This continued for the first few months of the project, until things began to go wrong. Then the board heard an earful, and did not know how to resolve the difficulties.

The first inkling that anything was wrong with the newly funded project came only three and a half months after the new director was hired. By then it was too late for the WSN board to do anything about it—even if they had known what to do. The minutes simply state: "Director resigned because of differences with [Project] Board. Two assistants are continuing on" (minutes, April 17, 1977).

The resignation was not good for the program, though one of the assistants eventually took over the directorship and did reasonably well for the rest of the project's first year. The next year, a third director was hired after the second one left for personal reasons. The third director was later joined by a WSN executive director (their first and last), neither of whom knew anything about community organizing or neighborhood safety. In fact, no one who came after the first director had the necessary training and experience for this type of program.

In the second year of the project—which now was called Neighborhood Safety rather than Crime Prevention—WSN assumed total control of the project after the other neighborhood group withdrew. They also moved their office to a new location—Westlawn Church on Copley Road, the same place where they had begun the organization. They decided to use the second-year grant money to hire a WSN director who would oversee the safety program and other WSN activities. "With a new location—new goals—and a place to publish our newsletter, we will be better able to serve the community" (minutes, June 11, 1978).

The new WSN executive director lasted less than a year, and was never replaced. At one point during his stay, he offered a $5,000 WSN reward for information about a killer of a neighborhood church secretary. WSN's board panicked. Their treasurer's report at that time read: "Liabilities—$7,533.89, Cash Balance—$47.08" (treasurer's report, Jan. 31, 1979). Half the reward fund was raised by the director and staff before he left, the other half was raised by the church that was the scene of the killing; the killer was found, and the reward was paid. But WSN was very uncomfortable during this entire time. Though they did indeed begin to recognize their responsibilities in having a funded project, they never again had a director.

A three-page chronology from August 1978 shows the sequence of events in WSN's first funded project. The reason for the preparation of the chronology was that subsequent new board members and new presidents had no idea of how that project came to be the responsibility of WSN. This, in fact, was what happened to other funded projects and some general WSN policies as well. Subsequent board members did not know what these earlier actions were about, and how WSN came to be involved with them. The story needed repeating constantly.

We can see why funded projects may have seemed to WSN a troublesome burden at that time. Though they were pleased to have the prestige that came with a funded program, and were grateful for the chance to operate a constructive program that benefited their area, they were clearly uneasy with the responsibility of managing such a program. In fact, they did not know how to do it adequately. Their lack of experienced organizational members and leaders became more and more apparent when the funded projects began. In addition, as long as a staff ran the program, the board never felt that it "owned" the program. Conflicts and misunderstandings were inevitable in projects that were underfunded, understaffed, ill-structured, and too little and too late.

Two more funded projects were soon to be WSN's responsibility. They had written and submitted a proposal for the funding of Project REACH, consisting of an internal program within the neighborhood (INREACH) and an external program focused on contacts outside the neighborhood (OUTREACH). These are both discussed in detail in the next section. Though WSN insisted that both programs had to occur simultaneously for maximum effect, they were unable to get funding from one source for the entire project.

They first submitted their proposal to the Ford Foundation in 1977, which was soliciting proposals from neighborhood stabilization groups across the country. When they were turned down by Ford, they rewrote the proposal and submitted it to the city of Akron, asking for $32,000 for a one-year demonstration program. They negotiated with the city for almost two years until an arrangement was made for the partial funding of the external program. This is one indicator of the city's unhelpful role. Meanwhile, when WSN learned that the city would not fund the entire project but might fund only the external portion, they divided the project's programs, rewrote them as two proposals, and submitted a separate funding proposal for the internal (INREACH) portion to a local foundation. To cover portions of the external program (UPON), they also submitted a proposal to another area foundation.

In somewhat dizzying succession, spaced some months apart, all proposals were eventually funded. But each was funded for only one year—and each by a different source—so the programs began and ended at different times, with different bookkeeping and report systems required for each. By 1980, the WSN treasurer had to name seven different accounts in the treasurer's reports. Small wonder that the board and its leaders, new and largely inexperienced in organizational matters, were confused and troubled by the funded programs.

Both of the subsequently funded projects posed further administrative difficulties for the inexperienced WSN board. By the time these projects were funded, from three different sources, the earlier safety project had ended and all personnel disbanded. But the WSN office (the third one in two years) and all the furniture and supplies were still available and had, in fact, been written into the funding proposals as in-kind contributions of WSN.

Most of the modest funds ($28,781) for the one-year REACH project were allocated for one full-time field representative and one part-time secretary. The WSN housing committee was to be the guiding body of the project, since they had been responsible for the writing of the original proposal. One founding board member and a member of the housing committee, Sara Milner, was written into the REACH funding proposal as a part-time consultant-director, to show that some expertise would be available for the administration of that program. A small consultant's fee ($4,800) was included, which Milner donated to an escrow account for WSN's future use. This she designated for part-time office staff to be used after the funded projects ended.

When the external program was finally funded by the city, Milner—who resigned from the board to become the project consultant—conducted an intensive orientation for the small staff and held weekly staff meetings. This worked very well until the second part of the project became funded a few months later from a separate source, and new staff (one part-time coordinator and one part-time block organizer) were added.

All were working out of the same tiny one-room storefront office with the same part-time secretary and the same part-time volunteer consultant-director. The internal and external parts of the project were now all operative, as they had been intended, but the administrative responsibilities and demands were excessively heavy for Milner. Each time new staff came on, they needed orientation and training from her. She devoted more and more of her time to the project during this period, and the difficulties continued to mount.

In 1980, when the UPON project's first year ended and part-time student interns were carrying on that program, the former project secretary became WSN's program coordinator—paid with the escrow fund established from the consultant's fee. A new full-time VISTA (Volunteer In Service To America) volunteer worker was added to the internal program (INREACH), which was now supervised by the part-time program coordinator. Though the staff and board were delighted to have a full-time person (the only such one) assigned for one year to the INREACH program, she soon caused a great deal of internal trouble for the organization. She seemed intent on changing WSN's goals, structure, program, and constitution.

Because the VISTA volunteer was the only full-time worker in the WSN office, she came to have tremendous power and influence over the other two part-time staff, and a brand-new WSN president. They formed an intense little office clique, with the VISTA volunteer as their leader. WSN's board, meanwhile, was largely ignorant of the inner dynamics of this office quartet. The VISTA worker conducted intensive nine-hour meetings with the other three, in which she practiced brainstorming—a skill she had recently acquired in a VISTA training session. After two terrible months in which the foursome wore themselves out, they learned that a second VISTA volunteer had been assigned to the INREACH program.

In came VISTA number two—this one meek, mild, and painfully shy. VISTA number one was assigned by the program coordinator to train her in block organizing (which number one had refused to continue doing). VISTA number two developed a distinct dislike of number one, and was too shy to do block organizing, so she was then assigned to help with the USE program, directed by another part-time coordinator. While this entire mess was continuing, few on the board were aware of it. Even if they had known, they would not have been able to handle it. The only relieving thought for those involved was that eventually the VISTA workers would leave. In fact, shortly after VISTA number one had accomplished her unbelievable chaos, she did leave—three months early. Few were sorry to see her go.

While the second VISTA worker finished out her year helping the part-time USE coordinator with that program, a third tiny grant of $1,000 from a private foundation was being used for the third year of the external program (UPON). In fact, that was the only funding for that program for its second and third years. Consultant Milner continued to supervise it as a volunteer, having gotten board approval to use the money for hiring occasional student interns and for copying and mailing expenses.

Though monthly reports about all the programs went to the board, they never really felt as though these funded programs were theirs. Whereas before funding, board members and committees had been the only ones involved in any of WSN's activities, now "outside" people were doing the work of the organization. What role did the board play—what role should it play—while all these others were running the show? They did not know.

Even more critical was the fact that the money from the escrow fund would soon run out, and then how would WSN run the office? And who would do all the work? By this time, the old dedicated leadership on the board had long since gone, and the remaining board members were not giving WSN their top priority in time, energy, or concern. They were "inclusive" rather than "exclusive" members (Zald & Ash 1966), with their involvement spread over other groups and activities.

When the board finally realized in 1982 that they had to cut the weekly hours of their program coordinator from twenty to ten, since they could not afford to pay for more, they lost their experienced program coordinator. Then they had to face, for the first time, the process of hiring a new one—with no funding to count on. They became involved in preparing various funding proposals to numerous sources for several different projects. All were turned down. WSN now faced the prospect of running their office and organization with little money and little help. So began phase three.

Phase Three: 1983–

From 1983 to the present, WSN existed with no external funding. Only membership dues and contributions kept the group going. But their membership was substantially lower than in earlier years. Whereas in phase one the average number of households supporting WSN was over 700, by phase three it was down to 450. Rapid turnover of residents was one reason for this. WSN never established a mechanism of quickly reaching out to new residents to enlist their support and involvement in the organization. Membership dues were still the modest five dollars per household, hardly enough to sustain an office and staff.

Their structure during phase three returned to what it had been during phase one, with the board setting policy and committees carrying out the program. There were, however, some important differences between phase one and phase three. In phase three, WSN maintained an office and had part-time secretarial help, which they never had in phase one. Also, in phase three the board was a tired one, as well as inexperienced. Even new board members became tired quickly. They suffered not only from fatigue, but also burnout, discouragement and a new malaise—internal bickering. None of these had occurred in phase one.

The WSN area had changed drastically since phase one, both racially and economically. The business area was unkempt and run-down, while awaiting a newly funded city rehabilitation program long sought by WSN. More vacant houses and unmowed lawns were evident, despite WSN's frenzied processing of housing complaints. By now, the area had been saturated with public housing tenants, despite WSN's vehement objections. Moreover, the WSN area was glutted with "group homes"—residential care facilities for various categories of needy people, such as disabled, delinquents, mentally ill, and so on. The board was affected by all of this. How, then, were they able to sustain an office and some staff with no funding, reduced membership contributions, weak leadership, and low morale?

One way was through the very low rent they paid ($50 a month) as a favor from a store owner, and later a church, who gave them space. A second way was through annual contributions from the five major banks of Akron. This was a clear result of sending out each year a volunteer field representative to discuss with bank presidents the annual WSN mortgage lending report and reinvestment—a carryover from phase two's UPON Project. And a third way was through the Senior Workers Action Program (SWAP), which offered free, federally funded part-time office help.

In 1983, when their second program coordinator left, WSN's personnel committee applied to SWAP for a senior office worker. For WSN, this was a heaven-sent arrangement. They were able to sustain the cost of their office, their newsletters, mailings and other modest expenses through their annual membership drives, and in addition could have twenty hours a week free office help. For a time this arrangement worked very well, but soon WSN found there was no free lunch.

Once more, they ran into confusion and anxiety with staffing, generated by the uneasy structural arrangement they had drifted into. Their arrangement of having a nonboard member (the chair of the personnel committee) supervise the office and staff only occurred because the president refused to accept this responsibility. No one on the board was willing to do it either. When trouble arose with staff, as it inevitably would, the president did not know how to handle it. Neither did the board.

The troubles with the SWAP worker did not surface until after some serene months had passed. The difficulties involved a series of trivial misunderstandings coming from poor communication between her and several board members, and confusion as to who said what and who was in charge. Finally, she asked for a transfer, and WSN lost their valuable free help. This was entirely due to inept management.

The exit of the SWAP office worker took place in the midst of the 1984 WSN membership drive, which required daily bookkeeping and mailings of monetary receipts and their acknowledgments. WSN handled that crisis by finding four office volunteers to help out until the membership drive was completed. After six weeks, one of the office volunteers became the new WSN administrative assistant, working ten hours a week at minimum wage. WSN continued with this arrangement, though with changing personnel, for the remainder of phase three.[2]

This crisis had one positive result, which continued for the rest of phase three. The weak president finally and reluctantly assumed the role of office supervisor—pushed into this by the personnel committee chair and one strong board member. The personnel committee and some other WSN members had by now prepared complete written details on office guidelines, membership drives, newsletter preparation, bulk mailings, and so on. But WSN for a long time was not able to quite overcome the image some others still held of nonboard members "running the WSN office." This was yet another reflection of the weak leadership WSN had in phases two and three. Only in 1987 was there a re-emergence of some skilled leadership, when a new president and new board were elected who were completely in charge of their office and programs—now all unfunded. By this time, however, some other serious events had occurred which threatened the existence of WSN.

In addition to the area's racial and quality changes noted above, which raised valid questions about WSN's long-standing goal of integration maintenance, two other organizations appeared on WSN's turf in phase three. These were intrusive movement organizations (Nelson 1974), with grave consequences for WSN. The first one was the re-formation in 1985 of a Westside Block Club Council, under the sponsorship of a newly elected city councilman from the WSN neighborhood.

Though publicly proclaimed at first as a partnership between WSN and the council, it was quickly apparent that this was a separate organization vying for recognition and funds as a legitimate representative of the west side of Akron. In fact, the councilman had already established a replica of the committee structure of WSN. His formation of a block organization committee and the subsequent block club council caused much dismay among WSN board members, and much confusion among neighborhood residents.

Though attempts were made by the WSN board to discuss and resolve this confusion with the councilman and his organization's leaders, no resolution was ever made. The unfortunate result was that in 1987 WSN's board decided to give up its block organization committee, since the councilman's group was doing that work with a full-time coordinator. This may have been good for the neighborhood, but certainly not for WSN. It was, however, a clear sign that others perceived WSN as waning once their grants expired. In fact, they had not done any new block organization for the past two years.

The second intrusive organization came in 1987, when a United Way grant was given to another group, located outside of the west-side area, to conduct a west-side program. Though WSN pleaded with United Way administrators to consider them for the funding, United Way's response was that capable, funded, staffed agencies should get the grant. This all came about because of the ending of another west-side United Way agency—the West Akron Community Services, a facility located south of Copley Road in a predominantly black neighborhood. When this agency's funds were terminated, pressure mounted in the black community for a replacement. When such a replacement was not seen as feasible, the United Way gave the equivalent funds ($43,000) to one of its existing agencies—the East Akron Community House—to conduct a community development program on the west side of Akron. The location of the program was to be south of Copley Road, in the black portion of WSN's area.

West Side Neighbors immediately contacted the East Akron administrators in an attempt to establish cooperative relations and a clear understanding of who was doing what. Amicable relations were established, and WSN's president was assured that whatever they wanted to do cooperatively could be arranged. This did not happen easily, however, and tensions mounted. The presence of this new group on WSN's turf further removed WSN's legitimacy as the spokesman for west Akron.

They continued to put up a valiant front, and approached their twentieth anniversary with a series of planned community events. A committee coordinator's report shows that their committees were not functioning very well in phase three (coordinator's report, June 1984). In fact, the only committee that continued to function throughout all three phases was the housing committee. By phase three, the schools committee was dead, though several attempts were made to revive it. Since the schools were now virtually all-black in the westside area, this was a sore point with many WSN members and was reflected in the inaction of the schools committee. The block organization function was taken over late in phase three by another group, as noted above. And the other committees were briefly resurrected after each board and officers were elected every fall. They were not able to sustain themselves very well. It became more and more difficult to recruit people to chair and serve on the committees.

At one point in 1986, the chairperson of the housing committee was also WSN's committee coordinator and chair of the business committee. This was all one and the same person, who was a long-time board member. News of her burnout and resignation in 1986 did not come as a surprise to those who knew what she was trying to do. She also resigned because she was disgusted with the bickering on the board. Her loss was a severe one for the WSN board, since she was one of the few remaining active, dedicated, and knowledgeable members.

The membership committee functioned only to plan and execute the annual WSN membership drive. The success of the annual membership drive became very critical, since all their operating funds came from it. The WSN annual membership drives brought in about $4,800 each year, including contributions from the five major banks of Akron. This contribution from the banks was one outcome of the mortgage lending studies first begun in phase one and continued annually thereafter. These are discussed more fully below in the section on WSN's program, to which we will turn after a brief review of WSN's stated goals during their three phases of development.

GOALS

Phase One: 1967–75

The purpose of the new organization was first stated in the proposed temporary bylaws, prepared three months after the group first met. That purpose was very simply stated: "To attain and maintain a stable, integrated community" (proposed bylaws, Oct. 3, 1967). Never again was that purpose so simply presented. The following month, a "Tentative Statement" of WSN's goals and plans was distributed to community leaders and organizations throughout the city of Akron as well as on the west side of Akron. This statement was one poorly duplicated sheet with six paragraphs explaining why WSN had formed and what they intended to do. It was used as their first proposal for funding, which was not granted.

To explain why they had formed, the first paragraph naively said: "As Negroes begin moving in greater numbers into areas outside the 'ghetto,' more and more neighborhoods in metropolitan areas will face the question of racial integration. These neighborhoods will have to decide whether they can stabilize on an interracial basis, or whether they will become resegregated as all-Negro areas." This was naive because it implied that any neighborhood could make an internal, autonomous decision to stabilize or not, without regard to outside forces. The next paragraph told who they were and what they believed. They described themselves as a "biracial interfaith" group of citizens who formed a voluntary "community stabilization" organization, believing that "positive constructive planning can lead to a peaceful, harmonious, stable integrated community."

The first issue of the WSN newsletter had its lead column devoted to "What WSN Is and Hopes to Do" (WSN *Bulletin*, Feb. 1968). Here, the goals were implicit in the first two questions which began the column: "Are you concerned about 'changing conditions' in your neighborhood? About maintaining good schools, city services, recreational facilities, your property values? Your neighbors are doing something about these things. You can help." The only graphic design on the first newsletter was of two clasped hands—one black, one white. No other design appeared until 1974—the end of phase one—when the official, artist-designed logo of WSN began to appear on all printed materials.

Two months after their first newsletter, a much more complex statement of purpose appeared in the first draft of WSN's constitution, most of which was retained for the rest of their existence. This document listed five purposes of the organization, with some changes made by the steering committee, which received, amended, and approved the new constitution on May 19, 1968. The five purposes were: to study the problems of successfully integrated communities around the country; to determine those things which tend toward the stabilization of the neighborhoods; to educate the members and others in the community on the means and methods of achieving a stable, integrated neighborhood; to arrange meetings, discussions, literature, and publications to educate the citizenry in the means by which a stable, integrated community can be maintained; and to take action to implement the aforementioned purposes. These five stated purposes or goals remained intact for the next twenty years.

An analysis of WSN's printed materials over the years also shows constancy of goals, though different emphases were made at different times. Their first printed brochure, developed in 1968 with the aid of a professional public relations expert who was a founding board member, was designed to promote the west side as a place to live. Only one small section referred to the organization:

"This message is a service of WSN, a biracial interfaith group of residents committed to the idea of working toward the best possible community. WSN plans for and acts to provide a peaceful, harmonious, stable, and integrated community." Ten committees were listed, as well as the names and addresses of five officers.

In no way does this first brochure reflect the deep thought and soul-searching that went into its development. Minutes of a board meeting at the end of WSN's first year are more revealing:

A discussion followed the committee reports as to a restatement of the purposes of WSN— What is stabilization? Is it to keep neighborhoods integrated? Is it to do something for the black people? Is it to do something for the white people? Is it our purpose to learn to live and work and play together and otherwise improve our particular community as a part of the larger whole of improving the city of Akron? Is it a matter of changing attitudes? It was agreed that it was all of these things and perhaps a restatement including these goals be worked out and put in a new brochure or flyer for WSN. (minutes, Dec. 15, 1968)

Neither the first nor second brochure said much about goals. A second brochure, developed in 1971, also promoted the west side but said little or nothing about WSN's goals. Again, the goals were implicit since reference to the organization in this brochure was only about what it did: "WSN is an organization of community residents who see to it that their neighborhood continues to offer more. They contribute time to committees that keep careful watch on schools and education, city services and neighborhood conservation and improvement efforts. They see to it that problems get solved in west Akron" (WSN brochure, 1971).

Two goal-setting workshops were held by and for the WSN board during phase one, two more in phase two, and one in phase three. These offer evidence of the ongoing struggles of the organization to fulfill their goals. They also reveal the differences in leadership and concerns in each of the three phases of WSN's development. The first workshop, held on January 31, 1970, was led by one of the board members, who was a social worker. The group broke into three small groups to discuss goals and ways of achieving them in three major areas: housing, education and conservation/city services. After lunch and reports from each group, the board was officially convened to consider and act on any of their recommendations.

The housing group strongly urged WSN to develop a more effective housing committee to "deal with such strong adversaries as the Board of Realtors, AMHA and Urban Renewal. How to block counterforces??? What other factors cause residents to flee???... Answer: lack of law enforcement and code enforcement" (minutes, Jan. 31, 1970). They also recommended that a housing fund be established to buy and rehabilitate houses in the WSN area before the AMHA bought them (this was never done, unfortunately). They further urged the formation of a listing service to sell homes and find buyers on the west side. Finally, they urged a two-pronged simultaneous attack on both housing and education fronts, since these were interrelated and must be dealt with together. Most of the recommendations made at this workshop were attempted or completed over the next decade.

The second board workshop on goal-setting took place one year later. It was to be the last one for seven years. This workshop was devoted primarily to the goals and functions of three committees: community education, housing, and schools. The recommendations from the schools committee were simple and benign; they wished to insure adequate resources for "high-level education to all children, particularly culturally-limited ones," and they wanted a "healthy racial atmosphere" in the schools.

Much less tranquil were the recommendations from the housing committee. This was a newly formed committee, which raised such searching questions as: "What, precisely, is meant by the term 'stabilization' in the WSN constitution? . . . What is meant by integration? . . . Do we integrate all of Akron, West Side, or a more limited area? . . . Shall we limit our endeavors to definite boundary lines?" (minutes, Jan. 23, 1971).

During phase one, the goals of WSN and their committees were discussed and thoroughly examined more intensively than in any other period of development. By the end of phase one, however, they were already showing signs of fatigue and discouragement. Both of these reactions reflected three things: (1) the rapid disquieting racial and economic changes that had taken place in their area; (2) the tremendous amounts of work they had to do—all as volunteers—to keep abreast of these changes; and (3) the enormous difficulties of maintaining adequate internal communication with no central coordination or staffing.

Phase Two: 1976–82

Ushering in phase two was a president who somewhat reluctantly assumed the presidency when no one else on the board would do it. He set the tone for his presidency with the motto: "Together—Best in the West" (minutes, Oct. 10, 1976). His first action was a call for goal-setting by the board and all WSN members and committees. This set a pattern for the rest of phase two and into three for attempted annual goal-setting by committees.[3] In 1978, the board held one four-hour planning session. Another was held the following year, in 1979. No others were held until eight years later, at the end of our study period.

The 1978 planning session covered the primary goals of WSN and the goals and objectives of seven committees: housing, schools, publicity, business, membership, safety, and churches. An entire newsletter (Winter 1978) was devoted to the results of this planning session, which heralded the future of the organization.

The housing committee stated two goals at the 1978 planning session: to maintain an integrated neighborhood, and to seek funding for three activities concerning block-busting, redlining, and block club maintenance. This was, in fact, their REACH proposal; it was finally funded after years of trying, and became WSN's most important funded project. The schools committee had three goals: to insure quality, integrated education for the Buchtel cluster (all the schools in the neighborhood); to influence and support the Buchtel cluster in the direction of quality, integrated education; and to have a personal monitor for each school in the cluster. Their one subgoal reflected their prime concern at that time: to seek community support for the pending school desegregation lawsuit, which they had mobilized (newsletter, Winter 1978).

WSN's major and enduring brochure, first printed with their official logo in 1978, specifies five general organizational goals. Goals two and five below are the only ones not contained in the constitution; these two new goals of promotion and physical and social maintenance reflect the sober recognition of their changing neighborhood:

(1) To maintain our area as a stable, attractive, integrated community, (2) To promote our area as a desirable place to live and work with charm, convenience, and diversity, (3) To study the achievements of other successful interracial communities across the country, and apply them here, (4) To involve the residents of our area in actions to implement these goals, and (5) To provide a sense of community and to make that community worth living in.

The 1979 board planning meeting—the last one for the next eight years— was also a four-hour session on a Saturday afternoon, taking place this time in one of the board members' homes rather than a church. Seven topics concerned them: schools, funding, businesses, public relations, housing, block clubs, and economic development. For each of these, they set forth what they hoped to do, how they planned to do it, and who specifically would be responsible for doing it. By this time, they had an office and staff to assist them so staff was named as an implementer in all but two of these concerns. The two were schools and housing.

For schools, what they said they wanted to achieve and maintain was quality integrated education. This was becoming more and more elusive in their westside schools. They saw their function as monitoring, receiving and responding to complaints, and serving as a link between the community and schools. But even then, the schools committee—once WSN's largest committee, with twice as many members as the board itself—had become inactive. So the mission here was to reactivate the schools committee, if they could find someone to chair it. They did, but this did not achieve integrated schools.

The goal for the housing committee was simply stated: to maintain quality integrated neighborhoods. Toward that end, they wanted to implement their REACH proposal. This called for publicizing their completed redlining study with bank presidents, and meeting with real estate companies and corporation executives. Though this positively would require staffing to achieve, they stated that if they were unfunded they would begin this task as volunteers. They did.

One important program idea for 1979 was to obtain external and internal financial support. They wanted to "write and submit proposals to foundations, government, etc." (planning meeting summary, Jan. 13, 1979). They also wanted to begin an intensive membership drive and have special benefit events. They did all of this, but results came very late.

Phase Three: 1982–

The only other extended goal-setting meeting of the WSN board took place in 1987, the end of our study period. By this time, much had happened to WSN, their board, and their neighborhood as we have already noted. A brief review of this last planning retreat reveals the status and morale of the board as they approached WSN's twentieth anniversary.

The 1987 planning retreat was the most extended one WSN ever had. One all-day meeting was held on a Saturday in January; a second half-day meeting was held the following month. Both of these meetings relied on outside professionals, sought out by WSN's president, for the planning of the sessions. This was a clear reflection of the president's sense of inadequacy in herself and the board as leaders of the organization.

A careful study of the subjects considered and the results shows that they were very different from WSN's earlier planning and goal-setting meetings. The earlier ones focused on long-term and short-term specific program objectives, and were internally led. The later one focused primarily on organizational problems, and was led by outsiders.

The 1987 retreat was preceded by a handmade invitation: "WE NEED YOUR MIND, BODY, IDEAS / Bring Your Smile." Consideration of board concerns took up most of the day. Two concerns were on their minds: WSN's approaching twentieth anniversary, and the new Westside Block Club Council and what to do about it. This was the intrusive organization promoted by the fourth ward councilman, which was duplicating WSN's efforts.

They successfully dealt with the coming anniversary by setting up a special committee and outlining four special events to commemorate the anniversary: an essay contest, a carnival, a parade, and neighborhood pot luck dinners. (Only the parade materialized.) These were to take place during the summer, preceding a gala celebration dinner in the fall which did occur.

Their second concern—the competing Block Club Council—was less successfully handled. WSN's board had good reason for concern. They were shaken and thoroughly threatened by this one-year-old rival. They raised eight questions about the council's purpose and territory, and what they should do about it. Their final poignant question, most revealing of all, was: "Do we want to continue organizing our Block Clubs within our boundaries?" (retreat agenda for Jan. 17, 1987). The sad fact was that WSN had not done any block organizing for over a year, and had no one to do it. By even raising this question, they were indicating their willingness to abandon the most vital aspect of their organization—the one they had begun with, now as much needed as ever.

They concluded by recommending that both block club organizing groups work together—the one from WSN and the newly formed rival one. They suggested making the newer one an affiliate of WSN's older one. This was to be handled by the WSN executive committee. Though later minutes show that this was followed through with a meeting of representatives from both groups, nothing was ever resolved. There was, however, one definite result: WSN stopped their work with block clubs, and the block club committee was finally and openly acknowledged as defunct in 1987. Thus, one of the original objectives and the prime tactic of the organization was abandoned.

The rest of their concerns were aired in the afternoon portion of this one-day planning retreat. The subject of one of the three discussion groups indicates organizational weakness: "The group discussed existing committees, non-functioning committees and the need to reactivate them . . . and the need to review the goals and objectives of the existing committees" (retreat report, Jan. 17, 1987). This was certainly a sign of distress; it reflected the inactivity of several key committees at the time—not only block organization, but also schools, church, and membership. So keen was the need for help with committees that a second board retreat was scheduled for the next month, which was to focus only on committees.

The day ended with the president commenting that a retreat was a "safe, quiet place, a withdrawal," and that the board had withdrawn and spent a day in reflection. She and they were pleased with the results, with the board leaving "rejuvenating and rededicated" (president's letter, Feb. 2, 1987). Though not even half of what they said they wanted to do ever came to pass, they felt in control of their actions, and they felt a little hopeful. How remarkable that the human spirit can find hope in the midst of adversity and decline. Weakened, threatened, demoralized, but still planning, the WSN board made ready for their twentieth anniversary and the preparation of a twenty-year chronology of their activities. We turn now to an analysis of their program over those twenty years.

PROGRAM

For the first ten years of their existence, WSN conducted the usual array of programs so typical of other organizations in this movement. We mark the end of the first phase before the end of the decade, however, because of the waning in 1975 of skilled leadership and the beginning of a recognition of the need for a serious pursuit of funding. The fun and games days were then over, and a grim search for money began. This came with the realization that all their hopes and dreams would never come to pass without sustained staffing and coordination. Volunteers simply could not deal adequately with the massive institutional forces confronting them. This realization came very late in WSN's development. Whether it came too late remains to be seen.

WSN's program in all three phases was carried out by volunteer committees approved by the board of directors. Not all committees survived the three phases, however. In phase one, for example, recreation, community education, and neighborhood conservation committees were very active but were nonexistent by phase two. The major committees for most of WSN's existence were schools, block organization, and housing, which we will examine in all three phases.

Schools

Phase One. Some of the committees in phase one were as large as or larger than the board itself. One such committee was the schools committee, with forty-eight members, one of WSN's most important committees during their first and second phases of development. The schools committee was "a key factor in stabilization . . . devoted to the maintenance of first-rate educational programs in the area schools" (goals and plans statement, Nov. 1967).

In the first year of WSN's existence, the schools committee invited the Akron school superintendent and fifty members of his staff to be dinner guests of the WSN board. A news report on that dinner meeting commented: "The meeting was a milestone in bringing together an almost equal group of top school administrators and neighborhood residents for a conversational approach to solving problems" (*Akron Beacon Journal*, March 20, 1968). That conversational approach did not last long.

In that first year of WSN's existence, the schools committee worked with elementary school PTAs to meet and welcome new residents of the community, prepared a statement to send to the Board of Education concerning its "Blueprint for the '70's," found adult sponsors for several high school clubs, and supported and worked for passage of the school levy. In addition, the committee also prepared public relations materials supporting and promoting west-side schools; invited all new teachers in west-side schools to small dinner meetings with residents; sent speakers to all west-side schools to explain WSN's concerns and support for quality education; established task forces in all ten west-side schools; and sent dozens of letters and held numerous public and private meetings with school administrators and teachers concerning the maintenance of quality education in west-side schools.

Though meetings with school administrators continued throughout phase one, they were progressively less cordial as it became apparent that school officials had no intention of doing anything about the growing racial concentration in the west-side schools. Minutes of board meetings and other WSN documents in phase one are filled with increasingly anguished references to the growing racial imbalance in west-side schools and the perception of an accompanying reduction in the quality of education.

Repeated meetings, letters, and public statements from 1968 to 1973, all expressing the same mounting concerns of WSN's board, schools committee and residents, had the same result—inaction on the part of school administrators. This culminated in two serious WSN actions in 1973: they presented a resolution on schools to the school board and to the Akron City Council, and they filed a lawsuit against the public schools. They did not have cordial relations with school administrators again.

The resolution on schools was first prepared in 1972 after widespread news publicity about the racial composition of Akron schools showed the extent of west-side racial imbalance. The resolution, presented jointly with Fair Housing Contact Service, called for the Akron school board and administration to "begin to study various plans and make recommendations for the desegregation of Akron's school system, utilizing professional consultants if necessary" (resolution on schools, Sept. 1972). After an angry, outraged reply from the attorney for the Akron schools denying that Akron schools "are now or ever have been segregated," WSN and FHCS filed an administrative complaint charging Akron schools with racial segregation with the U.S. Department of Health, Education and Welfare. They then took their resolution to the Akron City Council. There, they urged the city council to encourage the school administrators to begin to study plans for desegregation.

This time, an angry mayor responded that it was not the business of city government to tell the schools what to do. Thus WSN learned early that they would receive no help from either the school or city administrators. If they wanted to maintain racial integration in their neighborhood, they would have to do it themselves. They did not know then that this was impossible.

The lawsuit filed against the Akron schools in 1973 concerned a new careers program placed in Firestone High School—an all-white high school in the neighborhood adjacent to the WSN area. Parents of Buchtel High School students living in the WSN area sought repeatedly to persuade the school administration to place the program in another school where it was more needed. Signed petitions sent to Akron school administrators by the parents called the $75,000 program "ill-conceived, poorly presented, and undemocratic" (Akron Beacon Journal, Sept. 30, 1973). When the petitions, pleas, and discussions brought forth the usual inaction from Akron school administrators, a suit was filed by a WSN attorney in Cleveland District Court in November 1973. Lawyer's fees were $1,000, which WSN generated through some frenzied bake and garage sales. Out-of-court discussions between lawyers of both sides and the judge assigned to the case (Carson v. Ott) continued for almost one year before agreement was reached.

On October 15, 1974 a pretrial order proposed by U.S. District Court Judge Thomas Lambros was accepted by WSN and the Akron Board of Education and schools administration. The order removed the controversial program from Firestone and place it in another school, Central. It was a clear, though largely symbolic, victory for WSN. Their attorney was delighted with the outcome, and said: "It's a win. . . . Although the scope of the action and order is limited, discrimination in the Akron Public Schools was demonstrated and successfully challenged" (WSN newsletter, Dec. 1974). West Side Neighbors and Buchtel parents were pleased.[4] The school administrators were not. Relations between them were strained ever after.

Phase Two. The major activity of the schools committee in phase two involved their organized protest against Akron's school closure plan, culminating in a historic suit filed in 1978 (Saltman 1981). They also prepared a foundation grant proposal to fund a special creative education program in their high school. This prompted the school authorities to send their own proposal to the state, for which they received a million dollars for a demonstration magnet program for Buchtel High School, then 86% black. The magnet did not work.

By this time, other citizen groups had also begun to object to Akron's school racial isolation, facilitating WSN's organization of a protest coalition of thirteen organizations.[5] Their written protests charged the plan with being too little and too late, placing an unfair burden of transportation on black children, adding to racial imbalance at some schools, and leaving many racially isolated schools untouched. Akron school authorities were intractable as ever, refusing to modify the plan. West Side Neighbors consulted attorneys, who guided them and the coalition in one year of data gathering in preparation for a court challenge. When the Akron school board refused a hand-delivered letter from the coalition's attorneys requesting negotiation and settlement out of court, the battle began. WSN gave the first contribution for legal fees—$2,000, their entire bank balance—and then organized a citywide citizen group to raise more money.

The suit, filed on January 13, 1978, named as defendants the Akron school board and authorities, the city of Akron, the public housing authority, the state real estate commission, and HUD.[6] The three-week trial began nine months later, on October 16, 1978. Observers noted the contrast between the two teams of lawyers: the slick, skilled large team of school attorneys with their Brooks Brothers suits and polished mahogany file boxes, and the parent plaintiffs' four volunteer ACLU lawyers with their plain, baggy clothes and cardboard carton files. An impressive array of nationally known witnesses took the stand on behalf of the six parents who filed the suit.[7]

On April 11, 1980, the judge ruled that the Akron plan for school closures did discriminate against black children because they bore the sole burden of transportation; he ordered school authorities to submit a new plan, reopen a black school and close a white school. He ordered all school closures for the next five years to come before the court for approval, and he ordered the payment of costs and expenses to the parents' attorneys. This was essentially a victory for the parents. But on all other matters of the case, the ruling stated that claims of intentional housing segregation and intentional school segregation had not been established. This meant that the Akron school system did not have to change, and thus the predominantly black or white schools could go on as usual. This was terrible news for WSN, with their nearly all-black cluster of schools.

Though an appeal was immediately filed, the decision from the Sixth Circuit

Appeals Court seven months later was not based on the merits of the case, and simply let the ruling stand. The parents, their children, and WSN were back to square one. Their zeal and hope for achieving racial balance in west-side schools began to wane. Though they organized an open forum on the schools in 1982, they were further disheartened when their keynote speaker publicly stated her response to the racial statistics for Akron's west-side schools: "Not since my days in the deep south have I seen such racial segregation in public schools" (WSN schools workshop notes, Nov. 6, 1982). By the end of phase two, WSN's schools committee was barely functioning. In phase three, it died.

Phase Three. As long as the school suit was in process and until the final decision came in 1982, there was hope. Even after the decision, some west-side parents and WSN members continued to hope for several years that the Buchtel state-funded magnet program might succeed in attracting some white students to the program and the area. This did not happen, beginning as it did when the school was 86% black; the school continued to become blacker, reaching the 98% level in 1988. All the other seven schools in the west-side cluster also followed that trend, with statistics that could have represented Mississippi or Alabama or anywhere else in the Deep South. But it was Akron, Ohio, and it was the shame of the city and the despair of WSN.

Small wonder WSN had trouble finding members to serve on the schools committee, let alone to head it. They tried to work with the twenty-two objectives and goals left from the 1982 schools workshop, but nothing came of it. Brief frenzies of letter-writing in 1984, 1985, and again in 1986 pleaded with local and state school authorities to address the issue of racial isolation in west-side schools, but to no avail. West Side Neighbors did succeed in motivating the newspaper to write about the issue in an editorial (*Akron Beacon Journal*, Oct. 17, 1985). They also organized a small coalition of clergy in 1985 to persuade school authorities to deal with the issue, and they later mobilized a "lunch bunch" to take individual school board members out to lunch to discuss the issue and press for change. But nothing changed. The committee, now all-black, met occasionally and sporadically until early in 1986, after which no one could be found to chair it and it became defunct. The west-side schools then were virtually all-black, and with no functioning schools committee, WSN now faced a tactical dilemma: who would speak for WSN on school issues?

Block Organization

Phase One. When WSN began, block organization vied with the schools committee as the most critical program of the group. Originally intended to stem white flight and allay fears in newly integrated neighborhoods, this committee also played a vital role in membership recruitment, code enforcement, and crime prevention. The first WSN newsletter, printed when the group was only four months old, referred to block organization as "one of the most important functions of WSN . . . several block groups have already been formed and are operating" (newsletter, Feb. 1968). Two months later, the newsletter printed two pages of maps of the twenty-six newly formed block areas, with the names, addresses, and phone numbers of the new community liaison leaders of each area.

Though the goal of twenty-six area leaders was never reached, almost one hundred block groups were eventually formed. But because of the turnover of residents, there were never more than sixty functioning at any one time. Most of the block groups met only occasionally for social events—a picnic or holiday party—but they did provide a ready network for communication and community action. They were also an excellent base for assisting the city with code enforcement programs, one of the largest of which was conducted in a portion of the WSN area during phase one. The block clubs' impact on membership was dramatic, with the highest numbers of paid members occurring during this first phase. The 704 households that paid one dollar to belong to WSN in 1972 was a number not equalled again.

Phase Two. During this funded period, block organization was expanded as the focal point of two of WSN's newly funded programs; crime prevention and a neighborly service called the Useful Service Exchange (USE). The crime prevention program was designed to reduce crime through increased citizen involvement, and was based on a successful similar project in Seattle. Fulfilling their stated objectives in their first year, the staff organized sixty block clubs, reduced burglaries by 15%, and reestablished a block club council. At the end of the second year, the staff achieved another 10% burglary reduction, established thirty more block clubs, organized tenant security groups in fifteen apartment buildings, prepared and distributed monthly newsletters, and held four community fund-raising events. When crime prevention funds ran out, block organization and safety information continued under the USE program, described below. When that funding ended, volunteers took it over, and the program soon began to waver. As new block groups began, some of the old ones disintegrated, thus the task was a never-ending one.

The USE program was an outgrowth of WSN's earlier neighborhood concerns survey, conducted by ten volunteers in 1979 (Saltman 1980, 1986). One of the objectives of that survey of 312 residents was to obtain data for establishing a program for a household service exchange of residents in WSN's area. A majority of respondents (67%) said they would be interested in participating in such a service if WSN began one. A smaller number of respondents offered to host block meetings, if WSN organized and conducted them. WSN immediately sprang into action with this information, and began block meetings with ten volunteer organizers recruited for this purpose. They also began to organize a filing and referral system of neighborhood providers and users of household services, based on survey responses. While this flurry of volunteer activity was going on, the news came that USE had been funded for one year by a local foundation. It was funded for a second year by United Way. The USE program—one of only three like it the nation—was actually the internal part of WSN's REACH proposal, described above.

In their first funded year, USE staff organized eighty-eight block meetings, two block council meetings, offered 293 services by neighbors, coordinated 188 actual services, made 3,230 phone calls, and distributed 3,500 leaflets. They used the block meetings to continue their neighborhood safety information, to publicize the USE program, and to obtain additional providers and potential users of services. The second funded year resulted in an increase of 326 offers of services and 253 actual services provided, as well as nineteen additional blocks, forty-two block meetings, four quadrant meetings, and 828 mailings (reports, 1980, 1981). The USE program was a winner, and received much media praise as well as appreciation throughout WSN's neighborhoods.

Though WSN staff made intense efforts to conduct a self-sustaining membership drive, as their United Way proposal had promised, their 1981–82 returns were minimal—$1,966—and hardly self-sustaining. They submitted eight proposals for funding to various sources, but all were rejected. United Way informed WSN leaders that two reasons blocked their future funding: (1) their grant had not succeeded in producing self-sustaining membership dues; and (2) WSN had no one to give full-time direction to their programs. Both of these were true.

Phase Three. From 1983 to 1985, two WSN board members cochaired the block organization committee. In fact, they were the entire committee, since they could find no others to serve. They attempted to carry on the work of previous staff, dividing the WSN area into four quadrants, trying to find a leader for each, mailing letters to existing block contacts "trying to determine interest or disinterest," securing new block contacts to hold block meetings, and arranging socials for all block contacts. Though this had worked in phase one, it was not going to happen in phase three. By the end of 1983, only one of the cochairs remained as nominal head of this committee, which then consisted of one member—herself. She did try to organize new block groups on request, but was unable to do more than a few a year. Existing block group leaders who moved away were not replaced by new ones, and their groups dissolved. Slowly, the block organization structure that had been built by WSN during the previous fifteen years began to crumble.

Very much aware by now that they could not do an adequate job of block organization without paid staff, WSN submitted a funding proposal to the city in 1984 for a two-year neighborhood safety program based on an expanded block organization. When their proposal was rejected, WSN sent a letter of bitter disappointment to the mayor and the four city council members elected from their area. The letter stated that "our community will suffer an immeasurable loss," and pleaded for financial help: "We cannot do this alone. Some funding is essential" (letter from president, Nov. 7, 1984). None came.

Recognizing the void in WSN's block organization at that time, a newly elected councilman from WSN's area stepped in to fill it with his own organization of a new West Side Block Club Council, as noted above. After that it was uphill for that group, and all over for WSN's block work. The heart of the organization, and the pivot of their first two phases of development, was ended. Meanwhile, a different kind of block activity began to occur as part of housing rehabilitation by the city, in cooperation with WSN's housing committee, to which we turn next.

Housing Committee

Phase One. Confrontations with Akron's public housing authority and real estate agents began as soon as WSN began, since these were immediately recognized as threats to their goal achievement and so were overriding neighborhood concerns. Public housing concentration and real estate solicitation continued to plague the WSN area in all three phases, and the housing committee handled these issues consistently and vigorously.

Minutes, newsletters, and correspondence in phase one reflect WSN's increasing anguish as they tried to deal with the public housing issue. Two problems they faced were: (1) inability to obtain complete data on public housing locations and racial composition, and (2) refusal of public housing authorities to modify their practices of segregation. Repeated meetings, letter exchanges, and public statements throughout this phase brought no resolution of the public housing issues. But eventually, complaints filed with HUD did result in orders to the AMHA in 1972 to modify their policies on tenant and location selection. And personnel changes resulted in improved personal relations between WSN and the AMHA leaders. The battle for data, however, continues to this day, though it briefly abated after phase two's massive schools lawsuit.

The battle with real estate solicitation first began in 1971, when the housing committee chair asked for "board approval to present an ordinance to regulate solicitations by realtors" (minutes, March 7, 1971). Fanning this concern was the impending displacement of 350 families, mostly black, in the path of a new innerbelt highway. Real estate agents had publicly claimed that all the families about to be dislocated had expressed a preference for moving to the west side. The housing committee distributed hundreds of flyers warning west-side residents about unethical solicitation, and urging them to report any such encounters to the committee. So serious was the problem of real estate solicitation in 1972 that housing committee members formed a separate "friendly telephoning" subcommittee to counteract the ill effects, and by the end of 1972 had formed nine subcommittees to deal with all the problems facing them.

During this phase, the housing committee tape-recorded unethical real estate solicitations, sent letters of protest to offensive companies and their agents, filed complaints with relevant local and state agencies, held meetings with real estate board leaders, prepared legal affidavits, and filed and won two legal suits against specific agents and their companies.[8] Though only little more than four years old, they were becoming quite litigious. Events were forcing them to fight back, and they were learning how to do it.

The housing committee and WSN also initiated new laws and made an important public statement in 1972 to implement existing fair housing laws. The public statement, made to a packed council chambers as fifteen supporting nonprofit groups cheered, was given as a protest against human displacement and neighborhood segregation resulting from highway construction. The WSN statement also included some impassioned thoughts about racial segregation and eight specific proposals to reduce citywide segregation. Though only one of these was implemented by the city, it was an important one: the Fair Housing Service, sister organization of WSN, was eventually funded in 1975 to operate a fair housing agency to verify housing discrimination complaints (Saltman 1978).

Late in 1972, WSN proposed laws banning "for sale" signs and solicitation in their area, and had their councilman successfully present these for City Council passage in June 1973. Within two months, however, the sign ban's constitutionality was challenged by the local ACLU, and a fierce and protracted legal battle ended badly for WSN. On December 14, 1973, the law was declared unconstitutional and a chain of appeals from the Common Pleas Court to the county and state Supreme Courts were all lost. During the brief time the sign ban was in effect, WSN area residents were delighted with the calm uncluttered look of their neighborhoods. Less than a year after the law was passed, the blare and clutter of "for sale" signs reappeared in west Akron.

Phase Two. The housing committee's most significant activity during this phase was the guidance of the funded UPON project, which grew out of a mortgage lending study completed by WSN in 1978 (Saltman 1980). When the results of that twenty-seven-year mortgage analysis showed redlining in the WSN area, WSN knew they needed some paid staff to deal with this issue. They prepared a funding proposal for a full-time field representative to talk to bank presidents about reinvestment, and to work with real estate agents and corporate personnel to promote affirmative marketing of their neighborhood. This, in fact, was the external portion of their REACH proposal, and UPON was the acronym for United Promotion of Our Neighborhood (Saltman 1984). Until the project was funded (after two years of negotiation), WSN volunteers began to meet with bank presidents, guided by the housing committee.

In the project's first funded year, WSN's full-time UPON field representative visited eleven major bank presidents (in the first five months), met with thirty-three presidents of real estate companies, gave two-hour presentations to 170 real estate sales agents, made seventy-three other personal visits, and obtained sixty CARE agents.[9] The representative also sent 1,349 letters, made 1,439 phone calls, and arranged for the distribution of 3,000 CARE leaflets, 100 "no solicitation" posters, and 1,000 "no solicitation" flyers, 10,000 photo leaflets, 2,000 photo booklets, and 13,200 WSN newsletters, all promoting the west side as a desirable, diverse community.

The final project report, highly acclaimed in the press, ended with these prophetic words: "A massive ongoing effort will be required to realize any lasting results. . . . If this does not materialize, the WSN area will surely become re-segregated" (UPON report, Oct. 1980). When the funding ended, it was clearly impossible for WSN to maintain a "massive ongoing effort" of any kind. That is not to say they did not try. The project did continue the following two years (1980–82), with seven different successive part-time student interns taking the place of the former one full-time staff person. This at least ensured some follow-up to all the contacts established in the first funded year. But this, too, ended too soon.

Three unanticipated positive consequences of the UPON project were the formation of the Copley Road Area Merchants Association (CRAMA), the reference to UPON as a "pilot program" in a local proposal for a federally funded Community Housing Resources Board (CHRB),[10] and annual financial contributions from five major banks. CRAMA was formed through the efforts of the full-time field representative, fulfilling the city's requirement of this as a precondition for their planned $1 million improvement program of west Copley Road—part of the main business artery of the WSN area. The CHRB program was to be a regional extension of UPON's affirmative marketing program, with WSN's former field representative hired as the new CHRB program coordinator. And the annual financial contributions to WSN from banks were a little bit of blackmail extracted by the field representative as modest repayment for past disinvestment: "Is it guilt that is partially motivating lenders to give WSN money? We don't know. We won't ask" (UPON final report, Oct. 10, 1982).

The last UPON report ended with gratitude for the grants that made it possible, and these thoughts: "We believe we did affect some minds and hearts and actions. With or without funding, we hope to continue to work for constructive change." They did, but as we will see the effort was minimal after funding ended, in keeping with their lack of resources—both financial and human.

Phase Three. During this phase, the housing committee continued to process housing complaints to city agencies, prepare and distribute annual mortgage reports and visit lenders, assist the city with code enforcement efforts, obtain updated AMHA data and press for more positive policies, and evaluate federal funding applications as ongoing service on a citizen review panel, submitting social impact statements (see Appendix C). In addition, they developed and monitored a conciliation agreement with one discriminatory real estate agent and company, monitored the city's federally funded Urban Neighborhood Development Corporation (UNDC) for its integrative versus segregative impact, and lobbied on the state level for incentive payments for integrative moves as part of a new statewide mortgage revenue bond program. They undertook one new activity toward the end of this phase—annual house tours of noteworthy homes in their area. This was done by a small but determined volunteer committee of five people, with an occasional increase to six or seven.

Long before the city's code enforcement program began in blighted tract 5065 on Akron's west side, WSN's housing committee had been agitating for city aid there. Their public statement at a hearing in 1980 called attention to that specific area and was a clear cry for help:

If the City were more concerned with prevention than with cure, we might not have the extent of blight that we do in some of our neighborhoods . . . WSN invites the Mayor and the whole Planning and Community Involvement Department to come for a walk with us on Wildwood Avenue. . . . Come and see what the boarded up stores look like . . . come and look at the houses on that block. Tell us if you agree that this is an area of incipient blight. And are any funds allocated for the improvement of this area? We think not. (WSN statement, March 26, 1980)

In fact, they did have to wait till the city cure was offered, and as usual it was too little and too late. By 1982, when the first exterior code enforcement program began there, that area looked like a bombed-out, blighted wasteland. The former bars—which WSN had helped residents dry up at the voting booths—stood empty and boarded up, and so did the few former stores, which had moved away one by one, in disgust. The 1,400 remaining homes were run-down and unkempt, almost half of them now owned by absent landlords and AMHA, who had eagerly snapped them up.

This was the scene in which WSN's housing committee was asked to help the city promote home repairs and loan applications. With two small grants from two lenders, they managed to obtain two student interns and one resident to phone all tract residents to urge them to take advantage of the reduced interest rates on the repair loans. In the next eighteen months, they finally generated requests for more than $300,000 in repair loans from both lenders, and the program was judged a success. Toward the end of the second year of the program, the city announced its intention of including the Wildwood area as part of the next federally funded CDBG improvement program. This was ten years after WSN's housing committee first called the city's attention to this decaying neighborhood, and five years after they helped residents dry up the bars there, as a prerequisite for the city's help.

The struggle for securing current AMHA data was renewed and increased in this phase when a new director took over the public housing agency. When she filed an application for obtaining thirty-two west-side properties for additional public housing units, the housing committee objected with outrage through their citizen review panel, and the battle was on. After a protracted, dreary two-year confrontation with a barrage of letters, meetings, and protests to HUD, WSN finally obtained the data they asked for and promptly issued a public report. The report called attention to the extent of public housing impaction and segregation, and ended with two recommendations (see Appendix C). When a new director took over the AMHA at the end of this phase, WSN quickly established contact and renewed their two requests for changes. By this time, a new mayor had also given the AMHA a few guidelines for avoiding further impaction. But these came twenty years too late.

While this AMHA struggle drained their energy and time, the housing committee was fighting a simultaneous battle with a real estate company over a 1984 west-side housing discrimination complaint. Though they immediately called in their sister fair housing organization, FHCS, to assist them, that organization had its own troubles at that time, plus a new and inexperienced director. Together with HUD, they all worked out a conciliation agreement with the company, which was drafted by and required constant monitoring by the housing committee (see Appendix C). Since the complaint had involved steering and some minority agents, one of the "affirmative measures" in the agreement concerned minority agent assignments to majority locations. The housing committee suggested the CARE PAIR plan (white and black agents working together) from their UPON project,[11] but the real estate company's president had great difficulty implementing this and required constant prodding to do it.

The final agreement data analysis and report, prepared by the housing committee, showed a surprising higher proportion of integrative moves made by clients of the minority agents. This confirmed WSN's long-held belief that such positive affirmative marketing practices could result in wider housing choices for minorities. Unfortunately, when the agreement period ended, reports soon began to drift in of more black agents from the company being assigned to the west side and bringing only black clients there. The housing committee and FHCS sent the usual protest letters to the usual array of people and agencies, but no definitive change occurred.

To balance these draining, depressing activities was one positive housing committee action with positive results. In April 1983, WSN's housing committee became the first organization in Ohio to publicize the idea of a percentage of the state mortgage revenue bonds being set aside for integrative moves (see Appendix C). Their fifty-nine letters to many key state officials paved the way for the set-aside idea's incorporation in the recommendations of a statewide coalition of nonprofit groups,[12] who negotiated with the state housing financing agency for the next two years for its implementation. Ohio became the first state in the nation to have such a state-supported set-aside incentive payment for integrative moves.

Other WSN Activities

The recreation committee was extremely active and effective for the first four years of WSN's existence. Their major achievement was obtaining from the city three west-side neighborhood sites for recreation. This was no small victory, involving more than two years of negotiations with various city agencies and officials. The three sites provided two basketball diamonds, a football field, a baseball field, two tennis courts, and a tot lot. In addition to these, the committee established two other tot lots, formed three summer theater workshops for junior high school students, obtained evening classes for adults, secured tennis nets for high school students, sponsored annual drama productions at the west-side junior and senior high schools, blocked the removal of the city zoo from the west side, lobbied for city summer concert performances in west-side parks, formed a citywide Friends of Recreation committee, and developed a master plan for west-side recreation with the city Parks & Recreation Department. Just one of these actions required hundreds of volunteer hours, meetings, letters, and phone calls to achieve even modest success. Small wonder that by 1973 the recreation committee perished from exhaustion.

Other board members and committees continued the tradition of this early committee with "fun events," important to WSN's goals of providing a sense of community. Two outstanding recurring events during phase one were the Fun Arts Festivals and the International Smorgasbord Dinners, which drew large crowds and received much press coverage. The festivals, publicized as "Do Your Own Thing" and "Fun for Everyone" (*Akron Beacon Journal*, Nov. 14, 1968), were held for three consecutive years in the Buchtel High School gym. After 1971, no one could be found to chair them and they stopped. The International Dinners, however, continued as an annual spring event for fifteen years, throughout phases one and two and on into phase three. Held in the Buchtel High School cafeteria, they drew as many as 900 people, and were heralded as WSN's outstanding community event: "a mammoth eat-in . . . food and fun with an international flavor . . . music and dance . . . homemade dishes" (*Beacon Journal*, April 29, 1970). The dinners stopped in 1985, again when no one could be found to chair the committee. Other occasional events held by WSN in all three phases included Sunday picnics in the park, health and trade fairs, flea markets, political candidates' nights, house tours (begun in phase three), and fifteenth- and twentieth-anniversary dinners. Let us now see what impact WSN's activities and programs had.

IMPACT

As before, we use the same four criteria to evaluate the effectiveness or impact of WSN, Akron's movement organization. Each of these factors is relevant to the goals of the movement generally and WSN specifically: the extent of racial pluralism maintenance, quality maintenance, sense of community, and organizational influence. These four factors were analyzed both quantitatively and qualitatively through census data, interviews, visual surveys, news content, and published reports.

Integration Maintenance

Of the five census tracts in the WSN area, three are now predominantly black (see Figure 3, Appendix A). The two remaining white majority tracts in 1980 were 9% and 16% black. School racial data reflect these residential changes in racial composition over two decades, and also show a changing and differing demographic profile for whites and blacks during that time.

By 1980, that profile looked this way in the most integrated census tract of the WSN area. Two-thirds of the blacks had children under nineteen, while two-thirds of the whites had no children under nineteen. This is, of course, related to age differences according to race. Blacks living in the neighborhood were younger, with only 3% over the age of sixty-five, compared to 27% of the whites being over sixty-five (Saltman 1986). All of this is indicated in school racial data.

In 1957, Buchtel High School, the heart of WSN's area, was 6.4% black. At that time its attendance zone included northwest Akron—the present Firestone school zone. When between 1959 and 1962 the new Firestone cluster was built, less than a mile away from the Buchtel cluster, many white households moved away from the Buchtel cluster northward to that adjacent new school zone. We recall that this coincided with the time of urban renewal relocation of many black households to the Buchtel school area. It also coincided with the expansion of public housing in the west side of Akron. In 1963, Buchtel was 17.4% black; only three years later that proportion almost doubled to 32.5% black. In fact, this happened in one summer as a direct result of urban renewal relocation (Akron Planning Dept. Relocation Data 1975).

By 1970, Buchtel was 56.2% black, and its black population steadily increased until it was 84.7% black in 1977. After the school suit and the opening of the magnet program at Buchtel, its black enrollment continued to grow, and as of 1987 was 98% black. The junior high and elementary schools showed similar steady increases in black enrollment, going from 23% to 82% black from 1966 to 1986 in the junior high school, and from 20% to 98% black in the elementary schools.

Urban renewal relocation and public housing site location were the major initial causes of the shifting racial composition in neighborhoods and schools; these were compounded by real estate steering, bank redlining, and school administrative policies. Other factors contributing to racial change in the WSN area will be analyzed in the concluding section that follows. Here we merely state that racial integration in the WSN area has steadily declined over the past two decades, though the struggle to maintain it has been enormous, as we have seen.

Surveys conducted at three different points in time indicate some of the residents' perceptions of the changing neighborhood. West Side Neighbors' concerns survey, conducted in the summer of 1979 in one substantially integrated tract, was an in-depth study of how 312 residents felt about the WSN area. A briefer telephone survey in 1982 gave an updated picture of their views; it was more inclusive geographically, covering all five tracts. Finally, in 1987, letters solicited for WSN's twentieth-anniversary celebration, a series of neighborhood meetings, and a new survey in another predominantly black tract offer further insight into residents' most recent views about their west-side neighborhood and about WSN.

How people perceived the neighborhood was related to where they lived, how long they had lived there, and whether they were black or white. And all of these factors were related to their socioeconomic level. But there were a few perceptions held in common, regardless of these variables. The shared views concerned general satisfaction with the neighborhood and the most serious problems of the neighborhood.

A substantial majority of all respondents were either very satisfied or pretty satisfied with their neighborhood (Saltman 1986). The most serious problem of the neighborhood in 1979 was the run-down condition of the business area; half of all the respondents cited this as their most serious concern at that time. Some of their comments show the intensity of their feelings about the business area: "I'm planning to move because of the deterioration of the businesses" (white, over age sixty-five, tenure over ten years). "Some areas are beginning to deteriorate. We need to encourage good businesses to move in and get the liquor stores and beer halls out" (black, age forty-five to fifty-four, tenure three to ten years). "Copley Road is a hell hole" (white, age over sixty-five, tenure over ten years). "We need to fix Copley Road, get rid of the bars and chicken fast food places" (white, age over sixty-five, tenure ten years). "Neighbors advise me not to shop on Copley Road. It's dangerous—trashy people hang out there" (white, age fifty-five, tenure three to ten years). "The business area is my biggest concern. We should revoke liquor licenses and get rid of the bars" (black, age twenty-five, tenure three to ten years). "We need to add better shops" (black, age forty-five to fifty-four, tenure over ten years).

Reflecting these shared views of the business area are the data showing the extent of its use by residents. These show marked differences according to race. Only one-third of respondents used the grocery stores in the neighborhood, and those who did were primarily black. Other neighborhood businesses used were drug stores, cleaners, laundromats, and shoe repair shops, but again a majority of those that used these businesses frequently were black residents. Fifty-seven percent of the black respondents had high-user scores compared to only 24% of the white respondents (Saltman 1986).[13]

Comments about the public schools also indicate anxiety about racial composition and imbalance, reflecting the changing neighborhood. Though this ranked only tenth in order of importance in the 1979 survey, with only 16% of all respondents seeing this as a serious or somewhat serious problem, further analyses of the 16% showed significant racial differences. Twice as many whites (12%) saw this as a serious problem as blacks. The differences were magnified when controlling for type of school used, that is, public, parochial, or private. Four times as many of those using private or parochial schools (21%) saw the schools as a serious problem compared to those who used the public schools (6%). This was also related to race, since three times as many of the white respondents (43%) had their children in private or parochial schools compared to black respondents (14%). The most important factor in the public schools for whites was the racial composition, but some blacks also saw this as an important issue: "We need to fight for integrated schools . . . segregated schools lead to poorer facilities" (black, age over sixty-five, tenure three to ten years). "The schools worry me because we won't keep the good teachers if the neighborhood is black" (black, age thirty-five to forty-four, tenure over ten years).

Though residents still had hope in 1979, since the school suit had not yet been settled, most had lost it by 1986. Still agonizing over the glaring racial imbalance of the west-side schools, however, were a few respondents in 1987; most others had given up the struggle, believing that nothing more could be done. Several sad comments about this are noteworthy, first this one from a leader of the local League of Women Voters on the occasion of WSN's twentieth anniversary:

Congratulations on your 20th anniversary. You have done a splendid job in stabilizing and improving the neighborhood and proving that integration can work. It is unfortunate that despite valiant efforts and persistence the Buchtel cluster has not been integrated. It is our mutual wish that this result can be attained in the near future. Best wishes for the next twenty years. (WSN anniversary booklet, Oct. 1987)

Another anguished letter to the editor about the schools in 1987 asked: "Does anyone out there care that 5,793 black students—44% of all black students— in Akron are attending majority black schools, and that 75% of them are in west side schools?" (Akron Beacon Journal, Oct. 18, 1987).

Clearly, neither the west Akron schools nor the area they are in has maintained racial integration over the two decades of WSN's existence. Though when WSN began in 1967, only one portion of their area, south of Copley Road, was substantially racially integrated, in 1987 three out of five of the census tracts in the WSN area were predominantly black. And the schools are now virtually all-black. No one could say that WSN has achieved their major goal, despite valiant and persistent efforts with all the massive institutional forces that stood in their way: the schools, the city urban renewal programs, the public housing authority, and the real estate and banking industries.

We have seen how hard and long WSN worked to try to avoid the resegregation of their area. They did not succeed, though many still refer to the area as an integrated one, and statistically it is still integrated. It does follow the pattern of three neighborhoods as in the other cities we have analyzed. The northern portion is predominantly white, the central portion is integrated, and the southern portion is black (Figure 1, Appendix A). But the data show that the "integrated" areas are predominantly black, and are increasingly so, with no signs of stabilization (see Table 3, Appendix A).

Quality Maintenance

Having failed to achieve their primary goal, what about the next goal of preserving their area as a desirable area? Census and other data over the two decades show that some portions of the WSN community changed physically and socially toward lower socioeconomic levels. For example, in 1970 only one of the five tracts in the WSN area had a median housing value below that of the city's median value, and that one was only slightly below the city value. But in 1980, three tracts in the WSN area were below the city's median housing value, and substantially so, ranging from $4,300 to $19,130 less than the citywide value (U.S. Census 1970, 1980; WSN phone survey, 1982).

Another indicator of the changing socioeconomic levels of residents living in WSN's area is the proportion of persons below poverty level. In 1970 none of the five tracts contained people living below the poverty level. But in 1980, two tracts had poverty levels substantially higher than the citywide average. Data on median family income show similar trends. In 1970, four tracts had families with incomes that were above the city's median family income, and the fifth tract was only slightly below it. By 1980, however, two tracts contained families whose incomes were substantially below the city's median income for families, one was slightly above it and only two were substantially above it (U.S. Census, 1970, 1980).

These data, of course, reflect the growing numbers of public housing tenants who moved into the WSN area, at about the same time as and after urban renewal relocatees were also moving in—between 1967 and 1980. These were primarily black families, largely a result of the widespread racial steering, block-busting, and redlining occurring in the real estate and bank industries in those years.[14]

More than half of the respondents in the 1979 WSN survey complained that they had been repeatedly solicited by real estate agents who asked them to sell their homes. When asked how often, most (42%) said three to six times, a third (31%) said over six times, and a quarter (25%) said one or two times. Evidence of concern over the heavy real estate activity in the WSN area is seen is these comments: "I was solicited twenty-five times by real estate agents wanting me to sell!" "I'm very angry about agents who keep coming around wanting me to sell." "They [real estate agents] are a bunch of vultures" (WSN survey, 1979).

All of this contributed to the increasing racial imbalance in the public schools, further exacerbated by school administrative policies regarding attendance zones, optional zones, transfer policies, and so on. The end of this cycle is seen in the business district changes, which resulted in different types of businesses, personnel, and clientele.

City policies, and often the lack of them, also contributed to decline in neighborhood quality (Rabin 1987). Repair grants or low-interest loans for repairs were only available for persons in a few targeted areas of the city (CDBG sections), or for the elderly or handicapped. Thus, thousands of other hardship cases in need of help for home repairs could not get it. The most famous example cited by WSN housing committee members was the house at 750 Copley Road. Standing on a barren corner in Copley Road East—the most blighted but well-traveled business area on the west side of Akron—was this huge, three-story, rotting, old frame house. It stood like a pathetic landmark of decay, inhabited by its bankrupt, ill owner—who was neither elderly nor handicapped, however.

The home's siding had rotted away, its steps were gone, the windows were broken, and the porch was sagging. The first complaint on the house filed by WSN's housing committee with the city health department was in 1976. Repeated complaints over the next four years, with no results, finally brought the owner to the city's housing court.

This court made an arrangement with the owner that he could stay in the house if he promised to begin fixing it up to meet the city's code regulations. Fixing one door one year, one window the next, one step the third, the owner tried to fulfill his piecemeal arrangement with the city. The house continued to decay for the next ten years, while WSN's housing committee continued to scream in frustration to the city. Finally, when the owner moved out because of severe illness, the city took action and demolished the house—in 1986, ten years after WSN's first complaint. The housing committee, not sure whether to celebrate or mourn, wrote to the city then and sadly and wearily pointed out to them: "If you had acted ten years earlier, maybe the house could have been saved and restored and wouldn't ever have had to be torn down" (letter to city, Oct. 1986).

Despite the physical and social changes of the neighborhood and its residents over these two decades, a drive through the WSN area still reveals some residential areas of charm, excellent housing quality, and even beauty. The single most descriptive term for the entire area is diversity. Not only is the population diverse racially, it is also diverse economically, and this is reflected in the physical appearance and quality of the neighborhoods. Ranging economically from very low to upper income, the residents live in homes that vary from seedy to modest bungalows all the way to stately mansions in parklike surroundings. These are not always reflective of racial composition, however, as portions of the huge black tract below Copley Road are very handsome and contain fine older housing stock. This is known as "Sugar Hill," where some well-known black professional families live. Apart from this area, however, it would seem generally true that in the WSN area, the greater the proportion of black residents, the lower the socioeconomic level and housing and neighborhood quality. This is consistent with the findings in the four other cities studied.

Most respondents (94%) in 1979 were either very satisfied or pretty satisfied with their house, and ranked housing condition as only their ninth concern. But we must remember the survey was conducted in tract 5062—the area's integrated, middle-income neighborhood. By 1982, however, even that tract had its residents ranking housing as their third most serious problem, with only crime and streets outranking it (WSN telephone survey, 1982). And residents of all the other four tracts ranked housing as one their four most serious problems in 1982. So some internal perceptions of the neighborhood's quality seemed to be becoming more negative.

West Side Neighbors' role in housing rehabilitation and code enforcement was to prod city agencies to do their jobs by filing hundreds of housing and street complaints each year. They made numerous public statements advocating citywide repair loans for hardship cases regardless of location, age, or infirmity. They also cooperated and assisted with any and all city programs for physical improvement. And they assisted residents in getting rid of unwanted neighborhood bars by voting the precincts dry.

But in addition they occasionally raised funds to do a little rehabilitation work themselves, though they thought this was not the most effective way of maintaining neighborhood quality. Records show that the first external funding they ever received was a 1974 grant of $500 from IBM "to help paint homes of hardship cases found on the west side" (WSN anniversary booklet, Oct. 1987). And in 1979 they painted the outside of an eyesore cleaning shop on Copley Road with paint paid for by donations from thirteen neighboring businesses. The business district continued to worry WSN and many of the residents, because parts of it "looked so bad."

Long before the city finally decided to make some public improvements on Copley Road West, planners had described the area as "threatened," because old established businesses were being replaced with more marginal operations. And while the city procrastinated and considered the merits of an improvement program, the area continued to deteriorate. One reason given by the city for its long hesitation was the fact that only 30% of the businesses on Copley Road were owner-operated, compared with 50% to 65% in other city neighborhoods. Again, as with residential improvement, the city took too long to decide and act, and when they did it was too little as well as too late.

The prospects for Copley Road West are still uncertain today, with some city planners believing that its future as a neighborhood business district is doubtful.[15] Meanwhile, the eastern portion of Copley Road goes untouched, despite repeated cries of anguish from WSN. They have now become part of a neighborhood development group that will try to secure private funding to fix up that hideous blighted area, only a half mile away from a historic district.

Sense of Community

The things that WSN did purely for fun were those that created a sense of community—for themselves and for those that worked with them. These were the many community events that WSN arranged and sponsored. Some of them were fund-raising activities, some were fellowship activities, but all had the same result of creating a sense of community. In addition to these deliberate social events were those activities that were unintended as fellowship-builders but which, nevertheless, had the same result—they drew some west-side residents together into a unified group sharing a common activity relating to their neighborhood.

Typical of such social events were the annual International Buffet Dinners and the Fun Arts Festivals; the fund-raisers, such as garage sales and theater performances; school poster and essay contests; public meetings in rotating locations; political candidates' nights; the parties and picnics in the park; the health and trade fairs; the flea markets; and, much later, the house tours. But just as vital for building a sense of community were the many years of block organization, the hard, never-ending work of the housing and school committees, the neighborhood clean-up campaigns, the five consecutive years of unified effort to dry up the bars in the Wildwood-Madison neighborhoods, the monthly and later quarterly WSN newsletters going out to members and others living on the west side, the code enforcement programs, the concerns survey and later the telephone survey, the Useful Service Exchange, the membership drives and phone-a-thons, and even the general literature distribution. All of these served to create a sense of community on the west side, and a feeling of neighborhood.

Scores on neighboring in the 1979 concerns survey were considerably higher than anticipated; they were one of the most unexpected results of that study (Saltman 1986). The data showed that a majority of residents had quite extensive social ties with their neighbors, contrary to the common local perception of the west side as an area of great transition and turnover. A majority of respondents knew the names of six or more of their neighbors, 77% chatted with them often or sometimes, and 54% visited in their neighbors' homes often or sometimes. We can be certain that all the activities WSN sponsored over the years strengthened rather than weakened the sense of community in their area.

Some of the remembrances quoted in the twentieth-anniversary commemorative booklet support this view: "WSN organized one of the first neighborhood cleanup campaigns. Our children were very young then but we all participated. The effort was an excellent example of neighborhood responsibility and cooperation." Another comment:

I remember the Halloween party WSN sponsored in 1978 where hundreds of small children, black and white, gathered for a few hours of magic and fun. I often think of the Council of Block Club Presidents and admire the effort they put into bringing their different backgrounds and ideas together to make west Akron safe and attractive.

Two other contributions: "My favorite WSN memory is of the . . . Garage Sales . . . we attracted large crowds of treasure seekers who learned about us, our area, and our projects. . . . Most significantly, however, was the togetherness in a common, profitable, and enjoyable effort which the Sale fostered." "When our family looked for a home in Akron nine years ago we were drawn to west Akron. The qualify of life was and is so positive here; people work together no matter how diverse their life-style or background for the best interest of the neighborhood" (WSN anniversary booklet, Oct. 1987).

Despite the sense of community that WSN fostered, both deliberately and inadvertently, the racial and economic diversity of the area posed great difficulties for unification. This became more and more apparent as the socioeconomic level of some of the neighborhood residents declined with the advent of increased public housing tenants. As in the other four cities studied, the identification with WSN was less in the poorer and all-black areas of the WSN community. The integrated portion of the WSN area had the highest level of knowledge about the organization, and it also showed the most positive attitudes about the future (Saltman 1986).

The tangible evidence—through records and news clips—is that WSN held a greater number of community events in phase one than in phase two, and still fewer in phase three. In the late eighties, though, there has been a resurgence of leadership and vigor. The current reality is that they may now be forced into the position of giving up the largest portion of their community—the all-black area south of Copley Road, which contains some of the poorest housing and lowest economic levels in the entire area. If the two new intrusive neighborhood development groups succeed in obtaining funding for much-needed physical and social rehabilitation of that area, WSN will have to seriously consider redrawing their organizational boundary lines. Their community will indeed have shrunk. And given their shrunken resources—both financial and human—this may be appropriate.

Organizational Influence

What influence has WSN had on institutional forces and decision makers in their city and beyond? One social agency director said that WSN was seen by United Way as "the best thing since sliced bread" (interview, Aug. 11, 1986). And we know that in 1977 they won the prestigious Akron Area Brotherhood Award, on their tenth anniversary. What have they done to deserve these accolades? A brief review of two decades of their work in block organization, schools, and housing shows the influence they have had.

We recall that when WSN first began, block organization vied with the schools committee as the most critical and vital program of the organization. Their early work, resulting in the systematic organization of one hundred blocks—half of the huge WSN area—was phenomenal, considering that it was done by two volunteers. This block organization work soon caught the attention of the city, and in 1970 the code enforcement division of the Health Department made use of it in a new West Side Neighborhood Conservation Program.

The conservation program was the single largest housing code enforcement program ever enacted in the city, using twenty-one sanitarians, four supervisors and four clerks from 1970 to 1975. Obtaining the program for the west side was, in fact, a direct result of WSN's insistence and persistence, but the program depended on block meetings for much of its success. These were arranged by WSN's fledgling block organization committee, with excellent results: "We were successful in bringing 2,390 houses up to code at a cost to the residents of $1,009,291—quite a sum back then" (letter from director of code enforcement division, May 28, 1987).

Block organization was also the basis of two successive funded programs in phase two—the Crime Prevention/Neighborhood Safety Program and the Useful Service Exchange Program, both of which were analyzed above. In addition, block organization was the critical strategic factor accounting for the eventual successful voting campaign that forced the bars to close in the Wildwood-Madison neighborhood. And the closing of the bars was a precondition mandated by the city for any possible future improvement program in that area—wished for so long by WSN. This wish was granted, finally, in 1983—after ten years of agitation and protest—with the designation of the Wildwood-Madison area as a CDBG target area. Thus, much of the housing and neighborhood preservation of the enormous west-side area might never have occurred without the essential existence of WSN's block organization.

Turning to schools, we recall the constant diligent efforts of WSN from their earliest days to persuade school administrators to achieve racial balance in the schools. When the barrage of letters, private and public meetings, and strong public statements did not seem to work, WSN had to resort to the courts for coercive measures. As we saw, these were not always successful either. And yet, the influence of WSN as the constant gadfly, the eternal prodder, on the issue of school racial balance was unmistakable.

Theirs was the first public letter to the editor calling attention in 1970 to racial isolation in the schools. Their public resolution to the school board and later to the city council in 1972 was certainly the first of its kind in the city of Akron. And even though these were rejected by all recipients, who can say that this did not prick the consciences of some? Their letters of protest to the state board of education and to the U.S. Department of Health, Education, and Welfare—though seemingly falling on deaf ears—may have had some eventual impact on the state's development of school racial proportion guidelines. Their filing and winning the careers program suit in 1973 most certainly had an impact on school administrators—who had never lost a suit before, and who did everything possible to mask the results of this one from the public. Without WSN's drawing attention to the issue, reduction of school racial isolation might never have been cited as a goal by a 1974 blue-ribbon citywide task force. It might never have become a topic in the 1975 school board election campaign, and it might never have motivated an Akron youth group in 1976 to petition the local school board for a reduction in school racial isolation. These are no small achievements, when examined in their totality.

Had it not been for these preceding events, occurring persistently over nine years, the Akron school authorities might never have developed their "school decommissioning" Akron Plan by 1976, ostensibly to close some old school buildings, but actually to attempt some reduction of racial isolation, which they did. The state played a role in this as well, which may also have been a response to persistent pressure from WSN. And finally, of course, the massive lawsuit in 1978 against the schools and other significant public forces had a major impact—not only on the schools, but also on the city and public housing authority, named as codefendants in that suit. As Robert Sedler, the chief attorney for the parents in that suit, said: "They'll never be the same again" (notes, Aug. 18, 1978).

Before turning to the work of the housing committee, we must also briefly note WSN's influence on many west-side residents. In the 1979 survey, respondents were asked if they had heard about WSN before receiving the flyer announcing the survey. A substantial majority of them said they had (82%). Asked how they heard of the organization, 75% said from other members, 20% said from friends, and 4% said from publicized meetings or events. To find out whether they could correctly state the purpose of the organization, respondents were asked what they thought the purpose was. More than half the respondents (51%) gave the correct purpose, indicating that WSN was widely known in the area and their purposes were quite well understood.

What is more significant, however, is the association between some of those who knew about WSN and their optimism toward the future. For blacks, knowledge of the organization did not affect views of the neighborhood's future. But for whites, knowing about WSN made a statistically significant difference. When asked what they thought the neighborhood would be like in five years, twice as many whites who knew about WSN thought the neighborhood would be better than those who were not knowledgeable about WSN (Saltman 1986). Knowing or thinking that there was a "big brother" taking care of things might have offered hope and confidence in the neighborhood and its future. Thus, the impact of the organization was felt by some residents whose presence was critical to the maintenance of racial integration.

Reviewing the work of WSN's housing committee, that stalwart persistent small band of zealots, we find a similar array of happenings that all together added up to a tremendous influence. Beginning in 1969, their first protest to AMHA—the local public housing authority—about growing concentrations and segregation of public housing tenants on the west side was the onset of hundreds of such protests delivered over the next two decades. The influence of WSN on AMHA's policies was unmistakable, especially after WSN's housing committee became part of the citizen review panel for federal funding applications in 1976. By 1977, the AMHA was turning to WSN for opinions on site selection before ever submitting an application for federal funding.[16] When AMHA was named as part of the school lawsuit, their policies at that time changed consciously and deliberately in an attempt to reduce segregation and concentration.[17] West Side Neighbors' letters of protest to federal and regional offices of HUD certainly played a role in motivating AMHA to take corrective action.

West Side Neighbors' battle against real estate solicitation in their area ultimately produced some success; here, too, their influence was considerable. Beginning in 1971, they called attention to the relentless harassments west-side residents suffered from real estate agents urging them to sell their homes in the wake of massive urban renewal relocation. As we have already noted, they taped solicitation encounters, sent copies to the local real estate board and human relations commission, filed lawsuits against unethical realtors, made public statements to city council protesting unfair housing practices,[18] successfully urged city funding of a Fair Housing Agency, and by 1973 secured passage of a law—later removed—banning solicitations and "for sale" signs in their area. Twenty-four news articles about WSN and the solicitation issue appeared in the *Akron Beacon Journal* between January 26, 1972 and December 15, 1973.

The housing committee's first mortgage lending study, based on an analysis of twenty-seven years of data, paved the way for the funding of the UPON project—a program to encourage affirmative lending and marketing by bankers and real estate agents. When that funding was announced late in 1979, an unexpected news editorial appeared commenting on it and WSN:

For more than a decade, Akron's West Side has been fighting to keep its dignity in the face of numerous problems that threatened to turn the area into a slum. The fact that the community now proudly describes itself as the "largest interracial area of Summit County" is a tribute to successes attained by a number of individuals and organizations, particularly the West Side Neighbors. (*Akron Beacon Journal*, Nov. 5, 1979)

The editorial noted that WSN was the only neighborhood organization in the entire region "whose sole reason for being is to help create and preserve a stable, desirable integrated community." It also pointed out that achieving that goal depended in large measure on persuading real estate agents to stop soliciting sales and start affirmative marketing, on convincing banks to write conventional mortgage loans in the area, and not just government-insured ones, on pressuring government to provide good schools and city services, and on encouraging businesses to remain in the area and keep their properties attractive. All of this was achieved in the all-too-short time of the funded UPON project. And WSN, as we know, attempted valiantly to continue these efforts after the meager funding ended in 1982.

Thus, the housing committee's first mortgage lending study led to a continuing series of annual mortgage lending reports and to the funding of the UPON project. Out of that came the formation of the Copley Road Merchants Association, which paved the way for the $1 million city improvement program for Copley Road West. There is little question of the impact the UPON's program had on real estate solicitation in the west side area. As a result of the wide distribution of informational flyers about the illegality of solicitation in racially transitional areas (see Appendix C), and the constant educational efforts with real estate agents and brokers, such practices are now rare in the WSN area.

None of this could have been possible without the funding given to the UPON project, which enabled WSN to have full-time staff to conduct these efforts. The result has also produced a consciousness-raising for lenders, ongoing cooperative efforts between them and WSN, and some financial support from them to WSN. Another result has been the expansion of the WSN goals and program to a regional effort, now conducted through a HUD-funded Community Housing Resources Board (CHRB). Perhaps the most far-reaching result of

WSN's housing committee has been their impact on the state mortgage revenue bond issue. For the first time in the entire country, a state housing finance agency has set aside a portion of their funds for making incentive payments for integrative moves. WSN's letters in 1983 to state officials and agency leaders across the state, urging the set-aside, were the first in Ohio calling attention to this concept (see Appendix C). And WSN's Housing Committee drafted the set-aside letters in response to something I learned ten years earlier at a 1972 National Neighbors annual meeting.

When we try to assess the influence of WSN over two decades, we have much empirical evidence of practices and policies that were begun or changed as a result of their efforts. And we have said little or nothing in this brief review about their successful early attempts to secure several recreational sites for west Akron, their international student exchange program, or their serving as a training ground for public officials. Several outstanding public officials and community leaders first began their community work as a WSN board member, officer, or committee worker. They remembered and respected WSN as well-organized, dedicated, and persistent. The image that WSN created in their first two phases luckily carried over into the third phase, long after this earlier vigor had waned.

SUCCESS OR FAILURE?

What shall we say about WSN here? Did they succeed or did they fail? We have seen that their major goal of maintaining racial integration was not very successful, though there are still two tracts in their area which are only slightly integrated. We have seen, too, that some of the quality of their neighborhoods has declined along with the socioeconomic levels of some of their residents. We have also seen that their internal strength and leadership has subsided, as have some of their committees and programs.

Let us now analyze WSN's development over the years in terms of internal and external factors, as we have done in the other four cities. In those cities, however, the assessment of success or failure was much simpler. Those study neighborhoods had either stabilized and remained integrated, as in Model A, or they had become predominantly black, as in Model B. Their organizations also were either alive and well or they had died. But the situation in Akron—Model C—is less determinate. Akron's west side is now more transitional than the study neighborhoods in any of the other four cities, and its neighborhood organization, though weakened, is still alive and struggling. This mixture creates some evaluation difficulties. The picture is not as clear. It would be fair to say, though, that the neighborhood—as an integrated one—and the organization are fighting for their lives.

Internal Factors

These factors, as before, relate to the structure of the organization and its participants. But we quickly acknowledge that what is internal is highly affected by what is external and vice versa. Internally, we saw that WSN began with the stated goal of integration maintenance and worked zealously during their first two phases of organizational development to achieve this. The structure of their organization was similar to all the others studied, with one major difference. They were unfunded for their first ten years, then began a series of separate modestly funded projects that lasted only a short time within their otherwise totally voluntary life-cycle. Had this occurred in Indianapolis or Rochester or even Milwaukee, however, this might have been an insignificant factor. In Akron it may have been nearly fatal, because of what else was happening in the community and outside it.

None of the other study neighborhoods in Model A—the success stories— had to contend with a cluster of schools that became the only racially identifiable black schools in the entire city system. And none of those other study neighborhoods had to confront the colossal reality of having their community become home for more public housing tenants than any other portion of the metropolitan area. The only other study neighborhood that faced this double jeopardy was the failure in Model B—Hartford. The signs in Akron are ominously similar.

Why was the factor of funding so much more important in Akron? Because of the magnitude of the institutional forces facing the west side and the timing of them. Only a full-time effort could successfully deal with them. Had WSN's UPON project begun during their first phase and had it lasted longer, for example, they might have been able to stave off the public housing onslaught. It might have worked like this: if they had instructed and informed realtors earlier about affirmative marketing techniques and the illegality of solicitation in racially transitional areas, they might have retained more residents. If they had retained more residents, with fewer houses for sale, the public housing authority might not have been able to buy or lease as many units as it did on the west side for their leased and scattered-site programs.

Similarly, if they had been able to work with bankers sooner than they did, they might have averted some serious redlining practices which resulted in more FHA and VA mortgages on the west side than elsewhere, which in turn resulted in more fast foreclosures and abandoned houses. These, too, played into the hands of the public housing authority, who delightedly seized the opportunity to acquire these properties. If WSN had had adequate funding soon enough, then, they might have been able to retain more residents, who would have been more likely supporters and workers for the organization, unlike public housing tenants.

It is also possible that the retention of a substantial number of middle-class, educated residents might have had an impact on the schools. Even after the schools suit was lost for west Akron in phase three, there may have been more of a nucleus of fighters remaining who would have taken on the task of battling with the school authorities and continuing to press for racial balance. And if all this had happened, the leadership of the organization might not have begun to wane as it did—bereft of skills, resources, and hope. So a whole chain of events might have been averted if WSN had had funding and staffing early enough to deal with the forces affecting the life and death of their neighborhood and community. They did not begin to realize till very late—too late—that they had to have staffing to tackle the forces confronting them. And by the time they obtained such staffing, their leadership was such that they did not know how to deal with it adequately.

As it was, they did the best they could with the few resources they had. The fact that they still survive, in the face of enormous obstacles and institutional forces, is a testament to their courage, determination, and stubbornness. The remembrance I wrote for their twentieth anniversary recalled some early hopes and dreams: "Perhaps if we had known how hard a task . . . and what a constant struggle it would be, and the magnitude of the institutional forces we would have to confront—we might never have begun. So it's good that we didn't know all that then. . . . Because this has been a noble and a mighty experiment . . . with some noteworthy successes and some critical failures. The best part of it has been the sharing of a vision with wonderful people. If that vision was sometimes blurred, and if it was partially unfulfilled, it is not for lack of trying" (WSN anniversary booklet, Oct. 1987).

External Factors

Here we examine the same four variables as in the other cities: the amenities of the neighborhood, the role of the city, public housing concentration, and school desegregation. The amenities of the Akron west-side neighborhood are few: some physical attractiveness and good housing stock. But, as we have already noted, this is far from being uniformly distributed throughout WSN's five tracts. We have already referred to the diversity of the area and its residents; the amenities reflect that diversity. The tracts below Copley Road—that notorious Mason-Dixon line—house substantial numbers of residents of lower socioeconomic levels, along with those of middle and upper-middle levels. Their homes and neighborhoods reflect these differences.

The city golf course is located in one integrated tract, but is largely hidden from public view except along the expressway. One large, attractive park— Forest Lodge—is located at the northern edge of the same tract, adjacent to the campus of the St. Sebastian church, school, and convent. We have already referred to the Catholic school as an important stabilizing influence in the WSN area. One other major park—Schneider—is located in the same tract, also at the northern edge. Nothing else in the WSN area is noteworthy as an amenity. The business district is a disaster. Even after the million-dollar improvement program in the western portion, it remains unattractive because of quadrant parking next to all the stores, right up on the sidewalk, and because of some shoddy and vacant exteriors.

The role of the city mirrors the views of other institutional forces and the general society. It is one of long neglect, apathy, and selective policies that were harmful to the WSN area. Had the city played an early supportive role in WSN's stabilization efforts, so much of what happened to them might never have happened. For example, if the city had taken action to reinforce WSN's efforts with AMHA, this might have had profound positive consequences. Since it was the city that had to annually approve the public housing authority's plans for site locations and public housing programs for federal funding, all they had to do was make such approval contingent on the deconcentration and deseg-regation of public housing units, and AMHA would have capitulated. This never happened. The city continued to approve AMHA's plans each year, despite the growing intensity of WSN's protests.[19]

We have already referred to the lateness of the 1986 selection of the Wildwood-Madison areas for neighborhood improvement. Yet, ten years earlier, as we noted, WSN sent letters and made public statements describing that area and inviting the mayor and the city planning department to "take a walk on Wildwood Avenue." By the time it was designated as a target area, it was a cesspool and had been for a long time. This was, of course, all consistent with the city's triage policy of preferring to deal only with "good" salvageable areas. The Wildwood area, on the other hand, was the place snapped up by AMHA for public housing tenants, and this was the area that was unkempt, rundown, and blighted, with one of the highest crime rates in the city. By the time the city was persuaded to do something, it was too late.

Compounding this neglect was the underfunding allocated to the program, and the crippling stipulations placed upon it. The city stated that it would not proceed to the second phase of the program if the first phase did not produce a compliance rate of 70% of code enforcement for owner-occupied dwellings. After so many years of waiting for some help for this area, WSN's housing committee was understandably disheartened, discouraged, and angered about the city's actions.

What hurt even more was the city's excellent rehabilitation and improvement program in an adjacent area, Highland Square. The symbol of the difference was in the treatment of the business area: Highland Square was given old bricks for edging of sidewalks; WSN's Copley Road was given concrete or grass, which was difficult for storeowners to maintain. When WSN's president protested, he was told that the bricks were too expensive. Consistently, WSN felt that they received short shrift from the city—always too late, and always too little, with failure built into the program—as with impossible stipulations.

Another indicator of the city's negative role was in their policy of home repair assistance, which we have already noted. They preferred to work only in one target area at a time, for several years, and made loans and grants only in the target area. If housing needed rehabilitation in other areas, they could not receive city assistance. After much agitation and protest about this, the city finally set up a meager citywide repair grant program of $200,000—but only for elderly or handicapped persons. This did nothing to aid those in need who were neither elderly nor handicapped. Contrast this with Rochester's outstanding repair program.

The city of Akron was, furthermore, totally opposed to the concept of Neighborhood Housing Services—a nationwide program using the combined efforts of banks, the city, and neighborhood organizations to preserve and maintain housing and neighborhood quality. Chiefly responsible for these views and policies was the director of the city planning department, who was compared to the Pope in terms of power, and who remained as mayors and city councils came and went over the years.

Finally, we recall the work of the public housing authority in Akron—AMHA—and the work of the school authorities in Akron. Neither of these institutional forces needs further elaboration here. We have already presented detailed accounts of their policies and programs and actions, which destroyed the possibility of WSN ever maintaining a racially pluralistic community on the west side. The facts indicate that AMHA glutted the west-side area slowly and systematically with public housing tenants who were primarily black. And the facts show that the school authorities either did nothing to avert the racial imbalance of the west-side schools, or took deliberate actions that had the effect of increasing it. Since these and other Akron institutional forces show considerable executive interlocking,[20] it would have been relatively simple for them to agree on practices and policies to avert neighborhood resegregation. But they were not so inclined.

We must, then, in conclusion cite these three external factors as significantly blocking the possibilities of success for WSN and the west-side neighborhoods. The city was not helpful; its apathy and reluctance undermined the goals of neighborhood stabilization. The public housing authority's actions were extremely harmful to those goals by their concentration of low-income and black public housing tenants in the west-side neighborhoods. And the school authorities were vicious in their total neglect and denial of the issue of racial imbalance and isolation, to the ultimate end of having the west-side cluster remain the only racially identifiable black school cluster in the entire city system.

We end with one letter from a former resident, now an agency executive in another state, which is offered as a reminder of the intangible effects of WSN's work over twenty years. If the organization ultimately dies, what it stood for and the work it did may not.

By a strange twist of fate, I write this note from Reno, Nevada, over ten years since we left Akron. So often our thoughts turn to West Akron . . . our lovely homes, the tree-shaded streets, the International Dinners . . . WSN Board meetings, flowering shrubs on the lawns, riding bicycles up Sunset/Rose Blvd. Most of all I remember the warmth. I remember . . . our children's friends, football in our front yard and the neighborhood trick-or-treat days. . . . And I remember leaving. I was giving up a sense of belonging. I've never had the same feeling since, and I cherish the experience. . . . A part of me— a part of all our family—still remains in Akron. When people ask, upon learning of our odyssey of moving, "where did you like the best?" we all answer "West Akron."

So, my friends, I write as one who has not really left. Our children's sense of *hometown*, however brief, remains in Akron. Our sense of being part of something worthwhile, something significant—a statement to the world that our neighborhood, our community, our schools, our friendships—were all worthy of respect, a model, a bright light—all remain part of our memory. Eleven years after we left Akron, I write on behalf of Ralph, my husband, and Robin, Peter, Paul . . . thank you, West Side Neighbors, for still being there. We do remember you well. (WSN anniversary booklet, Oct. 1987)

But how long will they still be there?

NOTES

1. One black school-board member testified that he was told by the board chair, who was white, that it wasn't necessary to have a black person on the board since "the colored people were being taken care of, because South High School was built for the colored people" (Deposition, *Bell vs. Ott* 1978).

2. Another SWAP worker was obtained three years later in 1987, supervised by WSN's president. But she was paid by WSN for working an additional ten hours a week, so this was no longer a "free lunch."

3. This did not work very well, since committees were not often able to distinguish between goals and objectives.

4. But the decision came to haunt them when they later learned of junior high school counselors encouraging white students to go to Central High School instead of the west side's Buchtel High School. Parents' repeated complaints did not stop this practice.

5. These included local chapters of the Urban League, NAACP, League of Women Voters, and American Civil Liberties Union, plus the Fair Housing Service, East Akron Community House, two ministerial alliances and several church social action groups.

6. HUD was later removed from the case, after they agreed to furnish plaintiffs with valuable data concerning FHA and other housing segregation in Akron.

7. These included Martin Sloane (NCDH), Frank Schwelb (Dept. of Justice, Washington, D.C.), and Karl Taeuber (University of Wisconsin).

8. None of these cases involved settlements of more than two hundred dollars. Perhaps if more experienced fair housing attorneys had been available to press for serious monetary damages, WSN's suits would have had far greater impact on the real estate community. And, if Akron's fair housing agency had been more effective at that time, this too would have greatly aided WSN and the west side of Akron.

9. Acronym for Cooperating Agents, Recommended and Encouraged. Such agents agreed to do affirmative marketing of the west-side area, no solicitation, and prompt removal of "sold" signs, in exchange for WSN referrals and publicity.

10. This HUD-sponsored program brought $25,000 to Akron to have CHRB conduct part of the UPON project (affirmative marketing) on a regional basis.

11. This involved cooperating pairs of white and black agents, with white agents securing listings in white areas and co-broking these with black agents and their black clients. Fifteen such CARE PAIRS were obtained in UPON's second year.

12. This coalition was led first by the Cuyahoga Plan, a Cleveland area fair housing agency, and later by the Cleveland area Metropolitan Strategy Group, headed by NN's Chip Bromley.

13. Length of residence and race were the most significant background variables in this concern. People who lived in the neighborhood the longest had the highest percentage viewing this concern as a serious problem. And twice as many white residents saw this as a serious problem compared to black residents (Saltman 1986).

14. Audit results (Saltman 1975, 1979) and mortgage lending data (WSN Mortgage Lending Patterns annual reports, 1976–87) confirm this.

15. Only one branch bank has served the entire WSN area of 10,000 households. This one has just moved out of the area (December 1988). No other area of the city is so underserved by the lending industry.

16. Correspondence from AMHA authorities to WSN as late as 1979 confirms this.

17. Their own testimony and data at the 1978 school trial confirms this.

18. These statements were made singly by WSN, and in conjunction with other groups, throughout their twenty years.

19. This protest went all the way to HUD, who sent an investigator to Akron in 1987. One possible result of this is the announcement in 1988 that AMHA can now only acquire property in Akron in "some designated areas" (*Akron Beacon Journal*, Aug. 2, 1988).

20. This interlocking is shown in the following example of executive musical chairs in Akron: the newest executive director of the Akron Area Board of Realtors (AABR) is a former public schools administrator; the past executive director of AABR is now vice-president of Boebinger Realtors; two public schools administrators retired from the schools to take new executive positions with AMHA, the public housing authority.

7

PROFILES ACROSS THE COUNTRY, MODELS A AND C

"The real issue of the eighties is integration versus segregation . . . are the patterns that developed in the city . . . going to develop in the suburbs?"

"As the schools go . . . so goes the community. Schools have a position and importance in a community, and a legitimacy and responsibility for the integration process, that many other agencies don't have."

"When you get down to the grassroots, there is an element of long-term optimism which probably doesn't exist anywhere else in the world."

"They say it can't be done . . . but sometimes it doesn't always work."

This movement's geographical scope, contextual similarity, and program creativity and diversity are shown in the following examples of urban and suburban neighborhood efforts. These were not singled out because they are more noteworthy than any other efforts. They were selected, rather, as representing typical successful Model A and conditional Model C movement organizations and neighborhoods. There are, of course, many others just as typical, and still others

Unless otherwise noted, chapter quotes are from correspondence and responses to mailed questionnaires (Appendix B).

that show the failure of Model B. All of the three suburban efforts described here are success stories, as are four of the seven urban efforts. My conclusion is that suburban efforts have a greater probability of success than urban neighborhood efforts, because they are autonomous and are supported and reinforced by their municipal government.

SEVEN URBAN PROGRAMS

Prospect/Lefferts Gardens Neighborhood Association (Brooklyn, N. Y.)—Model C

Inception/Goals. The Prospect/Lefferts Gardens Neighborhood Association (PLGNA) was formed in 1968 "to build a stable interracial neighborhood to support U.S. freedom." Bill Tennyson, the founder, recalled that in 1968 he had just read the Kerner Report at the public library where he worked as a librarian. "I was moved by the report's prediction of Americans' loss of freedom as a price of angry blacks and fearful whites. So I decided to commit myself as a Christian to building an interracial neighborhood where I lived" (letter, 1985).

Martin Luther King's death was an additional catalyst for the founder. Five local "main line" churches were asked by Tennyson to form a board of directors with a constitution and bylaws to govern the new neighborhood association. The first board consisted of ministers and lay members of the five churches who were part of the new nonprofit membership corporation.

Prospect/Lefferts Gardens is an area of forty-six blocks with some 40,000 residents. Between 1960 and 1970, its black population rose from 30% to 70%. When the neighborhood association was formed, 300 deteriorated buildings were counted in the neighborhood. Three of them were abandoned. "Have you ever tried to turn around a decaying building as a volunteer?" asked Tennyson. It became clear very early that the housing problem was beyond the capability of volunteers, and funding was sought for a paid community organizer.

Between 1968 and 1973 funding grew from $5,000 to $16,000, gathered from churches, a local foundation, and a bank. Later, the New York State Preservation Society became the major source of support with an annual grant of over $100,000. Now a staff of four and a full-time community organizer carry on the work of the organization.

Program. Though black-white alienation and housing deterioration were the original issues around which the group was formed, four other problems quickly became apparent. As Bill Tennyson put it: "Three strong forces confront any interracial neighborhood: insurance, real estate brokers, and banks." The fourth is crime—or the perception of it. In sixteen years of PLGNA's existence, most of the active members' energies have been spent on these concerns.

The founder believed, however, that much of what was accomplished in the neighborhood was done by people who were not on the board of directors, which he thought "functioned poorly" over the years. So poorly, in fact, that eight executive directors came and went in nine years. Tennyson felt that the board members were not problem solvers; they were talkers, not doers, and they just "wanted a line on their resumes or political recognition." For this reason, "any achievement had to be organized outside the board." And much of it was done by the founder, who was in fact a member of the board. He described some of his efforts.

Concerning insurance:

I received a letter from Nationwide that my policy would not be renewed. What should I do? I wrote the company president, told him we were trying to build an interracial neighborhood and how important our effort was to moving America toward freedom, and he should support, not undermine, us. Sent a copy to Elizabeth Holtzman, our Congress representative, and the state insurance department superintendent. In two weeks I got a letter back from Nationwide's president saying the first letter had been a mistake.

Tennyson went on to say that without insurance, his mortgage would be in default even if he had made every payment. One business's rates went from $300 to $1,000 a year even though they had never submitted a claim. The result of the high insurance rates was that stores closed and were replaced by "fly-by-night operations that did not carry insurance. . . . Deterioration set in. . . . But then Representative Holtzman got our rates reduced, and that helped the neighborhood." She fought with the group to keep neighborhood insurance rates reasonable, and eventually succeeded.

In response to heavy racial steering by real estate agents, the PLGNA decided to form their own neighborhood real estate operation. Affirmative marketing was directed to white families through prepared displays and presentations taken to churches in surrounding areas. An annual spring house tour, conducted since 1969, was the main source of new buyers. "The tour was advertised in city-wide papers and generally 100 to 200 people turned out at $2 to $3 a ticket, some of whom eventually bought homes in the neighborhood" (letter, 1985). But racial steering by agents continued.

An audit of real estate practices was organized by Tennyson in 1973. Legal assistance was given by the NAACP and technical advice came from National Neighbors. Twenty people were recruited as "testers," and four major brokers were audited. The evidence of racial steering was substantial enough to file suit against the four brokers. The case was settled in federal District Court in 1974, with the brokers ordered by the court to report all rentals and sales by address and race for a stipulated period of time. "But since there are a thousand brokers in Brooklyn, and since the U.S. Department of Justice didn't expand our evidence, no major patterns were changed."

As for lending policies: "No university I ever went to—and I've been to a few—ever taught me how to force a powerful group to do something it didn't want to do. When Jane and I wanted to buy this house, seventeen banks refused to give us a mortgage" (Tennyson letter, 1985). Volunteer researchers were recruited to gather information on redlining in their neighborhood. After picketing and distribution of greenlining cards, the group was aided by passage of the Home Mortgage Disclosure Act and the Community Reinvestment Act (CRA). When a major bank, Greater New York Bank for Savings, was denied an additional branch because of noncompliance with the CRA, the Tennysons were granted their mortgage. The data used to establish noncompliance was gathered by neighborhood volunteers.

In addition to these specific activities, the PLGNA has developed an active crime prevention program through block patrols and special cars "with yellow flashers, walkie talkies, and magnetic signs" (letter, 1985). As a result of their funding by the state preservation department, a portion of their brownstone neighborhood has been declared a historic landmark area. One of their business strips, on Flatbush Avenue, has been improved, and another is under way. Though their local schools are nearly all-black, one of them has student reading and math scores above the national average.

Despite all these developments, the general perception of the neighborhood is a negative one. A visit to an urban sociology class at Brooklyn College—two miles south of the neighborhood—confirmed this. When the Prospect/Lefferts Gardens neighborhood was described to the students as "racially mixed," their written reactions revealed images of "broken glass, garbage piled on the sidewalks, and abandoned cars." Some of the students who actually visited the neighborhood were "amazed to find clean streets and beautifully kept houses and gardens" (letter, 1985).

The founder pointed, however, to continuing housing neglect and abandonment, the association's ineffective board of directors, continual staff turnover, and ongoing real estate discrimination.

So, with so much frustration and meager success why don't I move out to my farm in New Jersey or sell my six apartments here and move to the white suburbs? Because the God I worship, the interracial neighborhood I live in, and the work I do here form a deep integrity—a joy—that I would not exchange for all the prettified, empty homogeneous neighborhoods of this world. (letter, 1985)

This is a Model C movement organization—live MO, black neighborhood.

Belmont-Hillsboro Neighbors (Nashville, Tennessee)— Model A

Inception/Goals. BHN began informally in 1970, was incorporated in 1971, and by 1980 succeeded in having a major part of its area placed on the National Register of Historic Places. Further blessed by an excellent school desegregation program, no public housing concentration in its neighborhood, and the help of Neighborhood Housing Services, this is another example of Model A—the live

MO and successfully maintained integrated neighborhood. In its one hundred blocks, with 2,200 households, the racial composition has remained stable at 41% black since 1970.

Three reasons were given for forming the organization: racial panic, school desegregation, and slumlords and the need for code enforcement. "In the old, campus-oriented neighborhood in southwest Nashville, there was dissatisfaction with a rapidly changing area in transition. A 'chain of people acquainted with each other' began the organization with a public meeting in a school auditorium" (White 1973). As the organization gradually won a few victories—such as stopping unfair real estate practices against minorities—the esprit and solidarity of the group built up, according to the founder and first president (correspondence from Tilson 1985).

The original objectives of the group are intact, just as they were listed in their bylaws when the group first started. Eight objectives are stated in the bylaws, the first of which is "to unite all the residents of our neighborhood (boundaries given) in one interracial, multiclass organization, bring them into closer and more frequent contact with each other, and encourage them to plan and work together."

Other objectives included the preservation of the residential character of the neighborhood; helping residents maintain and improve their homes and grounds, encouraging in-movement "with continued diversity as the chief goal"; promoting good relationships between "people with different backgrounds"; working for equal housing opportunities; acting as a "channel of information" and advocate in public hearings and legal suits involving the neighborhood; and cooperating with other local, state or national groups having compatible goals. In fact, BHN was one of the charter members of National Neighbors.

The management of the affairs of the organization was through its steering committee, which consisted of chairpersons of committees, officers, and five members at-large elected by members at an annual meeting. They had no office or paid staff, and the only funding ever received was for the research and publication of a photographic booklet in 1975.

Building a Neighborhood: Yesterday, Today, and Tomorrow was the title of the sixty-page booklet, which focused on the architectural heritage of the neighborhood and its land use and zoning. Funded by a grant from the Tennessee Committee for the Humanities, an affiliate of the National Endowment for the Humanities, the booklet paved the way for the Belmont-Hillsboro neighborhood being declared a historic district five years later. BHN was the first neighborhood group in Nashville to receive an award from the Metro Historical Commission.

Program. The major source of operating funds came from a neighborhood fair, held for the first ten years of BHN's existence. The purpose of the fair was "to bring neighbors together" rather than mere fund-raising. A free newsletter, mimeographed and distributed by block volunteers six times a year, has also provided an ongoing network of communication in the neighborhood. The *Belmont-Hillsboro News* includes updates on issues affecting the neighborhood—

highway construction, drainage problems, proposed density of multifamily units—as well as announcements of new residents and births.

The earliest committees set up by the organization were zoning and code enforcement, traffic, and a housing listing service to recruit people interested in buying or renting in the neighborhood. The listing service was given up "when the neighborhood became desirable" (Tilson 1985). But the problems of absentee ownership and real estate speculation have continued throughout the BHN's existence. The group's early message was to the point: Belmont-Hillsboro would become a ghetto only if its residents let it happen.

One past chairman of the steering committee recalled their early activities to stabilize the neighborhood: "We began by trying to get accurate information to the people. Rumor is a very powerful thing" (*The Banner* 1974). Next came a campaign to encourage elderly residents in the area to keep their homes.

This is an old neighborhood so we have a considerable number of elderly people here. They were under tremendous pressure to sell, and one source of that pressure was the real estate agents. . . . They would come in and tell people that prices were going down, now is the time to sell, if you wait two more years you'll be losing money. (Banner 1974)

Another source of pressure was relatives, who urged elderly residents to move to the suburbs and "get rid of that big, old house that you don't need any more" (Banner 1974).

Gradually, the "for sale" signs that dotted the lawns in the neighborhood began to disappear. By 1974—just a few years after BHN began—there were more people wanting to move into the neighborhood than people wanting to sell, and property values were rising. Some of this was surely due to the MO's good work and the publicity it received. But some of it was also due, as we have seen elsewhere, to other factors external to the organization.

One of these was the school desegregation program—a countywide one—which began at about the same time that BHN began. This made it possible for the neighborhood to be affirmatively marketed, with an increase of young families with children moving in. This was also a stabilizing influence on the elderly, who were encouraged to remain in the face of this influx. The presence of an active Fair Housing Foundation in Nashville was an additional positive factor influencing real estate practices in the entire metropolitan area, and expanding the use of affirmative marketing in racially integrated neighborhoods.

Additional program concerns over the years have included zoning changes and land use modification, code enforcement and general rehabilitation, and proposed highway construction surrounding the neighborhood. The founder and first president explained the stance of the group: "We're not protectionists as many of the suburban areas appear to be. The area already has multiple dwellings, office and commercial uses. But it disturbs us when they [developers] are not content with the rezoning that's already taken place but always want to bite off just a little bit more" (White 1973).

Though BHN proposed an urban park and bikeways as an alternative to a proposed interstate freeway encircling their area, they lost that battle. But their victories far exceeded their losses over the years. Typical of their stubborn resistance to any encroachment is this public notice stating their policy:

Belmont-Hillsboro Neighbors, Inc. . . . hereby gives public notice to all owners . . . or potential investors . . . and all public agencies. . . . that it specifically opposes and will oppose any extension of commercial uses beyond the rear property line of [specified boundary]. . . . Copies of the present notice are being filed with the Mayor, the Metropolitan Clerk, the Metropolitan Board of Zoning Appeals, the Nashville Redevelopment and Housing Authority, and the State and Regional Offices of the Department of Housing and Urban Development. (BHN Public Notice 1973)

One newspaper columnist described BHN as having "gained a fair degree of notoriety ('Oh no, here they come again')" (White 1973). The founder gave his views on neighborhood organization:

Generally, neighborhoods do not get organized unless they feel they are directly under the gun in some way. It may be a freeway going through, or it may be sudden pressures for commercialization, re-zoning, or racial changes. But some way when people get disturbed enough. . . . If the planners feel they have to make certain areas the victims in order to accomplish something for the general good of the area, something's wrong. What effective citizen organization means is that nobody is going to get pushed around or victimized. (White 1973)

By their tenth anniversary in 1981, BHN had much to celebrate. Their area had been the first picked for a federally funded code enforcement program, they had been a target area for a rehabilitation program conducted by Neighborhood Housing Services, they were listed in the National Register of Historic Places, they had a "naturally integrated" school in their neighborhood that was exempt from busing, and they were slated for a continuing positive future under a new citywide Neighborhood Conservation Zoning plan to prevent redevelopment.

Yet, a recent newsletter revealed their own sense of fragility. Under the lead announcement of a Spring Fling ("Come and Meet Your Neighbors—Hot Dogs, Auction, Bake Sale, Green Thumb Booth, etc.") was News of the Neighborhood. The first item referred to the loss of "two more houses in our neighborhood—this time by fire," and continued:

[It] has made nearby residents aware of how fragile the texture of a neighborhood is. When a house goes down, and a new one is contemplated, there are many concerns that people have. One involves zoning: "How many units can they put there? How big will it be?" Sometimes the answer is that the big ideas of inexperienced investors are simply not legal, and we're able to reassure residents about that. But there are also questions about the appropriateness and scale of the new structure. . . . The momentum for a "neighborhood conservation district" is building, and there will be a presentation at our Spring Fling. . . . It would not stop redevelopment, and it can't solve all problems;

but it helps by reminding builders that they can do what they want to do in a way that fits in with the neighborhood. (*News*, May-June, 1985)

Directly under this news item was another noting that BHN had filed "another appeal of a variance by the Board of Zoning Appeals." The variance was to relax side-yard requirements, enabling the construction of two duplexes at an address in the neighborhood. Neighbors objected to the crowding, and to front-yard parking. The lawsuit had been filed by an attorney who was "a new resident of the neighborhood." So the struggle continues.

Though the founder in 1985 referred to some fatigue within the organization ("There has been a certain amount of loss of motivation from some people"), this may well be a result of the successes the MO and its neighborhood have had, as well as of some burnout. Compared to those neighborhoods in Models B or C, however, this one in Nashville is to be admired and cheered. Its future, though never certain, seems likely to continue in a positive direction.

Crenshaw Neighbors (Los Angeles, California)—Model C

Inception/Goals. In the early spring of 1961, a small discussion group of twenty black and white women was formed in a south-central neighborhood of Los Angeles. This neighborhood was in the area known as Crenshaw, which at that time was beginning to undergo racial transition. When the first black and Asian families began to buy homes in the high-priced Baldwin Hill areas, few residents panicked. "It seemed unlikely that enough minority families could afford the homes to make any significant impact on the area" (Crenshaw Neighbors 1972).

Calling itself United Neighbors, the purpose of the early discussion group was "to provide a much-needed opportunity for exploration, discussion, and under-standing . . . of our community's racial tensions" (CN 1963). They reached across the barriers of race and religion and discussed problems people have everywhere: mothers' concern for their children's welfare, playmates, school friends, and social partners; the quality of the schools; property values; and acceptance of new people. "One of the first discoveries was that all of us, regardless of race, seemed to share the same concerns" (CN 1972). This early discussion group was the predecessor of Crenshaw Neighbors (CN).

After holding monthly morning meetings for a year, with growing attendance, the discussion group changed to evening meetings to accommodate those men and employed women who had also expressed an interest in the discussions. The organization's newsletter noted many years later: "The group consisted of highly motivated, individualistic persons who preferred a loosely structured ar-rangement to permit freedom to act in pursuit of specific concerns" (*Crenshaw Notes*, July 1979). Even this loosely structured group, however, had weekly steering committee meetings to plan the larger discussion programs.

A committee structure was developed that allowed people who were interested in a particular issue to work together on it. Areas of major concern were: housing, schools, human relations, and standards. The primary goal was "to achieve integration of the Crenshaw community in a spirit of harmony and goodwill" (*Notes*, July 1979).

After three years of this informal structure, with evening meetings drawing more than one hundred people each month, a more formal structure and organization—Crenshaw Neighbors—was seen as necessary.

It became apparent that talking was not enough. As we talked, the panic and fear that had not come earlier began. Rumors of trouble in the schools became commonplace; block busting arrived at the same time; harassments and threats began for sellers and new arrivals. If Crenshaw was to avoid becoming a ghetto, like every other northern black area that was once an all-white neighborhood, action was needed. The dynamics of what was happening in Crenshaw gradually became apparent. The self-fulfilling prophecy had taken hold. If blacks live in an area, it is assumed that whites do not want to stay or move in because the area will become all black. Whites are then discouraged from moving in and sometimes frightened into leaving, and the area does become all minority. . . . The idea evolved that an organization devoted to stabilizing Crenshaw could work to do so by showing that predictions are not realities, that residents can make their community schools as good as they wish, and the standards kept high. Thus Crenshaw Neighbors was born. (*Notes*, 1972)

Another goal was added: "To work in every way possible to maintain this community as a desirable place to live for all people" (*Notes*, 1979). The corporation formed in July 1964 to do this work began with one hundred charter members each contributing ten dollars. A board of directors of twenty-five persons became responsible for the operation of Crenshaw Neighbors, aided by a staffed office.

They are still functioning, though somewhat fatigued and depleted in spirit. Their neighborhood has become predominantly black, and portions of their business and residential area are no longer bright and beautiful. Crenshaw Neighbors is an example of Model C—live MO, black neighborhood.

Program. According to the group's newsletter, "CN has established a widely accepted image as a respected community organization and has access to city officialdom as well as other responsible agencies and organizations" (*Notes*, July 1979). The support of CN is sought by other groups in pursuit of accomplishing their own objectives. It has contributed to upgrading the quality of life in the Crenshaw area by its special programs developed over the years. One of those programs concerned the affirmative marketing of their area. Crenshaw Neighbors became the first licensed real estate corporation in the country set up and operated by residents of a community for the purpose of maintaining integration (*Notes*, 1972). Annual home tours were conducted to publicize the area and to encourage more white homeseekers to buy or rent housing there.

To maintain the physical quality of their area, a standards committee served as "the watchdog of the neighborhood—ever concerned about abandoned vehicles, invasion of liquor stores and night clubs, merchants who had shoddy merchandise or dirty premises, poor street lighting, traffic problems, unswept streets, uncut grass, run-down housing" (Laura Damell 1984).

The CN program most often mentioned by those interviewed was a school integration attempt called APEX (Area Program for Enrichment Education). Alarmed by the rapidity of racial change in their schools, Crenshaw members appeared before the Los Angeles Board of Education pressing for an innovative approach to their need for integrated school experiences for their children. First conceived by the education committee of CN, APEX became federally funded in 1967, received a foundation grant one year later, and was eventually taken over by the Los Angeles Board of Education in 1970.

A joint community-school committee was established by the sympathetic Board of Education to create the program, involving five senior high schools and eight junior high schools in the Crenshaw area. Gradually the concept of subject centers at different schools evolved, which would enable students to voluntarily take classes that were not otherwise available. Any student in the participating schools could volunteer to participate, and would be bussed from his or her home school to one of the nearby APEX schools for two periods. Special guidance and counseling programs were devised, the University of Southern California agreed to provide consulting services, and bus transportation was arranged.

In September 1966, the package proposal was submitted to HEW for funding under Title III of the 1965 Elementary and Secondary Education Act. The proposal was approved by the federal government, and APEX began in the fall of 1967. The classes offered were varied, and included Chinese, Russian, Hebrew, aeronautics, data processing, anthropology, play production, ceramics, mass-media English, and constitutional law. Fifteen hundred students enrolled in the program during its first year, attending five senior high schools for two classes. Unfortunately, elementary schools were unaffected by the program, and they steadily increased in minority proportions. By 1973, few white families with children were moving in to the Crenshaw area, and the APEX program gradually dissolved.

Other programs CN developed included a community park, Jim Gilliam Park, which took seventeen years to achieve (interview, 1984); neighborhood watch and Operation Identification for crime prevention in about eighty organized block clubs; a "Shop Crenshaw" campaign to promote local business support; neighborhood coffees for fellowship; periodic clean-up campaigns; open forums on public issues; the neighborhood newspaper (*Crenshaw Notes*); and a constant twenty-year effort for business district improvement.

In 1983, CN was funded through block grant funds for a special youth services project. The proposal for the funding of CN Community Action Project was written by Laura Damell, a board member, who said: "since the original goal of CN—integration maintenance—could not be obtained in any way, CN should change its program to accommodate to the reality of the needs of its area. So the CNCAP project was conceived to try to achieve recognition for CN while at the same time doing something good for its area. It became harder to get volunteers to do anything, and harder for CN to find ways of gaining recognition after the area became predominantly black" (interview, 1985).

The brochure describing the CNCAP lists five aspects of the program: personal and career counseling for young people and adults; workshops on employment preparation; referral services for youth crisis intervention and temporary shelter; tutoring services; and safety and referral services for senior citizens. These were developed to meet the problems of education, crime, and unemployment in the Crenshaw community. As a 1983 brochure described it: "Operating under the auspices of Crenshaw Neighbors Inc., the parent organization with 20 years of service. . . . CNCAP also aims to serve as a catalyst for the coordination and partnership of services that are needed to preserve and promote the rich heritage and history that must continue to be a part of this growing community."

Despite this positive approach, the project seemed to be in difficulty when I visited Crenshaw in 1984, and again in 1985. Staff problems were referred to by both the office manager of CN and a long-time active board member. They spoke of trouble between the project director and the CN board and committee set up to oversee the project. "The second director wouldn't pay any attention to the board, and was asked to resign. So they're looking for someone else. The board and committee didn't seem to know what the project was really supposed to do, so they couldn't guide the director very well" (interview, 1985).

The same active member also spoke somewhat wearily of the planned and hoped for revitalization of the Crenshaw business district. She told of nine years or more of discussions, waiting, politicking, and no action on the business area improvement. Crenshaw was perceived as "laden with crime," she said, even though other areas had as much. She said that the building of a nearby shopping area took away much from the Crenshaw area, being only a little over a mile away. She thought it might help to revive the neighborhood if they built a bridge between the two major department stores and had some enclosed mall area. This, in fact, was "the latest plan," which appeared to be "certain of funding" from community development funds and private sources.

Internally, this long-time resident and CN member spoke of much turnover on the board, and how difficult that was for the organization. She also said that was reflected in her own neighborhood. She was going to a block meeting that week, and only knew now eight out of twenty-five or more of her neighbors. She remembered a time when she knew all of them.

A brief comparison of CN and the neighborhood on its tenth and twentieth anniversaries reveals some of the changes in both over the years. On its tenth anniversary, the lead newsletter article was titled, "Is It True That the First Ten Years Are the Hardest?" Four "Then and Now" items followed:

(1) THEN—We could not get our news releases in the local papers, NOW—Hardly a week goes by without news of CN in the local papers often with pictures, and on the front page; (2) THEN—The Chamber of Commerce did not recognize us, and our Ex-

Director's attempt to join the Women's Division met with polite but decidedly negative response; NOW—The Chamber is a good friend and cooperative partner in many of our community activities and our Ex-Dir. has been elected as an officer of the Women's Division; (3) THEN—We were considered radicals and troublemakers by local real estate brokers, members of the L.A. school administration and many officials, business establishments, etc.; NOW—Our support and cooperation sought by these same groups and recognition of our work is evidenced by the plaques, citations and resolutions that adorn our walls; (4) THEN—We were alive with a spirit of dedication and determination and a brotherhood of mutual respect and warm affection that brought us through ten years to—, NOW—Do we still have that spirit? Enough for another ten years? (*Crenshaw Notes*, July-Aug. 1974)

On its twentieth anniversary, in 1984, CN listed its achievements over the past two decades, and referred to itself as continuing to contribute "to the common good and benefit of all citizens" in the Crenshaw area. The printed program for its celebration (a lunch and installation of officers) included greetings from the president. He referred to the "dedicated network of volunteers," who for over twenty years kept the Crenshaw area a neighborhood of quality where all persons could live without regard to race or creed. He also asked for continued support in the effort "to keep Crenshaw a pleasant community in which to live."

Though its slogan is still "Serving an Integrated Community," the general perception is that Crenshaw is a black area. Statistics show this to be accurate. In 1960, the percent black in the Crenshaw area was 24%; in 1970 it was 70%. By 1984 it was over 80%. Though hardly stable, and certainly not integrated, city officials describing the area referred to it as having a "unique quality and range of housing stock," which continues to be recognized "as favorably comparable to the best in the city" (Gruen Report 1978). Yet, the negative aspects of the area—the run-down business district, and a dense multifamily rental area known as "the Jungle"—are well known and regretfully acknowledged by residents and nonresidents alike.

Still, the organization goes on—trying to bring about improvements in the "bad spots," and trying to maintain the good ones. Active member Laura Damell explained how she felt about CN and why she cared so much about them:

I know how sincere and honest they are. . . . I know how discouraged we have been and how at the bottom of the barrel we have been, and yet they have never given up. And to me that is a tremendous achievement. . . . We are constantly asked by people, "What are you doing, and what have you done?" And what we have done—well, is kind of like housework. You don't see it until it's not done. . . . The dirt shows if you don't do it. To me that is what Crenshaw Neighbors are all about. (interview, 1984)

Greater Park Hill Community, Inc. (Denver, Colorado)— Model A

Inception/Goals. Another example of Model A is the interracial Park Hill area of Denver. The genesis of the organization was in 1956, when the clergy of seven Park Hill churches preached sermons inviting minorities to their churches. At that time, as a 1979 pamphlet explains, the northwestern portion of Park Hill contained a growing black community, "created by housing, cultural, and economic discrimination."

Though the black community in Park Hill was less than 1% in 1960, by 1966 it was 38%, and it rose to 52% in 1970. The early sixties "saw a panic flight of whites out of Park Hill, and the influx of many black families." Real estate interests stampeded white owners into selling, and lending institutions illegally refused loans to blacks or whites who wanted to live in "other than commonly approved neighborhoods"—that is, white areas (GPHC pamphlet, 1979).

Faced with these circumstances, a coalition of blacks and whites was developed that began to work for open housing, equal educational opportunities, "and a general end to discriminatory practices" (GPHC pamphlet, 1979). This group was the forerunner of GPHC. Their shared concerns led to the formation in 1960 of the Park Hill Action Committee (PHAC) by Catholic and Protestant churches of Park Hill. Chartered then as a Colorado nonprofit corporation, it adopted corporate purposes that today remain those of Greater Park Hill Community, Inc. (GPHC). The six purposes of the organization are:

1. To foster better understanding between persons of different races, creeds and ethnic backgrounds through an educational program aimed at achieving and maintaining an integrated community.
2. To initiate and support projects designed to eliminate prejudice and discrimination both within and without the Park Hill community.
3. To work for better schools to assure that children of all races, creeds and ethnic backgrounds will receive high quality education.
4. To work for better cultural and recreational programs for both children and adults in order to enhance the desirability of living in an integrated community.
5. To work for the prevention of community deterioration in order to promote the advantages of an integrated community.
6. To carry out any other necessary activities through education, with the overall goal of eliminating prejudice and discrimination.

Program. A brief description of the area may increase understanding of the organizational programs described below. The Park Hill area is situated in the northeastern part of Denver, bounded on the east by an airport, on the north by a major industrial park, on the south by a commercial boulevard, and on the west by another arterial boulevard. The northern third of the community was developed after 1950, the southern two-thirds was the older section which developed gradually over the previous fifty years. The entire area contains over 535 city blocks, with 38,000 people.

In the fifties, the older area was characterized by brick homes, broad avenues with tall elm trees, and middle- to upper-middle-income households. The newer part of the community combined brick and frame construction of more moderately priced homes, with a significant number of duplexes, triplexes and higher density apartments. Middle to lower incomes characterized the newer area.

The newer and northern one-third of Park Hill was originally served by a neighborhood organization called North East Park Hill Civic Association, which was active in housing, real estate and zoning issues. This group cooperated with the earlier Park Hill group, the Park Hill Action Committee, to develop recreational facilities in north Park Hill, and in 1969 the two groups merged. The merged group was the immediate predecessor to Greater Park Hill Community, Inc.

GPHC is sponsored and financed by members of fourteen Park Hill churches and one synagogue. Members of these sponsoring religious institutions are automatically GPHC members, and membership is open to the public regardless of location or affiliation. The membership fee for those who do not belong to a sponsoring church is five dollars a year. In 1971, a survival budget was begun to sustain the staff and office of GPHC. This maintenance budget was sustained through Sponsoring Memberships at sixty dollars a year, payable at five dollars a month. "We encourage residents to make your community your favorite charity" (GPHC pamphlet, 1979).

Though it has one part-time staff person, GPHC is essentially a volunteer organization. Its neighborhood office receives an average of 1,000 phone calls each month, requesting information, assistance, and referrals for neighborhood and personal services. The group's pioneering human relations programs have brought it honors and awards.

One essential aspect of GPHC's programs is the blockworker, who is a volunteer and a major communications link with the community. Of the 535 blocks in Park Hill, 320 have blockworkers, who deliver the free monthly newspapers to 16,600 neighbors. The newspaper is professionally printed and has eight to twelve large format pages. Many of the blockworkers have performed this service for years, but new ones are constantly needed to replace those who have moved away or who can no longer perform this service. Each new resident of Park Hill receives, through the blockworker, information about the community and the organization in a welcome letter, which includes a membership form. One volunteer coordinates the work of the blockworkers, including a monthly volunteer crew of ten to fifteen people who prepare the newspaper for mailing and distribution.

The housing committee has existed since the inception of the organization. Segregation in public housing authority properties is an ongoing concern. Promotion of affirmative marketing of the Park Hill area to governmental and private agencies is also a continuing effort. Numerous meetings are held with officials of relevant agencies to encourage outreach to those least likely to seek housing in Park Hill and other areas. "These housing concerns have direct relationship to our schools" (report, 1985). This committee also monitors local, state and national legislation which may have an impact on the preservation of Park Hill as a racially integrated and economically diverse neighborhood.

For the past twenty years GPHC has operated a food bank for emergency assistance. Approximately 3,000 people each year are assisted with food, aside from annual Christmas baskets. A Park Hill Thrift Shoppe was founded by GPHC to further help those in need in the area. Supported by the area churches and residences, about $1,000 a year is given to needy residents in free clothing. In addition, a separate Christmas basket program is part of GPHC's total emergency community support services.

To raise money for these and other projects, GPHC conducts an annual home tour, a Festival Day, and an ongoing recycling program. Their home tour, which began in 1978, raised over $9,000 in 1984 and drew 1,500 people. Held in conjunction with it were an arts and crafts fair, a home idea exposition, and an open house at the nearby new law building of the University of Denver— all arranged by GPHC volunteers.

The Park Hill Festival Day includes such events as an all-day pancake cookout, sports contests, sales booths, musical entertainment, and so on. Money raised from this festival supports GPHC's Jobs for Youth summer program, which provides part-time work for teenagers on vacation from school. One special aspect of this program is the liaison with the city's Juvenile Probation Department, which wants job placement for youth who need to make restitution for crimes they have committed.

Other activities of GPHC include an active zoning committee, a parks and recreation committee, a crime prevention committee, a college advisory committee, and an airport committee. Each of these deals with a specific aspect of environmental monitoring. The college advisory committee, for example, is concerned with neighborhood parking problems relating to students at the adjacent college campus.

The airport committee focuses on noise from the adjacent airport, which in 1981 resulted in a lawsuit filed by GPHC. Though a settlement was still pending in 1985, the major terms of the agreement were: a commitment from the city "to insure that the existing noise environment is not further degraded"; a prohibition against the use of certain types of aircraft; the hiring of a noise officer to handle noise complaints and monitoring; and the refinement of the runway system limiting the amount of aircraft traffic over Park Hill (report, 1985). By 1985, the city had already enacted some of these measures, and was awaiting further confirmation from airport administrators.

The crime prevention program included the establishment of a neighborhood watch system and a community education effort. Special educational events focused in 1984–85 on rape assistance and awareness, a mobile crime prevention van, and an operation identification program.

Today, with these varied action programs, the Greater Park Hill neighborhood remains about half-black and half-white, and is regarded as one of the stable interracial neighborhoods in the country. However, four of its six census tracts are predominantly black, and only two tracts are from 10% to 29% black. They may remain stable, if the citywide school desegregation program continues. The court-ordered plan is still being modified, with the latest school pairing program having positive effects on the Park Hill neighborhood. This may be a strong and positive counter-effect to the concentration of some 400 units of public housing in one portion of Park Hill.

The GPHC sees itself as "a unique organization of people dedicated to making Park Hill the most desirable and interesting community in Denver" (pamphlet, 1979). They may have succeeded—aided by amenities, supportive institutions, and a citywide school desegregation program. In addition, an active neighborhood-school promotion program by the HUD-funded Community Housing Resource Board (CHRB) reinforces the affirmative marketing efforts of the GPHC.

Neighbors, Inc. (Washington, D.C.)—Model C

Inception/Goals. When Neighbors, Inc. (NI) celebrated its twenty-fifth birthday in 1983, the *Washington Post* recalled its beginnings in an editorial headed "Neighbors, Tried and True" (June 11, 1983). At a time when neighborhoods throughout Washington were in the midst of racial upheaval,

a group of self-conscious, slightly frightened but doggedly determined black and white homeowners in Northwest banded together . . . to battle the block-busting real estate speculators. In the tension of those times, they were looked upon by many of their own neighbors as dreamy-eyed do-gooders whose integrationist theme wouldn't play well or long.

The editorial went on to say that today, in the northwest part of the city, residents are "living proof of a good idea upheld—and of investments well protected."

The boundaries of the organization's program actually include seven distinct neighborhoods, containing a total of 40,427 people. Though the area is predominantly black, having gone from 36% to 70% black between 1960 and 1970, residents point with pride to their appreciating housing values and the attractiveness of their middle-class neighborhood. Today, the area is 82% black. This is another example of Model C, the live MO and the black neighborhood.

The twenty-fifth anniversary issue of NI's monthly newspaper, *Neighbors Ink*, contained seven commemorative statements from long-time residents and supporters of the organization. One of them was from the minister of the first Protestant church in the area to integrate in 1958—the year NI was formed. Recalling the beginnings of NI, he noted the tensions prevalent at the time of its inception. He remembered a phone call he had received from a black mother who worried about the safety of her child in his church's Sunday school. He wrote of the concern of those that met to consider what approach the community needed to take:

We met first in homes, and then as more people became involved, at the Church. Black and white people gathered to discuss many issues together. It became evident that a formal community organization should be planned. As we were all neighbors, we adopted "Neighbors, Inc." as our name.

In fact, it was this minister who gave NI its name (*Neighbors Remembering Neighbors*, 1983).

Another contributor to the anniversary issue noted that "NI's immediate purpose in June 1958 was to organize the residents of four neighborhoods to resist the scare tactics and block-busting of real estate speculators who sought to stampede white homeowners into selling cheap and to con black homeseekers into paying dear" (*Neighbors Remembering*, 1983). This contributor, a founder and past president of NI, also stated that the new group "soon realized that our essential task was to find ways to bring people together."

A 1985 brochure asks: "Why Neighbors, Inc.?" and explains that Neighbors was founded "in response to the tensions and pressures associated with the demise of segregation." Their purpose was "to promote the upper portion of what is now Ward IV as an integrated community. Neighbors continues to work to maintain our communities as a desirable place for people of different backgrounds to live together."

Program. An initial foundation grant of $10,000 began NI's program in 1958. Since the group was neither incorporated nor tax-exempt at that time, a local church received the grant and served as treasurer until NI's tax-exempt status was approved. They held "innumerable block meetings at which . . . arguments and statistics were supplemented before long by a less strenuous and more social occasion, the NI Open House" (*Neighbors Remembering*, 1983). The open house is a tradition that continues to this day, and helps foster the community spirit that is a distinctive feature of the area. It is a special house party and program open to the community, hosted by a different homeowner each year.

For a number of years, the most widely recognized event of NI was its annual art and book festival. Beginning in 1963 and for the next five years, NI took over an area high school for a weekend in June to display and sell arts and crafts, used books and records, and the community. Eminent area artists exhibited their work and took part in the events. One year Attorney General Robert Kennedy opened the festival, and another time Senator Hubert Humphrey began the event with personal greetings. One active member and resident recalled the 40,000 books sold, the professional art show, the juried show of amateur artists to promote new talent, the music and dance performances, and the dinners at the festivals. "It gave us a sense of what a truly great community we had become a part of, and that feeling has only deepened through the years" (*Neighbors Remembering*, 1983).

Other communal events in those early years were holiday serenades, family fun nights, a Neighborhood Commons, the Welcome Wagon, cabarets, theater parties, and international dinners. One member nostalgically recalled the holiday serenades: "a group of us tramped through cold and sometimes snowy streets singing Christmas carols, folk tunes, and Chanuka songs" (*Neighbors Remembering*, 1983). The family fun night was held each Friday night in a church, where a range of activities was provided for all age levels—games and crafts for children, workshops and discussion groups for parents. The discussion groups included "such esoterica as Japanese flower arranging and contemporary poetry" (*Neighbors Remembering*, 1983).

The Neighborhood Commons project was an unsuccessful attempt, under the direction of a "nationally known landscape architect," to salvage an abandoned lot and turn it into a playground and recreation area for residents on the block.

One former resident, still a dues-paying member of NI, recalled that when her family moved to the area in 1963, the NI Welcome Wagon was the first to welcome them to the neighborhood. Information was given to them about the neighborhood and NI, and "most of our doubts and fears were removed after we accepted membership and started attending their meetings . . . we were active members till 1981, when we moved away. I remember the Art and Book Festivals at Coolidge High School. Oh, what great fun and people, organization, and community relationships!" (*Neighbors Remembering*, 1983).

Neighbors, Inc. was involved in more than social events during its twenty-five year existence. Among its more serious activities were educational programs for youth, fair housing, campaigns, national and local civil rights demonstrations, law suits, and neighborhood preservation. One educational program, Democracy in Action, was organized by the wife of the first U.S. Ambassador to Zambia. The program functioned in a junior high school and sought to put students in touch with the "great resources of the nation's Capital—sessions of Congress and committee meetings, administrative hearings, court sessions, political rallies, etc." (*Neighbors Remembering*, 1983). The program was highly regarded and became a model for similar efforts elsewhere in Washington.

A more ambitious project was the Institute for Educational Development, in which schools in four neighborhoods participated. Financed by a federal grant, the institute made the resources of the University of Maryland available to all the schools in the NI area. In return, it offered training placements for the university's student teachers. "It ended after a few years when funds and stamina gave out" (*Neighbors Remembering*, 1983).

According to the founder of NI, the organization's impact on real estate practices was a strong one. Taking the lead in a campaign to persuade the District's three daily papers to drop racial designations from their real estate ads, NI finally succeeded in this effort. It also helped other neighborhoods in the city organize themselves to deal with block-busting. The executive director of NI was one of the organizers of Suburban Maryland Fair Housing, and of a similar group in Virginia, whose purpose was to help black families find homes in suburban neighborhoods generally closed to them. In addition, the fair housing groups offered friendly neighbors to welcome the black newcomers. Neighbors, Inc. also supported a fair housing regulation for the District of Columbia and a presidential executive order on equal housing opportunity.

Having recognized in its early days that freedom of residence was essential for the achievement of neighborhood stability, NI worked actively to bring it about. NI stimulated large-scale drives to end discriminatory practices and improve opinions about integrated communities... NI speakers talked to literally thousands of persons in civic and religious organizations in D.C., Maryland, and Virginia. (*Neighbors Remembering*, 1983)

Another long-term resident and member also referred to the fair housing activities of NI.

We educated people in our own community and elsewhere about block busting techniques and researched the records of real estate agents to see if they offered housing to everyone. Our struggle was to keep the neighborhood opened to white home buyers as well as black. This thrust is often misunderstood today, particularly when black and white families freely buy in our neighborhoods and when black and white agents sell to all races.

She recalled earlier househunting days:

Agents told us we wouldn't want to look in "that area anymore." They suggested a house in Shepherd Park would not be a good "long term investment." We could only get a twenty-year mortgage (and that was tough)... the neighborhood wasn't supposed to last even that long. Realtors would bombard us with scare postcards and late night phone calls suggesting that a cash sale was our best bet. A neighbor... was visited by an agent [who] placed thousands of dollars in cash on the coffee table... and warned the couple they had better move while they could. They did.

She concluded, "For those of us who have seen our homes quadruple in value ... when we have enjoyed our neighborhood and loved our neighbors, such predictions seem bizarre. It was not that way then... it was infuriating and racist" (*Neighbors Remembering*, 1983).

In 1963, under NI banners, about 300 residents and members participated in the national March on Washington for Jobs and Freedom. "They took part in that history-making confluence of persons from all over America who shared our concerns and hope for an America free of racial barriers and stigmas" (*Neighbors Remembering*, 1983).

One resident and NI supporter recalled being asked to sign an NI petition when she first moved into the area. The petition was to block the building of a new school, and the new resident signed on the advice of her neighbors. "Thus began our involvement with NI and the local issues." She remembered some amusing vignettes: "The donkey marching the picket line with slogans like 'I am only a donkey, but the new school gives me a pain', or 'Don't make an ass out of the taxpayer. It guaranteed coverage on every channel that night and added to the public awareness of our cause. It may not have changed the thinking at city hall, but it helped. We did win in the end." (*Neighbors Remembering*, 1983).

An NI suit against the D.C. government in 1974 involved broken waterlines, for which several residents had had to pay thousands of dollars. Protests were presented to the mayor, council members were lobbied, petitions were delivered from all parts of the city—and to no avail. Then, NI decided to go to court. Appeals for funds were made, and TV cameras helped by filming homeowners getting water with a garden hose from neighbors' homes after the city had turned their water off. Though they won the case in the lower court in 1976, the Court of Appeals ruled in favor of the city. Finally, however, in 1977 the city council passed a Water and Sewer Repair Act that made the city responsible for repairs and maintenance of water and sewer lines, with back reimbursement up to three years.

Neighborhood preservation efforts of NI were recalled by one resident who was "especially pleased to have been associated with the preservation of the Lucinda Cady House." When the house was scheduled to be torn down in 1974 and replaced by garden apartments, NI organized residents to testify before the Joint Congressional Committee on Landmarks. Neighborhood meetings were also held. Neighbors, Inc. offered a Community Improvement Project Award of $400 in support of efforts to preserve the home, which was finally designated as a historic landmark. It still stands as a continuing reminder of the efforts of residents and NI to preserve their neighborhoods.

A number of statements referred to a period in the late sixties and early seventies when NI was quite inactive. After a period of increasing significance during the Kennedy-Johnson years,

our fortunes declined when the mood of the nation changed. The Black Power movement affected philosophies and debates on the NI Board. While our commitment to integration did not waiver, Board members found their views subtly changing and disagreements increasing. The assassination of Dr. King and the ensuing riots challenged our somewhat rosy view of the kind of society we were building, and the belief in the progress we had made. As poverty became the focus of national concern, our middle class neighborhoods were less interesting to the foundations. We lost our staff and reduced our program. We were somewhat diverted from our goals. (*Neighbors Remembering*, 1983)

Another resident and member recalled: "At that time, NI had no office and most operations were conducted out of the president's home or were scattered throughout the neighborhoods. There were isolated pockets of activity, but NI as an organization had such a low profile that many old members thought it had disintegrated and died. Fortunately, that wasn't the case."

In 1972, NI opened an office again and began to reassert itself as a viable, important force in the community:

Moribund committees were revitalized, a new school was built, a library was renovated, a comprehensive zoning plan was developed, there were many zoning battles—most were won. NI created and funded a neighborhood improvement contest in each of the four neighborhoods. There were cabarets, arts and crafts fairs, extravaganzas, fund-raisers, and monthly open houses that were faithfully attended. NI had become, once again, that wonderful, unique organization I had anticipated. (*Neighbors Remembering*, 1983)

One comment of a long-term resident and member of NI spoke of more than protecting their investment:

As one who loves our neighborhoods and is proud of NI, I hope the focus of NI will never be simply one of protecting our investment. That would make us little more than a tax-payers' association. Our history demands we keep alive the memory of what we had to overcome and how much we had to grow in order to achieve an integrated living experience for ourselves and our children. We are privileged to know each other. (*Neighbors Remembering*, 1983)

Another member noted the many accomplishments of NI and observed: "As important as these activities and accomplishments are in themselves, they express something more—a coming of age for NI and the area it serves, a maturing of attitude, a real sense of community involvement, and responsibility, not only tolerance of diversity, but a unity of purpose" (*Neighbors Remembering*, 1983).

Finally, the founder said, "The greatest accomplishment, after all, is that NI still survives and still generates new ideas. Those of us who call the NI neighborhoods home can take pride in knowing that we have heeded Martin Luther King's admonishment. 'Integration,' he once said, 'demands life service, not lip service.' " (*Neighbors Remembering*, 1983). That life service has surely been given by NI in its quarter-century of existence.

East Mount Airy Neighbors/West Mount Airy Neighbors (Philadelphia, Pa.)

Side by side, two neighborhoods in Philadelphia represent the two models of success and failure in integration maintenance. Both have live, vigorous organizations dedicated to the same goal. One has now altered that goal to quality maintenance and service, since it has become a predominantly black community. East Mount Airy was 32.5% black in 1960, and changed to 56% black by 1970, and is now 75% black. East Mount Airy Neighbors began in 1966, during the height of racial transition. West Mount Airy Neighbors began sooner, and this made a difference.

East Mount Airy Neighbors—Model C

Inception/Goals. The official founding of East Mount Airy Neighbors (EMAN) was on January 18, 1966, but this was the aftermath of a series of meetings and an important, well-publicized sermon. The sermon, entitled "East Mount Airy: Slum, Ghetto, or Good Place to Live?" was given by the Rev. Rudolph C. Gelsey, who later became EMAN's first president. The sermon focused on the problems of the rapidly changing East Mount Airy neighborhood, and recognized that small neighborhood groups could not begin to solve the problems facing the area. An urgent need for an umbrella organization was seen.

Extensive coverage was given to the sermon in the *Philadelphia Evening Bulletin*, and a number of meetings were held, which led to the founding of EMAN. Two weeks after its first public meeting, EMAN had two hundred members and two strong committees: schools and real estate. The schools committee examined and reported on school conditions, and the real estate committee fought real estate solicitation. During that first month, the governing structure of EMAN was formed, bylaws were drafted, officers were elected, an executive committee was set up, and the first newsletter was sent out to all members. Their goal, then and now, was "Making a Good Community Better."

Program. The group's activities have varied throughout its twenty years, but the major emphases have been on educational quality and equality, housing and business area upkeep and development, block organization and security, and human services.

In its early days, the housing and community development committee reported on "sold" signs that had illegally remained up for more than seven days, and collected written solicitations received from realtors. They won victories in zoning, such as fighting the construction of apartment buildings and recommending zoning changes for the neighborhood. They surveyed substandard housing in their area, and developed plans for its upgrading and rehabilitation. They also promoted the development and improvement of their major business avenue. Housing in the EMAN area includes many row homes, and the density of population is considerably greater than in the West Mount Airy area. This single fact may account for the difference in integration maintenance in the two communities.

The housing committee's continuing and current activities involve ongoing home rehabilitation, finally culminating in a neighborhood rehabilitation office cosponsored and shared by two neighboring area associations. This office now oversees most of the activities concerning rehabilitation, and is run under the auspices of a Neighborhood Advisory Council, with representatives from each of the founding organizations. A homeowners' maintenance workshop offered ten weeks of free counseling in basic home repairs, and an "ask the experts" workshop focused on all the aspects of purchasing property. Residents of the area can receive help from the office with such problems as code violations, paving, lighting, street signs, dead trees, curbing, demolition, and sanitation.

Bank monitoring has also been a concern of EMAN's housing committee. When one of its neighborhood banks was accused of redlining, EMAN, along with the Philadelphia Council of Neighborhood Organizations, held public hearings to protect the interests of the neighborhood. When action was taken under the Community Reinvestment Act to block the opening of a proposed new branch of the bank, officials of the bank agreed to allocate more mortgage money and provide more services to the neighborhood.

When the ban on real estate solicitation in the EMAN area was lifted, EMAN mobilized an effective protest. They collected 2,500 signatures on petitions to protest this action, and presented these to the Human Relations Commission, all area real estate offices, and the City Council with the endorsement of all twelve council members.

School involvement was more intense during the early years of EMAN's existence. Educational equality and quality have continued to be a major goal of the education committee, though its activity has decreased with growing racial imbalance. Of the six elementary schools serving the EMAN area, three are black and three are majority black, though still integrated. The junior and senior high schools are black. The education committee formed an area Task Force on Public Education, concerned with integration and the physical safety of school buildings. They have sponsored public forums and have demanded accountability from school officials. The education committee developed a special project, called Paired Experience in Community Learning, to provide academic motivation and alternative learning situations for area high school students. Bond issues and tax support for the public schools have also been an ongoing concern of the education committee. The most recent efforts of the committee have involved the organization in 1981 of the Mount Airy Learning Tree, a joint program of East and West Mount Airy Neighbors. This program offers over 150 courses to more than a thousand adults and children throughout the year. It is self-sustaining, with the assistance of several churches and corporations providing space, supplies, and scholarships.

Perhaps the two most widely publicized and tangible results of EMAN's efforts are its group homes and daycare center. Concern for the mentally retarded was evident as early as 1968, when EMAN assisted in the establishment of a mental health center in its community. A few years later, EMAN began to explore the development of a separate corporation to run homes for mentally retarded local residents. By taking control, it was able to place its group homes on blocks where neighbors were sympathetic, and also avoid concentration in any one area. They now own four homes and rent eight apartments to deinstitutionalized adults, who participate in community living arrangements directed by EMAN Group Homes, incorporated in 1972. They are cautious in their future plans, having now reached a point where they fear oversaturation of their area may result with any further expansion.

In 1973, the daycare center opened its doors to preschoolers. A community center, funded with a foundation grant, now houses the daycare program, as well as a skill center and several other EMAN programs. The daycare center— with a $75,000 annual budget—is licensed by the state, with its facilities approved for up to forty-four children of working parents in the EMAN area.

In addition to these programs, EMAN—together with its neighboring organization WMAN—publishes and distributes the *Mount Airy Express* to each of the 12,500 households in East and West Mount Airy every month. The two organizations each provide $250 a month toward expenses, with the bulk of the budget coming from advertising. Together Blocks is a combined block organization and crime prevention program, originally funded by a federal grant and now maintained as an ongoing EMAN activity. Mount Airy Day is a special annual event, beginning in 1968 as Community Day, and continuing to the present with its flea market, art exhibits, games and films as a major social and fund-raising activity of the organization.

What of the future? Four concerns were cited by EMAN's president in the group's 1985 annual report: the defacement of property in the area, lack of involvement and participation by many members, abandonment of cars and houses in the area, and crime. The president pleaded for more involvement:

Your input is vitally needed if the organization is to continue to grow and provide needed services to our community at-large and in particular to our membership. You, as members, are an integral part of EMAN, and as such, you should be willing to participate actively on one of our committees and/or volunteer to assist on special projects.

Her plea went on to note that often the same faithful, dedicated and committed members go on doing the same tasks that need to be done for the organization and community, with these people rapidly facing burnout. She cited the three kinds of people in the world of volunteerism: those who make things happen, those who watch things happen, and those who say "What happened?" She begged members to "please put EMAN on your agenda and realize that time, energy, and concern will help to 'make a good community better.' "

Despite the expected drop in energy and participation after twenty years, the group seems stable and likely to continue with its major programs of rehabilitation and human services. Its original goal of integration maintenance is downplayed, but the goal of quality maintenance is as strong as ever. As an example of Model C—live MO in a black neighborhood—EMAN seems likely to go on as long as it can keep getting funding and community participation.

West Mount Airy Neighbors—Model A

In 1959, seven years before EMAN began, West Mount Airy (WMAN) was founded by fifty people who wanted to retain an integrated community. At that time, the WMAN area was 19% black. The earlier timing of their program, as well as the difference in their housing stock, may account for their successful maintenance of pluralism in the WMAN neighborhood. In 1970, WMAN's area was 38% black, and stability was achieved with a rise to only 46% by 1980. Their membership has grown from 300 to over 1,000 in their twenty years.

Program. The group's initial program focused on the real estate market, with freedom of choice in housing the main goal. This involved strong committee activities in the areas of real estate practices, zoning, and long-range planning.

They reached an agreement with real estate brokers on a code of ethics, obtained a solicitation ban in the area, and, in cooperation with EMAN, sought a citywide solicitation ban.

In 1975, WMAN began a cooperative effort with the city to remap the zoning of West Mount Airy, which was then passed as an ordinance in 1976. An active zoning committee monitors all zoning applications in the WMAN area to maintain a stable mix between industry, commerce, and residences.

Rehabilitation is also a major concern of WMAN, and their efforts have involved both commercial, multifamily rental, and single family properties. Like EMAN, they worked consistently for the revitalization of their major business street, Germantown Avenue. They planted over 200 trees along the avenue, provided paint for business owners, supplied planters for business fronts, erected fencing on the avenue, conducted a planning and market survey, and are now working towards the certification of the avenue as a historical sector. They are currently involved in the rehabilitation of a building on the avenue that will be used as a multipurpose community center.

Programs to support and improve the public schools of the WMAN area have been a constant concern. The group pressured for the inclusion of two area public schools in the city's desegregation plan, and each school received a grant of $150,000 for this purpose. The WMAN education committee sponsors an annual open house for parents of school-age children who have recently moved into the community. They also publish and distribute a pamphlet on their area's schools to prospective homebuyers through real estate brokers.

Social activities are important to WMAN, which sponsors an annual Walk 'n' Talk Night—a series of neighborhood block parties. In addition, New Neighbor Teas are given annually for all new residents, and Mount Airy Day is cosponsored with EMAN to provide fun, fellowship, and a sense of history about the area. Scout troops, athletic programs for youth, and summer day camp are some of the other activities that WMAN sponsors.

The group established a Community Services Corporation in 1978 as a separate entity authorized to provide services for the neighborhood. Childcare programs are offered through the corporation, offering daycare for preschoolers and after-school care for older children. These are operated on a fee-for-service basis, with some scholarship funds available. In addition, WMAN operates a Youth Employment Service, which places teenagers in jobs in the community. With EMAN, the Mount Airy Learning Tree is sponsored by WMAN, offering a program of neighbors teaching neighbors.

Success begets success. With the WMAN area remaining stably integrated, public school administrators in 1983 selected two elementary schools in the neighborhood for inclusion in the citywide school desegregation program. This, of course, attracts more homeseekers to the area and reduces flight from the area, thus generating still more stability and integration maintenance.

Four purposes are listed in the WMAN bylaws: (1) to eliminate prejudice, discrimination and neighborhood tension in West Mount Airy and its institutions, and to foster a spirit of harmony, peace and brotherhood among all people of all races, religions, ethnic groups and ages; (2) to encourage and promote projects, activities and improvements that will combat community deterioration; (3) to encourage and promote programs for youth and combat juvenile delinquency; (4) to provide a means of communication, understanding and information necessary to accomplish these goals. They seem to have succeeded in achieving these goals, and are another example of Model A—live MO in an integrated neighborhood.

SUBURBAN MUNICIPAL PROGRAMS—MODEL A

Quite different from the urban neighborhood programs we have described are the growing suburban efforts to maintain racial diversity. Many of these are sponsored and heavily funded by their municipalities. One program—in Shaker Heights, a suburb of Cleveland, Ohio—has the unique distinction of being funded by both the municipality and the school system. I believe these programs have a much higher probability of success than do those in urban neighborhoods. A brief review of several of these programs will show why.

Shaker Heights, Ohio

Shaker Heights, with a population of 31,776 people, is the site of one of the first suburban efforts to achieve and maintain racial diversity. In 1957, one of its nine school districts, Ludlow, formed the Ludlow Association to prevent white flight and the ghettoization of the community. In 1962, the Moreland Community Association was formed in another Shaker Heights school district to prevent white flight. A year later the Lomond Association began, followed in 1966 by the Sussex Association, each a separate school district in the Shaker Heights community. Meanwhile, the city of Shaker Heights banned "for sale" signs to aid in the growing stabilization efforts. Foundation grants paid for staffing the new associations. After ten vigorous years of stabilization programs, the city of Shaker Heights funded a community housing office to provide staffing and office space for the work of the Ludlow Association.

In that same year, 1967, Shaker Heights became the first suburb in the nation to undertake voluntarily a busing program to magnet schools. To maintain racial integration in the community, the school administration also contributed to the funding of the housing center, which now receives almost $200,000 yearly from both the city and the school system.

By 1974, other neighborhoods in Shaker Heights had formed associations, as did other suburbs around them, such as Cleveland Heights. Together they formed the Heights Community Congress, a coalition of suburban groups dedicated to the maintenance of racial integration. In 1974, they established the Cuyahoga Plan—a regional fair housing program funded by private foundations and municipalities in the Cleveland area. The newest effort in the Cleveland area is the East Suburban Council for Open Communities (ESCOC), a joint venture by three municipal suburban governments, their school systems and neighborhood associations to affirmatively market their communities and other suburbs in order to promote and maintain racial integration.

The statement of purpose of the Shaker Heights Housing Office includes an explanation of "true integration." According to the statement, it means that all the people of a given area, both minority and nonminority, actually compete for housing in numbers reflective of their purchasing power and proportion of the region's population. The statement acknowledges that the housing office "will concentrate the greater part of its efforts on attracting whites to areas of Shaker Heights where they are under-represented." They also apply similar affirmative marketing methods to blacks in areas where they are underrepresented. But there is no question that the major target population for Shaker Heights programs is white. The aim is to assist in "desegregating housing markets and not to contribute to patterns of segregation." Shaker Heights was 26% black in 1980, with an increase of only 5% since 1970 indicating its stability. Shaker schools are 44% black, however, indicating that white students are underrepresented in the public schools. This foreshadows housing resegregation, according to statements of the housing office. In 1986, a $250,000 Fund for the Future of Shaker Heights was established as a public-private partnership to provide financial incentives for pro-integrative moves.

Housing values in Shaker Heights rose 45% from 1976 to 1982, the greatest increase of any comparable community in the Cleveland suburban area. National media featuring the Shaker Heights housing program include the *New York Times*, NBC-TV, *Money* magazine, and *Nation's Cities*. Other communities across the nation who have sought advice from the Shaker Heights housing office include Oak Park, Illinois, Southfield, Michigan, Teaneck, New Jersey, Silver Spring, Maryland, and Fort Wayne, Indiana.

A staff of seven provides full-time affirmative marketing services, including tours, neighbor introductions, and real estate and mortgage lending liaison. They are also responsible for gathering, printing, and distributing all information pertaining to housing, schools, businesses, and the general community. The philosophy, expressed in Shaker Heights program literature is openly race-conscious: "Before James Farmer said it, before Martin Luther King said it, before Supreme Court Justice Blackmun said it, Shaker's leadership knew it—that IN ORDER TO GET BEYOND RACISM, RACE MUST BE TAKEN INTO ACCOUNT" (Shaker Lessons 1985). Their printed materials explain that integration does not just happen, it takes a race-conscious, antisegregative, pro-integrative effort to maintain it. Don De Marco, Director of Community Services and the Housing Office for Shaker Heights, claims that color-blind or race-neutral approaches simply do not work. They almost always result in resegregation, or what he terms "American apartheid." He believes that to maintain integration, quantity must be considered as well as quality. Numbers do count. For this reason, Shaker's affirmative marketing program must attract the racial group that is underrepresented in Shaker's housing market. Not because whites have some special added intrinsic human value, but because integration is good in both social and economic terms, and segregation is not. Whites are, therefore, a necessary ingredient.

And because Shaker leaders knew that they could not win the war for integration if it were fought only within the suburb of Shaker, they formed the East Suburban Council for Open Communities, referred to above. The special fund for the future of Shaker Heights, also referred to above, is based on the premise that the paramount challenge to be met is the avoidance of further racial imbalance in the schools and neighborhoods now threatened by resegregation. "Integration is good—the more the better . . . racially based programs must be justified by a compelling public interest and must be effected by option-expanding means" (Fund for the Future 1986).

Because of their clear purpose, their full-time coordinated effort involving both the city and the school administrators, and their regionally coordinated program (further supported by a new Ford Foundation grant), they have an excellent chance of continued success in maintaining Shaker Heights as an open, desirable, diverse, and stable community. Other municipally funded suburban programs show similar promise. We turn to some of these next.

Teaneck, New Jersey

Though the Housing Center of Teaneck was not funded until 1977, the efforts leading up to it began more than twenty years earlier. A book called *Triumph in a White Suburb* documents the events that made national headlines in 1955 (Damerell 1968). Subtitled "A bigoted town's progress to school integration and toward open housing," the book's introduction notes that this middle-class suburb's choice of progress in the mid-fifties was an "exciting, exasperating, and anxiety-raising experience" (Damerell 1968; introduction, R. J. Havighurst).

Teaneck is one of New York City's inner suburbs, with some 35,000 residents, located twenty-five minutes from Manhattan just across the George Washington Bridge. One of the Housing Center's full-color promotional booklets says the town is "close enough to the Big Apple to take a big bite, yet far enough away to grow your own apple tree."

Named a Model American Town in 1949, Teaneck was chosen by the U.S. Army Civil Affairs Division to represent the United States to the peoples of occupied Germany and Japan. Selected from among ten thousand communities, Army authorities said they chose it because of its "fine municipal spirit and the high quality of its governmental services." At that time the town was virtually all-white.

Located close to New York City, the "model town" also is next to Englewood, New Jersey, which had a black ghetto area adjacent to Teaneck by the early 1940s. When blacks began to move into Teaneck in the 1950s, some whites panicked and left, and others began stabilization efforts. In 1955, the Teaneck Civic Conference was formed; it was the predecessor of the 1977 municipally funded Teaneck Housing Center. In the twenty years between, the community was almost torn apart by the struggle to integrate its neighborhoods and schools.

The Teaneck Civic Conference was patterned after a similar group in Chicago—the Hyde Park–Kenwood Community Conference, formed in 1949—which Teaneck leaders had read about (Abrahamson 1959). After several small home meetings, the Teaneck Conference held its first public meeting, with nearly 150 people attending. The local newspaper described the meeting under the headline: "Interracial Section Fights Panic Sales" (*Bergen Record*, June 28, 1955). The lead paragraph was: "White and Negro residents packed the Town House last night in their first open-to-all discussion intended to prove that black and white can live side by side in the community." A general membership meeting was held a few months later, announced with the headline: "Teaneck Seen as U.S. Model in Race Unity—Civic Group Launches Integration Program for Community—Nation Watching" (*Bergen Record*, Oct. 4, 1955).

When the *New York Times* reported the meeting of the Teaneck group, a nationwide chain of publicity followed. Newspapers from all over the country told about the conference's work, NBC camera crews came to town to film a story for the "Today" show, and two national magazines sent reporters and photographers for feature articles.

Though this early national publicity was unusual for a stabilization group, their work was similar to most other such groups. They appointed twenty block captains and formed committees for membership, education, real estate and publicity. They started a monthly bulletin, called the *Good Neighbor*, and they tried to get whites and blacks to mingle. Interracial sewing, dancing and ceramic classes were formed, and an interracial bowling group began. They had dances in the spring and picnics in the summer, and they told their story to any civic, religious, fraternal, and educational groups in the area that would listen.

With the usual fear that the city might decrease its services and neglect the neighborhood because it was interracial, they initiated community betterment projects. They asked the town for improved street lighting and sidewalks where needed, encouraged leaf-raking and disposal, lobbied for new playgrounds, and requested traffic control on their streets.

They pressed the mayor and the city council to create a human relations commission to assist in their stabilization efforts. But it was not until 1960 that such a group was finally approved as the Mayor's Advisory Board on Community Relations. A sympathetic mayor gave his official support to the new group, which took over the work of the Civic Conference. Not all residents of Teaneck were pleased about the formation of the new group. They had not liked the work of the conference either.

One of the new board's most important and widely publicized activities was a six-week workshop designed to counter bias and suspicion, and to stimulate respect in race relations. The workshop, held in 1961, was developed and supported by New York University. Reports in the *New York Times* and the *Daily Mirror* were positive, with one headline reading: "Teaneck, N.J. Called

Model of Democracy" (Damerell 1968: 134). The mayor received commendations from state officials, and the state Commission on Civil Rights subsequently developed a similar ten-session, study-discussion series for leadership training in community relations for use all over the state of New York. Mayors from twenty towns across the country wrote asking for information. Teaneck was given full credit for having paved the way.

Not all Teaneck residents were happy about the workshop and the publicity it received. Counter groups that were anti-integration began to form in Teaneck, and other pro-integration groups were forming in and outside of Teaneck, recognizing that one community could not hope to stabilize by itself. One of these larger groups was the Fair Housing Committee of Bergen County, which had a local branch in Teaneck. These fair housing groups began to practice affirmative marketing in Teaneck and surrounding suburbs, hoping to encourage racial integration in other parts of Teaneck and other suburban communities. Again, many residents were not pleased with these efforts.

During this time, the school situation in Teaneck attracted growing attention and concern. Blacks in Teaneck were concentrated in the northeast quadrant of the town, and the schools there were becoming predominantly black. In 1961 blacks were only 4% of Teaneck's population. But all 1,700 blacks lived in one-half of the northeast section, which affected the school composition in that neighborhood and prompted more panic selling and white flight.

In 1961, a new school superintendent developed a plan for the voluntary integration of Teaneck's schools and the maintenance of racial balance. His plan was not well-received by many residents. Bitter conflicts marked the next few years, until in 1963 the State Commissioner of Education ordered three New Jersey towns to desegregate their schools under threat of losing state aid. One of these towns was neighboring Englewood; this gave the superintendent the reinforcement he needed.

Despite growing polarization in the community, with competing petitions, forums, meetings, candidates, and so forth, the new superintendent in 1964 began his plan. He had carefully prepared his school board and black leaders in the community for this, and had their support. Teaneck's was the first school board in the country to adopt a policy of prevention of racial imbalance. The wise guidance of the superintendent, a supportive mayor, and the persistent efforts of the Civic Conference, the Advisory Board, and the fair housing committee paved the way for this.

Today, Teaneck remains stable and integrated at 24% black, and the work of the municipally funded Housing Center is largely promotional. The earlier struggles made this possible. National recognition continues, with articles in the *Chicago Tribune* and *Newsday* praising this model diverse community, and the work of the center receiving notoriety on the Phil Donahue show in 1984 and earlier in a 1982 CBS-TV documentary.

Especially notable programs of the center are the annual "Discover Teaneck" weekend, featuring house tours, exhibits, movies, ethnic foods, and entertainment; the seminars and bus tours for realtors; and the Mayors' Exchange Conference. A typical year involves mailing 750 homeseekers' packets to prospective homebuyers, and assisting realtors with promotional materials and information about the community and its schools and public facilities.

Recent funding cuts have reduced the Housing Center's staff and efforts, however. Whether this will seriously affect their stabilization efforts remains to be seen. The next census will tell.

Oak Park, Illinois

Located next to a black ghetto on the western border of Chicago, this suburban village community of 54,887 residents passed a local fair housing ordinance in 1968, when it was almost all white. Realtors helped form the ordinance and worked closely with village officials to implement it. Oak Park's commitment to racial integration has been constant and successful since then.

In 1971, community trustees created one of the first community relations departments in Illinois to enforce the fair housing ordinance. A year later, when the first blacks began moving in, the Oak Park Housing Center was founded by the village trustees to ensure that the community maintained a mix of black and white residents. Today, fourteen years later, no one could claim they have not done so.

Some of the earlier history of Oak Park helps explain its positive image. After the Chicago fire, Oak Park was one of the first Chicago suburbs to prosper. It attracted people who worked in downtown Chicago, just ten miles east. The village's schools, libraries, mansions, and cultural offerings ranked among the nation's finest. In addition, the famous architect Frank Lloyd Wright lived there, and designed two dozen buildings for the village between 1890 and 1910. Author Ernest Hemingway was born and grew up in the village. This is the background that preceded its racial transition from all white to slightly integrated. Oak Park is now 13% black, having reached this point in the past decade with about 1% black increase each year. For the Chicago area, this is remarkably stable.

Using Shaker Heights and University City, Missouri as stabilization models, the Oak Park Housing Center in 1972 initiated programs to ensure economic and racial stability. Above all, the commitment to racial diversity and integration maintenance permeated their programs. In their first year of operation, they served 1,011 clients, of whom 266 moved to Oak Park. That first year was financed by two major foundation grants totalling $29,000, plus free space in a community church. They began production of a film, "As Time Goes By: Oak Park, Illinois," and initiated seminars for real estate personnel, residents, center staff, and others concerned about the community's future. They also formed a limited partnership to buy and rehabilitate a neglected nineteen-unit apartment building and two-family structure; they produced 10,000 copies of their brochure, *Oak Park: The People Place*, and began distribution to employers, medical center, and universities; and they placed ads in local and national publications to increase demand for Oak Park housing from underrepresented groups.

Each year since that first one, the numbers of those they counseled who actually moved to Oak Park grew larger. In their second year, with 2,157 clients served, 508 moved to Oak Park. Their third year had 989 clients who moved in, the fourth year had 1,227 clients who moved in, and that number has been maintained each year since then (Oak Park Housing Center Report 1983).

Other local and national foundations added their support to the center's work, and national media publicity grew. The seventy-four-minute color documentary film begun in their first year was completed in 1974; it received critical acclaim from Chicago newspapers and from *Variety*. In their third year of operation, they were chosen by HUD as one of the nation's top housing programs, and were listed in a new publication of the Real Estate Research Corporation, *Neighborhood Preservation*.

By the end of their first decade, the Oak Park Center had counseled over 40,000 clients, and had come to focus on rentals rather than sales. The center received CDBG funding through the village trustees, had an operating budget of $166,127.13 and a staff of seven full-time and five part-time people. They had won a Certification of Fair Housing Achievement award from HUD; had received coverage in national media, including *Time*, *Newsweek*, "60 Minutes," and the Phil Donahue Show; had been featured in a book called *The Oak Park Strategy* (Goodwin 1979); had initiated joint programs with surrounding suburbs and communities in the Chicago area; and had formed a nationwide federation of other suburb communities trying to achieve stable integration, the Oak Park Exchange Congress. In 1976, Oak Park was named an All America City in a national contest. The work of the center was cited as one of the outstanding reasons for this honor. But certainly sharing the credit for this blaze of glory is the municipal government of Oak Park.

The council-manager form of government, with its trustees, appointed commissioners, and staff, were able to develop and implement a variety of programs and ordinances directed at real estate practices, housing quality, public safety, economic strength, and community image. All of these supported, reinforced, and strengthened the work of the center. Finally, the village's actual funding of the center through community development block grants enabled it to have security and staff continuity.

Some of the specific programs undertaken by the village government were: (1) ordinances banning "for sale" and "sold" signs, and licensing inspection of multiple family dwellings; (2) an Equity Assurance Plan insuring homeowners against depreciation of market values of their homes; (3) construction of a 4-million-dollar Village Hall in a transitional neighborhood as a "vote of confidence"; (4) passage of a 1.5-million-dollar housing bond issue for rehabilitation of housing and clearance of neglected properties; (5) upgrading of housing inspection procedures, and initiation of neighborhood walks and alley inspections; (6) increased and improved police protection; (7) research and discussion of various approaches to guide racial diversity, and the establishment of a professional community relations department and citizen task forces; (8) contracting with a professional public relations firm to improve media reporting of Oak Park events and issues designed to increase confidence in the future of the community; (9) sponsorship of the Oak Park Exchange Congress as an annual forum for delegates from communities across the country with similar goals and programs; and (10) cooperation with school authorities in developing policies, plans, and programs to maintain racial balance in the public schools of Oak Park.

These approaches to community improvement were designed to destroy the myths associated with "changing" areas. Instead of decreasing services and accepting eventual economic decline and resegregation, Oak Park's government consciously decided to show that a racially diverse community could offer an excellent way of life. Their unflagging support and commitment to integration maintenance has enabled the Oak Park Housing Center to function with maximum effectiveness for the past fourteen years.

Yet, center leaders acknowledge that despite their optimism and record of success, they are not trouble-free. Black in-migration, though slow, has been steadily increasing. This makes the problem of maintaining white demand more difficult. In the face of this, center director Roberta Raymond wonders if diversity can survive in Oak Park:

We have had to add an escort service and apartment previewing to our affirmative marketing program to maintain continuing white demand. Now about half our clients are white and half are black. More buildings are in need of white demand, and these are the ones for which we do escorting and previewing. We also have had to intensify our advertising in radio, newspapers, and magazines. . . . We now have much more black visibility on the streets so it's much harder to market to whites overall. (questionnaire 1985, see Appendix B)

Community, staff, and government observers agree that Oak Park has gone beyond mere residential diversity. They point with pride to the fact that black residents are participating in both official and unofficial capacities in government, schools, business, and social and cultural affairs.

A visit to the Village Hall makes a deliberate and credible statement to the newcomer, for blacks are employed there . . . within the staffs of all major departments. . . . The schools employ blacks in positions ranging from administrative staff to teaching and custodial. Local businesses have followed the government's lead in equal hiring practices. From Little League to School Board selection committees, blacks are in evidence. (Illinois Advisory Committee 1982: 91)

A mixture of pride and concern prompted the center and the village government to involve surrounding suburbs in their efforts to expand housing choices for blacks. Formation of the West Suburban Housing Center is the result, with an active fair housing program operating there to open up housing opportunities for blacks in other suburban communities in the nearby Chicago area.

Outreach has involved not only surrounding suburbs, but also other suburbs across the country that share the common goal of maintaining racial diversity. In 1977, Oak Park's public relations consultant initiated the Exchange Congress to draw people from such communities together to share their experiences. Since then, the congress has become an annual event, with some 200 attendees from over fifty communities, including elected officials, city managers, municipal employees, business leaders, and interested citizens. Two founders of the congress explained its purpose: "to set up goals and strategies for economic development and racial diversity. . . . Economic development and racial diversity go hand in hand. If a community goes down the drain economically it won't be attractive to either blacks or whites" (Fraden 1983).

These communities not only share common goals and programs, they also share a common fear, according to center director Raymond.

They see themselves as an endangered species. They believe they have done more to end the long, sad history of racial segregation in housing than other communities, but are on the "firing line" more than closed communities. They feel isolated and vulnerable . . . and few voices are heard in support of their contention that individuals who want to live in diverse communities deserve a choice. They want desperately to succeed over a substantial period of time, yet they think the "cards are stacked against them." (Illinois Advisory Committee 1982: 92)

Three of the goals of the Exchange Congress are also the goals of all of its participating communities: (1) to promote the awareness that life in a racially diverse environment offers advantages over life in communities where black and white people live separately; (2) to stimulate the courage, commitment, and creativity of the leadership of American communities to work toward the greater realization of the goals of racially diverse yet economically vital communities; (3) to affirm the possibilities as well as the necessity for local initiatives, regardless of political trends in Washington, D.C.

The three suburban communities selected for description here were not chosen because of their unusual excellence or success in goal achievement. Rather they are typical of other municipally funded and supported suburban efforts such as these participating members of the Oak Park Exchange Congress: Bellwood, Illinois; Bloomfield, Connecticut; Cleveland Heights, Ohio; Forest Park, Ohio; Freeport, New York; Park Forest, Illinois; Southfield, Michigan; and Willingboro, New Jersey. All have the unique distinction of having their local government's financial and moral support for a committed, sustained effort to maintain racial diversity. All have ongoing coordinated programs designed to involve the key institutional forces in the community that affect the life and death of neighborhoods—the schools, the lending institutions, the business community, the real estate industry, and the public housing authorities. It is easy to see why such coordinated, sustained programs have a greater chance of success than the isolated neighborhood efforts within larger cities.

Part III
THE NATIONAL LEVEL

8

NATIONAL NEIGHBORS

"The magic of people coming together who have conquered old fears"

"An organization needs meetings, but for a national group on a limited budget, this can present problems"

"As we grow, we must deal with change. Sometimes, that change is difficult and painful"

"The times were tight and the pressures were almost overwhelming, but we were secure in our convictions and dedication"

"Believe me, Mr. Bromley, if this company had one ounce of commitment to equal opportunity, you would have the grant"

INCEPTION

The Carleton Conference

Though the date of the founding conference of National Neighbors is listed as May 25, 1970, in Dayton, Ohio (the Bergamo conference), the real formation of the organization took place one year earlier. On March 30, 1969, community leaders from twelve integrated communities across the country were invited to come to Carleton College in Minnesota to discuss a proposal to establish a national service agency for integrated neighborhoods. The participants' integrated communities were located in the cities of Chicago, Illinois; Cincinnati, Ohio; Denver, Colorado; Indianapolis, Indiana; Los Angeles, California; New Rochelle, New York; Oklahoma City, Oklahoma; Philadelphia, Pennsylvania; Shaker Heights, Ohio; University City, Missouri; and Washington, D.C.

The host for this conference was the National Committee on Tithing in Investment (NCTI)—later called the Sponsors of Open Housing Investment (SOHI)—a private, nonprofit, tax-exempt educational organization with 25,000 sponsors headed by Minnesota Congressman Donald Fraser and founded by Morris Milgram. Three foundation grants aided the NCTI in convening the conference.

At the Carleton College conference, participants expressed a clear need for a national agency to assist integrated neighborhood groups. They voted unanimously to request the NCTI to establish such an agency with an executive director, and offered to serve as an ad hoc advisory board until a national convention was held. They asked that the new agency be called "National Neighbors" (NCTI staff report, 1969). In fact, it was the NCTI that especially wanted this new service agency. They needed it to act as a clearinghouse for people wishing to live in integrated neighborhoods, since some of their sponsors were requesting information about areas where they could "live their beliefs."

In February 1969, one month before the Carleton conference, the NCTI had employed Jean Milgram to set up the new agency (NN fact sheet, Feb. 1970). Milgram was married to the chief executive of NCTI, Morris Milgram, the nationally known developer of integrated communities. It appears, then, that the voting for the new agency at the Carleton conference came after the fact.

At this earliest conference in 1969, discussion of terminology and semantics forecast themes and issues that have recurred throughout the history of this movement. For example, the word "stabilization" was distasteful to many of the participants, and most urged that it be avoided. The positive values of interracial communities were emphasized, along with dissatisfaction with "preservation of the status quo."

There was concern for the autonomy of local groups, expressed as a "strong feeling that each community group must feel free to respond pragmatically to its own situation." There was considerable discussion of the intentions of NCTI and the functions of the proposed advisory board. NCTI staff emphasized the willingness and desire of NCTI to be guided by the advice of conference participants in establishing the role of National Neighbors. They also expressed the intention of seeking such advice continuously on such major matters as applications to foundations, plans for the next convention, reports on the conference, and so forth. "By the same token, it was recognized that NCTI, in sponsoring a national agency, must have final responsibility in decisions" (staff report, NCTI 1969).

Some participants felt strongly that a national agency should be a service agency only, offering help when requested, as opposed to an advocate agency trying to get its own programs implemented. Others saw an advocate role for the new agency, especially on a national level and in cooperation with other organizations when appropriate. Some concern was also shown about the duplication of functions of other groups, "though this was not nearly so strong as the other concerns" (staff report, NCTI 1969).

A general session on the possible functions of a national agency produced many suggestions: develop communication among integrated community organizations; offer consulting services; sponsor conferences; compile a national directory of integrated communities; create a data bank for members; do research; educate others to the values of integrated living; provide information on legislation and urge implementation; publish manuals for new and existing groups on integration maintenance; assemble case histories of successes and failures; undertake public relations campaigns; and carry out action programs.

A panel and group discussion on real estate problems generated "some of the strongest reactions of the conference." Many felt that the survival of integrated neighborhoods depended on the development of an adequate and open supply of low- and moderate-income housing outside of inner cities. Conferees "were in agreement that no one is doing the job and many tools are needed" (staff report, 1969).

Though no firm conclusions were reached or recommendations made, "much food for thought was generated . . . all in all, the conference accomplished all we had hoped—and more. It was just a beginning—but it began a lot" (staff report, 1969). The staff evaluation was that the conference was valuable in itself, with the most immediate benefit being that the participants met each other. The success stories of various groups, the discovery of common experiences, the reaffirmation of conclusions and philosophies arrived at independently were all morale-boosters. "The conference reinforced the commitment of the people there to a course of action they believed to be the way to go, and this in itself, we believe, is a service to their communities" (staff report, 1969).

One participant's reaction to the conference shows something of the impact it had:

I was put in a position where I could actually see history in motion: right before my eyes were fifteen years of revolution in the United States . . . the revolution of Black America demanding to be allowed to flow into the mainstream of White American life . . . seeing the history of a social revolution in America pass before my eyes. (staff report, 1969)

Despite the positive response to this first conference at Carleton College, it was clear that much more thinking and planning were necessary before the final form of National Neighbors would evolve. Conference participants volunteered their help and set a maximum deadline of one year from the Carleton conference for a second and larger convention. At this second conference, a more defined national organization would be developed.

Preparations for First National Conference

Two advisory board meetings were held in May and June of 1969 to plan and prepare for the first national conference, to be held the following year. The first board meeting was held in Philadelphia, at the home of one of the members. Three other board members attended, plus the new National Neighbors executive director Jean Milgram, who had been hired by NCTI shortly before the Carleton conference.

The minutes of the first board meeting (May 24, 1969) indicate that there was no formal agenda, nor was there a chairman. Jean Milgram had a list of five items that she felt the advisory board needed to consider, and these were the subject of the meeting. This, in fact, was to be the format of many subsequent board meetings, though agendas and a chairperson were quickly established.

At the first board meeting, members heard a foundation proposal for funding that was then in a preliminary draft stage. The new board also discussed a proposed directory of integrated neighborhood organizations across the country, a proposed budget, which some thought was too meager, and the possibility of a national newsletter. The rest of the day was spent discussing the coming convention and the future organizational structure of National Neighbors. Some of the recommendations made during the discussion were carried out, and remained with the organization as part of its program and structure ever after. Others signalled differences of opinion, which also endured.

Discussion of structure focused first on who would be members. There was strong feeling that National Neighbors must be an organization of organizations, and that voting members would be grass-roots neighborhood groups having direct contact with a community. The consensus was that these need not be required to be "integrated" communities, since a clear wording of purpose would attract only groups who found this relevant. This proved quite soon to be a faulty assumption.

They wanted provision made for nonvoting associate members, such as individuals, umbrella organizations, coordinating groups, commissions, and so on. All applications for membership would be approved by the board of directors. Each voting member organization would appoint two representatives to a council of delegates, and the two would be of different ethnic groups wherever possible. The council would meet at annual conventions, and could also hold regional workshops. They would elect the board of directors and the officers of National Neighbors.

The board would consist of thirty-six elected directors, at least twenty-four of them to be members of the council of delegates. Each director would be elected for a three-year term, and terms would be staggered, with one-third elected at each annual convention. A nominating committee would submit a slate to the convention, and the method of selecting a nominating committee was to be included in the bylaws. Directors would serve as individuals, not as representatives of their organizations, and up to twelve directors could be nonmembers. The thinking there was that some persons could be elected to the board who might not be active in a local organization, but who might have other assets to contribute to the national organization (minutes, May 24, 1969).

The founding board of directors would be composed of the twenty-seven delegates and conveners who were at Carleton College, and this board would be expanded to thirty-six immediately after the first annual convention. This would be done by presidential appointment, with board approval. The twenty-seven original board members would draw lots to determine which would have one-, two-, or three-year terms.

Much discussion centered on possible geographic divisions, regional councils and regional meetings, but these were discarded in favor of the council of delegates, and possible regional workshops to be held at their discretion. The whole board of directors was to meet twice a year—perhaps a meeting of the old board immediately before a convention, and the new one immediately after, with one mid-year board meeting. Machinery for committees, conference calls, and so on would have to be developed by the board.

This skeletal outline of a workable national organization was developed at the first meeting of the advisory board, and more details were to be added at a second meeting in Chicago one month later. After that, tentative bylaws were to be prepared in time for each board member to respond before a September board meeting to be held in Los Angeles. Following the Los Angeles meeting, the organization could be formally established, and other groups notified of its existence and invited to join and attend the first annual convention (minutes, May 24, 1969).

The second advisory board meeting was held in Chicago on June 21, 1969, with many more board members attending: this time thirteen board members came, plus executive director Jean Milgram. The meeting was held in the office of the Hyde Park–Kenwood Community Conference, the nation's earliest successfully stabilized community (Abrahamson 1959).

At the Chicago board meeting, more details were proposed for the structure of National Neighbors. These came in response to a draft of the constitution and bylaws, prepared by one of the board members who had attended the first meeting one month earlier. One important change in the bylaws was the limitation of voting membership to "integrated organizations from integrated neighborhoods, approved by the board of directors" (minutes, June 21, 1969). Much discussion centered on this.

Strong feelings were expressed by some board members that they did not want membership to be open to all grass-roots neighborhood associations. They wanted the bylaws to state clearly that National Neighbors was an association of *integrated* neighborhood associations. One board member said: "If anyone can join, the whole concept of living together—not just talking about living together—would be watered down and lose its impact and meaning" (minutes, June 21, 1969).

Another subject that generated considerable discussion was the extent of power representatives should have at annual conventions. Consensus was reached that strong organizations would not join unless legislative and policy decisions were made by the council of delegates. Accordingly, an important change in the proposed bylaws was that "the Council of Delegates shall have the power to legislate and to determine the policies which shall govern the organization" (minutes, June 21, 1969).

However, the actual bylaws gave power to the board to amend the bylaws and, ultimately, to determine which actions should be carried out by the organization. So they, in fact, had the real power. But, since they were widely scattered geographically and did not meet often, it was the executive director who held the major responsibilities of the organization. This proved to be an unwieldy arrangement, and later caused much difficulty within the organization, as we will see.

The minutes of this second board meeting reflect some of the tensions of the time throughout the country coming at the peak of separatism in black-white relations. Several board members expressed anxiety about confrontation that might occur with black militants in their local communities who could challenge the ideology of integrationist associations. Others reported on coalitions that had formed between black separatists and integrationists in their communities (Denver and Cincinnati). Such coalitions worked for a common goal or a specific task that both groups agreed on. Despite differing and opposing philosophies, they recognized that they had a common enemy—white racism.

Flowing out of this discussion was the decision to hold workshops at the coming convention dealing with these issues. One workshop, for example, was to be on Pluralism in America—including coalition efforts. Another was to be on school centers, voluntary and mandated, dealing with effective ways of making integrated schools an option for those who wanted them. A third topic that led to a proposed workshop for the coming convention was the role of local governments in stabilizing integrated areas.

Executive director Milgram spoke of a visit to Dayton, Ohio, where the local government was involved in the prevention of deterioration and resegregation of a city neighborhood. Dayton had received several large federal and private grants for code enforcement, for innovative school programs, and for an experimental police district. Milgram noted that these could probably be obtained only by a governmental unit. Board members agreed that one workshop at the coming convention should be devoted to methods of involving local governments in stabilization efforts.

Other plans for the convention were only briefly discussed, "with general agreement that it should be somewhere in the Midwest" (minutes, June 21, 1969). It was, in fact, held in Dayton the following spring, at the Bergamo Center for Renewal, in the heart of the neighborhood undergoing stabilization by the city government. This was National Neighbors' first national conference—their founding conference.

The Bergamo Conference

On Friday, May 22, 1970, black and white representatives from thirty-three interracial neighborhood associations in twenty-four cities and seventeen states gathered to hear about and set direction for the new National Neighbors. They attended meetings, workshops, panels, plenary sessions, meals, and informal discussions from Friday evening until Monday afternoon, adjourning exhausted and exhilarated at 3:30 P.M. on May 25. One of the last motions passed at the new board of directors' meeting that final Monday afternoon was "that we not schedule meetings when people are tired or pressed to leave" (minutes, May 25, 1970).

Official minutes were taken of the opening session, the special board meeting, the plenary session, and the final board meeting by the new secretary of NN, Iris Bruce. She was a black delegate from Oklahomans for Neighborhood Equality in Oklahoma City, which she formed after her "inspirational experiences" at the Carleton College conference in 1969 (*Neighbors*, Nov.-Dec. 1970). The interim president was Joseph Hairston, a black attorney from Neighbors, Inc. in Washington, D. C. He introduced to the delegates the other interim officers, executive committee, and staff of NN and a newly appointed nominating committee. He gave the background of the formation of NN and spoke of the need for NN as a means of communication and information for member groups. He appointed a resolutions committee to receive current concerns from conference delegates to be presented at the plenary session. A committee for receiving proposed bylaws changes was also appointed.

Of the six resolutions adopted by the new council of delegates at the founding Bergamo conference, four were operational—relating to the structure of the new national organization—and two were programmatic—relating to ideology, goals, and objectives. Operational concerns included the location of the next annual conference (Atlanta was suggested), sending member organizations' mailing lists to NN for fund-raising purposes, sending news to NN, and having youth, lending institutions, and real estate boards on the next year's conference program. The two programmatic items adopted concerned equal educational opportunity and open housing. The education resolution read:

Be it resolved that NN strongly endorses equal educational opportunity for all children. It recognizes that segregated education is inherently inferior and recommends the most aggressive methods to achieve equal educational opportunity. NN hereby supports litigation to achieve the constitutional right of equal protection under the law with regard to education and hereby affirms achievement of quality education for all as a major priority of this organization. NN supports vigorous enforcement by HEW of the school desegregation decision. (minutes, May 25, 1970)

The council of delegates also agreed to telegraph this resolution to President Nixon, and the secretary of HEW. One of the delegates offered to pay for the cost of the telegrams. Another delegate asked that "we be sure that bussing is two-way, not just blacks to white schools, but also whites to black schools." Thus, the very early concern about integrated schools showed the awareness of the link between the maintenance of integrated neighborhoods and the maintenance of integrated schools.

The open housing program item was embodied in this resolution: "Be it resolved that National Neighbors select as this year's major program the challenging of agencies which control housing patterns to affirmatively and publicly promote open housing." A related resolution was referred to executive director Jean Milgram: "Be it resolved that NN engage in such projects as a Shoppers' Sunday where across the country National Neighbors members (with fair housing people) test the real estate practices of the local area and then concurrently file violation complaints."

One more implementing resolution referred to the board was: "Be it resolved that NN appoint a committee to coordinate this year's major program." The board officially requested the president and executive director to report to the board by September on the program to implement "our major thrust" (minutes, May 25, 1970). These resolutions show an early awareness of the link between the maintenance of integrated neighborhoods and equality of housing opportunity.

Indicators of financial difficulties, structural confusion, and semantic squabbles also appeared at the first conference. After the board unanimously voted to hire Jean Milgram as executive director of NN (which she already had been serving as for a year), they disagreed about her salary. One motion proposed that her salary be $1,100 a month, plus expenses, with details to be developed by the executive committee. Two board members immediately moved to table the motion. This failed.

Discussion of expenses revealed that the current office expenses and salaries were "running $1,600 a month. There is no rent because the office is in the Milgram home" (minutes, Bergamo conference, May 1970). Questions raised included the nature of the executive director's job, and NN's relationship in the future with SOHI—formerly NCTI, the original sponsor of NN, and how much money should be relegated to travel vs. phone. All of these were referred to the executive committee. Concern about finances is also reflected in a motion to appoint a chair of a finance committee and to expand the committee and establish its functions.

Terminology differences are seen in a motion "that the following words be used in place of 'integrated': pluralistic, multiracial, multi-ethnic, open, inclusive, one-world" (minutes, Bergamo conference, May 1970). This of course reflects the agonies of the times, with the growth of the black power and separatist movement fragmenting the civil rights movement. Though this motion carried, another one barring the use of the word "stabilization" in any further publications or correspondence failed. However, the minutes do note that the board "wishes the staff and others to avoid the use of the words 'integrated' and 'stabilization' in correspondence and future publications" (minutes, Bergamo conference, May 1970).

New officers elected at the Bergamo conference were Joseph Battle, a black realtor, member of the Ludlow Community Association of Shaker Heights, and head of Cleveland's Operation Equality, a funded fair-housing agency. Vice-president was Ruth Steele, white delegate and director of West Mount Airy Neighbors in Philadelphia. Secretary was Iris Bruce from Oklahoma, mentioned above, and the treasurer was Richard Kerr, white delegate and director of Denver's Greater Park Hill Community, Inc. Thus the officers were racially and geographically diverse. But the real leader of the new organization was its executive director.

At this first national conference, Jean Milgram was established as the inspirational leader of NN. When she gave her executive report, she said that an important factor in the success of the conference was "the magic of people coming together who have conquered old fears." She spoke of the future of National Neighbors as an organization different from others "in that it had no way to go but down one road," and that because of this it should be ready "to do battle with its identified enemies, particularly the real estate industry." She reported that finances were low at that time, and said that NN's only supporters were themselves. But for this reason, NN had less to lose than other groups by taking risks against the establishment. To much applause, she declared: "I'm ready and willing if you are" (minutes, Bergamo conference, May 1970).

When participants in the Bergamo conference returned home, they reported to their local organizations. Some excerpts from their reports reveal the kind of impact they experienced. One delegate from Baltimore's Social Security Administration, for example, said:

The basic theme was that the problems of integrated neighborhoods cannot be successfully attacked solely within those integrated neighborhoods . . . that the pressures within minority communities to find decent housing will overwhelm all presently integrated neighborhoods unless some means are found to effectively open existing white communities to minorities in practice as well as legal theory. . . . I believe National Neighbors will find a useful national role in promoting integrated housing and in attacking housing problems generally.

Jean Milgram reported: "There was complete consensus that the practices of real estate brokers, lending institutions, housing developers and property managers are the keystone to most of our racial problems. This is not to say that the real estate industry is the cause, but rather that if present segregated housing patterns are eliminated, the entire discriminatory structure will collapse" (*Neighbors*, Dec. 1970).

STRUCTURE

Phase One (1970–73): Unfunded, Zestful, Chaotic

We will examine NN's structure in terms of decision-making, membership, and finances. Since there were no changes suggested for the new constitution at the first national conference in Dayton, the structure earlier proposed was embodied in the bylaws. It remained to plague the organization, with its unclear decision-making mechanism and built-in conflicts. Misunderstandings and controversies eventually arose within staff, between staff and board, and among board members concerning communications, lines of responsibility and authority, and personnel practices. But these occurred mostly after the organization received funding. For the first three years, it operated very much like a volunteer effort.

The executive director, Jean Milgram, was the hub around which the organization functioned. She was a dedicated worker, who was given a title and the implied authority to build the organization and to raise and spend funds in the interest of commonly held goals. The five officers and ten board members were elected, with six more appointed by the president, but all were widely scattered geographically. There was no money to finance their travel to board meetings, and most could not afford extensive travel at their own expense. Their business between annual meetings was therefore conducted primarily by a seven-member executive committee, mostly through telephone conference calls.

Thus, the major responsibility for leadership, for marshalling financial resources, for generating programs, and for building the organization fell upon the executive director. The immediate issues of the first three years were fundraising, establishing communication with a farflung constituency, and initiating program activities that would provide the existing and potential membership with a sense of common cause and unity. The director had to make the most of what was at hand as she went along. An office was set up in her home. With so little money available for salaries, the staff was essentially volunteer. In time, some volunteers were paid small amounts for their services, but this was not done according to a salary schedule. There was no organizational chart, there were no job descriptions, and there were no guidelines or procedures governing board-staff relations. The bylaws were no help. They were, in fact, a source of confusion and conflict.

While the council of delegates was designated in the bylaws as the "supreme governing body" of National Neighbors, and had the power to determine policy, it had little or no control over management except through the election of board members. In reality, it also had little to do with policy-making, since it met only once a year and its composition changed from year to year.

The bylaws clearly vested the board of directors with the powers of management. Article IV also empowered the board to establish an executive committee whose "actions . . . shall stand unless rescinded within thirty (30) days after receiving the minutes." The specific duties of the board were listed as follows:

1. Carry out the policies and programs of the Association
2. Employ, direct and evaluate an Executive Director
3. Establish and monitor a personnel policy
4. Account for the funds of the Association
5. Determine the date and place for convening an annual meeting of the Council of Delegates
6. Determine the dues of the Association
7. Have the Bylaws reviewed prior to each annual meeting and recommend revisions as needed to the Council of Delegates
8. Perform such other duties as may be prescribed by these bylaws. (NN bylaws, 1970)

To add to this apparent conflict between the council of delegates' authority and that of the board of directors, a third authority named in the bylaws was the president of the association. The duties of this office were listed as being the principal executive officer of NN, who "shall act for the Council of Delegates and the Board of Directors with respect to the supervision and direction given the Executive Director." Up to six directors could be appointed by the president with the consent of the board of directors. Members and chairs of standing committees were to be appointed by the president with the consent of the board, "and shall serve at the pleasure of the President." The president was to be an ex-officio member of all standing committees. The president could establish such special committees "as deemed necessary." Finally, "the Executive Director shall receive direction and supervision from the Board of Directors through the President" (NN bylaws, 1970).

Thus, substantial executive powers were given to the president rather than to the executive director. The director's duties were specified as merely administrative, carrying out policies and activities subject to the approval of the president and following the guidelines established by the council of delegates and the board of directors. It was inevitable that confusion and conflict arose. As the organization grew and activities expanded, conditions in the home office became chaotic. Relations between staff and executive committee became strained, and the board was divided as to how to deal with the increasing tensions.

The difficulties of communication are seen in an early memo from the executive director to board members, which began with the sentence: "Summer is a difficult time for communication" (memo, Aug. 14, 1970). As it turned out, any season was a difficult time for communication, given the NN organizational structure and the geographical separation of the board members and the director.

Minutes of an executive committee seven-way telephone conference call show some of the early structural problems. How was the executive committee to meet and how often? This agenda item resulted in a decision to have "quarterly meetings, one to be the annual meeting, either in person or by conference call" (minutes, Sept. 13, 1970). Other agenda items concerned the number of reports to be sent to board members, and how NN should function between executive committee meetings. The consensus was that for the first year no committees would be set up, and that the executive committee would act as a committee for the whole. If decisions were required between executive committee meetings, the president and executive director would make them. Thus, many decisions of the new national organization were made by two people, and occasionally seven.

One executive committee meeting the first year was held in a Chicago airport, where members from Washington, Philadelphia, Atlanta, Cleveland, Oklahoma City, and Denver met the Chicago member for an all-day session. The difficulty of arranging meetings was publicly acknowledged in an item in NN's newsletter: "An organization needs meetings, but for a national group on a limited budget, this can present problems" (Neighbors, Jan.–Feb. 1972). The news item went on to describe how one NN committee, long-range planning, met the problem with a weekend retreat at one member's home in Philadelphia, and ended with a note on another marathon retreat planned by the committee the following spring.

Unaware of these problems, delegates to the third national conference voted approval of a proposal by the long-range planning committee to set up a series of task forces for NN. These were to be the nucleus of a nationwide self-help network on a variety of concerns facing member groups. The concept of task forces was seen as the most practical way to utilize fully NN resources, at the least expense to NN and member groups (Neighbors, June–July 1972). But the task forces proved to be as unwieldy as the rest of NN's structure.

Six task forces were established, one of which had three subcommittees; all were coordinated by a volunteer from Baltimore. Regional meetings were envisioned, and much enthusiasm was generated. But only one regional meeting was held during the entire year. Geographical dispersion was simply too great, and time and financial resources too limited, to do more. And the more difficult things became, the more committees were established to deal with them. Ultimately, all problems were dumped back on the executive committee, and from there on to the executive director—by now much overburdened and harried.

For the first three years of the organization's development, the board played a minimal role in policy-making and management. They mostly responded to suggestions brought to them by the president or the executive director, who was charged with finding funds for the organization and expanding its membership. She did both.

From the original twelve founding organizational members, the list grew from forty-one at the end of the first year to sixty-nine by the end of the third year.

Delegates were evenly divided racially, and their organizations were geographically dispersed. Voting membership was limited to integrated organizations having direct contact with an integrated neighborhood and "goals consistent with the purposes of NN" (bylaws, 1970).

But the question arose during the first year: what is an "integrated" neighborhood? This became an issue when several inquiries came from organizations that subscribed "whole-heartedly" to NN's purpose, but whose "integrated" status was "dubious to non-existent" (*Neighbors*, March-April 1971). The executive committee tried to clarify the issue with these guidelines:

If an organization is neighborhood-based; If the neighborhood has both white and black residents; If the organization has both black and white active members; If it has as a purpose the achievement of a viable interracial neighborhood; If it will send a black and a white delegate to NN's annual conference; Then it fills the qualifications for voting membership in NN. (*Neighbors*, March-April 1971)

Most of the organizations that did not qualify as voting members were fair housing groups, city agencies, or cities, which were encouraged to join NN for one dollar per 1,000 population. All of these became associate member organizations and remained an active and growing part of NN. At one time during phase one, in fact, of seventy-eight new members joining NN, seventy were individual associate members and four were group associate members. Only four were actual voting member groups from integrated neighborhoods (report, Oct. 12, 1972). This pattern continued into the next two phases.

As the membership grew, so did the financial contributions. Nearly all of this development was the work of the executive director. Increasing the financial support for NN meant not only more money for their program and office, but also more money for the sorely overworked and underpaid staff.

The very first budget proposed by the executive director and approved by the board was for $62,998. Of this amount, almost half was for salaries of a secretary, assistant director and a director. About a third was for program, including publications, the newsletter, travel, and the annual conference (totaling $23,400, of which $10,000 was just for the conference). The rest of the budget ($9,790) was for office expenses, including mailings (half the amount for this alone), postage, supplies, professional accounting and legal services, and miscellaneous ($1,000). No money was budgeted for rent, since the office was in the home of the executive director.

Of this budget, only $10,000 was on hand. The rest had to be raised. An obvious source was the dues of membership groups which were set at twenty-five dollars, with ten dollars for nonvoting individual members. But even with seventy group members, this only came to $2,450. Clearly, other sources had to be found. Foundation grants were to be applied for, and direct mail solicitation was planned. One other early idea was to have a national fund-raising project with a premiere of a new movie, with each member organization participating and splitting the profits fifty-fifty with NN (minutes, Sept. 13, 1970). This was never done.

The first budget was adopted with the stipulation that there be no deficit financing except for fund-raising projects. While they struggled on and wrote funding proposals to foundations and corporations, their bare survival budget was about $7,000 short, and they could not even make regular payments to their executive director. An ad hoc funds committee was appointed to deal with the financial problems, which were constant for the first three unfunded years of NN's existence. During most of this time, Jean Milgram was the only full-time staff member. In the fall of 1972, the newsletter editor was given the full-time position of coordinator of the new task forces, in addition to the work of being editor. Two part-time clerical workers assisted the two full-time staff.

The third annual NN conference, held in Baltimore in 1972, included five resolutions from the ad hoc funds committee, proposed to help the financially ailing organization. The resolutions, passed by the council of delegates, were: (1) have each voting member organization try to raise for NN a sum equal to at least 5% of their budget; (2) have all board members, delegates, and member groups pledge an amount they would personally be responsible for raising for NN during the following year; (3) have each member ask its local human relations commission to join NN as an associate member; (4) require voting member groups to give NN their mailing list each year for one financial solicitation a year; (5) have NN sell bumperstickers and buttons showing a NN logo (minutes, third NN conference, June 8–11, 1972). None of this ever happened.

A financial appeal in the fall of 1972 included a direct mailing from the treasurer, with a special message to the original founders of NN:

You are intimately aware of the need for NN. . . . [Its] tremendous . . . vital program . . . that can help in the fight for successful multiracial communities. . . . Many of the neighborhoods that need NN the most could not afford to join if dues . . . were set high enough to cover NN's operating expenses. The only effective way to cover the resulting financial gap is with income from associate memberships. That is why I am writing you today to ask that you consider joining NN as an individual. (NN Letter Nov. 25, 1972)

During the next year, NN raised $23,000 in contributions and memberships, but this was still not enough to pay the bills and conduct their program.

By the end of their third year of existence and struggle, the executive director rewrote one of their foundation proposals, and learned early in August 1973 that the Ford Foundation would fund them with $50,000 for two years. Though exhilarated by this news, NN recognized immediately that the grant would not enable them to do all they had originally envisioned. They were, however, assured of financial security for the next two years.

The grant, actually given on December 26, 1973, was retroactive to September 1, 1973, which happily covered some of the back salary owed to the executive director. One thing NN had to do, as a requirement of the funding, was to raise one-third—or $25,000—of their budget from small contributions. So their end-less quest for funds went on.

Phase Two (1974–81): Funded, Troubled, Unstable

Though the organization was now more secure, the executive director's salary was not. The executive committee approved an increase in Jean Milgram's salary to $20,000, of which half was to be paid from the Ford Foundation grant for half-time field service work. The other half was to be paid by NN from its general operating funds "if our funds permit" (minutes, Dec. 16, 1973). Her agreement to this arrangement is another mark of her dedication to her work. She remained with NN for three more years after it was funded. Then, dissension tore the organization apart, and she left. NN never recovered.

Conflicts arose when funding made additional staffing possible. By April 1975, controversy between two staff members and the executive director had erupted to the point of spilling over to several board members. These personnel problems became the subject of a special meeting of the executive committee in May 1975. The controversy dominated the attention of the board and staff at the June annual conference in Chicago "to such an extent that the spirit and quality of the conference was seriously dampened and many delegates became disenchanted" (consultant's report, April 1976).

The NN board, at its meeting in Rochester, New York in October 1975, decided to retain the services of an independent consultant to conduct a management audit. Interviews with the staff, executive director, and board and a review of pertinent documents indicated that the roots of the problems that appeared in the spring of 1975 "went back at least as far as 1973 and began to emerge at the time of the 1974 annual conference in Atlanta" (consultant's report, 1976).

The fifty-seven-page report of the consultant hired by NN included a brief hypothetical case study of another small, struggling organization. The imaginary case study was used as an illustration of some problems that were comparable to those of NN, especially the character of the founder (and NN's executive director). The most obvious parallel drawn by the consultant was that in each case "the organization became an extension of the character and personality of a strong individual. A second parallel is that in each case the 'enterprise' was initiated without any real capitalization and had to 'make-do' on a hand-to-mouth basis" (consultant's report, 1976).

As we have seen, NN began as a movement organization with high expectations and almost no financial resources. Their only real resources were the common commitment of the member groups to broad and somewhat vague goals, and an incredibly dedicated executive director, who was given a title and implied authority to build the organization according to the shared goals. Board members were widely scattered geographically, and the major responsibility for mobilizing financial resources, developing the program, and building the organization fell upon the executive director.

When she first put together a volunteer staff, they were drawn into a highly personal relationship with her because of mutual commitment to the cause, and their liking for each other. As the organization and its funding grew, its activities expanded and the staff became salaried. Production schedules and quality standards became necessary. The earlier subjective relationships had to submit to some discipline, and personal conflicts led to the breakdown of rapport between the staff and director. We have already noted that for the first few years of NN's existence, the board played only a minor role in policy-making and administration. When the time came for the board to assume greater responsibility in those two areas, it was not adequately prepared to act.

The searching, thorough analysis of the independent consultant suggested that if NN were to survive and prosper, two objectives should be pursued. One was that the management and procedure roles of both board and staff needed to be reshaped to meet the needs of the organization. The other was that the trauma of a radical change in leadership should be avoided. The report then offered a set of detailed principles of effective management and administration for NN's consideration.

But by the time the consultant's report reached the president of NN, executive director Milgram had already submitted her resignation. The controversies had been too intense and personal. She could no longer continue. A letter to all member organizations signed by the NN board secretary painfully dealt with this situation. It began: "As we grow, it is inevitable that we must deal with change. Sometimes that change is difficult and painful" (letter, May 3, 1976).

The letter went on to say that the board had regretfully accepted the resignation "of our well-known and widely admired Executive Director Jean Milgram, submitted March 28." In addition, the letter explained that both Milgram and the board agreed that NN was facing serious challenges and needed strong leadership to keep their budget balanced and to develop meaningful programs. The letter said that she was resigning because she felt that her leadership role had been weakened, while her continuing presence made it impossible for anyone else to exert the needed leadership.

This important letter also noted that the board had unanimously adopted the recommendations of the consultant, who said, "On balance, the achievements substantially outweigh the mistakes that have been made and stand to the credit of Board and staff alike" (consultant's report, 1976). Finally, the letter announced the appointment of an interim executive director while a search began for a permanent director to replace Jean Milgram.

The public announcement of Jean Milgram's resignation was in the summer issue of NN's newsletter: "The past year was a difficult one for NN leadership. . . . It had to deal with several changes in staff, including the resignation of Jean Milgram. Her leadership, guidance, and commitment to NN will be sorely missed" (Neighbors 1976).

The advertisement for NN's new director read:

Growing national community organization seeks executive director. Requires B.A. or equivalent experience plus three years administrative experience; demonstrated ability to relate well to diverse social and economic groups; strong commitment to integrated neighborhoods, open housing and civil rights; and demonstrated fund-raising ability. Responsibilities include moderate to heavy travel and direction of a three-person staff plus clerical workers and consultants. Salary negotiable within $15,000–$20,000 range. Send detailed resume. (board letter, May 3, 1976)

In the next three years, NN had a succession of five different executive directors, some of whom stayed only six or seven months. This was disastrous for both program and morale, though the organization plugged on. The one stable factor during this difficult time was the Ford Foundation funding, which made it possible to maintain a staff to keep things going for seven years.

Financial contributions during phase two included $50,000 each year from the Ford Foundation grant, plus annual member and other contributions of up to $40,000. The last two years of the Ford grant, however, reduced the amount by 20% and 40% in each of those years. The NN board was told to look for other sources of funding, as it was unlikely that Ford would continue to fund it beyond 1981. A HUD contract for $108,000 was awarded to NN in 1980 to conduct a study of housing discrimination against children in five selected geographical areas. This grant tided NN over the period of Ford's decreasing funding. Then, it too ended.

Increased staff necessitated larger office space, and NN moved to their first real office on November 1, 1974, at the beginning of phase two. Until then, they had worked out of Jean Milgram's home in Philadelphia. Three years later, after Jean Milgram left, they moved again to another Philadelphia office in February 1977. And less than a year later, on January 1, 1978, they moved their office to Washington, D.C. in order to gain national visibility.

In addition to the multiple changes in executive directors that plagued the organization during this second phase, other staff changes occurred. In 1976 a director of field services was hired, but this position also had a succession of people filling it for the remainder of this phase. One attempted change in structure was the addition of volunteer regional coordinators, but this proved to be an unwieldy arrangement, which eventually ended after a four-year struggle.

The last executive director hired during this phase remained with NN for several years, but his final months in 1981 were painful because of some unfilled contractual obligations relating to the HUD grant. This was to haunt the organization for the next five years, since HUD later sued NN for repayment of $20,000 because of undocumented time records overlooked by the unfortunate director. "He should have filled out his time sheets!" (minutes, Feb. 17, 1984). In the fourteen months preceding his resignation, this director worked only part-time for NN, while his salary was sporadically paid. Susan Learmonth also worked part-time as office coordinator, and she became the mainstay of the organization at the end of phase two. This continued for a time into phase three, even after a new executive director was in place.

Despite these constant personnel, staffing, and financial problems, however, member groups during phase two increased to seventy-six, with fifty-eight other associate memberships including cities, agencies, fair housing and other non-neighborhood groups. By the end of phase two in 1981, NN's member groups totaled 125 neighborhood organizations and 100 agencies and other associates, representing 25 states and 121 cities. They now all had equal voting rights, instead of only the neighborhood groups being eligible to vote.

The change in voting procedures required a bylaws amendment, first proposed by the executive committee in August 1979. A memorandum from NN's president to all member groups explained the reasons for the recommended change: the need for a broader base—in order to have a greater program impact and to secure "the funding essential to NN's continued existence" (memo, Aug. 28, 1979). No doubt the Ford directive to search for other sources of funding was a major impetus for this bylaws revision. It was one of many Ford directives that shaped NN.

Phase Three (1982–): Unfunded, Tired, Stable

When all funding ended at the end of phase two, NN returned to their earliest state of insecurity and impoverishment. But by this time, they had acquired a national reputation, an expensive office in the nation's capital, and a perceived need to maintain a national visibility. This was impossible without funds. The dilemma was intense, and their constant agonizing struggle for funds during phase three overshadowed all of their other activities in these years.

Ironically, though, the organization did have stability during this difficult period. This was possible only because of one dedicated board member, Charles ("Chip") Bromley, who became NN's president in 1982 and then in 1983 agreed to serve as their executive director and chief fund-raiser. One strong motivating factor in his search for funding was securing the payment of his own modest salary. But much more was at stake than that. He and the entire board knew that NN's survival was in jeopardy. Bromley devoted the next several years of his life to ensuring that survival.

Throughout his first few difficult years, the office was reduced to a bare-bones staff of one part-time person, who worked only fifteen hours a week, which was all the organization could afford. A small foundation grant provided initial funds for an intensive financial outreach program. Compounding these financial difficulties was the national climate of indifference and retrenchment in the field of civil rights. A painful fund-raising letter to NN supporters from six past presidents attests to this fact:

The commitment of persons such as you . . . led to the creation of National Neighbors thirteen years ago. . . . We fought hard and our successes grew. . . . Then times changed. The national commitment to civil rights, to open housing, to all aspects of integration fell off. Some former supporters . . . told us the goal was no longer relevant. As support fell off National Neighbors activities had to shrink. . . . We do not know where the money will come from to sustain us . . . but we are secure . . . that NN will endure . . . once the present national malaise lightens. (letter, April 6, 1982)

A message from the president in the July issue of *Neighbors* reveals some of the anguish felt by the board at this time. The message referred to severe apprehension about NN's ability to remain in existence. It also spoke of deep concern for maintaining NN's original goals and direction. "Spiritually we were millionaires, financially we were broke" (*Neighbors*, July 1982).

Three months later, NN received a $10,000 emergency grant from Cigna Corporation, the employer of one NN board member. The grant was "to cover the costs of developing a new plan of action and a fund-raising strategy aimed at $300,000 in support from corporations, foundations, community groups and individuals over the next three years" (*Neighbors*, Oct. 1982). The Cigna grant came soon after NN's annual conference in Chicago, where the question of survival dominated the meetings. "We had to face the question: 'Should we fold our tents and call it quits or face the very difficult funding requirements necessary to restore Neighbors to its former eminence?' " (*Neighbors*, Dec. 1982).

A second Cigna grant in September 1982 was a $15,000 challenge grant. One of the conditions of the Cigna grant was that NN had to raise at least $15,000 from other sources early in 1983. The Cigna challenge was met by April 1983, and jubilantly announced to the NN board by Bromley. But the struggle for funds was a never-ending one, as seen in this gold-colored letter to members four months later: "Finally, with a boost in funding and morale, NN is back on its feet. . . . Now more than ever, we need your support" (letter, Aug. 1983). The letter went on to say that in the first six months of 1983, NN had acquired twenty-five more member groups, opened a Midwest office in Cleveland Heights, Ohio, and increased their solicitation of corporations and foundations.

The opening of the new Midwest office was an important structural change for NN. The stated public reason given for this was to be closer to the 40% of member groups located in the Great Lakes region (*Neighbors*, Aug. 1983). But the real reason was that the new executive director—ex-president Bromley— lived in Cleveland Heights, and it was simply too costly and exhausting for him to keep travelling back and forth to the Washington Office. Not all NN board members were pleased with this decision.

A recurrent, underlying, unresolved theme of dissatisfaction with the two offices persisted throughout this phase, and revolved around two issues. The first issue was the cost of the Washington office. Some board members felt that it should be closed, since the organization simply could not afford to maintain two offices. The Washington office's monthly rental was $700, and much of the money that NN was raising went for office upkeep. The need for an address in the nation's capital was justified by some because of the need for national visibility and proximity to legislative contacts. One suggestion repeatedly made, and repeatedly rejected, throughout this third phase was to close the costly

Washington office and instead secure a mailing address or free space elsewhere in the capital. This was never resolved.

The second office issue concerned the fear that the Midwest office would consume a growing portion of the director's time and energy, and that NN's national program and visibility would then be weakened. In fact, this did happen in 1984, when three grants from Cleveland foundations were given to NN to support and sponsor a Cleveland-area program. The director went less and less to the Washington office. The part-time office coordinator there resigned because of lack of salary security, and another part-timer was secured, who later resigned. Meanwhile, a part-time office assistant was hired in Cleveland, an NN board office committee was formed of three Cleveland board members, and so it went.

Throughout this phase, however, the dogged persistence of the director slowly began to bring in more corporate contributions, more foundation grants, more individual contributions, and more member groups. Income rose from $27,593 in 1982, to $50,212 in 1983, to $53,522 in 1984, and to $72,092 in 1985 (report, Jan. 10, 1986). Some of this, however, came from annual conferences with little net gain to NN.

Internal memos and minutes during all this time show how discouraging and exhausting the entire process of fund-raising was. Only the NN newsletters were upbeat and publicly happy during these four years. The contrast between the internal (private) and external (public) printed materials is revealing throughout the remainder of this phase.

A 1984 treasurer's report to the board on March 10 "pointed out a very tight financial situation and was duly noted by those present." The report noted a cash balance of $1,345, with an average quarterly expense level of $4,400 (minutes, March 10, 1984). Publicly, the March newsletter said nothing about the financial crisis, and a spring solicitation letter to members also gave no hint of the really desperate situation NN was in:

With National Neighbors back on its feet, buttressed by recent foundation grants and renewed support . . . 1984 could be our take-off year. . . . But we need to keep our two offices running efficiently, with enough money to . . . free our energies for the big things. . . . Together, we can demonstrate that brotherhood in America is not dead. Send your contribution today! (letter to members, Spring 1984)

The fifteenth annual NN conference, held in Starrett City, New York, in June 1984, was to be used as a springboard for financial support: foundations were invited to attend, and the media were urged to publicize the nationally known civil rights leaders who would be speaking there including Coretta Scott King, James Farmer, and Roger Wilkins. The ever-optimistic executive director Chip Bromley, in his report to the board right before the conference, wrote: "Although our present financial situation is precarious, I strongly believe that we will emerge stronger and more vigorous than ever in 1984" (report, May 11, 1984).

Bromley's report also noted the difficulty in raising money during the first five months of that year. Bromley offered some insight into that difficulty with this revealing quote from a foundation officer of one of the country's largest corporations: "Believe me, Mr. Bromley, if this company had one ounce of commitment to equal opportunity you would have the grant" (report, May 11, 1984).

Another message to the board, two weeks later, noted that the average monthly income for NN during the first five months of 1984 was $3,580, but that monthly expenses were $4,129. So the deficit spending continued, in keeping with the national trend. The income total of $17,902 during those five months reflected $10,500 in grants and $7,902 in member support. But outstanding obligations in May 1984 included $5,000 in unpaid bills and $7,500 in unpaid salary to Chip Bromley. Also looming over NN was the HUD claim of $20,000 owed them from their last contract with NN. The treasurer's somber note at the end of his 1984 report was: "Current Projection is $0" (treasurer's report, May 30, 1984).

Despite a highly successful annual conference in June 1984, bringing over $8,000 to NN, the dreary fiscal situation continued. By July, all bills had been paid except Bromley's salary, who continued to work without it. Though NN made great financial strides since their fiscal death rattle in 1982, even with their increased income they were barely able to keep limping along. They paid some bills, but they withheld or reduced salaries, and above all they were unable to conduct any meaningful program for their interracial communities.

Bromley, usually indefatigable and up-beat, seemed worn out by August 1984: "Where is the money going to come from?... I haven't totally given up yet, but if we fail to persuade any donors of the urgency of making a substantial investment in NN, we have to consider some other alternatives" (memo, Aug. 3, 1984). The alternatives that he posed were three, but actually these were all just one option—to close both offices and continue as volunteers.

Despite the deep despair of this internal memo to the board, the NN newsletter appearing at that time was typically enthusiastic, optimistic, and filled with glowing reports about the recent fifteenth annual conference in New York. Headed "15th Annual Conference Called Best Ever," the newsletter referred to the conference as "an overwhelming success" (*Neighbors*, Aug. 1984). No hint of impending disaster was to be found in that issue.

This happy newsletter was followed one month later by a letter to all board members from a fellow board member informing them that NN had $1,400 left in the bank. Attached to the letter was a list of bills and operating costs for the next month, and a request that each board member contribute a minimum of one hundred dollars to NN: "This could keep the organization functioning until November" (letter, Sept. 26, 1984).

A board meeting three weeks later focused on nine agenda items, of which four related directly to the financial crisis, two were structural and three were program or goal related. The financial items included the need to decide whether to keep both offices open. The structural matters concerned the old problem of making board and committees work when members were dispersed throughout the country. Two of the three program/goal items were signs of general weariness and discouragement: one was the need for a statement of purpose that related effectively to the needs of housing groups, the other was "A *need to decide whether or not the organization should continue to exist*" (minutes, Oct. 20, 1984, emphasis added). The final program item concerned the general framework for the next annual conference, to be held in Baltimore the following June.

This agonized board meeting lasted all day. The last agenda item, concerning the coming conference, was disposed of first. The rest of the day was devoted to discussion about NN's critical financial situation and its future. The part-time Washington office manager announced that she was looking for another job, since she could not afford to continue as NN's unpaid staff indefinitely. The dissolution of NN and the closing of both offices were voted on and defeated. The stormy, desperate, prolonged meeting ended with no major changes in the structure or operation of the organization.

A somber letter from president W. Hairston to all board members went out six days after this meeting, telling them of their obligation to each raise $200 through solicitation or contribution in five days (letter, Oct. 26, 1984). Another memo to board members from Bromley, sent two months later, repeated the dismal financial picture: "We have not paid our employees since July and I have been working 'sans' salary since last February" (memo, Dec. 27, 1984). But this memo also contained the welcome news that $11,500 in expected grants had come in from three Cleveland foundations. These were to conduct a Cleveland area program (later called Metro Strategy), under the sponsorship of NN. For NN's operation, however, only $7,000 in contributions had been received. Bromley spoke with hope of a planned telethon fund-raising event for NN, to be conducted by a Chicago area volunteer.

The first board meeting in 1985 was a continuation of the discussion of all the old problems, and a continuation of not resolving them. Any suggestions for finding free space in Washington were dismissed by the president and a few others. Any suggestions for curtailing the Cleveland operation were rejected by the director, who felt it essential to continue the office there because of the funded programs NN was operating in the Cleveland area. So the impasse continued, as did the expenses and the ever-unbalanced budget.

One positive piece of financial news was the announcement by the treasurer that as of that moment, NN was $8,000 in the black and up-to-date with its bills. The telethon was succeeding after more than 650 phone calls made by Chicago volunteers. But now check-handling and record-keeping problems in the two offices became an urgent issue and the board could not agree on how to deal with them. Part-time, sporadic assistance was all that was obtained in the Washington office for the remainder of this third phase of NN's existence. But the $700 monthly rent went on, with no one there to adequately mind the store.

A fund-raising dance and the successful telethon enabled NN's solvency to continue, but this was done at the expense of salaried personnel and national program. Though the usual proportion of budget going to personnel in social agencies is 75%, in NN it was 32% (report, April 4, 1985). For the duration of this phase, NN's insecurity persisted. So, too, did the discrepancy between public and private statements about their true situation.

A public statement by the president, made at the Baltimore conference ten days later, praised the "tireless efforts of Chip Bromley" in moving NN to its then solvent position. "I am proud to be able to say to you that NN now has in place necessary resources . . . solvent, with paid staff successfully administering programs and delivering service" (statement to delegates, June 21, 1985). But five days later, a newly elected NN president's letter to board members spoke again of financial disaster: "The reality is that NN is in as much financial trouble as it was three years ago" (letter, June 26, 1985).

In 1986, the final year studied in this third phase of NN's development, events went on in much the same way: internal memos of woe, external proclamations of glee, the continual slogging for funds, an unstaffed, costly Washington office, and only a Cleveland-area program. The executive director continued to pay himself a meager salary of $400 a month. The cash flow early in the year was substantially below 1985: "The result has been that we have not been able to pay some of our bills" (memo, March 28, 1986). But a spring telethon yielded one hundred pledges and $3,500, which kept things going.

The issue of the two offices remained unresolved. Meanwhile, staff salaries and program suffered. Structural difficulties, along with the financial ones, continued to plague the organization, as minutes from the first 1986 board meeting revealed: "Do we lose pledges because of careless record keeping? . . . Do we send [dues] reminders? . . . Whose responsibility is it to give a report of the financial status of NN?" Discussion also included the method of distributing reports, and the need to hold committee meetings "in the same city [as the one picked for the board meeting] to save cost for members" (minutes, Jan. 18, 1986). The fact that the minutes were mailed out three months after this meeting is yet another indicator of the difficulties of geographical dispersion for adequate functioning. And along with waning efficiency was waning morale.

One more sign of structural problems is found in two bylaws changes proposed in the spring newsletter (Neighbors, Spring 1986). Both of these changes related to improving the functioning and fairness of the nominating committee, and both were approved by the board and later by the delegates in Los Angeles. Though they appear to be minor changes, they indicate some of the inner turmoil the board was experiencing and they forewarn of more turmoil to come. Especially, they are reflections of a weakening of trust and morale within NN's board, which still persists. Recent presidential power struggles confirm this.

A fall letter to potential contributors noted NN's goal for 1987 was "to quadruple our mailing list," and for 1988 "to quadruple our dues-paying membership" (letter, Sept. 15, 1986). Any hope for conducting an effective national program depended on securing more funding than they had had during this third phase. Such additional funding did not appear to be forthcoming. And the slick new brochure listing seven services provided by NN was a valiant attempt to

show that they were still doing something vital, when in fact they were not—
because they could not (*Something About National Neighbors*, 1986).

GOALS AND PROGRAM

Let us now look at the goals and objectives of NN over the years, to see
which of them remained constant and which changed. We will examine their
stated goals as revealed in minutes, reports, and printed materials. Then we
will study the actual services NN provided, to see how consistent they were
with their stated goals and objectives. We will look specifically at the resolutions
made at each annual conference to determine their content and their relationship to the stated goals. As with structure, we will analyze NN's goals and
program through the three phases of their existence and development.

Phase One: 1969–73

The founders of NN proposed at their first conference in 1969 that a national
service agency be established for integrated neighborhoods. The stated purpose
of the new organization was "to foster and encourage successfully integrated
neighborhoods" (bylaws, 1970). If we consider this as their first stated goal, we find
that it was retained throughout all three phases of NN's existence. What changed
were additional goals and some of the objectives—the means—for achieving them.

At the Carleton conference, twelve specific functions were suggested for the
new organization. Let us consider these as the first stated objectives of NN—
their first specified, intended program: (1) develop communication—among and
within integrated groups; (2) offer major consulting services; (3) sponsor conferences; (4) compile a national directory of integrated communities; (5) create
a data bank for members; (6) do research; (7) educate others to the values of
integrated living; (8) provide legislative information and urge implementation;
(9) publish manuals for new and existing groups; (10) assemble case histories
of successes and failures; (11) undertake national public relations campaigns;
(12) carry out action programs.

With perhaps one exception, all of these were eventually done. One of these
activities, the directory, was a one-time program item. All the others were
meant to be continuing activities, but only a few actually were. Some were
done during only one phase, others during another, and a few were carried out
during all three phases. But all were accomplished. The one exception is the
creation of a data bank, which may be a matter of interpretation. They did
acquire a file of case studies and descriptions of member groups across the country,
but there is no evidence that any systematic collection of data was ever done.

The two enduring program activities of NN throughout the three phases were
the national conferences and the newsletter publication. The frequency of newsletter publication varied according to funding and staffing. In phase three,

accordingly, it appeared only two or three times a year. But through these two enduring program activities—the national conferences and the newsletter—four of the other early stated objectives were met: developing communication, educating others, providing information, and assembling case histories.

The program activities that were not maintained in all three phases were: providing consulting services, doing research, publishing manuals, undertaking national public relations campaigns, and carrying out specific action programs. These were done primarily during phase two, but hardly at all in phase three. Thus, funding was the critical element enabling NN to conduct these five program activities, and it was only in phase two that they were funded.

What seems even more remarkable than the eventual accomplishment of all their stated objectives is the constancy of their primary stated goals. In the first seventeen years of their existence, NN's goals did not change very much, despite marked changes in their structure, staff, and leadership. For example, though the first printed brochure appearing during phase one, *Facts About NN*, did not list "Services Provided," as did subsequent brochures, it included six program activities that were essentially the same services mentioned in all of NN's subsequent printed materials. These included a clearinghouse service, newsletter, research, publications, field services and a real estate audit. In NN's most recent 1986 brochure, for example, six of the seven services listed are the same as the earlier ones, despite some changed wording. The only new service listed is "Joining with other national groups to promote common goals" (*Something About National Neighbors*, 1986).

Now let us examine the actual services provided—the program—during each phase of NN's development. In phase one, in the middle of all the early mobilization and organization and chaos, we find also the only evidence of a national action program in all of NN's history. This was the first real attempt to conduct a national housing audit in this country, and NN did it as "Shoppers' Sunday." In fact, they later tried to get substantial funding to repeat it on a much larger scale, but they were unsuccessful.

Planning for Shoppers' Sunday and trying to secure funding for a second expanded program consumed much of NN's time during phase one. This was very definitely a fair housing activity, and it encroached on the program and purpose of another existing national organization—the National Committee Against Discrimination in Housing (NCDH). How did this happen?

We must go back to the early leadership of NN to understand this important matter. At the 1970 founding conference in Dayton, half of the major speakers on the program were fair housing agency leaders or administrators. This panel of experts challenged the new NN to "utilize all its resources in a serious campaign to achieve totally open housing" (*Neighbors*, Nov.–Dec. 1970). Discussion groups that followed established the fact that conference delegates saw housing patterns as the keystone of continuing racial segregation. They also believed that housing patterns could be changed by challenging the institutions that controlled them—the real estate industry, the lending institutions, and governmental agencies. Fair housing laws, recently enacted by Congress in 1968, would make all this possible.

It is not surprising, then, that one of the first resolutions adopted at that conference was: "Be it Resolved that NN select as this year's major program the challenging of agencies which control housing patterns to affirmatively and publicly promote open housing." A second implementing resolution was: "Be it Resolved that NN engage in such projects as a Shoppers' Sunday where across the country NN members [with fair housing people] test the real estate practices of the local area and then concurrently file violation complaints" (minutes, Bergamo conference, May 1970). Elected as the first president of NN was Joseph Battle, a black realtor and the executive director of a Cleveland fair housing agency. This further reflected and bolstered the focus on fair housing at this conference.

In addition to the abundant fair housing leadership at this founding conference of NN, another factor within the fair housing movement itself made NN a ready candidate for fair housing action at this time. The only national organization devoted solely to fair housing then (or ever) was the National Committee Against Discrimination in Housing. Founded in 1950 as an organization of organizations, it was going through an internal crisis in 1970 at the time of NN's founding conference. Soon after its twentieth anniversary, NCDH faced the loss of its Ford Foundation and HUD funding. Its local networks were discontented, and it was in imminent danger of bankruptcy—financial, organizational, and spiritual.

National Neighbors' appearance at that time only added to NCDH's woes, casting even more doubt on its own effectiveness. Their anxieties about this new rival later mounted when NN began to seek Ford Foundation funding—NCDH's major source of financial support. Eventually, NCDH rallied after some structural and staff changes, but the time of NN's founding conference was at NCDH's lowest ebb. Thus, NN's adoption of a fair housing program as their first (and only) national action filled a vacuum left by NCDH's weakness in 1970.

I have described these events elsewhere as an example of an "intrusive movement organization" (Saltman 1978: 79). Though NCDH did attempt to establish friendly relations with NN, this never quite materialized, and the treading by NN on NCDH's ideological and program turf remained a problem. Sometimes this problem lay dormant while many other issues and worries prevailed. But throughout the existence of both movement organizations, this problem surfaced and was unresolved.

Since open housing and neighborhood stabilization are interdependent, the sorting out of priorities for the two organizations was eventually forced by their common funding source—the Ford Foundation. But the uneasy coexistence and semirivalry of both groups continued, even though NN had to give up their heavy emphasis on fair housing at the end of phase one as a condition of Ford Foundation funding.

Until then, however, fair housing was NN's major action program, with Shoppers' Sunday occupying much of the director's and executive committee's time and energy during phase one. Early memos from Jean Milgram to the board are filled with references to plans for Shoppers' Sunday. Two types of local action programs were urged—one for information gathering, the other for testing real estate practices. Questionnaires were to be sent to local groups asking for information on real estate practices in their area and laws governing them in their state. This was the "easy" project. The other one, testing the market, would "require greater commitment and more NN help" (minutes, Sept. 13, 1970).

For the first part of the project, NN distributed to their thirty-seven member groups a five-part questionnaire asking for information about local real estate firms and brokers, boards of realtors, real estate commissions and licensing agencies, property management firms, and builders and developers. Returns from member groups were spotty and incomplete, though responses from nine state real estate commissions were reported in 1972, almost two years after questionnaires were distributed (*Neighbors*, March-April 1972).

Reports on the testing of real estate practices on Shoppers' Sunday were given at NN's second annual conference, at Oberlin College in Ohio. Again, results were spotty and incomplete, despite efforts to insure uniformity of methods. Generally, the findings were that while black homeseekers were frequently treated politely, sometimes more so than whites, discrimination in housing continued despite the passage of the 1968 fair housing law. Some of the discrimination was blatant, as examples of these findings in a few of the cities tested indicate.

Hartford: "We learned that of the four largest real estate operations in the heart of our community, one has totally wiped out our interracial neighborhood as a place to do any transactions."

Baltimore: "We tested an integrated neighborhood and found that a white couple was shown three other all-white communities when they specifically asked for the integrated neighborhood. But the black couple was shown the area immediately."

Oklahoma City: "In one house they told me the same price as Clare [the black partner]. But in another I was told $24,500 with 10% down, and the blacks were told $25,900 and 20% down. At another house, he told the white couple $92,000 and the blacks $115,000."

The *Neighbors* issue that reported the Shoppers' Sunday findings (July-August 1971) had printed across its front page in bold large type these words: Sue the Bastards! (see Appendix D). This became the slogan for NN during the rest of phase one, as they continued to emphasize fair housing and the use of lawsuits to attain it.

The NN executive committee appointed an open housing project committee late in 1971. This project was envisioned as strengthening local groups through providing consultation and a specific strategy of testing, lawsuits, and negotiations for affirmative action. Needed was $300,000 to hire consultants, field representatives, publications editors, and legal counsel. A funding proposal was to be developed and circulated to potential funding sources as soon as possible, as well as to fair housing supporters. Meanwhile, NN would try to implement the project "in whatever ways possible" (*Neighbors*, March–April 1972).

The "ways possible" turned out to be a few field visits by a few selected staff and board members to a few neighborhoods, on request, in the next year. The preparation of the funding proposal, however, was done throughout the first phase. It was careful and thorough, written and rewritten many times, and ultimately did result in funding by the Ford Foundation. But the funding was not for the open housing project, nor was it in the amount hoped for. Thus, this expanded national action program was never implemented. The eventual NN total program was, in fact, shaped by their funding source's stipulations, as we shall see.

Until then, NN during their first phase were free to conduct whichever programs their limited funds and staff would permit. They made a valiant and monumental volunteer public relations effort in the summer of 1972. Bob Ketron, a member of a Baltimore neighborhood group and task force coordinator for NN, volunteered to drive 15,000 miles across the country to publicize NN. His trip was intended to reinforce contacts among member organizations, to interest new groups in joining NN, to accumulate information about the member groups, and to publicize NN's efforts from coast to coast.

In all twenty-one cities Ketron visited with his wife and baby daughter in their donated station wagon, he stayed with NN member group families and talked to local media and public officials. The eighty-day trip was judged a resounding success by NN, who widely publicized it (report, Oct. 12, 1972). The entire December 1972 issue of *Neighbors* was devoted to this cross-country tour and the findings and impressions of whirlwind tourist Ketron. His comments were moving and inspiring, and offered insight into the mood of NN, their member groups, and the country at that time. He ended with the sober recognition that "the magnitude and intensity of problems facing local neighborhoods trying to achieve or maintain stability almost defy description. Frankly, I had to realize that if these people—combining talent, good will, and energy— could produce so little a dent in the present situation, then we have a truly formidable task ahead of us" (*Neighbors*, Dec. 1972).

The editorial comment in that same issue referred to the similarity of problems facing interracial communities everywhere in the country—freeways, fear of crime, panic peddling, zoning, better public education. Internal problems also plagued many groups, ranging from apathy to dissension on how to resolve the problems. But throughout the account of Ketron's trip was one common problem, running "as a continuous thread"—the concern about racial steering practices used by real estate agents. As a result, interracial neighborhoods everywhere faced the fact that white homeseekers were either discouraged from living there, or not informed of available housing there. On the other hand, black homeseekers were encouraged to seek housing only in integrated or black areas.

Because of this deep concern and frustration of member groups about racial steering, NN decided to prepare a publication about steering, and about programs to combat it. So the Ketron trip spurred another program activity for the organization. Eight months later, the new publication was ready for distribution. Titled *Racial Steering: The Dual Housing Market and Multiracial Neighborhoods*, this was NN's first and major publication. One other publication in phase one was a twelve-page directory of thirty-four member groups, printed as a special issue of *Neighbors* at the end of their first year (June 1971).

Program activities of NN during this first phase of mobilization consisted of convening four national conferences, publishing their bimonthly newsletter sixteen times, sponsoring the cross-country tour in 1972, publishing the booklet on racial steering in 1973, and preparing and submitting their proposal for funding to diverse potential funding sources. In addition, they established among member groups task forces on housing, political power, public services, communications, education, and real estate practices. Within their board, they developed a long-range planning committee and an open housing project committee. And out of each national conference came a series of resolutions proposed by delegates for NN board action. We will examine these resolutions next, to see their content and the extent of their implementation.

Resolutions. We can divide the resolutions adopted by conference delegates into two types: operational and program. The operational resolutions related to the functioning of the organization and included such concerns as fund-raising; site selection and format or agenda for conferences; internal communication among member groups and between groups and NN staff; and any other matters unrelated to policies, goals, and program. The program resolutions concerned issues reflecting goals or ideology, and were intended to lead to some action or program.

We have earlier noted that the founding Bergamo conference in 1970 produced six resolutions, which clearly fell into these two types: four of the resolutions were operational, the other two were program oriented. All resolutions adopted at the conference were to be mailed to delegates and publicized in NN's newsletter, *Neighbors*. But all resolutions adopted at the conference were not necessarily implemented by the board. If they did not agree and could not pass a majority vote on a resolution already adopted by conference delegates, the resolution was never acted on.

One example of this is a resolution adopted at the Bergamo conference to change the word "integrated" in the bylaws and in the constitution's section on "Purpose of the Organization." The board later voted to reject this resolution after one board member reminded them of the expense and difficulties they would face if they made this change while seeking tax-exempt status from IRS.

The second NN conference at Oberlin in 1971 resulted in fourteen resolutions. Of these, only three were programmatic; all the others were operational. Two of the three program resolutions related to a second Shoppers' Sunday, which never materialized. The other program resolution urged NN to develop an advertising campaign, in conjunction with member groups, to promote multi-racial neighborhoods. This, too, was not implemented, since no such effort is reported in any subsequent NN records or newsletters. However, Bob Ketron's later whirlwind tour of the country might be seen by some as a national ad-vertising campaign.

Nineteen resolutions were adopted in 1972, at NN's third conference in Baltimore. Of the nineteen, six were programmatic and thirteen were opera-tional. The six program resolutions included two urging affirmative lending practices, one recommending metropolitan school desegregation, one supporting federal cash subsidies for pro-integrative moves, one relating to fair housing information, and one supporting funds for lead paint abatement programs.

Of these six, NN acted on the two relating to lending practices by sending a letter to appropriate agencies. The other program concerns were either referred to member groups for their consideration and action, or were not implemented. Most of the operational resolutions dealt with ways of increasing membership and funding, and development of a regional structure for NN. These were attempted, with successful results regarding more members, and generally un-successful results regarding the regional structure.

The fourth conference, in Rochester in 1973, marked the end of phase one of NN's development. Two months after the conference, NN received word of impending funding by the Ford Foundation. Since the funding mandated a change of objectives and program, some of the twenty-five resolutions adopted at the Rochester conference became untimely. They could only be implemented if they were consistent with NN's funding proposal and the conditions of the grant. First we will examine the Rochester resolutions, then we will analyze the Ford Foundation grant and its conditions.

Only seven of the twenty-five Rochester resolutions were programmatic. Four of these were directly related to fair housing practices, one concerned special education services for children, one urged mass transit development as an al-ternative to highway construction, and one recommended national advertising for NN. The eighteen operational resolutions focused again on regional structure development, improved internal communication between member groups and NN, and financial support from members.

A troubled memo from Jean Milgram to NN's executive committee explains the dilemma NN faced with the onset of Ford Foundation funding (memo, Aug. 8, 1973). The original proposal submitted by NN to the Ford Foundation had focused on an ongoing open housing and testing project, including a national Shoppers' Sunday. But the foundation was not interested in funding this pro-gram, since they were already funding another open housing agency—NCDH—and had been doing so since 1964.

The foundation was, however, interested in funding a program maintaining multiracial neighborhoods: "A proposal dealing with racial discrimination in housing cannot be sold to the Ford Board of Trustees . . . the proposal must deal with neighborhood 'stabilization' . . . not, of course, using that term" (memo,

Aug. 8, 1973). Jean Milgram's memo shows her concern that NN might be funded to do something they had not originally intended: "I think we are getting very close to a situation in which we turn in a proposal saying we are going to do one thing we know Ford will accept—while intending to really do something else, thinking that Ford understands this" (memo, Aug. 8, 1973).

Another memo from Milgram to the executive committee expresses her anxiety and concern over the purpose and program outlined in a revised Ford proposal. She describes two major problems. First, Ford was still committed to major support for NCDH, and they would not finance duplication of effort. Therefore, Ford's representative Bob Chandler had suggested NN use these words for their stated purpose: "To demonstrate the viability of multiracial neighborhoods" (memo, Aug. 12, 1973). But Milgram was worried that using those words and then helping member groups combat the dual housing market might not be suitable or ethical.

Her second concern was that $50,000 would not take NN as far as they had hoped to go. She asked the executive committee to come together on Sunday, August 12 to decide what they wanted to do with the Ford grant, and how they would do it (memo, Aug. 12, 1973). This all-day meeting produced a revised funding proposal to the Ford Foundation listing two goals: enhance the strength and viability of local interracial community groups; and help local organizations change real estate practices on a metropolitan level. Three objectives were to be met the first year: holding four to six regional conferences; creating and producing publications or films on auditing procedures and NN; and providing field services and consultant help to community groups on request.

The letter from the Ford Foundation officially notifying NN of the grant stated that it was "for a program to preserve the stability of racially mixed neighborhoods" (letter, Dec. 26, 1973). A newsletter announcement said the grant was "for the purpose of expanding services NN can offer interracial community groups. The grant is to cover some limited field and consultation services, a film on interracial living, a manual on real estate auditing, and additional resource people for regional conferences" (Neighbors, Nov.-Dec. 1973).

Thus NN's original goals and program were somewhat altered by their funding source. With the Ford grant, the focus on fair housing was curtailed, and a new emphasis on field services was established.

Phase Two: 1974–81

This phase of NN's existence must be analyzed in two segments: first, during Milgram's tenure, which was only until March 1976; and second, after she left, which was from March 1976 until the Ford grant ended in 1981. These final five years, we recall, saw a dizzying succession of executive directors, which did not make for very effective programming.

Though Milgram's presence during the first two years of this phase meant stability for NN, she was already under a great deal of stress with staff and board problems. But her drive and ability enabled her, nevertheless, to carry out the program outlined in the Ford Foundation proposal. In fact, she had already begun to provide some field services before the grant money arrived in January 1974. Of nine field trips to member groups made by Milgram from September through December 1973, three were to help with real estate auditing procedures, two concerned upcoming annual conferences, one was to attend a regional conference, two were as guest speakers, and one was to aid with a funding proposal to HUD. Five were in Northeast locations, one was in the Midwest, and one was in the South.

The first direct mailing to member groups about the new field services mentioned three types of assistance (January 8, 1974). One was help with any community or organizational need, another was consultant services on real estate problems by Joe Battle, NN's first president and also a realtor. The third (rarely called for) was an offer of volunteer consultant services from other experts with diverse areas of knowledge, to be arranged by NN according to particular need. Only the second type of consultation—real estate problems—was paid for completely by the Ford grant, but was limited to forty days a year. The first type, on general organizational and community concerns, was conducted primarily by Jean Milgram during the first funded year (1974). The second type of field service on real estate problems was done primarily by Joe Battle, especially during the second funded year, when Milgram was already preparing to leave.

Though NN's focus on fair housing was somewhat diminished, their field services and newsletters continued to reflect this concern. They justified their concern with fair housing at this time in a statement issued for distribution at an NCDH conference on "better ways of neighborhood stabilization" (March 15, 1974). The executive committee prepared the two-page statement, which explained in detail why a single housing market was so crucial for interracial neighborhoods. Supporting NCDH's stated concerns about this issue, NN's statement also recognized the unresolved problems of limited access of minorities to housing, and of limited opportunities for minority brokers to expand their business. The statement further explained that no policy had yet been established regarding the regulation of broker solicitation. They hoped to have better understanding of this issue after the next conference—NN's fifth. They had no way of knowing how stormy that next conference would be.

Though the Atlanta conference was packed with panels, workshops, speakers, parties, and other events and attractions, it came to be remembered forever after as the conference that saw the Oak Park movie. Following an hour-long presentation by Oak Park's leaders of "affirmative action for dispersed integration," their seventy-eight-minute film "As Time Goes By" was shown. It had previewed in Chicago earlier with favorable reviews in all but the black newspaper.

The film was a documentary account, beautifully photographed, of Oak Park's reaction to racial change as a comfortable middle-class suburb of Chicago. Oak Park was then 3% black, and had earlier proposed an ordinance—nationally publicized—that would have restricted their community to 30% black residency. Though the proposed ordinance had been withdrawn before the Atlanta conference and was no longer under consideration, delegates remembered it disparagingly as "a quota law." Many did not take kindly to the Oak Park movie, which was shown at 3 P.M. on the Friday that began the conference.

By Saturday morning, it was apparent to staff and Board that a lot of emotion had been generated that had to be ventilated. The feeling was that Oak Park's quota proposal and film were arguments for exclusion as a technique for maintaining integration, and that this in fact violated basic humanistic and democratic principles—thereby precluding any true equality. (*Neighbors*, Summer 1974)

In addition, the Oak Park program was seen by some as a violation of federal fair housing law.

A special 1 P.M session was called that continued throughout the afternoon, taking precedence over the scheduled agenda item—a panel on minority brokers and antisolicitation laws. Reactions to the film were mostly negative, and black and white racism was discussed in relation to the film, the conference, NN, and interracial neighborhoods. "Questions were raised about NN's purpose, its criteria for membership, its screening of conference programs" (*Neighbors*, Summer 1974). When buses arrived later that afternoon for a scheduled tour of Atlanta, followed by an evening party, delegates were unhappy that nothing had been resolved. So the issue was passed on to the resolutions committee, which was asked to recommend a resolution to the Sunday morning business meeting that would reflect the sense of Saturday's discussion.

The resolutions committee, however, despite hours of debate, could not agree on a resolution that fairly presented a consensus of the previous day's arguments. Since they had no resolution to present, the council of delegates spent two hours trying to agree on a resolution—postponing lunch twice. "Tears and anger and pleas broke forth in a debate over whether or not to oppose 'manipulations of the housing market such as quotas" (*Neighbors*, Summer 1974).

Finally, when departures began to deplete the quorum needed, the problem was referred to the newly elected board of directors. After lunch, they unanimously adopted a resolution supporting a single housing market and opposing quotas limiting the access of minorities to housing. However, the issue was far from resolved, and to this day continues to plague the movement.

The Atlanta conference prompted a reexamination of NN's goals by the board of directors when it met in early September 1974. Though their original purpose remained the same, seven stated specific goals were added to it. The purpose, we recall, was "to foster and encourage successful multiracial neighborhoods throughout the U.S." The seven newly stated goals were to achieve in all neighborhoods: a single housing market, that is, equal opportunity for whites and minorities to move into any community; improvement of local public schools; adequate public services; integration of nonintegrated neighborhoods;

greater participation by members of minority groups; an economic mix; and better ethnic and racial understanding through planned intergroup contact.

During 1974, the first year of Ford Foundation funding, NN not only inaugurated their field and consultation services, they also held three regional conferences, prepared and published a manual on auditing real estate practices, and produced a sixteen-millimeter color film on interracial neighborhoods. Thus, in addition to their ongoing bimonthly newsletter publication and annual conference, they fulfilled the terms of their contract with the Foundation.

Three more activities were begun by NN during their first funded year. First, communications and audiovisual training were provided by NN at selected regional and national conferences over the next two years, with the assistance of a special $2,000 grant from the Ford Foundation. Second, Mark and Oralee Beach from Rochester's member group volunteered to go on another cross-country trip visiting integrated neighborhoods. They contracted to produce a directory of interracial neighborhoods and their associations, as well as a bibliography on interracial neighborhoods, funded with an $18,500 Ford grant given to NN for this purpose. Third, NN agreed to serve as a review panel for the Ford Foundation in order to review applications for small demonstration grants to be given by Ford for projects to maintain interracial neighborhoods.

In 1975, the second year of Ford Foundation funding, with Jean Milgram still serving as executive director, NN continued to fulfill their contract with the Foundation, but with some diminishing results. Milgram explained why:

The frequency of the field visits shows a pronounced decrease from 1974. The reason is almost entirely due to internal problems that arose in April 1975 in the NN office and grew to create problems between Board and staff, as well as within the Board. Consequently, I found it necessary to devote far more time to administration than had been needed in 1974. (report to Ford Foundation, March 1, 1976)

Thus, only eight field trips were made by Milgram in 1975, plus eighteen by Battle. Though this is the same total number as the field visits in 1974, other program efforts of NN were not as successful. No regional conferences were held prior to the June conference, but after a plan was developed there for funding regional coordinators, one regional conference in 1975 was held in Baltimore for the Northeast region, and one in Akron for the Great Lakes region (see Saltman 1977). Bimonthly newsletter publication was intended, but only five newsletters were published in both 1974 and 1975.

The screening of local grant proposals for the Ford Foundation was a cumbersome, extremely time-consuming task. Though NN worked diligently to accomplish this through their review panel, their efforts were criticized by some as being faulty in both procedure and results. Of the five groups that received Ford grants through NN's screening, two were fair housing agencies and three were neighborhood stabilization groups. All were NN members (report to Ford Foundation, March 1, 1976).

The volume of work done in the first two years of the Ford grant was not duplicated in the next five years of funding—or ever again. Clearly, the organization was never the same after Jean Milgram left. The rapid succession of executive directors and office location changes did not bode well for NN's program. Though the national conference was held each year, newsletters were issued rather irregularly. In 1976 four newsletters were published, in 1977 there were five, in 1978 there were three, in 1979 and 1980 five, and in 1981 only one.

Field services and regional conference attempts continued, but sporadically. The field services were provided primarily by the executive director, aided occasionally by the president and volunteer consultants. These were given with diminishing frequency during the remainder of this phase, until they were largely conducted by mail or phone.

Regional conferences, too, were held irregularly and decreasingly for the rest of this phase. A new field services director was hired by NN in 1977, and a toll-free phone number was installed in NN's new Washington, D.C. office in 1978. With this increased outreach, five regional conferences were held that year. Shortly after this, the position of field services director was abolished, and regional activity reverted back to volunteer regional coordinators. As these regional coordinators slowly dwindled away, they were not replaced. There is no record of any more NN regional conferences being held in 1980 or 1981, or in fact ever again.

Other program activities during this second phase of development include two publications, preparation of a funding proposal to HUD, and implementation of some resolutions adopted at the annual conferences. The first publication was the long-awaited and overdue directory of interracial neighborhoods (1977). The funding proposal to HUD was for the purpose of conducting a national study of rental discrimination against families with children. The proposal, prepared and submitted by a former NN board member, was awarded a grant in December 1979 of $108,000, to be allocated during 1980. This is the contract that ended in bitter dispute, with HUD claiming that they were owed $20,000 by NN. The dispute carried over to phase three, and has still not been settled.

Resolutions. The annual resolutions adopted at each conference during phase two were implemented only as time, energy, resources, and other priorities permitted. The resolutions were not a major part of NN's program, even though they were very important to delegates and generated much interest and intensity at the conferences. Their impact outside NN was probably much greater than within NN's administrative leadership, as NN themselves acknowledged with the following statement in their newsletter: "Implementation of some [of these resolutions] will largely depend on the availability of funding and resources" (*Neighbors*, Summer 1975).

Though resolutions adopted by delegates at each annual conference reflected some changing events and concerns in the nation, there were a few issues that recurred each year. One was the concern with the dual housing market, and related fair housing issues, such as redlining, foreclosures, and affirmative marketing. Another recurring issue was equal educational opportunity, and anything related to maintaining quality education in racially integrated communities. Crime in racially integrated neighborhoods grew in importance as a concern during this phase, as did recognition of the need for coalitions with other groups and the need for influencing political leaders at all levels.

Analyzing the annual resolutions again as to whether they were program-related or operational, we find throughout this phase a greater proportion of the resolutions emphasizing program rather than NN's operation. This contrasts with the resolutions adopted during phase one, which showed a greater emphasis on operational issues. In 1974, for example, six resolutions were passed, of which only one was operational. From 1976 to 1981, seventy-one resolutions were adopted, of which only nineteen were operational. In only one year of this phase, 1975, was this proportion reversed. Thirty-four resolutions were adopted at the 1975 conference held in Chicago, of which twenty-one were operational.

Many of these operational resolutions called for more NN service to member groups, and greater visibility of the organization. For example, delegates in 1975 wanted NN to conduct special conference sessions and to provide consultation on redlining and racial steering; they wanted NN to collect and distribute information on exclusionary zoning, fund-raising techniques, crime prevention programs, and integrated schooling; they wanted NN to sponsor a national audit of relocation real estate firms, to set up regional task forces to combat racism, and to solicit funding for travel to annual conferences and board meetings. They wanted all of this, and more, in a year when there were "tumultuous . . . changes in organizational directions, priorities, staffing and leadership" (Neighbors, Summer 1975).

Implementation of resolutions was often lackadaisical and incomplete. In June 1974, for example, when delegates called for a strategy dealing with redlining, NN's board disposed of this three months later by asking a leader of another national organization to send them pertinent material and to run workshops on redlining at their next annual conference (minutes, Sept. 8, 1974). Perhaps this was all they could do at the time.

Of the ten resolutions passed in 1978 at the Indianapolis conference, the longest and most important one concerned affirmative marketing. This resolution, which occupied two full pages, defined the concept and called on NN to "mandate the housing industry, HUD, and the President of the United States to clarify, broaden and support affirmative marketing" (resolutions, June 11, 1978). Yet, one year later, the major action taken by NN on this resolution was to set up meetings to discuss the concept of affirmative marketing with the Congressional Black Caucus (response to 1978 resolutions, June 1979). But the focus on this issue at the conference did spur one local member group in Park Forest, Illinois to prepare a handbook on affirmative marketing, which was widely used as a reference by other groups (Wunker et al. 1979). National Neighbors themselves, however, did not do very much to implement this or many other resolutions adopted by their conference delegates.

As we have seen, NN's program during phase two floundered after Jean Milgram left in 1976. Then, the steady procession of executive directors, compounded by many changes in office locations, weakened NN's entire functioning and was disheartening to their board. This did not improve much in phase three, for despite their newly found stability in leadership, their monumental financial struggle for bare survival left little time, energy, or spirit for an effective program.

Phase Three: 1982–

Before we examine NN's program during phase three, let us review their reasons for moving their office from Philadelphia to Washington, D.C. on January 5, 1978. After two years of consideration, the move was made in order to give NN greater national visibility and to provide increased services to member groups (policy statement, Feb. 10, 1978). Such services were to include an expanded and computerized clearinghouse of neighborhood resources on pertinent topics, expanded consulting services to member groups, increased contacts with other national resources "to be plugged into the NN information network," and continued site visits and field services (policy statement, Feb. 10, 1978). Most of this never happened.

With the move to Washington in phase two there was, however, an increase in NN's contacts with other national organizations based in the capital. This was useful for an expanded visibility and influence on legislation, but could only continue with staffing that made it possible. During phase three, such staffing was unavailable.

Was there any program at all during phase three? A conference took place each year. Two newsletters were mailed each year, one before the conference to publicize the event and ask for money, and one after the conference to report on it and ask for money. In 1983, two additional newsletters were mailed, to report on funding progress. Besides the conferences and these few newsletters, there was little that could be called program on a national level. There was a regional program in the Cleveland area in the last two years of this phase, and there was some minimal office response to the resolutions passed each year at the conference. Let us turn to these to see what conference delegates were thinking about, and how NN responded to them.

Resolutions. Few resolutions were passed during phase three, and those that were received little attention from the deeply troubled director and board. In 1982, the "death rattle" year, only three resolutions were adopted at the conference held in Chicago. All were operational. One was the usual thanks for those who hosted the conference, another was a condolence for the death of a long-time supporter, and the third was a request that the "primary focus of NN in the forthcoming year should be assistance to grass-roots organizations" (minutes, Aug. 14, 1982). Such a focus was, of course, not possible at that time.

In 1983, delegates to the fourteenth annual conference in Bellwood, Illinois adopted four resolutions, of which only one was programmatic. This one asked NN to do an easy thing: endorse the statement of the Leadership Conference on Civil Rights opposing President Reagan's nominations to the U.S. Civil Rights Commission. This was done with a letter and legislative alerts to member groups, a typical disposition of many other resolutions adopted at NN annual conferences throughout the years.

Also urged was the creation of an NN advisory board, to be appointed by the president and approved by the board. The real purpose of the creation of this body was to enlist broader financial support, but the formation of this list of prominent people took three years, and was not officially announced until the end of this phase.

Of six resolutions adopted at the Starrett City, New York conference in 1984, four were related to program and two were operational. One of the program resolutions recommended that NN request the President and the secretaries of HUD and HEW to develop goals and a timetable for the desegregation of housing and schools. Another program resolution urged NN to support enactment of laws prohibiting discrimination in housing against families with children. The first of these resolutions was disposed of with letters. The second was not acted on other than passing it on to member groups. A third program resolution was that NN cooperate with the Oak Park Exchange Congress. In addition, an important policy statement was adopted as a major resolution that reaffirmed the principle of neighborhood integration. These last two resolutions are important enough to examine further.

The Oak Park Exchange Congress (OPEC), we recall, was a coalition of suburban municipalities devoted to integration maintenance. Vigorous, funded, well-staffed, and earnest, they posed a substantial threat to NN. Until the congress formed, NN had been able to say truthfully that they were the only national organization dedicated solely to neighborhood integration maintenance. Now there was another. Board members frankly discussed this issue at a meeting held eight months before the OPEC resolution was ever passed. At that meeting, when director Bromley announced that OPEC had just incorporated and received tax-exempt status, the first reaction to this was, "How will this affect NN?" (notes, NN board meeting Oct. 15, 1983).

After the resolution was passed in 1984, nothing much changed. The two groups continued to peacefully coexist, each having similar annual national conferences, with each attending the other's events and providing similar services to their constituents. But now the shoe was on the other foot. Having begun as "an intrusive movement organization" that moved on to NCDH's fair housing turf, NN was now facing a newer group with the same goals and program as theirs. Even though each addressed different communities, OPEC was seen as a serious potential competitor of NN for grants and other funding. Besides the difference in type of community each focused on, there was another essential difference between the two organizations: OPEC was highly successful, energetic, well-funded and staffed; NN was now none of these.

The last major resolution adopted at the 1984 conference was significant because of its subject matter and the length of time of its preparation. This resolution endorsed a prepared policy statement previously approved by the board. The statement, "Neighborhood Integration—a Reaffirmation," was first proposed at the same board meeting that prompted the OPEC resolution. At that meeting, plans were made for the 1984 conference to be held at Starrett City, New York, which was then embroiled in a major lawsuit challenging its policies and practices of "managed integration"—the recurring issue of this movement.

Managed integration, in fact, was selected as the theme of the conference. Board and staff were not in total agreement on this issue. Nor were the member groups of NN. How far can one go in maintaining integration without treading on fair housing principles? Are quotas acceptable? Are sign bans all right? What about solicitation bans? Two board members were enlisted to prepare a policy statement about this: I was one of the two; Don de Marco, from Shaker Heights, Ohio, was the other. It was a tough assignment. Comments of board members at that meeting reveal some of their feelings about the issue of managed integration: "We must deal with this issue. . . . Let's go into this boldly and kick it with our head . . . if we die, we'll do it taking a stand. . . . What are we saying by having our conference at Starrett City? . . . What means are justified in maintaining urban integration?" (notes, NN board meeting Oct. 15, 1983).

We exchanged and modified three different drafts of the statement before we agreed on what it should be. Then we sent it to the entire NN board, asking for their suggestions for revision. There were none. The statement was formally endorsed by the board on March 10, 1984. The statement next appeared in NN's March newsletter, with a request for comments. None came. Finally, the statement was presented to the conference delegates in June 1984, when it was adopted without revision (see Appendix D for complete text). There is no record of any other statement in NN's history receiving such scrutiny.

The irony of all this was that the theme of the Starrett City conference was later changed, making the statement there somewhat irrelevant. The need for the statement, however, shows that far from being something new, this was old wine in new bottles. The very same issue had presented itself in phase one of NN's existence. It was not resolved conclusively then, either. Perhaps the real difference in the later handling of this old issue lay in the public acknowledgment of the validity and integrity of diverse methods of achieving the same goal. In phase one, some of these methods had been summarily dismissed as unacceptable. But by phase three, when NN was older, wiser, warier, and much much wearier—almost anything that worked and was legal and seemed fair was okay.

Resolutions adopted by delegates to the 1985 conference in Baltimore were unique in that seven out of eight resolutions were programmatic. Two were direct mandates for extended NN action, the others were goal-related but readily accomplished through letters. The simpler goal-related resolutions concerned rejecting the nomination of William Bradford Reynolds as Associate Attorney General, urging local city and school officials to work together to reduce racial isolation in public schools, urging federal agencies to continue collecting data by race, urging increased federal financial support for low- and moderate-income housing, and urging pressure on the media to show successful interracial life.

The two extended program recommendations were to have NN create a $1 million endowment fund for member groups, and prepare funding proposals to develop a documentary showing successful examples and the values of racially diverse neighborhoods. No action was taken on the first one. The second one was attempted, and soon abandoned, when no funding could be found for it.

In 1986, resolutions were so ignored by staff and board that for the first time in NN's history they did not even appear in the newsletter that followed the conference. By this time, however, bitter internal conflicts between staff and the executive committee were tearing the organization apart. The smoldering unresolved issue of the two offices, one in Washington and one in Cleveland, and the regionalized program of NN in the Cleveland area finally erupted late in this phase, in December 1986. A new board president called together a new executive committee to gain their support in dismissing Executive Director Bromley. This was the same Chip Bromley who had saved the organization in 1983 by becoming its often unpaid director and chief funding solicitor. The charge was insubordination and lack of a national NN program. The new executive committee of five, most of whom lived in the East, listened to the president, also an Easterner, and voted unanimously to dismiss Bromley. They wanted the Midwest office closed, and promptly stopped payment on checks written by Midwest staff, that is, the director and his part-time office aide.

Immediately, several old-timers and ex-board members who heard about this sprang into action. Letters were sent, phone calls were made, meetings were held, and after a huge flurry of activity the president was persuaded to take the issue to the entire board, with Bromley present to tell his side of the story. After a long and stormy all-day session, the board voted on January 17, 1987 to rehire Bromley on a ninety-day probationary period, provided that he prepared two funding proposals for a national NN program. The Washington office remained open. So did the Midwest office. As usual, nothing was really solved.

The regional program effort conducted by NN's director in the Cleveland area during phase three was important, however. It served as a model for what could be done elsewhere in the nation to maintain integration. The formation of a Cleveland area Metropolitan Strategy Group began in 1984, and was strengthened by three small foundation grants awarded later that year. This was a coalition of city and suburban housing, community and economic development organizations, and municipalities, which met monthly to discuss collective strategies to promote fair housing, integration, and stronger communities.

Primarily, this group of over forty organizations and agencies promoted a state mortgage revenue program offering incentive payments for pro-integrative moves. Though the original idea of incentive payments for pro-integrative moves came from me, through Akron's West Side Neighbors (see Appendix C), Cleveland area groups pushed the idea along in repeated meetings with state officials. After two years of negotiations with the Ohio Housing Finance Agency, representatives of the Metropolitan Strategy Group finally and successfully in 1985 secured a set-aside of $7 million of mortgage revenue bonds to encourage pro-integrative moves in the Cleveland area.

The NN Midwest office and five Cleveland area fair housing groups monitored the program for the Metropolitan Strategy Group, issuing certificates to qualified homeseekers. To qualify for the 9.8% loans, blacks had to move to areas more than 90% white, and whites to areas more than 40% black. Early results of the bonus program showed that one-third of the black buyers located in predominantly white areas, and white buyers moved to five out of thirteen suburbs with approved neighborhoods. Requests for information from around the country began to pour into NN's Midwest office after news of the incentive program was printed in the NN newsletter (*Neighbors*, Winter 1985). Expansion of the program to other areas in Ohio occurred in 1988. If it were to spread to other states across the nation, this would greatly assist neighborhood integration maintenance efforts. It would be ironic, indeed, if this one regional effort of NN ultimately had greater impact than any of their other actions through the years.

IMPACT

Since NN's only two enduring program activities throughout all three phases were the national conferences and the newsletter, we will examine these more closely to see what they included and what effect they had. We will also analyze the impact of other program efforts of NN in each phase of their existence.

Phase One: 1969–73

We have already seen the impact of the first founding conference in 1969. With leaders of only twelve community organizations present, this first convening was a profound morale-booster and impetus for further action. We noted that one local group was formed soon after (Oklahomans for Neighborhood Equality) as a direct result of the "inspiration" found at the Carleton conference (*Neighbors*, Nov.–Dec. 1970).

In addition, the Carleton conference's panel and group discussion on real estate problems generated tremendous response, and paved the way for a similar emphasis at the next conference, in Dayton. Leaders and participants recognized early that the survival of integrated neighborhoods depended on an adequate supply of moderate-income housing outside of inner cities. Access to that supply was also critical. This theme was repeated the following year at the next conference, with a panel of experts in fair housing programs.

The first annual conference at Dayton in 1970 had four workshops, two panels, and five sessions devoted totally to presentations from the thirty-one community member groups there. No subsequent NN conference ever devoted this much time to member groups exchange. The workshops focused on fair housing programs, educational equality, local governmental programs, and intra-organizational programs. The two panels were about the national housing crisis, and about the Dayton View Project of city involvement in neighborhood stabilization.

The housing crisis panel focused on the need for fair housing and more dispersed housing. This panel of experts profoundly affected NN's future. They were the impetus for NN's first action program, and they inspired the first major resolutions on fair housing, which reappeared in various forms each year for the rest of NN's existence.

We saw that this first annual conference produced the only national action program NN ever had—Shoppers' Sunday, a testing of real estate market practices in various communities around the country. The conference also set the tone for the rest of the first phase of NN's development, and in some ways even affected NN's functioning in their second phase. We have already seen how phase one was marked by a heavy emphasis on fair housing, and we have explained why this was so. This focus on fair housing led to NN's preparation of a proposal for funding a national fair housing project—an expanded Shoppers' Sunday. This proposal was at first rejected by the Ford Foundation, which suggested instead field services and consultation on neighborhood stabilization. These, in fact, became the program of NN's second phase.

But the impact of this first conference panel was far greater than just the effect on NN and their program. In phase one, who knows how many local groups were affected by the bold theme "Sue the Bastards" after it appeared in an early issue of *Neighbors* (July-August 1971; see Appendix D). We do know that NN's newsletters at that time were appearing ten times a year, while NCDH printed none between 1971 and the summer of 1972. We also know that a wave of auditing real estate practices in communities throughout the country began at about this time, culminating in lawsuits that were later widely publicized by both NN and NCDH in their respective newsletters.

We know, too, that NN's annual conference in 1972 had a major session devoted to auditing techniques (I presented it). So there is little doubt that NN's heavy emphasis on auditing must have had an impact on member groups. However, the very first national publicity about auditing did not come from NN. It came earlier from NCDH's newsletter (*Trends*, May 1970) in their report of a 1969 audit in St. Louis. This makes it difficult to separate the influence of each organization on the various member groups around the country concerning auditing and litigation. Still, audits and lawsuits did receive a boost nationally by NN's focus on them during phase one. And these were a direct outgrowth of the panel presentation at NN's first annual conference in Dayton (Bergamo.)

Subsequent annual conferences during phase one continued to emphasize housing practices, school racial balance, and legal action to enforce fair housing laws. These affected the content of the resolutions proposed by delegates. Newsletters repeated and reinforced these themes in detailed reports about the conferences. In addition, NN's newsletters were filled with news and information from other communities—both member and nonmember groups—relating to the different strategies and programs for achieving the maintenance of racially integrated neighborhoods. Some examples indicate NN's impact on local groups during this phase.

The 1971 conference at Oberlin College inspired the formation of a new group in Nashville, Tennessee: Belmont-Hillsboro Neighbors was established in 1971 after a resident attended the second national conference. This conference (Sue the Bastards!) also generated much litigious activity by member groups, as we have noted. Three members of Hartford's Blue Hills Civic Association reported on their reaction to NN's second conference: "We have learned that Blue Hills is too middle-class, too nice. We are conciliatory and discussion focused, while the opposition is actually using all its powers to harm us. We must 'sue the bastards' to teach them that violations of the law are economically costly. We must continue to 'sue the bastards' until they realize it is economically necessary for them to adhere to the law" (Neighbors, July-Aug. 1971). Inspired and encouraged by the NN theme, the Hartford group soon did indeed "sue the bastards," becoming the first community group in the nation to be a plaintiff in a block-busting lawsuit.

Another first, also by an NN member group, was the winning of monetary damages by a community organization in a block-busting suit. The Broadmoor Improvement Association in New Orleans won $3,000 in the settlement of a lawsuit against a real estate firm they accused of block-busting. The firm consented to be permanently barred from soliciting by phone, mail, or in person in the Broadmoor interracial neighborhood. The headline about this news item was: "New Fund-Raising Technique" (Neighbors, Spring 1973).

Not only did existing groups learn about the need for and the strategies of litigation, but other groups applied for and received funding with NN's assistance. Oak Park, Illinois, for instance, prepared the funding proposal for their housing center using three NN member groups as resources, the Shaker Heights Housing Office, the University City Residential Service in Missouri, and West Mount Airy Neighbors in Philadelphia (Neighbors, March–April 1972). How did Oak Park people know about these other groups? Through NN's conferences and newsletters and the NN staff. And every time the newsletter reported the funding of another local group, this motivated still others to try to get funding for themselves. Many member groups eventually received grants ranging from small special awards to major funding for comprehensive programs.

Two local community actions, reported in early issues of *Neighbors*, affected other groups and encouraged them to try these in their own communities. The first local ordinance prohibiting door-to-door solicitation by real estate agents was announced in *Neighbors* as having been passed in Inglewood, California, and later replaced with an ordinance banning all commercial solicitation (*Neighbors*, March–April 1972). This idea spread across the country, with each report of another community adopting it fanning similar action elsewhere. Eventually, all such ordinances were struck down as being in restraint of trade. So, also, were "for sale" sign bans, which were first reported in early newsletter issues (*Neighbors*, Jan.–Feb. 1973).

Another significant idea first publicized by NN was incentive payments for pro-integrative moves. John Buggs, staff director of the U.S. Commission on Civil Rights, offered this idea as the keynote speaker at NN's third annual conference in Baltimore in 1972. He told the conference: "We're losing the fight against spreading ghettos . . . we need a massive dose of corrective action to reverse the trend toward an increasingly polarized and segregated society. . . . The federal government should adopt a plan to subsidize interracial living by paying cash to families making housing moves that would increase integration" (*Neighbors*, June–July 1972).

As an illustration, Buggs outlined a plan that would pay $1,000 to a white family moving into a 15–20% black neighborhood, and $1,000 to a black family moving into a 8–10% black neighborhood. The subsidy would progress up to $5,000 for a white or black family moving into a neighborhood 100% occupied by the other race. After outlining the far-reaching benefits of such a program, Buggs discussed the costs. If half a million families took advantage of this offer, it would cost about $1.75 billion—one-twentieth the cost of keeping the war active in Vietnam.

The boldness of this idea appealed to the eager listeners at NN's third conference, some of whom took it back to their communities, where it shocked some listeners and pleased still others. Ultimately, the concept of incentive payments for pro-integrative moves reached its fullest impact with Ohio's Housing Finance Agency mortgage program in 1985—thirteen years later. But before then, NN supporters and member groups spread the idea often enough that it eventually came to be more amicably received (for example, the Los Angeles Ferraro Resolution presented in 1982).

One notion publicized by NN—and not initially seen as outrageous—concerned panic-peddling. A news item in *Neighbors* described a San Bernardino, California group tactic. The group, Inland Neighbors, was disgusted and weary with real estate cards saying something like: "Dear Homeowner, Do you know what your neighbors at 2444 E. Victoria did? They sold their home through us to a fine family named Rufus Jackson. We would be happy to discuss listing your home, as we have many customers for this area." The group developed a response to the real estate agent: "Dear Sir: Do you know what the neighbors of 2444 E. Victoria did? They forwarded your card to the U.S. Dept. of Justice for action" (*Neighbors*, Sept.–Oct. 1973).

Another example of NN's impact in phase one is found in an August 1972 editorial in the *Denver Post*. Titled "How to Upset the System and Desegregate Housing," the article dealt with the common enemy—the real estate industry. Filled with optimism and hope, the author—an NN supporter—referred to National Neighbors' role and significance in the future of our cities.

Noteworthy relevant new books and articles were listed in most issues of NN's newsletter, and these too were influential. The few publications written by NN staff (primarily Jean Milgram) during this phase were also well-publicized in the newsletter, with distributions on request. Some of these were small in size and scope, and were either free or sold for ten cents apiece. Others were more extensive and more expensive, costing $1.50 each. The two major publications during this phase were the first directory of interracial neighborhoods and their associations, and the booklet on racial steering.

The directory was important as a resource and as a movement spur. When people saw what others in interracial settings were doing, and how they were pushing on, this was a morale-booster as well as an idea promoter. The directory was referred to for addresses and program ideas long after it became obsolete. The need for updating was constant, and eventually it became an impossible task to keep the information current.

The racial steering booklet was well received by member groups across the country, who ordered more than 200 of them. One group in Detroit—the Winship Community Council—used the illustrations in the booklet to make posters for a community meeting to discuss the subject. Comments from readers were positive: "Filling a widespread need," "Excellent new publication," "Very much impressed with your information and methods," "Rich in examples of the brave methods by which the dual housing market is opposed" (*Neighbors*, Sept.– Oct. 1973).

The whirlwind tour of Bob Ketron, sponsored by NN in the summer of 1972, had an impact on the communities he visited. His outreach in the twenty-one cities he visited resulted in the reactivation of some groups that had been faltering. The Wildwood Hills-Heights groups of Oklahoma City, founded in 1969, had been languishing, but was reinspired by Ketron's visit, and held its first meeting in a year right after he left (*Neighbors*, Dec. 1972).

Finally, the only national action program coordinated by NN very early in phase one had a swift and long-term impact in the communities that participated in Shoppers' Sunday. Many of the local member groups quickly developed more sophisticated and meticulous testing and auditing techniques of their own. Thus, many local communities felt the impact of NN's program long after it was over— well into phase two and beyond.

Phase Two: 1974–81

Again, we must divide this funded phase into two periods—with Milgram (1974–76), and without Milgram (1976–81). NN's program and impact remained vigorous during the two years that Milgram continued to serve as di-

rector. After she left, both program and impact dwindled—largely because of
the incredible staff turnover that plagued the organization. By the end of this
phase, and the end of Ford Foundation funding, we know that NN was in
seriously weak condition—financially, organizationally, programmatically, and
spiritually.

One measure of the impact NN had by 1974—the beginning of this phase—
is their designation as one of two national groups to receive monetary awards
given to plaintiffs in a historic lawsuit. In the famous case of *Trafficante v.
Metropolitan Life*, the decision held that tenants have standing to sue their
landlord for discriminating against minority applicants. The defendants in that
case signed a sweeping consent decree and made a large cash settlement. The
victors decided to donate $20,000 of the money to civil rights organizations
fighting housing discrimination. Though most of it went to local groups in the
San Francisco Bay area, site of the complaint, NN was honored to be named—
along with the NAACP Legal Defense & Education Fund—as a recipient of
$2,000 from the cash settlement.

Continuing effects of NN's annual conference on local groups and commu-
nities are seen in Project YSTB (Sue the Bastards!) in Hartford. Inspired by
NN's conference in Rochester in 1973, three member groups of NN in the
Hartford area teamed up in 1974 to attack steering and block-busting in the
greater Hartford area. All three groups acknowledged that the impetus for their
YSTB! project came from the NN conference the previous June in Rochester
(*Neighbors*, Jan.-Feb. 1974).

But suing the bastards did not always bring positive results. In Atlanta, a
1975 countersuit by Northside realty company frightened the entire neighborhood stabilization movement, and the open housing movement as well. Testers,
trained by NN consultant Joe Battle, were sued for damages totalling four million
dollars. In addition, Northside asked for a permanent injunction against testing.
This galvanized into action both the open housing and neighborhood stabilization movements; it took months of litigation to straighten the matter out.
Ultimately, the Northside countersuit was dismissed, and Northside was fined
for contempt of court orders. But until the case was resolved, auditing was in
jeopardy as a legitimate and necessary means of implementing fair housing law.
This did not seem to deter local groups from continuing to audit real estate
practices, however: NN's newsletters and conferences were filled with reports
of ongoing audits across the country.

Another example of the impact of NN's annual conferences is seen in an
array of seven audiovisual demonstration showings at the 1975 Chicago conference. Each showing, as part of the program named "Park Bench Sessions,"
was repeated on a different day of the conference to allow for maximum outreach
to delegates. The audiovisuals came from member groups in Dallas, Cleveland
Heights, Philadelphia, Hartford, and Chicago. They featured specific local programs and community events as well as broader movement topics, such as the

causes of segregated housing and the relation between open housing and stable neighborhoods.

These seven audiovisual presentations were an inspiration and invaluable source of information to those who saw them at the Chicago conference. As a result, NN included audiovisual expansion in their next Ford funding proposal so that the impact could grow. And the first plenary session of the 1976 conference, presided over by Bob Chandler of the Ford Foundation, was devoted to two presentations dealing with innovative use of media—both of which had been funded by the Ford Foundation.

Field visits by Milgram and Joe Battle early in this phase received evaluations by more than forty different local groups. Responses indicated that the most helpful aspect of these visits was the national perspective the groups gained on their problems and efforts, "the feeling that they were not alone, and that others had faced similar problems and had success" (report to Ford Foundation, March 1975). Whether the field visits produced tangible benefits for the maintenance of local interracial neighborhoods was difficult to judge, according to Milgram. But NN staff felt that those benefits had occurred, and Milgram cited four instances of positive impact of NN's field visits.

The Greater Dallas Housing Opportunity Center reported that Battle's visit gave them added confidence, which helped get a written agreement with their local realty board. Atlanta fair housing people developed both an audit and a housing locator service after a visit from consultant Battle. Milwaukee's Sherman Park Association also felt that Joe Battle's advice "moved them into a new and much more productive approach with their local realty board." And the Prospect/Lefferts Gardens group in Brooklyn, New York "began an ambitious audit with Joe's help" (report to Ford Foundation, 1974).

Supportive personal contact was, as we have seen, abundantly provided at the annual conferences. "Delegates report that they go home 'psyched up,' 'high,' enthusiastic about new ideas they have heard. *But they do not usually attend from any single community in enough numbers, usually, to be able to communicate that feeling to the entire local group*" (report to Ford Foundation, 1974; emphasis added). For producing local group contagion, the regional conferences were more effective.

Regional conferences were mandated by the Ford Foundation funding, and their effect was sometimes even more significant than the national conferences. But as we have seen, the regional conferences did not continue for very long. Local groups—beset with problems of their own—became more and more unwilling to put them on, even with NN's offer of help.

We saw that NN's impact in the early part of this phase was enhanced by their Ford Foundation grant, and we have already noted that the grant conditions affected NN's program. But NN also had an impact on the Ford Foundation. The foundation's funding of other local neighborhood stabilization efforts across the country was an outgrowth of NN's influence. Their repeated contacts with

Ford officials and administrators were filled with accounts of their struggle and the local neighborhood struggle, their reasons for it, their need for funding, and their determination to continue. In addition, a Ford-sponsored NN publication provided ready information about interracial neighborhoods, their organizations, and their problems (*Desegregated Housing and Interracial Neighborhoods: A Bibliographic Guide*, 1975).

Ford's decision to fund other groups with similar efforts came partially as a result of NN's consciousness-raising, since they had never before funded these types of organizations. The designation of NN as the screening panel for the local demonstration grants from the foundation further increased NN's visibility and impact. Fifty-six proposals from local groups throughout the country were given to NN in 1975 by the Ford Foundation to evaluate and prioritize; NN's status and fame were immeasurably increased as a result. A second round of grants from Ford to neighborhood stabilization groups was offered the following year, with NN publicizing these in their newsletters, but this time not doing the screening.

Each of the first two years of Ford Foundation funding had a double cumulative effect on NN. At the same time that they were able to expand their services and increase their effectiveness and impact, their internal conflicts grew as their structure became more complex and their problems more difficult to resolve. Jean Milgram, at the end of the second year of funding and shortly before she resigned, wrote:

The Ford Foundation grant to NN has undoubtedly had profound effects on the organization itself, most of which are still to be assessed. One clear effect is that . . . both individuals and groups are turning to NN for information and assistance at a faster rate and over a broader scope than the organization has so far been able comfortably to absorb. (report to Ford Foundation, March 1, 1976)

After Jean Milgram left, we saw that NN's program receded steadily and unmistakably for the rest of this phase and beyond. Annual conferences and newsletter publication continued, as they always have, but the newsletters were issued irregularly and the conferences varied in their spirit. Though NN tried hard in 1976 to get a HUD contract to conduct a national audit, the million-dollar contract went instead to NN's semirival, NCDH.

Only six months later, a staff member reported that some member groups felt that NN had lost touch with them. A spring board meeting in 1977 was filled with concerns about this: "M. K. reported that West Mount Airy Neighbors has a feeling that NN has lost touch with member groups. C. H. STATED THE BASIC PROBLEM: WHAT CAN NN DO WITH SPREAD-OUT BOARD . . . AND A LIMITED BUDGET. WHAT SERVICES CAN WE DO WELL?" (minutes, April 1977; emphasis added). This question was never answered—not at that meeting, not ever. An organizational goals review was conducted by board members at the same meeting where the above concerns were expressed. Seven NN activities were identified and analyzed as to current and future impact (minutes, April 1977). The board's judgment of their program's current impact ranged primarily from low to fair. Thus, using the NN board's own judgment as to which of their activities were effectively being done, we see a spotty picture of NN's program and impact one year after Jean Milgram left. This did not improve, despite their positive projections for the future.

A few other positive indicators of NN's impact at this time were hangovers from Milgram's time as director: The producers of "60 Minutes" called NN's office to discuss affirmative marketing, NN received the William L. Hastie Award from the Fund for an Open Society (led by Morris Milgram, ex-husband of Jean), Baltimore's successful Northeast Real Estate Center was the outgrowth of an earlier field visit by Joe Battle, and Indianapolis's new school desegregation plan was developed with the aid of an NN consultant. But despite these positive results, NN's impact did not continue to grow after Milgram left.

Though a letter sent out by a new field services director to all member groups and individual supporters promised a "comprehensive information and resource system for interracial neighborhoods" within one year, this never materialized (letter, Nov. 7, 1977). The new field services director left before the year was up, and only one other was hired to replace her for a short time before this staff position was abolished.

During this time, NN moved twice—once to another office in Philadelphia, the second time to the nation's capital—"to improve their national visibility." This was done despite the fact that the Ford Foundation had informed NN's board in 1978 that next year their funding would be reduced by 20%, and the following year by an additional 40%. With their typical optimism, the NN board took a five-year lease on the new office in Washington, D.C. They could not have known that at the end of those five years, NN would be close to death.

We have already reviewed the reasons NN gave for moving their office to Washington, and we have noted that there was an increase in NN's contacts with other national organizations based in the capital. This did achieve an expanded visibility, it did provide some influence on national legislation, and it did have an impact on local groups. For example, in 1978 NN was one of over 150 organizations invited to a White House briefing on the neighborhood initiatives available under the new urban policy of President Carter. First Lady Rosalynn Carter announced a new partnership between neighborhoods and agencies of government at all levels. Seven neighborhood assistance programs were listed and explained in NN's next newsletter following the briefing. The Neighborhood Self-Development Act of 1978, with its provision for federal funds to help neighborhood groups, was also widely publicized in NN's newsletter (Neighbors, Nov. 1979).

All of these were highly relevant to NN's member groups struggling to maintain themselves and their changing neighborhoods. Early knowledge of these programs had a positive impact on the local groups, and ultimately on their neighborhoods. Had NN not been located in the nation's capital, they might not have known of these programs until much later, and the information about the programs might have come down to the local level too late to be of any value.

In addition, NN formed linkages with other civil rights groups based in the capital, and gave testimony in public hearings before congressional committees. Lasting ties were made with the Leadership Council of Civil Rights, a coalition of civil rights groups; the Center for National Policy Review; the Low-Income Housing Coalition; and the National Commission on Neighborhoods. National Neighbors joined with some of these groups and the Center for National Policy Review in a lawsuit against federal agencies regulating lending institutions. The suit resulted in an important consent decree affecting lending policies and practices in neighborhoods across the country.

But the impact of NN's increased visibility in the nation's capital was short-lived. Only continued staffing and funding could sustain it, and these were soon gone. A sobering meeting in June 1979 with a Ford Foundation administrator heralded the coming disaster. At that meeting, Bob Chandler of the foundation told the NN board of a recent study they sponsored evaluating the major groups funded by the foundation. Though the study found five positive effects of NN's work, it also reported six negative factors.

The positive factors were: (1) NN did provide a rallying-point for interracial neighborhoods; (2) their annual meetings were useful and important for information exchange and communication; (3) their field services were helpful on legislation, real estate practices, and auditing; (4) their regional structure development was useful; and (5) they had excellent publications, especially the newsletter and manual on auditing.

The negative factors were: (1) NN had not "put interracial neighborhoods on the federal map" as the recognized representative organization; (2) NN had not capitalized on the wide array of federal grants available; (3) NN had "very low-level results," despite being represented on task forces and committees in Washington; (4) NN had not served as a conduit of information to its neighborhood groups about private and public dollars that were available "in the wake of rising national interest in neighborhoods"; (5) NN's leadership had not made itself felt "and particularly suffered from a lack of continuity"; and (6) NN remained heavily dependent on the Ford Foundation and continued to have a minimal dues structure (report of meeting with Chandler, June 15, 1979).

Chandler "made it quite clear" that neither he nor the foundation would try to tell NN what to do, but he urged the board to take these "outside perceptions" seriously. He said bluntly that NN did not need the Ford Foundation to provide services to neighborhoods "with only a minimal impact on the national scene." Finally, he said NN should not count on Ford's support in the future unless "new thrusts and impetus to its programs" were developed.

The NN board did indeed take these perceptions and comments seriously. The meeting with Chandler took place during an annual conference in Denver, right before the election of a new board. After a long, intense discussion following Chandler's remarks, the president asked a committee of three to prepare recommendations to the new board to serve as a guide and point of reference during 1979–80. They had one day to prepare this report, before the new board took over the responsibility of leading the shaky organization.

The report to the new board said NN had to make a determination: whether it should remain a service organization maintaining programs that respond primarily to the needs of member groups, or whether it should expand current operations to involve new, major, and intensive efforts to become a "more effective, national organization" (report, June 1979). They said that a decision not to change their focus would mean that the new board's first priority, and immediately, would have to be raising the money for survival.

Once more, they acknowledged the structural difficulties and operational problems "inherent to a national voluntary Board with extremely limited opportunities to meet together. Neither this outgoing Board nor previous Boards have been able to satisfactorily resolve these problems." The problems they outlined included the ones we have already noted, such as maintaining communication between board members and between board and staff; the urgent fund-raiding needs and budget revisions caused by cash flow difficulties; the continuing need for careful appraisal of current programs in terms of productivity, effectiveness and need; securing the support of the existing membership; and the need for active board participation between infrequent meetings.

These thoughts, reflections, and recommendations were carefully and caringly prepared. One of the three who prepared this report became the next president of NN. But all the care and caring could not put NN together again, for when the Ford funding ran out at the end of 1980, the organization was unable to secure other adequate funding to replace it. The continued vacillation between wanting to maintain a national image and serving the member groups, and not being able to do both or either successfully, haunted the worried, weary group for the rest of their existence—which, miraculously, continues.

A 1980 letter from Jean Milgram in response to one from the new president offers some perceptive insights. Apparently, the president had invited her to come to a board meeting to help the new board reach some decisions about what to do. She declined, saying she did not think she would be helpful: "It has been too long and I know too little of what has happened. More than that, I think that I see between the lines indications that NN has gone off on a tangent I would bemoan excessively." She also regretted hearing of the resignation of the latest executive director: "Frankly, I wouldn't blame all of you if you throw in the towel. Four executive directors in four years is a pretty good indication that something basic is awry." She then offered her opinion as to the choices that lay before the board, noting that "NN cannot be a presence until it has first been a successful coalition of multiracial neighborhoods" (letter, Nov. 28, 1980).

Statements from member groups on the occasion of NN's tenth anniversary show NN's impact. From a delegate from the Hyde Park-Kenwood Community

Conference in Chicago: "Coming together, sharing, and learning with committed people was exciting. Love permeated the group. I always got a go-back-and-work transfusion." From a delegate from the Butler-Tarkington Neighborhood Association in Indianapolis: "NN is one of the best things that ever happened, even though it is not a cure-all." A delegate from the Ludlow Association in Shaker Heights, Ohio: "I saw the potential of NN as a vehicle for communicating the concerns of multiracial communities. It has established itself in this regard." And a delegate from West Mount Airy Neighbors in Philadelphia: "I came to NN in complete ignorance about life-and-death issues that related to multiracial communities. . . . Learning was exhilarating; developing friendships across the country continues to be enriching" (Neighbors, July 1979).

For the remainder of phase two and on into phase three, NN's program and impact dwindled steadily, while their funding appeals mounted incessantly. Signs of their growing despair we have already seen in some internal memos and even a few newsletters. Particularly, the remarks of the past director who served until 1981 reflect honest appraisals of organizational weakness: concerning relations between NN and member groups, "Communication between NN and member groups is definitely lacking" (Neighbors, Nov. 1979). With regard to building their national image: "We are not presently capable of delivering completely." Concerning office inquiries: "Unfortunately we have not finalized the . . . network needed to follow through on these calls." And with regard to service to member groups, "Changing leadership has resulted in some confusion in record keeping" (report to Ford Foundation, June 1980).

An editorial headed "Integration vs. Disintegration" bemoaned the national climate's low priority for civil rights and NN's low morale: "The future looks bleak . . . mobilizing a national force is not an easy task. NN could easily be one of the powers behind such an effort *but realistically we can barely keep our structure intact, our member constituency involved and our supporters informed.* Nevertheless, *frail as we are,* NN must exist" (Neighbors, Dec. 1980; emphasis added).

Two months later, a grim NN Executive Committee meeting resulted in the decision to terminate the office worker and accept the resignation of the executive director due to lack of funds. The office, however, remained open. (minutes, Feb. 7, 1981). A memo from NN's president a few days later was headed "Current Status of NN," and was sent to all board members and past presidents. It told of the drastic cost-saving measures decided on, and insisted that:

the need for NN is more important now than ever before because of federal cuts in beneficial programs and increasing racism . . . the small group of the Executive director [soon gone] and officers cannot save this organization by ourselves. We need the effort of board members, past board members and member groups to become a viable and effective organization again. We need both programmatic and financial support. (letter, Feb. 16, 1981)

All of phase three was spent in trying to get such support.

Phase Three: 1982–

When the question was raised at the 1981 annual conference in Washington, D.C. as to whether NN should continue, delegates answered with a resounding yes. They gave three reasons why NN should go on: (1) NN was "a good source of information exchanges and should continue to be a clearinghouse; (2) personal growth derived from NN conferences enabled people to feel good about themselves and what they were doing; and (3) NN was the best in the area of problemsolving and problem-sharing" (minutes, July 18, 1981).

A letter to the president and all board members from two people who could not attend a scheduled board meeting also voiced the need for NN to continue. One of their suggestions was that the main focus of NN in the next two years should be development of a neighborhood organization foundation to provide yearly grants of $1,000 to all NN members who were willing to work toward implementing NN goals, pay an initial fee, and provide NN with a proposal for using the money and a summary of the results. They offered a plan to make this program work, based on a similar program in Cincinnati (letter, Sept. 30, 1981).

Though the board voted to adopt this report, there is no indication that they ever took it seriously. Perhaps if they had, there might be more to include under "impact" during phase three. But instead of implementing a program that would strengthen member groups across the country, NN's mighty efforts during phase three were concentrated on raising money for their own operation. Instead of making the office in Washington a mailing address and concentrating on program, they kept the office open, which drained their meager resources so that any hope of a visible program was impossible. They did continue their annual conferences and their sparse newsletters, and these continued to provide an impact on those who attended and read. But these could have been done out of any place in the country, with far less money than they spent on the Washington office to maintain their "national image."

A simple alternative to the year-round Washington office might have been holding their annual conferences in the capital. Many other groups have had substantial impact on national legislation by convening their members in Washington, even though their base of operation is not there. The powerful National People's Action group, for example, is based in Chicago but meets annually in Washington for a well-organized conference and dynamic meetings with key legislators. This is the group that pushed through the Home Mortgage Disclosure Act, which gave neighborhoods a lasting tool to combat bank redlining. Clearly, groups do not have to live in Washington to have a national impact. But, once having made that move, NN's board could not bring themselves to undo it when their funding ended, and their program and impact suffered accordingly. Only their conferences and newsletters remained of their earlier program. Let us finally examine these during phase three to see what they contained and what effect they had.

Conference content during phase three was consistent with that of past conferences. The theme of the 1982 conference in Chicago, for example, was "Neighborhood Issues and Options: A Need for Commitment to Multi-racial and Multi-ethnic Neighborhoods." During the three-day meeting, delegates heard experts on the issues of displacement, fair housing, maintaining diverse communities, corporate citizenship, and options in education.

The 1983 four-day conference in Bellwood, Illinois—a suburb of Chicago—had six "Action Workshops" focusing on: (1) open/closed communities—perceptions and reality; (2) fair housing—law and human dignity; (3) integration and the family—prejudice and preference; (4) commercial revitalization—role of city and business leaders; (5) integrated schools—education for life; and (6) integration maintenance—facts and controversy. Costs were relatively low (seventy-five dollars for meals and registration, forty to fifty dollars a day for lodging at Triton College) to attract maximum numbers of delegates, with 230 people actually attending. Many of these, however, were from the Chicago area. This was a typical result at the annual conferences; areas closest to the conference site had the largest attendance, though typically more than seventy cities throughout the country were represented.

While the impact of the conference was felt by those attending, the post-conference press releases reached many more. After the Bellwood conference, for example, the NN press release, headed "Conference Brings Together Civil Rights Vanguard," began with a quote from keynote speaker James Farmer. "Farmer, quoting Rabbi Hillel—'If not now, when?'—brought the audience . . . to its feet" (press release, June 24, 1983). A statement from Chip Bromley, NN's new director, referred to the unsympathetic national climate at the time: "With . . . institutional racism still threatening to undermine our interracial communities throughout the country, we needed to reaffirm our unity and pave the way for the civil rights movement of the 1980s" (press release, June 24, 1983).

Articles about the conference appeared in the *Chicago Tribune*, *Chicago Sun-Times*, *Washington Post*, *Indianapolis Recorder*, and several other weeklies and publications. Though all conference delegates were urged to use the press release locally, obviously not all did. Still, the impact of the conference was greater than just on those who attended.

The most glamorous conference ever held by NN was in 1984 at Starrett City, New York. Organized by professional public relations people who worked for the corporation that operated Starrett City, this conference was quite out of character for NN. Coming at a time when the organization was gasping for survival, the advertised conference "package" was almost unbelievable, including cocktail receptions, continental breakfasts, lunches, a dinner-dance, Sunday brunch, a trip to Manhattan, and "full use of the Pool, Health and Tennis Club facilities at Starrett City" (*Neighbors*, March 1984).

Aside from the slickness of this package, the program was an outstanding one, with nationally known people as key speakers: Coretta Scott King, Roger Wilkins, Mayor Koch of New York City, Kenneth Clark, Mayor Harold Washington of Chicago, and again James Farmer. Not only was there superb advance publicity, but the conference itself was covered by national media—all arranged by the public relations professionals. With the prominence of the key speakers, the expertise of the panel participants and workshop leaders, and the glossiness of the whole event so close to the Big Apple, the impact could not fail to be great.

More than 500 people participated in the 1984 conference at Starrett City, which included fifteen workshops focusing on issues as specific as "Gentrification" and "The Effect of Integration on Senior Citizens," and as general as "Integration: Perceptions and Misconceptions." The conference theme was "Brown vs. Board of Education: 30 Years Later," and a major panel focused on integration maintenance and the controversial Starrett City lawsuit.

Though the headline in Neighbors heralded this as "the best conference ever," in many ways it was so atypical that it seemed almost an anomaly to those who knew the inner turmoil of the organization. One fear expressed during the conference was that this was so fancy an affair it might frighten local groups away from ever agreeing to sponsor another one. Who could match this glamor?

But the 1985 conference at Johns Hopkins University in Baltimore dispelled this fear. This one was back in character; not so glamorous, and it was filled with solid, informative workshops and vigorous speakers. With costs down to $150 for the three days, including room, meals, and registration fee, this one made up for lack of glamor by its affordability. The conference theme was "Integrated Neighborhoods: America's Living Future," and workshops dealt with resources, realtors, affirmative marketing, communication, schools, the role of government, gentrification, and "what does integration mean to me?" Though only 150 delegates attended the Baltimore conference, the atmosphere was warm, friendly, and stimulating. Keynote speaker Senator Mathias pointed out that the struggle for equality had to continue, even though civil rights had low priority at that time and did not "summon the energizing outrage" of earlier years (Neighbors, Summer 1985).

The 1986 annual conference—NN's seventeenth—held in Los Angeles, California on the campus of the University of Southern California, was organized, as usual, by local groups. This time, they were all fair housing groups. The conference theme was "Racial Diversity in a World City," and several workshops focused on special concerns of Western cities: "Growth in the Asian Community," "Growth in the Latino Community," and "Integrating the Old and New Immigrants." Other workshops dealt with more standard issues, including "What Is a World City?" Black-Jewish Relations," "Media: The News from Whose Perspective?" and "Fair Housing Today." A "Night on the Town" was designed to "give participants a taste of Los Angeles' spicy nightlife" (Neighbors, Spring 1986).

This conference and its workshops reflected two different factors: location and type of host. Being held in the West, many of the topics covered were especially relevant to the Los Angeles area. And being hosted by fair housing groups, the conference content was more characteristic of their concerns than of neighborhood concerns. News of the 1987 conference being held in Boston and hosted by a coalition of community development corporations prompted some expressed anxieties about NN "drifting far afield."

We end this analysis of NN's impact by noting the continuing excellence of the newsletters. Though less frequent than in other phases, they continued to offer vital information on neighborhood groups and their activities across the country, on legislation and national programs affecting neighborhoods, and on publications of interest to member groups everywhere, as well as occasional excerpts from letters and comments regarding controversial issues relevant to integration maintenance. Each newsletter was mailed to over 3,000 recipients, including individuals, organizations, and government agencies.

Though the newsletters and annual conferences were the mainstay of NN's program during phase three, the impact of these two activities should not be underestimated. Those who were exposed to them were enriched with vital information and renewal of spirit. If some of this came back ultimately to the neighborhood level, it was reason enough to continue. National Neighbors' future remains questionable, with many of their troubling problems unresolved. At this point, they seem to be barely coasting along on their previous momentum and reputation. How long this can continue is unknown.

Postscript

At their twentieth anniversary conference in Washington, D.C. in June 1989, NN changed their name to "National Federation for Neighborhood Diversity." The reason? To state their purpose more clearly for funding sources.

Part IV

CONCLUSIONS

9

SUMMARY AND POLICY
IMPLICATIONS

In this final chapter, I will first present thirteen hypotheses concerning movement success. I will then summarize our findings on the community level of this movement. We will review the case studies of the three models of MOs and their neighborhoods and the briefer profiles across the country. Then we will turn to the national level and review those findings, and discuss the ongoing ideological conflict in this movement. Finally, I will use all the findings to develop policy recommendations for achieving success in this endangered movement—a precious remnant of the civil rights movement of the past.

Before we begin this summation and draw some conclusions, let us consider once more the meanings of our three analytical models. These represent the various kinds of combinations of movement organizations and neighborhoods that I actually found in this research. When I say "success," I am referring to the prime movement goal of maintaining stable racially integrated neighborhoods. I am also referring to survival of the MO. When I say "stable," I mean a neighborhood showing relatively little racial change in the past decade.

And when I say "integrated," I am not using this term to mean blacks and whites necessarily socializing together. I acknowledge that in every one of the so-called success examples there were identifiable racial neighborhoods within each target community. The term integrated, as I use it, suggests pluralism rather than amalgamation or assimilation, that is, blacks and whites living

amicably and equitably in the same territory, some of whom are joined together
in common pursuits. This I did find in all three models. What marked the
differences among them, however, were the proportions of blacks, the survival
of the movement organization, and the potential for stability in the future. If
Hartford's MO had survived, I would classify that effort as a conditional one
rather than a failure. This is because I believe, as I must, that it is always possible
to effect change.

"Conditional" I am using to mean something that is neither total failure nor
yet success. If the neighborhood is predominantly black but the MO lives, I am
classifying this as a conditional example. If the neighborhood is still statistically
integrated (as with Akron's 48% black level), and the MO is alive (although
weakened), but the future stability and degree of integration is doubtful, I am
calling this a conditional example. The particular factors that led me to the
conclusion of relative certainty or doubt about the future in each case are offered
below. These are first presented in the form of hypotheses to be tested further
by other scholars. I have developed them only from the knowledge gained and
a good deal of reflection generated in this study of a limited sample. They are
expanded in the final section on policy implications and strategies for change.

HYPOTHESES OF STABILIZATION MOVEMENT
SUCCESS

On the Community Level, the probability of success, that is, a stable racially
integrated neighborhood, is greater:

1. The greater the amenities of the target neighborhood
2. The more supportive the role of the city
3. The more comprehensive a school desegregation program
4. The more deconcentrated the location of public housing
5. The more extensive an affirmative marketing program
6. The more effective a regional fair housing program
7. The greater the regional housing supply for all income levels
8. The earlier the timing of the movement effort, that is, before the target neighborhood
   is racially identifiable
9. The more securely and adequately funded the MO.

On the National Level, the probability of movement success is greater:

10. The greater the commitment of the national government to undoing racism through
    implementing and enforcing existing civil rights laws, and establishing a national
    neighborhood integration maintenance policy
11. The more effective a national movement organization is in establishing a national
    presence

12. The more coordinated the efforts of the MOs in both the fair housing and neighborhood stabilization movements

13. The more securely and adequately funded a national MO is.

THE COMMUNITY LEVEL: COMPARATIVE SUMMARY
OF CASE STUDY MODELS

Model A—Success (Live MO/Integrated Neighborhood)

All three study neighborhoods in Indianapolis, Rochester, and Milwaukee had pervasive long-standing racism in their cities, manifested in housing and school segregation. All three had massive urban renewal projects in their inner cities, which dislocated blacks, forced their migration to new neighborhoods, and led to the formation of the movement organization in each neighborhood studied.

In all three communities, the goal of integration maintenance remained consistent throughout the existence of the MOs. Though the words differed over time, the intent was the same. Indianapolis's BTNA was the only group in this model that remained essentially unfunded and totally voluntary throughout its existence. Rochester's WCA and Milwaukee's SPCA were eventually well-funded for housing rehabilitation projects and other special programs requiring offices and staffing.

All three organizations had elected boards of directors consisting of officers, committee chairs, and area representatives. In all three communities, however, the real power and control lay in the executive committee and the president. Standing committees conducted much of the work of the organization in all three study areas. Leadership in all three was primarily white and middle-class, though intensive efforts were made to recruit black leadership—with minimal success. All three groups had great difficulty in securing representation from lower socioeconomic portions of their neighborhood, which were predominantly black.

All three study neighborhoods had three areas within them, racially defined: one area was predominantly black, one was racially integrated, and one was predominantly white. Leadership and membership came mostly from the racially integrated area in all three communities. However, program boundaries in all three neighborhoods consciously included black areas from the outset. In fact, most of the housing rehabilitation funds in each neighborhood were spent in the predominantly black area.

Common concerns in the three MOs were housing, schools, and zoning. Common enemies were real estate agents who practiced block-busting and racial steering, owners who did not maintain their properties, and special interest groups who attempted to alter the zoning of the neighborhood from residential to other uses. Housing strategies in all three organizations included correcting real estate practices, promoting affirmative marketing of their area, and securing funds for rehabilitation of deteriorated properties. One real estate practice that plagued all three communities was solicitation by agents. As a result, all three MOs successfully obtained bans on "for sale" signs and on solicitation through their city councils or state legislatures. These strategies required extensive contacts with local and state governmental representatives and agencies, private corporate executives such as lenders, businesses and industries, and all the media.

All three MOs were consistently involved in efforts to desegregate the schools in the city and their neighborhood. Additional program activities common to all three MOs were membership drives, community social events, newsletter preparation and distribution, and other special projects, such as youth recreation in Indianapolis and Rochester, and senior outreach in Milwaukee. Crime prevention programs were more recently conducted in Rochester and Milwaukee's study neighborhoods. Block organization was not prominent in Indianapolis or Rochester, but began to be a major program in Milwaukee in very recent years.

Though the level of racial pluralism was not the same throughout any of the three communities, integration maintenance and stability were achieved in all with varying degrees of success. The physical quality of the housing was generally good, but there was some deterioration of the business areas in all three study neighborhoods. The lower-income sections of each study area were less well-maintained than the middle- and upper-income portions, despite the fact that these were the areas that had received special rehabilitation funds. Evaluation of the sense of community showed that all three MOs devoted considerable time and effort to fostering fellowship in their neighborhoods, but in all three communities, the racial difference in three portions of each study neighborhood detracted from a total sense of community.

The influence of the MO in all three study neighborhoods was considerable. In each of their major program areas, the three MOs sought to influence institutional policies and practices, with substantial degrees of success. All three neighborhood associations, throughout their existence, presented unified, strong, stubborn images and succeeded in influencing key decision makers on local and state levels. Some of those decision makers were former MO leaders— a positive factor for each MO and its neighborhood.

Considering internal factors of success, organizational structure does not appear to be a significant factor in accounting for the successful stabilization of the three areas. The Indianapolis MO had no staff or sustained funding; the Rochester group had part-time staff from its inception, and separate staff and offices for other funded projects; and the Milwaukee MO had extensive staffing for funded projects, but no separate staffing for the operation of the organization itself. Of the two funded groups, the Rochester structure was more successful in maintaining harmony within the group. The Milwaukee structure was much less conducive to internal peace; Indianapolis, unfunded, remained internally congenial.

One internal factor—the participants in the MO—is intertwined with an external factor. Both the Indianapolis and Rochester study neighborhoods had significant amenities, which attracted people to the area. In Indianapolis's Butler-Tarkington neighborhood, for example, the presence of a major private university in its central tract was a major stabilizing force. Indianapolis's MO was also aided by having an active adjacent neighborhood organization, which shared some common goals and boundaries. This provided double strength and energy in mutual efforts, which benefitted both neighborhoods. Similarly, Rochester's nineteenth ward was very close to two major universities, which attracted professional people to the neighborhood, providing abundant human resources for the neighborhood association. Milwaukee's Sherman Park did not possess such amenities, and its human resources were waning in its third phase of development.

Turning to external factors of success—those outside of the organization and its participants—we saw the importance of the role of the city toward neighborhood organizations. One specific example of the city's helpful role in both Indianapolis and Rochester was their participation in the neighborhood statistics program offered by the U.S. Census Bureau. In Indianapolis, the city assigned specific city program planners to work with each neighborhood organization for constant liaison. In Rochester, the city had an outright grant program for housing rehabilitation anywhere in the city. In addition, the Rochester MO received a special grant from the city for affirmative marketing and promotional efforts. In Milwaukee, the city government began a vigorous neighborhood development program in 1977, which was beneficial for the study neighborhood.

The economic base of the city of Indianapolis was banking and manufacturing, and as a county seat it was not as adversely affected by economic decline in the late 1970s and early 1980s, as was Milwaukee. Rochester, too, was fortunate in maintaining employment during those periods of recession, because of its high technology focus. These were positive factors for the two study neighborhoods and their MOs. Major economic recessions would have threatened the success of many of their programs. In Milwaukee, however, the study neighborhood and the MO did feel the pinch of economic decline, and their more run-down business areas showed it. This was partially offset in Milwaukee by the secure source of funding from United Way for the operation of the organization. State funding of special rehabilitation projects also seemed secure, and offered hope for the maintenance of the group's programs, despite the city's and the neighborhood's economic problems.

All three communities had citywide school desegregation programs, which were beneficial to the study neighborhoods in their struggle for racial pluralism maintenance. Citywide bussing in Indianapolis began in 1971, and later expanded to countywide bussing, so the neighborhood school was no longer a meaningful concept there. The result of this was that residents in any neighborhood of the city could expect two things—racially integrated schools everywhere, and neighborhood schools nowhere. This effectively removed one stigma from racially integrated neighborhoods, since their schools were no more racially identifiable than those in any other neighborhood.

Thus, families could be encouraged to move to the pluralistic Butler-Tarking-ton neighborhood, for example, without worrying about their children attending racially isolated schools there. This enabled BTNA's housing information service and affirmative marketing programs to succeed. Similarly, in Rochester, though not as effective a school desegregation program as in Indianapolis, there were numerous options for residents of the nineteenth ward in choices for their children's schooling. Rochester's citywide open enrollment policy, with special elementary and junior high magnet programs, was supported by state mandates for school racial balance for over twenty years.

In Milwaukee, with the least effective school desegregation program of the three, court-ordered school desegregation removed from the study neighborhood the burden of having racially identifiable schools, though they did exist elsewhere in the city. Thus, affirmative marketing programs for the study neighborhood had some chance of success. In Milwaukee, too, the presence of an active and effective metropolitan fair housing center was a significant positive force for the maintenance of racial pluralism in Sherman Park.

One more external factor was important in the successful maintenance of pluralism in the three study neighborhoods—the absence of public housing concentration in the neighborhood. This was true for Indianapolis and Roch-ester, somewhat less so for Milwaukee. There, some scattered-site subsidized housing was beginning to have an impact on one of the sectors of the study area—the one with the most low-income and minority households. However, a city plan for regional mobility of public housing residents—developed through the SPCA's influence—was being actively considered to reduce the subsidized housing concentration in the city.

In conclusion, all three MOs played a critical role in preserving their neigh-borhoods as desirable, stable, pluralistic communities. They each performed a "holding" action while stabilization was sought through a vigorous combination of programs and strategies. But other forces—external to the organization— were essential to the success of their efforts. The amenities of the neighborhood, the city's supportive role, the absence of public housing concentration in the study neighborhood, and the school desegregation program for the city were the four major external forces in the neighborhood's success and the organization's survival. Without these, it is not likely that either the neighborhood or the organizations would have successfully survived as pluralistic communities.

Model B—Failure (Dead MO/Black Neighborhood)

Hartford's MO, despite equally dedicated and vigorous participants and lead-ers, was unable to maintain racial pluralism in the Blue Hills neighborhood. In Hartford—insurance capital of the nation—the beginning of the north-end ghetto could be seen even before World War I. In 1900 almost half of the city's blacks lived in the city's densely populated north end, near where the Blue Hills study neighborhood is located. In the postwar period, the black movement to north Hartford gathered momentum.

Urban renewal programs in Hartford added to the black population movement within the city and the white movement out of the city. Between 1950 and 1970, city neighborhoods had whole new populations on their doorsteps almost overnight, and by the end of those decades Hartford lost over 25,000 residents and businesses. Of the eighteen neighborhoods in Hartford that experienced change, seven had most (83%) of the demographic shift. Blue Hills was one of the seven. It had the third largest population change in the city—4,800 non-whites replaced 4,282 whites in Blue Hills between 1960 and 1970.

In 1962, the Blue Hills Civic Association was formed; it was the only MO studied which did not begin with the stated purpose of maintaining a racially integrated neighborhood. This came three years later, after the organization changed in leaders, membership, and direction. With this change came a new ideological position and new fervor, making the group a true MO rather than just an interest group.

A voluntary fifteen-member board of directors and six committees carried out the work of the organization, which remained essentially unfunded throughout its twenty-year existence. Though they submitted numerous proposals for funding that would have enabled them to have some staffing for their operation, the only operational funding they received was for the printing of their newspaper and for a few special projects.

Four major committees conducted the work of the organization: housing, education, neighborhood improvement, and recreation. Later, youth services and a senior center became part of the program, and finally were the only remnants left of the BHCA. One special annual unique event was the Freedom Seder, begun in 1968 as a community dinner and continuing for eight years as a symbol of the universal struggle for freedom throughout human history.

The earliest activities of BHCA were related to housing and the housing committee, which functioned actively from 1965 to 1969. Then, a separate housing services corporation was formed and continued until 1972, when it dissolved after the most bitter internal conflict in the organization. The conflict centered on affirmative marketing tactics, an issue that still plagues this movement in the neighborhoods and in the courts.

As important as the early housing committee was the vital education committee of BHCA, which completed nine activities during the first two phases of the BHCA's existence. These were accompanied by a constant effort to secure racial balance and quality education in the public schools. After the spring of 1973, the activities of the education committee dwindled, until general organizational decline led to its extinction. By then, the schools were 81% to 93% black in the Blue Hills neighborhood.

Blue Hills did not remain racially integrated; between 1970 and 1980, it became predominantly black. As to quality maintenance, the Blue Hills area is still pleasant looking, with decent housing and well-kept grounds. However, its business strip is not well-maintained, has considerable litter in full view of most stores, presents parking difficulties, and is generally unattractive. This, despite a supposedly successful revitalization and beautification program under-taken by the city in the late 1970s. In addition, the large neighborhood park appears unkempt and quite deserted. Census data reveal some of the changes in median income and stability in the Blue Hills neighborhood between 1960 and 1980. Though percent of owner occupancy remained stable at 55%, median income and permanency declined, and the neighborhood was considered in incipient decline by 1980.

Analyzing the MO's impact, the BHCA's provision of a sense of community offers an unqualified positive record. If there was anything that BHCA succeeded in, it was this. Over and over again, respondents cited their feelings of fellowship and camaraderie when nostalgically recalling their affiliation with the MO. The largest single category of newspaper items in all the years of publication of the Blue Hills News was related to recreational events sponsored by the organization.

The most compelling evidence of influence is found in the major programs of the organization during the first two phases of the MO, up until 1976. Neighborhood improvement, housing, and education each left records of ded-icated volunteers repeatedly contacting key decision makers and officials to express their concerns about issues affecting the Blue Hills neighborhood. They were able to prevent some major and minor decisions, change others, and bring about still others by influencing the appropriate officials, some of whom lived in or were former residents of the Blue Hills area.

Some examples of this influence include blocking a chamber of commerce multimillion-dollar proposal for a low-cost housing project in Blue Hills. Instead, a school was built on the site, which the organization wanted. Every zoning change resisted by the MO was successfully stopped during its first phase. Their early efforts to promote their area and attract new homeseekers were successful, until ideological differences tore them apart. Nevertheless, the successful pro-motion of their area led to Blue Hills later being selected as a pilot target site for the national Neighborhood Housing Services, which later expanded to other cities and states across the country. Their educational efforts led to the passage of a State Racial Imbalance Act, which had broad ramifications for schools in the entire state, though implemented too late for Blue Hills Schools.

Why, then, did Blue Hills fail—as an organization, and as an integrated neighborhood? Internally, we saw that this was the only organization that did not begin with the stated goal of integration maintenance. By the time new leaders and members openly acclaimed that goal in 1965, the neighborhood was already almost half-black, and the schools there were predominantly black. Though the zeal and commitment during their first two phases of organizational development were unsurpassed anywhere else, this came too late to bring sta-bilization to Blue Hills. Recognition of this led to deep burnout, fatigue, and discouragement. This, plus the fact that they were unable to secure funding for the staffing they so much needed for their monumental task, led to even more burnout of the already overworked and overburdened volunteer board and committees.

The bitter internal conflict over affirmative marketing tactics further weakened them, and the spin-offs of two other organizations staffed by ex-BHCA leaders seriously splintered the group, resulting in fragmentation of talent and energy. To add to this, rapid continuing white flight continually drained the remaining leaders and members of their friends, allies, coworkers, their support—and hope.

The most serious internal weakness was the lack of a clear program and objectives from the outset. They seemed to move from one crisis to another, and were unable to come to grips with actual policy statements concerning racial integration maintenance. Finally, in their third phase, their leadership was unable to muster much support even for attendance at monthly meetings. Their senior center program ultimately diverted the few remaining leaders and supporters away from any other BHCA programs to the mere maintenance of the small, ramshackle, sparsely attended senior center.

Externally, the Blue Hills neighborhood was surrounded with the most massive public housing project in the city of Hartford. Fourteen hundred residents, more than half of whom were black, were also included in the BHCA boundaries and in their school cluster. Inevitably, this was not helpful to the goal achievement of the MO.

The school funding base was inadequately structured, following state mandates. The implications of this weakness for Blue Hills are seen in several critical decisions made in the mid- and late sixties by the Hartford School Board. With a gigantic study team's recommendations before them offering details for keeping the city's schools racially balanced and academically enriched, the school board rejected the plan that would have achieved this. State funding difficulties were cited as the major reason for this rejection. Instead of adopting the plan, the school board spent the next ten years implementing piecemeal segments of the plan, avoiding others, and circumventing still others. The results of this for the Blue Hills schools were disastrous. By the time school officials seriously began to devise ways of achieving racial balance in the city schools, it was too late. The single most cited factor by those who moved away was the racial isolation in the public schools.

Thus, internal and external factors led to burnout, decline and death. If they had not had the internal ideological split as early as they did, and if they had retained their promising affirmative marketing program, they might have been able to also perform the "holding action" we found in the success model. But Hartford had something those communities in Model A did not—massive segregated public housing projects surrounding their neighborhood. Had these been racially integrated, Blue Hills still might have maintained integration until the citywide school desegregation plan finally went into effect. But none of this happened, and they failed to survive—as an organization, and as an integrated neighborhood.

Model C—Conditional (Live MO/Transitional Neighborhood)

Akron's West Side Neighbors had dedicated, vigorous, skilled participants and leaders in their first two phases, and won many skirmishes and achieved much throughout their existence. By their third phase, however, they were losing the war of integration maintenance and their strength was waning.

Akron—named an all-America City in 1980—is indeed typical of other cities of this country in being home for both racists and civil rights activists. Akron is where the Ku Klux Klan flourished in the 1920s, when blacks were only 2.4% of the city's population. This, also, is where the local public housing authority by 1950 had established eight totally segregated projects. Blacks, making up 13% of Akron's people by 1960, were largely confined to the central city.

Protests against Akron's racism surfaced in 1945 and 1950, and again in 1963 when the first of three lawsuits was filed against Akron's school authorities, charging intentional segregation. Those protests continue to this moment. In 1967 riots in the heart of an urban renewal area—ironically called Opportunity Park—rocked the city and called out the National Guard. By this time, too, both Fair Housing Contact Service and West Side Neighbors had been formed to deal as volunteers with the twin problems of fair housing and integration maintenance. Thus, vigorous racism and equally vigorous civil rights action coexisted in Akron, as in other cities. It is a typical American city. And this conditional model may well be the typical and prevailing model of integration maintenance in this country.

Urban renewal land clearance in Akron, as in other cities across the nation, devastated more than 5,000 housing units by 1960. This affected blacks by destroying their neighborhoods, decreasing their housing supply, and forcing their relocation in a hostile and segregative housing market. Their relocation into west Akron prompted the formation of West Side Neighbors (WSN).

WSN began in 1967 for three reasons: reaction against racism, desire for neighborhood control, and the wish to serve as a demonstration model of successful integration. The purpose of the new biracial group was "to attain and maintain a stable, integrated community . . . and to promote community harmony and improvements." They did not know how incredibly difficult it would be.

A biracial, twenty-one member board of directors and nine committees carried out the work of WSN, whose structure changed in the three phases of their development. Their first ten years were unfunded and a totally volunteer effort, culminating in their winning the prestigious Akron Area Brotherhood Award shortly after their tenth anniversary. Their second phase of development included five years of funded projects, and a staff. At the same time, this second phase of development was marked by a weakening of leadership and organizational skills. The combination of these two situations was an unhappy one, and led to confusion, irritation, and rapid burnout.

In their third phase, WSN reverted to unfunded, unstaffed status, and the responsibility of maintaining an office with part-time office help. Their existence was threatened in their twentieth year by the intrusion of two other new all-black neighborhood groups vying for programs, funding, and recognition as the true spokespersons for Akron's west side.

Three major committees conducted most of the work of the organization during all three phases: block organization, schools, and housing. By the end of the third phase, however, only the housing committee survived, along with a newly revived business committee.

The block organization committee in phase one organized one hundred blocks and ten neighborhood meetings, obtained 704 household memberships, and assisted the city with a massive code enforcement program in one tract. In phase two, block organization expanded during WSN's first funded project—a two-year crime prevention program, and in another funded project, the Useful Service Exchange. Funded programs expanded the block clubs into a block club council, and assisted the city with another code enforcement program in a blighted tract. After funding ended, WSN tried to sustain a block organization program as volunteers, but gave up their faltering attempts toward the end of phase three, when another block club council was formed by a west-side councilman.

The education committee, WSN's largest and most vigorous committee during phase one, consistently tried through persuasion and then legal coercion to obtain and maintain first-rate, racially balanced schools in their area. Though their efforts were monumental, they failed. Three lawsuits, two major and one minor one, resulted in overall citywide reduction in school racial segregation, but an almost totally black west-side school cluster. The schools committee stopped functioning in 1986.

The enduring housing committee's major efforts were directed against real estate solicitation and block-busting, and against public housing concentration and segregation on the west side. At the beginning of phase two, their first mortgage lending study—a twenty-seven-year analysis—led to a one-year funded project UPON, an affirmative marketing and reinvestment program directed to real estate, banking, and corporate institutions. When all funding stopped, the annual mortgage lending reports continued to bring some small financial contributions to WSN from the banks. As volunteers, their battle against segregative forces continued.

In addition to these focused activities of the three long-standing WSN committees were the many special events and activities WSN sponsored and conducted over the years through other committees. These provided interracial fellowship, fun and relief from grim tasks, and a sense of community when that community seemed to be crumbling. Akron's MO went into their third phase as they had begun—unfunded and unstaffed. But by this time, their energy and hope were depleted; they and their substantially integrated community were fighting for their lives. Volunteers could no longer do what needed to be done. The forces were too gigantic.

Integration maintenance in Akron's west side has steadily declined over the past two decades. Of the five census tracts in the WSN area, two are now predominantly black, one is substantially integrated, and two are predominantly white, yielding an overall ratio of 48% black. Though WSN neighborhoods can still be considered racially integrated, the schools cannot. The schools in the WSN area are almost totally black, ranging from a low of 80% black in one elementary school to 98% black in the high school. Even more dramatic is the fact that now this school cluster is the only racially identifiable black cluster of schools in the entire city.

Quality maintenance is variable: quite fine in some streets, shoddy in others, with homes ranging from low-income-level modest bungalows to high-income mansions. Census data show that some portions of the WSN community changed over time toward lower socioeconomic levels, largely through the influx of more public housing tenants in leased and scattered-site units. The main business street has predominantly black clientele, and its eastern portion is a disaster area.

Three neighborhoods are evident on Akron's west side, as in the other communities studied: one is white, one is integrated, and one is black. Some sense of community still exists in the WSN area, though population turnover has been great in three of the five tracts. Most recently, however, two new neighborhood groups have focused attention on the black portions of the WSN area. This may weaken the sense of unity in the area, and may shrink the actual community boundaries for WSN's activities.

This MO's influence is found through an analysis of their programs and results over two decades. Their vigor and creativity during their first two phases brought enduring results that extended into their third phase, when that earlier energy had declined. Some of those enduring results are: a citywide master recreational plan; a standing zoo; two massive code enforcement programs with a third under way; no bars in two tracts; a citywide reduction in school segregation; a funded fair housing agency; a $1 million improvement of a major business street; and heightened awareness and policy changes in housing, banking, and city government institutions. Their influence went beyond their own neighborhood boundaries, reaching out into the state and the entire country with their idea for incentive mortgage payments for integrative moves. The influence of WSN over two decades was unquestionably considerable and most definitely admirable. So why aren't we smiling?

In Akron, we saw that historically the same factors of racism, segregation, and massive urban renewal relocation we found elsewhere led to the formation of the MO. Internally there was nothing unique about the Akron MO's structure, goals, or programs in their first phase of development. One difference, however, was that they were unfunded for their first ten years, and then began a five-year series of very modestly funded projects, returning to a totally volunteer status in their third phase.

We observed that this sequence of events might have been insignificant in other communities of Model A, but that in Akron it may have been nearly fatal. This is so because of the external institutional forces creating a double jeopardy in the study neighborhood: an all-black school cluster, the only one remaining in the entire city, and more public housing tenants than any other city neighborhood. The only other place that faced this double jeopardy was Hartford, the case study of failure in Model B. Will Akron become another case study of Model B? All the signs are ominously familiar. In the absence of any new intervening forces changing the current picture, we must predict yes.

We also referred earlier to the timing of events. Had WSN been substantially funded earlier, they might have been able to avert the crushing disasters that came to engulf them. They simply did not realize the need for funding and staffing until too late. They naively believed for most of their first phase that they could continue indefinitely to do whatever they had to do as volunteers.

Only when they were finally funded were they able to see how much more a full-time effort could accomplish—even with just one full-time and one part-time staff person. In all three funded programs—the crime prevention project, the UPON affirmative marketing/investing project, and the Useful Service Exchange—they were able to accomplish in one year what they could never have done in ten years as volunteers. This was so, despite the confusion and misguided management of the then inexperienced board. But the funding was over all too soon.

Had the funding continued, even meagerly as it had been, that too might have enabled the MO to qualify for other programs that later came their way. As it was, they were perceived by others as being unable to handle any substantive program, since they had no staff. That was a correct perception. And this lack of staffing was directly responsible for the formation of two new intrusive organizations on their turf, one of which was linked to a heavily funded and well-established social agency in another part of the city.

We have established the link between the timing of the funding and the potential for staving off the public housing onslaught, bank redlining, real estate steering, residential turnover, school turnover, commercial turnover, membership turnover, and finally deep organizational fatigue. This whole chain of events might have been averted if the MO had had staffing early enough and adequate enough to deal with these monumental forces. By the time they obtained it, their leadership was such that they did not know how to best deal with it. Despite this, they did manage to achieve excellent results in the short period of their very modest funding. But they could not sustain these efforts as volunteers.

We also examined the role of two other external factors—the amenities of the neighborhood and the role of the city—and noted the paucity of both.

Convenience, some good housing stock, and some physically attractive streets and a few parks were not enough amenities to make this an unusually desirable neighborhood. When home sale prices dropped, it did become a very desirable neighborhood for those who had lower incomes. But this did not help the MO's goal.

The role of the city we saw as one of long neglect, apathy, and hurtful selective policies. These were apparent in actions relating to public housing, home repair assistance, selection of neighborhood improvement target areas, comparative underfunding of west-side programs, and restrictive stipulations which built in failure.

Finally, we cite once more our two remaining external factors, the "killer variables"—school racial isolation and public housing concentration. These are initially linked to urban renewal relocation, we may recall, in the fateful few years before the MO began. When a new all-white school cluster was built in 1962 adjacent to the Akron study neighborhood, many white households moved away from the MO's area. This coincided with the time of some urban renewal relocation and the expansion of some public housing in the study neighborhood. This was surely an unbeatable combination for the defeat of the MO's goal attainment.

Still, the figures of racial proportions at that time (56% black in the high school in 1970) show that with wise policies and practices, both stability and integration could have been maintained. We know that they were not. And we know that no wise external policies or practices were undertaken to prevent the current reality of Akron's study neighborhood: an all-black school cluster and the largest number of scattered-site public housing units in the entire city. I call these "killer variables" because when they exist in an MO's neighborhood, I maintain this movement's goal of integration maintenance cannot be achieved there.

We turn now to a brief summary of other MOs in other places across the country, as contained in the profiles of Chapter 7. We again divide these into urban neighborhood efforts and suburban municipal efforts; this difference in type of effort strongly affects goal achievement in this movement. The greater probability of success lies in the suburban municipal efforts.

ACROSS THE COUNTRY

Urban Neighborhood MOs

Model A. Our three examples of "success" stories are in the cities of Denver, Colorado; Nashville, Tennessee; and the West Mount Airy section of Philadelphia. Of these, Nashville's Belmont-Hillsboro Neighbors may be the luckiest. Endowed with an excellent citywide school desegregation program, historic register listing, neighborhood housing services, and no public housing concentration, their neighborhood has the greatest probability of maintaining its stable racial integration of 41% black if all these positive factors continue.

Denver's Greater Park Hill Community stability is threatened by 400 units of public housing in one portion of their area. But this is counterbalanced by a citywide school desegregation program, which is having positive effects on the Park Hill community's racial integration. Their fifty-fifty ratio is likely to be maintained if no additional units of public housing come to their area. Their support structure also assures continuing security, based as it is on financing by members of fourteen Park Hill Churches and a synagogue.

The West Mount Airy Neighbors area in Philadelphia maintains a 46% black population, with the aid of a citywide school desegregation program and secure funding for their community service programs. Because of their prior success in maintaining stable racial integration, their area was recently selected for special school magnet programs, which further aids their affirmative marketing efforts. Success begets success. In addition, they are fortunate in having an excellent housing stock and a lower population density than their Model C neighbors in adjacent East Mount Airy. Also, they began seven years before East Mount Airy's MO, with a much smaller black population (17%) than East Mount Airy had when it began (48%). Timing and proportions do make a difference.

Model C. East Mount Airy is now 75% black, and its MO has altered their operative goal to service and quality maintenance rather than integration maintenance. Their stated goal has remained the same: "Making a Good Community Better." Housing in their area includes many row houses, resulting in greater population density than neighboring West Mount Airy. One of their service programs was to provide residential care facilities for deinstitutionalized mentally retarded persons. They now own four homes and rent eight apartments in their community to retarded adults, but they have become cautious in their future plans, fearing oversaturation. Their junior and senior high schools are predominantly black, and their six elementary schools are either black or integrated with a black majority. Their future as an ongoing organization in a black neighborhood seems secure, with adequate funding for staff and program maintenance.

Brooklyn, New York's MO is also securely funded, operating in a stable, predominantly black (80%) neighborhood. Their schools are virtually all-black. Though when the MO began twenty years ago the neighborhood was already close to 60% black, their stated original goal was "to build a stable interracial neighborhood." With a portion of their brownstone neighborhood now declared a historic landmark area, the improvement of several business strips, and an active crime prevention and housing rehabilitation program, the area is likely to continue as a stable, desirable black community with a well-funded and staffed neighborhood program.

Los Angeles's Crenshaw Neighbors still retain their twenty-year slogan, "Serving An Integrated Community," though their area's black population has climbed from 24% in 1960 to 85% in 1988. They have nevertheless steadily contributed to the improvement of the quality of life in their area, and continue to do so even though weary and often discouraged from their struggle. Theirs was the first licensed real estate corporation in the country set up and operated by community residents to do affirmative marketing for integration maintenance. Their early junior and senior high school racial balance program was a valiant effort to retain school integration, but the exclusion of elementary schools resulted in failure and eventual abandonment of the program. By the time the city of Los Angeles received court orders to desegregate, it was too late for Crenshaw. They continue to function, largely as volunteers with minimal office assistance, and they continue to press for quality maintenance in their community. They are battling a huge city bureaucracy externally, a run-down business district and a local area appropriately called "The Jungle," and they are very, very tired.

Our final example of this model is Washington, D.C.'s Neighbors, Inc., MO for an attractive, stable, middle-class, now 82% black neighborhood. When they began in 1958, their area was 36% black, and in their first decade rose to 70% black. There was a time at the end of that decade when the MO was barely functioning, having lost some foundation funding and staffing, and their reason for existence. But they revived in 1972 and began to reassert themselves as an important community force. But by that time the neighborhood was predominantly black, though the MO continued to press for both quality and integration maintenance. That pressure continues to this day, with great pride in their high quality community expressed by MO participants.

Suburban MOs

Model A. I have two qualifying statements concerning success and MOs in suburban municipal efforts. Though I report here only three success stories of this type of movement effort, there are some examples of organized suburban efforts that failed—but they were not municipally sponsored and conducted. We also know of other suburbs that became predominantly black, but they were not part of this movement.

Second, applying the term MO to these suburban efforts may stretch this concept somewhat. All these efforts are municipally funded, with ongoing heavily financed programs and staffs, some directed by city employees. They did not begin as volunteer efforts, but they are nevertheless surely a part of this movement. They may, in fact, offer the greatest chance of success in achieving the movement's prime goal—stable racial integration.

The three suburban communities selected as examples of this type of movement effort were not chosen because of their unusual excellence or success in goal attainment. Rather, they are included because they are so typical of other municipally funded and supported suburban efforts. Now united through the national organization of the Oak Park Exchange Congress, these suburban integration maintenance programs share one distinction. All have local government financial and moral support for a committed, sustained effort to maintain racial diversity. All have ongoing coordinated programs designed to involve the institutional forces in the community that affect the life and death of neighborhoods. This is precisely why I think they have the greatest chance of success in this movement.

The Shaker Heights, Ohio, program is unique in that it is funded not only by the municipal government but also by the school administration. As far as I know, this is the only such program in the nation. It seems important to remember, however, that this program began as a grass-roots movement. Starting in 1957, one after another of the Shaker Heights neighborhoods formed groups to stem white flight and ghettoization. The city government of Shaker Heights then responded positively to these stabilization efforts by banning "for sale" signs, and later funding a community housing office to provide staffing and office space for this work.

At the same time, this small city of just over 30,000 people became the first in the country to voluntarily undertake a busing program to magnet schools. And finally, the school administration joined the city in funding the housing office to retain racial integration. Most recently, Shaker Heights has followed the path of Chicago fair housing and neighborhood stabilization groups in forming a metropolitan, regional approach to affirmative marketing and racial integration. They have also formed a public-private partnership to provide financial incentives for integrative moves.

Teaneck's program, also municipally funded, began too as a grass-roots integration effort, some twenty years earlier. When blacks began in the 1950s moving to this New Jersey town of 35,000, some whites fled and others who remained began stabilization efforts. The Teaneck Civic Conference of 1955, patterned after the earlier Hyde Park-Kenwood Community Conference of Chicago, was the predecessor of the 1977 municipally funded Teaneck Housing Center. In the twenty years between, the town was torn apart by the struggle for integration. They too came to eventually realize that one town could not hope to achieve stable racial integration by itself, and they joined regional efforts in affirmative marketing and racial integration.

The village of Oak Park, with 55,000 people located next to a black ghetto on the Chicago border, began to fund its nonprofit housing center with community development block grant funds when it was three years old. The center, supported also by foundation and corporate grants, used Shaker Heights, University City, Missouri, and West Mount Airy as models for its programs to ensure economic and racial stability. Oak Park's housing center has also linked its affirmative marketing efforts to a regional approach to expanding housing choices for blacks, further improving its chances for continued success in maintaining stable racial integration.

The village government aided and reinforced the center by implementing a variety of ordinances and policies directed at real estate practices, housing quality, public safety, economic strength, school racial balance, and community image. The government also initiated its renowned Equity Assurance program for homeowners, and sponsored the national exchange congress, which still serves as a forum for other municipally funded programs across the country.

Though the exchange congress was first seen as an "intrusive" MO by National Neighbors, for years the only national voice for the neighborhood stabilization movement, these two national organizations have more recently worked cooperatively and may even one day merge. We turn now to a brief summary of National Neighbors, which represents the national level of this movement. We also consider some current national issues and concerns in this movement.

THE NATIONAL LEVEL: NATIONAL NEIGHBORS

Formed in a centripetal way by MOs already in existence, National Neighbors since their inception maintained two enduring activities—annual national conferences and a newsletter, Neighbors. Their very first conference in 1969, with only twelve community groups represented, was a profound morale booster and impetus for further action on the local level. Subsequent conferences inspired the formation of new local groups, in centrifugal fashion, and affected local programs and action across the nation.

The only national action program NN ever had was Shoppers' Sunday in 1970, a testing of real estate practices in various communities. Ill-designed, poorly managed and coordinated, and altogether inadequately handled, this was nevertheless the first national real estate audit in the country. It was the forerunner of the $1 million HUD audit seven years later. It also became the motivating force behind the famed NN slogan, "Sue the Bastards!" two years later, which prompted a wave of local auditing and litigation by member groups across the nation. Another first was the winning of monetary damages by a community organization in a block-busting suit. The headline and news item about this in the Neighbors newsletter motivated other groups to try the same "fund-raising" technique.

Not only did MOs learn about the need for and strategies of litigation, they also applied for and received funding with NN's assistance. Oak Park's first funding proposal, as we noted above, used three NN member groups as resources. And Oak Park and other groups learned about these groups from NN's conferences, newsletters, and staff. Every time NN's newsletter reported the funding of another local group, this motivated others to try to get funding for themselves.

Two local community actions—bans on real estate solicitation and "for sale" signs—reported in early issues of Neighbors, affected other groups and encouraged them to try these tactics in their own communities. Another highly significant movement strategy—incentive payments for integrative moves—was first publicized by the NN at their third annual conference in 1972. The idea took hold, surfacing in other places and times across the country, finally crystallizing in 1985 in Ohio, with the first state-supported integration incentive payment program in the nation. This could grow into a bold national movement strategy in the future, with the right combination of people, politics, and perseverance. Let us continue to dream.

Publications of NN also had an impact on local groups, such as their directory of interracial neighborhoods and their booklet on racial steering. These were definite movement spurs, boosting morale, providing ideas and strategies for local action programs, and offering contacts. Additional impact on the local level came from staff and volunteer field trips, which helped form new groups, reactivate others, and strengthen the work of existing ones.

We saw that though the Ford Foundation grant greatly enhanced the work of NN, the grant conditions affected and shaped NN's program. We also saw that NN had an equally significant impact on the Ford Foundation, which came to fund other local MOs. This occurred primarily because of the foundation's repeated contact and involvement with NN leaders, and their growing understanding of the difficulties in achieving the goals of this movement.

Much of NN's impact on the local level, however, was felt during their first two phases of existence. Their program remained vigorous, as we saw, during the first two years of phase two while their first director was there. When she left, NN's program and impact dwindled, primarily because of the incredible staff turnover that plagued the organization. By the end of phase two, when their Ford Foundation funding ended in 1980, NN was very weak—financially, organizationally, programmatically, and spiritually.

Though their annual conferences and newsletters continued to have an effect on local MOs, that effect steadily declined throughout phase three. The major activity of NN's leaders in phase three was raising money to stay alive, despite repeated attempts to set goals and establish program priorities. Their earlier office move to Washington to "gain a national presence" resulted in neither a national presence nor financial solvency, since the cost of maintaining an office in the capital was one they simply could not afford. The timing of their loss of foundation funding coincided with the onset of a federal administration apathetic and destructive to the civil rights struggle. The combination of internal and external disaster factors was a miserable one.

Finally, because their president came from Cleveland and could no longer afford the time, energy, and money to travel back and forth to the Washington office, NN set up a second, Midwest office in Cleveland. Now with two offices to support, their search for funding became even more frantic. They would not give up the Washington office. And they had no funds to maintain the Midwest office. Moreover, since they now had no ongoing program with which to appeal to potential funders, their grant proposals yielded slim returns.

Beset with repeated financial crises and continuing program losses, they were further weakened by internal power struggles, which continue to this day. Miraculously, their annual conferences are still invigorating and productive. These, however, are produced by the talents and efforts of local groups, with minimal aid from NN. Their seldom-appearing newsletters, however, have decreasing utility. How long NN can go on, we do not know. They approach their twentieth year with plans for an annual conference in Washington, D.C. If they can find a local group or groups to put this event together, it will happen. And after that?

What will happen to the movement if NN dies? Probably the same thing that happened when NCDH died. The National Committee Against Discrimination in Housing—the only national organization of the fair housing movement—lost its funding from the Ford Foundation in 1987, after thirty-five years of effort. Another sign of the low priority of civil rights in the 1980s. But this sister movement's MOs, all funded fair housing agencies, have now formed a new group to take NCDH's place.[1] They will go on to provide their own forum for discussion of issues and concerns affecting movement participants. My guess is that neighborhood stabilization MOs would do the same if they lost NN.

Or, they may link themselves with the Oak Park Exchange Congress, also comprised of funded agency MOs like the fair housing movement. I know of no unfunded groups left in that movement; there are, however, many unfunded groups in this movement. Using resource mobilization theory terminology, here we would have a new "social movement industry" replacing NN as the single organizational hub of this movement.

What would this mean for the ideology, fervor, creativity, and vision of the older, unfunded MOs? With few resources, we saw they had little or no national power. Therefore, all their fervor and creativity were not able to be put to maximum use. "Only if survival is insured can other goals be pursued" (Zald & McCarthy 1987: 28). With the resources derived from some of their own funded agencies as part of the exchange congress, all the MOs, funded and unfunded, could gain strength and power in this new movement "industry." This would, however, depend on the extent of unity of purpose they could develop and their structural ability to implement this.

We have already seen how extremely difficult it was for NN to achieve a national presence, largely because of their structure. This segmentary, polycephalous, reticulate body had a board of directors from various parts of the country, who met occasionally in between annual conferences. The real work of NN as a national MO, or industry, fell on the director, who did not have the autonomy or the resources to carry it out. In all their years, NN never really worked this out. Whether a new social movement industry would succeed in doing this will have to be seen. Undoubtedly, new structural problems would arise in any new arrangement.

It may be that the Exchange Congress would do no worse than NN as a national force for this movement, and might even expand that force if they began to hold their annual conferences in Washington. There, they could take conference resolutions directly to Capitol Hill, and lobby for movement goal-enhancing actions on the spot before they went home. This would surely be no worse than NN's record, and might in fact improve it considerably as an effective national voice for this struggling movement.

In any case, ongoing efforts must continue on the local level in this movement, and here the scattered MOs need guiding policies, new ideas, and strategies to nurture and revitalize them. This is perhaps the greatest role NN has played over the years, despite their own internal weaknesses and inadequacies. Whether they continue to serve this function, or whether another organization assumes this role, it is necessary to the life of this or any movement.

Recurring Issues

On both the national and local levels of this movement, a fundamental debate simmers. It is not a new one. We saw it twenty years ago when NN first began, and we saw it surfacing periodically throughout their existence. We saw it in Indianapolis much earlier, later in Hartford and Milwaukee, and in Akron both early and late. We see it in current lawsuits of national significance involving Starrett City and south Chicago suburban fair housing agencies. We are referring in simplest terms to the meaning and intent of "stabilization" or "integration maintenance." There has not been a time in this movement when this issue has not been present.

Some refer to this issue as one of "freedom of choice" versus "integration maintenance," as if they were opposed to each other. This position suggests that efforts to maintain integration deny freedom of choice to blacks, and are thus fundamentally in conflict with fair housing laws and equal housing opportunity. The implication is that in order to preserve integration, blacks have to be restricted. My long research for this book has shown this to be a false and damaging assumption. The truth about integration maintenance is that it relies on affirmative marketing, which is an *expansion* of housing choices for all— blacks and whites alike. Affirmative marketing is a moral, effective and essential movement strategy, consistent with fair housing laws. I elaborate on this in the concluding policy section of this chapter.

Those like Starrett City, who had quotas limiting black or minority occupancy in order to preserve racial integration, have now in 1988 received the final court decision on the illegality of their programs. In fact, it was a venerable open housing agency that supported the historic suit against Starrett City, together with the NAACP. Those who have active programs of affirmative marketing, showing blacks and whites geographical areas they had not usually considered, have just received a court decision affirming their program's legality and morality.[2] But isn't affirmative marketing the same as racial steering? What is behind this whole issue?

One view is that today, in the late 1980s, the national climate is so dismal in the field of civil rights that both the Department of Justice and the National Association of Realtors have seized the moment to wipe out any integration efforts they see as nontraditional and questionable (Galster 1987; Rabin 1987). It is a fact that the original legal decision and settlement on Starrett City was a wise and fair one, but was then challenged by the Department of Justice and hauled back into court. There, the original settlement decision was overturned and the case was then lost on appeal.

That original settlement decision was wise and fair because it recognized existing entrenched racism and the intensely difficult struggle to break it by fostering stable integration. The decision of the settlement, *with all parties agreeing*, was to retain a slightly increased (37% instead of 35%) minority quota in Starrett City and to *simultaneously expand* similar area housing opportunities elsewhere. Specifically, the decision was that an additional 175 units in Starrett City's 5,800 units would be made available to minority families over the next five years. More important, eighty-six other state-supported, predominantly white housing developments in New York City would increase their minority occupancy by 20% within the next fifteen years. This would surely be an expansion of housing access for blacks throughout the metropolitan area, rather than all in one housing development. This decision was wise, just, legal, and in the best civil rights tradition. It also recognized the "precious rarity" of stable integration.

One major editorial that praised this settlement was headed "Common Sense for Starrett City," and it began this way: "In most of America, whites and minorities who go to school, work and even spend leisure time together still live in segregated neighborhoods. A housing development like Brooklyn's Starrett City is a precious rarity. The 46-building, publicly financed complex laudably sustains a commitment to racially integrated housing." The editorial continued with the statement that Starrett City maintained that commitment "only by maintaining racial quotas. Sensibly, the proposed settlement of a lawsuit challenging this practice would retain a quota and stimulate efforts to expand housing opportunities mostly in other places. . . . Regrettably but realistically, there is in integrated housing a . . . point at which whites begin to flee and leave a segregated community behind" (*New York Times*, May 6, 1984).

Understandably, blacks have been suspicious of "stabilization," "integration maintenance," and "managed integration" from the very beginning of these efforts, because of the legacy of racism they know too well.[3] Some ardent fair housing supporters have shared their concerns. I am one of those. But I also share the anguish of those who have tried to achieve stable racial integration against all odds. And, with my conclusion being that it is easier to attain integration than to maintain it, I must support programs that address both issues simultaneously. The first settlement decision for Starrett City was such a program. I deeply regret that the Department of Justice found it necessary to intervene in that case, and in the suburban Chicago case where no quotas are involved, when it has shown no such zeal in implementing fair housing laws for the last eight years. Instead of actively pursuing the countless cases of segregation and active housing discrimination in this country, they are now hounding the few models of stable integration. Thus the tenor of the national administration strongly affects movement efforts, and currently eats away at them.[4]

CONCLUSIONS

From our comparative analysis on the community level, we can see that racially transitional urban neighborhoods do not inevitably become resegregated. Whether they do or don't depends on a number of critical factors; some are related to internal organized efforts, but more are external to those efforts. We saw that racism in all study neighborhoods accounted for the initial black concentration in each city. When urban renewal in each city displaced these black enclaves, their movement to new neighborhoods was the precipitating factor leading to movement formation in each neighborhood studied.

These "defended" neighborhoods (Suttles 1972) then became "conscious communities" (Hunter 1978) committed to the goal of neighborhood stabilization—the maintenance of racial integration. They were movement organizations rather than mere interest groups because their goal was a change-oriented, nontraditional one. They were "swimming upstream" against the usual pattern of white flight and integration avoidance (Farmer, in Saltman 1977).

The mobilization of resources in each community and on the national level involved tangible and intangible sources of support (Freeman 1983). The intangible resources were found in people's skills, time, and commitment; the tangible resources were spatial, financial, and political assistance. Of the three possible strategies of persuasion, bargaining, and coercion (Wilson 1973), all MOs used the first two, and some used all three—adding coercion in lawsuits (for example, Akron, Hartford, and Milwaukee).

Though independently formed, each with no knowledge of the other until they met through National Neighbors, their specific strategies were similar since they confronted common problems that threatened their shared goal. These common problems were rooted in a legacy of racism that prevailed in each community. All the community-level MOs had a constant struggle with proposed zoning changes that threatened the nature of their existent land use. These proposed zoning changes were not trivial. In Indianapolis, for example, we recall that one proposed change would have converted the only neighborhood park in Butler-Tarkington into a parking lot. In Milwaukee, a giant freeway would have cut through the heart of the Sherman Park neighborhood. In Hartford's Blue Hills, a new public housing development would have been built in addition to the 1,400 existing units surrounding the neighborhood. In Akron, more group homes would have been added to the forty already existing within a two-mile section of their west-side neighborhood.

Besides zoning changes, all the MOs confronted real estate practices that included racial steering, block-busting, and panic selling. They all faced lending institutions reluctant to grant conventional mortgages in their racially heterogeneous neighborhoods. As a consequence, some of them became inundated with vacant houses and fast foreclosures. They all saw some or much of their commercial areas change from prosperous, well-kept, diverse, interesting, pleasant business districts to shabby and declining ones. They all watched their

schools become increasingly racially isolated. And they all experienced continuing turnover of neighbors, with the resulting loss of friends and supporters.

In response to these shared situations, it is not surprising that they developed
some common strategies. All firmly and successfully resisted zoning changes,
promoted their neighborhoods through affirmative marketing techniques, sought
rehabilitation funds for deteriorating properties, organized varied community
and recreational events, and established newspapers with mass distributions. All
promoted fair and open housing in their metropolitan regions, and all (except
Hartford) sought bans on "for sale" signs and real estate solicitation. Finally,
all worked intensively for racial balance and quality education in their public
schools.

Yet, despite these intensive efforts and their successes, we see how fragile
this movement is. We know that Hartford's MO didn't survive, and its Blue
Hills neighborhood did not remain integrated. We know, too, that even though
the MOs are still alive in Brooklyn's Prospect/Lefferts Gardens, Los Angeles's
Crenshaw area, Washington, D.C.'s northwest area, and Philadelphia's East
Mount Airy, those neighborhoods have become almost all-black. Yet the efforts
there were just as intense, and the people were just as committed, just as caring
as those in the MOs that succeeded.

Above all, we know that each of the other successful and conditional MOs
and their neighborhoods are also vulnerable. People in all of them were appre-
hensive about the future, and not at all certain that their gains would last. But
it was in Milwaukee that I first heard the term "fragile" applied to this movement.
Four days after I returned from that field visit, I wrote these reflections in my
journal: "What struck me was how many different people connected with the
organization kept referring to their achievements as 'fragile.' The same word,
used independently by different people—and repeatedly. What they meant, on
my probing, was that everything could be lost very quickly if they let down
their guard or weakened their attention." I noted, for example, that they were
distressed and disgusted about the recent flurry of real estate solicitation and
activity in their area—they had thought that battle was over. And after all their
frenzied and successful five-year efforts in stopping a freeway from going right
through their neighborhood, there was now new talk of a light rail system cutting
through their area—a new battle over an old issue.

The special fragility of this particular movement of neighborhood stabilization
stems from the sociohistorical legacy of racism. Drawing on theoretical perspectives from the field of race relations, I suggest that just as the offspring of
black-white matings are socially defined as black in this country (Lieberson
1983: 32), so too when neighborhoods become racially integrated, they initially
assume the same status that the incoming minority group has in the society at
large. As such, they—the neighborhoods—are subject to the same levels of
domination, discrimination, and segregation in the local community as the
minority group experiences in the larger society.

This occurs especially through institutional racism, which operates impersonally to foster and maintain segregation in housing, schools, and businesses. These three vital aspects of any neighborhood are interlinked in a circular pattern, so that racial change in any one of them leads to further change in the other two, and eventually to total resegregation of the neighborhood—unless dramatic intervention occurs.

This is an additive model of neighborhood change. Its cycle can be broken only with organized efforts to intercede in any one of the three interacting links. Such intervention is the substance of the neighborhood stabilization movement. But, we have seen that organized efforts—though necessary—are sometimes insufficient for achieving successful neighborhood stabilization.

Four External Factors Reconsidered

In our comparative analysis on the community level, we noted four external factors that affect a movement organization's effectiveness in achieving neighborhood stabilization. These four factors are the amenities of the neighborhood, the role of the city, the school racial composition, and public housing location. We now further divide these four factors into those that are very important, and those that are absolutely critical—the "killer variables."[5]

From our study of this movement in different places and times, there is no question about the importance of the amenities of the neighborhood. The quality and type of housing stock and any special features of interest are surely important in being able to affirmatively market the neighborhood. And we have certainly established the importance of affirmative marketing as a tool for both achieving and maintaining racial integration. So any positive amenities of the neighborhood will make it easier to market that neighborhood and attract diverse people to it. However, it does not follow that the absence of positive amenities makes it impossible to market the neighborhood.

In this day of slick public relations, it is not always necessary to have an item of high quality in order to sell it as such. I am suggesting, then, that a reasonably decent neighborhood with no special features can still be sold and marketed affirmatively.[6] The factor of amenities is an important one, but I do not believe it alone is critical to the success of this movement in any one community. Any fairly adequate neighborhood can still be successfully marketed to both whites and blacks, provided some other conditions are present.

The second external factor—the role of the city—I also classify as very important, but not critical. As with amenities, it is far better to have than not to have city support, but I believe it is still possible to have success on the local level of this movement even without city help. Their cooperation and special nurturing policies and programs can most surely benefit the local movement effort, but they are not essential. Looking at our study of failure and five conditional examples, we see that the reasons for the failure were not particularly related to the role of the city, although it would indeed have been comforting and helpful in Hartford and Akron to have some special nurturing actions taken by the city for neighborhood stabilization.

Examining each of our movement success stories in the urban neighborhoods of Indianapolis, Rochester, Milwaukee, Denver, Nashville, and Philadelphia, we can see that success would undoubtedly have occurred there even without city support. And this is so because of the presence in each of these communities of the two other external factors. Because I believe these are absolutely essential to local success in the movement, I call these two other external factors "killer variables." Without these, I maintain that the movement for neighborhood stabilization cannot succeed in any community. I refer, of course, to system-wide school desegregation and the deconcentration of public housing.

In each of our success examples, we found a systemwide school desegregation program. In our failure and conditional examples this was absent. The reason this is a critical factor is that affirmative marketing of an integrated neighborhood cannot occur effectively without it. Unless racial balance is empirically present in a neighborhood's public schools, a majority of whites with children will not perceive that neighborhood as a desirable one and will not move into it. We have countless studies that verify this.[7] The smaller number of whites who may be persuaded to move into a neighborhood having predominantly black schools would simply not be enough to maintain the racial integration of the neighborhood. The presence of a systemwide school desegregation program removes from the target integrated neighborhood the onus of having a racially identifiable black school or schools. Since that integrated neighborhood is then no different from any other in the school system, affirmative marketing can proceed with maximum potential for success.

In summary, a systemwide program for achieving and maintaining school racial balance affects the racially integrated neighborhood in this movement positively in five ways. First, the integrated neighborhood is no longer identified as "the one with black schools," since blacks are now distributed equitably in schools throughout the city, or metropolitan area, depending on the unit of the system. Second, there is a greater incentive for whites with children to move into the integrated neighborhood, since the schools there are not substantially different from those in other neighborhoods. Third, there is less reason for whites with children to move out of the integrated neighborhood, since wherever they might move within the region there is likely to be some integration in the schools.[8] Fourth, there is renewed hope for stabilization success within the MO, and a greater motivation to push for whatever is needed to further achieve this. Fifth, the chances for organizational survival and retention of the original goal are greater, and the chance for ultimate success in maintaining integration is thereby greater.

The other killer variable—deconcentration of public housing—operates in much the same way as school desegregation. Because of the common *perception* of public housing as associated with poverty, welfare, and blackness,[9] a concentration of public housing in a neighborhood will make it impossible to effectively and affirmatively market that neighborhood. In each of the success examples, we found no evidence of public housing concentration. In Milwaukee and Denver, however, there were such situations developing, and steps were being taken to correct this.

In the failure and some conditional examples, there were repeated situations of public housing concentration. Though not having public housing concentration in a target neighborhood certainly does not guarantee success in this movement, having it almost surely does insure failure.[10] That is why it is one of the two "killers" for this movement. And with both killer variables present in a neighborhood, the only possibility for avoiding failure in this movement is to have one of those two situations change. Of the two, I believe the school situation is the more critical.

With these four external factors in mind, we now turn to the policy implications of our findings, and a suggested comprehensive strategy for achieving success in this fragile movement.

IMPLICATIONS FOR SOCIAL POLICY AND STRATEGIES FOR SOCIAL CHANGE

The policy implications of these findings are clear. An interventionist approach is necessary, and the timing is critical. Massive affirmative intervention must occur before the neighborhood is racially identifiable, or the chance of success will be minimal. Such intervention would be designed to focus on the three links of the additive process, to strengthen the MO, and to enable affirmative marketing to work most effectively for maintaining racial integration.

But we know that only focusing on a single neighborhood will not be effective. We must attack the racism and segregation in the larger community in order to reduce it in the smaller one. Therefore, I divide these strategies into external and internal ones, according to whether they take place in the neighborhood or outside of it. I offer four comprehensive external, regional strategies and three internal ones for intervening positively in the struggle to maintain neighborhood racial integration. I also offer examples of creative strategies that have succeeded elsewhere.

External Strategies

Coordination of Housing and School Metropolitan Planning. Especially critical in any policy implementation would be the coordination of school and housing strategies. As many others have noted (Orfield 1981; *Society* 1979), school and housing policies and patterns interact at many levels. We need only to search the real estate ads in any local newspaper to see how often the schools are noted in the housing ads. While it is true that originally it was segregated neighborhoods that led to segregated schools, this causal sequence has been reversed. People, especially those with children, now choose their neighborhoods on the basis of the *perceived* quality of the schools (Hochschild 1984; Orfield 1984; Pearce 1981; *Society* 1979). And their perception of quality is strongly associated with the racial composition of the schools. They do this not only because of their concern for their children's education and social contacts, but also because of their perception of the resale value of their homes. And as we know from W. I. Thomas's old sociological dictum about self-fulfilling prophecies, "if people believe situations are real, then they are real in their consequences."

Potential policy changes affecting housing and schools involve many agencies and interests. In most cities across this nation, city and regional planners and school authorities do not work together on matters that vitally affect them and their constituents (Orfield 1984). It is essential that they do so for the success of this movement, and for some simple justice and humanity toward the people affected by their decisions. Such matters would include highway construction, homesteading, regional mobility plans, public housing site location, new construction, demolitions, and neighborhood rehabilitation. Any situations that involve the shifting of people because of city or school actions should be considered in tandem by both sets of authorities. And here is where our four external factors come together. Let us consider the impact of the following four examples of coordinated comprehensive strategies involving two or more of these four factors.

First is the Cleveland, Ohio suburban, regional approach linking municipal governments and public school authorities in a joint program to achieve and maintain racial integration in neighborhoods and schools (ESCOC). Funded substantially by a local foundation in 1985, it is modeled after the much older Chicago suburban regional effort (now in court), but is potentially even stronger than that one since the Cleveland area program includes the schools. This, indeed, recognizes the crucial link and reciprocal effect of neighborhoods and schools. And it is an outgrowth of the realization in Shaker Heights that they could not retain their success in integration maintenance unless they expanded into a regional program. This is precisely the same realization that occurred earlier in the Chicago area, where thousands of minority families have moved to the suburbs under the Gautreaux program.[11] Thus, a combination of several institutional forces and a broad geographical approach are necessary for success in this movement.

A second example of a comprehensive regional strategy is the one in Louisville, Kentucky, which links schools, neighborhoods, and public housing. Conducted by the state-funded Kentucky Commission on Human Rights, this program began in 1976 immediately after the county school system had been ordered by the courts to desegregate. It ties housing desegregation to school desegregation. The director of the commission, who designed this strategy, first produced a clever little pamphlet called *Six Ways to Avoid Busing*, which actually focused on expanded housing choices throughout the county. "If you lived here or here, your child wouldn't have to ride the bus" was the message to parents. Then, he set up an escort service to assist minority homeseekers in searching for housing in unfamiliar suburban areas. Finally, he worked with the local public housing authority to find 1,500 scattered Section 8 housing units through the county, and encouraged low-income minority families to apply for these. This program has been in effect more than ten years, and it works. In the first three years, six hundred black families moved to the suburbs of Louisville, Kentucky as a result of this creative comprehensive strategy (Kentucky Commission on Human Rights 1983).

A third example of a creative regional strategy, focusing only on housing this time, is the Minority Broker Program of Washington. This was a joint effort of the regional Council of Governments and the Washington Area Board of Realtors and Realtists' Association, which gave matching funds to the Ford Foundation-funded project. Together, they recruited, trained and employed forty minority brokers in suburban real estate offices throughout the Washington, D.C. metropolitan area. Knowing that minority brokers have major access to black homeseekers, they paved the way for expanding housing choices—through skilled affirmative marketing—for minorities in the Washington, D.C. area.

This was an innovative real estate training program, far different from the traditional one in most communities, which simply advises minority brokers to work in the neighborhoods they are most familiar with. We all know which neighborhoods those are: primarily black or substantially integrated neighborhoods—the legacy of the dual housing market. This has the effect of racial steering, though not the intent. So the Washington program, in contrast, paved the way for expanded housing choices for blacks in that area by recruiting minority brokers to work in outlying nontraditional areas, and training and assisting them in affirmative marketing techniques when they got out there (Ford Foundation 1978).

Finally, our fourth example of a comprehensive regional strategy, again focusing only on housing, is the Ohio Bonus for Integrative Moves. This program, conducted by the Ohio Housing Finance Agency (OHFA), was the result of two and a half years of intensive negotiating effort conducted by fair housing and neighborhood groups throughout the state. Finally, OHFA agreed in July 1985 to set aside 10% of their $20-million state mortgage revenue bond program for buyers making integrative moves. The bond program was for first-time home-buyers, and the set-aside was to be a demonstration program in the Cleveland area, and then expanded to other Ohio areas.

After a massive publicity and counseling effort by the fair housing and neighborhood groups involved in the Cleveland program, 81% of the mortgage applicants made integrative moves. Half of these were black. Three different suburbs and their neighborhoods and schools, formerly all-white, became racially integrated because of this program. And other integrated neighborhoods and schools were stabilized with the move-ins of white homebuyers (Metropolitan Strategy 1987).

Though this Ohio state program gave the financial incentives directly to the homebuyer, other types of bonus programs could offer financial incentives to real estate agents whose clients make integrative moves. These and other types of incentive payments were suggested in 1982 in the Los Angeles City Council (Farrell-Ferraro Resolution), and much earlier in 1972 at a NN annual conference, as we recall. Lenders and insurance companies, too, could be drawn into this strategy by offering them financial incentives for giving conventional mortgages and insurance in racially integrated neighborhoods. The objective is to change the norm by making it financially worthwhile to assist communities in remaining racially integrated in their neighborhoods and schools.

We see the common factors in each of these four successful strategies: use of affirmative marketing techniques to expand housing choices, involvement of several key institutional forces, and a metropolitan approach. We must note here the ever-present need to show institutional leaders why it is important and desirable to maintain stable racially integrated neighborhoods. The fact that such neighborhoods have been written into three national laws, two executive orders, and three Supreme Court decisions[12] may not be convincing enough.

One effective way to make this point is to cite the costs of racial segregation— not just to the blacks involved, but to the whole community (Leadership Council 1987). If segregated blacks have higher dropout rates from school, lower lifetime earnings, and higher unemployment rates, this hurts everyone. And if segregated neighborhoods result in divided, weakened, and isolated communities, facilities, and resources, we all pay the price. Also, if segregated neighborhoods and schools make it more difficult to attract businesses and investment to the city and the downtown, everyone loses there too. This may be the most strategic argument to gain the support of community decision makers in the struggle for neighborhood stabilization.

Perhaps the most compelling study that confirms the cost of racial segregation in neighborhoods and schools is a recently completed Hartford study. Financed by the National Institute of Education (1986), this longitudinal study shows the tremendous positive effects of desegregated schooling on inner-city black children. The study examined the adult lives of 661 black students who were in school from 1966 to 1970. Of these students, carefully matched as to family backgrounds and socioeconomic levels, 318 went to predominantly white schools and 343 remained in black schools as part of Hartford's Project Concern.

What happened to these children? Those who went to the predominantly white schools were significantly more successful as adults academically, economically, occupationally, and socially than those who stayed in black schools. Those who went to predominantly white schools had a higher rate of college attendance, completed more years of college, had fewer incidents with police, fewer fights as adults, had fewer children by the age of eighteen, and were more likely to live in integrated neighborhoods as adults.

This is a most powerful argument for ending racial isolation in schools and neighborhoods, and might even seem compelling to municipal officials and other institutional leaders. Such officials and institutional decision makers also need to be reminded that ending racial isolation is strongly supported by laws and federal regulations, even if they are not currently enforced. What are some of the laws which support this goal? Title 8 of the Civil Rights Act of 1968, which we all know as the national Fair Housing Act, provides for fair housing and freedom of housing choice throughout the United States.

Less well-known is the fact that in addition to free housing choice, the goal of the fair housing act is "to replace ghettos with truly integrated and balanced living patterns for persons of all races" (*Zuch v. Hussey* 1975). This goal is confirmed and reinforced by Executive Order 11063. It is also reconfirmed and expanded in the Housing and Community Development Act of 1974, which has provided millions of dollars for downtown development (UDAG) programs in recent years. This act calls for "promoting maximum choice within the community's total housing supply, lessening racial and economic concentrations and isolation, and facilitating desegregation and racially inclusive and diverse neighborhoods and use of public facilities, through the spatial deconcentration of housing opportunities" (U.S. Commission on Civil Rights 1979: 8). This is very clear and unequivocal.

In addition, the federal regulations of the act state that HUD will consider the following three factors in determining if a community has achieved "reasonable results" in providing equal housing opportunities: (1) the extent to which housing units promote the geographical dispersal of minority families outside areas of minority concentration; (2) whether housing choice is being promoted in all neighborhoods through participation in an area-wide affirmative marketing effort or other fair housing activities; (3) whether relocation has expanded housing opportunities for minorities outside areas of minority concentration. The fact that HUD did not implement these regulations during the Reagan administration is less significant, perhaps, than the fact that these principles are there. They are embedded in laws and regulations which are enforceable. The tools are there. The sanctions are there.

Now that we may have the ear of municipal and institutional leaders, let us consider what else might be done externally to help achieve stable, racially integrated neighborhoods. Additional external efforts in a public-private partnership should include strengthening *regional* fair housing programs, providing an adequate supply of housing for people of all income levels throughout the metropolitan area, and securing social impact statements that cite the effect of governmental expenditures on housing and school integration maintenance.

Strengthening Regional Fair Housing Programs. Elsewhere, I and others have written extensively about the need for ongoing auditing of housing availability for blacks.[13] It is not enough to do an annual audit to satisfy local funding requirements. The auditing must be continual, at the very least monthly, for old and new housing opportunities, both sales and rentals, and throughout the metropolitan area. And conducting the audit is not enough. The preparation for the audit, the training of the auditors and supervisors, the meticulous analysis of the audit results, and the careful dissemination of those results are critical for the success of this important tool in achieving fair housing.

There is little question of the importance of an ongoing, vigilant, regional fair housing program to the success of the neighborhood stabilization movement. Since racial steering is one of the surest ways of destabilizing racially integrated neighborhoods, its reduction and elimination must be sought. Ongoing auditing, analysis, dissemination of results, and litigation, or the threat of it, is the surest way to uncover and reduce racial steering in any area.

Let us here consider the difference between steering and affirmative marketing, a point which has often been misunderstood.[14] Affirmative marketing encourages people of the race least likely to consider moving to an area to do so. This would mean blacks to white areas and whites to integrated ones. The move would be to a nontraditional area for that racial group. Steering, on the other hand, encourages those most likely to move to an area to do so. This would mean whites to white areas and blacks to black or integrated ones. The move would be to a traditional area for that racial group. Affirmative marketing is supported by law, results in an integrative move, and expands housing choice. Steering is against the law, results in a segregative move, and restricts housing choice. The difference between the two is fundamental. Referring to affirmative marketing as "reverse steering" or even "benign steering," as some have done, is simply incorrect. It is like saying a fish is a chicken without legs.

In addition to ongoing auditing and vigorous exposure of results, regional mobility programs and incentive payments could be administered by effective funded and staffed regional fair housing agencies. In the 1970s, regional mobility programs were part of HUD-funded housing assistance programs. Though dormant now, they could be resurrected under a new administration, and could then be implemented by regional fair housing organizations in conjunction with local MOs and public housing authorities. Likewise, state funding for incentive payments for integrative moves could be administered by regional fair housing groups, in cooperation with neighborhood stabilization groups and public housing authorities.

The funding for the fair housing groups currently comes from local, regional, state, and federal sources, as well as some private foundations and corporations. The reason for the continuing funding, despite national apathy and inaction on civil rights issues during the eight Reagan years, is the local official recognition that a city might lose federal funding for a wide variety of development programs if it does not show some official support of fair housing. The simplest way of doing that is to fund a local fair housing group. Whether that group is effective or not is another question, and one which I have considered elsewhere (Saltman 1978). Such funding is, nevertheless, one of the supreme enduring gains of the fair housing movement. This is an important issue, because it paves the way for neighborhood stabilization group funding. We see here the vertical links that affect local communities, and impinge on this movement.

A most important adjunct to regional mobility programs and integration incentive payments is the involvement of public housing authorities. Not only are public housing units concentrated in certain locations in all metropolitan areas across the nation, they are also notoriously racially segregated. Few exceptions exist.[15] Regional mobility programs involving public housing tenants, such as was done in Louisville, Kentucky, should be implemented everywhere. And they, too, should receive incentive payments for integrative moves. These could be in the form of paid utilities, reduced rent for a stipulated time, free rent for the first two months, or cash bonuses. Since public housing location has an impact on neighborhoods and schools, and since existing public housing policies and practices have resulted in racially segregated units all over the country, they must be part of any comprehensive strategy to bring about constructive change.[16]

Regional Housing Supply for All Income Levels. This, too, is an important related issue. If the only housing available for low- and moderate-income people is in the inner city, and if there are greater proportions of black people who are in those income categories, this relegates large numbers of poor blacks to the inner city, with racially segregated results for both neighborhoods and schools. This must change. One way to provide an adequate supply of housing for people of all income levels throughout the metropolitan area is through fair share programs, such as those implemented in the Dayton, Ohio metropolitan area.[17]

This is done through the cooperation of suburban governments and jurisdictions within a metropolitan area. Such a program begins with a determination of the total need for housing within a defined housing market area, based on criteria of land availability, facility of employment access, and other pertinent factors such as sewers, drainage, transportation, and school facilities. The housing is then allocated by number of units of various types and prices to the various parts of the planning jurisdiction. Within five years of the time the Dayton Plan began, over twenty-five other metropolitan areas undertook housing allocation planning. Though only about half of these plans were officially adopted, and though it takes years to reach the point where the jurisdictions agree on their "fair share," this still remains a valuable and needed strategy to reduce racial isolation in metropolitan regions. In Dayton, for example, more than 7,000 housing units were built in a five-county area that previously had no minority or moderate-income residents. These counties for the first time experienced racial integration in their neighborhoods and schools.

Social Impact Statements. Our fourth and last external strategy for social change is securing social impact statements from all levels of government for any expenditures they make. There must be a public commitment from government officials at all levels—local, county, regional, state, and federal—that government money will not be used to promote or sustain racial segregation. Not in neighborhoods, not in schools, not in shopping areas, not in recreational areas. Not from highway construction, urban renewal, public housing, or any other housing construction.

Any use of government money, on any level, should be accompanied by a social impact statement as to the effect of that project on racial segregation in neighborhoods and schools. If we can require such impact statements for environmental agencies, why not with any other government funding? Surely neighborhoods and schools are also vital parts of the environment? Local, regional, state, and federal officials should announce and implement a mandate that all relevant government spending must be supported by an impact statement detailing how those expenditures will decrease existing residential and school segregation and increase residential and school integration in any given community or region. All the laws exist to legally support this action; this is just one way of implementing them.

One tactical tool that relates to this strategy is found in regional intergovernmental reviews, formerly A–95 reviews. These involve community organizations and funded agencies, and offer an opportunity to those citizen groups to review any applications for federal funding within their region. The application summaries are distributed by a regional agency, with provisions for citizen acceptance or rejection of such future funding. Though most citizen groups do not respond, or routinely accept these proposals, this is an opportunity for more thoughtful groups to reject some and state why (see Appendix C).

For example, if a public housing authority wishes to purchase more land in a specified area to build more public housing units, an effective response from a citizen group might be: "No. This location is already oversaturated with public housing units. Government money must not be used to foster or maintain racial segregation." Or: "Tell us how you plan to make and keep these units racially integrated." This simple device has, in fact, stopped some powerful interests from securing federal funding, at least in the days when the federal government paid attention to it.[18]

That day will come again, we fervently hope. Meanwhile, such statements alert the agencies wanting the funding, as well as those giving the funding, and also those reviewing the comments, about the continuing issue of racial segregation and its harmful effects on neighborhoods and schools. Requiring social impact statements of all applicants for government funds would be an important and helpful strategy for this movement and for the general civil rights movement.

Internal Strategies

Within the target stabilization neighborhood, there are three general ways to facilitate integration maintenance. These internal methods are extensive affirmative marketing campaigns, special programs to achieve and preserve quality and stability, and MO assistance. These alone might be successful in some communities, but for maximum long-term impact and more enduring success, they should be implemented in conjunction with the external strategies.

Affirmative Marketing. Clearly, the common denominator for both external and internal strategies is affirmative marketing, which we defined and explained earlier as encouraging homeseekers of a race least likely to consider an area to do so. Specifically, affirmative marketing involves an expansion of housing choice for everyone, since whites are encouraged to seek housing in integrated areas, and blacks are encouraged to seek housing in white areas. Each of these would be a nontraditional move for those involved. This is a corrective attempt to counteract hundreds of prior years of racial steering and denial of housing opportunity. It may be the single most important tool for neighborhood stabilization.

Affirmative marketing must ultimately involve the entire housing industry—real estate practitioners, lenders, appraisers, and insurers. These are the same institutional forces that affect fair housing, and indeed fair housing and affirmative marketing are significantly related. They complement and reinforce each other. Fair housing law supports and requires affirmative marketing. And affirmative marketing is a tool to achieve fair housing as well as integrated neighborhoods. It is an extremely effective way of eliminating the dual housing market, implementing fair housing laws, and maintaining integrated neighborhoods.

Unfortunately, it is a concept not well understood by many in those very institutions that are involved. The misunderstanding has been increased by HUD's VAMA program, which has consistently equated affirmative marketing with freedom of choice in housing.[19] Given the long, painful legacy of denial of choice for blacks, and of racial steering for whites and blacks in this country, merely extending free choice will do nothing to counteract the past. "The right to open housing means more than the right to move from an old ghetto to a new one" (Zuch v. Hussey, 1975). Much more is needed to diminish the effects of the past before mere freedom of choice can be enough. "Because of racism in this nation's culture, the nation would continue to be segregated if left to freedom of choice alone" (Farmer, in Saltman 1977). Freedom of choice in housing is not enough now for most homeseekers—black or white—given the extent of racial steering and discrimination that persists in our society. We must go beyond it. Affirmative marketing is that step beyond.

Educating local real estate, appraising, and lending industries with affirmative marketing seminars is the first step in an extensive affirmative marketing campaign.[20] A second part of this effort would be preparing and distributing printed promotional materials on nontraditional neighborhood choices for blacks, along with a different set for whites.[21] A third program focus would be dealing with the minority agent issue, noted above (Ford Foundation 1978). A fourth would concentrate on mortgage lending practices in integrating neighborhoods.[22] And a fifth focus would be on appraisers and insurers and corporate personnel managers.[23] Each of these institutional forces has in the past played a devastating role in racially integrated neighborhoods across this country. They must be brought into a partnership to promote and maintain those very kinds of neighborhoods they helped to destroy in the past.

But, in order to affirmatively market a neighborhood, it should be worth marketing. This brings us to special programs to improve the physical quality, security, safety, and racial balance of integrated neighborhoods.

Special Programs for Special Neighborhoods. Three types of neighborhood programs would greatly enhance any affirmative marketing efforts in those neighborhoods. These are not new in concept or design. First, maintenance of quality housing, lawns, streets, and business areas is important in retaining existing residents and attracting new ones. I am referring to clean, well-kept units, including any that may be vacant. This seems a simple matter, yet it is inadequately handled in many cities and thus paves the way for many shoddy neighborhoods. These cannot be successfully marketed, whether they are or are not racially integrated. But our concern is with the integrated neighborhood, which has an especially difficult marketing task. It is essential for cities to enforce their housing, building and zoning codes and to pass bond issues creating low-cost home improvement loans and grants for residents in those neighborhoods. Many other programs for housing maintenance and rehabilitation are available, but these are not within the scope of this study.[24]

In addition to physical quality, we must also focus on social quality, which involves security. Neighborhood safety and low crime rates are surely one aspect of neighborhood quality. It is a fact that the *perception* of crime is higher in racially integrated neighborhoods than in one-race neighborhoods.[25] This is one more stubborn remnant of racism. Any affirmative marketing effort must take this into account, and must be able at least to point to specific safety or crime prevention projects that exist in the target neighborhood.[26] These are special neighborhoods, and they require special physical and social maintenance programs to assist them in overcoming past inequities. City and state governments can and should be drawn into a partnership with neighborhood MOs to preserve and promote such neighborhoods.

Second, in addition to physical quality and security, racial balance in schools and business areas must be sought and maintained. We have already named the schools as a killer variable in the struggle for neighborhood stabilization. But achieving school racial balance is not easy in any community. Some school authorities and funding structures are much more amenable than others to plans for racial balance. Much depends, too, on the state board of education's mandate for reducing racial isolation. We saw this in contrasting Rochester with Akron and Hartford.

There is little question about the advantage of a metropolitan or system-wide plan for achieving school racial balance (Hochschild 1984). But legal decisions[27] have made it virtually impossible to obtain cross-district desegregation programs, and some communities have already been to court and lost even the possibility of a citywide program. What can a neighborhood do to affirmatively market itself if it has the only racially identifiable black school cluster in the city?[28]

One possible solution is to enlist the aid of the local school board in opening a citywide elementary magnet school in their neighborhood, emphasizing a special curriculum (creative arts, science, basics, and so on). This would be by application only, with public assurance of racial balance, and with massive publicity about the excellence of the academic program. Once parents from all over town are beating down the doors to get their children into the new program, a second elementary magnet school could be opened in the same neighborhood a year or two later, emphasizing a different academic program.

This strategy has worked in a number of communities, and offers promise as one way of improving the perception of the target neighborhood and its schools.[29] One tactical way of motivating local school authorities to do this is for an MO or some other nonprofit organization to write a magnet school grant proposal to a foundation or other funding source. They do of course let the local school authorities know they are doing this, and even seek their advice in preparing the grant proposal. Since most local school authorities would find it embarrassing to have an outside group funded to do a school-related program, they might be inspired to write and submit such a proposal independently in order to get the money and control themselves. This, in fact, happened in Akron, though not for an elementary magnet.[30] We emphasize the elementary level, because research has shown this is most desirable for the children involved (Hochschild 1984). It is also obviously the most strategic way of encouraging new people to look at and move into the target neighborhood.

Achieving racial balance in the business district of a racially integrated neighborhood also requires special, intensive, affirmative marketing efforts. But again we must have something worthwhile to market. Once the good physical quality of storefronts and businesses and their streets is obtained and maintained, the second concern here too is security. The neighborhood safety program should include the business area, and also the churches, for maximum effectiveness in actual crime prevention. Meanwhile, special efforts must be made to attract and retain businesses in the target neighborhood that cater to both a white and black clientele. Once the business district is perceived as black only, this will seriously weaken any possibility of successfully marketing the rest of the neighborhood to both whites and blacks (Clay & Hollister 1983; Aldrich & Reiss 1976).

A final special program for our special neighborhood would be one that alleviates any fears about financial loss on resale, and at the same time promotes stability. Such a program is an equity assurance program, now operating in Oak Park, Illinois, one of our municipal suburban examples. This is a local government program that reimburses residents for up to 80% of any losses incurred in the sale of their homes after five years. It is a model for integrated communities faced with potential flight of their existing homeowners.

The only cost to residents who enroll in the program is that of a property appraisal by a certified appraiser approved by local government officials. This is about $100, but could be reduced to half by having the homes appraised in groups. The money to pay for the program would be about $300,000 a year, obtained from tax revenues. Most of the money would go to a cash pool for reimbursing homeowners, as needed. The theory behind this program is that if a municipality can guarantee that housing values will not drop below a certain level in an integrated neighborhood, panic selling will not occur, affirmative marketing can succeed, and racial integration and stability can be maintained.

MO Support. It should be apparent by now that the lifeline of integrated neighborhoods is found in indigenous movement organizations devoted to stabilization. Residents respond to such organizations with a trust and motivation that makes it possible to effect small and large changes that might not happen otherwise.

But the problem with many such groups is that they lack adequate day-to-day coordination of their programs. Some minimal municipal and state funding should be provided to enable such organizations to continue to exist more effectively. It is they who should be given the subcontracts to carry out all or some of the programs outlined above. In addition, they should be assisted with funding source information and technical assistance in writing grant proposal applications, to better enable them to obtain additional funding from nongovernmental sources. This is a critical skill often lacking in MOs.

In the fall of 1976, the National Neighborhood Policy Act was passed by Congress. It was the first piece of legislative action since the middle sixties that tried to define the needs of our urban neighborhoods. That act included this statement: "City neighborhoods are a national resource to be conserved and revitalized wherever possible. Public policy should promote that objective." This is true for all neighborhoods, whether racially integrated or not. Any neighborhood organization is a critical link between often isolated individuals and the larger mass society. The neighborhood organization is a buffer between the little folks and city hall, the schools, or any other large formal structure. The neighborhood organization gives people a sense of belonging and a sense of community that is often missing in our hurried, impersonal urban life. The neighborhood organization can provide a helping hand and problem-solving mechanism.

Building up a sense of community in a neighborhood and developing the capacity for effective problem-solving is important for the welfare of the entire city and region. For healthy neighborhoods make healthy cities and metropolitan regions—they create an atmosphere where businesses can flourish, and where government can provide needed services and facilities for its people. This is so important that it should be the foundation of an enlightened and meaningful national neighborhood policy—as well as a wise local governmental policy.

But if this is true of neighborhoods in general, what shall we say of the integrated neighborhood? Here we have a special phenomenon. Though all neighborhoods are products of their history, integrated neighborhoods are products of a national history that makes them an endangered species. Spawned by a legacy of racism which created black enclaves in each central city, displaced by urban renewal and shunted by denial of free choice to other neighborhoods, there met by small stalwart bands of idealists fired by the wish to welcome and remain side by side with them, such neighborhoods must surely be considered a national treasure. They are the living result of the civil rights movement.

Are they not worth saving? Might this not be the final payment of retribution by a government that was chiefly responsible for their plight? Logically, since government was one of the first institutional forces responsible for both racial concentration and then racial displacement through urban renewal, it should be government—at all levels—that becomes the major force responsible for undoing its past effects. This could be done in cooperation with adequately funded MOs on the local level.

Our neighborhood link with the vertical chain ends here. A renewed national policy focusing on neighborhoods is necessary, and a special national, state, and local policy cherishing and preserving the endangered species—the integrated neighborhood—is urgently needed. This integrated neighborhood must be nurtured and cared for. The role of the public sector is to initiate this process, to implement the external and internal programs outlined above. This would create a national, regional, and local civil rights environment that encourages the maintenance of integrated neighborhoods through private and public sector investment, and a commitment matching that of residents and their movement organizations.

We have seen that the maintenance of an integrated urban neighborhood is not likely with only a neighborhood movement organization at work—no matter how dedicated, creative, and effective it may be. An MO is a necessary but insufficient condition for success. It is clear that external forces and institutional processes affect all neighborhoods, and that these must be included in any strategies for neighborhood stabilization. Specific policies to achieve stabilization of urban integrated neighborhoods depend on these seven conditions:

External

1. Coordinated school and housing strategies to maintain racial balance.
2. Funding of a metropolitan fair housing agency, with well-designed regional mobility programs and incentive payments for integrative moves.
3. Provision of an adequate supply of housing for people of all income levels throughout the metropolitan area.
4. Public commitment by city, county, state, and federal officials for neighborhood integration maintenance, with social impact statements required for all relevant government expenditures.

Internal

5. Encouragement of stable racial balance in the neighborhood through extensive affirmative marketing campaigns.
6. Implementation of special physical, social, and financial programs in these special neighborhoods for maximum affirmative marketing effectiveness.

   a) Maintenance of physical quality and safety of housing, streets, and businesses to insure pride in the area as a desirable integrated neighborhood for existing and potential residents.

   b) Provision of financial assurance to alleviate fears of loss of equity on resale.

7. Funding of neighborhood MOs to enable them to function more securely and effectively in conducting stabilization programs.

These conditions are essential to counteract all the previous years of stereotyping and misconception about racially integrated neighborhoods. These

efforts are urgently needed because of the sociohistorical past of these neighborhoods. They have unique histories, and require unique programs to overcome
past practices, policies, and perceptions. Together, public and private sectors,
local MOs and the national MO should mount a vigilant ongoing effort to
influence the major institutional networks dealing with housing, schools, and
businesses. The understanding and cooperation of these institutional forces must
be secured to achieve constructive changes in policies and practices affecting
the life and death of integrated neighborhoods.

As we have seen, such integration is maintained with enormous difficulty.
Special and extraordinary efforts are required to sustain it. Whether such efforts
will receive the necessary commitment and support will determine the future
of our urban neighborhoods—and will tell us whether this nation made a constitutional promise it cannot keep.

NOTES

1. This is called the National Alliance of Fair Housing Organizations.
2. *Greater South Suburban Board of Realtors and NAR v. South Suburban Housing
Center* (1984).
3. See, for example, Leigh & McGhee 1986, and Lake & Winslow 1981 for minority
perspectives on this issue.
4. The most recent example of this in Akron is HUD's refusal in December 1988
to allow the AMHA to enter into a voluntary desegregation plan with the fair housing
service and West Side Neighbors.
5. This term was coined by Anthony Downs; I first heard it used by James Hudson
of Penn State at an annual meeting of the American Sociological Association in Washington, D.C., August 1985. There, Hudson referred to Downs's three "killer variables"
in neighborhood upgrading: mixed land use, high rise public housing, and distance from
central city.
6. Evidence of this is seen, for example, in Milwaukee's Sherman Park, where their
predominantly white section has no special amenities and very modest housing, yet
maintains a high demand.
7. Orfield (1985: 192), for example, states: "Schools change racial composition before
neighborhoods, and racially identifiable schools become key factors in ending the migration of white families to integrated areas." Among others who have cited the schools
as significant factors in housing choices are Hochschild 1984; Taylor 1981; Foley 1973;
and thirty-seven additional social scientists in *Society* (1979).
8. This is especially true in a countywide system.
9. National opinion surveys show that Americans think most people on welfare are
black, and public attitudes associate public housing with welfare (HEW 1970, 1972).
10. I would qualify this by distinguishing among the various types of public housing,
that is, scattered-site, leased, Section 8, family projects, and elderly projects. Since
elderly projects are almost always predominantly white, it is possible that this type of
public housing might not adversely affect an integrating neighborhood. It is also possible
that the rare example of a racially balanced and maintained and well-kept family project
might overcome the usual negative perceptions. But public housing segregation being

what it is and has been, and public perception of it being what it is and has been, any concentration of it will continue to be a "killer variable" for an integrating neighborhood.

11. For details on this court-mandated program, see HUD's *Gautreaux Housing Demonstration*, Washington, D.C., 1979.

12. See Potomac Institute 1976 and U.S. Commission on Civil Rights 1975 for a detailed account of these laws.

13. Saltman, 1975, 1977, 1978, 1979; Keating et al. 1987; Galster 1986; and Yinger 1984.

14. This is true on both local and national levels. Even at a recent National Neighbors conference in Philadelphia (June 1988), I heard real estate agents refer to affirmative marketing as "reverse steering." The same misconception exists among realtors in Akron, where I learned that a realtor serving with me on CHRB thought that affirmative marketing involved quotas.

15. One such notable exception is Providence, Rhode Island's Valley View Homes (*Nation*, April 9, 1977).

16. See National Housing Task Force 1988; Jones et al. 1988; Kofron & Mendelson 1988; and Kivisto 1986.

17. See Saltman 1977 for more details, and Miami Valley Regional Planning Commission, *Housing Plan for the Miami Valley Region*, 1970.

18. See Appendix C for Akron's West Side Neighbors' notice of intent to file social impact statements.

19. The Voluntary Affirmative Marketing Agreement is a major ingredient of the Community Housing Resources Boards established by HUD in 1980 to develop cooperative relations between real estate practitioners and fair housing agencies and advocates.

20. West Side Neighbors' UPON project in Akron used this approach.

21. Each promotional effort must be aimed at the racial group least likely to seek housing in a particular geographical area.

22. Neighborhood groups throughout the country have used the Home Mortgage Disclosure Act and the Credit Reinvestment Act to secure data to study lending patterns in their own areas, and then to pressure lending institutions to invest more equitably in their communities (Saltman 1980).

23. Insurance studies are now increasing, and should be an important future focus in neighborhood stabilization (see Squires and Velez 1987, and DeWolfe 1981; HUD's *Insurance Crisis in Urban America*, 1978, and *Full Insurance Availability*, 1974). Appraisers and corporate personnel have not yet been targeted for serious affirmative marketing efforts, but they should be as they too play a vital role in where people choose to live.

24. A few of the many sources of information on rehabilitation are: the Enterprise Foundation (505 American City Building, Columbia, MD); LISC (666 Third Avenue, New York, N.Y.); and the Neighborhood Reinvestment Corporation (1325 G Street NW, Washington, D.C.). See also Clay & Hollister 1983; 21–35).

25. See Taub et al. 1984: 15; and R. Bratt in Clay & Hollister 1983: 144–45.

26. "There is little evidence that such programs reduce crime. Instead, the programs give residents a feeling of security because they believe their crime problem is being confronted" (Taub et al. 1984: 185).

27. Court decisions in *Milliken v. Bradley* 1974, the Detroit school desegregation case, and *Keyes v. Denver* 1973, the Denver school case, imposed serious obstacles to metropolitan school desegregation.

28. This is the situation in Akron's west side neighborhood.

29. One excellent model is in the Capitol Hill neighborhood in Washington, D.C., where a determined group of about one hundred parents turned a predominantly black elementary school into an integrated one by establishing an outstanding citywide magnet program in that school.

30. West Side Neighbors wrote a grant proposal to the Ford Foundation for a special creative curriculum for Buchtel High School; this prompted the Akron school authorities to write one of their own, which received over $1 million from the state for a magnet program in Buchtel High School.

Appendix A

TABLES AND FIGURES

Table 1
Population of Case Study Neighborhoods/Cities, 1980 (Models A, B, C)

Neighborhood	Households	Persons	%Black	City	Persons	%Black
Model A (Success)						
Butler Tarkington	3273	10,975	55	Indianapolis	476,258	22
19th Ward	9011	21,287	49	Rochester	241,700	26
Sherman Park	3927	52,822	34	Milwaukee	741,324	23
Model B (Failure)						
Blue Hills	3834	13,698	81	Hartford	135,000	34
Model C (Conditional)						
West Side	9884	32,900	48	Akron	237,177	22

Table 2
Percent Black in Case Study Neighborhoods, 1950–80 (Models A, B, C)

Neighborhood	MO Began*	1950	1960	1970	1980
Model A					
Butler-Tarkington	1956	08	30	41	55
19th Ward	1965	00	00	14	49
Sherman Park	1970	00	00	05	34
Model B					
Blue Hills	1962	00	07	40	81
Model C					
West Side	1967	00	04	24	48

*Year Movement Organization began.

Source: U.S. Census 1950–80, Dept. of Commerce, Washington, D.C.

Table 3
Percent Black in Neighborhood and Subareas, 1960–80 (Models A, B, C)*

Neighborhood	1960 Sub-area	1960 Whole	1970 Sub-area	1970 Whole	1980 Sub-area	1980 Whole
Model A						
Butler-Tarkington		30		41		55
North	00		05		10	
Central	15		29		34	
South	75		79		80	
19th Ward		0		14		49
East	00		24		63	
West	00		04		32	
Sherman Park		0		05		34
East	00		16		63	
Central	00		00		21	
West	00		00		04	
Model B						
Blue Hills		7		40		81
East	00		39		78	
West	07		40		85	
Model C						
West Side		4		24		48
North	00		02		12	
Central	00		19		66	
South	23		77		85	

*Percentages for whole areas are not always consistent with those of

 sub-areas because of averaging of sub-area groupings.   See Figures 1–3

for exact sub-area trend data.

Figure 1
Racial Composition of Subareas of Neighborhoods, 1970, 1980—Model A

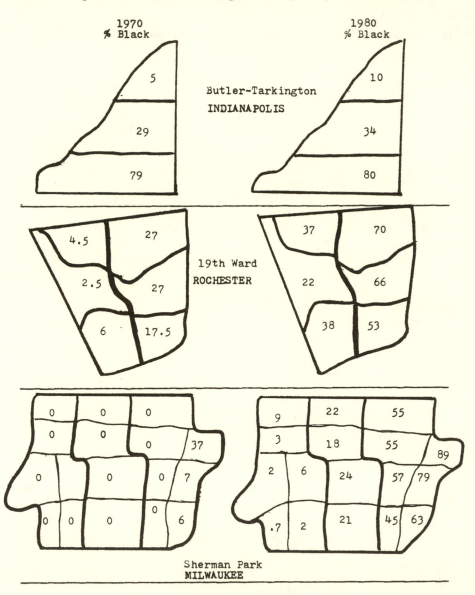

1970
% Black

1980
% Black

Butler-Tarkington
INDIANAPOLIS

5   10

29   34

79   80

19th Ward
ROCHESTER

4.5   27   37   70

2.5   27   22   66

6   17.5   38   53

Sherman Park
MILWAUKEE

Figure 2
Racial Composition of Subareas of Neighborhoods, 1970, 1980—Model B

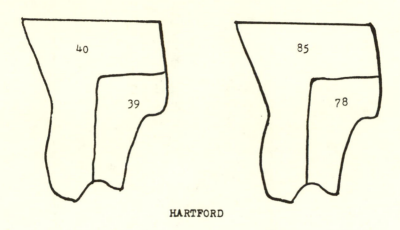

1970

%. Black

1980

% Black

Blue Hills

40

85

39

78

HARTFORD

Figure 3
Racial Composition of Subareas of Neighborhoods, 1970, 1980—Model C

1970

% Black

1980

% Black

West Side

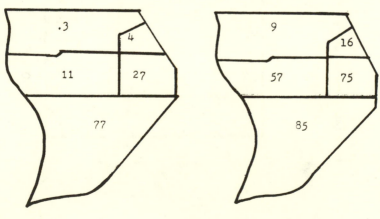

.3

4

9

16

11

27

57

75

77

85

AKRON

Figure 4
Percent Black in Case Study Neighborhoods, 1960–80, Models A, B, C

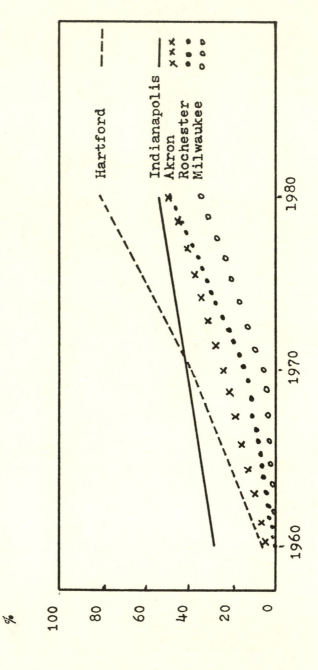

Appendix B

INTERVIEW SCHEDULE

Neighborhood   Stabilization Movement

FIELD   INTERVIEW GUIDE *

<u>Face Sheet</u>

City _____

Date _____

Place _____

Name of Group_____

Person Interviewed _____

Position _____

Time _____

Category: Org. Leader   _____
          Org. Member   _____
          Neighborhood Resident   _____
          Non-Resident _____

How referred _____

Name of neighborhood _____

*This guide (interview schedule) was also used as a mailed questionnaire
for organizations discussed in Profiles Across the Country, Chapter 7.

Neighborhood   Stabilization   Movement

FIELD   INTERVIEW GUIDE

1. When did your group first get started?
2. How long have you been involved? How? Time in neighborhood?
3. Why did the group first form an organization?
4. Did they know of any other groups anywhere else, like theirs?
5. What were the geographical boundaries of their area of concern, i.e., where is the "neighborhood"?
6. How many blocks and households does it include?
7. Which schools are in the area?
8. Which shopping area is included?
9. Which churches are in the area?
10. When the group first formed, what structure did they have?
11. Who was in the first group?
12. Are any of them still around? Who? Names & addresses?
13. Who were the most influential members of the original group?
14. Who do you think they are now? Names & addresses?
15. What committees were first set up?
16. Which of thes are still used?
17. Why do you think the others didn't survive?
18. Is there a copy of the first constitution? Where?
19. Who has all the early records & news clips? Where are they?
20. What were the original goals of the organization?
21. Are there any old printed materials of the gorup? The first brochures?
22. Which programs were developed to achieve the goals?
23. Do you think any of the goals have changed over the years? Which?
24. What about programs? Have any of these changed? Which? How? Why?
25. Has the business area changed in any way over the years? How? Effects?
26. Have the schools changed? How? Results?
27. How about the general neighborhood, any changes? How? Results?
28. What successes has your organization had? When? Why?
29. What obstacles has your group faced? When? How were these handled?
30. What failures has the group had? When? Why do you think these happened? What was done about these?
31. Have you had any special projects? What? When? How funded? Results?
32. What do you see as the future of this neighborhood?
33. Future of the group?
34. Do you have some current brochures of the group? Newsletters? History? List of Board members? Committees? Where are these?
35. Does your group have an office? Where? Staffed? Funded? By whom?

36. How do you think the organization differs now from the old days?
    Why?
37. Are any of the problems of today the same as the old ones? Which?
38. Would you say your group has or has not succeeded in achieving its
    original goals?
39. How do you think your neighborhood is perceived by non-residents? By
    City officials? By school administrators? By public housing officals?
40. What do you think is the single most important need of this area
    today? What is your group doing to obtain this? When do you think
    you'll have it?
41. Any coalitions with other groups? Any local fair housing group? Any
    involvement with them ever?

Appendix C

THE COMMUNITY LEVEL—MODEL C

cc: Gov. Celeste, A. Celebrezze, M.E.
Withrow, Sen. Ocasek, L. Fisher, Reps.
T. Sawyer, C. Skeen, V. Sykes, M. Boyle
A. Smith/OAR, J. Boebinger/AABR,
Bds. of Ed./ Ohio, Akron, L. Meeks,
R. Sawyer.

West Side Neighbors, Inc.

April 7, 1983

Mr. Alfred S. Dietzel, Chairman
Ohio Housing Finance Agency
30 E. Broad St.
Columbus, Ohio 43215

Dear Mr. Dietzel:

Now that the mortgage revenue bond (MRB) program is about to
begin, we urge you to take preventive measures against the potentially harmful racial consequences of this program for all Ohio
communities. We offer several suggestions which might help to
avoid further racial concentration of neighborhoods and schools
in Ohio:

1. Instruct the Ohio Association of Realtors to require affirmative marketing plans from all participating real estate agents.

2. Develop a review system to determine the adequacy of such plans
   in avoiding further racial impaction of neighborhoods and schools.

3. Require participating lenders and real estate agents to keep
   records of MRB grantees by location and race.

4. Develop a system of reporting so that the actual racial impact
   of the MRB program on neighborhoods and schools can be analyzed
   and made available in written summaries.

5. Set aside 5% of the revenue bonds for financial incentives for
   pro-integrative moves. These funds could be used in the following
   ways:

   a. Revolving loans for assisting minority homebuyers in moving
      to non-traditional areas (white) and majority homebuyers
      in moving to integrated areas.

   b. Cash bonus payments to real estate agents who accomplish
      pro-integrative moves with their clients.

   c. Tax credits for homebuyers whose moves result in decreased
      racial concentration of neighborhoods and schools.

We urge you to do everything possible to prevent government
funds from being used to foster and perpetuate racial segregation
of neighborhoods and schools. These suggestions, we hope, will help.

Sincerely yours,

M. Sommerville, President

946 Frederick Blvd.
(At Copley Road)

Akron, Ohio 44320

(216) 864-8850

424

march 23, 1981

West Side Neighbors, Inc.

MEMORANDUM

TO: Those Concerned About Real Estate Solicitation In The WSN Area

ABOUT: Judge Damon Keith's Decision (Zuch vs. Hussey, 3-14-75)

A complete copy of Judge Keith's decision in the Zuch vs. Hussey case is now available in our office. We invite you to stop in to read this historic decision, or we will gladly make and send ($2) copies on request. Meanwhile, we offer a few pertinent exerpts from the decision, for your information:

p. 14,491 - "Uninvited solicitations for the sale of homes in racially transitional areas are unlawful under the Fair Housing Act."

p. 14,493 - "Areas in transition seem to experience rapid population turnover which in large part results from panic selling."

p. 14,494 - "The real issue is whether the real estate industry should be allowed to enter into the process and, for commercial advantage, artificially hasten or at least accelerate the rate of population turnover and the pace of racial change."

p. 14,491 - "If the real estate industry is allowed to operate unchecked, the pace of racial transition will be manipulated in a way that will irreparably distort any chance for normal and stable racial change."

p. 14,507 - "Section 3604 (of the Fair Housing Act) is aimed at both overt blockbusting and other uninvited solicitations in racially transitional neighborhoods where it can be established 1) that the solicitations are made for profit, 2) that the solicitations are intended to induce the sale of a dwelling, and 3) that the solicitatiins would convey to a reasonable man, under the circumstances, the idea that members of a particular race are, or may be, entering the neighborhood."

p. 14,508 - "The right to open housing means more than the right to move from an old ghetto to a new ghetto. Rather, the goal of our national housing policy is to 're- place the ghettos' with 'truly integrated and balanced living patterns' for persons of all races... "

946 Frederick Blvd.   **Akron, Ohio 44320**
  (At Copley Road)

(216) 864-8850

Judge Damon Keith's Decision (cont'd)

p. 14,510 - "In view of the foregoing conclusions of law and
findings of facts, the Court concludes as matter
of law that the racial atmosphere in the area in
question is such that a solicitation for a listing,
made for profit and with the intention of inducing
the sale of a dwelling, would convey to a reasonable
man the idea that members of a particular race
are or may be entering the area in question, and
thus violate 42 U.S.C. 3604 (e). This is so even
though race is not mentioned in the solicitation.
Therefore, the solicitations by H.W.R. Realty,
Inc., and H-W Realty Co. constituted violations
of 42 U.S.C. 3604 (e). "

p. 14,511 - "Racially integrated neighborhoods can evolve and
sustain themselves... Such neighborhoods can only
exist when the black and white inhabitants of
those neighborhoods develop mutual respect and
tolerance. Such respect and tolerance is more
likely to thrive in an atmosphere where people
who affirmatively desire to live in a community
are not continually subjected to .. pressures..."

p. 14,512 - "Compounding this situation is the fact that because white homeowners do not generally patronize
black realtors, the black realtor is limited in
his operations to either predominantly black communities or transitional communities... In a
sense, therefore, this injunction, while necessary,
is also somewhat unfair ... Its effect will be to
limit again the areas in which they can operate
with any hope of being successful."

p. 14,508 - "The interest of both the black and white citizens
in stable communities outweighs any minor incon-
venience of having to utilize alternate methods
for advertisement and information gathering...

It is clearly consistent with the Constitution and
federal housing policy .. to pursue a policy of
encouraging stable integrated neighborhoods and
discouraging brief integration followed by prompt
resegregation.."

Distributed by West Side Neighbors, Inc.

West Side Neighbors, Inc.

September 8, 1981

Mr. Sylvester Angel, Director
U.S. Department of Housing & Urban Development
Region V, Area Office
200 N. High St.
Columbus, Ohio 43215

Dear Mr. Angel:

      As non-profit citizen group A-95 Reviewers for the Akron area, we would like to acquaint you with the following action plan. Since federal funds should not be used to promote or maintain racial or economic segregation, we intend to request a Social Impact Statement from all area applicants for federal funds. The purpose of this is to assess the possible impact of any project on the racial and economic composition of neighborhoods and schools, so as to guard against their resegregation.

      We believe your office could assist us in this effort by notifying applicants early in their application process, so as to avoid unnecessary delay later when their proposals reach us for the A-95 Review procedure. We would appreciate a response from you, indicating your reaction to our plan and your willingness to help, if possible.

Sincerely yours,

Cazzell Smith, Director
EAST AKRON COMMUNITY HOUSE

D. Pinkerton, President
WEST SIDE NEIGHBORS

Darryl Tukufu, Director
FAIR HOUSING CONTACT SERVICE

E. Landsberg, President
LEAGUE OF WOMEN VOTERS (Akron Area)

Vernon Odom, Director
AKRON COMMUNITY CENTER & URBAN LEAGUE

cc: Akron Area Board of Realtors, Akron Board of Education, Akron Metropolitan Housing Authority, City of Akron Planning Dept., City Council, COG, Congressman John Seiberling, NEFCO, Summit County Commissioners, Summit County Planning Department. Senator Glenn, Senator Metzenbaum, Samuel Pierce (HUD, Washington, D.C.), Akron Home Builders Association, Mayor Roy Ray.

946 Frederick Blvd.   **Akron, Ohio 44320**
(At Copley Road)

(216) 864-8850

Appendix D

THE NATIONAL LEVEL

FRONT PAGE, EARLY NEWSLETTER

Neighbors

A bi-monthly publication on interracial living

July—August 1971

Vol. 1 — No. 5

aker Man Reports on Neighbors Reelect Battle

IN THIS ISSUE

Discriminatio... ...Stance on Hous...

Still Bars Homes to Bla...

"SUE THE BASTARDS!"

A Report on National Neighbors' Second Annual Conference

Survey shows bias is more subtle now

The Cleveland Press. Wednesday, June ... 1971

THE OBERLIN CONFERENCE, JUNE, 1971

When National Neighbors began in May 1970, delegates from interracial neighborhoods adopted an action goal of achieving an open housing market in fact as well as in law. A year later, June 11-14, 1971, approximately 100 people met at NN's second conference, at Oberlin College in Ohio, to survey the current scene and plan how to proceed. The theme that clearly emerged was legal action to enforce the law, succinctly put by an attorney speaking to the conference, "Sue the bastards!"

Delegates Respond to Nixon

About midway through registration Friday afternoon, Joe Wine of the Dayton View Project stormed in with word of President Nixon's statement on housing policy (on racial discrimination in housing - committed to end it; on economic integration of the suburbs - against forcing it.) This news precipitated an issue no one had forseen. Where do the middle-class interracial neighborhood organizations that make up National Neighbors stand on economic integration? The carefully planned agenda was quickly in disarray - special sessions were scheduled, committees appointed, and stirring speeches made!

While delegates were unable to speak for home organizations on the unscheduled topic, they were virtually unanimous as individuals that economic as well as racial exclusion must end.

Their final resolution stated that although the President is right in saying "poor" and "black" are not synonymous, the two kinds of discrimination are inextricably intertwined. Regretting the President's failure to recognize this, delegates also called for prompt enforcement of existing fair housing laws to end all racial discrimination in housing.

Conference Action

The convention, after responding to the President's bomb, went about the business of setting its own house in better working order through. . .

- - The adoption of new bylaws designed to improve communications within NN;
- - The creation of a task force to plan realistically for future action;
- - The recommendation that regional conferences be held to broaden participation;
- - The recommendation of a second and more comprehensive Shoppers' Sunday followed by legal action.

Reelected were Joseph Battle of Cleveland as President of NN, Ruth Steele of Philadelphia as Vice President, and Iris Bruce of Oklahoma City as Secretary. John Michener of Baltimore was elected Treasurer, and Claudia Morgan of Rochester was elected to the newly created post of Assistant Secretary.

Neighbors is published bi-monthly by National Neighbors, an organization of interracial neighborhoods. Organizational memberships are $25 a year; individual associate memberships are $10 a year. Memberships include copies of all publications. Subscriptions to Neighbors, 6 issues a year are $5 for 12 issues. Material from this newsletter may be used as long as NN is credited. Co-editors: Phyllis Insull and Jean Bullock. National Neighbors, 5 Longford St., Philadelphia, Pa. 19136 - (215) 338-2905.

431

NATIONAL NEIGHBORS POLICY STATEMENT , 1983

Neighborhood Integration: A Reaffirmation

(This statement was unanimously adopted by the National Neighbors Board of Directors. The House of Delegates will vote on this issue at our June conference. Please let us know your opinion. Contact Susan Learmonth at 815 15th Street, N.W., Washington, D.C. 20005, phone (202) 347-6501, or Charles Bromley, 3130 Mayfield Road, Cleveland Heights, OH 44118, phone (216) 371-4285).

National Neighbors has been devoted to the principle of neighborhood integration since its formation in 1970. Its purpose, stated in its constitution, is to foster and encourage successful multiracial neighborhoods throughout the U.S. and to perform all acts consistent with this purpose. Its publication and policy statements since 1970 have reaffirmed its commitment to neighborhood integration and the preservation of diversity.

Periodically, many organizations find it helpful to re-examine their goals and purposes. The National Neighbors (NN) Board of Directors has recently done this soul-searching, and offers this statement for the review and consideration of all members, supporters and friends. We will welcome your thoughts and views on this subject - so vital and dear to all of us.

Neighborhood integration is directly related to fair housing. Fair housing law was enacted to achieve two goals: 1) equal access to housing, and 2) replacement of ghettos (monoracial neighborhoods) with integrated and balanced living patterns. Equal access to housing makes integration possible. But once neighborhoods become integrated, they can only stay that way with continuing equal housing access throughout a metropolitan area. Without this, racial concentration will occur, making integration impossible.

The main reason for residential segregation in this country is racial discrimination. We have a long legacy of racism in the courts, the housing industry, the lending institutions, government at all levels, and public housing. These have all been responsible for neighborhood segregation, which has led to school, economic, and social segregation. These segregated institutions all reinforce each other and perpetuate and increase neighborhood segregation.

There are two major ways of achieving neighborhood integration: 1) enforcement of fair housing laws which prohibit racial discrimination in housing, and 2) affirmative marketing. Affirmative marketing goes a step beyond equal housing opportunity. It involves the use of positive information and education to encourage pro-integrative housing choices. Affirmative marketing is a remedy for the long accumulated effects of past institutional racism in housing.

Without fair housing law enforcement and without affirmative marketing, integrated neighborhoods would not likely remain integrated for long. This is because of the long legacy of racism in this country. As James Farmer said:

"An integrated society will not automatically happen. We've got to take deliberate counter-measures to create it...it won't create itself...If left to freedom of choice alone, because of racism in this nation's culture, the nation will continue to be segregated...that is certainly true. And many of these counter-measures we must take will have to be extraordinary measures...because, in a way, we are jumping up-stream...running against the prevailing trend (of segregation). I can't think of anything more important than this counter-trend of working for integration."

(1975, NN Great Lakes Regional Conference)

2

Affirmative marketing may take different forms and use different approaches depending on the local housing market conditions, the community relations environment, the type and price of housing, and the degree of existing segregation in the metropolitan area. What may be necessary, effective, and justified in one area may be unnecessary or ineffective in another. Whatever the strategy used, however, affirmative marketing does not limit housing choices. Rather choices are expanded for all homeseekers to include areas that might not otherwise be considered because of past practices of denial and racial discrimination. With affirmative marketing, then, whites are especially encouraged to seek housing in areas of minority concentration, and minorities are especially encouraged to seek housing in areas of white concentration. But, after all information is given and all areas are shown, final choices are ultimately left to the individual homeseeker.

Affirmative marketing does not use quotas and does not require specific numerical goals. But for monitoring and planning, numbers are used and are necessary. Data used for monitoring and planning are legal and essential. They should not be confused, however, with quotas used to limit choices.

We need to remember that integration may be any one of many points along a continuum. It may range from a very low level of integration (a few whites or minorities) to a very high level of integration. Beyond this level, we may move into the situation of concentration and resegregation, depending on the circumstances of the community's environment. Each level may require different programs to preserve diversity.

In our country, 15 years after the passage of fair housing law, most neighborhoods are still segregated – either all minority or all white. This represents a failure of the government, the courts and the housing industry to eradicate racism. But there are some neighborhoods, municipalities, and school districts that are working affirmatively to promote and preseve racial diversity and integration. They are working to enforce fair housing law, to attract people of all types, and to maintain diversity where it exists. National Neighbors is proud to represent them. They - and we - all need support and reinforcement, and each other. We respect diversity of programs, as we recognize diversity of areas and problems.

National Neighbors reaffirms its commitment and dedication to neighborhood integration - to its promotion and to its maintenance. We call on all relevant private and governmental sources to work with us toward more effective fair housing law enforcement AND legally valid, morally responsible affirmative marketing programs for achieving and preserving integrated, balanced living patterns.

433

BIBLIOGRAPHY

BOOKS AND ARTICLES

Abrahamson, Julia. 1959. *A Neighborhood Finds Itself*. New York: Harper & Row.

Abrams, Charles. 1965. *The City Is the Frontier*. New York: Harper & Row.

Ahlbrandt, Roger, and James Cunningham. 1978. *A New Public Policy for Neighborhood Preservation*. New York: Praeger.

Aldrich, H., and J. A. Reiss. 1976. "The Race Composition of Neighborhood Businesses." *American Journal of Sociology* 81:846–866.

American Institute of Real Estate Appraisers. 1977. *Affirmative Action Program*. Chicago.

Aukofer, Frank. 1968. *City with a Chance*. Milwaukee: Bruce Publishing Co.

Bailey, Kenneth. 1978. *Methods of Social Research*. New York: Free Press.

Baron, Harold. 1969. "The Web of Urban Racism." In *Institutional Racism in America*, by L. Knowles and K. Prewitt. Englewood Cliffs, N.J.: Prentice-Hall.

Barth, James, and Donald Noel. 1972. "Conceptual Frameworks for the Analysis of Race Relations." *Social Forces* 50: 333–348.

Bennett, Lerone. 1966. *Before the Mayflower*. Baltimore: Penguin Books.

Blalock, Herbert. 1982. *Race and Ethnic Relations*. Englewood Cliffs, N.J.: Prentice-Hall.

Blumberg, Rhoda. 1984. *Civil Rights: The 1960s Freedom Struggle*. Boston: Twayne Publishers.

Bolduc, Vincent. 1976. "Association and Community: A Case Study." Ph.D. Diss. Stamford: University of Connecticut.

Bradburn, N., S. Sudman, G. Glockel. 1971. *Side by Side: Integrated Neighborhoods*. Chicago: Quadrangle Books.

Cameron, William. 1966. *Modern Social Movements*. New York: Random House.

Campbell, John. 1976. "Contributions Research Can Make in Understanding Organizational Effectiveness." In *Organization Effectiveness*, by Lee Spray (ed.). Kent, Ohio: Kent University Press, 1976.

Chapin, F. Stuart. 1974. *Human Activity Patterns in the City*. New York: Wiley.

Chase, Stuart. 1953. "We Can Do Something About It." In *Triumph in a White Suburb*, by Reginald Damerell, New York: William Morrow, 1968.

Clark, Thomas. 1987. "The Suburbanization Process and Residential Segregation." In *Divided Neighborhoods*, edited by Gary Tobin. Beverly Hills, Calif.: Sage, 1987.

Clay, Philip, and Robert Hollister. 1983. *Neighborhood Policy and Planning*. Lexington, Mass.: Lexington Books, D.C. Heath & Co.

Crain, Robert. 1975. "School Integration and Occupational Achievement of Negroes." In *Racial Discrimination in the U.S.*, edited by Thomas Pettigrew. New York: Harper & Row.

Damerell, Reginald. 1968. *Triumph in a White Suburb*. New York: William Morrow.

Darden, Joe. 1987. "Choosing Neighbors and Neighborhoods." In *Divided Neighborhoods*, by Gary Tobin (ed.). Beverly Hills: Sage, 1987.

Davis, F. James, ed. 1979. *Understanding Minority-Dominant Relations*. Arlington Heights, Ill.: AHM Publishing Corporation.

Dawson, Carl and W. E. Gettys. 1934. *Introduction to Sociology*. New York: Ronald Press.

Douglass, Frederick. 1966. *Life and Times*. New York: Crowell.

Farley, John. 1982. *Majority-Minority Relations*. Englewood Cliffs, N.J.: Prentice-Hall.

———. 1987. "Segregation in 1980." In *Divided Neighborhoods*, edited by Gary Tobin, Beverly Hills, Calif.: Sage.

Farley, Reynolds. 1984. *Blacks and Whites: Narrowing the Gap*. Cambridge: Harvard University Press.

Feagin, Joe. 1978. *Racial and Ethnic Relations*. Englewood Cliffs, N.J.: Prentice-Hall.

Fischer, Claude. 1976. *The Urban Experience*. New York: Harcourt, Brace.

Foley, Donald. 1973. "Institutional and Contextual Factors Affecting the Housing Choices of Minority Residents." In *Segregation in Residential Areas*, edited by A. H. Hawley & V. R. Rock. Washington, D.C.: National Academy of Sciences.

Ford Foundation. 1978. *New Approaches to Fair Housing: The Local Dimension*. New York.

Francis, E. K. 1976. *Interethnic Relations*. New York: Elsevier.

Freeman, Jo. 1975. *The Politics of Women's Liberation*. New York: Longman.

———, ed. 1983. *Social Movements of the Sixties and Seventies*. New York: Longman.

Galster, George. 1986. "More than Skin Deep." In *Housing Desegregation and Federal Policy*, edited by John Goering. Chapel Hill: University of North Carolina Press.

———. 1987. "Federal Fair Housing Policy in the 1980s." Cambridge: MIT Center for Real Estate Development.

Gerlach, Luther. 1983. "Movements of Revolutionary Change: Some Structural Characteristics." In *Social Movements of the Sixties and Seventies*, edited by Jo Freeman. New York: Longman.

Gist, Noel, and Sylvia Fava. 1974. *Urban Society*. New York: Crowell.

Goering, John. 1978. "Neighborhood Tipping and Racial Transition." *Journal of American Institute of Planners* 44: 68–78.

———, ed. 1986. *Housing Desegregation and Federal Policy*. Chapel Hill: University of North Carolina Press.

Goodwin, Carole. 1979. *The Oak Park Strategy*. Chicago: University of Chicago Press.

Grant, Ellsworth, and Marion Grant. 1969. *Passbook to a Proud Past and a Promising Future*. Hartford: Society Bank.

Grismer, Karl. 1952. *History of Summit County*. Akron, Ohio: Summit County Historical Society.

Gusfield, Joseph. 1968. "The Study of Social Movements." In *International Encyclopedia of the Social Sciences*, edited by D. Sills. New York: Collier and Macmillan.

———, ed. 1970. *Protest, Reform, and Revolt*. New York: Wiley.

Hallman, Howard. 1984. *Neighborhoods*. Beverly Hills: Sage.

Heberle, Rudolf. 1951. *Social Movements*. New York: Appleton-Century.

Helper, Rose. 1979. "Social Interaction in Racially Mixed Neighborhoods." *Housing and Society* 6 (1): 20–38.

———. 1986. "Success and Resistance Factors in the Maintenance of Racially Mixed Neighborhoods." In *Housing Desegregation and Federal Policy*, edited by John Goering. Chapel Hill: University of North Carolina Press.

HEW. 1970. *Welfare Myths vs. Facts*. Washington, D.C.: National Center for Social Statistics.

———. 1972. *Public Welfare: Myth vs. Fact*. Washington, D.C.: Social and Rehabilitation Services.

Hochschild, Jennifer. 1984. *The New American Dilemma*. New Haven: Yale University Press.

Hoyt, Homer. 1933. *One Hundred Years of Land Values in Chicago*. Chicago: University of Chicago Press.

HUD. 1979(a). *Measuring Racial Discrimination in American Housing Markets*. Washington, D.C.: Office of Policy Development and Research.

———. 1979(b). *Gautreaux Housing Demonstration*. Washington, D.C.: Office of Policy Development and Research.

Hunter, Albert. 1974. *Symbolic Communities*. Chicago: University of Chicago Press.

———. 1975. "Loss of Community." *American Sociological Review* 40: 537–552.

———. 1981. "Persistence of Local Sentiments in Mass Society." In *City Scenes*, edited by J. John Palen. Boston: Little, Brown & Co.

Illinois Advisory Committee. 1982. Report to U.S. Civil Rights Commission. *Housing: Chicago Style*. Chicago, Ill.

Janowitz, Morris. 1961. *Community Press in an Urban Setting*. Chicago: University of Chicago Press.

Jones, Michael et al. 1988. "Rethinking Large City Public Housing Projects." North Central Sociological Association Meetings, Pittsburgh, Pa.

Kain, John. 1986. "Housing Market Discrimination and Black Suburbanization in the 1980s." In *Housing Desegregation and Federal Policy*, edited by John Goering. Chapel Hill: University of North Carolina Press.

Kain, John and John Quigley. 1975. *Housing Markets and Racial Discrimination*. New York: National Bureau of Economic Research.

Keating, Dennis et al. 1987. "Racial Integration in Three Cleveland Suburbs." Preliminary Report. Cleveland State University: Department of Urban Studies.

Keller, Suzanne. 1968. *The Urban Neighborhood*. New York: Random House.

Kentucky Commission on Human Rights. 1983. *School and Housing Desegregation Are Working Together*. Louisville.

Killian, Lewis. 1964. *Handbook of Modern Sociology*. Chicago: Rand McNally.

King, C. Wendell. 1956. *Social Movements in the U.S.* New York: Random House.

Kivisto, Peter. 1986. "A Historical Review of Changes in Public Housing Policies." In *Race, Ethnicity, and Minority Housing in the U.S.*, edited by J. Momeni. Westport, Conn.: Greenwood Press.

Knowles, Louis, and Kenneth Prewitt. 1969. *Institutional Racism in America.* Englewood Cliffs, N.J.: Prentice-Hall.

Kofron, Charles, and Robert Mendelson. 1988. "Changing Patterns and Strategies in Public Housing Management." Paper. North Central Sociological Association Meetings, Pittsburgh, Pa.

Lake, Robert. 1986. "Unresolved Themes in the Evolution of Fair Housing." In *Housing Desegregation and Federal Policy*, edited by John Goering. Chapel Hill: University of North Carolina Press.

Lake, Robert, and J. Winslow. 1981. "Integration Management: Minority Constraints on Residential Mobility." *Urban Geography* 2 (4): 311–326.

Laska, Shirley, and D. Spain, eds. 1980. *Back to the City.* New York: Pergamon.

Lauer, Robert. 1976. *Social Movements and Social Change.* Carbondale: Southern Illinois University Press.

Leadership Council for Metropolitan Open Communities. 1987. *The Costs of Housing Discrimination and Segregation.* An Interdisciplinary Social Science Statement. Chicago, Ill.

Lee, Barrett. 1985. "Racially Mixed Neighborhoods during the 1970s." *Social Science Quarterly* 66 (2): 346–364.

Leigh, Wilhemina, and James McGhee. 1986. "A Minority Perspective on Residential Racial Integration." In *Housing Desegregation and Federal Policy*, edited by John Goering. Chapel Hill: University of North Carolina Press.

Leven, Charles; James Little; Hugh Nourse; R. Read. 1976. *Neighborhood Change.* New York: Praeger.

Lieberson, Stanley. 1980. *A Piece of the Pie.* Berkeley: University of California Press.

London, Bruce et al. 1986. "The Determinants of Gentrification in the U.S. *Urban Affairs Quarterly* 21: 369–387.

Madison, James. 1982. *Indiana through Tradition and Change.* Indianapolis: Indiana Historical Society.

Mangione, Jerre. 1974. *Mt. Allegro.* New York: Columbia University Press.

Mason, Philip. 1970. *Race Relations.* London: Oxford University Press.

McEachern, William. 1976. "Education Finance in Connecticut: Equity vs. Efficiency." In *Issues in Financing Connecticut Governments*, edited by John Sullivan. Hartford: Capitol Region Council of Governments.

McMichael, Stanley. 1952. *A Manual for Appraising.* Englewood Cliffs, N.J.: Prentice-Hall.

Milgram, Morris. 1977. *Good Neighborhood.* New York: Norton.

Miller, Loren. 1965. "The Protest Against Housing Segregation." *The Annals of the Academy of Political and Social Science* 357:73–79.

Milofsky, Carl. 1988. "Predicting Survival among Neighborhood Based Organizations." Paper. North Central Sociological Association Meetings, Pittsburgh, Pa.

Molotch, Harvey. 1972. *Managed Integration.* Berkeley: University of California Press.

National Institute of Education. 1986. *Project Concern.* Washington, D.C.

Nelson, Harold. 1974. "Intrusive Movement Organizations: A Preliminary Inquiry." Paper. American Sociological Association Meetings, Montreal, Canada.

Noel, Donald, and Carla Wertheim. 1987. "The Continuing Significance of Race in the Housing Market." Paper (Unpublished). Milwaukee: University of Wisconsin.

Olson, Marvin. 1989. "Participation in Neighborhood Associations." *Sociological Focus* 22: 1–17.

Orfield, Gary. 1981. Toward a Strategy for Urban Integration. New York: Ford Foundation.

——— et al. 1984. "Neighborhood Change and Integration in Metropolitan Chicago." Report to Metropolitan Leadership Council. Chicago: University of Chicago.

———. 1985. "Ghettoization and its Alternatives." In *The New Urban Reality*, edited by Paul Peterson. Washington, D.C.: Brookings Institution.

Pawlowski, Robert. 1973. *How the Other Half Lived*. Hartford: Northwest Catholic High School.

Pearce, Diana. 1981. "Deciphering the Dynamics of Segregation: The Role of Schools in the Housing Choice Process." *Urban Review* 13 (2): 85–102.

Pettigrew, Thomas. 1975. *Racial Discrimination in the United States*. New York: Harper & Row.

———. 1980. *The Sociology of Race Relations*. New York: Free Press.

Phillips, C. J. 1968. *Indiana in Transition*. Indiana Historical Bureau.

Polikoff, Alexander. 1986. "What's in a Name? The Diversity of Racial Diversity Programs." In *Issues in Housing Discrimination*, U.S. Commission on Civil Rights. Washington, D.C.: Government Printing Office.

Potomac Institute. 1976. *Equal Housing Opportunity*. Washington, D.C.

Rabin, Yale. 1987. "The Roots of Segregation in the Eighties: The Role of Local Government Actions." In *Divided Neighborhoods*, edited by Gary Tobin. Beverly Hills, Calif.: Sage.

Roberts, Ron, and Robert Kloss. 1979. *Social Movements*. St. Louis: C. V. Mosby Co.

Rossi, Peter, ed. 1972. *Evaluating Social Programs*. New York: Seminar Press.

Rush, Gary, and Serge Denisoff. 1971. *Social and Political Movements*. New York: Appleton-Century Crofts.

Saltman, Juliet. 1971. *Open Housing as a Social Movement: Challenge, Conflict and Change*. Lexington, Mass.: D. C. Heath.

———. 1975. "Implementing Open Housing Laws Through Social Action." *Journal of Applied Behavioral Science* 11:39–61.

———. 1977. "Three Strategies for Reducing Involuntary Segregation." *Journal of Sociology and Social Welfare* 4:806–821.

———, ed. 1977. *Integrated Neighborhoods in Action*. Washington, D.C.: National Neighbors.

———. 1978. *Open Housing: Dynamics of a Social Movement*. New York: Praeger.

———. 1979. "Housing Discrimination: Policy Research, Methods, and Results." *Annals of the Academy of Political and Social Science*. 441:186–196.

———. 1980. "Action Research on Redlining." *Urban Affairs Papers*. 2:20–33.

———. 1981. "The Special Significance of Akron's School Case." *Integrateducation*. 18 (1–4): 12–15.

———. 1984. "Neighborhood Stabilization Strategies as Social Interventions." *Journal of Voluntary Action Research*. 13: 37–45.

———. 1986. "Neighborhood Change: Facts, Perceptions, Prospects." *Housing and Society* 13:136–159.

Schelling, Thomas. 1972. "A Process of Residential Segregation: Neighborhood Tipping." In *Racial Discrimination in Economic Life*, edited by A. Pascal. Lexington, Mass.: D. C. Heath.

Schermerhorn, Richard. 1970. *Comparative Ethnic Relations*. New York: Random House.

Schoenberg, Sandra, and P. Rosenbaum. 1980. *Neighborhoods That Work*. New Brunswick, N.J.: Rutgers University Press.

Schwab, William. 1982. *Urban Sociology*. Reading, Mass.: Addison-Wesley.

Schwab, William, and B. Ringel. 1988. "The Role of Voluntary Associations in Neighborhood Revitalization: A Social Movements Approach." Paper. North Central Sociological Association Meetings, Pittsburgh, Pa.

Smelser, Neil. *Theory of Collective Behavior*. 1963. New York: Free Press.

Society. 1979. "A Social Science Statement: School Segregation and Residential Segregation." July/August: 70–76.

Spray, Lee, ed. 1976. *Organization Effectiveness*. Kent, Ohio: Kent State University Press.

Squires, Gregory, and R. DeWolfe. 1981. "Insurance Redlining in Minority Communities." *Review of Black Political Economy* 11 (3): 347–364.

Squires, Gregory and W. Velez. 1987. "Insurance Redlining and the Transformation of an Urban Metropolis." *Urban Affairs Quarterly* 23(1):63–83.

Stave, S. A., ed. 1979. "Hartford, The City and the Region." Hartford: University of Hartford.

Still, Bayrd. 1948. *Milwaukee, The History of a City*. Madison: State Historical Society of Wisconsin.

Suttles, Gerald. 1968. *The Social Order of the Slum*. Chicago: University of Chicago Press.

———. 1972. *The Social Construction of Communities*. Chicago: University of Chicago Press.

Taeuber, Karl, and Alma Taeuber. 1965. *Negroes in Cities*. Chicago: Aldine.

———. 1975. "Racial Segregation: The Persisting Dilemma." *The Annals of the American Academy of Political and Social Science* 422: 87–96.

———. 1979. "Housing, Schools, and Incremental Segregative Effects." *Annals of the American Academy of Political and Social Science* 441: 157–167.

———. 1988. "Residence and Race: 1619 to 2019." Madison: University of Wisconsin Center for Demography and Ecology.

Taub, Richard et al. 1977. "Urban Voluntary Associations: Locality Based and Externally Induced." *American Journal of Sociology* 83: 425–442.

Taub, Richard, D. Garth Taylor, and Jan Dunham. 1984. *Paths of Neighborhood Change*. Chicago: University of Chicago Press.

Taylor, D. Garth. 1981. "Racial Preferences, Housing Segregation, and the Causes of School Segregation." *Review of Public Data Use* 9: 267–282.

Thornborough, Emma Lou. 1965. *Indiana in the Civil War Era*. Indianapolis: Indiana Historical Society.

Tobin, Gary, ed. 1987. *Divided Neighborhoods*. Beverly Hills, Calif.: Sage.

Turner, Ralph, and Lewis Killian. 1957. *Collective Behavior*. Englewood Cliffs, N.J.: Prentice-Hall.

U.S. Commission on Civil Rights. 1967. *Racial Isolation in the Public Schools*. Washington, D.C.: Government Printing Office.

———. 1974. *The Federal Civil Rights Enforcement Effort*. Washington, D.C.: Government Printing Office.

———. 1975. *Twenty Years after Brown: Equal Opportunity in Housing*. Washington, D.C.: Government Printing Office.

———. 1979. *The Federal Fair Housing Enforcement Effort*. Washington, D.C.: Government Printing Office.

———. 1986. *Issues in Housing Discrimination*. Washington, D.C.: Government Printing Office.

Warren, Rachelle and Donald Warren. 1977. *Neighborhood Organizer's Handbook*. Notre Dame, Ind.: University of Notre Dame Press.

Warren, Roland. 1963. *The Community in America*. Chicago: Rand McNally.

———. 1977. *Social Change and Human Purpose*. Chicago: Rand McNally.

Wellman, Barry, and Barry Leighton. 1979. "Networks, Neighborhoods, and Communities." *Urban Affairs Quarterly* 14 (3): 363–390.

Wells, Robert B. 1970. *This Is Milwaukee*. New York: Doubleday.

Whyte, William F. 1982. "Social Inventions for Solving Human Problems." *American Sociological Review* 47 (1):1–13.

———. 1984. *Learning from the Field*. Beverly Hills, Calif.: Sage.

Wilkinson, Paul. 1971. *Social Movements*. New York: Praeger.

Williams, Robin. 1964. *Strangers Next Door*. Englewood Cliffs, N.J.: Prentice-Hall.

Willie, Charles, ed. 1979. *Caste and Class Controversy*. Bayside, New York: General Hall.

Wilson, John. 1973. *Introduction to Social Movements*. New York: Basic Books.

Wilson, Thomas. 1983. "White Response to Neighborhood Racial Change." *Sociological Focus* 16: 305–318.

Wilson, William. 1978. *The Declining Significance of Race*. Chicago: University of Chicago Press.

Wood, James, and Maurice Jackson. 1984. *Social Movements*. Belmont, Calif.: Wadsworth.

Woodward, C. Vann. 1963. *The Strange Career of Jim Crow*. New York: Oxford University Press.

Wunker, Judy et al. 1979. *Affirmative Marketing Handbook*. Park Forest, Ill.: South Suburban Housing Center.

Yin, Robert. 1984. *Case Study Research*. Beverly Hills, Calif.: Sage.

Yinger, John. 1984. "Measuring Racial and Ethnic Discrimination with Fair Housing Audits." Paper. HUD Conference, Washington, D.C.

Zald, Mayer, and John McCarthy. 1973. *The Trend of Social Movements in America: Professionalization and Resource Mobilization*. Morristown, N.J.: General Learning Press.

———. 1977. "Resource Mobilization and Social Movements: A Partial Theory." *American Journal of Sociology* 82 (6): 1212–41.

———, eds. 1987. *Social Movements in an Organizational Society*. New Brunswick: Transaction Books.

Zald, Mayer and Roberta Ash. 1966. "Social Movement Organizations: Growth, Decay and Change." *Social Forces* 44 (3): 327–40.

DOCUMENTS AND PERIODICALS

Affidavits of John Goering, Oscar Newman. 1986. Starrett City vs. U.S.A.

Akron, Arnold et al. vs. Board of Education et al. 1968.

Akron, Bell et al. vs. Board of Education et al. 1978.

Akron Beacon Journal. 1967–88. Akron, Ohio.

Akron City Planning & Urban Renewal Department Reports, 1964–87.

Akron Community Audit, 1952.

Akron Mayor's Task Force on Human Relations Report, 1962.
Akron NAACP Civil Rights Committee Report, 1961.
Akron Urban League. "Brief on Urban Renewal," 1961.
Banner, The Nashville. 1971–78. Selected issues. Nashville, Tenn.
Belmont-Hillsboro Neighbors. 1970–85. Brochures, newsletters, reports. Nashville,
    Tenn.
Blue Hills Civic Association. 1962–1980. Newsletters, minutes, reports. Hartford, Conn.
Brayfield, C. and W. Brayfield. 1975. "Public Education and Desegregation in the
    Hartford Region." Mimeographed.
Bush, Mim, and Margaret Weiss. 1979. "19th Ward Community Association: A History."
    Rochester, N.Y.
Butler-Tarkington Neighborhood Association. 1960–84. Annual reports, history, min-
    utes, newsletters, policy statements. Indianapolis.
Champ, Thomas. 1975. "Compromised Efforts at Desegregation," Hartford. Mimeo-
    graphed.
Crenshaw Neighbors. 1963–85. Newsletters, reports. Los Angeles, Calif.
Cuyahoga Plan. 1988. "New Dimensions in School and Housing Desegregation Policy."
    Preliminary Report. Cleveland, Ohio.
Democrat-Chronicle. 1968–84. Rochester, N.Y.
East Mount Airy Neighbors. 1985. Annual Report, Documents. Philadelphia, Pa.
East Suburban Council for Open Communities. 1986–88. Documents, reports. Mayfield
    Heights, Ohio.
Fradin, Dennis. 1983. "Housing and Harmony in Oak Park." Illinois Issues. February.
    Springfield: Sangamon State University.
Greater Park Hill Community. 1979–84. Reports, brochures. Denver, Colo.
Hagedorn, John. 1983. "Dreams of the Seventies, Facts of the Eighties," Milwaukee,
    Wis. Mimeographed.
Hartford City Planning Commission. 1978. A Neighborhood Strategy for Hartford. Hart-
    ford, Conn.
Hartford City Planning Department Report, 1983.
Hartford Courant, 1969–79.
Hartford Times, 1963–71.
Hartford Public Schools Racial Statistics, 1965–84.
Harvard Graduate School of Education. 1965. Schools for Hartford. (Harvard Plan) Cam-
    bridge, Mass.
Indianapolis Star, 1958–84.
Johannsen, Marilyn. 1980. "A Brief History of Sherman Park Community Association."
    Milwaukee, Wis.
Letters and Correspondence. 1984–89. Selected respondents: Brooklyn, Denver, Hart-
    ford, Indianapolis, Los Angeles, Milwaukee, Nashville, Oak Park, Philadelphia,
    Shaker Heights, Teaneck, Washington, D.C.
Los Angeles City Council. 1982. Farrell-Ferraro Resolution.
Magazine. 1984 (March). United Airlines.
Meadows, Doris. 1984. Neighborhood as Community. Rochester, New York: Sesquicen-
    tennial Committee, City Department of Community Development.
Metropolitan Strategy Newsletters. 1984–88. Cleveland Heights, Ohio.
Miami Valley Regional Planning Commission. 1970. "A Housing Plan for the Miami
    Valley Region." Dayton, Ohio.

Milwaukee Journal. 1970–84.

National Housing Task Force. 1988. "A Decent Place to Live." Washington, D.C.

National Neighbors. 1969–88. Board minutes, correspondence, newsletters (*Neighbors*), publications, reports. Philadelphia, Pa., Washington, D.C.

Neighbors, Inc. 1983. "Neighbors Remembering." Washington, D.C.

Newman, Oscar. 1983. "Integration Equals Intervention." (Testimony in Arthur et al. vs. Starrett City et al.). New York: Institute for Community Design Analysis.

Nineteenth Ward Community Association. 1965–84. Minutes, newsletters, reports, statements. Rochester, N.Y.

Nyden, Philip et al. 1987. "Perceptions of Neighborhood Quality in South Evanston." Report. Chicago: Loyola University.

Oak Park Housing Center. 1972–87. Annual reports, brochures. Oak Park, Ill.

Obermanns, Richard. 1980. "Stability and Change in Racially Diverse Suburbs." Cleveland Heights, Ohio: Heights Community Congress. Mimeographed.

Ohio Housing Finance Agency. 1985–1988. Report on Mortgage Revenue Bonds. Columbus, Ohio.

Shaker Heights Housing Office. 1983–86. Documents, reports. Shaker Heights, Ohio.

Sherman Park Community Association. 1970–84. Annual reports, brochures, funding proposals, minutes, newsletters, reports. Milwaukee, Wis.

———. 1960. Policy on Integration and the Schools.

Soifer, A. 1975. "The Supreme Court's Desegregation Decisions: Unresolved Questions for the Hartford Desegregation Suit." Hartford: University of Connecticut School of Law. Mimeographed.

State of Connecticut. 1969. Regulation Section 10–22.6, C.

State of New York. 1968. Integration and the Schools. Albany, New York: State Education Department.

Teaneck Housing Center. 1982–85. Brochures, reports. Teaneck, N.J.

Times-Union (Rochester). 1968–84.

Transcripts. 1984–85. Hartford, Indianapolis, Los Angeles, Milwaukee, Rochester Respondents (names altered).

U.S. Census Reports. 1940–80. Akron, Brooklyn, Denver, Hartford, Indianapolis, Los Angeles, Milwaukee, Nashville, Oak Park, Philadelphia, Rochester, Shaker Heights, Teaneck.

West Mount Airy. 1983–85. Brochures, Constitution, Reports. Philadelphia, Pa.

West Side Neighbors. 1967–88. Board minutes, committee reports, constitution, newsletters, project reports.

White, Joe. 1973 est. "Who Says You Can't Fight City Hall?" *The Nashville Banner.* Nashville, Tenn.

INDEX

About the Author

JULIET SALTMAN is Professor Emerita of Sociology at Kent State University, and an urban programs consultant. Educated at the University of Chicago, Case Western Reserve University, and Rutgers University (Douglass College), she has published three books and numerous articles in the fields of housing discrimination, racial segregation, neighborhood change, and urban social movements. She has been involved in the open housing and neighborhood stabilization movements at all levels, and has served on the national boards of directors of National Neighbors, the National Committee Against Discrimination in Housing, and OPEN. In production is her co-edited book on international housing segregation *Comparative Housing Segregation*.